D0989430

PUBLICATIONS OF THE NEW CHAUCER SOCIETY

THE NEW CHAUCER SOCIETY

Officers and Board of Trustees

President 1998–2000 PAUL STROHM, Oxford University

Executive Director SUSAN CRANE, Rutgers University

Trustees 1996–2000 DAVID AERS, Duke University
JOHN GANIM, University of California, Riverside
LINDA GEORGIANNA, University of California, Irvine
ANNA TORTI, University of Macerata

Trustees 1998–2002 C. DAVID BENSON, University of Connecticut
CAROLYN DINSHAW, New York University
ROBERT W. HANNING, Columbia University

Editor, Studies in the Age of Chaucer LARRY SCANLON, Rutgers University

Book Review Editor CHRISTINE CHISM, Rutgers University

Editorial Assistant SUSAN ARVAY, Rutgers University

Bibliographer MARK ALLEN, University of Texas, San Antonio

Assistant Bibliographer BEGE K. BOWERS, Youngstown State University

Studies in the Age of Chaucer, the yearbook of The New Chaucer Society, is published annually. Each issue contains substantial articles on all aspects of Chaucer and his age, book reviews, and an annotated Chaucer bibliography. Manuscripts, in duplicate, accompanied by return postage, should follow the *Chicago Manual of Style,* 14th edition. Unsolicited reviews are not accepted. Authors receive free twenty offprints of articles and ten of reviews. All correspondence regarding manuscript submissions should be directed to the Editor, Larry Scanlon, Department of English, Rutgers University, 510 George Street, New Brunswick, NJ 08901-1167. All correspondence regarding subscriptions to The New Chaucer Society and information about the Society's activities should be directed to Susan Crane, Department of English, Rutgers University, 510 George Street, New Brunswick, NJ 08901-1167. Back issues of the journal may be ordered from the University of Notre Dame Press, 310 Flanner Hall, Notre Dame, Indiana 46556; phone (219) 631-6346; fax (219) 631-8148.

PR
1901
.S88

Studies in the Age of Chaucer

Studies in the Age of Chaucer

Volume 22
2000

EDITOR

LARRY SCANLON

PUBLISHED ANNUALLY BY THE NEW CHAUCER SOCIETY
RUTGERS, THE STATE UNIVERSITY OF NEW JERSEY

The frontispiece design, showing the Pilgrims at the Tabard Inn, is adapted from the woodcut in Caxton's second edition of *The Canterbury Tales.*

Copyright © 2000 by The New Chaucer Society, Rutgers, the State University of New Jersey. First edition. Published by the University of Notre Dame Press for The New Chaucer Society.

ISBN 0-933784-23-6

ISSN 0190-2407

PR
1901
.S88
(v.22)

CONTENTS

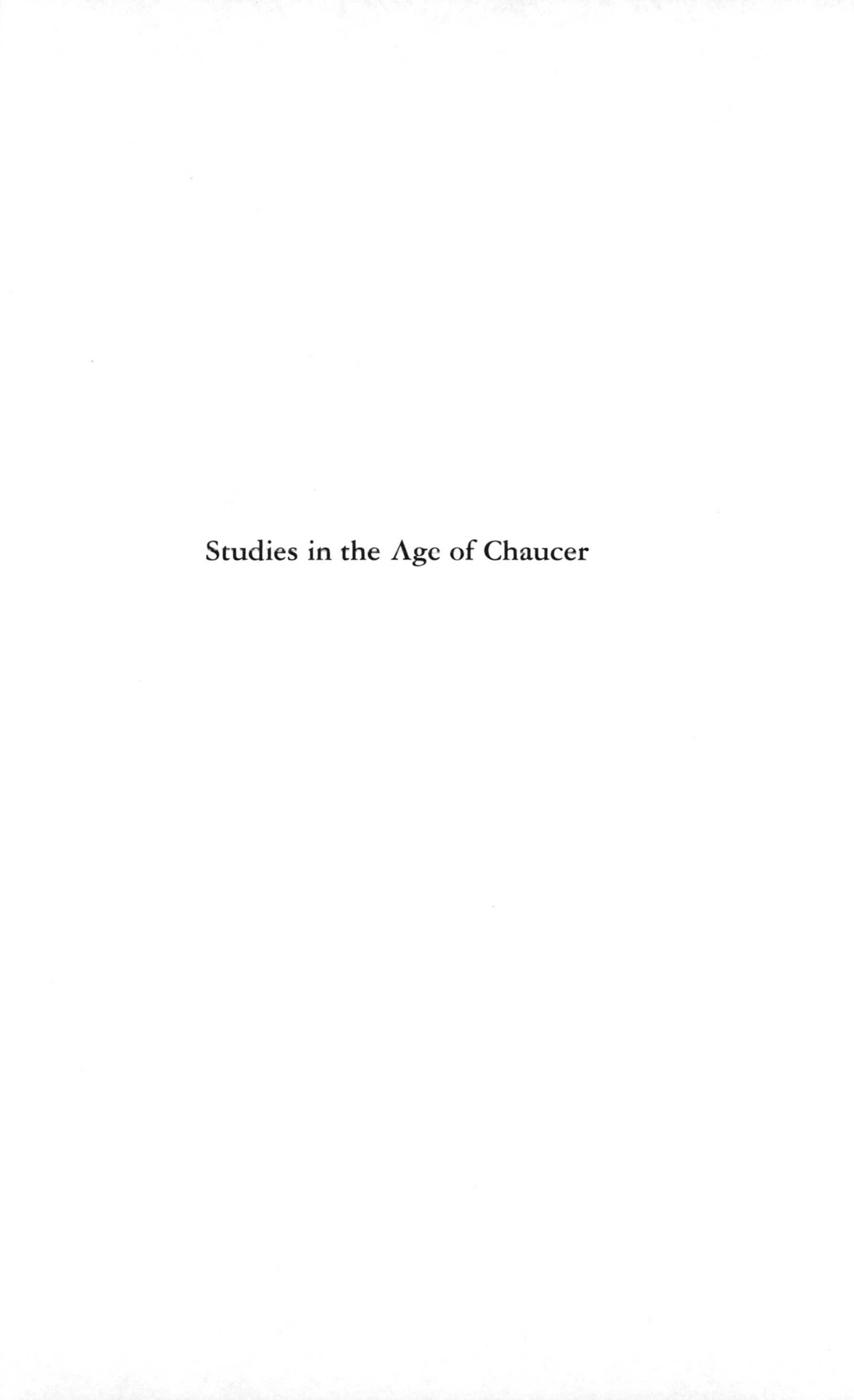

Studies in the Age of Chaucer

White

Peter W. Travis
Dartmouth College

"a word is elegy to what it signifies . . . "

—Robert Hass

WHAT'S IN A NAME? What's in a noun? And what's in a pronoun? Each of these three nominal signifiers manages somehow to acquire significance within a larger linguistic system, and each apparently succeeds in pointing beyond its descriptive meanings toward a discrete and unique referent in the real world. But how are these connections between word, meaning, and thing actually achieved? Consider, first, the proper name, which strives to designate and define an individual even though the name originally carries no "meaning" and the referent is itself "unknown" until after it is actually named. About the unusual semantic complexity of proper names linguist David Kaplan has written, "Proper names may be a practical convenience in our mundane transactions, but they are a theoretician's nightmare. They are like bicycles. Everyone easily learns to ride, but no one can correctly explain how he does it."[1] These theoretical nightmares would appear to intensify whenever a newly minted proper name appears inside a work of literature. "What a dictionary gives us about a word," writes literary theorist Paul Pickrel, "is the meaning or meanings it has accumulated through years . . . ; but a [fictional] character resembles what students of language call a 'nonce word,' something formed for and used on only one occasion. He or she has no accumulated meaning."[2] And of course, in

I am grateful for the advice and assistance of Brian Reilly, Becky McLaughlin, Joel Kaye, Darrel Mansell, Monika Otter, Davida Wegner, Susan Bibeau, and especially Sylvia Tomasch.

[1] David Kaplan, "Dthat," rptd. in A. P. Martinich, ed., *The Philosophy of Language,* 3d ed. (New York: Oxford University Press, 1996), p. 294.

[2] Paul Pickrel, "Character as Nominal: A Sketch for a Theory," *Novel* 22 (1988): 66.

addition to having no "accumulated meaning," literary names rarely claim to enjoy extra-literary reference. If this referential absence is normal for fictional proper names, does it not perforce follow that those two other fictive nominals—literary nouns and pronouns—likewise refer to nothing present or once present in reality? Further, although it seems counter-logical, is there possibly something incomplete about the relationship of *all* nominals to the realities they wish to designate? Such linguistic questions have been a central concern of many philosophers and poets, ancient, medieval, and modern, including, I would suggest, Geoffrey Chaucer. In this essay I intend to argue that the controlling metalinguistic program of Chaucer's elegy, *The Book of the Duchess,* is located in its own problematic nominal signs and most specifically in their complex relationship to an already-absent object which apparently can never be adequately known or named.[3]

Although supported by no incontrovertible empirical evidence, it seems quite credible that Chaucer's premier elegy was first performed on a ceremonial occasion to eulogize Blanche, John of Gaunt's wife, who died in September 1368. In Chaucer's *Retraction,* this poem is simply called "the book of the Duchesse" (line 1085), but the *Prologue* to *The Legend of Good Women* entitles it "the Deeth of Blaunche the Duchesse" (F 418), leaving not much doubt as to the poem's historical object of grief. Within the elegy itself, however, the lamented woman remains unnamed until, near the poem's end, she is identified merely by the descriptive *nomina* "good fair white." Likewise, her mourning lover, the man in black, is never explicitly identified as John of Gaunt, known al-

[3] Rather than providing a long list of studies of Chaucer's elegy to which I am indebted, I rely upon Alastair Minnis's ample critical review to serve as a reliable representation of the major appraisals of the poem: see A. J. Minnis, with V. J. Scattergood and J. J. Smith, *The Shorter Poems,* Oxford Guides to Chaucer (Oxford: Clarendon Press, 1995), pp. 1–160. The studies I have most depended on and whose interests are most approximate to mine are Maud Ellmann, "Blanche," in Jeremy Hawthorn, ed., *Criticism and Critical Theory* (London: Arnold, 1984), pp. 105–12; Elaine Tuttle Hansen, *Chaucer and the Fictions of Gender* (Berkeley: University of California Press, 1992), pp. 58–86; Gayle Margherita, "Originary Fantasies and Chaucer's *Book of the Duchess,*" in Linda Lomperis and Sarah Stanbury, eds., *Feminist Approaches to the Body in Medieval Literature* (Philadelphia: University of Pennsylvania Press, 1993), pp. 116–41; Kathryn L. Lynch, "The *Book of the Duchess* as a Philosophical Vision: The Argument of Form," *Genre* 21 (1988): 279–305; and (although not specifically on *The Book of the Duchess*) Louise Fradenburg, "Voice Memorial: Loss and Reparation in Chaucer's Poetry," *Exemplaria* 2 (1990): 169–202. I came across Cyndy Hendershot's excellent "Male Subjectivity, *Fin Amor,* and Melancholia in *The Book of the Duchess,*" *Mediaevalia* 21 (1996): 1–26, only after completion of this essay.

so as the earl of Richmond and duke of Lancaster. Yet for a privileged subset of readers—those who are "already in the know"—the historical identity of these two literary figures is made diegetically discernible at the very end of the poem in Chaucer's cryptogrammatic description of King Octavian's castle: "A long castel" (read "Lancaster") "with walles white" (read "Blanche"), "Be Seynt Johan" (read "John"), "on a ryche hil" (read "Richmond") (*BD* 1318–19).[4]

Thus, once they have been identified by knowing editors, it is clear that several occulted names are embedded in *The Book of the Duchess* awaiting the reader's readiness to acknowledge their hidden existence.[5] But I want to make a much stronger argument concerning the complexities of the elegy's nominal program as well as the significance inside this program—linguistic, philosophical, and psychological—of what it means to be, or not to be, "in the know." In order to do this, I mirror in my method some of the complexity of the poem itself. *The Book of the Duchess* is a highly structured work that has been much admired for the way it nestles frames within interiors within frames: the Black Knight's talking cure sited within the narrator's dream vision next to Ceyx and Alcyone's tragedy inside a bad case of insomnia surrounded by a poetic fiction beyond which proper words gesture in the direction of the real. Inspired by the poem's articulation of tangentially related discourses, my analytical techniques are several, some linguistic, some philosophical, some psychoanalytic, some formalist, some pedagogical—all of which I believe are discourses utilized by Chaucer in his poem. Because I intend to emulate what I consider to be the elegy's most significant strategy, that is, the spotlighting of confusion, incomprehension, and *méconnaissance* as profound responses to the mystery of linguistic signs, a brief précis clarifying in advance the framing elements of my argument may be in order.

In Section One I focus upon three moments of linguistic confusion, each of which foregrounds the problematics of nominal reference and signification. The first is the contested reference of the pronoun "I" as employed by the Black Knight in his elegiac lament; the second is the confused meaning of the noun "fers" in the Black Knight's allegory of

[4] All citations of Chaucer are from Larry D. Benson, gen. ed., *The Riverside Chaucer*, 3d. ed. (Boston: Houghton Mifflin, 1987).

[5] A considerable amount of attention has recently been paid to the matter of titles of, and historical names in, *The Book of the Duchess.* See especially Steve Ellis, "The Death of the *Book of the Duchess*," *ChauR* 29 (1995): 249–58.

a game of chess; and the third is the poem's deployment of "white" as a paronymic name (an accident used to signify a substantive) for a longed-for but absent object. Relying on the conflicting nomenclatures of medieval chess and on classical debates concerning "white"'s instructive indeterminancy, I argue that each of these three linguistic conundra is designed not to be "solved" but rather to be examined as a compact case study in the puzzling nature of linguistic signs. In Section Two I move to a panoptic survey of nominal signs and of their place in the rule-governed order of language. In order to situate Chaucer's interrogation of "white" in relation to the ideas of his philosophical contemporaries, I summarize the work of Duns Scotus, William Ockham, and Jean Buridan on the logical notion of "being white." Then, in order to develop a contemporary critical language appropriate to further analyzing Chaucer's linguistic signs, I turn to the twentieth-century sign-theory of Ferdinand de Saussure and specifically his semiology of chess as an instructive gloss to the metalinguistic game of chess played out in *The Book of the Duchess.* Finally, because the descriptive adjective "white" is transformed by Chaucer into a proper name, I conclude with Slavoj Žižek's bold attempt to resolve the descriptivist/anti-descriptivist debate concerning the question of whether there is something (or nothing) *in* the proper name that also inheres in the object so named. Serving as a philosophical framework to the entire essay, this section thus reconsiders the elegy's three nominal cruces through the development of interrelated linguistic treatises which either informed Chaucer's intellectual milieu or more recently have informed our own.

What is notably lacking to this point, however, is any consideration of the dynamics of those human desires being expressed in the intellectual analysis of linguistic signs. One of the innumerable qualities that distinguish Chaucer from his philosophical contemporaries is his readiness as a dream-vision poet to explore the complex set of needs and drives, both conscious and unconscious, that are at the core of the human pursuit of signs. Therefore, working with the psychoanalytic topography of Jacques Lacan, a discourse deriving directly from the logico-linguistic tradition already reviewed, I inaugurate in Section Three a sustained psycholinguistic study of the poem's speaking subject, an individual identified only as "I." The restive yearnings of the poem's depressed and riven "I" gradually disclose themselves to be inchoate longings for an indeterminate "nothing" imagined to reside both within and far beyond his own psychical identity. In the poem's semiotic discourse, the ideality of this sublimely absent "nothing" finds its most nearly adequate name in the powerful paronym "white," which, I contend, corresponds to what Lacan has called *l'objet petit a,* an absence grounded in an object never fully imagined to have been lost. Finally, in Section Four I address the feminine gender of this lost object and the place of white as the phantasmatic object of semiotic/erotic desire. Using the work of Julia Kristeva, Slavoj Žižek, and Vicky Kirby, I interrogate the significance of white's one spoken word, "Nay." Returning to the subject of nominal signification, white's negative assertion may actually embody a trace of the real, thus serving as the elegy's most nearly adequate proper name.

In *Language and Death,* Giorgio Agamben asserts that there is a "fracture in the plane of language" which "traverses the whole history of [Western] metaphysics."[6] I believe Chaucer places *The Book of the Duchess* precisely on this linguistic and metaphysical faultline, an aporia where absence displaces presence, where signification (a sign's pointing toward a concept) separates from indication (a sign's pointing toward a thing), where accidence ("white") is disengaged from substance (white), and where reality (as defined by Lacan) is barred from the real. That this rich site of semiotic rivenness resists interpretation and understanding is, I believe, part of the elegy's talking-cure wisdom. In an uncharacteristic immodesty trope, the elegy's narrator boasts of the uninterpretability of his dream: "Y trowe no man had the wyt, / To konne wel my sweven rede" (lines 278–79). Like the dream it contains, much of the meaning of Chaucer's poem resides in the uninterpretability of the absence, negation, and lack at its center. Therefore, I take the much-mocked misunderstandings of Chaucer's narrator to be instead a positive sign, an example that I strive to honor by insisting that acknowledging our *méconnaissance* is, necessarily and purposely, at the heart of the elegy's strategies of consolation.

What's in a name? The title of this essay is itself a troublesome name, for it apparently fails to include those qualities requisite to identifying the ideas it seeks to constitute. The very title of Chaucer's elegy (there are several titles, including no title at all) is problematic as well, serving as a temporizing place-holder for the yet-to-be-encountered thing-in-itself. It may therefore be the case that every word is ultimately a place-holder, an unsuccessful calling forth of an object that language itself ren-

[6] Giorgio Agamben, *Language and Death: The Place of Negativity,* trans. Karen E. Pinkus and Michael Hardt (Minneapolis: University of Minnesota Press, 1991), p. 18.

ders absent. As Richard Stamelman notes, "The law that language obeys is that of negation. . . . [for merely] to speak of something, to name it, is to recognize that as a thing it is now lost."[7] In this regard, then, what is most memorable about Chaucer's *The Book of the Duchess* is not merely that each of its words is (to use Robert Hass's haunting phrase) an "elegy to what it signifies,"[8] but that the entire poem is a work of mourning powerfully interrogating the nature of its own linguistic foundations.

I: Nominal Issues

An initial indication that *The Book of the Duchess* is concerned with foregrounding nominal problems is the dreamer's seemingly inept response to the Black Knight's first words. Wandering inside his dream vision, the narrator comes across a solitary man in black standing in a terrestrial paradise and uttering a lyric lament to himself (lines 475–486):

> "I have of sorwe so gret won
> That joye gete I never non,
> Now that I see my lady bryght,
> Which I have loved with al my myght,
> Is fro me ded and ys agoon.
> "Allas, deth, what ayleth the,
> That thou noldest have taken me,
> Whan thou toke my lady swete,
> That was so fair, so fresh, so fre,
> So good that men may wel se
> Of al goodnesse she had no mete!"

Although the narrator overhears these words of sorrow quite accurately, his subsequent low-affect response seems to indicate that he fails to understand the knight's actual meaning, which is: "I, the Black Knight, am mourning the tragedy of my beloved lady's death." There have been two prevailing explanations of the narrator's *méconnaissance* of the Black Knight's words: either the narrator is woefully thickheaded and thus he is meant to serve some kind of "comic" purpose, or else his interpretive dunderings are actually a deliberate ruse meant to assist the Black

[7] Richard Stamelman, *Lost Beyond Telling: Representations of Death and Absence in Modern French Poetry* (Ithaca: Cornell University Press, 1990), pp. 38–39.
[8] Qtd. (without citation) in ibid, p. xi.

Knight in his own talking cure.[9] Rather than getting caught up in this characterological debate, I think it is more important to interrogate the linguistic status of the Black Knight's words themselves. The narrator's "neutral" response may indicate that he has understood the Black Knight's lament as being a conventional poem of lovelornness (which of course it is) and thus a nonliteral utterance spoken in that linguistic modality that medieval logic called the improper, or figural, level of supposition.[10] After all, having unexpectedly come upon a man standing under an oak tree and reciting a *planh* for a lost lady, how many of us would immediately be convinced that his words are a direct expression of personal grief and a veridical chronicling of historical events?[11] A half-hidden clue to the unusual nature of the Black Knight's speech-act lies in his vocal inflections: "He *sayd* a lay, a maner song, / Withoute noote, withoute song" (lines 471–72; emphasis added). But failing to understand that the very same words may have quite different meanings if spoken or sung, the narrator apparently interprets the complaint's grief-stricken "I" as a pronoun belonging inside double quotation marks. Most readers of *The Book of the Duchess* have been fully persuaded that the "I" in this particular song signifies on the discrete level of supposition, that is, it serves as an indexical sign of the Black Knight him-

[9] For a brief review of scholarship on this matter, see *Riverside Chaucer,* pp. 970–71.

[10] In this essay I employ the medieval levels of supposition (especially figural, material, discrete, and determinate) in such a fashion that their meanings, in context, should be immediately clear. Paul Vincent Spade provides examples of six different levels of supposition enjoyed by the one word "man":

(1) the "improper" (figural) level of supposition: "After six moves the Russian chess player was a man down."
(2) the "material" level of supposition: "Man is a monosyllable."
(3) the "discrete" level of supposition: "That man is my brother."
(4) the "simple" level of supposition: "Man is a species."
(5) the "determinate" level of supposition: "A man is at the door."
(6) the "merely confused" level of supposition: "Every *masseur* is a man."

See Spade, "The Semantics of Terms," in Norman Kretzmann, Anthony Kenny, Jan Pinborn, eds., *The Cambridge History of Later Medieval Pilosophy* (Cambridge: Cambridge University Press, 1982), p. 196. J. Stephen Russell discusses the various levels of supposition in *Chaucer and the Trivium: The Mindsong of the Canterbury Tales* (Gainesville: University Press of Florida, 1998), pp. 39–51.

[11] This, I need to emphasize, is not a new idea. A. J. Minnis, in his full summary of critical studies of *The Book of the Duchess,* cites Donald Howard's "vivid modern analogy": "If you came upon a cowboy in a field singing to himself a typical cowboy song about death, would you conclude that someone had really died?" See Minnis, *Shorter Poems,* p. 125.

self, just as the fictive figure of the Black Knight serves as a sign pointing toward an historical person with a real name outside the poem. But it could well be that Chaucer's hermeneutically challenged narrator has arrived at an alternative yet still logical way of discriminating between the knight's use of a positivist "I" and his use of a nonreferential "I."

In calling attention to the referential uncertainties of the pronoun "I," *The Book of the Duchess* is announcing its general commitment to exploring the problematics of nominal signs. As is well known, "I" is an unusually complex nominative. Unlike a noun or a proper name, the pronoun "I," according to Emile Benveniste, is an "'empty' sign" nonreferential to reality or to any "'objective' positions in space or time."[12] Only when the word "I" is spoken does it suddenly discover its momentary referent and come to signify that "person who is uttering the present instance of the discourse containing I."[13] Outside of the unique context of its local utterance, Benveniste insists, the only referent of "I" is nothing more nor less than "the reality of discourse" itself.[14] The Black Knight's use of "I" would seem to validate Benveniste's thesis: the first-person singular of his complaint has no external referent until he, as speaker, says "I." But the narrator's implicit counterinterpretation underscores a phenomenon not considered by Benveniste: in many contexts we are obviously quite capable of uttering first-person pronouns so as not to take full possession of them. Indeed, numerous contemporary theorists have gone much further in their interrogation of the noncoincidence of the I that is and the I that speaks: according to some of these theories, while uttering this "'empty' sign" a speaker succeeds only in pointing in the direction of an already absent referent: the speaker's own riven subjectivity.[15] Even the conservative conventions of Chaucerian

[12] Emile Benveniste, *Problems in General Linguistics,* trans. Mary Elizabeth Meek (Coral Gables, Fla.: University of Miami Press, 1971), p. 219.

[13] Ibid., p. 218.

[14] Ibid.

[15] Derrida, for example, has argued at length that the self is not a coherent ground but only the product of the language that seeks it out. Rather than the originator of language, the "I" is an "effect" of language; in other words, the "I am" that seems to present itself simultaneously with the "I think" comes "after," not before or during, thought itself. The real meaning of "I am," then, proves to be merely "I will have been represented." Because "[t]he presence that is thus delivered to us in the present is a chimera," Derrida reasons, this means not only that "I" represents the absence of I, but that language itself has been deprived of its essential "first principle"—the present indicative of the verb "to be"; see Jacques Derrida, *Of Grammatology,* trans. Gayatri Chakravorty Spivak (Baltimore: Johns Hopkins University Press, 1974), p. 154. See also Karen Mills-Courts, *Poetry as Epitaph: Representation and Poetic Language* (Baton Rouge: Louisiana State University Press, 1990), pp. 218–30.

criticism have managed to illustrate some of the difficulties of the first-person singular pronoun: "Chaucer the man," "Chaucer the poet," and "Chaucer's literary *persona*" are often seen as partial identities, each vying for primacy of referential place whenever that voice we call "Chaucer" utters the pronoun "I." Thus, if for no other reason than that it is a telling parody of our critical practice, the problematics of "I" in *The Book of the Duchess* are issues of more than minor literary-critical concern.

A second nominal crux foregrounded in *The Book of the Duchess* is a semantic riddle embedded in a game of chess. The Black Knight, in an attempt to inform his interlocutor of the cause of his grief, explains that he once played a disastrous game of chess against Lady Fortune (lines 652–58):

> "At the ches with me she gan to pleye;
> With hir false draughtes dyvers
> She staal on me and tok my fers.
> And whan I sawgh my fers awaye,
> Allas, I kouthe no lenger playe,
> But seyde, 'Farewel, swete, ywys,
> And farewel al that ever ther ys!'"

The narrator's response to the mourning Black Knight, who has fallen so deeply into sorrow that he wishes he might "deye soone" (line 690), is—once again—curiously unsympathetic. First he warns the knight that were he to commit suicide it would be a grievous sin. His death would be equal in gravity to Medea's slaughter of her children, or the suicides of Phyllis, Dido, Echo, and Sampson. Next he argues that even had he lost "the ferses twelve," his killing himself would still be unforgivable: "Thogh ye had lost the ferses twelve, / And ye for sorwe mordred yourselve, / Ye sholde be dampned in this cas" (lines 723–25). In fact, he concludes, losing but one fers is such a minor setback that no normal person would feel much in the way of grief: "But ther is no man alyve her / Wolde for a fers make this woo!" (lines 740–41).

The narrator's misprision of the Black Knight's intent has left a strong impression on readers, many of whom agree with Talbot Donaldson that the narrator "seems at times almost too stupid to be true."[16] What has not been obvious, however, is that part of his misreading specifically

[16] E. Talbot Donaldson, ed., *Chaucer's Poetry: An Anthology for the Modern Reader*, (New York: Ronald, 1958), p. 952.

involves (for a second time) the complex interplay between figural and discrete levels of supposition. Whereas earlier in his dream the narrator may have mistaken the Black Knight's complaint for his lost lady as a mere literary artifact, here he may have mistaken the chess metaphor as referring to an actual game. There is no doubt that the narrator is capable of comprehending the rules of allegory; he readily recognizes that Lady Fortune represents the abstract idea of fortune. But poised between two contestants, one figural (Lady Fortune), the other material (the Black Knight), the narrator has chosen to read their chess game *ad litteram.*

The fundamental reason the narrator does not view the Black Knight's game as a personal allegory would appear to be centered in the nominal construction "my fers." Modern editors explain in their notes that "fers" was a technical word used in Middle English to denote that chess figure which was also called the "quene"; therefore, when we read "fers" we should think "queen."[17] If the lexical situation were this straightforward, the only difficulty would rest in the linguistic competence of Chaucer's narrator: either he is less than a fully competent native speaker of Middle English, or he is handicapped by an imperfect understanding of the standard names used in the game of chess. In point of fact, however, the semantic field of "fers" in fourteenth-century English, both in its significance and in its reference, was a site of telling ambiguity. In his magisterial study *A History of Chess,* H. J. R. Murray explains that in the original Arabic game, *firzan* denoted that chess figure whose movement was very restricted (one square diagonally) and which normally kept close to the king. While losing its original Arabic meaning of "wise man" or "counselor," *fers* was one of three Arabic names retained in parts of Europe when the game of chess was adopted, the other two being *al-fil* (aufin) and *rukh* (rook). Murray details how "two well-

[17] See, for example, *Riverside Chaucer,* p. 972. Minnis, in *Shorter Poems,* agrees that "fers" means "queen" (p. 127). There are several studies of the role of chess in *The Book of the Duchess* that Minnis cites in his bibliography in *Shorter Poems,* pp. 145–46. To that list should be added Margaret Connolly, "Chaucer and Chess," *ChauR* 29 (1994): 40–44: Connolly argues that because of "the confusion surrounding Chaucer's use of the chess metaphor," we should conclude that "[his] knowledge of chess comes therefore at second-hand" (p. 43). In contrast, Guillemette Bolens and Paul Beekman Taylor, in "The Game of Chess in Chaucer's *Book of the Duchess,*" *ChauR* 32 (1998): 325–34 succeed in proving that Chaucer was very knowledgeable about chess. After accurately tracing out the history of "fers," they then conclude that "Chaucer is the first writer in English to make the fers feminine" (p. 330). My position is that Chaucer deliberately leaves the gender, the referent, and the significance of "fers" open to interpretation.

marked systems of nomenclature" developed on the continent and how both of these two systems took hold in England. The first system called its chess figures *king, fers, aufin, knight* (*horse*), *rook,* and *pawn;* this set of names was characteristic of Spanish chess, "the older French chess," and "the English game of Norman times."[18] The second nomenclature system called its figures *king, queen, bishop* (*sage, count, fool*), *knight, rook* (*margrave*), and *pawn;* this system (using Latin *regina* or vernacular equivalents of "queen") is characteristic of German chess "and to a less degree of the oldest Italian and English chess."[19] Thus, in the game that spread from Spain into France and Norman England, the name "fers" was retained (Sp. *alfferza;* OFr *fierce;* ME *fers*). In Italy and Germany, however, as well as in early medieval England, the figure called *firzan* in Arabic was called the "quene" (It. *reina;* MLG *koninginne;* ME *quene*). As Murray's study further explains, not only did these two nomenclatures enter England at different times but also both systems were maintained, neither displacing the other; moreover, in the latter part of the Middle Ages, both in England and in France, these two variants "overlapped and became confused."[20]

The co-existence of two contending nomenclatures in Chaucer's England begins to explain the communication block between the narrator and the Black Knight. What, for each of them, does "fers" actually mean? Part of their problem has to do with a distinctive morphological feature of Middle English itself—the nongenderedness of the typical English noun. Because ME *fers* has no gender inflection (in contrast to its Romance and Germanic language equivalents), the gender of the Black Knight's "fers" could be understood in various ways. It could be understood as a feminine signifier, equivalent (if only in gender) to the "queen." It could be understood as a neuter noun, directly designating that "neuter" chess piece that can move only one diagonal square. It could also be understood as a masculine noun, since all the other "men" on the board were male. That Chaucer was fully aware of the existence of these three possibilities is revealed by the great care he takes *not* to give away the gender of the word "fers" in *The Book of the Duchess:* that is, he never allows the Black Knight to refer to his fers as "he," "she," or "it." The Black Knight appears to be a product of both systems of

[18] H. J. R. Murray, *A History of Chess* (Oxford: Clarendon Press, 1913), p. 425.
[19] Ibid.
[20] Ibid.

nomenclature: for him, "quene" and "fers" are interchangeable names for the same chess piece. The narrator, however, appears to be a product of only one chess dialect: he is therefore incapable of perceiving anything feminine or queenlike in *his* meaning of the word "fers." "Fers," in the narrator's speech community, is a neuter or masculine name for that figure on the board which keeps close to the king and moves one diagonal square at a time. It is anything but a synonym for "quene."

There is, however, still another partially clarifying explanation. In the original Arabic game, as Murray explains, the pawn that reached the eighth line instantly became a *firzan,* whether or not the original *firzan* (that is, "wise man, counselor") was still upon the board. However, while

> the same promotion awaited the Pawn in European chess, . . . the new European game introduced unforeseen difficulties. Not only had the Pawn to change its sex, a contradiction to which attention was directed by Neckam and others, but by its becoming a Queen when the original Queen was still upon the board the moral sense of some players was outraged. . . . The boldest attempt was the prohibition of promotion so long as the original Queen was untaken. . . . [But this prohibition] never commanded universal acceptance. . . . More usually, the difficulty arising from the possible plurality of Queens was evaded by an alteration in the nomenclature. Thus at quite an early date we begin to meet with a more general name for the Queen than *Regina,* e.g., *Femina, Virgo,* and later *Mulier.* The usual practice, however, was to use a different name for the promoted Pawn from that of the original Queen, and in France and England where there was a possible choice between Reine (Queen) and Fierce (Fers), many players tried to restrict the use of Reine (Queen) to the original Queen, and Fierce (Fers) to the promoted Pawn.[21]

Murray's paragraph might almost have been written to defend Chaucer's "obtuse" narrator from his critics. Simply put, the narrator may have been one of those "many players" in medieval England who straightforwardly called the queen the "quene" and who reserved the name "fers" for the promoted pawn. If Chaucer's narrator belonged to this particular chess community, then his low estimation of the value of one lost pawn makes a greater amount of sense: "ther is no man alyve her / Wolde for a fers make this woo!" By recuperating the competing and overlapping nomenclatures of medieval chess, we can begin to comprehend the lin-

[21] Ibid., pp. 426–27.

guistic foundation of Chaucer's allegorical game. This highlighting of linguistic matters is not meant to devalue the Black Knight's grief nor erase the narrator's troubling *méconnaissance.* Instead, the elegy's board-game of miscommunication is, I believe, a scene of semiotic confusion directed toward a knowing reader who is invited to re-interrogate the sliding significations of "fers" at a higher level of linguistic and philosophical theorizing.

Perhaps the most problematic act of naming in *The Book of the Duchess* appears near the end of the Black Knight's dialogue with the narrator, as he discloses his lady's proper name (lines 948–51):

> "And goode faire White she het;
> That was my lady name ryght.
> She was bothe fair and bryght;
> She hadde not hir name wrong."

One of the many striking features of these lines is the unusual emphasis given to the activity of naming itself. Here a proper name is implicitly assumed to carry a high degree of signification: a "right" name successfully identifies the essence of its subject; a "wrong" name either fails properly to identify its subject, or the resisting subject refuses to reify the substantive meaning of its given name. Equally remarkable is the oddity of the given name itself. What kind of name is "good fair white"? Unlike a proper name such as "Geoffrey Chaucer," it does not appear to contain either a first name or a surname; nor does it even contain what we would now call a noun. Rather, as a collocation of three adjectives, it seems to be searching for some substantive to adhere to. It is the reader who feels obligated to perform an act of grammatical alchemy by transmuting one of these three adjectives into a noun ("white" being the least counterintuitive choice). But, we must ask, can "white" serve as a *nomen,* and if so, how? Is it possible for "white" itself to identify *any* person, place, or thing? While modern readers are likely to grow impatient with seemingly trivial queries such as these, Chaucer's educated contemporaries would have recognized in "white" a conflation of questions medieval schoolmen had been asking for centuries: Does the word "white" indicate anything that is essential in reality? Is "white" capable of subsisting independently of its adherence in some noun-substance? Do qualities of accidence enjoy a form of categorical being in their own right?

The text primarily responsible for initiating these questions is the first work of the *Organon,* Aristotle's *Categories.* Aristotle begins the *Categories,* a text that is essentially a study of names, by defining three kinds of names: homonyms (which name equivocally), synonyms (which name univocally), and paronyms (which name derivatively). *Grammaticus* (or "having-knowledge-of-language") and *albus* are both paronyms, he explains, because they derive their names from other names: "grammar" and "whiteness." As paronyms they are also accidents, because they are incapable of existence apart from their subjects; in other words, they are not predicates of their subjects and are thus not essential to their subjects' being *qua* subjects. Aristotle explains how paronyms (b) differ from other words (a, c, and d):

Of things there are: (a) some are *said of* a subject but are not *in* any subject. For example, man is said of a subject, the individual man, but is not in any subject. (b) Some are in a subject but are not said of any subject. (By 'in a subject' I mean what is in something, not as a part, and cannot exist separately from what it is in.) For example, the individual knowledge-of-grammar [*grammaticus*] is in a subject, the soul, but is not said of any subject; and the individual white [*albus*] is in a subject, the body (for all colour is in a body), but it is not said of any subject. (c) Some are both said of a subject and in a subject. For example, knowledge is in a subject, the soul, and is also said of a subject, knowledge-of-grammar. (d) Some are neither in a subject nor said of a subject, for example, the individual man or individual horse—for nothing of this sort is either in a subject or said of a subject.[22]

In other words, what is basically at issue in the status of the paronym is the question of being, or *ens.* Substantial being (*esse per se*) is categorically distinct from accidental being (*esse per accidens*): although *albus* may be "in" the linguistic sign "the body" and *grammaticus* may be "in" the linguistic sign "the man," neither of them is essential to that noun's nature. Neither of them is a defining predicate (without which the noun would not exist); neither of them has being in its own right (they are not substantives); thus (and this is very important for our study) neither of them alone is able to indicate (or "appellate") the object in which it may occasionally, or "accidentally," inhere. In the *Topics,* and still later in *The Metaphysics,* Aristotle carefully explains how a categorical *nomen* (his primary examples are the proper name "Callias" and the common noun

[22] Aristotle, *Aristotle's* Categories *and* De Interpretatione, trans. J. L. Ackrill, Clarendon Aristotle Series (Oxford: Clarendon Press, 1963), chap. 2, p. 4.

"man") indicates the essence, the being, of that which it names. For Aristotle, therefore, a proper name clearly contains in itself all the attributes essential to the individual so named. Words such as "mortal" or "rational" are likewise predicates essential to the identity, the being-man, of "Callias" and "man." By contrast, however, paronymous attributes such as *albus* and *grammaticus* are not necessary predications of anything, and thus they fail to name the being, or essence, of any subject.

As a way of illustrating the basic nature of paronyms, medieval logical primers sometimes employed dramatic scenes to teach the first principles of "attributive being." For instance, in his late-eleventh-century instructive manual appropriately entitled *De Grammatico,* Anselm of Canterbury has a student ask his tutor to clarify, once again, how the paronym "white" "doesn't signify that which it in some sense does signify." The tutor imagines an interactive drama (deriving from a similar scene in Aristotle's *Topics*),[23] where the student is told only that a "white is in this building":

> Tutor: Suppose that, unknown to you, a white horse were enclosed in some building or other, and someone told you, "A white is in this building"—would that inform you that the horse was inside?
>
> Student: No; for whether he speaks of a white, or of whiteness, or of that within which the whiteness is enclosed, no definite circumstance is brought to my mind apart from the essence of this colour.
>
> Tutor: Even though you did happen to understand something over and above the colour, it is at least definite that the name in question conveys to you nothing as to exactly what that something is in which the colour is to be found.
>
> Student: That is quite definite. True, that name brings to mind a body or a surface, but this is simply because my experience has shown me that whiteness is usually found in such things: but of itself the name *white* signifies none of them, as was

[23] Aristotle imagines in the *Topics* (1:9) a scene where the linguistic constructions "a man," "an animal," and "a white colour" are all set before an individual: "For when a man is set before him [as a subject of a dialectical discussion] and he says that what is set there is a man or an animal, he states what it is and signifies a substance; but when a white colour is set before him and he says that what is set there is white or is a colour, he states what it is and signifies a quality. . . . Likewise, also, in other cases." Aristotle, "Topics," in Jonathan Barnes, ed., *The Complete Works of Aristotle* (Princeton, N.J.: Princeton University Press, 1984), p. 172.

> shown in the case of *literate* [*grammaticus*]. And now I'm waiting for you to show me what it does in fact signify.
>
> Tutor: Suppose you were to see a white horse and a black bull standing together, and someone gave the order, "Give it a thwack!", thereby meaning the horse, but without giving any indication as to which he intended: would you then know that he was referring to the horse?
>
> Student: No.
>
> Tutor: But suppose, while still in ignorance, you were to ask "Which?", and he were to reply, "[The] white!", would you then gather his reference?
>
> Student: I would gather from the name *white* that he meant the horse.
>
> Tutor: Thus for you the name *white* would signify the horse.
>
> Student: It certainly would.
>
> Tutor: And do you notice that this would be in a fashion other than that proper to the name *horse?*
>
> Student: I quite see that. I notice that even before I know the horse to be white, the name *horse* signifies to me the substance *horse* precisively, not obliquely.
>
> On the other hand, the name *white* signifies the substance *horse* not precisively, but only obliquely, that is, thanks to my being aware that the horse is white.
>
> Now the name *white* is equisignificant with the phrase *having whiteness;* similarly, the precise effect of this phrase is to bring to my mind the understanding of whiteness, but not of the thing which has the whiteness, so that the word *white* has the same effect.
>
> However, because I know, otherwise than by means of the name *white*—by sight, for example—that the whiteness is in the horse, when whiteness has been thus conveyed by means of that word, I also gather the reference to the horse because I know that the whiteness is in the horse.[24]

Although simplified for classroom use, Anselm's understanding of the basic nature of paronyms is quite similar to Aristotle's: because a paronym is the name for an accidental property of some otherwise unknown

[24] Desmond P. Henry, ed. and trans. *The* De Grammatico *of St. Anselm: The Theory of Paronymy* (Notre Dame, Ind.: University of Notre Dame Press, 1964), pp. 67–69. We need here to note the obvious: in Modern English the adjectival qualities "white" and "black" have also become full substantives.

thing, it carries at best only a minimal amount of information concerning the nature of the thing itself. Anselm emphasizes that what is primarily at issue in the study of paronyms is the different signifying powers of morphologically related words, such as "white" (*albus*), "white thing" (*album*), "whiteness" (*albetudo*), as well as "white man" (*homo albus*) or "white horse" (*equus albus*). But unlike Aristotle, Anselm shows no interest in suggesting that a categorical *nomen* names a certain subject whose essence, or being, rests *inside* the symbolic order of language.[25] Instead, in a somewhat reductive fashion he illustrates how a categorical *nomen* such as "white horse" directly indicates an object that actually exists in reality. All the same, by collapsing *essentia* into *substantia,* by bringing a real horse into the regime of linguistic signs, Anselm succeeds in clarifying a feature of nominal signification that remains somewhat elided in Aristotle. A concrete *nomen* (a noun, that is, working on the discrete level of supposition) is understood to signify in two interrelated directions rather than one: it gestures first toward its meaning (*significatum*), and then points through its meaning toward its empirical referent (*designatum*). Thus the noun "horse" points toward the general idea of horse (its universal connotation, or "type") as well as toward an individual horse (its particular denotation). What makes "white," as a paronym, a peculiar *nomen* in this regard is that it points successfully only toward the idea of whiteness, while failing to point in the direction of a particular white something-or-other. Is it therefore ever possible to compensate for the inadequate referential and individuating powers of the paronym? Anselm's implicit answer arrives via the paralinguistic sign: if the speaking subject were able to *point* in the direction of the intended object, or at the very least have that intended object brought from behind the building's wall and into full view, then the identity of the thing his paronym fails to name will finally be revealed.

Perhaps the most striking parallel between Anselm's primer and Chaucer's poem concerns their shared interest in the *méconnaissance* of the paronym's clueless interpreter.[26] Anselm's student is unable to ascertain "white"'s referrent because there is an actual wall between verbal sign

[25] That all of Aristotle's categories are exclusively *linguistic* categories has been clearly shown by L. M. de Rijk in his six *Vivarium* articles entitled "On Ancient and Mediaeval Semantics and Metaphysics" published between 1977 and 1982; see especially de Rijk, "On Ancient and Mediaeval Semantics (3)," *Vivarium* 18 (1980): 1–62.

[26] To my knowledge the only study to discuss the philosophical importance of "white" in *The Book of the Duchess* is Lynch's "*The Book of the Duchess* as a Philosophical Vision." Lynch briefly shows how "white" was a key term in Ockhamist epistemology; she does not, however, address "white"'s paronymic inheritance.

and physical object. In Chaucer's elegy it is suddenly the reader (and not simply the narrator) who is incapable of moving from verbal sign to empirical reality. Unless that reader somehow already "knows," the word "white" locates no discernible *designatum* beyond the wall of the poem's linguistic discourse. Despite the possibility that the innocent reader might be able to intuit the presence of proper names hidden in the elegy's final lines, there is in fact no word within the poem's discursive system which is *intrinsically* capable of revealing the identity of the elegy's referent.

The problems posed by "white" are similar in certain ways to the indexical and individuating problems of "fers": both fail to identify the object they are meant to designate. In their particular failures, however, they are different. The paronym "white" is a word whose powers of designation are overly generalized, whereas the homonym "fers" is actually two words, each with a different meaning and a different referent, thus creating confusion on the level of both *significatum* and *designatum.* Perhaps if the Black Knight had remembered to bring his chess set into the bosky dell he could have pointed toward his fers at the crucial moment; but even with fers in hand he would still have had to explicate its meaning, the piece itself being nothing but a conventionalized material sign. Chaucer's chess analogy thus gestures in several theoretical directions at once, reminding the reader that the primary achievement of language is precisely its ability in most circumstances to conjure forth images of things which are *not* immediately present to the senses.

The semantic problems posed by "white" and "fers" are also, to a certain degree, similar to the indexical and individuating problems of the pronoun "I." Enjoying but a small amount of intrinsic meaning, "I" is a nominal that appears to be in urgent need of an absolute referent. But the presence of that referent is apparently no guarantee of the pronoun's successful connection with reality. As we have seen, just as the Black Knight's personal utterance is indistinguishable from a formal lament, in certain cases the determination of the identity of "I" appears to be beyond both the speaker's and the auditor's control. Even were the Black Knight to have pointed with his finger toward himself as he uttered his grief-stricken words, the referent of his enunciated "I" might still have remained ambiguous. Furthermore, "I" as a signifier in Chaucer's elegy is made even more complex by the fact that the Black Knight's "I" is actually spoken by the voice of another, the "I" which enunciates the entire poem.

In contrast to my insistence on the problematic nature of these three little words, editors and other readers have generally assumed the opposite: when the Black Knight says "I," that word definitely points to himself; when the Black Knight says "fers," that word certainly points to his queen; and when the Black Knight says "white," that word surely points to Blanche. My major purpose in this section has been to deconstruct these nearly universal assumptions and to suggest that, in light of the preeminence of logical study in England throughout the fourteenth century, Chaucer's educated contemporaries would have recognized in these key words an instantiation of a variety of sophisticated debates concerning the nature of *nomina* and the significance of these signs within their broader linguistic environment. Accordingly, the next section opens with a discussion of some important late medieval studies of the semantic status of "white," the paronym's placement among morphologically related words, and its degree of "attributive being." While providing a useful critical vocabulary, these treatises also raise questions concerning the naming powers of *all* words and the ontology of *all* linguistic signs. The most fundamental questions addressed in each study concern the interplay among the three elements of Aristotle's semiotic triangle: *vox, conceptus,* and *res.* That is, is there anything in a word, either its sound or its conventional meaning, that connects it "naturally," "categorically," or "non-arbitrarily" to the thing it is assumed to signify? And if there is nothing actually *in* the word's sound or *in* its meaning that is actually also *in* the thing, how can words link us with reality and bring us knowledge of the world, either in the present or in the past? These problems, some raised only obliquely and "paronymically" in the Middle Ages, are addressed more directly and skeptically in the twentieth century, by Saussure and Žižek, among others. Taken as a whole, these medieval and modern studies reveal the extraordinary complexity of the metalinguistic program of *The Book of the Duchess.* That is, they illustrate how it is that "I," "fers," and "white," rather than being rogue signs in an otherwise seemingly stable field of signifiers, are actually symptoms of the elegy's overall linguistic malaise. They underscore how the difficulties in comprehension provoked by these problem words stand in for a more general *méconnaissance,* our less-than-full understanding of the meaning of all signs. Finally, they lead toward the poem's interior, which we enter by undertaking a sustained analysis of the elegy's "I" and the absence this "I" passionately desires yet nevertheless is unable to name.

II: Philosophies of the Sign

The thirteenth-century philosopher Duns Scotus in his treatise *Ordinatio* defines the relationship of the spoken word (*vox*) to its referenced object (*res*) as a sign that recalls the signified idea (*conceptus*): *vox est signum rememorativum respectu conceptus.*[27] For Scotus, as for all medieval logicians, the human *vox* is a conventional *signum* whose meaning depends on its original *impositio,* a once-upon-a-time "baptismal" act from which a word's *significatio* emerged. Where Scotus distinguishes himself from many of his peers is in insisting that both a word's *impositio* and its *significatio* presuppose a "memory" of the reasons that determined the original choice of the name. This memory proceeds along two different routes: first, the intellect has an "etymological" knowledge of why the word had been originally selected; second, it has an "extensionalist" knowledge of the properties of the thing that the word names. The former kind of knowledge honors the Aristotelian precept that every *vox* is an immediate sign of its *significatio;* the latter kind supports Scotus's fairly radical, nomenclaturist, notion that a *vox* also signifies its *res* directly. But how then is the human intellect capable of knowing (retroactively, so to speak) the signifying code? And why is it actually necessary to know this code if *vox* somehow is able to refer directly to *res?*

Scotus addresses these questions via a capacious definition of "universal," wherein a universal is seen as a product of the intellect as well as being grounded in reality. Universals for Scotus are not only *in intellectu* (as products of abstraction) but they are equally *in re* (as grounds of our knowledge-in-objects). By identifying the meaning of words as things-that-are-understandable, as *res ut intelligitur,* Scotus is able to show how individual things can be signified by singular terms or by proper names as well as be understood through intuitive cognition. Likewise, he is able to argue that the *impositio* object and the *significatio* object coincide in such a way that the individually named object is a concrete universal, a thing whose name, as Costatino Marmo explains, is "assumed as a *type* in virtue of the characteristics it shares with individuals which are *tokens* of the same type."[28] In order to illustrate his understanding of the semiotic triangle of *vox-conceptus, vox-res,* and *conceptus-res* as it relates to the

[27] On Scotus, see Costantino Marmo, "Ontology and Semantics in the Logic of Duns Scotus," in Umberto Eco and Costantino Marmo, eds., *On the Medieval Theory of Signs* (Amsterdam: John Benjamins, 1989), pp. 143–93.

[28] Ibid., p. 164.

difference between concrete and abstract terms, Scotus uses paronymy as an all-purpose case study. Returning to Aristotle's paronym *albus,* Scotus argues (contra Aristotle) that only by reference to ontology is it possible to distinguish concrete terms and abstract terms or substance names and accidental names. He therefore outlines a continuum of attributive being using "white" as the best example. Among substance terms, there is only one type of abstract term (such as *humanitas*). Among accidental terms, however, there are two kinds of abstract as well as two kinds of concrete *nomina. Album* (white thing) is the only "pure concrete" term, as it signifies the quality connoting its inherence in a *substratum* (i.e., an individual thing). *Albedo* (being white) is both the "first abstract" term and the "second concrete," since it "signifies the quality of whiteness while connoting its *supposita.*"[29] The "pure abstract term" is *quiditas albedinis. Albedineitas,* in turn, is the form signified by all these terms, the "common nature of whiteness in its absoluteness."[30] From this absolute abstract term, *albedineitas,* derives the first denominative, *albedo.* And finally, coming full circle, deriving from *albedo* is *album* (white thing), which "signifies the formality of whiteness and its exemplifications, connoting their inherence in *substrata.*"[31]

Scotus's thirteenth-century continuum of attributive being helps situate Chaucer's "white" within a highly nuanced ontology. Scotus has developed those grammatical endings that for Aristotle had simply been markers of morphological difference into indicators of "the ontological distinction between a formality in its absoluteness and its contraction or accidental inherence."[32] These formalities Scotus arranges according to a hierarchical ladder or tree, whereby the greatest amount of "ontological density" subsists on the level of the concrete individual (*album*) and the greatest amount of essential formality, and thus "communicability," is found at the level of the greatest abstraction (*albedineitas*). What matters most here is that all of these accidental forms enjoy a measurable degree of being. Admittedly, there remains for Scotus a real distinction between absolute and relative accidents: in the strictest sense of the term, only substances for Scotus are real (*res*), but in a slightly broader sense, each and every form of the accident "white" is an *ens reale et absolutum.* Thus Chaucer's "white," even if it did not claim to be an absolute

[29] Ibid., p. 166.
[30] Ibid.
[31] Ibid.
[32] Ibid.

name, would nevertheless in a Scotist ontology be the name of some being rather than the name of nothing. Since Scotus believes that every *vox* is a *res ut intelligitur* and that every *res* by definition is not *nihil,* it follows that every possible form of accidental being, including *albus,* is necessarily something and "not nothing."

In his early-fourteenth-century treatise the *Summa logicae,* William Ockham approaches the issue of "white" 's ontological status from a different vantage point.[33] In a general way he agrees with Scotus that there are two kinds of terms in language: all abstract terms are "absolute" terms and all concrete terms are "connotative" terms. An absolute term enjoys a one-to-one relationship with the thing it signifies; in fact this privileged mode of unmediated nomination is close to what Saul Kripke, centuries later, calls a "rigid designator." In accordance with the basic tenets of fourteenth-century nominalism, Ockham maintains that every absolute term is an abstraction that realizes its ontological being only through individuation in particulars: thus the abstraction "man" is conceptually derived from our experience of individual men, and as an absolute *nomen* it signifies each and every individual man. But the signifying process of a concrete or "connotative" term is considerably more difficult for Ockham to define. Using "white" as his principal example, Ockham argues that the accidental term "white" signifies in at least two different ways.[34] It can signify via "primary signification" just the way an absolute term does: like "man" for individual men, "white" signifies (and thus "supposits" for) this and that and every other white something-or-other. However, via "secondary signification," it is also able to signify individual and inherent "whitenesses."

As several of his commentators have shown, Ockham's definition of the duplex signifying powers of "white" runs into considerable problems. It is obviously conceptually challenging to comprehend the existence of "individual whitenesses." But equally challenging is comprehending how the connotative term "white" can enjoy primary signifying powers no different from the signifying powers of an absolute name. In the *Summae logicae,* Ockham explains that the nominal definition of white (i.e., *album* in the nominative case) is "something [*aliquid*] having

[33] William Ockham, *Ockham's Theory of Terms: Part One of the* Summae logicae, trans. and ed. Michael J. Loux (Notre Dame: University of Notre Dame Press, 1974).

[34] Michael J. Loux argues that "white" for Ockham actually signifies in three distinctly different ways: "generally," "primarily," and "secondarily." See "The Ontology of William Ockham," in ibid., pp. 6–7.

whiteness."[35] But this *aliquid,* as John Boler has explained, is an "ambiguous" choice that "makes it hard to spell out just what the 'primary signification' of the term 'white' is."[36] What is this *aliquid?* And why shouldn't the *aliquid* that "white" signifies instead be a *res* or *corpus?* "It is a natural reading," writes Boler, "to identify the primary signification of 'white' as 'white things' (or 'bodies that happen to be white')," but unless we were to blur Ockham's basic distinction between absolute and concrete, it simply "won't do to equate the primary signification of 'white' with the signification of the absolute term 'body' in its explication."[37]

Thus the refinements Ockham adds to Scotus's analysis of attributive being do not succeed in granting "white" a status entirely equivalent to the ontology of a thing, or a body, or a substance. Nevertheless, it is clear that Ockham is committed to ameliorating the naming powers of "white" and to moving the term further inside the set of objectively existing entities. The discretely different terms Ockham uses to distinguish ontological states (such as "object," "being," "thing," and "existence") are admittedly sometimes difficult to decode. For example, Ockham maintains that a *fictum* such as the unicorn is an "object" that has "existence" even though it is an "unreal entity," because every idea represented in language has to be about something rather than nothing: "just as it is impossible that there should be a vision and nothing be seen," Ockham reasons, "or that there should be a desire and nothing desired, so also it is impossible that there should be a cognition and nothing be cognized by that cognition."[38] How then might an Ockhamist reading of *The Book of the Duchess* cast light on the cognizable status of Chaucer's "white"? First, the fact that "white" necessarily signifies innumerable *significata* may assist in the communicability of "white"'s identity to more, rather than fewer, readers: because the property of whiteness is shared by analogy with all white things, the individual reader who has not cognized this individual "white" will nevertheless participate in an oblique knowledge of its referent.[39] Second, even if she were a *fictum* of the imagination and thus an "unreal entity," Chaucer's "white" would

[35] Ibid., p. 70.

[36] John Boler, "Accidents in Ockham's Ontological Project," *Franciscan Studies* 54 (1997): 85, n. 20.

[37] Ibid., pp. 86–87.

[38] Qtd. by Marilyn Adams, "Ockham's Nominalism and Unreal Entities," *Philosophical Review* 86 (1977): 147, n. 12.

[39] See Deborah Brown, "The Puzzle of Names in Theory of Ockham's Mental Language," *Review of Metaphysics* 50 (1996): 79–99.

still have the status of an "object," because the ideational power of her concrete/abstract name summons the *conceptus* of "white" into existence. Finally, "white"'s imperfect degree of "ontological density" is a partial quality that helps to catalyze, both in Ockham's philosophy and in Chaucer's elegy, a yearning for the absolute in signification—a desire for a body that, once cognized, will become united with the name of its accidental *inherent.*

The late medieval proclivity toward upgrading the status of accidental being reaches its apex in the work of Jean Buridan. In his *Quaestiones,* a commentary on Aristotle's *Metaphysics,* the mid-fourteenth-century French philosopher advances no fewer than eight arguments in support of the idea that "white" has just as proper a title to being called a "being" as any substance. Buridan bases his argument initially on a fundamental article of Catholic belief: Christians are able to know by faith that accidents are separable from their substrates because the whiteness of the eucharistic bread remains in existence after the act of transubstantiation. The remainder of Buridan's commentary is a sequence of logical arguments designed to prove that "an accident 'has being' (or 'is truly an *ens*') just by itself, independently of its actual inherence in some substance."[40] To validate his position, Buridan finds he must redefine the traditional Aristotelian distinctions between *album, albedo,* and *esse album.* Buridan's general aim is to uphold Aristotle's discriminations between *album* and *albedo* while rejecting Aristotle's willingness to equate *esse album* and *albedo.* "What exactly does *esse album* (being white) mean?" Buridan asks. He agrees that *esse album* formally implies that some thing is actually white (according to Aristotle, *esse album* should be read as "that-*something*-is-white").[41] But he rejects Aristotle's assertion that *albedo* (whiteness) also requires a substrate to exist (although in the natural order of things, it always *de facto* inheres in something). Whereas Aristotle had been ready to conflate the semantic behaviors of *album* and *albedo,* Buridan's understanding of *album* as a concrete term and *albedo* as an abstract term helps him determine that the concrete term *album* only "supposits for the subject that is white" while it "connotes the whiteness inhering in the subject."[42] Thus, by the end of his commentary on Aristotle's *Metaphysics,*

[40] L. M. de Rijk, "On Buridan's View of Accidental Being," in E. P. Bos and H. A. Krop, eds., *John Buridan: A Master of Arts; Some Aspects of His Philosophy* (Nijmegen: Ingenium, 1993), p. 48.

[41] Ibid., p. 45.

[42] Ibid., p. 46.

Buridan is certain he has demonstrated how accidents *can* exist in their own right, independently of any subject-substrate, although he grants that he would not have been able to arrive at a logical understanding of this metaphysical truth without the assistance of his faith.

This selective representation of late medieval ideas concerning the issue of attributive being indicates "white"'s extremely rich and rigorous intellectual environment: the logico-linguistic ramifications of "whiteness," the issue of paronymy, and the nature of accidental being are matters to be found everywhere in lae medieval philosophy. In the opinion of the premier authority on these issues, L. M. de Rijk, the general "upgrading of 'accidental being'" is without question one of "the most striking characteristics of late medieval metaphysics."[43] In my view, therefore, as soon as the Black Knight discloses his beloved lady's name, for a well-educated contingent of Chaucer's readers a host of refined interrogatives would likely have tumbled forth. What is the nature of her being? How does her name manage to grant her individuation? Is her *nomen* an abstract term, an absolute term, a connotative term, a concrete term? Can she exist outside the body in which her name suggests she inheres? How does she relate to "whiteness"? How does she relate to "being white"? And what does her being a "being" actually mean? Furthermore, how does one "cognize" a white object? How does one "cognize" a past object that no longer exists? And finally, how can any word used within a figurative discourse lead us to an accurate knowledge of the world, either in its present state or in the past? These questions, explored by philosophers in Chaucer's intellectual environment, have also been fully addressed, albeit within different cultural paradigms, by twentieth-century thinkers. Since it is the work of these intellectuals that directly informs our own linguistic training and literary-critical practice, I turn in the remainder of this section to certain modern language theories that broaden and deepen our understanding of Chaucer's metalinguistic program.

Often considered the single most influential linguistic study composed in the twentieth century, Ferdinand de Saussure's *Course in General Linguistics* is probably best known for its emphasis on the arbitrary nature of all linguistic signs. Saussure begins his study by attacking the nomenclaturist assumption that language is a straightforward naming-process wherein words are linked up with preexisting things and/or

[43] Ibid., p. 41.

ideas: "We might conceive of an act by which, at a given moment, names were assigned to things and a contract was formed between concepts and sound-images; but such an act has never been recorded. The notion that things might have happened like that was prompted by our acute awareness of the arbitrary nature of the sign."[44] Instead, as is well known, Saussure argues that the linguistic sign is "a double entity" that unites "not a thing and a name, but a concept and a sound-image."[45] The "concept" within the sign Saussure chooses to call the "signified," and the "sound-image" (the mental reception of the sound and not the sound itself) he names the "signifier." These two elements are "intimately united"; in the "psychological entity" of the sign, "each recalls the other."[46] The "intimate unification" of signifier and signified Saussure illustrates by the use of diagrams, such as of the sign *equus*[47]:

For all its immeasurable influence, there are nevertheless certain problems with Saussure's definition of the linguistic sign. Uninterested in semantics (for him, every variety of word is equally a "sign"), Saussure claims to be equally uninterested in the "reality question," the relationship of signs to "things-in-themselves." But as many of his critics point out, in the course of his analysis there is a telling slippage between ideas and things, between the signified conceived as a concept and the signified conceived as a referenced object. Saussure's conflation of *vox*, *conceptus*

[44] Ferdinand de Saussure, *Course in General Linguistics,* trans. Wade Baskin (New York: McGraw-Hill, 1966), p. 71.

[45] Ibid., pp. 65, 66.

[46] Ibid., pp. 66, 67.

[47] Ibid., pp. 65–67. I have made two modifications to the original, correcting "equos" to "equus" (presuming Saussure would prefer the nominative case) and adding the surrounding circle and arrows, which I borrow from Saussure's tree illustration.

and *res* is visible in the diagrammatic horse itself, wich Saussure significantly places above rather than below the word *equus.* Strikingly reminiscent of Anselm's iconic *equus* in *De Grammatico,* this graphic image presumes a privileged, *a priori* relationship between an already existing idea and an equivalent thing existing in an already "divided-up" reality. Thus, as Vicky Kirby notes, by presuming that the signified element of the sign has direct "recourse to the substance of reality," Saussure "is ironically allowing a major nomenclaturist error to return and serve as a foundation for his own semiological system."[48]

A closely related problem is contained in that all-important line Saussure draws between "concept" and "sound-image." For Saussure, this line (supported by the two complementary arrows) indicates how each of the two parts of the sign "recalls" the other. However, since Saussure insists that the entire sign is *arbitrary,* one must ask: What is it that makes the "recollection" between the sign's two inner parts anything *less* than arbitrary? It would appear that Saussure is torn between two equally powerful linguistic ideologies. He maintains that the verbal sign is arbitrarily (or conventionally) blocked off from any connecting link with signifiable reality. On the other hand, he believes that within the sign itself there is a co-presence of meaning shared by both parts: a certain immanent X in the signifier "recalls" a Y in the signified, and a certain immanent Y in the signified "recalls" an X in the signifier. However, as Kirby astutely notes, Saussure's telling use of the word "recalls" concessively acknowledges "that the signifier and signified are indeed differentiated both spatially and temporally."[49] Thus, the all-powerful "connecting" bar by which Saussure means to "unite" signifier and signified reveals itself to be a sign, both in space and in time, of a potential linguistic *impasse.* Saussure's inconsistent interpretation of the verbal sign, I would suggest, is homologous to the *nomen*/paronym dialectic at work in *The Book of the Duchess.* The Black Knight ardently believes there exists in the best of names an essence shared by signifier and signified alike, and that, via a kind of baptismal speech-act performed some time in the past, the "intension" of the name is now married to the "extensional" attributes in the one so named. However, simply by invoking

[48] Vicky Kirby, *Telling Flesh: The Substance of the Corporeal* (New York: Routledge, 1997), p. 17.
[49] Ibid., p. 11.

the paronym "white," the Black Knight conjures up the Anselmian wall and the linguistic *impasse* that was understood to separate at least this kind of verbal sign from the object it is assumed to represent.

Saussure's second major contribution to modern linguistics is his insistence that language is a synchronic, complete and rule-bound system whose discrete units find meaning solely in terms of their difference from all other units. This means that a sign's "sound-image" comes into phonemic being only by dint of that requisite "negative" space of silence between one potentially meaningful sound and the next; similarly, a sign's "content" is determined not by some internal or essentialized meaning, but only by its difference from the various meanings in contention among all the other signifieds in the language. Thus Saussure sees language as an interplay among lexical units which constantly shift about both in relation to their individual meanings and in their relation to each other. As Saussure states, the "most fruitful comparison" to this complex interplay of signs is the game of chess, where the pieces have no significance until they become part of the game. "Take a knight, for instance," Saussure writes. "By itself is it an element in the game? Certainly not . . . ; it becomes a real, concrete element only when endowed with value and wedded to it. Suppose that the piece happens to be destroyed or lost during a game. Can it be replaced by an equivalent piece? Certainly."[50] Yet for all this movement among arbitrarily determined signs, Saussure insists that at any given moment the entirety of language is in a state of orderly "equilibrium": "there is no general rummage."[51]

Saussure contends that there is nevertheless one major difference between chess and language: whereas a chessplayer *intends* "to exert an action on the system," changes in language are effected "spontaneously and fortuitously." Therefore, in order to make chess perfectly analogous to language, "we would have to imagine an unconscious or unintelligent player."[52] What he means here is that as native speakers we have already submitted to the abstraction called language (*langue*), and even though we are granted a modicum of free choice in the way we fashion our indi-

[50] Saussure, *Course,* pp. 153–54. Ludwig Wittgenstein makes an almost identical point, using the king of chess rather than the knight as his example; see *Philosophical Investigations,* 3d ed., trans. G. E. Anscombe (Englewood Cliffs, N.J.: Prentice Hall, 1958), Passage 31, p. 15. For an extensive analysis of the chess-game analogy as employed by both Saussure and Wittgenstein, see Roy Harris, *Language, Saussure and Wittgenstein: How to Play Games with Words* (London: Routledge, 1988).

[51] Saussure, *Course,* p. 88.

[52] Ibid., p. 89.

vidual *paroles,* we can do so only according to the pre-established rules of the game. But Saussure's memorable image of the unconscious or unintelligent player also refers to the indecipherable cause of linguistic changes *over time.* Because the diachronic movement of language is an irrational phenomenon, historical linguistics can tell us nothing about the present state of a language. This means, in turn, that the present state of a language is radically unrelated to its state in the past. Saussure's uncompromising (some have said "draconian"[53]) position on the synchronicity of all signification strongly implies that language, trapped as it is in the absolute present, is incapable of recapturing any significance that was once constituted in the past.

Saussure's exploration of the linguistic ramifications of the game of chess provides further assistance in examining the symptomatic role of "fers" in Middle English and in Chaucer's poem. Having lost its Arabic significance, "fers" conventionally takes on more than one meaning in Europe. But no matter what chess nomenclature it belonged to, "fers" acquires significance only in relation to all the other signifiers in that system. Further, in the version Chaucer probably knew best, the fers does not "exist" at the game's beginning but rather only comes into being in the course of the game in the guise of a promoted pawn. What these analogies illustrate is that, precisely because of its arbitrariness and its mobility, "fers" is an absolutely typical linguistic sign: both parts of the sign, signifier and signified, find their semiotic location within a rule-governed system of nomenclature and even then only in relation to the "negative" spaces between those momentarily fixed positions assumed by other signs moving about on the board.

If there were to be any possible exception to Saussure's generalizations about the linguistic sign, it would have to be that peculiar *nomen* that Saussure chooses not to address: the proper name. Surely the proper name enjoys unusual powers in its uncanny ability to identify its unique referent. And surely—especially in the case of "descriptive" proper names such as "good fair white"—those qualities inhering in the name constitute or recollect the identity of the named individual. Aristotle was absolutely certain about the categorical substantiality of the proper name (recall his confident use of the name "Callias"), and such certainty might well be expected to have held fast throughout the Middle Ages. But in point of fact disagreements concerning the proper name

[53] This is Roy Harris's assessment in *Language, Saussure and Wittgenstein,* p. 87.

abounded. Ockham and Peter of Spain were what we would now call anti-descriptive referentialists (for them there is no descriptive "meaning" in a proper name); Boethius and Roger Bacon granted a very minimal *significatio* to the proper name; while Anselm, Abelard and William of Sherwood were all ardent descriptivists (believing there *are* descriptive attributes subsisting in the proper name).[54] One of the fullest analyses was Buridan's. In his discussion of "complex singular referring expressions" and "vague singular referring expressions" (proper names, demonstratives, pronouns, etc.), Buridan notes that it is possible for a proper name to name anything and everything imaginable (human, animal, vegetable, inanimate)—one could even impose a proper name on an accident by naming this "whiteness" "Robert."[55] In the twentieth century, these medieval disagreements become, if anything, even more heated and complex so that presently the debate over proper names between the descriptivist camp and the anti-descriptivist camp would seem absolutely resistant to any kind of synthetic resolution. It is therefore remarkable to discover an ambitious thesis recently advanced by Slavoj Žižek in *The Sublime Object of Ideology* that attempts a full deconstruction of both positions, descriptivist and anti-descriptivist, by the ingenious integration of the psychological with the philosophical analysis of nominal signs. Žižek's theoretical breakthrough requires our attention because Chaucer in *The Book of the Duchess* appears to have fully imagined an analogous breakthrough six centuries earlier.

In "Proper Names," the descriptivist John Searle proposes that, as with every common or concrete noun, every proper name is "a kind of shorthand description" associated with a more or less fixed set of attributes that determine, if only indirectly, what object is designated by that name.[56] Searle believes it is essential that the "meaning" of a proper name contain some of the attributes belonging to the object so named, or else the name is not naming anything at all. He supports his belief by describing an unusual "primitive tribe": in this community everyone

[54] See Mauricio Beauchot, "La Semantica de los Nombres Propios en la Filosophia Medieval," *Analisis Filosofico* 10 (1990): 69–88.

[55] Peter O. King, "Jean Buridan," in Jorge J. E. Gracia, ed., *Individuation in Scholasticism: The Later Middle Ages and the Counter Reformation, 1150–1650* (Albany: SUNY Press, 1994), p. 426. See also Jorge J. E. Gracia, *Introduction to the Problem of Individuation in the Early Middle Ages* (Washington, D.C.: Catholic University of America Press, 1983), p. 63, n. 79.

[56] John Searle, "Proper Names," rptd. in A. P. Martinich, ed., *The Philosophy of Language,* 3d ed. (New York: Oxford University Press, 1996), p. 251.

knows everybody else; every feature of their world is learned by ostension; newborns are baptised in ceremonies attended by every member; and "there is a strict taboo in this tribe against speaking of the dead, so that no one's name is ever mentioned after his death."[57] The significance of this tribe, Searle explains, is two-fold: first, "[e]very use of the name in this tribe . . . satisfies the descriptivist claim that there is an Intentional content associating the name with the object"; and, second, "this tribe has an institution of proper names used for reference in exactly the same way that our names are used for reference."[58]

In *Naming and Necessity,* the anti-descriptivist Saul Kripke argues the validity of precisely the opposite position. A proper name, he believes, has absolutely no descriptive meaning and no intentional content whatsoever. At some moment in time the meaningless name is simply attached to a thing through an ostensive act of "initial baptism,"[59] and that name serves thereafter as a "rigid designator"[60] of the identity of its fixed referent.[61] In fact, Kripke makes the powerful claim that proper names are no different from all other nouns. *All* nouns and pronouns are non-descriptive denoters of their referents because there is absolutely

[57] John Searle, "Proper Names and Intentionality," rptd. in ibid., p. 311.

[58] Ibid.

[59] Saul Kripke, "Naming and Necessity," rptd. in ibid., p. 266.

[60] Ibid., p. 258.

[61] The anti-descriptivist *locus classicus* is John Stuart Mill's study. In his landmark nineteenth-century treatise *Systems of Logic,* Mill maintains that certain words are "connotative": words like "white," "long," and "virtuous" are all "connotative" terms because they denote their subject and imply an attribute. But other, "nonconnotative" terms signify their subject only and do not imply any attributes of that subject. The proper name is a prime example of this kind of signifying, nondescriptive name. Even if it may originally have been intended to carry "descriptive" significance, Mill believes, a proper name is nothing but "an unmeaning mark which we connect in our minds with the idea of the object," and this "idea" must always be understood to be *in the object,* and never *in the name:*

> [I]t is no part of the signification of the word John that the father of the person so called bore the same name, nor even of the word Dartmouth to be situated at the mouth of the Dart. If sand should choke up the mouth of the river or an earthquake change its course and remove it to a distance from the town, the name of the town would not necessarily be changed. . . . Proper names are attached to the objects themselves and are not dependent on the continuance of any attribute of the object.

Thus Mill would utterly disagree with the Black Knight concerning the significance of the proper name "white": precisely because it is a proper name, "white" is an "unmeaning mark"; but had it been an adjective and not a proper name, "white" would ironically have been a fully connotative term. Mill, *Systems of Logic,* rptd. in ibid., pp. 247, 246.

nothing in the name that is inherent in the object, just as there is absolutely nothing in the object that is inherent in the name.[62] Thus the essential/substantial relationship between every name and every thing-so-named is absolutely arbitrary. Nevertheless, the object having once been "baptised" ("gold" and "unicorn" are his favorite examples), Kripke admits there must be something—either in the name, the thing, or the act of naming itself—which grants the name the power to denote that object at all times and in every possible world.[63] This essential something remains in place even when, as so often happens, that cluster of attributes imagined initially to determine the name's "meaning" were to change beyond all recognition. Yet precisely how the transmission of this "something" over space and time actually works remains (at least for Kripke's critics) an absolute mystery.

At this juncture in the debate Žižek intervenes. He begins by asking a simple question: How is it possible to overlook the "libidinal contents" at work in each theory? Searle's fantasy is transparent. Even though his imaginary primitive tribe lives in a utopian world where absence, lack, and death are unnameable, Searle wishes to believe that their "institution of proper names" is no different from our own. And even though Kripke's argument may be the more persuasive of the two (Žižek finds it so), there remains a fundamentally "libidinal" desire at work in Kripke's theory as well. What precisely is it that determines the identity of the Kripkean object "beyond the ever-changing cluster of descriptive features"?[64] How can a name denote the same object in all counterfactual situations? What exactly is *in* the object that serves as the "objective correlative" to the "rigid designator" which is its name? According to Žižek, Kripke's unnameable "something" *in* the object has to be recognized for what it actually is. And what it is is "nothing."

Unpacking the significance of this "nothing" is Žižek's central undertaking. The basic strategy of his argument addresses the most sacrosanct rule of Western logic, the law of non-contradiction. The list of contradictory, mutually exclusive philosophical categories is seemingly

[62] Kripke, "Naming and Necessity," p. 260. Derrida deconstructs the privileged category of the "*so-called* proper name" by contending that the proper name is "always already common" by virtue of its being named as that which belongs to the category "proper." See Derrida, *Of Grammatology,* pp. lxxxiii, 109.

[63] Saul Kripke, "A Puzzle About Belief," rptd. in Martinich, *Philosophy of Language,* pp. 382–410.

[64] Slavoj Žižek, *The Sublime Object of Ideology* (London: Verso, 1989), p. 94.

inexhaustible, but includes name vs. thing, subject vs. object, essence vs. substance, intension vs. extension, signifier vs. signified, paronym vs. proper name, descriptor vs. rigid designator, meaning vs. ostension, Being vs. being, Being vs. Nothingness. Žižek quite simply refuses to carry on with these binaries, arguing that there is actually a split on each side of the dialectic itself—a fissure both in the domain of the subject and in the domain of the object. The nature of this fissure, and the theorizing that supports its plausibility, Žižek extrapolates from the work of Jacques Lacan: "[T]he most radical dimension of Lacanian theory lies not in recognizing" that the "subject is divided, crossed-out, identical to a lack in a signifying chain . . . but in realizing that . . . the symbolic order itself, is also *barré,* crossed-out, by a fundamental impossibility, structured around an impossible/traumatic kernel, around a central lack."[65] There is something in the object itself, in other words, which resists being named, a "kernel of the real" that resists all symbolic representation. This kernel, Žižek insists, does not in fact exist. It is the asymbolizable "Thing," the unattainable X, the object-cause of our desire to which Lacan gives the name *l'objet petit a.* Using a mixture of Lacanian and Kripkean terminology, Žižek explains that "the Real is the rock upon which every attempt at symbolization stumbles, the hard core which remains the same in all possible worlds (symbolic universes); but at the same time its status is thoroughly precarious; it is something that persists only as failed, missed, in a shadow, and dissolves itself as soon as we try to grasp it in its positive nature."[66] Where then is this "impossible/traumatic" kernel of the object's identity to be found? Paradoxically, it is to be found nowhere else but in the signifying subject, in the subject's incompleteness, its own "lack-of-being." In Žižek's judgment, therefore, both descriptivism and anti-descriptivism miss the same crucial point, namely, the "radical contingency of naming"—the fact that naming *retroactively* constitutes the X in the thing itself. This X is the "sublime object" which exists only (if it exists anywhere) in the ego of the riven subject. It is only by means of the very failure of naming the essence of the object that "we can have a presentiment of the true dimension of the Thing."[67]

No matter at what point in history one intervenes, therefore, it is

[65] Ibid., p. 122.
[66] Ibid., p. 169.
[67] Ibid., p. 203.

obvious that the nature of a sign's relation to its meaning and to its referent is understood to be an extremely complicated affair. The philosophers surveyed in this section are generally assured that the relationship between *verbum* and *res* is purely conventional, or arbitrary. While acknowledging that a word's steady-state meaning would seem to depend on an original *impositio,* "the act of a mythical linguistic lawgiver which fixed correspondences between expression and things,"[68] most of the thinkers we have surveyed concede that this moment of verbal baptism is a supreme fiction. Medieval logicians like Scotus, for example, recognized that the "etymological" knowledge of the *imponens,* the original name-giver, could well have been imperfect in the first place.[69] Yet while recognizing these realities, the very same thinkers, even "scientists" of language such as Saussure, have a profound need to believe that the signifier is also (if only in part) a sign, meaning that the reality-effect of the referenced object is somehow contained in the sign's conceptual meaning.

We can now see that the linguistic problems foregrounded in *The Book of the Duchess* dramatize a tension between two equally powerful traditions in Western thought. On the one hand there is the all but insuperable persuasion that the conventions of language successfully connect verbal signs with the reality they signify. On the other hand, there is the recognition that at least with certain signs an in-place wall or bar renders a word's full representation of a thing impossible. The confusion, miscommunication, and *méconnaissance* created by the readerly experience of the collision of these two traditions constitute one of Chaucer's major heuristic purposes. But what makes the linguistic program of Chaucer's elegy remarkable to the extreme is its development of a second powerful site of signification which proves to be equally barricaded, riven, and resistant to explication. So far, we have focused on "white" as a sign that does not succeed in adequately representing an absent or lost *object.* But, following Žižek following Lacan, "white" is also a fully developed, albeit riven, sign of the desiring *subject.* The foundation of this idea is introduced by the Black Knight himself when he acknowledges that, well before he meets white and learns her name, "white" had pre-existed in his mind (lines 775–84; emphasis added):

[68] Marmo, "Ontology and Semantics," p. 160.
[69] Ibid.

"And this was longe, and many a yer
Or that myn herte was set owher,
That I dide thus, and nyste why;
I trowe hit cam me kyndely.
Paraunter I was therto most able,
As a whit wal or a table,
For hit ys redy to cacche and take
Al that men wil theryn make,
Whethir so men wil portreye or peynte,
Be the werkes never so queynte."

What is remarkable here is not only "white"'s inherence within an image of that very wall that traditionally represents the paronym's partial failure to signify,[70] but also "white"'s placement inside the human psyche itself. Equally striking is that this psychological wall apparently serves as some kind of universal *tabula rasa,* a blank canvas primed to "cacche and take" whatever curious colors and figures men may wish to project upon it. Whether this wall of whiteness is a site of the signified object or a barrier to the fulfilment of erotic desire, its functionality comes "kyndely" to all men—not only to the Black Knight but to the "I" in whose dream he appears. Therefore, in order to analyze the psycho-semantics of the elegy's subject, and to connect the poem's object-oriented linguistics with the "unconscious" language of its dream, we need to return to the third problem signifier highlighted by Chaucer. With extended reference to the work of Jacques Lacan, we can now enter *The Book of the Duchess* and begin tracing out the "semantic" needs and desires of its speaker, starting of course with his first word: "I."

III: The Signifying Subject

Georgio Agamben has claimed that the twentieth-century fascination with the dynamics of the signifier "I" grew out of medieval linguistic concerns with drawing distinctions between significance and reference:

[70] "White"'s inherence in a wall, however, is another standard example used in medieval philosophical textbooks; see Ockham, "On Inherence and Being In," in *Ockham's Theory of Terms,* pp. 112–13.

In its intuition of the complex nature of indication and its necessary reference to a linguistic dimension, medieval thought became aware of the problematic nature of the passage from *signifying* to *showing,* but does not manage to work it out. It was the task of modern linguistics to take the decisive step in this direction, but this was possible only because modern philosophy, from Descartes to Kant to Husserl, has been primarily a reflection on the status of the pronoun *I.*[71]

An important matter Agamben overlooks, however, is that the signifying status of the pronoun "I" was actually extensively explored in the Middle Ages, but these explorations were for the most part embedded in confessional, mystical, and literary works rather than philosophical texts. The supreme fiction of Dante's authenticating "I" in the *Commedia;*[72] the "dichotomous" "I" in the poetry of Machaut, Froissart, Deschamps, and Christine de Pizan;[73] the "radically unstable" "I" of Chaucer's dream-vision poems[74]: these are but a few instances of how the subject-position of "I" afforded medieval literary artists the opportunity to explore the social, psychological, and philosophical complexities of that most labile signifier of their own identities.

I want to argue in this section that *The Book of the Duchess* is in many ways a linguistic, literary, and psychological interrogation of the status, being, and meaning of the pronoun "I." "I" in this poem is not only a first-person singular nominal, but also the sign of a fissured subject whose incomplete identity is fashioned in large part by the incomplete identity of that sublime object which it desires. The only long Chaucerian poem whose very first word is "I," *The Book of the Duchess* invites interpretation as an individual quest undertaken by a subject whose primary knowledge is that he does not know himself. The elegy opens with an extended Proustian monologue where "I" confesses he comprehends

[71] Agamben, *Language and Death,* p. 23; as evidence of "the privileged status the pronoun has occupied in the history of medieval . . . thought" (p. 20) Agameben cites Priscian: "Therefore, if pronouns lack demonstraton or relation they are null and void, not because they change in appearance but because without demonstration or relation they posit nothing certain and determinate" (p. 22).

[72] See Jessica Levenstein, "The Pilgrim, the Poet, and the Cowgirl: Dante's Alter-Io in Purgatorio XXX–XXXI," *Dante Studies* 114 (1996): 189–208.

[73] See Catherine Attwood, *Dynamic Dichotomy: The Poetic "I" in Fourteenth- and Fifteenth-Century French Lyric Poetry* (Amsterdam: Rodopi, 1998).

[74] In *Chaucer's Narrators* (Cambridge: D. S. Brewer, 1985), David Lawton refers intermittently to the speaking subject of the dream visions as "radically unstable," an "open persona," an "apocryphal voice" (pp. 36–75).

almost nothing about himself—not the reason for his long-lasting insomnia, nor the precise dynamics of his emotional ennui, nor the ultimate cause of his physical exhaustion. In fact, the poem's subject seems to come closest to naming his present state of being by repeatedly invoking the word "nothing" (lines 1–15; emphasis added):

> I have gret wonder, be this lyght,
> How that I lyve, for day ne nyght
> I may nat slepe wel nygh noght;
> I have so many an ydel thoght
> Purely for defaute of slep
> That, by my trouthe, I take no kep
> Of *nothing,* how hyt cometh or gooth,
> Ne me nys *nothyng* leef nor looth.
> Al is ylyche good to me—
> Joye or sorowe, wherso hyt be—
> For I have felynge in *nothyng,*
> But as yt were a mased thyng,
> Alway in poynt to falle a-doun;
> For sorwful ymagynacioun
> Ys alway hooly in my mynde.

Physically so disequilibrated by his strange kinship with "nothing" that he is in danger of falling down, his senses so numb he is unable to discriminate between pleasure and pain, the speaker's opening words seem to indicate an advanced state of identity dissolution. A bewildered and "mased thyng," the speaker is consumed by a pervasive *melancholia ex nihilo,* a powerful yet indeterminate form of "sorwful ymagynacioun" that has paralyzed his consciousness with mournful longings, aphasic thoughts, and specters of nothingness. His "felynge in nothyng" may possibly signal the originary cause or the desired end of his melancholic torpor. But analytical conjectures of this nature are beyond the subject's dysfunctional mind to pursue. Rather, his overwhelming desire is simply to fall asleep to find relief from the emptiness, lassitude, and *méconnaissance* that plague his psyche (lines 16–29):

> And wel ye woot, agaynes kynde
> Hyt were to lyven in thys wyse,
> For nature wolde nat suffyse

To noon erthly creature
Nat longe tyme to endure
Withoute slep and be in sorwe.
And I ne may, ne nyght ne morwe,
Slepe; and thus melancolye
And drede I have for to dye.
Defaute of slep and hevynesse
Hath sleyn my spirit of quyknesse
That I have lost al lustyhede.
Suche fantasies ben in myn hede
So I not what is best to doo.

For all the words he has spoken to this point, what is noticeable is how little headway "I" is making toward identifying the root cause of his problems. He is able to point toward various symptoms of his depression: his vitality is gone; he is exhausted, moody, and troubled by fearful thoughts of death; so many fantasies ravage his brain he lacks the desire to describe any one of them. But the cure of his *anomie* is apparently beyond his powers to apprehend. If pressured to unravel his mental state, he can either repeat himself, saying once again he does not understand, or else conjure up some idiosyncratic theory with no apparent conviction that it is anywhere near the truth (lines 30–43):

   But men myght axe me why soo
I may not slepe and what me is.
But natheles, who aske this
Leseth his asking trewely.
Myselven can not telle why
The sothe; but trewly, as I gesse,
I holde hit be a sicknesse
That I have suffred this eight yeer;
And yet my boote is never the ner,
For there is phisicien but oon
That may me hele; but that is don.
Passe we over untill eft;
That wil not be mot nede be left;
Our first mater is good to kepe.

Searching for an adequate diagnosis, the narrator eventually proposes, "trewly," that he is suffering from an unnamed sickness that has lasted precisely eight years, and that the cure for this sickness lies in the hands of a single (albeit unnamed) "phisicien." But only a moment earlier, and just as "trewely," he has admitted that for the life of him he "can not telle why" he is suffering. As sleep-deprived as before, the narrator would now prefer to cease brooding over his mental condition and return with his auditor ("Passe we over") to the poem's "first mater"—whatever that first matter might be.

The poem's "first mater," I am suggesting, is precisely the same matter that has been addressed at the outset by the poem's speaking voice: the inability of this fragmented subject to understand himself. One aspect of the narrator's disunified identity may well be convinced that the remainder of his narration—as he reads Ovid, falls asleep, and dreams a many-layered dream—is entirely unrelated to the personal anxieties with which the poem begins. But it is my contention that Chaucer's elegy is the projection of a single, albeit riven, consciousness that is seeking some form of "other" that will address, perhaps even cure, his own sense of fragmentation and self-alienation. *The Book of the Duchess* is often appreciated as an elegiac love poem that has found a way to successfully express the lovelorn grief of another—a figure who may be identified as the Black Knight or John of Gaunt. While not wishing to undo this reading, I believe the loss and longing given voice throughout the poem more fundamentally constitute an urgent quest by the poem's "I" for a consoling wholeness of Being the "nothingness" of his fractured being lacks.

One way of understanding the dynamics of the subject's quest for wholeness is Jacques Lacan's analysis of the formation of the "I."[75] For Lacan, the idea of an internal, natural, and unified self is a myth created by the romantic ego. Beginning life as a fragmented cluster of drives and attachments, the male child acquires an imaginary sense of unity by assuming his mother is himself and his primary desire for her is continuous with her primary desire for him. In the crucial mirror stage, however, the child traumatically discovers that he is in fact a separate and

[75] The follow analysis is based on Jacques Lacan, "The Mirror Stage as Formative of the Function of the I as Revealed in Psychoanalytic Experience," in *Ecrits: A Selection,* trans. Alan Sheridan (New York: Norton, 1977), pp. 1–7. Throughout this essay I have often used Dylan Evans's highly responsible *An Introductory Dictionary of Lacanian Psychoanalysis* (London: Routledge, 1996); unless otherwise noted, all translations from the original French edition of *Ecrits* (Seuil) are Evans's. I am also very indebted to Bruce Fink's excellent *The Lacanian Subject: Between Language and Jouissance* (Princeton: Princeton University Press, 1995).

separated entity. As partial compensation for this loss of wholeness, the child imagines in his mother's gaze an idealized image of himself, a unified body of mastery and control. At the same moment, however, the child is forced to acknowledge his own lack of unity through a fragmented counterimage, *le corps morcellé,* the body in bits and pieces. Thus the Lacanian "I" comes into being at an originary point of fissure and separation: wrested from an imaginary sense of fullness, the infant is torn between two aggressively competing self-images, one producing exhilaration, the other depression and despair. Throughout life, the self-deluding ego identifies itself with its specular ideal, even though an alienated part of the subject may resent that ideal, equating it with the "omnipotent" maternal Other because it reminds him of his own incompleteness and lack. Even while repressing the foundational truth of its lack-of-being (*manque-à-être*) by identifying with the imaginary fullness of the ego-ideal, the subject is not, Lacan explains, engaging in an act of pure ignorance. Rather, the ego's *méconnaissance* is a mistaken form of self-knowledge—a misrecognition of the symbolic determinants of subjectivity that are to be found elsewhere, namely, in the discourse of the Other and in the unconscious.

When the child enters the domain of language and the law, he moves into the symbolic order (although the imaginary is never left behind). Lacan captures the Oedipal, linguistic, and cultural regulations of the symbolic order through a characteristic play on words: letting go of its symbiotic and preverbal relation with the mother, the child must learn to accede both to *le "non" du pere* and to *le-Nom-du-Pere.* That is, enjoining the incest taboo and all other forms of social proscription, the first word of the symbolic father is "*Non!*" The symbolic father's first word is simultaneously "*Nom!*" because the Name-of-the-Father (Lacan's capitalizations) is the symbolic order's fundamental signifier, conferring identity on the subject by naming and positioning him within the order of all other linguistic signifiers. The symbolic order itself, based as it is on Saussure's binary opposition of linguistic signs, is epitomized for Lacan by Freud's famous account of his grandson's *fort/da* game. The basic phonemic difference *o/a,* substituting verbal sounds for an absent object (the child's mother), is a microcosmic illustration of how all language is a presence made of absence: in the symbolic order, Lacan explains, "nothing exists except upon an assumed foundation of absence."[76] Thus, in his radical revision of Saussure, Lacan argues that all words are merely

[76] Jacques Lacan, *Écrits* (Paris: Seuil, 1966), p. 392; trans. in Evans, *Dictionary,* p. 1.

signifiers (rather than signs), and therefore the absent and displaced signified must always be sited beneath rather than above the bar, and the signifier above rather than below, as in $\frac{S}{s}$. Concerning the identity of the subject, what this means is that the I-as-signified is rendered absent by the "I"-as-signifier. Or, to put it another way, the universal symbol of all signs in the symbolic order, $\frac{S}{s}$, serves equally well as an index of the subject's identity, the impassable bar representing what Lacan calls "the self's radical excentricity to itself."[77]

In *The Book of the Duchess,* as we have seen, Chaucer's subject is profoundly "excentric to itself." That indeterminate "nothing" of which the subject repeatedly speaks can be understood as a metonym for a certain absence or lack–of–being in himself. In fact, when we consider the linguistic difficulties foregrounded in the rest of the poem, the narrator's opening complaint makes even more sense as an internalized dialectic between reference and significance, being and nothingness, signifier and signified. The very same bar severing signifier from signified is seen again in the bar blocking the subject from knowledge of himself. Lacan's "$\$$," the sign of the barred and fissured subject, thus serves as an efficient indicator of the Chaucerian "I" as well as of the inability of that "I" to align signifiers with signifieds, whether the signifier points outward toward part of the world or inward toward part of himself. Just as later, in the case of the Black Knight's use of "I," "fers," and "white," he is unable to unify the word's signified with its referent, so from the outset he is perplexed by the very "I" of which and with which he himself begins to speak. Because the pronoun "I" is a "shifter" (to use Roman Jacobson's term), and it is both a signifier acting as the subject of a statement and an index that designates, but does not signify, the speaking subject. What this means for Lacan (in thunderous response to Descartes) is that the "I" is constitutionally incapable of knowing the essence, or being, of its absent self: "I think where I am not," Lacan declaims, "therefore I am where I do not think."[78] Or, in an equivalent prescription that neatly captures the inability of Chaucer's "I" to locate or comprehend its signified, repressed, or "other" self: "I am not wherever I am the plaything of my thought; I think of what I am where I do not think to think."[79]

If the elegy's "I" is unable to arrive at self-knowledge from within his

[77] Lacan, *Écrits,* p. 204, trans. in ibid., p. 77.

[78] Lacan, "The Agency of the Letter in the Unconscious, or Reason Since Freud," in *Écrits: A Selection,* p. 166.

[79] Ibid.

own speaking position, another discourse in the poem, the elegy's refrain, provides analytic assistance, even though the subject's ego may be incapable of decoding its meaning. Immediately after the Black Knight completes his allegorical story of the chess game, he finds he must reprove his interlocutor because he does not understand what that story was actually intended to mean (lines 743–44):

> "Thou wost ful lytel what thou menest;
> I have lost more than thow wenest."

Much later in the poem, the Black Knight details his long history of the courtship of his beloved, only to have the narrator ask him to repeat the story so that he might be able to understand "what ye have lore" (line 1135). For a second time the Black Knight reproves his auditor (lines 1137–38):

> "'Yee!' seyde he, 'thow nost what thow menest;
> I have lost more than thou wenest.'"

Finally, very near the elegy's end, the narrator fails once again to understand the explicit import of the Black Knight's history of personal loss ("'Sir,' quod I, 'where is she now?'" [line 1298]), and the Black Knight for a third time finds its necessary to critique the narrator for his misprision (lines 1305–6):

> "Thow wost ful lytel what thow menest;
> I have lost more than thow wenest."

Although refrains in elegies normally provide psychical energy in advancing the poem's work of mourning, giving rhythmic voice to communal grief and providing the possibility for consolation and change,[80] in no obvious way is Chaucer's refrain doing the work of communal mourning or consolation. Rather, these lines focus on the narrator himself and his inability to comprehend words that give expression to another's personal loss. In this regard, what is most troubling about the

[80] Concerning the role of repetition in the elegy, see Peter Sacks, *The English Elegy: Studies in the Genre from Spenser to Yeats* (Baltimore: Johns Hopkins Press, 1985), pp. 22–23.

refrain is that the words whose meaning the narrator does not understand are not in fact his own words, but rather the words spoken by another; yet that other speaker, the Black Knight, attributes the meaning of his words to his listener rather than to himself: "Thow wost ful lytel what thow menest."

The strangeness of the Black Knight's repeated reprimand has caught the attention of various critics. In *Chaucer and the Fictions of Gender,* for example, Elaine Hansen exclaims: "[W]hat the Knight says here, after all, is not, 'You don't understand what *I* mean,' but, 'You don't understand what *you* mean.'"[81] Hansen wonders whether this "apparently illogical or impossible statement" could have some meaning other than its overtly contradictory meaning, but after consulting *The Middle English Dictionary* she finds she "cannot explain away the fundamental problem."[82] Unable to make sense of the troubling couplet, Hansen leaves it as an unresolved conundrum, allowing only that Chaucer's poem "seems to express as deep an anxiety about the possibility of certain knowledge and true interpretation as any twentieth-century deconstructive reading could wish to impute to it."[83] I agree that there is a "deep anxiety" in the poem "about the possibility of certain knoweldge," and I would suggest accordingly that Lacan's representation of the symbolic construction of the subject provides a pertinent though extremely complex rationale as to why the meaning intended by "I" must reside in the words of another, and why "I" is unable to understand what those words actually mean. The interdisplacement of "I" and "thow" in Chaucer's insistent refrain can be explained by Lacan's remarkable thesis that the symbolic determinants of subjectivity are actually located in the discourse of the Other and in the unconscious.

Je est un autre, Rimbaud's famous pronouncement, has served as a watchword for many twentieth-century theorizers of subject-identity, including Lacan. From 1955 onward, Lacan actually discriminated between two kinds of other: the big Other, or *l'Autre* (symbolized by *A*), and the little other, or *l'autre* (symbolized by *a*). The big Other, one of the most complex terms in all of Lacanian thought, designates a radical alterity, an otherness which the subject cannot in any way assimilate through identification. Lacan equates this radical alterity with language

[81] Hansen, *Fictions of Gender,* p. 79.
[82] Ibid.
[83] Ibid., p. 80.

and the law. Thus, insofar as it is particularized for each subject, the Other is equivalent to the symbolic order. Like the symbolic order itself, the Other is the place of the signifier, the site from which all language originates. This means that the subject, which comes into being through the naming powers of the symbolic father, is very much under the sway of the Other: as Lacan explains, "[T]he subject is a subject only by virtue of his subjection to the field of the Other."[84] It also means that the words spoken by the subject are not actually "his," but rather—returning to Saussure's contention that all language is a self-contained system beyond the regulating intent of any single consciousness (recall Saussure's reference to the "unconscious or unintelligent player")—that all language is in fact "the discourse of the Other." Speech, in other words, does not originate from the ego (which is part of the imaginary order), nor even from the subject (which is constructed by the symbolic order); it derives instead from a locus which is placed beyond the *cogito,* beyond human consciousness. Lacan's name for this locus is, unsurprisingly, the unconscious. In striking contrast to Freud's unconscious, however, Lacan's unconscious is neither primordial nor instinctual nor internal. Rather, it is a synchronic, intersubjective, and quasi-linguistic structure made out of repressed signifiers that return, or unfold, in the form of symptoms, jokes, parapraxes, and dreams. Therefore, insofar as it is structured as a language "the unconscious is the discourse of the Other."[85] What this means in psychoanalysis is that the analyst, while attending to the words of the analysand's ego, must listen for the voice of that repressed subject which has been barred by the symbolic order. In the "empty speech" of the ego there are likely to be elusive and partial breakthroughs of "full speech," cryptic signs that Lacan's *sujet,* the subject of the unconscious, is speaking.

"Thow wost ful lytel what thow menest; / I have lost more than thow wenest": within the context of Lacanian psychoanalytic thought these illogical words are capable of carrying a good deal of meaning. At the most basic level of this address, what the Other, the Black Knight, may be understood as saying to the subject (the narrator in whose dream the Black Knight exists as a sign) are of course many things. But one strain of the refrain could sound like this: *You do not own your own language, you*

[84] Jacques Lacan, *The Seminar: Book II. The Ego in Freud's Theory and the Technique of Pyschoanalysis, 1954–55,* trans. Sylvana Tomaselli (New York: Norton, 1988), p. 188, cited in Evans, *Dictionary,* p. 196.

[85] Lacan, *Écrits,* p. 16; trans. in Evans, *Dictionary,* p. 133.

do not know what it is that you have said, nor is your intention capable of determining the meaning of your words; you are subject to the language of the Other, your being exists only in the realm of the Other, and yet your being in the Other constitutes a loss greater than anything you are able to understand. That loss, although represented in the symbolic order, is also repressed by the symbolic order; the only place language may address your loss, your absence, your lack-of-being, is through the unconscious, an intersubjective place that neither of us owns or understands.

There are many ironies about the placement of this diagnostic refrain in the psychoanalytic dynamics of the poem. As several commentators have noted, the protracted exchange at the poem's center between depressed speaker and patient listener is in many ways similar to a typical therapy session. Yet, if only at these moments of refrain, it is the depressed speaker himself who takes on the role of the explicating therapist. At most other moments in this talking cure roles appear to be reversed: it is the narrator who is called upon to understand the deep meaning of the Black Knight's words, to sympathize with his emotional pain, and to provide therapeutic counsel for his loss. While the narrator's failure to provide any of these humane services may be troubling, in Lacanian psychoanalytic practice such shortcomings are actually valued as professional virtues. Lacan liked to compare his ideal psychoanalyst to the "dummy" in the game of bridge, that nonparticipating player who lays down his cards and is thus "out of the game." Appearing to the analysand as passive, uncomprehending, enigmatic, and nonsupportive, the Lacanian analyst resists being read, resists transference, resists becoming what he is desired to be, the "subject-supposed-to-know" (*sujet supposé savoir*). So whether or not he knows, Chaucer's narrator is an accomplished Lacanian "dummy," providing salutary resistance to the ego's desire to find reflected in the Other a narcissistic image of his own self-grieving.

Insofar as *The Book of the Duchess* is a simulacrum of the talking cure, therefore, it is important to remember that, rather than a dream being recounted in a therapy session, here a therapy session is re-enacted in a dream. What this suggests is that the poem's subject has internalized and fictionalized signifiers of his ongoing process of self-analysis. When we recall how condensed, disguised, and inverted dream-symbols normally are, within the psychomachic *allegoresis* of the subject's unconscious both the figure of the dreamer and the figure of the Black Knight are best understood as "barred," shifting, and at times interchangeable signifiers of the dreamer's multiple and subjective *personae.* These symbolic shifters lead to one more problematic in the subject-position of "I". Because, at least in part, the poem's "I" has preempted the role of diagnostic analysand, the position of the analyst ("the subject-supposed-to-know") is being proffered to the silent and inscrutable dummy "outside the text": i.e., the reader. In Lacanian terms, therefore, the primary responsibility of Chaucer's reader-as-dummy is to attend to those verbal symptoms in the poem's discourse which seem to indicate the existence of a reality beyond the symbolic order, on the other side of the bar of linguistic signification.

The presumed existence of a reality beyond the symbolic order brings us to the last of Lacan's three interdependent orders: after the imaginary order and the symbolic order there is the order of the real. For Lacan a clear distinction needs to be drawn betweeen "reality" and the real. While "reality" denotes all of our imaginary and symbolic representations of the world, the real is "the domain of whatever subsists outside symbolisation."[86] Thus the real is asymbolic: like the Kantian thing-in-itself, it is the unknowable *X*, the impossible Thing. But the asymbolia of the real does not mean that it is unamenable to calculation and logic. In direct contrast to the symbolic order, which is constituted in terms of opposition (phoneme/phoneme; signifier/signified; presence/absence), the real is known to be full, without fissure, and without absence ("There is no absence in the real"[87]). The real also has connotations of matter, death, and the physical body, implying a material substrate underlying the imaginary and the symbolic, and includes as well such things as hallucinations and traumatic dreams. The real is thus "extimate" (another of Lacan's neologisms): like the unconscious, which is inside and outside, the real both is and is not in the subject. In this way Lacan is able to contend that things only exist in the real, yet just as readily he will maintain that things only exist, or have being, in the symbolic. What this paradox appears to mean is, since there is no prediscursive reality (there is nothing "outside social discourse"), only that which is integrated into the symbolic order fully "exists." But since everything within the symbolic order is signifiable only because that which it signifies is putatively absent, "[n]othing exists except insofar

[86] Lacan, *Écrits,* p. 388; trans. in ibid., p. 159.
[87] Lacan, *The Seminar: Book II,* p. 313.

as it does not exist."[88] Whereas existence in the first sense is synonymous with Lacan's use of the term Being, existence in the second sense is its near opposite (Lacan signifies this sense via a different spelling, *ex-sistence*): by the material substance, or the Real, or Nothing. Lacan's psychoanalytic placement of the existence of the real inside the subject is another way of his asserting that the most significant part of the human subject is "radically unassimilable to the signifier."[89] The real, in other words, is the "nothing" of the unconscious, the indiscernible signified which is repressed under the bar of "I."

Up until this point we appear to have been studying two different orders of names in *The Book of the Duchess.* The first comprises the elegy's "philosophical" attempts to discover whether the symbolic order of linguistic signifiers can make present, or embody, the materiality of the real. The second order comprises those "psychological" attempts made by the elegy's "I" to discover an unnameable and unknowable "nothing" within himself. With the assistance of Lacan's idea of the "extimacy" of the real, it is now possible to appreciate how these two discourses, one "objective" and the other "subjective," are as intimately related as the "two sides" of a Moebius strip. The poem's search for a name that will properly constitute its lost and longed-for "material" object is a variant of the attempts by the poem's "I" to name the inscrutable desires of its own unconscious. The unsuccessful attempts of the poem's language to reach beyond its own signifying powers in order to actualize the real shed light on the poet's sense of the limitations of his own linguistic powers. These limitations are, in turn, connected to (in fact, continuous with) the chimerical objectification of the real that inheres in the narrator's psyche, a phantasmatic object that Lacan calls the little other, or the *object petit a.*

Consider first two "empirical"/interpretive cruces found in two Chaucerian poems other than *The Book of the Duchess.* The so-called incomplete poem *The House of Fame* comes to a sudden halt with an out-of-the-blue gesture in the direction of an otherwise unidentified "man of gret auctorite" (line 2158). Many attempts have been made to discover the intended external referent for this infamous signifying teaser, with sugges-

[88] Jacques Lacan, *Écrits,* p. 392, trans. in Evans, *Dictionary,* p. 58.

[89] Lacan, *The Seminar: Book III. The Psychoses, 1955–56,* trans. Russell Grigg (London: Routledge, 1993), p. 179; cited in ibid., p. 58.

tions ranging from Chaucer's contemporaries Richard II and John of Gaunt all the way to Boccaccio, Boethius, and Christ.[90] The same indexical trick occurs in the antepenultimate line of *The Nun's Priest's Tale,* where, in his mysterious aside "As seith my lord" (line 3445), the narrator suddenly points in the direction of a diegetically unknown and never-to-be-identified person. Various scholars have tried to ground the Nun's Priest's "my lord" in historical reality—for instance, by equating him either with Chaucer's contemporaries the archbishop of Canterbury, William Courtenay, or the bishop of London, Robert Braybrooke.[91] In both cases, I would contend, these scholars have fallen into a trap carefully set for them: the groundlessness of the ungroundable signifier.[92]

In *The Book of the Duchess,* a striking instance of the ungroundable signifier is the narrator's disorienting allusion (noted earlier) to "the ferses twelve." In his review of attempts to explicate this strange piece of nomenclature (strange because of the knowledge presupposed in the ostensive force of *the*[93]), A. J. Minnis concludes that "Chaucer's reference to *twelve* 'ferses' remains an intractable problem."[94] But I would contend that the intractability of the problem is precisely the point. Just as with the Nun's Priest's "my lord" (who "exists" fully neither inside nor outside the symbolic order of the poem) and just as with *The House of Fame*'s "man of gret auctorite" (who is also at the outermost edge of the poem's discursive body), we must conclude that, for "the ferses twelve," there simply is no locatable referent. In fact, each of the aforementioned literary/"empirical" cruces is designed to call attention to its nature as an unsuccessful linguistic signifier within the symbolic order of the poem. And, further, each of them calls attention to the awkward nature of *all* linguistic signifiers within the symbolic order of human language itself.

[90] *Riverside Chaucer,* p. 990.

[91] Ibid., p. 941.

[92] See the full note on this crux in Derek Pearsall, ed., *The Nun's Priest's Tale,* pt. 9 of *A Variorum Edition of The Works of Geoffrey Chaucer, Vol. II:* The Canterbury Tales (Norman: University of Oklahoma Press, 1983), pp. 257–58.

An "internal" example of the same literary/"empirical" instructive crux is found in *The Merchant's Tale,* where the fictional character Justinus cites as one of his authorities the Wife of Bath, an extradiegetical figure whom, because she is a "fiction," he could never "actually" have known.

[93] For the importance of articles in the analysis of language, see E. M. Barth, *The Logic of the Articles in Traditional Philosophy* (Dordrecht, Holland: D. Reidel, 1974). Although I have found no evidence to support this position, it is possible that Middle English "the ferses twelve" (the discrete level of supposition) was actually equivalent to "ferses twelve" (the determinate level of supposition).

[94] Minnis, *Shorter Poems,* p. 146; his emphasis.

Just as these groundless signifiers "call out" for a real world referential object which fails to present itself, so, in a corollary fashion, it may be that all verbal signifiers "call out" for an "absent" material object that is ultimately unpresentable and unknowable. In the unfissured fullness of the real, of course, "the ferses twelve" may enjoy a signified and meaningful existence. But, within the symbolic order itself, the verbal construction "the ferses twelve" stands as a challenging reminder that *every* word is an incomplete sign. There is *no* sign that contains within itself the material fullness of its absent referent. There is *no* word that is capable of conjuring into being the yet-to-be-experienced existence of the real.

Furthermore, just as "the ferses twelve" gives expression to an anxiety that the synchronic substance of the real might not prove answerable to its being named *in the present,* other episodes in the elegy underscore the diachronic inability of names to bring things into the present which are absent and lost *in the past.* Two closely related experiences in the poem illustrate language's mortifying touch. Having fallen asleep, the narrator in his dream wakes up within a room whose stained-glass windows depict the story of Troy and whose painted walls depict *The Romance of the Rose.* These graphic illustrations provide the poet an ideal occasion for an ekphrastic display of his own linguistic powers (lines 326–34):

> For hooly al the story of Troye
> Was in the glasynge ywroght thus,
> Of Ector and of kyng Priamus,
> Of Achilles and of kyng Lamedon,
> And eke of Medea and of Jason,
> Of Paris, Eleyne, and of Lavyne.
> And alle the walles with colours fyne
> Were peynted, bothe text and glose,
> Of al the Romaunce of the Rose.

And that's it. In the ekphrastic exercises that adorn so many major works of literature—such as Homer's Shield of Achilles in book 24 of the *Iliad,* Dante's program of marble carvings in canto 10 of the *Purgatorio,* Chaucer's *oratories* in *The Knight's Tale,* and Keat's "Ode on a Grecian Urn"—great poets have been only too eager to demonstrate how their verses are able to transform the mute stillness of art into the movement, speech, and drama of three-dimensional life enacted in the unfolding process of time.[95] What Chaucer has chosen to do in *The Book of the Duchess* is quite the opposite: the magnificent history of Troy is nothing more than a roll call of the dead, while the characters of *The Romance of the Rose,* perhaps because their names are generic, descriptive, and "fictional," are not even granted an existence in the world of the imagination. Thus the brilliant failure of Chaucer's ekphrasis gives additional support to the elegy's exploration of the restricted power of naming. Unless one already knows what they signify, proper names ("Ector," "Priamus," etc.) are unable to grant even phantasmatical being to that which is not already and presently "there."

The inability of the narrator's chamber of poetic memory to vivify the past is subconsciously inspired by the Ovidian narrative of Ceyx and Alcyone, which the dreamer had been reading just before falling asleep. In Chaucer's version of the tale, Juno asks Morpheus to "crepe into" the "dreynte body" (lines 144, 195) of Ceyx and appear before his grieving wife Alcyone. But the only words of consolation Ceyx's phantasm can provide his wife are: "I am but ded. / Ye shul me never on lyve yse" (lines 204–5). Thus the voice of a pagan god may summon a body from the vasty deep, but no divine language is able to inspirit that matter with being. In a corollary maneuver, Chaucer calls attention to the limits of his own linguistic powers by concluding Ovid's tale quite differently from Ovid. Rather than being benevolently metamorphosed into a new form of life, Ceyx's grieving wife Alcyone is provided nothing but the frigid comfort of a solitary and sudden death: she "deyede within the thridde morwe" (line 214). In the overall program of *The Book of the Duchess,* therefore, each of these episodes is a monitory sign concerning the seeming impenetrability of the real by the symbolic. The longed-for metamorphosis that does not happen, the lifelessness of a failed ekphrasis, the unlocatable referent of "the ferses twelve": each of these is a linguistic articulation of the subject's desire to quicken an object that does not exist; each demonstrates the limits of human language to make the absent present; each fails to penetrate or embrace the fullness of the real.

Yet the fullness of being—and perhaps this totality is equivalent to the fullness of the real—is precisely what the poem and its subject most

[95] For a full study of these and other ekphrases, see James A. W. Heffernan, *Museum of Words: The Poetics of Ekphrasis from Homer to Ashbery* (Chicago: University of Chicago Press, 1993).

deeply and persistently desire. The poem's quest for unity of being is expressed most directly in the poem via the narrator's promise that he will do all within his power to make the Black Knight whole (lines 548–54):

> "But certes, sire, yif that yee
> Wolde ought discure me youre woo,
> I wolde, as wys God helpe me soo,
> Amende hyt, yif I kan or may.
> Ye mowe preve hyt be assay;
> For, by my trouthe, to make yow hool
> I wol do al my power hool."

This desire for psychical wholeness, this search for some Other that might fill the profound lack with which the subject initiates his talking cure, is, as I suggested, the "other" side of the Moebius strip of language. And this desire can now be defined with considerable precision by further reference to Lacan's understanding of the *objet a.*

According to Lacan, since it is the mother who first occupies the position of the Other, the child's first trauma occurs when it discovers that the mother's desire is incomplete: there is already a lack, an absence, in the Other. Throughout the subject's life, there are several meanings to the lack in the Other (which Lacan represents by striking a bar through its sign: Ø). Since that bar can never be crossed, the subject's original desire is placed under the bar of the signifier, which means that it enters the subject's unconscious. The barring of the Other also determines that all the signifiers that the subject thereafter pursues as fillers for an unfillable lack can be traced back to the originary and imagined completeness of the mythical Mother. Linguistically, this means that because a crucial signifier is forever absent from the treasury of signifiers constituted by the Other, the subject will slide from one signifier to the next, each standing in for, but failing to provide, the sought-for whole. The desiring subject is thus forever condemned to move along a metonymic chain of linguistic names, ignoring the "lack-of-being" in each, unwilling to acknowledge language's inability to arrive at the real, fantasizing that somewhere in the symbolic order there may be an ideal object that will fill that inner void of "nothing."

To this all-powerful object of fantasy Lacan has given the name *l'objet petit a.* Put rather simply, the *objet a* denotes the desired object that can never be attained. Phantasmatic in nature, a lost object that never was, it is an absence that is paradoxically asked to fill a void. The *objet a* is inscribed entirely in the imaginary order because it is a product of the fantasizing ego; yet what it strives to do is fill the absence created by the inadequate assimilation of the real by the symbolic. In its fantasized fullness, therefore, the *objet a* is actually part of the real; more precisely, it is the "stuff" of the real which cannot be symbolized yet which can be acted on by the imaginary. The cause rather than the effect of desire, the *objet a* sets into motion those drives which seek it but which never quite wish to attain it (attainment equaling annihilation), preferring rather to circle around, never getting too close nor too far away. The *objet a* is unquestionably the single most important idea in Lacan's complex system. Without it, he explains, the orders of the imaginary, the symbolic, and the real would drift apart from each other, the ultimate effect in the subject being hysteria and psychosis. Were it not for the *objet a,* as Bruce Fink clarifies, the subject would be incapable of achieving even "a phantasmatic sense of wholeness, completeness, fulfillment, and well-being."[96]

In light of the subject's quest for well-being, I propose that Lacan's elusive idea of the *objet a* accords coherence to the entirety of Chaucer's elegy. From beginning to end, the poem is driven by the search for a phantasmatic object, never adequately identified, but granted numerous surrogate names ranging from "phisicien but one" to "fers" to "good fair white." This phantasmic object "ex-sists" on the other side of the universal bar of signification—that fissure in Western thought symbolized before and after Chaucer's time by the image of an impermeable wall upon whose surface readers, like the narrator and the Black Knight, paint the color of our desires. Epistemologically, therefore, as well as philosophically and psycholinguistically, the poem's subject continuously seeks to approach this wall, to cross that bar which divides signifier from signified. But because the poem's subject is driven by a conflicted desire both to know and not to know the nature of this bar, his *méconnaissance* propels him erratically along the poem's chain of signifiers as he approaches but never touches his temporary substitutes for the Other. For all of the above reasons, therefore, the semiotic rivenness of *The Book of the Duchess* must be understood as being many things at once: it is the bar slashed through the symbolic order; it is the fissure between the Other and the

[96] Fink, *Lacanian Subject,* p. 60.

objet a; it is the ragged fold between the symbolic and the real; it is the difference between "white" and white. This fault line has already been given many names in this essay, but surely the name that bears most urgently on the agenda of Chaucer's elegy is close to hand and deserving of special study. The Other, the barring of the Other, the other-than-the-Other, as well as the rupture between reality and the real: all of these have been given a single name in the West, and that is the name of Woman.

IV: The Name of Woman

In a brief but brilliant essay published in 1984 with the no-nonsense title of "Blanche," Maud Ellmann focuses on the sexual politics of Blanche's name:

> In loving her own name, Blanche logically must love her namelessness, her own blancheur: it is as if the name must be erased in the perfection of its own propriety. But is it not through whiting out the name of woman that patrilineal proprieties must always institute themselves? Namelessness enables women to circulate between the names and properties of men. Blanche herself, as her name implies, has no intrinsic properties: she represents the currency through which names, places and proprieties are realigned. . . . [Thus t]he "walles white" of Blanche's chastity defend the castle of propriety against the threat of woman's *jouissance.* It is as if male discourse and its dream of meaning could commence only through her bloodless body and her whitened signature.[97]

Ellmann's sharp attack provides a critique of more than one phallocentric thinker. One of her primary targets is Claude Lévi-Strauss, the structuralist anthropologist whose "Saussurian" coding of the role of women as "empty objects of exchange" appears to be complicit in the very subordination of women that it purports merely to explicate. Another target is Jacques Lacan, whose reinscription of several Lévi-Straussian ideas helped point him in the direction of uttering such seemingly absolutist proclamations as "The Woman does not exist." It is also possible that Chaucer falls within range of Ellmann's critique. For the homoerotic drama at the center of *The Book of the Duchess* is a seemingly ageless archetype: two men producing a cornucopian text praising the beauty

[97] Ellmann, "Blanche," pp. 105–6.

and virtue of an absent/dead woman. Moreover, there is little doubt that the "whitened signature" of this absent woman bears, as Ellmann says, almost "no intrinsic properties." Precisely because of this lack/absence, one of the qualities of white's name is its availability as a blank wall upon which any freelance lover may project his individual erotic fantasies. Because it is a paronymic name, "white" also calls attention to its role as a lexical sign linked to the entire synchronic order of signifiers. Finally, because it is a proper name, "white" helps expose the "patrilineal proprieties" and homoerotic competition that men share as they contend for ownership of the sign of Woman.

Since the mid-1980's feminist studies have critiqued Chaucer's sexual politics even as they have striven to protect the so-called Father of English Literature from allegations of phallocentricism. The temptation to whitewash Chaucer's good fair name is compelling, but of course highly problematic. If it were possible to essentialize Chaucer's intent (there are as many Chaucer-the-signifieds as there are Chaucerians), I would concur with Sheila Delany's view on the matter. When considering the centuries-old question, "Was Chaucer 'friend to woman'?" Delany answers simply: "yes and no"—"Chaucer's attitude toward women" "remains an ambivalent attitude."[98] My concern is not with Chaucer's relation to women *per se,* but rather the Chaucerian subject's "yes and no" relation to Woman, the sign of the idealized feminine Other. White is clearly the elegy's *objet a.* For the Black Knight, for the narrator, as well as for the imaginary reader, she is the absolute "All" with which every courtly lover wishes to be united. This universal desire to merge into the oneness of All is poignantly narrativized in the unification of those two seemingly immiscible lovers, black and white (lines 1289–97; emphasis added):

"*Oure* hertes wern so evene a payre
That never nas that oon contrayre
To that other for no woo.
For sothe, ylyche *they* suffred thoo
Oo blysse and eke oo sorwe bothe;
Ylyche *they* were bothe glad and wrothe;
Al was *us* oon, withoute were.

[98] Sheila Delany, *The Naked Text: Chaucer's Legend of Good Women* (Berkeley: University of California Press, 1994), pp. 12, 240.

> And thus *we* lyved ful many a yere
> So wel I kan nat telle how."

What is quite remarkable in this passage celebrating the absolute unification of two erotic identities is that the Black Knight not only uses the plural pronoun, rather than the singular, but actually shifts his pronominal references back and forth between the first person and the third. These linguistic indications that the two lovers remain subject and object, both "we" and "they," clearly challenge the very sentiments of love the speech-act asserts as having been true. In "Love and the Signifier," Lacan argues that "the idea of love begins with 'We are but one.'" Yet, he contends, this universal sentiment only gives voice to an impossible fantasy: "The One everyone talks about all the time is, first of all, a kind of mirage of the One you believe yourself to be."[99] By imagining that he and his beloved are One ("Al was us oon"), the elegy's lover is thus projecting upon white a desire for his own "lost" unity of being, displacing the barred Other with the imaginary *objet a.* In other words, the very blankness of "white" noted by Ellmann suggests that if the Black Knight were not in love with white's absolute perfection, he would be in love with another's.[100] In the subject's imaginary, therefore, what white has in common with all other possible Ones is their shared function as inadequate surrogates for a lost original. The ultimate One is of course none other than *prima Mater,* which Chaucer punningly refers to as "Our first mater" (line 43), the unitary state of being to which the poem's depressed "I" seeks to return.[101] But since the primary referent of "Our first mater" is the poem's first matter, that is, the text itself as a linguistic construct of signifiers and signifieds, our focus is returned once again to the interrogation of discrete linguistic signs.

In a Lacanian linguistic analysis, of course, language leads to—indeed determines—gender. When the symbolic order destroys the imaginary unity of child and Mother via the phallic interjection of the Father's "No!" the subject's gender-choice is either to align itself with the law of

[99] Jacques Lacan, *On Feminine Sexuality, The Limits of Love and Knowledge 1972–1973: Encore, The Seminar of Jacques Lacan, Book XX,* trans. Bruce Fink (New York: Norton, 1998) [hereafter cited as *Encore*], p. 47.

[100] And he will do the same, Lacan cynically cautions, with his next One and the next: "There are as many Ones as you like—they are characterized by the fact that none of them resemble any of the others in any way" (ibid., p. 47).

[101] Lacan warns that the issue of woman must "never be taken up except *quoad matrem.* Woman serves a function in the sexual relationship only qua mother" (ibid., p. 35).

the phallus (and thus be constructed under the banner of the masculine) or to align itself with the non-phallic Other (and thus be constructed under the banner of the feminine). Man, therefore, "has" the phallus because the subject-as-masculine succumbs to the authority of the first signifier and immerses himself in the alienation, yet mastery, of language. And since the totality of man falls under the phallic function, alienated man is "all": "He can be taken as a whole," Bruce Fink logically explains, "because there is a definable boundary to his set."[102] However, for woman, the feminized object rather than the masculinized subject of language, the case is quite the reverse. In the symbolic order of reality, rather than "all," woman is "not all":

> [W]hen any speaking being whatever lines up under the banner of women it is by being constituted as not all that they are placed within the phallic function. It is this that defines the . . . the what?—the woman precisely, except that *The* woman can only be written with *The* crossed through. There is no such thing as *The* woman, where the definite article stands for the universal. There is no such things as *The* woman since of her essence—having already risked the term, why think twice about it?—of her essence, she is not all (*pas-toute*).[103]

Since only that which is part of the symbolic order has being, Lacan is able to claim that that part of the feminine that denies the phallus does not in fact *exist:* "For to exist is to have a place within the symbolic register."[104] Since the symbolic register allows nothing to exist which says "No!" to it, in her powerful negation of the phallus, the abstraction Woman, according to Lacan, may only *ex-sist* on the other side of being, outside of language.

In terms of *The Book of the Duchess,* it is not surprising to note then that the Black Knight, although he expends close to four thousand words describing his courtship of white, grants her only one word, and that word is "Nay" (lines 1236–45):

[102] Fink, *Lacanian Subject,* p. 109.

[103] Lacan, "God and the *Jouissance* of ~~The~~ Woman," in Juliet Mitchell and Jacqueline Rose, eds., *Feminine Sexuality: Jacques Lacan and the école freudienne,* trans. Jacqueline Rose (New York: Norton, 1985), p. 144. We might connect Lacan's discomfort with his own conclusions with the Black Knight's awkward representation of the sign of woman, as noted below.

[104] Fink, *Lacanian Subject,* p. 113.

"And whan I had my tale y-doo,
God wot, she acounted nat a stree
Of al my tale, so thoghte me.
To telle shortly ryght as hyt ys,
Trewly hir answere hyt was this—
I kan not now wel counterfete
Hir wordes, but this was the grete
Of hir answere: she sayde 'Nay'
Al outerly. Allas, that day
The sorowe I suffred and the woo."

While "Nay" is the only word white is allowed in her rejection of this representative of the phallic order, we must note that her heroic stance is necessarily compromised from the start. "Nay" is, after all, not apparently her own speech but rather a ventriloquized representation of it. How awkward is the Black Knight's articulation of white's rejection of his amorous suit! Although he wishes to recount her rebuff "shortly," "ryght," and "[t]rewly," he is apparently unable to "counterfete" her words accurately, so he instead generalizes the gist, "the grete," of her intent. This squirmy linguistic performance surely signals a male discomfort with the penetration of the phallic order by the threat of feminine language (whatever that may be). Whether or not white's "Nay" belongs ultimately to white or to her rejected lover, this negative "edgewise" sign from/of woman is obviously positioned very carefully right on that gendered faultline between the symbolic and the nonsymbolizable. Therefore, determining the meaning of white's "Nay" may prove to be the most challenging problem posed in the entire elegy, a problem made even more complex by the male subject's iteration of white's "Nay" in the final stage of his therapeutic dream. Indeed, defining the significance of white's "Nay" is comparable, perhaps identical, to resolving the ontological problem of "white" itself.

On the subject of the negation of woman, Lacan, of course, does not have the final word. Julia Kristeva attempts to redress Lacan's psychoanalytic masculinism by revalorizing the negativity he attributes to woman. While agreeing that the speaking subject is always already riven, Kristeva contends that language itself is constituted by a dialectic between the symbolic—"an always split unification"—and what she calls the "semiotic"—"a negativity introduced into the symbolic order." For Kristeva, the semiotic *chora* (a term deriving from the *Timaeus*) is both the revolutionary place of "poetic language" and a "negative" maternal and feminine space that has logical and chronological links to somatic drives and primary processes.[105] In itself, however, the semiotic (which in several of its features approximates Lacan's imaginary order), and thus its effects are registered only in and through disruptions within the symbolic order itself. Rather than with a positivity that is able to function elsewhere, therefore, Kristeva is only able to equate the semiotic with a radical negativity that finds limited expression and "complex articulation" in those occasional "thetic" breaks in the symbolic order. It is in these gaps of transgressive rupture at the threshold of language that Kristeva believes a revolutionary poetics and a reconstruction of the (feminine) subject's identity are possible. As Barbara Will explains, Kristeva's "revolutionary poetic practice [is] always 'in process,' always engaged in constituting itself in and through the 'impossible dialectic' of the symbolic and the semiotic. [Her p]oetic practice, in short, exposes the fantasy of identity, and places the symbolic order 'under attack.'"[106]

Seen through the agenda of Kristeva'a poetics, white's "Nay" would appear to embrace several negative meanings at once: it signifies the resistant "emptiness" of the semiotic *chora* to the hegemony of the phallic signifier; it foregrounds the poem's dialectic between the symbolic order and the presymbolic (characterized as either the semiotic or the imaginary); it dramatizes the power of feminine negativity as a radical counterpoetics, saying "no" to *le "non" du Pere.* None of this, however, changes the fact that, for all of her significance, white's "reality-effect" would appear to have scant presence in the elegy. White-the-signified is still an absence, on the other side of the bar of signification, outside the text, "Nay" serving as a sign of her nonpresence. "In 'woman,'" Kristeva avers, "I see something that cannot be represented, something that is not said, something above and beyond nomenclatures and ideologies."[107] From a Kristevan perspective, therefore, the identity, reality, and agency of white remain hypothetical or nil.

Kristeva's pioneering attempt to open a "feminine" space of difference

[105] Julia Kirsteva, *Revolution in Poetic Language,* trans. Margaret Waller (New York: Columbia University Press, 1984), pp. 68, 69.

[106] Barbara Will, "(Mis)reading Krisreva," *Feminist Review,* forthcoming (I am grateful to her for sharing her essay before publication).

[107] Julia Kristeva, interviewed in Elaine Marks and Isabelle de Courtivron, eds., *New French Feminisms* (Amherst: University of Massachusetts Press, 1980), p. 137.

inside the gap between the symbolic and the nonsymbolizable has been provided a somewhat surprising response from Žižek, a Lacanian exegete not usually concerned with feminist poetics. Taking as his major text another of Lacan's famous aphorisms, "Woman is symptom of man," Žižek maintains that, rather than relegating Woman to the realm of nonbeing, Lacan, at least in his later writings, is actually arguing that the entire being of man exists only in his symptom, and only because of his symptom, which is Woman:

If . . . we conceive the symptom as Lacan did in his last writings and seminars, namely as a particular signifying formation which confers on the subject its very ontological consistency, enabling it to structure its basic, constitutive relationship towards enjoyment (*jouissance*), then the entire relationship is reversed, for if the symptom is dissolved, the subject itself disintegrates. In this sense, "Woman is a symptom of man" means that man himself exists only through woman qua his symptom: his very ontological consistency depends on, is "externalized" in, his symptom. In other words, man literally *ex-sists:* his entire being lies "out there," in woman. Woman, on the other hand, does *not* exist, she *insists,* which is why she does not come to be through man only. . . . Lacan attempted to capture this excess by the notion of a "*not-all,*" feminine *jouissance.*[108]

To take this reading further would be to argue a reversal in the relationship between subject and object, man and woman, the symbolic and the symptom. White's insistent "Nay" then becomes a positive sign, a "particular signifying formation" saving man from the nothingness and disintegration of mere exsistence. In a manner that comes close to reinscribing the negative theology of courtly love, the adoring male subject—be he the dreamer or the Black Knight—discovers psychical wholeness via that *jouissance* residing in the "symptomatic" realm of woman. At the same time, however, for Žižek the bar between the phallic subject and the symptomatic object remains what it had been for Lacan, an impervious and undeconstructible barrier utterly resistant to the passage of the linguistic signifier. As a sign, "Nay" must reside *inside* the symbolic order, under the banner of the masculine. Therefore, white's "Nay" cannot be white's but must be man's.

A third way of responding to that feminine "Nay" sited in the apore-

[108] Slavoj Žižek, "Rossellini: Woman as Symptom of Man," *October* 54 (1990): 21.

tic gap between language and the Other has been developed by Vicky Kirby in her brilliant study, *Telling Flesh: The Substance of the Corporeal.* Reevaluating the epistemic framework informing Saussure, Lacan, Kristeva, Žižek, and other postmodern thinkers, Kirby contends that the principle of noncontradiction that underpins Western metaphysics has necessitated that philosophers of language maintain an impossible position: even while positing that there is nothing "outside the sign," they must also posit that there is "something" outside the sign. This something, variously called materiality, substance, body, or woman, is also provided the anti-name of "nothing" because it is presumed to be unknowable. Kirby convincingly argues that some of the most important anti-essentialist thinkers in this past century have been consistently guilty of an unselfcritical essentializing of matter itself. If, however, the essence of the so-called asymbolic other were itself deessentialized, then the world of the referent might come into being as an integral part of the game of language, a place where movement and difference between partially embodied signs would produce a more playful and labile relationship between signifiers and signifieds:

> If we extend the play of the signifier "in the world" to "the game of the world," then the generative substance of matter, the body of feminized nature, is no longer a solid ground as immutable essence and origin. If difference motivates matter, incorporating transformations thought to be incorporeal, knitting signification within representation within substance, then the body as nature as woman as other involves a *différance* for which oppositional logic can give little account. What is required here is a sense that ideality and materiality are enmeshed and empowered by what Derrida might call an inscriptive efficacy, a "writing together of traces." This productive entanglement is so entire that ideality and materiality, as they are commonly conceived, are profoundly altered.[109]

Deconstructing the aporetic gaps in deconstruction itself, Kirby's methodologies can also be employed to revalorize the status of white's "Nay." In such a reading, rather than a radical rejection of the patriarchal "no," or a metaphysical support-symptom for masculinist being, white's "Nay" may constitute the promise of a "productive entanglement" of essence and substance, the feminine and the masculine, signifiers and signifieds. Much of the power of Kirby's argument is located in her insistence that the Saussurian bar between the verbal signifier and things "in

[109] Kirby, *Telling Flesh,* p. 55.

the world" need never have been considered an absolute, even though Lacan, Žižek, and others have barred the bar from scrutiny. And Chaucer would seem to have agreed with Kirby's revisionism. By granting "Nay" such dramatic attention, by placing this one word of prohibition on the cusp between the symbolic and the Other, and by insisting that the subject of the talking cure reiterate white's negative command at the very end of the poem, Chaucer makes the gendered faultline of Western metaphysics available for sustained critical analysis.

The poem's interrogation of this faultline comes to rest at nearly the same moment that the narrator's dream comes to its end. The dreamer's closing appraisal of the semiotic faultline, symbolized by the gap in his psyche between "white" and white, need not of course be the poem's fully considered appraisal nor the reader's. In fact, while the dreamer's "unconscious" resolutions are instructive, the poem's resolutions, unsurprisingly, are considerably more capacious. *The Book of the Duchess* ultimately grants its readers the responsibility to determine for themselves the nature and import of this gendered, linguistic, and metaphysical bar between the symbolic and the Other. While this insistence on hermeneutic freedom and readerly agency is a signature of Chaucer's art, equally typical of Chaucer's poetic strategies is the "disappointing" and nontriumphal manner with which he brings both the dream and the poem to an end.

The dream begins its ending with the third and last appearance of the "I/thow" refrain, after which the narrator and the Black Knight finally succeed in communicating, agreeing to the elementary but essential fact that white is dead (lines 1305–13):

> "'Thow wost ful lytel what thow menest;
> I have lost more than thow wenest.'
> God wot, allas! Ryght that was she!"
> "Allas sir, how? What may that be?"
> "She ys ded!" "Nay!" "Yis, be my trouthe!"
> "Is that youre los? Be God, hyt ys routhe!"
> And with that word ryght anoon
> They gan to strake forth; al was doon,
> For that tyme, the hert-huntyng.

The abrupt *finale* to the dream's talking cure has, unsurprisingly, troubled many readers. "For a climax to a long apotheosis of love and the lady," protests Minnis, "is not this rather disappointing?"[110] In an attempt to improve upon this ending, various exegetes have exercised their ingenuities by ameliorating the dialogue's quick-dispatch *conclusio* into some kind of transcendent *consolatio.* But their apotheosizing efforts do not seem to succeed; indeed, the dreamer's talking-cure stops "too fast," and the perfunctory reappearance of the all-but-forgotten hunters does nothing to decrease our readerly dissatisfactions. Anything—solace, false surmise, epiphany, "truth," or "a-little-bit-more"—would be better than this. But all we are given is a minimalist swap of fact for feeling—"She ys ded!" "Nay!" "Yis, be my trouthe!" / "Is that youre los? Be God, hyt ys routhe!"—before the dream is gone.

Cheat, loss, disappointment—"That is not enough, that's not what I wish/need to know"—these emotions are deliberately evoked by the elegy's closing strategies. And these strategies may be intended to be therapeutic. Having projected his personal fantasies of erotic union with the *objet a* throughout the poem, at poem's end the ego is confronted finally, and suddenly, with what Freud called the "hard kernel of truth." This hard kernel (Žižek calls it "the Rock of the real") emerges as the ineffable Thing which the censoring powers of the unconscious have successfully repressed until the very end of the dream. It is only at the *unexpected* end of the therapy session, Lacan believed, that the "true speech" of the unconscious subject is likely to break through.[111] Thus the depressed dreamer may have accomplished the hard work of self-analysis precisely because the non-elevating end to his talking cure refuses to keep the ego protected in a delusory state of gratification. Therefore, in all likelihood, were it not for the facticity and simplicity of this recognition, "She ys ded!", the real could never have surfaced into the symbolic plane of language.

Despite its adamantine hardness, the core statement "She ys ded!" appears to provide the potential for symbolic release. In fact, if we look at them more carefully, these three words clearly incorporate issues central to the psycho-semiotics of the dream and of the entire elegy. "She" is a pronoun that invokes once again—but now in the third person—the conundrum of pronominal reference. As such, it foregrounds the resistance of all pronouns to the pressures of individuating reference: How does "she" represent white, and does "she" represent white only? "Ys" is the foundational copulative of language, upon whose meaning our

[110] Minnis, *Shorter Poems,* p. 84.

[111] Evans, *Dictionary,* p. 191.

understanding of Being and Nothingness, presence, and absence, rests. As such, "ys" invokes one of the elegy's major questions: How does the referent of any sign have, or lack, being? "Ded" would seem to speak to both of these questions, for it is a signifier which has the power to strike through both preceding signs, negating their claims to significance and truth. As such, it is intimately linked to the narrator's own response, "Nay!," another instructive, even metaphysical, sign. Although technically a negative, this "Nay" would seem to affirm the core statement's equation of Being ("ys") with Negativity ("ded"). Indeed, it is possible to imagine between affirming negation ("Nay") and negating affirmation ("Yis") the emergence of an evolving and expanding dialogue. Juxtaposed, stichomythic, these logical opposites—"Nay"/"Yis"/ /"ded"/ "ys"—appear to be entangling, even converging, as if the Western law of noncontradiction were itself undergoing a poetic deconstruction. Rather than Lacan's "impassable bar," rather than Kristeva's "impossible dialectic," the faultline between Being and Nothingness, symbolic and feminine, reality and the real, may be closer to what Kirby calls a "productive entanglement." Yet, for all this, the hard kernel of truth is now acknowledged: the material actuality of white's death has been unambiguously stated, for the first and last time in the poem.

Since, in my reading, it is the narrator and not the Black Knight who is the subject of the talking cure, it is the narrator's search for truth and his acceptance of loss that are at issue throughout the dream. Why, we then need to ask, is it precisely these words—"Yis, be my trouthe!" / "Is that youre los? Be God, hyt ys routhe!"—that serve as the dreamer's cue to awake from sleep? Minnis does not like their sound: "there is a hint of something . . . which feels uncomfortably like bathos. The chime of the rhyme diminishes the emotional force of the exchange, making it sound inappropriately pat and curt."[112] But surely the chiming rhyme is meant to suggest a near-identity between "trouthe" and "routhe," each a subjective correlative to the same efficient cause, the recognition of "los." In fact, at this moment, it appears that the subject's psyche actually moves beyond the Black Knight's. In the psychoanalytic grammar of the dream, in other words, the Black Knight represents but one part of the dreamer's fractured identity, and while this part stays locked in melancholia, the "I" of the dream, internalizing the "trouthe" of death, moves from the paralysis of depression into the sadness of "routhe." This movement from depression to mourning matters. "Depression freezes,

[112] Minnis, *Shorter Poems,* p. 84.

but sadness flows," writes Terrence Real about men and depression, "It has an end."[113] Acknowledging the reality of "los," feeling the force of "routhe," the dreamer has apparently transformed the "nothing" with which his therapy began (no thought, no feeling) into the affirmative maturities of "Nay."

But where is white in all this? In a perfect rhyme that resonates throughout the poem, the dreamer's "Nay" echoes the "Nay" of the feminine Other. But does the dreamer's "Nay" likewise empower white herself? One could argue that Chaucer's poem presents white's "Nay," and not the dreamer's, as its most powerful sign and its most proper signifier. Indeed, as we have noted, white's "Nay" could be seen to effect a "thetic" break in the poem's symbolic surface, putting its cultural ideology "under attack" (Kristeva). White's "Nay" could be interpreted as an enabling symptom of masculine identity, without which man's being, his ontological consistency, would cease to exist (Žižek). And white's "Nay" could be appreciated as a dialogized sign deconstructing the bar's principles of opposition, effecting a mutual exchange between subject and object, "knitting signification within representation within substance" (Kirby). These three readings of the gap between "white" and white are not embraced by the dreamer, but may be by the poem's readers.

When we suffer tragic loss, one of our profoundest responses is to cling to the dream that we might be able to reverse the course of time, undo history, and make the past present. Much of the work of mourning is thus given over to the pain of emotions evoked by signs of the past, as the sorrowing subject accedes gradually but never wholly to history's refusal to be revivified. Like other elegies, *The Book of the Duchess* gives expression to the human hope of undoing time and to our refusal ever fully to accept irreversible loss. And, in fact, these desires are manifested in the poem's all-inclusive temporal design. *The Book of the Duchess* opens in the present tense as the narrator complains about his sleeplessness; at line 44, however, the tense of the poem abruptly shifts into the past; the elegy remains in this tense until the poem's last four words, where, 1290 lines after its movement into the past, it shifts back into the present: "now hit ys doon."[114]

[113] Terrence Real, *I Don't Want to Talk About It: Overcoming the Secret Legacy of Male Depression* (New York: Scribner, 1998), p. 285.

[114] Specifically, the poem opens (line 1) with "I have gret wonder," shifts into the past (line 44) with "So whan I saw," and returns to the present (line 1334) with "now hit ys doon."

The elegy's breaking of its own linguistic plane, working from present to past and to present again in a motion unaligned with the events it narrates, may be critically glossed by invoking one final Lacanian term, the *point de capiton.* Translated as "quilting point" or "anchoring point," the *point de capiton* is literally an upholstery button: just as a mattress-maker's needle is inserted to hold down a shapeless mass that would otherwise move too freely about, so *points de capiton* are points in the free-floating discourse of language where "signified and signifier are knotted together."[115] In the constant slippage of language, Lacan suggests, it is necessary to believe there is at least a minimal number of holding-points where a signified is attached, if only momentarily, to a signifier. While these linguistic attachments guarantee us a much-needed measure of sanity, they also allow us to quilt retroactively, so to speak, as the signifier works against the course of time in the direction of a signified which is lost, repressed, and past.[116]

Like a *point de capiton* writ large, Chaucer's poem may thus be viewed as a single linguistic sign, an elegy whose signifiers quilt retroactively into a field of historical signification, a field they themselves are (re)constituting. While this master gesture of "presentifying" history is consoling, it is at the same time another cause for grief, for of course the signified contains only the image and *conceptus* of the sign, and not the thing itself. It may be for this reason that Chaucer's choice of "white" as his premier nominal proves so satisfying. A paronym signifying not a substantive but an accident, "white" gestures toward some *aliquid* somewhere in space and in time with an imprecision that is in fact consoling in its indeterminacy. (Is it mere coincidence that elegists, from Theocritus to Whitman, substitute a nonce-name for the name of the lost beloved?) A more proper sign would surely be too determinate, too final: to utter that rigid designator would be like naming death itself. Thus, both for Chaucer's immediate audience and for his modern readers, part of "white"'s perfection as a name is that it names so imperfectly. Nevertheless, at any moment, readers have the freedom to perform a baptismal act of (re-)naming in an attempt to cross the bar of our *méconnaissance.* At any moment, that is, we have the option of pointing the linguistic sign of *The Book of the Duchess* in one direction, toward a woman whose name is White.

[115] Lacan, *Seminar. Book III,* p. 268; cited in Evans, *Dictionary,* p. 149.
[116] See Evans, *Dictionary,* p. 149.

For the poem's dreaming subject, however, effecting his own talking cure, white seems not to have acquired any greater definition of identity or agency: she remains for him a paronym, a general and incomplete signifier of absence and lack. Because white-the-signified is now signified as "ded," it can be understood that the talking cure is complete, as the subject finally acknowledges both his own lack and the lack in the Other. For this reason, at dialogue's end, for the first and final time in the poem, this "I" feels sorrow: "Is that youre los? Be God, hyt ys routhe!" As the subject of Chaucer's elegy, he is finally able to mourn. Yet the object of his grief proves not to be white's body nor the Black Knight's loss, but that part of his own ego that has just passed away.

Chaucer and Rape: Uncertainty's Certainties

Christopher Cannon
St. Edmund Hall, Oxford

Rape is a brutal crime and implies a degree of depravity which should make us cautious in fixing such a charge. There is really no evidence for it. That he seduced Cecilia we may well believe; that she was angry with him, and still more with herself, is extremely probable. She may have honestly thought that because it all happened against her better judgment, that therefore it was without her consent. Her scandalized family would naturally treat that as an irrebuttable presumption. But there is nothing to suggest that Cecilia could have convicted Chaucer of felony.

—T. F. T. Plucknett (1948)[1]

GONE ARE THE DAYS when conjoining Chaucer's name to the crime of rape seemed repugnant even to those scholars who would address its possibility. In place of Plucknett's insistence that the very gravity of such a crime converts uncertain guilt into certain innocence—where the very documents that raise the issue provide "no evidence"—we now have Carolyn Dinshaw's demonstration that the conjunction makes us better readers: as it "invites us to consider causal relationships between gendered representation and actual social relations between men and women," we may acknowledge that there are "real rapes" as

Elizabeth Scala and Elizabeth Robertson created the different, but simultaneous, opportunities that occasioned this piece, and I thank them for these invitations as well as for their helpful responses to my earliest attempts. I would also like to thank all my interlocutors at the University of Texas at Austin and, for careful and extremely useful readings, Juliet Fleming, H. A. Kelly, Jill Mann, and James Simpson.

[1] T. F. T. Plucknett, "Chaucer's Escapade," *Law Quarterly Review* 64 (1948): 35. This epigraph has more than incidental status in framing an exploration of the Chaumpaigne release. With the exception of the first sentence I quote, these words are also repeated for their authority in the standard source for the Chaumpaigne release, the *Chaucer Life-Records,* ed. Martin M. Crow and Clair C. Olson (Oxford: Clarendon Press, 1966). For the release, see p. 343 in this volume; for Plucknett's words, see pp. 345–46.

well as "fictional rapes" and thereby learn to see what is and is not "figurative" in Chaucer's "sexual poetics."[2] That on May 4, 1380, Cecily Chaumpaigne had enrolled in Chancery a document releasing Chaucer of "all manner of actions such as they relate to my rape or any other thing or cause" ("omnimodas acciones tam de raptu meo tam de aliqua alia re vel causa") is a fact that few now would try to put by: it is, as Dinshaw also says, "perhaps the one biographical fact everyone remembers about Chaucer."[3] And the resilience of that memory, we have also learned to recognize, is not simply due to the gravity of the released crime. As Jill Mann has shown, the subject is one that Chaucer himself does not shrink from: throughout his writing, "rape remains a constant touchstone for determining justice between the sexes."[4]

But if we have arrived at a stage where considering Chaucer and rape together no longer seems dangerous, if we are even able to make that consideration critically enabling, we are not yet at a stage where the Chaumpaigne release seems able to teach us anything more than we are willing to presume. Clearer understanding of the role rape may play in Chaucer's poetics has not resulted from any clearer understanding of what precisely the Chaumpaigne release refers to, largely because the release is so parsimonious of description and the language and procedure of medieval English law so frequently ambiguous as they pertain to *raptus.* Although I have argued elsewhere that this word in the Chaumpaigne release must refer to forced coitus, central to that earlier argument was the claim that mention of a *raptus* in fourteenth-century law was itself an attempt to achieve clarity in the face of a legal tradition that had become hopelessly confused about the naming of sexual violence and its punishment.[5] That confusion will always make it possible to say that "raptus" *might* have been used to describe an "abduction" in the Chaumpaigne release, as has been said in the past—although I think not because the term has always had wide reference in Latin (as past claims for *ambiguity* have maintained), but because, first, a legal document in the fourteenth-century as well as now is necessarily an instrument at some

[2] Carolyn Dinshaw, *Chaucer's Sexual Poetics* (Madison: University of Wisconsin Press, 1989), p. 11.

[3] Ibid., p. 10.

[4] Jill Mann, *Geoffrey Chaucer* (Hemel Hempstead, UK: Harvester Wheatsheaf, 1991), p. 45.

[5] See my "*Raptus* in the Chaumpaigne Release and a Newly Discovered Document Concerning the Life of Geoffrey Chaucer," *Speculum* 68 (1993): 74–94, esp. pp. 76–89.

remove from "what happened" and, second, because sexual violence is itself a crime wherein "what happened," the very act that might constitute the crime, can be variously defined even by those who have identical "facts" in hand.[6] The first point is clear enough even to the casuist Plucknett: although he is certainly wrong to suppose that uncertainties about the Chaumpaigne release's historical witness are themselves necessarily absolving, he is certainly right in suggesting that even if *raptus* refers to "rape" in that release (which he believes), this does not demonstrate that Chaucer raped Cecily Chaumpaigne. Plucknett gets at the second point too when he explains how different parties in a rape case can position the act in question on different sides of the line that marks crime: the "irrebuttable presumption" of Cecily and her "scandalized family" is a presumption that Plucknett, taking Chaucer's part, is perfectly willing to rebut. But the relation of this second point to the first—whether an event that Chaumpaigne would call "rape" and Chaucer would call something else is or is not rape, either to fourteenth-century courts or to us—is an issue that has not been explored. What definition will we use for rape, in other words, when we ask what *raptus* means? What does the Chaumpaigne release really say if the *raptus* it refers to is an act that, according to the vigorously defended affective states of both those involved in it, is *at once* rape and not rape? What does the Chaumpaigne release teach *us* if that act is one that we would now call "rape" (because, say, Chaumpaigne felt it was but Chaucer did not) but that fourteenth-century law was entirely happy to throw into a category it understood as "abduction"?

[6] For a survey of the various positions that have been adopted on the meaning of *raptus* in the Chaumpaigne release, see, again, ibid., p. 75 and nn. 5–7. To these may be added the more recent remarks of Derek Pearsall: "Quite commonly in legal documents of the time, *raptus* means 'abduction'"; *The Life of Geoffrey Chaucer: A Critical Biography* (Oxford: Blackwell, 1992), p. 135. For exploration of other fourteenth-century legal records that mention *raptus,* see Henry Ansgar Kelly, "Meanings and Uses of *Raptus* in Chaucer's Time," *SAC* 20 (1998): 101–65. Kelly attempts to reconstruct the events that led to the use of this term, and he finds evidence that those events were sometimes more like abduction than rape. His evidence certainly extends the gray area in the record, particularly as it relates to one case (Yeuelcombe/Mann), which I have relied upon to argue that *raptus* means "rape" in the legal milieu in which the Chaumpaigne release was drafted. On the other hand, Kelly's important deepening of our knowledge of legal language should be read against my exploration here of the problems involved in either believing or understanding what that legal language "means." If *raptus* may mean "abduction," then what does *abduction* mean? For my discussion of the Yeuelcombe/Mann case as well as the beginnings of my claim that the "persistent gray area" in legal records must be related to the "complex continuum of behavior" that constitutes acts of "abduction" and "rape," see my "*Raptus* in the Chaumpaigne Release," pp. 86–89.

This essay claims that, while many questions about the Chaumpaigne release will never be answered, answers are available for the questions I have just posed; its implication, therefore, is that we are wrong to assume that the release's witness allows us only to reconstruct possibilities, and that "beyond that, all is speculation."[7] We have not yet been fully schooled by this document, I will suggest, because our worry that we will be wrongly certain has prevented us from realizing that uncertainty is itself something we may be certain about. The fault in our method of inquiry relates directly to its object here, since definitions of rape necessarily occupy the very gray area we have refused to define: we mistake what this wrong *is* when we insist that it has only occurred under conditions of absolute agreement between accuser and defendant or when it has been named and punished by the law. The improvement of our understanding is given an imperative, moreover, in the ways that Chaucer's writing shows him to have defined such grayness with precisely the situational and philosophical specificity we have lacked. It may not constitute proof of the biographical relevance of either the Chaumpaigne release or of rape to describe the great imaginative and intellectual energy Chaucer devoted to such definition in his poetry and prose. But it should be relevant that Chaucer understood rape better than we have done in our scrutiny of the Chaumpaigne release, that he answers questions we have not as yet really posed. As I will argue in what follows, understanding the Chaumpaigne release and reading Chaucer ought to be identical endeavors precisely because a more careful definition of the conditions that constitute an act as rape shows Chaucer knowing those conditions and carefully delineating them for us.

Since, as I have suggested, any definition of rape we discover in fourteenth-century law is necessarily subject to reevaluation according to modern definitions, it would be well to make clear from the start what these modern definitions are themselves both certain and uncertain about. "Rape defined" in the modern criminal code turns at every junc-

[7] Pearsall provides an admirable reconstruction of this kind in the *Life of Geoffrey Chaucer* and nearly ends with the phrase I quote here, which he calls the "safest conclusion" in a case for which "there is not enough evidence to come to a conclusion." On the other hand, Pearsall does not forgo speculation, some of which usefully defines the uncertainties in question ("the actual offense . . . is not necessarily the offense named in the charge"), but some of which obscures what "violent physical rape" might be, as it suggests that problems would be ameliorated if this were a case of "violent physical passion"; see Pearsall, *Life of Geoffrey Chaucer,* pp. 135–38.

tion on "consent" and the "victim's will."[8] The principal matter of this definition is the set of conditions or rules by which an "act of sexual intercourse" can be judged to have been accomplished without consent, against the victim's will: the specificities of these rules go, in every case, to the *circumstances* that would indicate nonconsent at the moment of an act. Where an act of sexual intercourse occurs and there is mental disorder, developmental or physical disability, force or violence, fear of bodily injury either immediately or as threatened for the future, unconsciousness of the nature of the act, intoxication or anesthetization, or an artificially induced belief that the person committing the act is the person's spouse, then consent is deemed not to have been given and the act is judged to be "rape."

The modern law's strength is, therefore, the extent to which it determines consent on the basis of clear rules, but the mode of that determination is also this law's most serious weakness: while the copiousness of conditions specified makes rape detectable and prosecutable in an extraordinarily wide variety of modern circumstances, acts inevitably occur for which no rule has as yet been devised. Rules about conditions inevitably leave some conditions out; the law can therefore not be certain about consent to acts committed under those conditions; and the law necessarily renders such uncertainty legally equivalent to consent

[8] I will take the code of the state of California as paradigmatic of the "modern" here, because it is progressive (and so its definitional failures are the more interesting and significant) and lengthy (providing substantial text for the detailed analysis I undertake). The issues I will take up in relation to this American code are also raised in modern English provisions (in particular, the crucial relation between sexual violence and "consent"), but these issues are less easy to ventilate because the detail of English provisions is spread so much more diffusely through the case law. The framework for this law is set out, however, by section 1 of the Sexual Offences Act of 1956 (as amended by section 142 of the Criminal Justice and Public Order Act of 1994): "(1) It is an offence for a man to rape a woman or another man. (2) A man commits rape if—(a) he has sexual intercourse with a person (whether vaginal or anal) who at the time of the intercourse does not consent to it; and (b) at the time he knows that the person does not consent to the intercourse or is reckless as to whether that person consents to it. (3) A man also commits rape if he induces a married woman to have sexual intercourse with him by impersonating her husband." For the text of the California Code, see California Penal Code, sec. 261, in *West's Annotated California Codes* (St. Paul, Minn.: West Publishing, 1997), vol. 48 (supplement): 50–51. Here and subsequently I cite the version of the code in the "Cumulative Pocket Part" supplementary to the 1988 volumes of *West's Codes*. For the text of the English law, see Alan Reed and Peter Seago, *Criminal Law* (London: Sweet and Maxwell, 1999), p. 387. I am grateful to my colleague in St. Edmund Hall, Adrian Briggs, for guidance on points relating to the English law.

(insofar as the acts then in question are excluded from criminal punishment). Indeed, as Susan Estrich has shown, what might appear to be relatively small gaps in these rules can still render most acts of forced coitus undefinable as "rape": until relatively recently, the modern law required nonconsent to be manifest in some corroborating physical evidence of "resistance" (that is, by the visible harm of bruises and torn clothing), and so it could not define as nonconsensual those acts of sex that had themselves been forced but that were not accompanied by evidence of violence of some *other* kind.[9] It is true that the rigor of these rules has recently been dramatically increased, particularly as they now specify conditions that allow for nonconsent within marriage (making spousal rape prosecutable).[10] But even the newest rules still ignore some conditions: where, for example, mental or physical disability or intoxication bars the very giving of consent—where unconsciousness of the nature of the act precludes agreement to sex—it is still maintained that, for such an act to be "rape," that disability or that unconsciousness must be *known* to the perpetrator.[11] And the conviction that assures that some limitations will always remain in the modern law (that some rapes will go "undefined" and therefore unpunished) is clearly set out in that law's most careful definition of "consent":

> In prosecutions under Section 261 ["rape defined"] . . . in which consent is at issue, "consent" shall be defined to mean positive cooperation in act or attitude pursuant to an exercise of free will. The person must act freely and voluntarily and have knowledge of the nature of the act or transaction involved.[12]

Our law is simply unwilling to make judgments about the status of an interior faculty (as both this section and the section on "rape defined" name this faculty, it is the "will") unless that faculty can be transformed into an activity (so the "free will" is "exercise[d]" and "consent" takes

[9] See Susan Estrich, *Real Rape* (Cambridge, Mass.: Harvard University Press, 1987), pp. 29–56.

[10] On "rape of spouse," see California Penal Code, sec. 262, in *West's Codes* 48 (suppl.). For the addition of this definition by statute in 1979, see the 1988 volumes of *West's Codes* 48:160–61. The English law, it should be noted, does not take the possibility of spousal rape into explicit account (for it only makes the "impersonation" of a spouse unlawful), although a decision of the House of Lords in 1992 has made prosecution of spousal rape possible under the Sexual Offences Act. See Reed and Seago, *Criminal Law,* p. 388 nn. 95 and 98.

[11] See California Penal Code, sec. 261 (subsecs. 1, 3, and 4), in *West's Codes* 48 (suppl.).

[12] California Penal Code, sec. 261.6, in ibid.

the form of "positive cooperation"). In its need to externalize the inner territory that is the acknowledged site of its investigations, in other words, the modern law ensures definitional failure: if "cooperation" must be indicated by "act," then any conflicting "attitude" (a concomitant reluctance of the "will") may itself be hidden *by means of* a cooperative act. Where certainty about consensual states is necessary for an act to be defined as rape and conditions of consent cannot be rendered certain, there must be acts that are rape that remain unknown to the law—and therefore unpunished by it—because the law's own definitions make it impossible to know what they are.

If such severe definitional problems remain for modern understandings, we should hardly be surprised to find that definitions of rape in the English Middle Ages were troubled. But what makes the lens of modern problems particularly apposite for understanding earlier confusions is the extent to which, even in the context of very different legal and social circumstances, those definitions can be analyzed by exactly the terms I have just used. The codes in question here—that is, those with most direct relevance to the legal circumstance of the Chaumpaigne release—are the notoriously difficult chapter 13 of Westminster I (1275), the equally difficult chapter 34 of Westminster II (1285), and the so-called Statute of Rapes (1382).[13] There are, indeed, a host of problems yet to be solved in relating the language of these statutes to the complex court procedures that arose in their name, but fundamental to these problems is, again, the determination of nonconsent as a means to defining the acts these laws would punish.[14] The first phrases of chapter 13 in Westminster I make this clear in themselves, for they have the king prohibiting "that none do ravish nor take away by force any maiden

[13] The "Statute of Rapes" follows the Chaumpaigne release, of course, but its close proximity in time gives it relevance. For text and translations of these statutes, see *The Statutes of the Realm,* 12 vols. (London, 1810–28; rpt. [London: Dawsons], 1963), 1:29 (Westminster I, ch. 13), 1:87–88 (Westminster II, ch. 34–35), and 2:27 ("Statute of Rapes"). I have been aided greatly in my research on these statutes by Henry Ansgar Kelly's "Statutes of Rapes and Alleged Ravishers of Wives: A Context for the Charges against Thomas Malory, Knight," *Viator* 28 (1997): 361–419.

[14] For crucial examinations of the procedural ramifications of these statutes, see two articles by J. B. Post: "Ravishment of Women and the Statutes of Westminster," in J. H. Baker, ed., *Legal Records and the Historian* (London: Royal Historical Society, 1978), pp. 150–64, and "Sir Thomas West and the Statute of Rapes, 1382," *Bulletin of the Institute of Historical Research* 53 (1980): 24–30. See also Sue Sheridan Walker, "Punishing Convicted Ravishers: Statutory Strictures and Actual Practice in Thirteenth[-] and Fourteenth-Century England," *Journal of Medieval History* 13 (1987): 237–50.

within age, *neither by her own consent,* nor without" ("le rey defent qe nul ne ravie ne prenge a force damoysele dedenz age, ne par son gre ne saun son gre").[15] It is not surprising to find that the phrase *by force* (or, *a force*) comes and goes in the manuscript tradition of this statute, since, when present, it proposes a circumstance in which force is required to accomplish a "ravishment," even though the victim *agrees* in the first place.[16] On the other hand, the presence of the phrase only intensifies that odd proposal, since even without it we have a statute prohibiting *consensual* "ravishment"—whatever that might be. Although, as J. B. Post has noted, Westminster II seems to have returned to the matter of Westminster I to clear up language that "was considered wholly inadequate," definitions grow no clearer there.[17] Chapter 34 of Westminster II prohibits "ravishment" where a woman "did not consent, neither before nor after" ("ou ele ne se est assentue ne avaunt ne apres"), but also where that "ravishment" occurs "with force, although [a woman] consent *after*" ("a force, tut seit ke ele se assente apres").[18] In the first clause we find a newly rigorous attention to consent, in which a victim's nonconsent actually creates the wrong; in the second clause, however, the law uses this attention to imagine, yet again, circumstances in which a woman would consent to something that it still thinks might appropriately be called "ravishment" (because it here disallows her from withdrawing her consent). Time has become an issue in this statute, because it remains possible to conceive of a woman as still in some measure responsible for her own ravishment. What would motivate such imaginings in both Westminster I and II finally becomes clear if we look to the next clauses in chapter 34 of Westminster II, which, first, describe the suit required when "women [are] carried away with the goods of their husbands" ("de mulieribus abductis cum bonis viri") and, second, describe how a woman may be punished for her own ravishment:

> if a wife willingly leave her husband and go away and continue with her advouterer, she shall be barred forever of action to demand her dower that she ought

[15] *Statutes* 1:29 (emphasis mine). The chapter further prohibits this for "any wife or maiden of full age, nor any other woman against her will [ne dame ne damoisele de age, ne autre femme maugre seon]."

[16] For an edition of this chapter of Westminster I that leaves "a force" out, see the appendix to Post, "Ravishment of Women," pp. 162–63. For the salient differences between the edition of this chapter in the *Statutes* and Post, I rely upon Kelly, "Statutes of Rapes," pp. 364–66.

[17] Post, "Ravishment of Women," p. 156.

[18] *Statutes* 1:87 (emphasis mine).

to have of her husband's lands, if she be convict thereupon, except that her husband willingly, and without coercion of the Church, reconcile her and suffer her to dwell with him; in which case she shall be restored to her action.[19]

The Westminster statutes try to determine the status of a woman's consent *not* because they are interested in *non*consent and the prohibition of acts accomplished under this condition, but because they are worried that a woman's consent has the power to accomplish acts—in particular, to threaten her husband's financial interest in the act that is marriage. Lest we wonder how unmarried women might fit into this logic, we need only look at chapter 35 of Westminster II, which concerns "children, males and females, whose marriage belongeth to another," where the "ravisher" has "no right in the marriage."[20] It is therefore clear that, in Westminster I, consent can be given when a ravishment occurs "by force" because ravishment is not generally committed against the person ravished but against those, either husband or guardian, who have an interest in the marriage; the "force" in question, therefore, is exerted against that husband or that guardian.[21] What confirms this logic and testifies to its strength in the later decades of the fourteenth century is the more explicit effort in the Statute of Rapes (1382) to include those persons who have been ravished in its definition of the *perpetrators* of this wrong. Under prohibitory scrutiny in this statute are not only "ravishers" ("raptores") but the women who "after such rape do consent to such ravishers" ("post huiusmodi raptum huiusmodi raptoribus consenserint"); such women are dispossessed of "all inheritance, dower, or joint feoffment" ("omnem hereditatem, dotem, sive conjunctum feoffamentum"), and, what is more, in such cases the statute actually transfers "the suit to pursue" ("sectam prosequendi"), in the event of the act (now called *raptus*), to the husband, fathers, or next of blood of the person ravished.[22] A woman's consent in this statute is examined no longer for conditions that will make a "raptor" culpable—to determine in which cases she is the victim of a wrong—but in order to determine *her* culpa-

[19] "Uxor, si sponte reliquerit virum suum et abierit et moretur cum adultero suo, amittat imperpetuum accionem petendi dotem suam que ei competere posset de tenura viri, si super hoc convincatur, nisi vir suus sponte, et absque cohercione ecclesiastica, eam reconciliet et secum cohabitari permittat; in quo casu restituatur ei accio" (*Statutes* 1:87).

[20] "De pueris, sive masculis sive femellis, quorum maritagium ad aliquem pertineat, raptis et abductis, si ille qui rapuerit, non habens jus in maritagium" (*Statutes* 1:88).

[21] See Kelly, "Statutes of Rapes," p. 366.

[22] *Statutes* 2:27.

bility in the accomplished act and to make her, finally, one of the perpetrators of her own *raptus.*

Particularly as they worry about an *enabling* consent on the part of women, what all these statutes seem most concerned with is the act that we (and the women in question) might call "elopement" or "marriage choice" but which the law calls "ravishment" and seems to imagine as a kind of "seizing" in order to prohibit it; forced coitus is not the medieval law's concern.[23] I have argued elsewhere that such an emphasis in the statutes must be understood in relation to the case law contemporaneous with it, for in the latter, the language and logic of the statutes were often ignored, and explicit definitions of *raptus* as forced coitus were often set out.[24] But it is, in fact, the definitional method employed in medieval statutes and not the intention behind them that commands our attention, for "consent" is, in this sense, also the overwhelming concern of the older law. To compare the role of consent in medieval and modern definitions of rape (or "ravishment" or *raptus*) is also to see, however, that while both laws are fundamentally concerned with this condition, the modern code is so concerned in order to make consent the single condition determining the criminality of the act, whereas the Westminster statutes and the Statute of Rapes are so concerned in order to make the victim's consent *irrelevant* to that act: the medieval statutes define "ravishment" or *raptus* as punishable acts even when the "victim" consents to them. Most pertinent to any attempt to understand the Chaumpaigne release in terms of medieval statutes, then, is the way that medieval definitions disregard—and therefore inevitably render uncertain—precisely the condition that our own definitions of rape require us to be certain about.

We might try to mitigate such a drastic definitional difference by looking at "what happened" in individual medieval cases, by applying our own definitions of crime to acts regardless of the names the medieval law gives them. The problem with such an investigation, of course, is that any record we have of such acts is itself everywhere infected by those very rubrics for determining "consent" that ignore precisely the information we require: where "consent *after*" is of most interest in such records, and where a victim's "consent" is adjudged a problem (and might therefore be unreported or hidden), how will we find out what *we*

[23] Kelly, "Statutes of Rapes," pp. 380–81.

[24] See my "*Raptus* in the Chaumpaigne Release," esp. pp. 84–89.

need to know? A more profitable method, I think, is to explore the different definitional judgments the medieval statutes and our own must make of a single hypothetical act: applying the logic of both rubrics to even an imagined scenario should help us to see how differing rubrics for consent's relevance will affect the crucial designation (is the act rape, or is it not?). A scenario imagined in literature offers us as good a site as any for such a definitional experiment, and if we choose, say, the *raptus* of Helen of Troy, we find a very useful exchange in Ovid's *Heroides,* in the imagined letters of Helen and Paris, where the nature of the act and the consensual state that preceded it are precisely the matters under discussion.[25] Paris's letter, which begins this exchange, makes the issue explicit when he enjoins Helen not to fear the *raptus* he plans ("nec tu rapta time" [16.341]). And he very clearly defines the acts that he would fit under this designation when he recalls Helen's previous *raptus* by Theseus and Pirithous and, in that recollection, describes what he would have done had he been the *raptor:* "vel mihi virginitas esset libata, vel illud / quod poterat salva virginitate rapi" ["Either your virgin flower I should have plucked, or taken what could be stolen without hurt to your virgin state"] (16.161–62).

Paris promises Helen marriage (she will be "nupta" [16.370] and "coniunx" [16.374]), but he does not see marriage as necessarily distinct from conquest either, since, as his bride, Helen will still be his "prize in a mighty contest" ["pretium magni certaminis"] (16.263). Helen's reply to Paris is even more interesting, however, for she focuses at length on the status and evolution of her own consent. She begins by making clear that she is affronted by Paris's suggestion that a previous instance of *raptus* should make her seem to be generally "rapable": "an, quia vim nobis Neptunius attulit heros, / rapta semel videor bis quoque digna rapi?" ["Because the Neptunian hero employed violence with me, can it be that, stolen once, I seem fit to be stolen, too, a second time?"] (17.21–22). Her main line of defense stresses her nonconsent in the previous act, which, she says, she should not be reproached with precisely because, as a *raptus,* it was against her will: "crimen erat nostrum, si delenita fuissem; / cum sim rapta, meum quid nisi nolle fuit?" ["The blame were mine, had I been lured away; but seized, as I was, what could I do, more

[25] In what follows I take both letters and their translations from the Loeb edition of Ovid, *Heroides and Amores,* trans. Grant Showerman, rev. ed. G. P. Goold (Cambridge, Mass.: Harvard University Press, 1977). Quotations hereafter will be cited by epistle number (16, "Paris to Helen"; 17, "Helen to Paris") and line number within the text.

than refuse my will?"] (17.23–24). The change in what Helen says she wants over the course of this letter, from allowing that Paris's offer might be attractive ("a woman might well wish to submit to your embrace" ["potestque / velle sub amplexus ire puella tuos"], 17.93–94) to admitting her own desire ("Grant, none the less, that I desire to become your bride at Troy" ["ut tamen optarim fieri tua Troica coniunx"], 17.109–10), to anticipating her capitulation ("I perchance . . . [shall] yield in tardy surrender" ["aut ego . . . fortasse . . . dabo cunctatas tempore victa manus"], 17.259–60), might be understood to lend Ovid's representation of consent the kind of titillating humor we do not much enjoy anymore: even Helen's claims of guiltlessness in the earlier *raptus* are progressively impugned by her steady progress toward consenting to this one. But, however we read Ovid's tone, what may very much interest us in the subtlety of these letters is the way both consent and nonconsent are made inherent to the accomplishment of this act of *raptus:* were Helen to withhold her consent, it is suggested, the *raptus* would not happen, but even when she *does* consent, as it is clear she will, the act will not be categorized by her choice, but, still, *as* a *raptus.* Indeed, when we finally find Helen capitulating to Paris's persuasion in her letter, she imagines herself agreeing to an act that she still imagines as a "surrender" to conquest (she will be "victa" [17.260]).

By way of analyzing what this complicated set of conditions might mean to either the modern or medieval law, we may turn at this point to Chaucer, whose thinking about these issues, I have said, can instruct our own, and who in addition takes up the *raptus* of Helen of Troy at precisely the point any law must encounter it: that is, *after* the act. I do not refer here to the "teeris of Eleyne" mentioned in the Introduction to *The Man of Law's Tale* (line 70), although it is Chaucer's location of those "teeris" in "Ovide['s] Episteles" (lines 54–55) that, if there be any doubt, makes clear Chaucer knew the passages just examined.[26] More interesting for the definitional investigation in progress here is the ex post facto portrayal of Helen in *Troilus and Criseyde,* where there is no doubt that both the grounds of the war and the grounds of Helen's presence in Troy is a "ravishment": the narrator tells us in the poem's first

[26] All quotations from Chaucer are from Larry D. Benson, gen. ed., *The Riverside Chaucer,* 3d ed. (Boston: Houghton Mifflin, 1987). Subsequent citations will be made parenthetically in the text.

few lines that the Greeks have laid their siege "The ravysshyng to wreken of Eleyne" (1.62), and, when Pandarus instructs Troilus much later to "Go ravysshe" Criseyde (4.530), Troilus points out that "this town hath al this werre / For ravysshyng of wommen" (4.547–48). It is of equal interest, then, that within such a frame we actually meet Helen and, also, that when we do, she is just one member of the big, happy, Parisian family (2.1555–60):

> The morwen com, and neighen gan the tyme
> Of meeltid, that the faire queene Eleyne
> Shoop hire to ben, an houre after the prime,
> With Deiphebus, to whom she nolde feyne;
> But as his suster, homly, soth to seyne,
> She com to dyner in hire pleyne entente.

Helen, now indeed Paris's "wif" (1.678), exhibits nothing but enjoyment of her status as (in Pandarus's words) "lady queene Eleyne" (2.1714). Helen's regal and domestic comfort here, her placidity, might simply be taken at face value, but the "ravysshyng" that is their stated predicate also makes the exhibition of these qualities ostentatious, shocking evidence really of the "consent after" that the medieval law would notice on the way to discounting it. It is just here, moreover, as he notices an acquiescence that would transform "ravysshyng" into marriage choice and continues to call that choice "ravysshyng" that Chaucer follows both the interest of the medieval law and its judgment ("consent after" still equals "ravishment"). It is in the shock of the juxtaposition, however, that he also registers the conditions of such consent that the modern law would depend upon for its own claim that such an act was rape. To better see how this complex double movement is present in *Troilus and Criseyde,* we can gloss Helen's depicted acquiescence there with a worry Ovid shows her having before her *raptus:* "quis mihi, si laedar, Phrygiis succurret in oris? / unde petam fratres, unde parentis opem?" ["Who will succour me on Phrygian shores if I meet with harm? Where shall I look for brothers, where for a father's aid?"] (17.227–28). Chaucer cannot allow Helen to voice such worries given the comfort he envisions for her, but he can envision them for Criseyde, since, on Phrygian shores, she is in precisely the condition Helen was in before her *raptus* (1.92–98):

> Now hadde Calkas left in this meschaunce,
> Al unwist of this false and wikked dede,
> His doughter, which that was in gret penaunce,
> For of hire lif she was ful sore in drede,
> As she that nyste what was best to rede;
> For bothe a widewe was she and allone
> Of any frend to whom she dorste hir mone.

The extent to which Criseyde's choices are themselves glosses on Helen's (and, for that matter, Helen's are a gloss on Criseyde's) is an interesting issue that I will turn to below, but it is enough to note here that Chaucer also frames our witness of Helen's comfort in a Trojan "brother's aid" with acknowledgment that having one's protectors on the other side of a siege is a proper source of petrifying fear ("of hire *lif* she was ful sore in drede"). By modern definition, of course, "fear of . . . bodily injury" or a "threatening to retaliate in the future against the victim" establishes nonconsent and makes an act rape,[27] but we do not even need to press the issue this far to realize that what Chaucer is giving us, alongside the definition of "ravysshyng" current in the medieval law, is the means we need to realize what that definition leaves out.[28] Once she has been ravished, Helen's resistance would not merely have been useless but would very likely constitute a positive harm to her, and in that circumstance how can we equate "consent after" with "consent?" If medieval definitions of an act of "ravishment" can imagine (as Chaucer daringly does here) a woman *happily* married to her *raptor,* what Chaucer helps us to see is how such definitions ignore precisely those conditions of consent that make such an act wrong. The very terms of Chaucer's portrayal, in other words, invite us to wonder about all the acts of sex between Paris and Helen from the "ravysshyng" up until the "meeltid" at Deiphebus's house. If that sex is now consensual (as Helen is Paris's "wif"), *when* did it become consensual, and what were the precise conditions of Helen's consent at the moment of *raptus?* Moreover, if the act of that *raptus* was itself "merely" abduction, and sex, when it followed, was indeed consen-

[27] California Penal Code, sec. 261 (subsecs. 2 and 6), in *West's Codes* 48 (suppl.).

[28] It should be emphasized that Chaucer alone is responsible for the subtle portrayal of Helen I have traced here; he is not absorbing these distinctions from Boccaccio's *Filostrato:* the key stanza I quote in this paragraph on Helen's domestic comfort (2.1555–60) has no direct parallel in Boccaccio's poem. See the *en face* comparison in Geoffrey Chaucer, *Troilus and Criseyde,* ed. B. A. Windeatt (London: Longman, 1984).

sual, how can we admit that consent, since after the abduction, Helen has been placed in conditions of "force" and "fear" that make her will unfree?

Chaucer's portrayal understands what modern rubrics will only intensify and confirm, which is that, while the act of Helen's *raptus* might be categorized as a "ravysshyng," "mere" abduction, the conditions that must govern any consent given subsequent to that abduction make such consent equivalent to nonconsent: as Chaucer implies and we may safely say, Helen of Troy is Helen raped. It is in this harsh light, moreover, that we may find all attempts to discover whether Chaumpaigne released Chaucer from *either* rape or abduction, forced coitus or consensual sex, deeply misguided. To be sure, there was a forum in the medieval law that was deeply concerned with investigating and protecting the freedom of a woman's consent. As Gratian had it, "no woman should be coupled to anyone except by her free will,"[29] and the canon law on marriage was everywhere alive to the ways "force" and "fear" could make the will unfree: it did declare that "a marriage contracted under duress could be subsequently dissolved,"[30] and that "where [consent] was wanting, there was no marriage."[31] In the forum of the criminal law, however, such insights about the potential for coercion to qualify consent did not operate: that legal thinking, accepting on the one side that a woman such as Helen was, first, as in Ovid, "a lawful wife" ("legitima nupta" [17.4]) and, second, as in Chaucer, the "wif" of another, could not have cared less about the consensual states that intervened between these two "marriages." Interested above all in protecting the interests of the Menelauses of its world, the medieval English law on *raptus* and "ravishment" lumped together nonconsent before and consent before and gathered consent after together with these, prohibiting *as a single wrong* categories of act that we would call, on the one hand, marriage choice, and, on the other hand, rape. A woman raped in medieval England did have an option besides the law set down by the statutes we have examined: she could employ an older form of appeal that allowed her to come

[29] "Nisi libera voluntate nulla est copulanda alicui"; Gratian, *Decretum in Corpus iuris canonici,* ed. E. Friedberg (Leipzig: Bernhard Tauchnitz, 1879–81), dictum post c. 4, cited and trans. in John T. Noonan Jr., "Power to Choose," *Viator* 4 (1983): 422, 422 n. 6.

[30] R. H. Helmholz, *Marriage Litigation in Medieval England* (Cambridge: Cambridge University Press, 1974), p. 90. On force and fear as impediments to consent in marriage generally, see pp. 90–94, 178–81, and 220–28.

[31] Noonan, "Power to Choose," p. 425.

into court and assert, above all else, that she had not consented to an act of sexual intercourse (that it was "contra voluntatem suam"); where these cases appear in court records contemporaneous with the Chaumpaigne release, they call that act *raptus.*[32] But, in the context of the statutes, knowing that such acts fit the modern definition of rape does not help us know what most acts of *raptus* mentioned in contemporaneous documents were, simply because consensual states are *not* specified there. All the medieval law makes certain to us is that we cannot know precisely what we need to know to categorize most of its mentions of *raptus.* Where the extended portrait of affective states that Ovid and Chaucer give us for Helen is wanting—which is, according to its concerns, in nearly *every* case in the medieval law—all we know for certain is that we are uncertain. It is in this sense that saying the Chaumpaigne release does not prove Chaucer was a rapist does not measure our current, even temporary, ignorance, but our knowledge: the document is not incomplete evidence for judging between two different crimes ("rape" or "abduction") but complete evidence of the medieval law's commitment to joining those crimes so thoroughly that modern rubrics will never distinguish them.

As I have been suggesting, Chaucer knew this—if not by the rubric of the modern law, then at least in the terms of the uncertainty that would have surrounded the Chaumpaigne release as implacably in the fourteenth century as it does now. But we do not see this only as Chaucer raises questions about consent's determination in the case of Helen's "ravysshyng." The large significance of the Chaumpaigne release and our need to understand its witness is most strenuously proved by the extent to which an exploration of the conditions of consent that may attend acts of sexual intercourse finally becomes, in Chaucer's thinking, a consideration of the conditions of consent that attend all human acts. It is, in fact, the exploration of this much larger penumbra that was Chaucer's means for investigating the crucial distinction between an act and the names that might be given it, a distinction we too must make in order to read the Chaumpaigne release aright. Less central to this exploration, then, are those acts of forced coitus in Chaucer's writing where consent's conditions are clear and indisputable by any rubric (i.e., the rapes in *The Legend of Philomela, The Legend of Lucrece,* and *The Wife of Bath's Tale*). Cen-

[32] These are the cases and legal forms I connect to the Chaumpaigne release in "*Raptus* in the Chaumpaigne Release."

tral to it, however, is the consideration of consensual states where the nature of the act ("what happened") is either indeterminate or varying according to those states.

Acts that we would call rape still matter, but according to the terms of Chaucer's investigation, we must expect his observations to be most acute when he does *not* call an act "rape." A useful paradigm here is the representation of acts of sex at the conclusion of *The Reeve's Tale.* There is, first, the simplest form of such nonconsent when Aleyn sneaks into bed with Malyn (lines 4194–97):

> This wenche lay uprighte and faste slepte,
> Til he so ny was, er she myghte espie,
> That it had been to late for to crie,
> And shortly for to seyn, they were aton.

There is, second, a more complicated kind of nonconsent when the Miller's wife thinks she is getting into bed with her husband but is tricked into having sex with John[33] (lines 4228–31):

> Withinne a while this John the clerk up leep,
> And on this goode wyf he leith on soore.
> So myrie a fit ne hadde she nat ful yoore;
> He priketh harde and depe as he were mad.

In Malyn's case what is most significant to the representation is the way that clear nonconsent before the act ("it had been to late for to crie") quickly becomes consent after: once she is "aton" with Aleyn (a phrase that conflates both physical and affective acquiescence) he becomes, in her own words, her "deere lemman" (line 4240). But in both these cases what is significant is the way this tale details the conditions that govern these acts of sex but then knows nothing more at its conclusion than that those acts were accomplished: that the Miller's "wyf is swyved, and his doghter als" (line 4317). That these acts are *not* rapes by this tale's measure are judgments that we may fold back into the Reeve's "ire"

[33] That the wife remains certain that she has had sex with her husband both during and after is made clear when the fight between Aleyn and Symkyn breaks out and Symkyn falls on the wife: her cries show that she believes this person is someone *else* ("'Awak, Symond! The feend is on me falle'" [*RvT* 4288]) and that it is the clerks, arisen from their bed, who are fighting ("'Help, Symkyn, for the false clerkes fighte!'" [*RvT* 4291]).

(*RvP* 3862), the violence of a vengeful poetics whose aim is the "bleryng of a proud milleres ye" (*RvP* 3865) or the "cherles termes" of fabliau (*RvP* 3917), but we may not, I think, attach these judgments to Chaucer. As relevant to the tale's final ignorance of the conditions of consent that might define a particular kind of "swyving" here is the fact that we, as readers, are made to know all that we need to know about those conditions to call this "swyving" rape. Most important for the concerns addressed here, then, is the way that Chaucer's representation of these acts not only goes straight down the line of the rubrics of the medieval statutes (Symkyn's belief that a wrong has been done to Malyn because her "lynage" has been "disparage[d]" [*RvT* 4271–72] despite her "consent after" is the logic of a medieval law obsessed with marriage rights) but also investigates consent sufficiently to satisfy definitions of rape (like our own) that care about a woman's nonconsent.[34]

The Reeve's Tale is, however, only a small example of how attentive Chaucer can be to the conditions that the modern law cares about, and it is to *Troilus and Criseyde* that we must look to see Chaucer's understanding, not just of the relevance of consent's certainties, but of the crucial nature of its uncertainty—here, in fact, in all the complexity that still troubles the modern law. At issue in this respect is not the determination of Helen's consent in her "ravysshyng" but of Criseyde's in whatever we will call the act that consummates her relations with Troilus. The difficulty is pointed by the way we are everywhere given careful detail about Criseyde's consensual states, even as Criseyde is haunted by what Louise Fradenburg has called the "specter of rape."[35] Such haunting is sufficient to make the story of Troilus's "wooing" equally well a story about the difficulties Criseyde must have in acceding to his blandishments in circumstances where even her agreement is compelled by a variety of forces. Relevant here are descriptions of Criseyde's physical vulnerability in Troy (as Pandarus introduces her to Deiphebus, she is one "Which some men wolden don oppressioun, /

[34] In the instance of Malyn a modern judgment of rape would be easy by legal standards of "force," but even the more complex nonconsent of the wife is expressly covered in the California code concerning acts of spousal rape ("where a person submits under the belief that the person committing the act is [her] spouse"). See California Penal Code, sec. 621 (subsec. 5), in *West's Codes* 48 (suppl.).

[35] Louise O. Fradenburg, "'Our owen wo to drynke': Loss, Gender, and Chivalry in *Troilus and Criseyde*," in R. A. Shoaf, ed., *Chaucer's* Troilus and Criseyde, *"Subgit to alle Poesye": Essays in Criticism* (Binghamton, N.Y.: Medieval Renaissance Texts and Studies, 1992), pp. 88–106; for the phrase, see p. 99.

And wrongfully han hire possessioun" [2.1418–19]), Troilus's relative strength (as Criseyde fears it, that her refusal would lead to his "dispit" and her "worse plit" [2.711–12]), Pandarus's extensive trickery in manipulating Criseyde into Troilus's bed, as well as the extensive imagery of rape that immediately surrounds the consummation scene (songs of nightingales, dreams of violent bodily invasion).[36] But the conditions barring Criseyde's freedom are nowhere more clear than when she must be free if sex with Troilus is not to be coerced and the act of sex is not to be rape (3.1205–11):

> This Troilus in armes gan hire streyne,
> And seyde, "O swete, as evere mot I gon,
> Now be ye kaught; now is ther but we tweyne!
> Now yeldeth yow, for other bote is non!"
> To that Criseyde answerde thus anon,
> "Ne hadde I er now, my swete herte deere,
> Ben yolde, ywis, I were now nought heere!"

The indications of force in the instant (Troilus "gan hire streyne," Criseyde "kaught" without "other bote") as well as the terms of Criseyde's consent make clear that her "yielding" can no longer be simple agreement under conditions where a decision has already been embodied in a set of compulsions, where a "no" would be a meaningless gesture toward an act whose accomplishment is already settled. And yet the claim made by the complex tracing of these conditions is not, I think, that this *is* rape, but that we must *wonder* if it is, even as we are encouraged to decide it is not. Fradenburg suggests that "we cannot 'decide' whether Criseyde has consented or not, whether she has been raped or not,"[37] but the opposite judgment has been made by Jill Mann in an equally compelling argument.[38] Crucial to Mann's case is the sensitivity to Criseyde's predicament that Chaucer has Troilus show: so worried is he, in fact, that he

[36] Fradenburg carefully traces these images and their ramifications in ibid., pp. 98–101.

[37] Ibid., p. 100.

[38] Jill Mann, "Troilus' Swoon," *ChauR* 14 (1980): 319–35. In this article Mann shows how the "developing relationship between Troilus and Criseyde is conceived and described in terms of power" so that "the shifts and transformations in the way each of them either exerts or refuses to exert power over the other lead to the achievement of a mature and complex relationship on which the consummation can fittingly be based" (p. 320).

swoons and thereby relinquishes his own "will" at the very moment that this will is really about to coerce Criseyde.[39] As the "specter of rape" proposes this crime for our consideration, the careful handling of consent in this scene keeps the crime just beyond our judgment; we *may* accept Criseyde's "yielding" as consensual even as that consent is qualified to the very edge of freedom. But it is also in this double movement that we can see Chaucer acutely aware of the very definitional requirements for rape that preoccupy us—because, that is, the definition of the act here is not made to turn on consent given or denied but on the conditions of the consent, on the constraints and qualifications that interact with agreement. The material of the scene, in other words, is that vast gray area between consent and nonconsent that the medieval law had created, but its interest is to identify the fine line between rape and not-rape that the modern law understands consent to make. Chaucer's aim is, with infinite care, to place Troilus and Criseyde on neither side of but just *on* that line.

At the same time, we may notice that, even if rape is shaded away from definitional possibility in the consummation scene, it is not finally dismissed from consideration in this poem. The crime returns by name still later as Pandarus denies that it will have any relevance on relations between Troilus and Criseyde: "It is no rape, in my dom, ne no vice, / Hire to witholden that ye love moost" (4.596–97). And, insofar as this poem raises the threat of rape in this earlier scene by defining the crime as a function of constrained consent, we may also observe that the crime *occurs,* according to the poem's definition, when Criseyde finally is "in the snare" of the Greeks (5.748), really caught now in Diomede's "net" (5.775), again "allone" and in "nede / Of frendes help" (5.1026–27), coerced by circumstance with no protector as sensitive as Troilus to protect her from compulsion. Of the presumed act of sex between Diomede and Criseyde, the poem says that Criseyde "falsed" Troilus (5.1053); but where it also makes all the constraints on Criseyde's decision so clear, where it describes Diomede's very consolation as an act that "*refte*" Criseyde "of al hire peyne" (5.1036; emphasis mine), it also makes clear that the act that constitutes this falseness is forced. The poem's analysis gives us the material to know, in other words, that just as certain condi-

[39] On this crucial relation between the swoon and the consummation, see ibid., pp. 325–30.

tions will make being "kaught" and "streyne[d]" no act of rape, other acts, differently named, *are* rape nonetheless. If we focus, for example, on the extended anatomy of Criseyde's "slydynge of corage" (5.825), we may also recall that there are two characters in this poem notable for such "slydynge," and, furthermore, that we have already seen how the first of these "slidings" is called "ravysshyng." Criseyde's will changes as a direct result of what is called her "chaungynge" (4.231) for Antenor, as she does not initially agree to it but, as the poem puts it, is "yelden" ("yielded") by the Trojans to the Greeks (4.347). If Helen's "ravysshyng" is a rape by modern measure, what then can the act resulting from Criseyde's unwilled exchange otherwise be? Since in the former case we are only urged to ask the questions that would result in this classification and never given the classification itself, it is irrelevant by this poem's logic that Criseyde's rape is not so named. Indeed the anatomy this poem offers of rape's definition emphatically proposes that an act accomplished under the conditions of "force" and "fear" that make it rape may well be described by other emotional languages, languages that would figure the crime instead as the giving of a "herte" (5.1050) or, even, as a "betrayal." If it should seem preposterous that "rape defined" could ever be so outrageously named, we need only pause to consider (as I think this poem asks us to) what word the Greeks can have been using at this point to characterize Helen's acquiescence in *her* "ravysshyng."

The truly general importance of Chaucer's thinking about the definitional problems posed by the Chaumpaigne release is best approached, however, through a much more simple connection between the matter of the release and the matter of Chaucer's writing. Indeed, it is so simple to suggest that the "lyf . . . of Seynt Cecile" (*The Legend of Good Women* 426) was meant to count as some kind of pious reparation for wrong done to Cecily Chaumpaigne that the connection has hardly ever been proposed.[40] Still, the date of the poem's original composition may be made to work,[41] and, that aside, we know the poem was again in Chau-

[40] To my knowledge the connection has only been made once, by George H. Cowling in *Chaucer* (New York: E. P. Dutton, 1927), p. xviii, cited in P. R. Watts, "The Strange Case of Geoffrey Chaucer and Cecilia Chaumpaigne," *Law Quarterly Review* 63 (1947): 491–515.

[41] The uncontroversial chronology offered by Larry D. Benson in "The Canon and Chronology of Chaucer's Works" (*Riverside Chaucer,* pp. xxvi–xxix) places the "lyf" between 1372 and 1380 and, within this group, notes that its date is "possibly later" (p. xxix).

cer's mind as it became *The Second Nun's Tale* during composition of *The Canterbury Tales.* The notion that a *poem* could have even been thought reparatory had Chaucer raped Cecily Chaumpaigne might itself cause us to wonder whether Chaucer understood anything about the terrifying realities of *raptus* when he wrote this "life." And yet it is precisely the generality of the poem's investigation of the conditions of consent that show its understanding of what is at stake in the release to be very complicated indeed. If we look to the poem's detail, for example, we may note that the first thing Cecilia must overcome is the sexual compulsions imposed by marriage: she must live in "pure chaastnesse of virginitee" (*SNP* 88) by protecting herself from the "touche" of "vileynye" (*SNT* 156) that is, in this case, the touch of her husband. In its detailing of the kind of force that even the sanctioned act of marriage might represent, this poem also investigates the more general forms of unfreedom that a lack of concern for consent's conditions produced in the medieval period. But it is, in particular, the language Chaucer uses to describe what Cecilia achieves that connects the analysis of this poem to a more general investigation of consent in much of Chaucer's other writing. When Valerian finally agrees to leave her "body clene" (*SNT* 225), he also acknowledges that she is as undefiled in attitude as in act, that her "will" has been the instrument of her resistance, that it is her "*thoght*" above all that is "unwemmed" (VIII, 225). For Chaucer, "unwemmed" is the condition of a woman whose consent is uncoerced: he uses it to describe a Mary whose "maidenhede" is also preserved, "unwemmed," in marriage (*ABC* 91), and also to describe a Constance whom divine intervention has just saved from rape ("And thus hath Crist unwemmed kept Custance" [*MLT* 924]). But for Chaucer this word also connotes the general conditions of *any* person whose will remains free: in the *Boece,* in particular, the "arbitrie" of such a person is also said to be "hool and unwemmed" (2.pr4.21).[42]

To see how a consideration of the human will in Chaucer's writings might bear upon consideration of the problems entailed in understanding the *raptus* mentioned in the Chaumpaigne release, it will be helpful to make a brief and preparatory detour through the *quaestio* in Thomas Aquinas's *Summa Theologiae,* where *raptus* and the "will" are carefully ex-

[42] In addition to the instances I cite here, Chaucer also uses this word on one other occasion in *The Second Nun's Tale* (as Cecilia prays to preserve her chastity in marriage [line 137]). See Larry D. Benson, *A Glossarial Concordance to the Riverside Chaucer* (New York: Garland, 1993), *s.v.* "unwemmed adj."

amined together.[43] *Raptus* in this context is probably best translated as "rapture," for what Aquinas is puzzling over here is Paul's claim that he knows "a man in Christ who was caught up to the third heaven" ("Scio hominem in Christo. . .raptum usque ad tertium coelum" [2 Corinthians 12:2]), and what he wants to analyze is how, by *raptus,* a man may be "raised to divine things" ("ad divina elevetur" [2a2ae.175.1]). Even if this *raptus* is not forced sex, Aquinas remains very much alive to the way force must be part of an act so described: "Raptus violentiam quandam importat. . . . Violentum autem dicitur cuius principium est extra, nil conferente eo quod vim patitur" ["Rapture does imply a certain violence. . . . Violence . . . is done when the principle is external and the sufferer confers nothing to it"] (2a2ae.175.1). And in a nuanced analysis that may remind us of the analysis of "consent" in the modern law, Aquinas also explores ways that, under pressure of such violence, what we regard as "free" about the "will" depends entirely on how we involve that will in our definition of the act itself (2a2ae.175.1):

> Ad ea quae excedunt liberi arbitrii facultatem, necesse est quod homo quadam fortiori operatione elevetur: quae quidem quantum ad aliquid potest dici coactio, si scilicet attendatur modus operationis, non autem si attendatur terminus operationis, in quem natura hominis et eius intentio ordinatur.
>
> [For what exceeds the capacities of the free-will, a man needs to be uplifted by a more powerful source of action. This source might be termed coercive if we consider the mode of action, not so however if we consider the term of the action, namely the end to which man's nature and tendency is ordered.]

Focus on the act itself, Aquinas says, and you will find violence, but focus on the end toward which that violence is directed and you will find "order." Aquinas can finally dismiss the coerciveness of violence in this *raptus* because its end is God—"divine love causes ecstasy" ["divinus amor facit extasim"] (2a2ae.175.2)—but at the same time he shows how the exigencies of *any* "order" may be made to justify a "certain vio-

[43] St. Thomas Aquinas, *Summa Theologiae,* vol. 45, "Prophecy and Other Charisms (2a2ae.171–78)," ed. and trans. Roland Potter (New York: McGraw-Hill Book Company, 1970), 2a2ae.175, 1 (pp. 94–117). All subsequent quotations and translations from the *Summa* are taken from this edition and will be cited within the text. I have made a few silent alterations in the translation for the sake of clarity.

lence," how the higher claims of a "term of action" (*terminus operationis*) can redefine the state of freedom that is ostensibly its "mode" (*modus operationis*). Such a description is itself a gloss on the logic of the medieval English law, for that law ignores a woman's will at the moment of an act of "ravishment" or *raptus* in favor of the higher order of marriage, which it understands as a "right" of fathers and husbands. But the gloss is even more general than this, since Aquinas also helps us to see that *raptus* in any period (or by any name) may be investigated by considering not only the state of the will (its "consent," simply put) but the nature of the order that could define the violent compulsion of that will as "freedom." The conditions that make an act *raptus,* Aquinas teaches, may be described apart from definitions of crime, as a pure consideration of the "will" and the scheme and method by which that "will" may be said to be "free."

That Chaucer considered this issue in just such schematic terms hardly needs to be pointed out, for it is well known that the main concern of books 4 and 5 of the *Boece* is the freedom and constraint of the "will." Still, it is probably worth noting for the purposes of the connections I want to stress here that in the *Boece,* the "unmoevable purveaunce," which "constreyneth the fortunes and the dedes of men by a bond of causes nat able to ben unbownde" (4.pr6.154–58), has as one of its forms of constraint a kind of "ravishment": "This atempraunce norysscheth and bryngeth forth ale thinges that brethith lif in this world; and thilke same attempraunce, ravysschynge, hideth and bynymeth, and drencheth undir the laste deth, ale thinges iborn" (4.m6.34–39).[44] The dreamer's extensive worries about what freedom the "will" can have in the context of such constraint are, at least here, pointed directly at the category of act whose relation to the will occupies us. In this light, what we find when we examine how "philosophy" can find "any liberte of fre wille in this ordre of causes" (5.pr2.3–4), is an order that, again, dismisses the nonconsent that "ravishment" would seem to propose, defining the "will" as "free" *even in such cases.* And the dreamer learns to understand such constraint in terms that exactly parallel the effect constraint is shown to have on Criseyde's character: as "the destinal

[44] Chaucer here is not inventing this image but discovering it, for the figuration is already present in Boethius's Latin: "Haec temperies alit ac profert, / quicquid vitam spirat in orbe; / eadem *rapiens* condit et aufert / obitu mergens orta supremo"; *Philosophiae Consolationis Libri Quinque,* ed. Karl Büchner (Heidelberg: Carl Winter, 1977), 4.m6.30–33 (emphasis mine).

cheyne constrenith the moevynges of the *corages* of men" (5.pr2.5–7; emphasis mine), so do Trojan movings constrain the "corage" of Criseyde. The dreamer is made to agree that the "corage" is rightly constrained in this way—that "corages" *necessarily* "slide"—because Lady Philosophy shows that what is called force by the "resoun of mankynde" is *not* force when named in the "symplicite of the devyne prescience" (5.pr4.9–15). Philosophy's claim—that the "will" in such cases is "free"—is of course Aquinas's claim, but this position becomes directly relevant to Chaucer's consideration of consent in marriage, as it is couched in the language I have also said Chaucer uses to describe such a woman:

> "And syn that thise thinges ben thus . . . , thanne is ther fredom of arbitrie, that duelleth *hool and unwemmed* to mortal men; ne the lawes ne purposen nat wikkidly medes and peynes to the willynges of men that ben unbownden and quyt of alle necessite; and God, byholdere and forwytere of alle thingis, duelleth above, and the present eternite of his sighte renneth alwey with the diverse qualite of our dedes, dispensynge and ordeynynge medes to gode men and tormentz to wikkide men." (5.pr6.286–98; emphasis mine)

The insight is also deepened here, for rather than claiming that a "term of action" or an "ordre of causes" such as marriage does not constitute compulsion, what we learn is that this higher order may compel by a "certain violence" and yet the "mode of action" is still "free." Put the medieval law that enforces marriage "rights" in the place of the "devyne prescience" and you will be able to define as consensual ("free") even the marriage that begins in rape. By this same definitional insight, of course, put the *modern* rape law in the place of that "devyne prescience" and you will also be able to define many medieval marriages as rape. Chaucer, I would also suggest, offers just such judgments when, in his poetry, he unsettles Philosophy's neat scheme and puts personal agents in the crucial position of the "devyne prescience." When Theseus, for example, stands in for God and imposes order at the end of *The Knight's Tale,* marrying Emelye to Palemoun without even consulting Emelye's wishes, we are made to see Theseus defining her "arbitrie" as "unwemmed" even as we are also made to see that this will is compelled. When Griselde's will is made everywhere to cleave to Walter's as if he were God—"But as ye wole youreself, right so wol I" (*ClT* 361)—we are also made to see how this general yielding results in a series of acts to which Griselde ostensibly consents but to which the very terms of her marriage bar any other response. It is in these instances (as well as many others) that we may say that Chaucer is concerned with considering the issues at stake in understanding the Chaumpaigne release to precisely the extent that his poetry is Boethian—that is, to a very great extent indeed.

Less stressed in the *Boece* but emphatically explored in Chaucer's Boethian poetry are the implications to the quotidian world of the claim that an act is only ascertainable as it is referred to the order that defines (ignores or credits) the conditions of consent that allow it to happen: such a claim suggests that, as that order alters—as, say, rubrics of the modern law are substituted for the rubrics of the medieval law—the *act itself* will change. Where that act might be rape, Chaucer also shows his awareness of this possibility by exploring the conditions of consent so fully that we may see how what is not rape by the medieval law may still be rape by our own definition. Moreover, as we come to understand the medieval law in light of Chaucer's incisive diagnosis of definitional possibility, we also learn to see how the "order" of that law guarantees that we will never have the means to know whether Chaumpaigne's *raptus* was her rape. And it is here—as he shows us this—that Chaucer also establishes his relation to this *raptus.* What we do not know and cannot know about the act the Chaumpaigne release names as *raptus* is what Chaucer knew was not and could not be known about any such act in circumstances that routinely co-opted or ignored a woman's consent. It is the uncertainty of such consent in the fourteenth century that is also all we may count as our own certainty in determining what the Chaumpaigne release "really means." But, as I have been arguing, this does not convert all we may say about the release into "speculation." If we do not know what act prompted the Chaumpaigne release, we do know precisely why and precisely how the medieval law carefully put our particular uncertainty in place.

Infantilizing the Father: Chaucer Translations and Moral Regulation

David Matthews
University of Newcastle

RETURNING FROM ONE of his lecture tours abroad in the 1880s, the Reverend Hugh Reginald Haweis looked down on the steerage passengers from the upper deck of the Atlantic steamer on which he traveled and thought of how much better off they would be if they had cheap books to counteract their idleness. Back at home in graceful Cheyne Walk, Chelsea, he planned a series of condensed cheap classics that would cost threepence in paper and sixpence in cloth. As he further explained,

> When I think of the long, gossiping, yawning, gambling hours of grooms, valets, coachmen, and cabmen; the railway stations, conveniently provided with bookstalls, and crowded morning and evening with workmen's trains—the winter evenings in thousands of villages, wayside cottages, and scattered hamlets—the brief, but not always well-spent leisure of Factory hands in the north—the armies of commercial and uncommercial travellers with spare half hours—the shop assistants—the city offices with their hangers-on—the Board Schools—the village libraries—the Army and Navy—the barrack or the dockyard—again the vision of "**Routledge's World Library**" rises before me, and I say, "This, if not a complete cure for indolence and vice, may at least prove a powerful counter-charm."[1]

I would like to thank Steve Ellis for sharing his extensive knowledge of Chaucer modernizations with me, and Ruth Evans, Allen Frantzen, and Ian Hunter for reading this essay in draft and commenting on it.

[1] From the unpaginated general editor's preface to Routledge's World Library; see Mrs. H. R. Haweis, ed. and intro., *Tales from Chaucer* (London: Routledge, 1887).

Haweis's description of himself on the upper deck is presented as a moment of benevolent enlightenment, betraying no consciousness of how eloquently it functions as a metaphor for the hierarchizing of class. His concern, in the context of the passing of the third reform bill in 1884, mirrors reactions to the passing of the second bill in 1867, when it was thought that literacy and education needed to be extended to the now dangerously empowered lower classes.[2] Haweis looks favorably on the increased democratizing of British society, but his concern about the condition of the lower classes does not extend to questioning existing conceptions of class and hierarchy.

I. Chaucer in Steerage

When the volumes of Routledge's World Library began appearing it was natural that Chaucer should appear in an early publication in the new series. This was because Haweis's wife, Mary, an accomplished illustrator and early feminist, had already published two versions of Chaucer; her *Chaucer for Children: A Golden Key* (1877) was specific in its address to very young children, with asides to the mother who it was assumed would be reading the book out loud, just as Haweis herself had read Chaucer to her own son Lionel. *Chaucer for Schools* (1881) was essentially the same work simplified and aimed at a slightly older reader. Reconfiguring these books for "grooms, valets, coachmen, and cabmen," Mary Haweis pitched the tone at an older audience, but not specifically at adults. The kind of "talking down" that Haweis had found appropriate in her Chaucers for the young she now employed in *Tales from Chaucer* (1887), a Chaucer for the lower classes, as if the workers were simply large children.

The book consists of a selection from *The Canterbury Tales* in translation (using some existing translations and some by Haweis herself) along with others of Chaucer's poems in normalized rather than translated form. The selection was calculated to correct the impression of Chaucer as a morally unserious writer: "Chaucer was a serious man, and . . . his tales were chiefly serious," Haweis wrote; "his good feeling and good taste were so much above any of his Renaissance successors that on

[2] On the spread of literacy in the nineteenth century, see R. K. Webb, *The British Working Class Reader, 1790–1848: Literacy and Social Tension* (London: Allen & Unwin, 1955), and Richard D. Altick, *The English Common Reader: A Social History of the Mass Reading Public, 1800–1900* (Chicago: University of Chicago Press, 1957).

no occasion he puts an unseemly expression in the mouths of his characters. No high-born maid or dame uses a coarse word, no 'gentil' priest, even in the sharpest satires, criminates himself."[3]

This view of what constitutes "seriousness" is related to class; Chaucer is serious when he writes of upper-class people. The selection of verse, naturally, does nothing to contradict this view. *The Knight's Tale,* a perennial favorite in the nineteenth century, is included, but most of the fabliaux are not. The *Tales* of the Wife of Bath and Pardoner appear, but not their *Prologues.* However, in a bold and, for the time, unusual move, Haweis included *The Miller's Tale,* perhaps the most obvious example of Chaucerian nonseriousness in Victorian eyes, in a prose modernization of her own. In this highly sanitized version, Nicholas and Alison are "great friends" who team up to teach the carpenter a lesson; when they leave the carpenter asleep in his tub in the ceiling, "in high spirits [they] made ready for a real good time—it was the first time they had ever had a moment's freedom." Absolon comes to the window seeking a kiss and "the mischievous Alison rushed at him with a broom of no great purity, which he received on his face with considerable force." The insulted Absolon returns with a hot coulter and Nicholas loses "whole patches of skin" from an unspecified area of his body.[4]

Describing what she has done here, Haweis writes only that she has "made a very slight alteration in this tale."[5] Just as she did with her younger readers, Haweis patronizes her new audience, everywhere exhibiting great care about what her readers can have and cannot have of Chaucer. Specifically, the dangerous immodesty of the fabliau and its threat to the morally serious construction of Chaucer are mitigated by the infantilizing of the tale. Nicholas, Alison, and Absolon have become children; the carpenter, an oppressive master. In their larking about, the children do no great damage, and the carpenter, when he tumbles from the roof, is punished as a bad parent-figure rather than as a jealous husband. In this attempt to bring *The Miller's Tale* into line with a *morally* serious vision, the cost is a relatively *un*serious narrative by comparison with the tale's original structure of retribution. Chaucer himself, in short, is also infantilized, the author of an intricately plotted fabliau becoming the producer of an anodyne and slightly foolish children's

[3] Haweis, ed., *Tales from Chaucer,* p. 16.
[4] Ibid., pp. 55, 60, 62, 63.
[5] Ibid., p. 64.

story. Most interestingly, the readers are infantilized as part of this process. Haweis, already used to the demands of rendering Chaucer for children, here infantilizes readers whom she knows to be adults (because her own husband has constructed them for her), treating them as she had previously treated childish readers.

It was a short step for Haweis from deciding what was appropriate for her own young son to know of Chaucer to deciding what was appropriate for her son's generation. It is a much bigger step to make the decision for her fellow adults. It is to decide that what one person can read without damage to her moral well-being might nevertheless be harmful to others, embodying the paradox of censorship that one person must decide a text is morally corrupting while being empowered to make the decision precisely because he or she is not morally corrupted by the text. The notional equality that the extension of the franchise was seen to bring was political, not intellectual: Chaucer, read in steerage, might have an adverse effect on readerly morals that he did not have on the upper decks.

It was the mission of many Chaucer enthusiasts of the late nineteenth century to try to establish Chaucer alongside the greats: Spenser, Milton, and Shakespeare. While this move gave the appearance of being an aesthetic judgment, the actual critical deployment of Chaucer usually placed the poet and his work in a *moral* role. The linguistic problems of Chaucerian language—not presented to readers of the other writers—meant that whenever Chaucer's work was translated, as it frequently was with the ostensible purpose of increasing the poet's popularity, there was always a largely unacknowledged expurgation. No translator could resist the urge to moralize the Chaucerian text. This meant that the aesthetic object, Chaucerian verse, was hidden from view while an ethical function was foregrounded.

This split between the two poles, aesthetic/original and ethical/translation, is most starkly evident in the edition with facing-page verse translation published by Frederick Clarke in 1870. The versos present the text of MS Harley 7334 (probably plundered from an earlier *Canterbury Tales* edition by Thomas Wright), the rectos Clarke's own translation. The parity between original and translation implied by the facing-page format is, however, belied by the nature of the translation, as *The Miller's Tale* again effectively shows. Having translated *The Miller's Prologue* quite competently into Modern English rhyming couplets, Clarke shifts without explanation to blank verse for the tale itself, presumably to heighten the style:

> Dark was the night as pitch or coal, and at
> The window with stern outermost she stood;
> And Absalom knew neither more nor less,
> But kissed her as she stood full savourly.
> Now when the parish clerk was 'ware of this,
> Back went he, thinking there was something wrong;
> He had felt something roughly hirsute, and
> Considering that a woman hath no beard,
> Said, Fie, alas, alas! what have I done?[6]

The clear implication is that those who can read the Middle English are somehow immune to the moral danger inherent in the text while those who cannot need to be protected from it. The modern reader is, once again, an infant protected from the reality of the medieval text by a concerned parental figure.

The early tradition of translating Chaucer, especially as practiced by Dryden and Pope, created new aesthetic artifacts (many complaints about the translations by these poets focus not on the fact of translation itself but on the way in which they created new poems). Similarly, the explosion of Chaucer translation in the late 1940s and 1950s involved several clear attempts to create new aesthetic objects, as in Nevill Coghill's *Canterbury Tales.* Translations between 1870 and the 1940s, almost all of which infantilize Chaucer, are less obviously driven by aesthetic concerns, and the moral role is correspondingly privileged.

In this essay I will examine the link between the infantilizing of Chaucer and the construction of Chaucer in a morally regulatory role. I look first at the infantilizing trope and then the specific translations of Chaucer for children before turning to the changed assumptions of the post–World War II Chaucer translations. This inquiry pursues all forms of translated Chaucers, from minimal normalizations to genuine translations and paraphrased retellings, but it is not evaluative: I will not attempt to assess their relative aesthetic merits and neither will I try to arbitrate on the question of the value of translating Chaucer.[7] As it is only in the second half of the twentieth century that translations have

[6] Frederick Clarke, ed. and trans., The Canterbury Tales *of Geoffrey Chaucer: Done into Modern English* (London, 1870), 1:211–13. Only one volume was published of what looks to have been projected as a complete *Canterbury Tales.*

[7] For the case against, see Marvin Mudrick, "Chaucer as Librettist," *PQ* 38 (1959): 21–29; Peter G. Beidler, "Chaucer and the Trots: What to Do about Those Modern English Translations," *ChauR* 19 (1985): 290–301. Arguing the case for is Giles Sinclair, "Chaucer: Translated or Obliterated?" *College English* 15 (1953–54): 272–77.

had the aim of being as close to Chaucer as possible, translating with the fidelity we would expect of translations of works in foreign languages, there has been a longstanding split between translations and editions of Chaucer, a split that sees the translations failing to reflect what is there in the edited text. I am not concerned to privilege the more faithful translations. The main concern here is the stark way in which the work of Chaucer is severed from its original aesthetic being and reconfigured as an aesthetic artifact in order to be projected as an agent of moral regulation. The nature of the gap between the translations and the edited text of Chaucer has much to tell us about the deployment of Chaucer (especially *The Canterbury Tales*) as a moral and ethical technology and an ideology.

In this respect this essay privileges the account of English given by Ian Hunter over that which sees English as fundamentally an ideology, as in the work of Terry Eagleton and Chris Baldick. Hunter's Foucauldian reading of the study of English sees it as "a hybrid ethical technology," one that is potentially liberating as it encourages the development of the self.[8] Hunter counterposes this view to what might be called the repressive hypothesis, in which English is read as an ideological mechanism designed to have its outcome "in controlling and incorporating the working class," as Eagleton puts it, at a time when, "If the masses are not thrown a few novels, they may react by throwing up a few barricades."[9] By contrast, Hunter proposes that the techniques of literary pedagogy do *not* produce "the individual as the subject of a true or illusory consciousness." Instead, "The self that emerges from literary pedagogy . . . is positively constructed when the techniques of incitement and supervision—spontaneity and normativity—focused by the teacher-student relation *create* specific capacities for self-monitoring and self-shaping."[10]

Despite the influence of Hunter's reading here, however, the material ways in which Chaucer is reconstructed for moral purposes do seem to me to have an inescapably ideological dimension. For the Haweises, for

[8] Ian Hunter, "Learning the Literature Lesson: The Limits of the Aesthetic Personality," in Carolyn D. Baker and Allan Luke, eds., *Towards a Critical Sociology of Reading Pedagogy* (Amsterdam: Benjamins, 1991), pp. 49–82, at p. 72.

[9] Terry Eagleton, *Literary Theory: An Introduction* (Oxford: Blackwell, 1983), pp. 24, 25; see Ian Hunter, *Culture and Government: The Emergence of Literary Education* (Basingstoke: Macmillan, 1988), pp. 121–22.

[10] Hunter, "Literature Lesson," pp. 59–60.

example, there is no trace of an idea that there should, ultimately, be an abolition of the distinction between steerage and the upper deck. The point of Routledge's World Library is that there should be cheap books for people who are *never* going to have much money. In fact, the workers are supposed to make room in their lives for literature by self-denial: "I am not one of those who 'wish to rob the poor man of his beer,'" Haweis writes, "but I cannot help thinking that should this fly-leaf flutter down upon the frugal board at the right time, there may be many who would be willing to substitute a glass of water for a glass of beer once a week, in order to secure a Life of Nelson, Garibaldi, De Foe's Plague of London, Scott's Marmion, or Goethe's Faust."[11] Here, as a necessary prelude to aesthetic work on the self, some more material self-shaping, through temperance and financial prudence, is quietly recommended (and is appropriate to the envisioned "frugal board"). The better-cultivated selves that will be produced by the aesthetic work will ideally have undergone some engineering from above intended to maintain the hierarchical status quo.

This example suggests that moral technologies and ideological mechanisms can coexist. In this analysis I am principally interested in the way in which Chaucer translations have been situated as morally regulatory. But I want to retain the sense that such situating is ideological. The development of the study of Chaucer's writing in the period under examination was intricated with various ideological considerations, of gender, nationalism, and class in particular. At the same time, Chaucer is certainly part of a project of self-formation; reading Chaucer, as far as the great Victorian/Edwardian proselytizer Frederick Furnivall was concerned, would ensure that better Englishmen and -women would be shaped. One does not, in Furnivall's formulation, read Chaucer for his aesthetic value (beautiful though much of his writing is); Chaucer is to be read because he was one of the finest men of the English Middle Ages (as his writings demonstrate) and reading him will cultivate the self of the reader.[12] What drove translation in the late nineteenth century and the first half of the twentieth was less the perceived need to recreate an

[11] Hugh Reginald Haweis, unpaginated preface, in Haweis, ed., *Tales from Chaucer.*

[12] Despite his vast output, Furnivall wrote no books or critical articles as such and the utterances that illustrate this point are scattered in fragments across his work. For one of the more coherent summaries of his views on Chaucer, see Frederick J. Furnivall, *Trial-Forewords to My "Parallel-Text Edition of Chaucer's Minor Poems"* (London: Chaucer Society, 1871).

aesthetically valued object in terms all could understand than the desire to make accessible the work of an ethically exemplary figure.

II. The Infantilized Father

As Seth Lerer has argued, the original construction of Chaucer as the father of English poetry involved a corresponding infantilizing of themselves by Chaucer's fifteenth-century successors. Such poets as Hoccleve and Lydgate repeatedly constructed Chaucer as a poet far greater than they could hope to be, creating a cult that Lerer sees as nostalgia generated in a culturally insecure era. Abjecting themselves before the figure of father Chaucer, these poets became childlike.[13]

When John Dryden reinvented the trope of Chaucer's literary paternity, he did so in a culturally secure context, from a position of superiority rather than abjection. Most critics of the eighteenth and early nineteenth centuries wrote in the knowledge that theirs was a superior time; to them, though he is a great poet, Chaucer, far from living in the linguistic golden age imagined by the fifteenth-century poets, was condemned to struggle with a poor language and to live in a time of religious superstition. Chaucer's literary paternity now relies on his re-creation as a poet who somehow transcended his medieval context. In Dryden's appropriation of Chaucer, as Lee Patterson has noted, "Chaucer escaped [the Middle Ages]. . . . And he was not merely a Renaissance rather than a medieval poet: more to the point, he was the first poet who lived in our own, postmedieval time—the first modern poet and hence the father of English poetry."[14]

This paradox, of a medieval poet who was somehow not a medieval poet, is evident throughout eighteenth- and nineteenth-century writings, which repeatedly construct Chaucer as standing outside his time. To some extent, Chaucer is seen as imprisoned by his time, particularly its morality: Thomas Warton is representative when he writes "that Chaucer's obscenity is in great measure to be imputed to his age." But Chaucer also observes his time as one who is timeless himself. "We are surprised to find," Warton adds, "in so gross and ignorant an age, such talents for satire, and for observation on life; qualities which usually

[13] Seth Lerer, *Chaucer and His Readers: Imagining the Author in Late-Medieval England* (Princeton, N.J.: Princeton University Press, 1993), intro., esp. pp. 15–16.

[14] Lee Patterson, *Chaucer and the Subject of History* (Madison: University of Wisconsin Press, 1991), p. 15.

exert themselves at more civilised periods."[15] Similarly, the many writings on Chaucer that see him as having refined the language of his time propose, at least implicitly, that he alone somehow stood above or outside his own time in order to perform the renovation of language of which no one else was capable.[16] In William Thynne's 1532 edition of Chaucer it was thought marvelous that Chaucer had achieved what he did at a time "wha*n* doutlesse all good letters were layde a slepe throughout ye worlde," either because of the "disposycion & influe*n*ce of the bodies aboue / or by other ordynaunce of god." Later writers might have taken a less cosmic view of Chaucer's place, but the notion that Chaucer had to surmount the problems of "a half-formed language," in Robert Southey's words, was a commonplace.[17]

Eighteenth-century writers do not and cannot abject themselves before Chaucer because they know their cultural world to be manifestly superior to Chaucer's; it is fundamental to the edifice of post-Reformation, Enlightenment Britain that it excludes the medieval, the other. For Warton's brand of literary Whig history, the problem is to retrieve Chaucer from a cultural world so inferior that he cannot be regarded as having been a great poet unless he can be seen as in some way transcending his context. This had its outcome in a further paradox of Chaucerian reception: the fatherly poet is himself infantilized. Chaucer's anchoring role in the history of English verse caused some writers to refuse to look further back than his lifetime, in the belief that there was no earlier English verse worth considering. Chaucer, along with Gower, therefore belonged to "the first age" of English poetry, as George Puttenham thought, and this childhood of poetry emerged more fully with Dryden, who, believing that much of Chaucer's verse was metrically faulty, responded by conceding, "We can only say, that he liv'd in the Infancy of our Poetry, and that nothing is brought to Perfection at the first. We must be Children before we grow Men."[18] In this respect the father was also a child.

[15] Thomas Warton, *The History of English Poetry,* 3 vols. (London and Oxford, 1774–81), 1:431, 435.

[16] Occasionally Gower is seen as having joined Chaucer in this lonely work, as for example in George Ellis, *Specimens of the Early English Poets,* 3 vols. (London, 1801), 1:131.

[17] William Thynne, ed., *The Workes of Geffray Chaucer* (London, 1532), sig. A2v; Robert Southey, *Select Works of the British Poets* (London: Longman, Rees, Orme, Brown and Green, 1831), p. 1.

[18] [George Puttenham], *The Arte of English Poesie* (London, 1589), p. 48; John Dryden, *Fables Ancient and Modern* (London: Jacob Tonson, 1700), sig. B2v.

The later project of claiming a new seriousness for Chaucer was therefore related to retrieving him from childishness. Chaucer is at his best when most original, Thomas Tyrwhitt argued; when he stays too close to his sources he is "jejune."[19] Tyrwhitt also argued, contra Dryden, that Chaucer "was not ignorant of the laws of metre"; great numbers of Chaucer's verses are regular, so it must be assumed "that he intended to observe the same laws in the many other verses which seem to us irregular." If Chaucer *meant* his verses to be regular, then, "what reason can be assigned sufficient to account for his having failed so grossly and repeatedly, as is generally supposed, in an operation, which every Balladmonger in our days, man, woman, or child, is known to perform with the most unerring exactness, and without any extraordinary fatigue?"[20] Metrical correctness, in short, is child's play; to continue to see Chaucer as metrically incorrect would make him, as a poet, less than a child.

In the later nineteenth century some scholars, especially those behind the Chaucer Society and the program of editing and publishing Chaucer's work under way in the last third of the century, strove to create for Chaucer a newly dignified poetic persona, a kind of moral guide. The so-called Hoccleve portrait of Chaucer in MS Harley 4866 was used constantly in Chaucer productions of this period as part of a concerted campaign to project Chaucer as a poet of moral seriousness and gravity who, despite such worrying lapses as the fabliaux, was essentially a benign *fatherly* figure. In this period, Chaucer as a man was invested with a gravity and seriousness unparalleled since the fifteenth century. For Furnivall and Walter Skeat, and others such as Henry Bradshaw and James Russell Lowell, there is little of the childish wonderment in the face of Chaucer's achievement that can be seen in Lydgate and Hoccleve.[21]

However, precisely at this time when Chaucer was being constructed as newly serious and fatherly, a countering move occurred in the production of the deliberately infantilized, translated Chaucer. The two things were by no means opposed strands of the appropriation of Chaucer but were often closely linked. Mary Haweis, for example, was an associate

[19] Thomas Tyrwhitt, The Canterbury Tales *of Chaucer,* 5 vols. (London, 1775–78), 1:143.

[20] Ibid., 1:91.

[21] On the portrait and the moral construction of Chaucer, see further David Matthews, *The Making of Middle English, 1765–1910* (Minneapolis: University of Minnesota Press, 1999), chap. 7. On popular appropriations of Chaucer in this period, see also Steve Ellis, *Chaucer at Large* (Minneapolis: University of Minnesota Press, 2000).

of Furnivall's and shows in her work that she is abreast of the newest scholarship. Her Chaucers for children are obvious dilutions of scholarly work for the young in which the poet is seen, appropriately, as a fatherly writer. At the same time, he is infantilized, not simply in the obvious sense that his work is reconfigured for children but because of the specific transformations performed on his text.

III. Chaucer in the Nursery

William Forster's Education Act of 1870, which created a national, governmentally supervised elementary schooling system, is no longer credited with creating a new readership so much as consolidating the literacy rates that had been improving in the course of the century.[22] But the Act certainly had an effect on publishers, who increased their publications in children's literature after its passage in anticipation of a new market among young readers. An efflorescence of Chaucers for children followed on the passage of the Act, continuing until at least 1930 and peaking in the Edwardian period. Many of these publications, given numerous and frequent reprintings, were obviously commercially very successful and presumably much read. All link the infantilizing of Chaucer to a desire to reproduce the poet as an agent of ethical self-shaping.[23]

The founding text of this subgenre appeared long before the Act. Charles Cowden Clarke produced his *Tales from Chaucer in Prose: Designed Chiefly for the Use of Young Persons* in 1833, probably inspired by the Lambs' *Tales from Shakespear* (1807). This was by no means the first expurgated Chaucer, but it was the first of the modern era to present a moralized Chaucer specifically for the young. It is also the first major rendition of Chaucer in prose; prior to this it was simply assumed that anyone translating Chaucer would want to do so in verse. The work was well received but did not provoke immediate imitators. Chaucer did not have anything like the prominence of Shakespeare, and there was correspondingly little perceived need to generate a "Family Chaucer."

[22] See Altick, *English Common Reader*, p. 171; Alan J. Lee, *The Origins of the Popular Press in England, 1855–1914* (London: Croom Helm, 1976), p. 181; Louis James, *Fiction for the Working Man, 1830–1850* (London: Oxford University Press, 1963), p. 2.

[23] I do not discuss here the verse translations produced by Walter Skeat. These were not specifically aimed at children but nevertheless present a sanitized *CT.* Skeat produced, in three separate volumes, *The Knight's Tale;* the *Tales* of the Prioress, Clerk, Second Nun, and Canon's Yeoman; and the *Tales* of the Man of Law, the Nun's Priest, and Squire (all published London: De La More Press, 1904).

While Tyrwhitt's edition had created new interest in Chaucer, it was still possible for Walter Pater to say, in reference to an 1841 translation, "Of course . . . I have heard of the *Canterbury Tales,* but did not know that they were considered of sufficient importance to be modernised."[24]

When the second edition of *Tales from Chaucer* appeared in 1870, it became a staple of children's literature. Publishers incorporated it into their series for children such as the Everyman's Library for Young People, in which it appeared in 1911, and William Collins's Illustrated Children's Classics (1931), giving the work an active life of more than a century. Cowden Clarke's immediate successor was Mary Haweis, a more learned and scholarly writer who produced, as we have seen, three Chaucers from 1877 to 1887. The first two of these were more technical and difficult than Cowden Clarke's; the level of proficiency she seems to have expected from parents, teachers, and children alike was probably unrealistic. Nevertheless, her first two books saw new editions in the later nineteenth century.

Cowden Clarke's and Haweis's Chaucers produced many imitators in the late-Victorian and Edwardian periods in England and in America. These tended to be highly simplified prose retellings of *The Canterbury Tales,* often in the small octavo format that became common for children's literature at this time. They include Francis Storr and Hawes Turner's *Canterbury Chimes, or, Chaucer Tales Retold for Children* (London, 1878); Mary Seymour's *Chaucer's Stories Simply Told* (1884); Janet Harvey Kelman's *Stories from Chaucer told to the Children* (1905), aimed at the very young; J. Walker McSpadden's *Stories from Chaucer* (London and New York, 1907) and *Tales from Chaucer* (1909); Eva March Tappan's *The Chaucer Story Book* (London, Boston, and New York, 1908); R. Brimley Johnson's *Tales from Chaucer* (London and Glasgow, 1909); Ada Hales's *Stories from Chaucer* (London, 1911); Emily Underdown's *The Gateway to Chaucer* (London, Edinburgh, Dublin, and New York, 1912).[25]

The trend continued, if at a slightly decreased rate, after World War

[24] Thomas Wright, *The Life of Walter Pater,* 2 vols. (London: Everett & Co, 1907), 2:268.

[25] Though ostensibly aimed at adults, John S. P. Tatlock and Percy MacKaye's *The Complete Poetical Works of Geoffrey Chaucer: Now First Put into Modern English* (New York: Macmillan Company, 1912) should perhaps also be included here; the completeness is belied by some strategically placed asterisks. Margaret C. Macaulay, the daughter of the Gower editor, produced *Stories from Chaucer: Re-told from* The Canterbury Tales (Cambridge: Cambridge University Press, 1911), a more scholarly version of the children's genre.

I, with Mary Sturt and Ellen C. Oakden's *The Canterbury Pilgrims, Being Chaucers {sic} Canterbury Tales Retold for Children* (New York, London, and Toronto, 1923) and Eleanor Farjeon's *Tales from Chaucer* (London, 1930). This apparent falling away in production is deceptive. Most of the Edwardian Chaucers were reprinted or reedited several times in the 1920s and 1930s, McSpadden's *Stories from Chaucer,* for example, being reprinted fourteen times up to 1930 before appearing in a revised edition in 1932. This means that the slowing down in the appearance of *new* Chaucers for children after World War I does not indicate that the material was not there to be read.

Apart from rendering Chaucer into simple English for children, these works share several consistent trends reflecting the moral refashioning of Chaucer. First, *The Canterbury Tales,* though privileged over Chaucer's other works, was represented in limited form. Cowden Clarke presented, in prose paraphrase, *The General Prologue* and the *Tales* of the Knight, Man of Law, Wife of Bath, Clerk, Squire, Pardoner, Prioress, Nun's Priest, Canon's Yeoman, and Cook (in the shape of *Gamelyn*). He furthermore allocated subtitles to each tale, *The Knight's Tale* gaining the additional title of *Palamon and Arcite; The Man of Law's Tale, The Lady Constance;* and the remainder, *The Court of King Arthur, Griselda, Cambuscan, The Death-Slayers, The Murdered Child, The Cock and the Fox, The Alchymist,* and *Gamelyn.* This group of tales, with some additions and subtractions, more or less constituted the *Canterbury Tales* canon where translations were concerned for the rest of the nineteenth century and well into the twentieth. The Victorian and Edwardian periods drew principally on the tales of the Marriage Group along with other domestically focused stories, often throwing *Gamelyn* into the mix (usually without acknowledging its spurious status). The fabliaux, *The Wife of Bath's Prologue, The Pardoner's Prologue,* and the prose tales were rarely included.

Subtitling the tales in the way Cowden Clarke did became common, and sometimes the original titles were dropped altogether. This heightened the focus on character that made *The Canterbury Tales* so appealing to the nineteenth century, and allowed a certain flexibility of emphasis: *Palamon and Arcite* could and did become *Emilye* at times. Correspondingly, the relation of tales to tellers is deemphasized, in line with a move to make the *Tales* more narratively coherent. In favor of this coherence, the children's Chaucers suppress generic diversity and narrative interplay between pilgrims, privileging by contrast Chaucer himself as a guiding central narrator. This is part of a generic relocation of the tales, begun by Cowden Clarke and espoused by most of the children's versions, whereby *The Canterbury Tales* is reinvented as a coherent collection of linked short stories or an episodic novel. The individual genres represented by the tales, already smoothed out by the loss of the fabliaux, are subordinated under the master-genre of the moralistic and episodic novel for children. The process is assisted by what became the standard practice of providing illustrations, which further homogenize the tales by casting diverse material into the same style: the courts of Theseus in Athens, Arthur in Britain, or Walter in Saluzzo all have the same look about them.

Cowden Clarke collapsed author and narrator together to provide a stable point of view around which to construct the collection: "At this time of the year, I, Geoffrey Chaucer, the writer of these Tales, was remaining at the sign of the Tabard, in Southwark, ready to set forth on my pilgrimage to Canterbury."[26] This straightforwardly unironic reinvention of the narrator and elision of any author/narrator distinction is typical of later children's versions. It makes the *Tales* more novelistic (anchored by a unifying central narrator with a correspondingly diminished role for the secondary narrators) and documentary (the realism of the *Tales* guaranteed by a writer who is giving an unironic eyewitness account of fourteenth-century life). Equally importantly, a morally irreproachable controlling narrator is created, quite unlike the frequently licentious pilgrims or the actual Chaucer himself. This figure then becomes a staple: "luckily for us," one later version has it, "one of those twenty-nine Canterbury pilgrims was a quiet, observant, elderly gentleman called Geoffrey Chaucer. Nothing escaped his eyes."[27]

Much ingenuity is shown in the deployment of this narrator. While *Gamelyn* was often supplied for the wholeness and coherence it added, Sturt and Oakden came up with a different device. When the Cook begins his tale, the pilgrims reach a patch of bad road and have to proceed strung out in a line. Chaucer is at the end of the line and so does not hear the Cook's tale or any of the others told that day. Later, the Squire's tale is interrupted by lunch. Gaps are explained in a realistic way, without compromising Chaucer's powers as observer. In this version the pilgrims are brought to Canterbury and a picture of the cathedral follows

[26] Charles Cowden Clarke, *Tales from Chaucer in Prose* (London: Effingham Wilson, 1833), p. 51.

[27] J. Walker McSpadden, *Stories from Chaucer,* new rev. ed. with intro. by Dorothy M. Stuart (London: Harrap, 1932), p. 10.

the text. Likewise, in the most extensive and ambitious of the novelizations, *Tales of the Canterbury Pilgrims: Retold from Chaucer & Others* (London, 1904), F. J. Harvey Darton filled in gaps and allocated each of the tales to one of five days (a common strategy), adopting the Bradshaw Shift to smooth out the pilgrims' itinerary.[28] In this version too the pilgrims reach Canterbury, spending the night there and leaving the following morning, with episodes supplied from *The Mery Adventure of the Pardoner and the Tapster,* the prologue to *Beryn* found only in the Northumberland MS of *The Canterbury Tales.* John Lydgate joins the pilgrims in Canterbury and tells the story of the destruction of Thebes, and the tale telling then continues with *Beryn* as the Merchant's second tale.[29]

In 1930 Eleanor Farjeon, the noted children's author, produced her *Tales from Chaucer,* an extensive, novelized *Canterbury Tales;* ostensibly, all the tales are to be found in it, though of course some of them are reduced in prose paraphrase to a few lines. Unusually, versions even of *Melibee* and *The Parson's Tale* make their appearance. There were fewer new Chaucer translations by this time, though reprints continued to appear; Farjeon's book was reissued, for example, several times up until as late as 1959.

From Clarke and Haweis to Farjeon, then, the basic shape of translated Chaucers was the coherent, novelistic narrative with a guiding central narrator and moral observer. These "novels" were illustrated and were often principally about exemplary figures, particularly women (Griselda and Constance are favorites), undergoing a period of suffering and sometimes achieving domestic bliss. The churls among the pilgrims, and their churls' tales, are correspondingly deprivileged, elided altogether or pushed to the margins. What is rendered up is the kind of narrative coherence that, at least by implication, the infantile mind (whether truly childish or working-class) can understand and identify with. Victorian and Edwardian translators in particular view Chaucer as having a unique sympathy with the childish mind. Haweis, for example, was "encouraged to put together" her book "by noticing how quickly

[28] The Bradshaw Shift, largely repudiated by twentieth-century editors, has had a remarkable afterlife in translations: Coghill used it in 1951 and so the current Penguin Classics edition espouses it still.

[29] A notable exception to the novelizing trend is the work of Haweis. Her first two Chaucers, those for children and schools, represent the texts in several different forms: the original, the modernization, and her own phonetic rendering, designed to help the reading mother pronounce Chaucer correctly.

my own little boy learned and understood fragments of early English poetry. I believe that if they had the chance, many other children would do the same." The reason for this quick uptake of Chaucer is a natural sympathy on the part of the child for Chaucer's English: "I think that much of the construction and pronunciation of old English which seems stiff and obscure to grown up people, appears easy to children, whose crude language is in many ways its counterpart."[30]

What is exploited here is the always infantile character of Chaucer's verse, which has the beneficial side effect of making his poetry a particularly useful medium for the passing on of ethical truths to the infantile, and the rendering of a period of history in a morally acceptable way. The early practitioners, Cowden Clarke and Haweis, made these aims clear. Cowden Clarke outlined the dual aesthetic and ethical imperatives at work in his volume, fully conceding the occlusion of the aesthetic role as a result of the transposition into prose and the corresponding privileging of the ethical role. Addressing "My Young Readers," he wrote of the tales that the "object in presenting them in this new form was, first, that you might become wise and good, by the example of the sweet and kind creatures you will find described in them: secondly, that you might derive improvement by the beautiful writing."[31]

Aesthetic considerations can only come second; Cowden Clarke records that he has attempted to preserve "the poetical descriptions, and strong natural expressions of the author," but inevitably the translation can function only as a foretaste for the eventual reading of the *Tales* "in their original poetical dress."[32] Some of the tales are "coarse and indelicate," he concedes, adding that "as a distaste for vice will assuredly keep pace with a love of virtue, so a well regulated and delicately instructed mind will no more crave after and feed upon impure writings, than a healthy and natural stomach will desire and select carrion or dirt."[33] In other words, for all the greatness of Chaucer as trumpeted by scholars, his aesthetic merits cannot be seen simply or uncomplicatedly; readers must be shaped by the ethical work the text performs before they can be exposed to the original aesthetic artifact. That work is enabled by the infantilized Chaucer.

[30] Mrs. H. R. Haweis, *Chaucer for Children: A Golden Key* (London: Chatto & Windus, 1877), p. ix.

[31] Cowden Clarke, *Tales from Chaucer in Prose,* p. iii.

[32] Ibid., pp. iii–iv.

[33] Ibid., p. iv.

Mary Haweis's Chaucers similarly embody the notion that Chaucer must be infantilized in order to be rendered ethical and therefore readable. Haweis was interested less in extolling Chaucer's aesthetic beauties than in the historicism his work afforded, which characterized the more official versions of Chaucer promulgated by Furnivall and the Chaucer Society. The appearance of her *Tales from Chaucer* in Routledge's World Library locates it in the civilizing, ethical role, one that she emphasizes in all three of her Chaucers by stressing Chaucer's seriousness, purity, and religious character. Chaucer, she states, "was a very wise and good man," an echo of Cowden Clarke's sentiment that his readers would become "wise and good" as a result of their exposure to Chaucer. Haweis also believes that "There is no clearer *or safer* exponent of the life of the fourteenth century, as far as he describes it, than Geoffrey Chaucer,"[34] a statement that combines the commonplace faith in Chaucer's realism with an emphasis on the ethical character of his representations of fourteenth-century life (it is in this respect that Chaucer is a "safe" writer).

There is some irony in Haweis's claim for Chaucerian realism. Like most modernizers, she in fact devotes a great deal of energy to taking the fourteenth century out of Chaucer. In the absence of the fabliaux, the "world" of Chaucer for great numbers of readers up until the 1930s was the Athens of Theseus, the Mediterranean and pagan Britain of Constance, and the Saluzzo of the Marquis Walter. *The General Prologue* and the pilgrims themselves, occasionally along with *The Nun's Priest's Tale,* have to stand in for Chaucer's much-vaunted realism.

In Haweis's *Chaucer for Schools,* it becomes easy to see the attractions the late fourteenth century held for a Victorian readership. Just as Chaucer is to some extent out of his time, that time can look uncannily like the Renaissance and Reformation. Chaucer's "religious character," for example, is that of a Protestant, given the "Wicliffism and true Protestant feeling" of *The Parson's Tale.* Chaucer the proto-Protestant, a creation of the sixteenth century, was not much believed in by Haweis's time, but in her view nevertheless Chaucer strove "to propagate with his pen the pith of the new religious views . . . long before Luther sounded the note of victory."[35] The true character of *The Parson's Tale,*

[34] Mrs. H. R. Haweis, *Chaucer for Schools* (London: Chatto & Windus, 1881), p. x; my emphasis.

[35] Ibid., p. x.

furthermore, is obscured by the tampering of a Catholic scribe. Pointing to aspects of Chaucer's writing to note, she recommends "the well thought out individuality of Chaucer's characters, shewing a knowledge of human nature, Shaksperian as far as it goes, such as Palamon, Arcite, Walter, and many more."[36] All that is best in Chaucer is actually that which belongs to a later time.

Like Cowden Clarke, Edwardian and later compilers repeatedly assert their hope that readers will be led on to the original Chaucer when they grow up. "This little book now put into your hands is not meant to be an end in itself," writes Ada Hales in 1911, "and will lamentably fail in its purpose if it does not make you want to read Chaucer's own Prologue and Tales presently, for yourselves, as he wrote them." This sentiment is linked with Hales's explanation that "it is with some care that this particular little group [of tales] has been chosen, as those which are most likely to appeal to you, and, again, as those which serve as illustrations of the very different kinds of tales he wrote."[37] These sentiments are typical, though other compilers more candidly state that their selections have been made on the basis of taste or propriety. When the young readers do eventually turn to the real thing, they will "learn to love one who has been dear for his humanity, kindliness and humour to poets and ordinary folk alike, from 1370 to now," and find that while the original will amplify what they read as children, it is "not a contradiction of their old story-book."[38]

In these rationales yet again is the view that Chaucer is a wise and kind writer whose work improves us, yet which also contains inexplicably vicious material that readers must be taught to negotiate. Chaucer is always best approached through a mediating, moralized experience before a less-mediated exposure takes place, an exposure that will then simply confirm the impression given by the moralized version. Chaucer—to assemble some of the common ideas about him—is safe, healthy, pure, humane, kindly, humorous, shrewd, spiritual, and religious. And yet he is also none of those things until we learn how to

[36] Ibid., p. xiii.

[37] Ada Hales, *Stories from Chaucer* (London: Methuen, 1911), pp. xi, vii.

[38] M. Sturt and E. C. Oakden, *The Canterbury Pilgrims, Being Chaucers [sic] Canterbury Tales Retold for Children* (New York: Dutton, [1923]), p. 8; Francis Storr and Hawes Turner, *Canterbury Chimes or Chaucer Tales Retold for Children* (London: Kegan Paul, 1878), p. vii.

handle him; in order for Chaucer to assume a morally regulatory role, he must be infantilized.

IV. Adults-Only Chaucer

In the 1930s Chaucer began to grow up. In the immediate postwar years translated Chaucer suddenly looked very adult after decades of infantilized versions. In 1930 Frank Ernest Hill produced a translation of a selection of Chaucerian verse including *The General Prologue* and the *Tales* of the Knight, Prioress, Nun's Priest, and Pardoner. This was followed by a complete *Canterbury Tales* in 1934, lavishly produced for the Limited Editions Club. These were verse translations in rhyming couplets, an old tradition but one not much seen in the twentieth century to that point. Hill's motivation was the much-used one that Chaucer is a great poet but not nearly well enough known, for the reason that his language is harder to learn than it looks (most Victorian and Edwardian translators insisted that it was *easier* than it looks). Therefore, Hill argued in an essay entitled "The Unknown Poet," a translation was warranted for Chaucer just as it was for Virgil or Homer.[39]

In 1930 Hill wrote that his selection of poems "represent[s] . . . most of Chaucer's significant moods, though some readers may find the collection short in ribaldry."[40] This was remedied in the 1934 complete *Tales,* where the problem of Chaucer's "bawdy" was addressed. Some of the tales would offend the "morally censorious," Hill suggested, but as this was because of their general characteristics, if they were translated at all it was no great matter how individual words were dealt with. Such words, Hill wrote, "have their descendants in modern English, well known to most little boys of ten years or more. . . . It has sometimes seemed to me that these monosyllables have been in the custody of little boys from generation to generation. Some, I believe, would to-day be used only by men in the company of men when they wished to produce an effect of unusual 'toughness.'"[41]

[39] Frank Ernest Hill, trans., The Canterbury Tales: *The Prologue and Four Tales with the* Book of the Duchess *and Six Lyrics,* illustrated by Hermann Rosse (London, New York, and Toronto: Longman's Green and Co, 1930), pp. xi–xviii.

[40] Ibid., p. xvii.

[41] Frank Ernest Hill, The Canterbury Tales *of Chaucer Rendered into Modern English Verse,* 2 vols. (London: Limited Editions Club, 1934), p. xx.

In this neat reversal Hill in effect says that it would now be infantile to expurgate Chaucer because the offending parts are already in the possession of the infantile themselves (whether boys, or men being childish). "The frankness of Chaucer can hurt no one," Hill proposed, "children included. Boys and girls, whether their parents like it or not, get at the 'facts of life' early, and I know no better source than Chaucer. For he has put vulgarity and bawdiness into that natural setting of fun and casual life which makes us feel it not only as something inoffensive, but also justly and humorously a part of human experience."[42] Suddenly the aspect of Chaucer from which children had been most protected, far from posing a threat to their moral sensibilities, is potentially a source of instruction. Nevertheless, Hill's complete *Tales,* a lavishly produced and illustrated two-volume work, was obviously not destined for the eyes of children. It is deemed perfectly safe for children who are not going to see it; the argument about children's reading is here obviously designed to persuade *adults* that the book is acceptable.

A more completely adult appropriation of Chaucer occurred in the late 1940s and early 1950s with a spate of translations, some of which are still in use today. In the second half of the 1940s the Oxford academic and theatrical producer Nevill Coghill broadcast translations of *The Canterbury Tales* on BBC radio. Around Christmas 1950 his translation of *The Nun's Priest's Tale* was published under the upmarket Penguin imprint, Allen Lane, in an illustrated edition of one thousand copies on thick paper. This was a foretaste of the complete *Canterbury Tales,* which appeared in 1951 under the Penguin Books imprint. The paperback *Tales* is still part of the Penguin Classics list today, and Coghill's is probably the best known, and certainly the most durable, of recent translations. Explaining his principles, Coghill noted, "My translation is unexpurgated; the barbarous and (one is almost tempted to say) hypocritical practice of Victorian times in the matter of expurgation has lapsed in our lifetime, and what our greatest authors chose to mean and write need no longer be obscured by dashes, gaps and asterisks."[43]

In the U.S., R. M. Lumiansky's prose translation of the *Tales* appeared in 1948; it is not expurgated but uses modern American colloquialisms where required in the fabliaux. In the same year, Vincent F. Hopper's

[42] Ibid., p. xxii.

[43] Nevill Coghill, trans., *Geoffrey Chaucer:* The Canterbury Tales *Translated into Modern English* (Harmondsworth: Penguin Books, 1951), p. 18.

selection of *Tales* with an interlinear translation appeared, and in the following year the much reprinted *Portable Chaucer,* edited by Theodore Morrison, was published. Like Coghill's, each of these productions displays a turnaround in attitudes to Chaucer's bawdy tales. "What once would have been called obscenity in Chaucer," Morrison wrote, "is not likely to ruffle many sensibilities in the latter twentieth century." He adds that Chaucer "does not have the air of defying convention or exploiting forbidden ground. Partly this effect comes from his naturalness and health of temperament, but no doubt it was also due in part to the social conditions of his time."[44] In a new edition of his interlinear translation in 1970, Vincent Hopper added the *Tales* of the Miller and Reeve to his selection, creating some sort of landmark by glossing *queynte* (as noun) with "cunt."[45]

This reversal of attitudes reflects the beginnings of liberation from censorship and a general loosening of attitudes in the postwar period, along with the expansion of higher education in America and Britain. In this climate a new appreciation for the fabliaux as critical objects became evident, especially the Miller's and Reeve's *Tales.*[46] These Chaucer translations are the first complete unexpurgated Chaucers, reversing a trend of expurgation going back to 1795.[47]

Needless to say, although children's Chaucers still exist, there has been no going back on this particular trend in translations of Chaucer in the now highly competitive world of classics in translation. Although widespread academic acceptance is still lacking—many academics would share Derek Pearsall's belief "that translation of Chaucer is not only unnecessary but undesirable"[48]—the new trend marks a convergence of the aims of translations and scholarly editions of Chaucer: in

[44] Theodore Morrison, selected and trans., *The Portable Chaucer,* rev. ed. (New York: Viking Press, 1975), p. 26.

[45] Vincent F. Hopper, *Chaucer's* Canterbury Tales *(selected): An Interlinear Translation,* rev. ed. (Woodbury: Barron's Educational Series, 1970), p. 208.

[46] This is clear in bibliographies and first became evident to me in work undertaken for T. L. Burton and Rosemary Greentree, eds., *Chaucer's Miller's, Reeve's and Cook's Tales: An Annotated Bibliography, 1900 to 1992* (Toronto: University of Toronto Press, 1997).

[47] William Lipscomb's The Canterbury Tales *of Chaucer: Completed in a Modern Version,* 3 vols. (Oxford and London, 1795), was an expurgated Chaucer produced for avowedly moral reasons. But even before then, Dryden had avoided translating the fabliaux saying that he would "no more offend against Good Manners" (*Fables,* sig. C1v). On eighteenth-century Chaucer modernization apart from Dryden's and Pope's, see Betsy Bowden, ed. *Eighteenth-Century Modernizations from the* Canterbury Tales (Woodbridge: Brewer, 1991).

[48] Derek Pearsall, rev. of David Wright, trans. and intro., *The Canterbury Tales* (Oxford and New York: Oxford University Press, 1985) [*SAC* 9 (1987): 199–203, at p. 203].

his own way, Coghill wants to present an authentic Chaucer just as the editors of *The Riverside Chaucer* do.

This convergence begins with a renewed commitment to the translated Chaucer as an agent of ethical regulation, now through access to his unexpurgatedly healthy approach to sex and the human body, which might among other things be instructive about the facts of life. It also coincides with a renewed sense of the importance of Chaucer as an object of scholarship, and of the translated Chaucer as an aesthetic artifact in its own right. With the appearance of Manly and Rickert's *The Text of the Canterbury Tales* in 1940, and F. N. Robinson's second edition of the complete works in 1957, this is a period comparable to 1868–94, when the Chaucer Society was established and Walter Skeat's magisterial *Complete Works of Geoffrey Chaucer* published. At the same time, translations of Chaucer take on new aesthetic forms, especially in "fine press" versions. Coghill's *Canterbury Tales* was republished, illustrated with woodcuts, by the Folio Society in 1956–57; in addition to the special edition of *The Nun's Priest's Tale* mentioned above, his *Shipman's Tale* and *Merchant's Tale* both appeared in deluxe editions.[49]

A new, adult readership is implied and constructed by these texts. It is not the (literally) infantile audience of the early years of the century. It is not being told that there are parts of Chaucer it cannot have. There remains, perhaps, a trace of the trope of infantilization to the extent that these readers are told that Chaucer is just a bit too difficult for them. But what is most obvious is a new anxiety, no longer over ethical considerations (as the belief in literature's power of moral instruction declined in the second half of the century) but sheerly pragmatic ones. This is the anxiety over whether Chaucer will be read at all. Where the Edwardians had blithely asserted that reading Chaucer was easier than it looked (because Chaucerian poetry was simply the childhood of modern poetry), Chaucer is now modernized in a context in which some believe *Shakespeare* will have to be translated to be understood.[50] Chaucer has grown up, and finds himself in a harsh adult world.

[49] Nevill Coghill, trans., *Geoffrey Chaucer's* The Shipman's Tale (Department of Printing, College of Art of Wolverhampton, [1962]); Nevill Coghill, trans., *Geoffrey Chaucer:* The Merchant's Tale*, with illustrations by Derek Cousins* (London: Lion and Unicorn Press, 1960).

[50] E.g., Gary Taylor, *Reinventing Shakespeare: A Cultural History from the Restoration to the Present* (London: Vintage, 1991), p. 378.

The Engaged Spectator: Langland and Chaucer on Civic Spectacle and the *Theatrum*

Lawrence M. Clopper
Indiana University

SPECTACULA ARE PROBLEMATICAL in a number of ways for medieval people, for they are the sites of social, political, and religious strain. Spectacles assert the power and dominance of their sponsors and participants; they evoke social relations and create hierarchies. They are lay rather than clerical; indeed, clerics used the Latin term *spectacula* to refer to the obscene entertainments and the *theatrum* of the ancient world. Within clerical culture, *spectacula* were considered to be worldly and thus forbidden to clerics, for *spectacula* were thought to be conducive to pride, lechery, gluttony, and sloth; they were wasteful and superfluous. The way to control *spectacula* was to ritualize them—as in Corpus Christi processions. But civic and royal spectacles contended with clerical ritual for their own spaces in order to legitimate lay identity and prestige.

Thus far I have stressed the division between lay and clerical cultures with regard to spectacle. Now I want to move into the more equivocal space of practice in order to see how we might read instances of spectacles as statements about social relations.

Recent scholarship on medieval civic spectacle has emphasized the ideological content of mayoral and Corpus Christi processions.[1] On one

This essay is dedicated to Martin Stevens, mentor and friend.

Parts of this paper were presented at the Ninth and Tenth International Congresses of the New Chaucer Society at the University of Dublin (Chaucer) and the University of California at Los Angeles (Langland) in 1994 and 1996, respectively.

[1] Charles Phythian-Adams, "Ceremony and the Citizen: The Communal Year at Coventry 1450–1550," in Peter Clark and Paul Slack, eds., *Crisis and Order in English Towns* (London: Routledge, 1972), pp. 57–85; Mervyn James, "Ritual, Drama and Social Body in the Late Medieval English Town," *Past and Present* 98 (1983): 3–29; Sheila Lin-

side of this debate are scholars such as Charles Phythian-Adams and Mervyn James who emphasize the utopian agendas of these spectacles: the processions are said to contain an image of the whole body of the city or of the mystical body of Christ. Sheila Lindenbaum, on the other hand, points to the dysutopian consequences of elitist productions; for even though a Corpus Christi or civic procession is intended to create an image of unity, the procession itself is made up of discrete units arranged in hierarchical fashion, which as a consequence makes a statement about lesser and greater degrees, and distinguishes the feet from the head of the body.[2] And then there are those nonparticipants who are excluded from the procession altogether. These spectacles have been made to speak about the relationship not only between audience and participant but also among participants, though usually only in generalized ways, that is, in terms of groups, the producers and their intended audiences. Because we have few eyewitness accounts of late-medieval spectacles, we can only imagine the diversity of reception that Claire Sponsler has suggested we should look for in any evaluation of public spectacle.[3]

Langland and Chaucer are diverse witnesses whose testimony has been little used as registers of the problematics of public spectacle. Both give us powerful representations of London spectacle, yet both narrate these events in ways that suggest they were conscious of the clerical critique of spectacle, and, in Chaucer's case, of the *theatrum.* Langland reports two spectacles, Richard II's coronation procession and the 1366 Pageant of the Lady of the Sun. The first of these is presented approvingly because it is edificatory, yet it is interesting to note that the poet focuses not on the spectacle, which presumably was costly, but on the words

denbaum, "The Smithfield Tournament of 1390," *Journal of Medieval and Renaissance Studies* 20 (1990): 1–20, and "Ceremony and Oligarchy: The London Midsummer Watch," in Barbara A. Hanawalt and Kathryn L. Reyerson, eds., *City and Spectacle in Medieval Europe* (Minneapolis: University of Minnesota Press, 1994), pp. 171–88; many of the other essays in *City and Spectacle;* and Gordon Kipling, *Enter the King: Theatre, Liturgy, and Ritual in the Medieval Civic Triumph* (Oxford: Oxford University Press, 1997).

[2] See also Miri Rubin, *Corpus Christi: The Eucharist in Late Medieval Culture* (Cambridge: Cambridge University Press, 1991), pp. 266–71.

[3] Claire Sponsler, "The Culture of the Spectator: Conformity and Resistance to Medieval Performances," *Theatre Journal* 44 (1992): 15–29. See, in addition, Kathleen Ashley, "Sponsorship, Reflexivity and Resistance: Cultural Readings of the York Cycle Plays," in James J. Paxson, Lawrence M. Clopper, and Sylvia Tomasch, eds., *The Performance of Middle English Culture: Essays on Chaucer and the Drama in Honor of Martin Stevens* (Cambridge: Boydell and Brewer, 1998), pp. 9–24.

spoken. By contrast, he condemns the 1366 pageant for its conspicuous waste and misuse of regalia. He reports no words from it, only the sight. Chaucer's tournament in *The Knight's Tale* links contemporary jousting to the ancient *theatrum.* His classicizing tactic, however, moves the tournament into the pejorative realm of clerical discourse against the *theatrum* and things associated with it. I think Langland's and Chaucer's strategies in reporting spectacle register the impact of clerical attempts to control the ludic and to channel inappropriate game and display into purposeful ritual, but they also raise the question of what kinds of spectacle are appropriate for lay people.[4]

I wish to discuss Chaucer's and Langland's representations of urban and royal spectacle within the arena of competing discourses to which such spectacles were subjected. Both must have been aware of clerical suspicion of spectacle and attempts to suppress *ludi inhonesti,* but Chaucer and Langland occupied different niches in London, an eventuality that colored their reception of the public spectacles they saw. Chaucer was a resident of London who also served at noble and royal courts; during his productive literary years, he resided in London, acting for a twelve-year period as collector of customs for the city at the same time that he was presenting his poetry to persons within court circles. We might see Chaucer, then, as one of those advantaged persons who could move easily between city and court.[5] Despite the absence of the city from his work, we may presume that Chaucer had some identification with London through his birth, his residence, and his occupations therein.[6] And we may also assume that his relations at court and his dealings with the nobility made him conscious of the different interests of London and the royal court and the difficult relationship that exists when a city granted freedoms by a monarch also at times had the monarch (not to mention John of Gaunt) in its midst. Langland, by contrast, neither was born in London nor apparently did he reside there in his youth. Like Chaucer,

[4] I discuss clerical attempts to control the ludic in my essay "English Drama: From Ungodly *Ludi* to Sacred Play," in *The Cambridge History of Medieval English Literature,* ed. David Wallace (Cambridge: Cambridge University Press, 1998), pp. 739–66. See also Glending Olson, "Plays as Play: A Medieval Ethical Theory of Performance and the Intellectual Context of the *Tretise of Miraclis Pleyinge,*" *Viator* 26 (1995): 195–221.

[5] Paul Strohm, *Social Chaucer* (Cambridge, Mass.: Harvard University Press, 1989); and Lee Patterson, *Chaucer and the Subject of History* (Madison: University of Wisconsin Press, 1991), pp. 194–98 (on Chaucer's relation to the community of honor).

[6] See David Wallace, "Chaucer and the Absent City," in Barbara A. Hanawalt, ed., *Chaucer's England: Literature in Historical Context* (Minneapolis: University of Minnesota Press, 1992), pp. 59–90.

he was from a prosperous and important family, but if we may assume his persona bears some resemblance to the poet, he either voluntarily abandoned the secular world or was reduced to poverty, whereupon he seems to have taken up some sort of quasi-religious occupation.[7] Wille, as I will try to show, is represented as a spectator of the London scene, one who is more attracted to it perhaps than was his maker.

When Langland and Chaucer record their responses to London's civic and royal spectacles, they reveal their expectations and judgments of them. Their responses are not apt to be simple or even alike because the status of the two writers differs and they may have conflicted emotions about specific events. In addition, the ideological content of the three kinds of ceremony to be discussed—the Lord Mayor's Midsummer Show, the royal entry, and the royal procession or pageant—differs one from the other with the result that the urban Chaucer, for example, might respond more favorably to one kind of spectacle than another. Chaucer's presentation of urban spectacle in *The Knight's Tale* functions as both an evocation and a critique of court culture within the city of London. Langland had mixed feelings as well, for he represents the spectacle associated with Richard's coronation as an opportunity for educating the monarch, a potential feature of the reception of royalty, yet indignantly condemns the royal pageant of 1366. In the case of both poets, I suspect that their conflicted responses to spectacle and their sometimes equivocal presentation of them is occasioned by the moral questions clerics raised about *spectacula* in general.

Clerical discourse frames the problematics of spectacle in numerous ways. It not only condemns sights and entertainments of certain kinds but also links spectacle to immoderate behavior and even excessive bodily movement. There is, as we shall see, an "antitheatrical" tradition in Western medieval Europe that has little to do with the drama and everything to do with what was associated with the *theatrum.*[8] Because of antagonism in the late empire to the *theatrum* and other *spectacula,* the clerical culture of the medieval Christian West officially condemned

[7] These two scenarios are suggested by the biography of Wille in the poem; for more detail, see my essay "The Life of the Dreamer, the Dreams of the Wanderer in *Piers Plowman,*" *SP* 86 (1989): 261–85. The most recent discussions of Langland's life and family are Ralph Hanna III, *William Langland,* Authors of the Middle Ages 3 (Aldershot, Hants.: Variorum, 1993), and my *"Songes of Rechelesnesse": Langland and the Franciscans* (Ann Arbor: University of Michigan Press, 1997), the final two chapters.

[8] I will discuss this antitheatrical tradition in more detail in my forthcoming book, *Drama, Play, and Game: English Festive Culture in the Medieval and Early Modern Period* (Chicago: The University of Chicago Press, 2001).

clerical participation in a wide range of *ludi* and at various times attempted to restrict lay engagement in games and *ludi* the church felt to be pagan in origin or conducive to lechery and gluttony.[9] Even after the *theatrum* physically disappeared, things thought to be extravagant in gesture, given to pomp, lascivious, or immoral might be labeled "theatrical."[10] And since there was an early tendency to identify *theatrum* with *spectaculum,* indeed, at times, to equate the two, there was suspicion of anything that drew people to behold and to delight in the pageantry of this world. But medieval people, both lay and cleric, were very much given to spectacle because dress, action, and presentation express status and identity; consequently, the clerical opposition to a wide range of *ludi* had the potential to problematize recreation and spectacle for many individuals.

For Isidore of Seville, the *theatrum* was a place for spectacle; indeed, the very word itself came from the Greek *apo tes theorias,* which means "spectacle."[11] His etymological comment is one of the more neutral things Isidore has to say about the *theatrum,* for to him, Tertullian, Chrysostom, Augustine, and numerous others—including ancient Roman writers themselves—the *theatrum* was a place of immorality, its institution a sign of, and complicit in, the degeneration of the empire, and its denizens *infames,* persons who could neither be full citizens of the empire nor Christians.[12] When Augustine, for example, turns to the theater in *The City of God,* he mounts an attack on not just the institution and its occasioning of sin but the whole theological foundation for the use of *spectacula* within the empire.[13] What kind of gods, he asks, would demand that theatrical games be instituted on their behalf when these shows depict their own immoralities? The pagan gods do not instruct their followers in the moral life; rather, they provide them with sacrilegious entertainments and spectacles. Citing the games in honor of

[9] Mary Marshall, "*Theatre* in the Middle Ages: Evidence from Dictionaries and Glosses," *Symposium* 4 (1950): 1–39, 366–89; and Millett Henshaw, "The Attitude of the Church toward the Stage to the End of the Middle Ages," *M&H* 4 (1952): 3–17.

[10] Dino Bigongiari, "Were There Theatres in the Twelfth and Thirteenth Centuries?" *Romanic Review* 37 (1947): 201–24.

[11] Isidore of Seville, *Etymologiarum,* ed. W. M. Lindsay, 2 vols. (Oxford: Clarendon Press, 1911), 18.42–53; and see Joseph R. Jones, "Isidore and the Theatre," in Clifford Davidson et al., eds., *Drama in the Middle Ages: Comparative and Critical Essays* 2d ser. (New York: AMS, 1991), pp. 1–23.

[12] On ancient pagan attacks on the theater, see Catharine Edwards, *The Politics of Immorality in Ancient Rome* (Cambridge: Cambridge University Press, 1993), pp. 98–136.

[13] Saint Augustine, *The City of God,* 1.32–33, 2.4–14. Nicholas Trevet (d. ca. 1334) glossed these passages with information gleaned from Isidore.

the virgin Coelestis and Berecynthia (= Rhea, Cybele), mother of the gods, Augustine describes the lewd actions played and sung before the mother of the gods—so lubricious, he says, they would shame a chaste matron—yet these shows are performed publicly in words no one would ever say before one's mother. Even the performers are despised. But this is illogical: if the plays are demanded by the gods, then why are the performers stigmatized and refused citizenship and barred from all honors and offices? Given the tirades against the obscenities of the *theatrum* by Augustine and others, it is not surprising that the words most commonly connected with *theatrum* in the Middle Ages are *impudicitia, spurcitia, impuritas, turpitudo, licentia, luxuria, foeditas,* and *obscenitas.*[14]

Because the church fathers were so offended by the *theatrum,* church councils enacted legislation to effect as much of a divorcement of Christians from the surrounding pagan culture as possible. Although the early councils did not prohibit converts from going to the games, except on Sundays and church festivals, it condemned associations with actors and those who were engaged with the *theatrum.* Christians were not permitted to be *scenici* or to marry them; if an actor sought baptism, he had to abandon his profession. Much of this early legislation was incorporated into Gratian's *Decretum* and the various continuations of it (together the *Corpus iuris canonici*).[15] Clerics were forbidden to be amid *spectacula* and other pomps (dist. 23, cap. 3); all clerics, and the laity, were to avoid games of chance (which might include everything from gambling to martial contests), and the clergy were not to observe or attend performances by *mimi, ioculatores, et histriones* (dist. 35, cap. 1); clerics were not to go to taverns or engage in feasts or entertainments with the laity or in activities that involved singing or the wearing of distorted masks (*larvae;* dist. 44); the clergy were not to give things to *histriones* (dist. 86, cap. 7). In this legislation we can see the desire to physically separate both laity and clergy from pagan culture; however, within this impulse we can also discern an interest in clerical decorum per se. The clergy are to absent themselves from all *ludi* and amusements; they are to be sober in action and dress.

As the ancient theater faded into the past, the word *theatrum* came to stand for any public space; it was the marketplace or the site of civic and

[14] Bigongiari, "Were There Theatres," p. 217.

[15] *Corpus iuris canonici,* ed. Emil Friedberg, 2 vols. (Leipzig, 1879–81).

royal spectacle. But always there hovers around *spectacula* the stench of the *theatrum;* engagement in the *theatrum* (= the world), attendance at *spectacula,* is a sign of pomp and indulgence, an exhibition of too much concern for the *saeculum.*

In the later Middle Ages, as evidenced particularly in episcopal letters and sermons, some clerics tried to extend clerical decorum to lay activities by suppressing the more outrageous, lascivious, and violent ones.[16] Bishop Grosseteste attempted to extirpate "somergames," "scotales," tilting at quintains and wrestling in churchyards and cemeteries, and other activities that he regarded as more pagan than Christian. The writer of the *Tretise of Miraclis Pleyinge* echoes canon law and other clerical discourse when he condemns these *ludi* for their incitement to lust and gluttony. In his *Summa predicantium,* under the rubric *Ludus,* John Bromyard attacks games of chance: dicing and tournaments.[17] Tournaments are to be condemned not only because they endanger life but also because of their expense and the vices that attend upon them. Since *ludi inhonesti* are activities that imperil one's soul, they are to be avoided entirely. Therefore, we might read the institution of lay religious processions, indeed all the phenomena associated with Corpus Christi and the like, as alternatives to various kinds of *ludi inhonesti;* they are decorous expressions of piety and of communion in the body of Christ.

Within this broad antitheatrical and antiludic tradition, there was the more pointed papal legislation against tournaments in the twin interests, at least initially, of controlling violence within Christendom and directing it toward the Muslim enemy in crusade.[18] Innocent III at the Council of Clermont, in 1130, forbade tournaments and ordered that those killed in them not be given Christian burial. Popes reissued the condemnation with some frequency but with little apparent effect until it was rescinded by John XXII in 1316. The campaign against tournaments was carried out largely by preachers. One of the better-known examples is Jacques de Vitry's sermon exemplum about his conversation

[16] Glynne Wickham, "Robert Grosseteste and the Feast of Fools," *Sewanee Mediaeval Colloquium Occasional Papers* 2 (Sewanee, Tenn.: University Press, 1985), pp. 81–99; and my "*Miracula* and the *Tretise of Miraclis Pleyinge,*" *Speculum* 65 (1990): 878–905.

[17] John Bromyard, *Summa predicantium* (Venice: D. Nicholinus, 1586), fols. 454–55v.

[18] Maurice Keen, *Chivalry* (New Haven, Conn.: Yale University Press, 1984), pp. 44–63, 94–97. Monarchs also attempted at times to control tournaments because they were thought to be occasions when the barony might bond in potential conspiracies against the monarchy. But monarchs also tried to control tournaments in order to promote those under their own aegis.

with a tournament enthusiast in which the preacher shows the knight how a participant engages in each of the seven deadly sins.[19] Among other things, he says that tournaments are undertaken out of pride, rather than for military practice, as often claimed by the participants; are given to all manner of excesses, including lecherous encounters with meretricious hangers-on; and are conspicuous in their waste of goods and lands. Although the condemnation of tournaments per se was rescinded in 1316, preaching against them and their excesses continued, as we see in John Bromyard's *Summa predicantium.*[20]

The link between tournaments and the *theatrum* was made in the interests of buttressing the legitimacy of jousting. The most common rationale for tournaments was the argument that knights needed practical training; if the state were to be preserved and Christendom protected, then knights had to prepare themselves. But another argument was that jousting was an ancient practice (when in actuality tournaments dated only from the eleventh century). Perhaps it was the interest in the *roman antique* that fostered this claim; in any event, some authors suggested that tournaments were descendents of the gladitorial games of Rome.[21] The link between tournaments and the *theatrum* undermines the argument in their favor—though perhaps most of these writers were unknowing that it did so. Boccaccio, on the other hand, was completely aware of the contradiction. In the *Teseida* he presents the tournament as a noble sport, yet in his glosses he repeats many of Isidore's damning comments. When he describes the seating arrangements in the amphitheater, he refers to the participants as gladiators and gives an account of the building.[22] These passages are indebted to Isidore. The first sort of gladiatorial game Isidore describes is the "ludus equestrium":

[19] The text is reprinted and translated by David Carlson, "Religious Writers and Church Councils on Chivalry," in Howell Chickering and Thomas H. Seiler, eds., *The Study of Chivalry* (Kalamazoo, Mich.: Medieval Institute Publications, 1988), pp. 152–55.

[20] See further G. R. Owst, *Literature and Pulpit in Medieval England* (Oxford: Basil Blackwell, 1966), pp. 333–38. One should note, however, that tournaments often appear in exempla without there being any condemnation of them and that the sacralization of knighthood in part countered the depiction of knightly activities as immoral and vainglorious. See Keen, *Chivalry,* pp. 97–101, for some examples.

[21] Guy Raynaud de Lage, "Les Romans antiques et la representation de l'Antiquité," *Le Moyen Age* 67 (1961): 247–91.

[22] James McGregor, "Boccaccio's Athenian Theater: Form and Function of an Ancient Monument in *Teseida,*" *Modern Language Notes* 99 (1984): 1–42. The translations of Isidore cited below are McGregor's, pp. 34–36.

Two horsemen, with military insignias preceding them, one from the eastern side, the other from the west, advance on white horses with golden swords . . . [,] struggling until one suddenly arrives at the other's death, so that the one who falls has death, the one who conquers glory.[23]

It is easy to see how a medieval reader of this text would link jousting to these gladiatorial games. But Isidore's readers would also know that equestrian games, indeed all *ludi* associated with the *theatrum,* were in honor of demons:

The games of the Circus were instituted as rituals and for the celebration of the pagan gods. . . . Now equestrian matters were formerly carried out simply . . . but when the natural use of horsemanship is bent towards the games, it is changed into the worship of demons.[24]

Boccaccio celebrates the tournament in his text and points to its immorality in his glosses.[25]

Despite the clergy's attacks on the *theatrum* and *ludi inhonesti,* early Christians no more stopped going to the games than nobles ceased to have tournaments or lay men and women gave up parish ales. Spectacles are statements of who and what individuals and institutions are and thus are not apt to be abandoned easily. Yet some spectacles are more decorous than others. John Lydgate scripted verses for royal entries and pageants and mummings for royalty and the London mercers and goldsmiths, but he never wrote a fully scripted drama. His generic choices undoubtedly reflect the interests of the classes for whom he wrote; nevertheless, they also suggest that he was wary of things that might be identified with the *theatrum* or frivolous spectacle and chastened his verse with allegory and moral sentiment. My point is that it would be difficult for laity or clergy to engage in *ludi* without being sensitive to

[23] "DE LVDO EQVESTRI. . . . Duo enim equites praecedentibus prius signis militaribus, unus a parte orientis, alter ab occidentis procedebant in equis albis cum aureis galeis . . . dimicantes quousque alter in alterius morte prosiliret, ut haberet qui caderet casum, gloriam qui perimeret" (*Etym.* 18.53).

[24] "DE LVDIS CIRCENSIBVS. Ludi Circenses sacrorum causa ac deorum gentilium celebrationibus instituti sunt: unde et qui eos spectant daemonum cultibus inservire videntur. Nam res equestris antea simplex agebatur . . . sed quum ad ludos coactus est naturalis usus, ad daemoniorum cultum translatus est" (*Etym.* 18.27).

[25] Scholars do not believe that Chaucer was familiar with Boccaccio's glosses; see William E. Coleman, "Chaucer's MS and Boccaccio's Commentaries on *Il Teseida,*" *Chaucer Newsletter* 9 (1987): 1, 6.

the issues of appropriateness; indeed, there is a large body of literature on the value of recreation, a discourse that in itself suggests that the notion of recreation was problematical.[26]

Appropriateness in such matters is bound by status (lay or clerical), degree (noble or common), location (London, provincial cities, or the countryside), and by one's sense of oneself and one's milieu. In the fifteenth and sixteenth centuries, the oligarchies in some northern cities—York, Coventry, and Chester—expressed their prestige by, among other things, mounting expensive sequences of biblical dramas. Since London had a similar guild oligarchy, an even larger population, and the willingness to consume wealth in spectacular display, we might expect it also to have produced biblical plays. In fact, we do not find such a phenomenon within the walls of London; instead, the city seems to have preferred extravagant processions of corporate bodies or of the court.[27]

It is perhaps significant, then, that Chaucer provincializes the few references he makes to biblical drama, as if to say that he does not regard them as appropriate *spectacula* for his city.[28] It is the drunken Miller who insists on intruding himself into the storytelling contest by crying out in "Pilates voys" (*MilP* 3124), and within the tale we are told that among Absolon's other talents, he "pleyeth Herodes upon a scaffold hye" (line 3384). The Wife of Bath, we find, is in the habit of going to vigils, processions, sermons, pilgrimages, and "to pleyes of myracles" (*WBP,* 558). Chaucer does not associate these activities with London or its environs; rather, he places them at Oxford and Bath.[29] Equally significant,

[26] Glending Olson, *Literature as Recreation in the Later Middle Ages* (Ithaca, N.Y.: Cornell University Press, 1982).

[27] There are references to biblical plays produced by the *clerici* of London at Clerkenwell, outside the city; Ian Lancashire, *Dramatic Texts and Records of Britain: A Chronological Topography to 1558* (Toronto: University of Toronto Press, 1984), pp. 112–14 (items 543–49). These records are problematical, and the tradition that biblical plays were performed regularly is further complicated by the antiquarian reception of the tradition. I believe that the records include sufficient antiquarian embellishments and possible misreadings—both medieval, early modern, and modern—to induce skepticism. My analysis of the data, to be published in *Comparative Drama* 34 (2000), suggests there was only one performance of biblical plays at Clerkenwell in Chaucer's lifetime.

[28] As Alexandra Johnston has demonstrated, Chaucer's apparent references to the mystery cycles are among the earliest we have; see her "Chaucer's Records of Early English Drama," *Records of Early English Drama Newsletter* 13 (1988): 13–20. For a discussion of Chaucer and the theater that complements the present essay, see Seth Lerer, "The Chaucerian Critique of Medieval Theatricality," in Paxson, Clopper, and Tomasch, eds., *Performance of Middle English Culture,* pp. 59–76.

[29] However, we do not have records for biblical drama of the type required in either place in the fourteenth *or* the fifteenth centuries, so Chaucer's remarks may not be historically accurate.

he links Pilate with the loud-mouthed and uncouth Miller; Herod with the effeminate Absolon, the object of the Miller's ridicule; and the "plays of miraclis" with the other peregrinations of the shrewish Wife. My point is that not only are the allusions provincialized but they are associated with people who are not refined, who are not urbane.

By contrast, Chaucer gives us a picture of a noble spectacle—that is also urban—in his lavish description of the tourney in *The Knight's Tale.* Theseus, Hippolita, Emelye, and other members of court—ordered in their degree—ride through the city to the lists constructed outside the town. They are followed by the one hundred knights in Palamon's and Arcite's retinues. The exotic dress and armor of the knights is described in considerable detail. There are musicians to create a splendid noise. If one reads the descriptions of the great Smithfield tournament of 1390, one is reminded of Theseus's, and it is particularly important to recall that Chaucer was Clerk of the Works and the supervisor for the building of the lists at Smithfield for the tournaments in May and October 1390.[30] The 1390 event began at the Tower; there were sixty squires of honor on coursers; sixty ladies of honor on palfreys, each of whom led a knight by a gold chain. The company processed through the center of the city—accompanied by trumpeters—and rode out to Smithfield, where Richard had had the lists built and where the company retired to specially constructed rooms to watch the tournament.[31]

Theseus's procession and great theater may recall Chaucer's experience in 1390 or at some earlier event, but I do not think it correct to say that Chaucer presents us here with an idealization of a London urban spectacle, because it is centered on the royal court, not the city. To illustrate the difference, we might contrast this royal pageantry with two other kinds of urban ceremonial, the later, annual Lord Mayor's Midsummer

[30] Lindenbaum, "Smithfield Tournament"; Martin M. Crow and Clair C. Olson, eds., *Chaucer Life-Records* (Austin: University of Texas Press, 1966), pp. 456, 472. We cannot be certain that Chaucer is drawing upon the Smithfield tournament in his description of Theseus's tourney because the first version of *The Knight's Tale* was written before the tourney and we do not know whether Chaucer made any revisions when he placed the tale into *The Canterbury Tales.* For a succinct discussion of the matter of dating, see Patterson, *Chaucer and the Subject of History,* p. 169 n. 10. Patterson implies that the 1390 tournament is still relevant, since he believes Chaucer continued to revise the tale after 1390. In any event, Chaucer could have seen tournaments like the Smithfield one before he wrote the first version of *KnT.*

[31] Scholars have noted that Chaucer deviated from Boccaccio's *Teseida* in having the lists specially constructed for the event, a detail that is true of England whenever there were these great tournaments, but not at all true of Boccaccio's Italy, where Roman amphitheaters were ready to hand. See, for example, V. A. Kolve, *Chaucer and the Imagery of Narrative* (Stanford: Stanford University Press, 1984), pp. 105–12.

Show and the occasional royal entry or reception of the monarch by the city in Chaucer's day. The politics, or ideological structure, of these three ceremonies differ because the participants within them make up different groups and because the audience for each, and hence the relationship between the participants and audience, differs. On the other hand, all three ceremonies share the same structural feature: they are discontinuous scripts that include allegorical or idealized scenes sometimes with speeches from historical, personified, or biblical figures. When the goldsmiths, drapers, and other wealthy guilds created spectacles, they did not follow the example of their northern counterparts in producing biblical plays; instead, they seem to have imitated royal processions, establishing perhaps through their own lavishness that they were a political presence to be reckoned with.

The Lord Mayor's Midsummer Show, like its predecessor, the Midsummer Watch, was very much a statement of corporate identity and oligarchic power whether in London or elsewhere.[32] The Watch was originally a safety precaution against the dangers of bonfires during Midsummer celebrations; however, the members of the watch were usually the principal landholders of each part of the city. Dressed in livery and accompanied by musicians, they patrolled the city, in effect, to protect "their" city from the present danger. During the fifteenth century, this ancient custom in many instances developed into a more elaborate Show in which the elites of the city marched in procession with pageants and other displays. Wherever we find these merchant guild processions, we usually find evidence of a concern for appropriate and hierarchical order. Mayoral books—or the orders for the procession of Corpus Christi—list the participating guilds in their proper places, with the lesser ones, the victuallers for example, at the beginning and the more prestigious and older guilds, often the merchants and drapers, toward the end. The content of the shows varies from place to place, but the London "Mayres Watche" of 1521—for which we have an eyewitness account as well as records—gives a good sense of its ideological program. The pageants honor the mayor and the sheriffs, and the procession privileges the twenty-four aldermen and the masters of the merchant guilds who constitute London's ruling elite. Their movement through the city asserts their rights over the local terrain. Although they do not literally own the city of London, they symbolically take possession of it

[32] Lindenbaum, "Ceremony and Oligarchy."

by marking its bounds and liberties. The London Midsummer Watch assembled at Smithfield and marched into the city, a kind of mock invasion of the city that imposed order on the urban space.

If the Lord Mayor's Show is seen as a statement about the power of London's oligarchic government, the reception of royalty into the city is a celebration of negotiated power, for a monarch, especially a new monarch, is not only a granter but a maintainer of a city's liberties.[33] Even though a city has a charter granting rights of self-governance, the charter is theoretically revocable, since all possession and justice presumably descend from the king's person. On the other hand, once certain freedoms are granted, the city wishes not only to maintain but to enlarge them as well as to lower any fee farms that may have been instituted since incorporation. When a monarch enters "his" city, consequently, there is a confrontation between the freemen of the city, who must acknowledge their monarch—the source of their freedom—and the monarch, who is the source of even greater freedoms if he is properly cajoled. But a city already having freedoms may feel incumbent to restate its "ancient" political corporateness. Most provincial cities were probably at a greater disadvantage in this kind of contest; consequently, their receptions of monarchs and other dignitaries were likely to be primarily complimentary. London, which could claim the monarch as its "premier citizen," had sufficient power—both from the ancientness of its freedoms and its economic importance—to contest royal domination more successfully. We can see how this dynamic works from a passage in Langland's Prologue to *Piers Plowman* that is generally regarded to be a reflection of the activities surrounding the coronation of Richard II.[34]

Richard's coronation was preceded by the London reception of the young monarch on the day prior to his installation. The greeting of the monarch was part of a political reconciliation between the city of Lon-

[33] Lorraine Attreed, "The Politics of Welcome: Ceremonies and Constitutional Development in Later Medieval English Towns," in Hanawalt and Reyerson, eds., *City and Spectacle,* pp. 208–31. Martin Stevens has provided us with a wonderful illustration of how the reception of Christ into the city of York works on the level of the sacred; see his chapter "The York Cycle: City as Stage" in *Four Middle English Mystery Cycles: Textual, Contextual, and Critical Interpretations* (Princeton, N.J.: Princeton University Press, 1987), pp. 17–87.

[34] E. Talbot Donaldson, *Piers Plowman: The C-Text and Its Poet* (New Haven, Conn.: Yale University Press, 1949), pp. 116–18. Technically Richard's procession was not a royal entry (he was already in the city at the Tower); however, since it shares features with the entry—the erection of pageants along the route by the city—it has the dynamics of an entry.

don and John of Gaunt, Richard's uncle and a feared antagonist of the city.[35] On the evening before his coronation, Richard, attended by a large company of knights and men-at-arms, progressed from the Tower to Westminster Abbey, where he stayed the night. Along the route the city had arranged a number of elaborate pageants, among which, according to Walsingham, was a castle from which a golden angel descended to place a crown upon Richard's head.[36]

We can see the dynamic of the spectacle in Langland's representation of the event. He opens with a statement of the social contract:

> Thanne kam þ*er* a kyng: knyȝthod hym ladde;
> Might of the co*m*munes made hym to regne.
> And þanne cam kynde wit and clerkes he made
> For to counseillen þe kyng and þe co*m*mune saue.
> The kyng and knyȝthod and clergie boþe
> Casten þ*a*t þe co*m*mune sholde [hire communes] fynde. (Prol. 112–17)[37]

This statement asserts that there are three estates: that of the king, who rules with the aid of his knights in order to protect the kingdom; that of the clergy, who advise the king and protect the kingdom through their wisdom; and that of the commons, who protect the kingdom through the manual labor that provisions the two ruling estates. This statement of the trifunctional image turns out in the lines that follow to be not just an iteration of a theoretical commonplace but the justification for advising the king in his obligations. Immediately after this construction, a lunatic speaks "clergially" to the king when he says, "Crist kepe þee, sire kyng, and þi kyngryche, / And lene þee lede þi lond so leute þee louye, / And for þi riȝtful rulyng be rewarded in heuene" (Prol. 124–27). This succinct statement moves from a call for Christ's blessings on this kingdom to the advice that the king should provide his people with land (which implies that the king is sole possessor of it) as a consequence of which the king's people will love him (for his largesse) with the ultimate result that the king will be saved (for his "riȝtful rulyng").

Next an angel of heaven descends to warn the monarch—in Latin so

[35] May McKisack, *The Fourteenth Century: 1307–1399,* Oxford History of England 5 (Oxford: Clarendon Press, 1959), pp. 397–99.

[36] Thomas Walsingham, *Historia anglicana,* ed. H. T. Riley, 2 vols. (London: Rolls Series, 1863), 1:331.

[37] *Piers Plowman: The B Version,* ed. George Kane and E. Talbot Donaldson (London: Athlone Press, 1975).

that the "lewed" will not misconstrue the message—that the king may not be king in future. The implication is that a king who does not administer the laws of Christ may feel the vengeance of God. He is admonished to clothe himself with a sense of duty to God, and, if he does not, then let judgment be measured out to him according to his deeds. The angel's admonition evokes the response from a "goliardys" that insofar as a king takes his name from ruling (i.e., *rex* from *regere*), he is a king only in name if he does not rule righteously. The scene closes with the commons' acclamation: "*Precepta Regis sunt nobis vincula legis!*"

Langland has captured the contestive atmosphere that exists at the reception of royalty. The speeches honor the king and acknowledge his lordship, but every one of them is made conditionally, with the result that each statement advises and educates the king. The statement of the social contract tells him that there is a hierarchy and that he is at the top of it, but it also asserts that the welfare of the kingdom is predicated upon mutual dependence: the commons provide "communes" for their superiors, but the superiors in turn have obligations to the commons. Even a lunatic knows that a king must make provision for his people if the kingdom is to prosper and the king is to secure personal salvation. The "angel of hevene," a title commonly used to denote a cleric, warns, like a prophet of old, of the dangers of bad rulership of God's people. The "goliardys" can tell the king that his regnancy consists not in his name (his coronation) but in his proper rulership. And the acclamation of the commons, which to the modern reader might seem to indicate complete and abject surrender, turns out to contain a warning as well. The Latin phrase would seem to suggest that the commons should be utterly submissive to the laws of the king no matter what they might be, but the phrase actually recalls the legal maxim that all power ultimately derives from the people, or, as Langland puts it in the trifunctional image just mentioned, the "might" of the commons made him, the king, to reign.[38] Langland's version of the reception of Richard II by the city of London is shot through with statements of the king's obligations to the city and his kingdom.

The presentation of Richard to London, as orchestrated by John of Gaunt, was apparently intended in part as a means of making a reconciliation between the city and Gaunt as much as it was a political move to gain the acceptance of the child as monarch. But the city took the

[38] See J. A. W. Bennett's ed. of *Piers* (Oxford: Clarendon Press, 1972), p. 100, n. to line 145.

opportunity of the procession, as it often did in royal entries, to educate the monarch—and in this case, his guardian—on the appropriate relation between the monarchy and the city. Since Richard was but a child at the time and under the care of Gaunt, we may see London as the father instructing a minor child but also addressing the feared "faux-father," John of Gaunt, about the nature of legitimate kingship. Thus it is not surprising that Langland's text immediately proceeds to the fable of the rat parliament with its warning against leashing the legitimate monarch and allowing a rat to rule in his stead.

At least as Langland presents it, this royal procession became a potentially beneficial dialogue; however, Langland is elsewhere critical of royal display. His initial description of Lady Mede can be read in part as his reaction to Alice Perrers's appearance as the Lady of the Sun in the pageant of 1366.[39] The apparent purpose of such royal display was to excite the local populace to an awesome respect for majesty, but in this case what Langland, though not his persona, Wille, registered was outrage at this embodiment of misgovernance and conspicuous waste. The difference in these two responses illustrates quite well a point that recent critical literature on spectacle has not addressed: the ability of a spectator, here Wille, to be awed at the same time that he is excluded or marginalized.

When Wille asks to know the False, Dame Holy Church directs his attention to his left, where he became

> . . . war of a wo*m*man wondirliche cloþide,
> Ipurfilid wiþ pelure, þe pureste [o]n erþe,
> Icorounid in a coroune, þe king haþ non bet*er*e.
> Alle here fyue fyngris were frettid wiþ rynges
> Of þe pureste p*er*reiȝe þat p*r*ince werde eu*er*e;
> In red scarlet robid & ribande wiþ gold. (A.2.8–13)[40]

Scholars have long thought that this passage contains a pun ("perreiȝe") that identifies Lady Meed with Alice Perrers (see the Bennett ed. notes, pp. 119–20). I would like to suggest that Langland plays off the royal, desired response—awe and admiration in the case of Wille—against the poet's reaction to the Pageant of the Lady of the Sun. Wille's descrip-

[39] As far as I know, *Piers*-scholars have not made this connection between Meed and Alice as the Lady of the Sun. Sheila Lindenbaum and I hope to do more work on this pageant.

[40] *Piers Plowman: The A Version,* ed. George Kane (London: Athlone Press, 1960).

tion of Lady Mede is morally revealing, though not to him, for he is "rauysshed" by the display of wealth (B.2.17).[41] He does not see the usurpation symbolized in Alice's wearing of royal "pelure" and a crown good enough for any king. Nor does he associate the red robe with the image of the Whore of Babylon. Insofar as Langland the poet's construction functions as an account of a critical spectator, we are made aware of the usurpation and of Lady Mede as a sign of some dire apocalyptic ending. Since we are presumably better readers of this spectacle than Wille, we might see much of the action that follows as a commentary on the significance of Alice Perrers as Lady of the Sun. This "marriage" between Alice and Edward is illicit; the jewels, perhaps appropriate as insignia for true kingship, are here displaced to an interloper. But perhaps even more significant is that while Langland elsewhere in the poem would seem to allow kings and knights to have quantities of wealth appropriate to their stations and their office, Conscience preaches the stern message that even kings should be restricted to their needs (B.19.465–79). The king may have whatever is necessary to maintain and exercise his authority, but he should not accumulate superfluous wealth for the mere sake of having it or because he can take it by force, as does the rapacious Lord in the confrontation with Conscience (19.459–64). Langland's depiction of Alice Perrers links corruption, greed, and illegitimacy with superfluity. As was intended by the producers of this pageant of the Lady of the Sun, Wille, a kind of London Everyman, is seduced by the display. Langland was not.[42]

The three ceremonials I have described thus far represent three different ideological constructs. The Midsummer Show is intended to symbolize the unified body of London and its corporate freedoms, even though, as we have seen, it also asserts that a ruling oligarchy is natural and that the rights of citizens vary within the hierarchy. The royal entry constitutes a dialogue about power; indeed, in 1392 the reception of Richard was used as a means of reconciling him to his principal city and his subjects.[43] The royal pageant or procession is the riskier venture of

[41] The A-passage cited above establishes the allusion to Perrers; there Langland establishes Will's awe by having him remark that she was "wonderliche cloþide." He intensifies the reaction in B and C by having Will say he was "rauysshed."

[42] Lady Mede on the Cart of Liar may be another image of this pageant.

[43] Glynne Wickham, *Early English Stages,* 3 vols. (London: Routledge & Kegan Paul, 1959–72), 1:64–72. By contrast, Henry VII rejected the rebel city of Worcester's attempt to reconcile themselves when he refused to attend to their speeches and pageants that were to welcome him. See *Herefordshire/Worcestershire,* ed. David N. Klausner, Records of Early English Drama (Toronto: University of Toronto Press, 1990), p. 406.

the three because in a sense the monarch and his court usurp the city to act out their social drama. The action is exclusionary even though it is intended through display and majesty to create a bond between the ruler and the ruled. Some, like Wille, are ravished by this display, but some in the audience may have been less moved.

Although Langland's responses to London spectacle are filtered through his persona, his and Wille's relationships to these events are relatively straightforward and easy to read. Chaucer's representation of Theseus's tournament is less so because he does not report an English tournament directly and because his description of Theseus's is a rewriting of his source, Boccaccio's *Teseida,* in the interests of creating an antique narrative that differs in a number of ways from Boccaccio's.[44] We might read Chaucer's presentation of Theseus's tournament, then, as a celebration of urban and noble culture—but one that is shot through with an inappropriate worldliness, one that signals an inordinate carnality filled with danger. It is a royal spectacle tainted by the *theatrum.*

My approach builds on the tradition that Chaucer allows a critique of chivalry by having the Knight speak this particular narrative.[45] It would seem that the Knight is attempting to create a noble picture of the chivalric life in his tale, but as many commentators have noted, the tale, its moral, and its attempts to impose order on chaos move beyond the control of the teller and the chief protagonist, Theseus, so that the disorder, the happenstance, that lies beneath the show is revealed. I wish to further this argument by claiming that Chaucer constructed Theseus's "theatre" in the image of the *theatrum* of late antiquity, that he altered Boccaccio not only to achieve an antique effect but also to recall the early Christian view that the *theatrum* was a place in which games were played in honor of demons, that is, the gods. My argument requires some deep archaeology.

It is difficult to know how much Chaucer might have known about

[44] David Anderson has argued that Chaucer did with the *Teseida* what Boccaccio did with Statius's *Thebaid;* he thinks that "Chaucer's alterations generally reflect a concern with preserving and accentuating the *Thebaid* like structure and themes of Boccaccio's narrative"; *Before the Knight's Tale: Imitation of Classical Epic in Boccaccio's Teseida* (Philadelphia: University of Pennsylvania Press, 1988), p. 201.

[45] Lee Patterson gives a succinct review of this critical tradition in his chapter on *The Knight's Tale* in *Chaucer and the Subject of History,* pp. 165–68. I have used the phrase "allows a critique" in order to echo Patterson's argument that Chaucer does not criticize chivalry in a polemical fashion but rather stands aside to allow the reader to see chivalry's self-contradictions.

the *theatrum,* yet we can be certain that he knew where to find the information. There are numerous Latin works that would have provided him whatever he wished to know, the chief one being Isidore's *Etymologies.*[46] After describing the shape of the *theatrum,* the elements within it, and the variety of participants, Isidore condemns it all as immorality:

> These spectacles of cruelty and displays of vanity were created not only by the vices of men but also by the commands of devils. Hence the Christian should have nothing to do with the foolishness of the Circus, the immorality of the theater, the cruelty of the amphitheater, the atrocity of the arena, the lust of the show.[47]

He adds that after the games were concluded, the *theatrum* functioned as a *lupanar,* a brothel.

Although I cannot produce definitive proof that Chaucer read Isidore or any text dependent upon him, there is some evidence in his translation of the Boethius that he knew the reputation of the ancient theater. Dame Philosophy rebukes Boethius for having suffered the approach of "thise comune strompettis of swich a place that men clepen the theatre" (1.pr1.48–50, to translate *scenicas meretriculas*). Scholars now believe that Chaucer used the Latin text and Jean de Meun's French version for his translation, so it is important to note Jean does not translate *scenicas* even though he retains the notion that the muses are whores ("communes putereles").[48] The Latin text that Chaucer used, we also know, contained the commentary of Nicholas Trevet, who defined the *scena* as a place in the *theatrum* and pointed to *Etymologies* 18 as his source.[49] Chaucer would know where to go if he wanted to know more about the *theatrum.*

[46] Marshall, "*Theatre* in the Middle Ages," and Jones, "Isidore and the Theatre." Isidore is quoted in some form or other by virtually everyone who glosses the *theatrum* or terms associated with it.

[47] Jones, "Isidore," p. 39. *Etym.* 18.59: "Haec quippe spectacula crudelitatis et inspectio vanitatum non solum hominum vitiis, sed et daemonum iussis instituta sunt. Proinde nihil esse debet Christiano cum Circensi insania, cum inpudicitia theatri, cum amphitheatri crudelitate, cum atrocitate arenae, cum luxuria ludi."

[48] V. L. Dedeck-Héry, "Boethius' *De Consolatione* by Jean de Meun," *Mediaeval Studies* 14 (1952): 173. On the texts that Chaucer used in his translation, see the notes in Larry D. Benson, gen. ed., *The Riverside Chaucer* (Boston: Houghton Mifflin, 1987), pp. 1003–5. All citations from Chaucer are from this edition and are cited parenthetically in the text.

[49] *Nicolas Trevet on Boethius: Expositio fratris Nicolai Trevethi Anglici Ordinis predicatorum super Boecio: De Consolatione,* ed. Edmund T. Silk (n.p.: John K. Silk, 1966), p. 25: "Scena autem secundum Isodorum, Ethimologiarum libro 18, capitulo de ludo scenico, erat locus infra theatrum in modum domus instructas cum pulpito" (The *scena* according to

My first observation, therefore, may appear paradoxical: that Chaucer knew the traditions associated with the ancient *theatrum* but thought his audience might not. I judge that Chaucer may have been concerned with his audience's knowledge of the *theatrum* from the fact that "theatre" is rare in Middle English (though not Latin) and from the way Chaucer introduces the word into *The Knight's Tale.* Prior to *The Knight's Tale* (first recension ca. 1385; the *Canterbury Tales* recension in the 1390s), there are only two recorded usages: in the Wycliffite Bible, Acts 19:29, where *theatrum* is internally glossed as a "comune beholdyng place"; and in Trevisa's translation of Higden's *Polychronicon* (1387), where Higden relates the story of Scipio's construction of the *theatrum* (with the Isidorean glosses embedded in the narrative).[50] The word remained rare in Middle English (see the later *MED* entries), which may account for why some later scribes substituted "entre" and "sercle" for "theatre" at line 1885 and "auters" and "gates" at line 2091.[51]

Equally suggestive of the rarity of the term in the vernacular is the way Chaucer places it in his text. When he introduces the structure, he uses a term that his audience would understand before he moves on to the unfamiliar term (*KnT* 1881–86):

> I trowe men wolde deme it necligence
> If I foryete to tellen the dispence
> Of Theseus, that gooth so bisily
> To maken up the lystes roially,

Isidore, *Etymologies,* book 18, in the chapter conderning ludic games, was a place within the theater built in the manner of a house with a pulpit [for the poet to recite from]). Trevet's gloss on "tragedy" may also have influenced Chaucer's reshaping of *The Knight's Tale* since it links the mutability of fortune with the tragedies performed in the *theatrum;* see A. J. Minnis, *Chaucer and Pagan Antiquity* (Cambridge: D. S. Brewer, 1982), pp. 26–27. The gloss also points to *Etymologies* 18.

[50] Trevisa, in *Polychronicon Ranulphi Higden,* ed. C. Babington and J. R. Lumby, 9 vols., Rolls Series 41 (London, 1865–86): 4:98–103; the term also appears in a reference to Oedipus at 3:243. Higden was widely distributed in the later Middle Ages and may have been known to Chaucer. The passage in question describes the first founding of the Roman *theatrum,* with a gloss from Isidore about its layout followed by the comment that "Ludy scenici" were first "i-ordeyned by excitinge of þe devel." James McGregor indicates that "teatro" is rare in fourteenth-century Italian as well; see "Boccaccio's Athenian Theater," p. 9. Although there is no evidence that Roman amphitheaters were used for jousts in the fourteenth century, Boccaccio places Theseus's there.

[51] The substitution of "auters," however, may mean that that scribe knew the *theatrum* to be a place for the worship of demons in dramatic representation; this emended description would be similar to those in Boccaccio and his sources.

> That swich a noble theatre as it was
> I dar wel seyen in this world ther nas.

First the arena is called a "lystes," a royal list, which is the terminology of Chaucer's day; second, it is renamed a "theatre," a term derived from antiquity.

Perhaps it was because he imagined his audience would be unfamiliar with the theater that Chaucer elaborated Boccaccio's description of the amphitheater.[52] He also made it more pagan and more foreign. When Chaucer used the word "lystes," his audience would have recalled that lists in England are usually rectangular and built for the occasion (whereas in Boccaccio the theatre is a permanent structure). The constructions for the Smithfield tourney were typical; there was a rectangular, wooden framework, the lists, placed before housing for the king and court. As Chaucer drops the notion of the English lists from his story, he reverts to Boccaccio's description of a round, stone structure. He places it on an astrological axis to achieve an image of a *theatrum mundi* in order to suggest that the "theatre" is a micro-universe.

Unlike Boccaccio, Chaucer brings the temples of the gods into his theater.[53] In the *Teseida,* each of the principals visits a variety of temples around the city before going to the temple of the patron deity to make his or her plea. The temples are associated with the city, not the "theatre," which is said to be outside town. Moreover, Chaucer significantly changes the descriptions of the images painted on the walls of the temples.[54] Although Chaucer, like Boccaccio, makes use of personifications in his representation of the realms of the deities, his pictures are more graphic, violent, and unsettling. Chaucer's temple of Mars is closer to that in the *Teseida* than is his temple of Venus, though Chaucer added

[52] Chaucer radically cut Boccaccio's narrative but increased the amount of space given to the description of the "theatre" and the temples; proportionately, then, Chaucer's presentation is not only longer than Boccaccio's but takes up more of his narrative.

[53] I rely here on Piero Boitani, *Chaucer and Boccaccio* (Oxford: Society for the Study of Mediaeval Languages and Literature, 1977), and N. R. Havely, ed. and trans., *Chaucer's Boccaccio: Sources of Troilus and the Knight's and Franklin's Tales* (Cambridge: D. S. Brewer, 1980).

[54] The representation of the personifications associated with each of the deities is handled entirely differently in *Teseida.* The prayers of Arcite and Palamon are personified as birds that fly to the locations of the gods' residences and there meet a series of personifications in the *locus* of the God. After hearing the prayer, the deity comes to the Athenian temple to make the sign of his or her willingness to aid the knights. See Boitani, *Chaucer and Boccaccio,* pp. 79–95, and Havely, ed., *Chaucer's Boccaccio,* pp. 125–28.

the image of Mars in the cart with the ravenous wolf before him from Bersuire's *Ovid moralizatus.*[55] There is no glorification of war in the temple of Mars; we see hideous murders, unprovoked violence, arson, felony, the slit throat, the nail driven in the head, and Conquest above sitting in great honor beneath a Damoclean sword. Although many of the same personifications that are in Venus's temple in the *Parlement* appear here, there is a shift toward the woe that Venus brings (lines 1951–54), and the stories mentioned are ones in which the lover suffers great disaster or is led to his death. The temple of Diana, for which there is no counterpart in the *Teseida,* is one where chastity, a virtue presumably to be honored, is the occasion for violence. The dominating image is of Diana coldly looking down on a woman in the agony of a never-to-be-completed childbirth (lines 2075–86). These are gods who represent the dark forces, the irrationalities within human existence. Augustine, Isidore, and others had said that the pagans had constructed their *theatra* as places to honor the gods through blood sports and dramas that depicted the immoralities of the gods. Chaucer's temples are filled with the obscene consequences of those under the influence of these gods.

Chaucer not only moved the temples from the city into the "theatre" but also associated the gods with astrological signs. Boccaccio had used the pagan gods much as they had been in epic: they were deities who exhibited human feelings and failings and who intervened in the affairs of men and women. The deities in *The Knight's Tale* remain personages but they have been "astrologized." We are made aware, through the astronomical plan of the "theatre" and the heavenly bodies with which the gods are associated, that they are fatal forces beyond human control. Chaucer's representation of the gods creates a fearful pagan world in which human action seems pitifully inconsequential.

I have been trying to suggest that all of these moves centered on Theseus's "theatre" were made in the interests of historical authenticity, but also that they may have been motivated or framed by Chaucer's knowledge of the ways that Christians in late antiquity and the Middle Ages (in learned sources) had represented the *theatrum* of the ancients. Even if we cannot document Chaucer's knowledge of the *theatrum* with the certainty we would like, it could still be argued that his reshaping of Boc-

[55] Minnis, *Chaucer and Pagan Antiquity,* p. 110. Chaucer had used the description of the temple of Venus from the *Teseida* in his *Parlement of Foulys,* but provides a different image of Venus here.

caccio indicates his awareness of the polemic against the *theatrum* of late antiquity.

In negotiating between the demands of his story for historical verisimilitude and his own appropriation of English aristocratic and chivalric culture, Chaucer opens a rift that permits a critique of the very culture he would seem to celebrate. His representation of the tournament itself might seem to move the narrative toward romance and away from the epic tradition he has attempted to create elsewhere; however, Chaucer seems to have historicized this part of the narrative by describing archaic tournament practice.[56] Chaucer's presentation of the tourney differs both from the practice of his day and from Boccaccio's depiction. Although both poets say that each of the sides is to have a hundred champions, Boccaccio describes a series of epic encounters between pairs of fighters.[57] Chaucer describes a mêlée, a kind of tournament combat that was no longer used and one that more nearly approximated the conditions of war. Although Theseus initially declares the tournament to be a fight to the death (lines 1845–69), he subsequently decides that since mortal combat would cause the destruction of "gentil blood," no one is to carry into the lists arrows, battle axes, short knives, or short swords, and no one is to joust more than once with a sharp lance (lines 2537–57).[58] Instead of killing their foes, those who are victorious are to take their captives to a stake where the latter are to await the outcome of the battle. Despite the attempt to contain the battle, it is bloody as the combatants fight with swords, maces, and truncheons; there is no animal in the forest so wild, the Knight tells us, as Palamon, who desired "to sleen his foo Arcite" (line 2633).

This tournament is an odd combination of archaic and semicontemporary practice. The mêlée had finally been suppressed because it so closely enacted the conditions of war that great numbers of fighters were seriously injured or killed, either of which would subvert the artic-

[56] Bruce Kent Cowgill, "The *Knight's Tale* and the Hundred Years' War," *PQ* 54 (1975): 670–79; and N. Denholm-Young, "The Tournament in the Thirteenth Century," in R. W. Hunt, W. A. Pantin, and R. W. Southern, eds., *Studies in Medieval History Presented to Frederick Maurice Powicke* (Oxford: Clarendon Press, 1948), pp. 240–68. See also G. A. Lester, "Chaucer's Knight and the Medieval Tournament," *Neophilologus* 66 (1982): 460–68.

[57] Havely, ed., *Chaucer's Boccaccio,* p. 137.

[58] Boccacio's Theseus modifies the battle into ceremonial games in honor of Mars. There are to be no lances—because they are more dangerous—only swords and maces (Havely, ed., *Chaucer's Boccaccio,* p. 124).

ulated purpose of a tournament: to prepare knights for battle (and the crusades).[59] Edward I sought to control the mayhem and to turn the tournament into a social and chivalric institution. In a joust, which opposed individuals rather than armies, swords and lances were blunted; one's skill was evaluated rather than having all depend upon the victory. Theseus's second set of instructions seems intended to move the mêlée toward the conditions of a joust: as in Chaucer's day, the knights were to have one pass on horseback with a lance and then to continue, if that were the condition prescribed, with swords on foot. Theseus's half-measures do not entirely succeed (Palamon, for example, is seriously wounded [lines 2638–40]), and one wonders whether Chaucer's audience would see Theseus's changes as a move toward the tournaments of their own day. In any event, the audience listening to *The Knight's Tale* would undoubtedly compare Theseus's tournament with those they had seen. Would they consider their own effete by comparison with the manly battle at Athens? Or would they consider their own more "civilized"? Given the antagonisms Lee Patterson describes toward the knightly class in late-fourteenth-century England, some might see the Smithfield tournament and others like it as empty forms—and extravagantly expensive ones at that.[60]

If we focus on Chaucer's naming, first the "lystes" and then the "theatre," we might see the first as a familiarizing tactic and the second as a classicizing and alienating one. A lists would not have to be described; a "theatre" does. We have also seen that these words have two rather different valences for his culture—noble and ignoble, respectively—that also reflect two different sets of cultural values: aristocratic and clerical. When Chaucer uses the word "theatre," he obviously does so with his source in mind and with the intent to construct the historical illusion of antiquity; nevertheless, given the clerical assault on the *theatrum* and tournaments, he could not have been utterly ignorant of the sea of connotation into which he launched the word "theatre."

In romance, our most aristocratic genre, and in actuality, the lists are arenas in which noble persons establish their honor when they enter them and maintain it by conquering other men of honor. Jousting is a noble sport, one that excludes all but the greatest of rank and, under

[59] Denholm-Young, "Tournament"; and Juliet R. V. Barker, *The Tournament in England, 1100–1400* (Woodbridge, Suffolk: Boydell Press, 1986).

[60] Patterson, *Chaucer and the Subject of History,* pp. 179, 189–98.

certain circumstances, young squires who are attempting to establish their own prowess. When Chaucer constructs his lists for us, they seem a *theatrum mundi,* a realization of a noble conceptualization of the world and the way it operates—though, like the 1390 lists, Theseus's "theatre" allows none but the noble to operate within its walls.

In medieval clerical culture, the "theatre" has associations only with obscenity; it is not only non-Christian but anti-Christian. Although Isidore indicated that the *theatrum* was a place for games, sports, and other entertainments—all of which might seem either neutral or recreative—he ultimately condemned them as lubricious and asserted that after the games were over the theaters became places of prostitution. Given the antagonism of the Latin Fathers toward the *theatrum* of late antiquity—and this material would be known through the original sources as well as in the antitheatrical canons of the *Decretum*—it is not surprising that for late medieval culture, *theatrum* does not designate a place for dramas but, rather, names a place where men engage in worldly activities. The *theatrum* is the marketplace; it is the arena. The *theatrum* is separate from the sacred precincts of the true God. For the Dominican John Bromyard, tournaments, like dicing, are games of chance. Participants who misguidedly engage in them subject themselves to fortune; they implicitly reject God's grace when they submit themselves to the fortunes of the world. The *theatrum* is the garden of Fortuna, a place of "caas" and "aventure." In such a garden, the sudden appearance of an imp from hell is not surprising because imps and demons are the rulers and inhabitants of such places. Theseus's "theatre" is just such an arena; indeed, it is ruled by the deities placed in the towers that are located at their appropriate astrological positions, and the paintings within these temples depict obscenities and immoralities.

Chaucer's assessment of spectacle seems equivocal at best. When he creates Theseus's lists, he does not seem to evoke an ideal urban spectacle perhaps because, as with the 1390 Smithfield tournament, the nobles use the city as a space—a set, as it were—to enact their own social drama rather than successfully engaging the entire populace. Yet Chaucer, an associate of the court, is more subtle than those makers of royal entries and other shows that attempt to compliment and educate—and to claim—the monarch all at once; Chaucer compliments the court with his rich painting of the tournament, but he also reveals the fateful machinery that lies beneath the show.

Sir Orfeo and the Flight from the Enchanters

Alan J. Fletcher
University College, Dublin

NOTHING IN EXTANT early Middle English romance quite matches the extraordinary chamber of horrors that awaits Orfeo in the glittering castle of the fairy king:

> þan he gan bihold about al
> & seigh liggeand wiþ-in þe wal
> Of folk þat were þider y-brouȝt,
> & þouȝt dede, & nare nouȝt.
> Sum stode wiþ-outen hade,
> & sum non armes nade,
> & sum þurth þe bodi hadde wounde,
> & sum lay wode, y-bounde,
> & sum armed on hors sete,
> & sum astrangled as þai ete;
> & sum were in water adreynt,
> & sum wiþ fire al for-schreynt.
> Wiues þer lay on child-bedde,
> Sum ded & sum awedde,
> & wonder fele þer lay bisides:
> Riȝt as þai slepe her vnder-tides
> Eche was þus in þis warld y-nome,
> Wiþ fairi þider y-come.[1]

This passage is not the only shadow cast across the bright surface of *Sir Orfeo,* but it is one of the longest. Thrust suddenly into view, the sordid

[1] A. J. Bliss, ed., *Sir Orfeo,* 2d ed. (1966; rpt. Oxford: Clarendon Press, 1971), p. 34, lines 387–404. All further citations are to this edition of the poem.

eventualities catalogued here disrupt the ease of the reader in wonderland. Their appearance is perhaps not entirely unexpected; earlier in the poem, the deformation of Heurodis's formerly tranquil and beautiful body with scars of self-inflicted violence, too graphically obtrusive for the reader to avoid, plus the generic expectations aroused from outside the poem, that fearful things may lurk under a fair aspect, may already have put the reader on the alert.[2] But why this particular waxworks of the undead? It is a reminder of the world of hideous realities that the romance genre more usually puts on hold. Interpretation can choose to back off from it; it can be left alone as part of the "irreducible mystery" that A. C. Spearing finds in the poem.[3] Yet mystery exerts its force precisely because it persists in defying human reason. In the case of lines 387–404, the challenge is to try to organize their apparently random contents into a consolingly intelligible shape: why is this medley of unfortunates here, not to mention the question of how it can be that they bear all the signs of mortality yet are dead, or dying, only in seeming? Such questions, for the reader provoked to ask them, return no fully adequate answers, or at least none that the text is prepared to vouchsafe. Rather, the reader is fobbed off with an answer so superficial and paltry that, in leaving more unexplained than it reveals, advertises its fundamental *indifference* to the demands of intelligibility in the very moment that it stimulates them: "Eche was þus in þis warld y-nome, / Wiþ fairi þider y-come" (lines 403–4). There is nothing more disclosed than that. The fairy folk have brought them there. Only two things, then, are clear: first, that these people have been collected in their agony and taken to their eternal gallery "wiþ-in þe wal" of the castle upon some inscrutable whim of fairyland;[4] and second, that the fairy folk, to whatever extent they can be said to have a legible motive, seem to be as much the connoisseurs of chaos as they are of beauty, and to have followed their collec-

[2] Robert W. Hanning, *The Individual in Twelfth-Century Romance* (New Haven: Yale University Press, 1977), p. 108 and n. 4, has observed in certain early romances scenes that, while having the veneer of a *locus amoenus,* nevertheless betray the application of the beauties of human craft to disguise a latent danger.

[3] A. C. Spearing, *Readings in Medieval Poetry* (Cambridge: Cambridge University Press, 1987), p. 77.

[4] Strictly speaking, their location was simply "wiþ-in þe wal" of the castle (wherever exactly that was), so my use of the term "gallery" throughout this article is tendentiously metaphorical, calculated to emphasize the sense of their being displayed like so many statues in an exhibition. Indeed, it is precisely this tableaulike quality that has struck some modern readers (for example, Felicity Riddy, "The Uses of the Past in *Sir Orfeo,*" *YES* 6 (1976): 5–15; see p. 6).

tor's instinct. For what the gallery's exhibits all share, that common quality which appears to have made them eligible for collection in the first place, is their all having being touched by a violent or fearsomely unpredictable fate. Thus the gallery, fundamentally inexplicable, constitutes a site of resistance within the text to the reassurances of explanation, and this resistance, as I hope further to demonstrate, is conducted on at least three different fronts.

At least three authoritative medieval discourses, the cognitive models whereby (otherwise unmanageable) aspects of human experience may be squared into a rational picture, are mobilized and challenged. We have already observed that the gallery's contents are the casualties of a baffling universe that obviates prediction or explanation: no reasons are explicitly ventured within the terms of the text itself that would make their fates at least understandable, and hence reassuringly circumscribable, within known schemes of things. At the purely narrative level of plot advancement too, the introduction of the gallery is inexplicable, indeed gratuitous; not surprisingly, some commentators have avoided its challenges by dismissing it as an interpolation.[5] It is even hermetically sealed within the narrative as a presence unto itself, a place within a place, since it exists in temporal stasis, untouched by the processes of change to which the rest of the narrative is subject.[6] So any attempt to explain it, which means, in effect, trying to contain the danger of its threat to intelligibility, must be imported from outside the text. It is here that the trope of madness within the text assumes a truly frightening proportion, as unintelligibility is extended to touch those very cognitive models by means of which the horrifying aspects of reality are customarily grasped and domesticated. *Sir Orfeo* enacts an enchantment of unreason in two overlapping domains: in the intratextual domain of narrative, Orfeo struggles to negotiate a flight from this enchantment,

[5] Bruce Mitchell, "The Faery World of *Sir Orfeo*," *Neophilologus* 48 (1964): 155–59. But the drastic shift of gear in lines 387–404 is, I believe, a symptom of the poem's complexity, not evidence of interpolation. Riddy, "Uses of the Past," p. 6, minimizes the lines in a different way, finding them mere "images of grotesquerie rather than suffering." It will become clear that I do not concede their diminution in these terms either.

[6] While it may be on account of the fairy folk that interruptions occur in the linear world, and while they fraternize with an altered time scheme through association with the people in the gallery, since they are caught up in the process of narrative, they are nevertheless touched by linear time in a way that the gallery folk never are (or are never seen to be, Heurodis excepted). Therefore, the timescape inhabited by the fairy folk is qualitatively different from the stasis of the gallery. While fairyland somehow encompasses that timescape, it is not coterminous with it.

salvaging intelligibility, in his case, by recuperating the stability of his marriage and hence the social stability that his marriage figures; in the extratextual domain of late-thirteenth-century England, readers formed in that historical circumstance have to negotiate a flight of their own from an enchantment of unreason and the spell of existential disorientation that it is able to cast.

I will argue, then, that early audiences of *Sir Orfeo* had three principal discourses familiarly at their disposal in their everyday lives and in their terms they might have tried to make sense of the chaos accumulated in lines 387–404. Three (ordinarily stable) cognitive models were available to them for making sense of the damaging human experiences that these lines evoke. I will also suggest that some of the remarkable imaginative power long acknowledged to inhabit the poem depends upon the compelling invitation that these lines extend to audiences to join in a contemplation of the entropy of both the human and of the discursive master narratives by which human beings live. However, this contemplation, thrilling in its scope and richness, is also frightening in bringing readers to the brink of being unrewarded with the prospect of salvaging any settled meaning from entropy after the adventure of contemplation is over.[7] *Sir Orfeo*'s readers, too, were invited to become, momentarily, the connoisseurs of chaos. And the poem goes about purveying its entropic vision in a sophisticated way: the three discourses in question have been absorbed and then dislocated in the moment of their expropriation into the text. The very artistry of *Sir Orfeo,* therefore, like the fairy folk populating its narrative, may be seen as both beautiful and dangerous, capable of carrying off discourses from the real world of its readers away into itself. The lesson would seem to be that discourses too, like the people who live by them, may be *taken.*[8] The poem's capacity in this respect to digest and transform the familiar fosters a subtle symbiosis between its status as literary fiction and the historical reality of late-thirteenth-century England (perhaps, more specifically, late-thirteenth-century London) that it will also finally be my purpose to trace. In *Sir*

[7] That is, at any rate, not as far as the text itself is concerned. Of course, readers might have resorted to their own resources for explanations, but in such self-recourse the text does nothing to assist. Rather, it is more likely to confuse, for reasons that will become clear (and see also nn. 40 and 63 below). The only "settled meaning" that will eventually be derived from *Sir Orfeo,* as will be seen, will simply bracket entropy, not negate it.

[8] In italicizing *taken,* I allude to the influential reading of lines 387–404 by Dorena Allen, "Orpheus and Orfeo: The Dead and the *Taken,*" *MAE* 33 (1964): 102–11.

Orfeo, the consolations of intelligibility, the trophies that the mind returns with after its quest to search out reassuring reasons behind events—perhaps grounding those events in a stable "Providence," but in any case tidily pigeon-holing them into some known category—are to be temporarily lost from view. Early readers, I will suggest, would have found whatever explanations for chaos that they could arrive at starting to shimmer like a mirage; hence the disturbing imaginative power of the text. Thus, as the text refracted unitary explanation into variegated possibilities—here were many explanations and yet no one explanation—beauty and danger would once again have found a way in.[9] After explanations have come close to exposure by the poem as human constructs, vulnerable because negotiable, the reader's world could never as a result be quite the same again, just as Orfeo's was not, even though by the end he had done his utmost to repair, stabilize, and shore it up.

Since the three discourses alluded to were historically contingent, they will need elucidation before the nature of their dislocation can be clearly grasped and appreciated. To anticipate, the consequence of their collection within the gallery "wiþ-in þe wal" is to reify chaos as an object of aesthetic contemplation, a project that seems to me unusual not just within the early Middle English romance corpus but also within the canon of early Middle English poetry in general.[10] One of the dislocations contributory to this reification has in fact already been identified at a formal, narrative level—*Sir Orfeo* presents a plot that accommodates the puzzling paradox of both linear (that is, humanly familiar and comprehensible) and nonlinear (that is, humanly unfamiliar and incompre-

[9] The pleasure that Roland Barthes associated with the abandonment of prescriptive meaning may serve as a modern analogy for what I have construed in *Sir Orfeo* as "beauty" and "danger"; see Roland Barthes, *Le plaisir du texte* (Paris: Éditions du Seuil, 1973), p. 103: "Le plaisir du texte, c'est ça: la valeur passée au rang somptueux de signifiant." "Beauty" and "danger" were qualities also identified in the poem (if less formally) in the useful reading of Peter J. Lucas, "An Interpretation of *Sir Orfeo,*" *Leeds Studies in English,* n. s. 6 (1972): 1–9.

[10] Even later when Chaucer, in *The Knight's Tale,* came close to catching the dark temper of *Sir Orfeo* when he made a frightening fresco out of the turmoil caused by Mars, or when he made Saturn rehearse his baleful catalogue of effects (Larry D. Benson, gen. ed., *The Riverside Chaucer,* 3d ed. [Boston: Houghton Mifflin Co., 1987], pp. 52–53, lines 1975–2038; and p. 58, lines 2454–69, respectively), he still grounded human disaster in an efficient cause, namely, in these cases, in astrological influence. We will see that while *Sir Orfeo* may have prompted readers to consider astrological causality a possible explanation, it has stopped short of actually naming it. This textual gap has important interpretative consequences that will subsequently become clear.

hensible) time—but there are others that our distance from the poem's cultural matrix has rendered obscure. These will be examined next in the context of the three discourses in which they are effected. Finally, we will consider the nature of the refuge from chaos that *Sir Orfeo* ends by constructing, and how the poem's attempted quarantine of beauty and danger witnesses to, and underwrites, a distinctive social praxis, characteristically current in aristocratic circles. In the *Sir Orfeo* poet, then, we must prepare to face not only a writer well versed in a literary tradition but also a fluent reader of the various sets of ground rules by which his culture operated.

I. The Discourse of Late-Medieval Christianity

In the real world surrounding *Sir Orfeo,* that is, in the London region in the late thirteenth century, the human casualties listed in *Sir Orfeo*'s catalogue of the *taken* were already sadly familiar. One of the church's most pressing social enterprises was the explanation of what deaths and disasters like these might be thought to signify and how in spite of their awkwardness they might nevertheless be reconciled within the providential order, thereby salvaging from the human debris some comforting sense of a divine, if in the last analysis unfathomable, rationale. Indeed, the very power of the church over temporal affairs was in part coextensive with the trust reposed in its authority as an arbiter of matters such as these. In view of this sociotheological mandate, it is interesting to note that the deaths and disasters installed in *Sir Orfeo*'s gallery have not been randomly assembled. On the contrary, they appear to have been deliberately selected for their maximum sensitivity within the discourse of late-medieval English Christianity. They were (acknowledged) irritants that goaded that discourse into action by provoking within it considerable anxiety. In the later Middle Ages, the ideal form of Christian death—one might say the normative death—was the death well prepared for. This death was most typically codified and celebrated from the late fourteenth century within the *Artes moriendi* tradition, yet it was a death already coveted when *Sir Orfeo* was composed.[11] To die in one's

[11] Bliss, ed., *Sir Orfeo,* p. xxi, dated the composition of the poem on linguistic grounds to any time in the second half of the thirteenth century. A date at the beginning of the fourteenth century is also conceivable, but in any event, it was necessarily before the production of the Auchinleck manuscript, generally dated ca. 1330. On the *Artes moriendi,* see M. C. O'Connor, *The Art of Dying Well* (New York: Columbia Univ. Press, 1942). For an example of the value implicit in a meticulously ordered deathbed scene in a text composed before *Sir Orfeo,* compare the account of the death of William Mar-

bed, in a controlled environment where one could be fortified, as death's door swung perilously open, with the last sacramental rites of confession, extreme unction and viaticum, was a consummation devoutly to be wished. The converse, a *mors improvisa,* was greatly to be feared.[12] It lacked the reassurance of a neat Christian closure. The crisis of confidence within the discourse that the *mors improvisa* was liable to precipitate found expression in the grave concern often voiced as to how the exequies of those dying in less well governed circumstances should be conducted. As their deaths were difficult, so too were their burials. Similarly, the "dead" in *Sir Orfeo,* who were in no position to enjoy any of the benefits *in extremis* that the church would otherwise have conferred upon them, would likewise have been focuses of anxiety and perceived by the poem's early audiences as problematic. Since for all classes in society the fate of the soul was felt to be linked to that of the corpse,[13] what became of those who, like most of the casualties in the gallery of horrors, died beyond the pale of church and churchyard? These were uncomfortable deaths, ones at which the technocrats of death, the clerics, were not in ministering attendance.[14] So, in terms of the ideals of dying that late-medieval Christian discourse promulgated, most of the casualties in *Sir*

shall in *L'histoire de Guillaume le maréchal,* ed. Paul Meyer, 3 vols. (Paris: Société de l'histoire de France, 1891–1901). This biographical poem was written between 1219 and 1226. Also, compare the story of the goldsmith who went to purgatory because death had caught him unawares, in *The Vision of the Monk of Eynsham,* in H. E. Salter, ed., *The Cartulary of the Abbey of Eynsham,* Oxford Historical Society 49 and 51, 2 vols. (Oxford: Clarendon Press, 1907–8), 2: 319–20; this *visio* of the monk Edmund of Eynsham is recounted in a work of Adam of Eynsham, who died sometime after 1233; Edmund's *visio* is dated to 1197. In this case, a daily tracing of "Ihesus Nazarenus" on the brow and breast would have protected against a *mors improvisa.*

[12] Paul Binski, *Medieval Death: Ritual and Representation* (London: British Museum Press, 1996), p. 36. Compare the anxiety implicit in the popular belief that anyone seeing a consecration at Mass was safeguarded that day against violent death. Though later than *Sir Orfeo,* John Mirk's *Instructions for Parish Priests* (probably composed some time in the last quarter of the fourteenth century) bears witness to this long tradition. Mirk attributed it to St Augustine: "As seynt austyn techeth a-ryȝt,— / þat day þat þow syst goddes body, / þese benefyces schalt þou haue sycurly: / . . . Soden deth that ylke day, / The dar not drede wyþowte nay"; Gillis Kristensson, ed., *John Mirk's Instructions for Parish Priests,* Lund Studies in English 49 (Lund: CWK Gleerup, 1974), p. 85, lines 315–17 and 322–23.

[13] R. C. Finucane, "Sacred Corpse, Profane Carrion: Social Ideals and Death Rituals in the Later Middle Ages," in Joachim Whaley, ed., *Mirrors of Mortality: Studies in the Social History of Death* (London: Europa, 1981), pp. 40–60; see p. 60.

[14] The late-twelfth-century Paris theologian John Beleth expressed the view in his *Rationale divinorum officiorum* that if the dying person had made a final confession, it might act as a guide to the living as to how the body should be disposed of (see Patrologia Latina 202, col. 159). That is, the confessed person would be accorded the benefit of any doubt and buried with the full circumstances of Christian exequies.

Orfeo would have been regarded as dying out of a secure context. They would already have been perceived as dislocated, therefore, because their counterparts in the real world repeatedly challenged the discourse to negotiate their safe reintroduction into the fold of Christian intelligibility. It seems appropriate to consider *Sir Orfeo*'s "dead" and *taken* in order, indicating where the anxieties that they galvanized lay deepest, and how the discourse strove to sedate those anxieties with consolations tailored to the circumstances.

The tour of the gallery begins with a standing group of headless bodies (line 387). It is not explained how their decapitations came about. In theological literature, decapitation was a common form of martyrdom and hence a relatively positive exit from this world, one implying a happy heavenly resolution.[15] But in *Sir Orfeo,* colored by association with the next two groups of persons, people without arms and people wounded in their bodies (lines 388–89), the headless of line 387 may have beckoned the reader's imagination toward a bleaker prospect, the carnage of war. Here, by contrast, Christian anxiety about how to dispose of the bodies of those slain in battle was acute.[16] More often than not it happened that they received no adequately supervised Christian burial at all. Alternatively, were the decapitations of line 387 the results of execution?[17] In which case, by an association of judicial ideas, the armless state of the people listed next to the decapitated might suggest the dismemberment inflicted on certain capital traitors.[18] Or were the

[15] As Christopher Daniell points out, Christ's athletes often suffered violent deaths, among which decapitation was a favorite; *Death and Burial in Medieval England, 1066–1550* (London and New York: Routledge, 1997), pp. 78–9.

[16] Ibid., p. 107. Also, note the view of the thirteenth-century canonist William Durandus that people killed in a just battle might be buried in the cemetery but their bodies must be kept out of the church, "ne pauimentum sanguine polluatur" ("lest the [church] pavement be polluted by blood"); A. Davril and T. M. Thibodeau, eds., *Gvillelmi Dvranti Rationale Divinorvm Officiorum I–IV,* Corpus Christianorum Continuatio Mediaevalis 140 (Turnhout: Brepols, 1995), p. 62, lines 150–52. His *Rationale* was written between 1285 and 1291.

[17] Compare F. Pollock and F. W. Maitland, *The History of English Law before the Time of Edward I,* 2d ed., with new intro. and select bibliography by S. F. C. Milsom, 2 vols. (Cambridge: Cambridge University Press, 1968), 2:496, for instances of thirteenth-century executions by decapitation in cases of manifest grand larceny (an alternative was to hurl the convict from a rock into the sea). For other crimes punished by decapitation, see further below.

[18] Compare the case of Simon de Montfort's dismemberment after the battle at Evesham in 1265. His head was cut off (as were his testicles, one inserted into each nostril) and sent to the wife of one of his enemies. Other members were sent to various parts of the kingdom; J. O. Halliwell-Phillipps, ed., *The Chronicle of William de Rishanger, of the Barons' Wars,* Camden Society 15 (London: J. B. Nichols, 1840) pp. xxxi–xxxii. Similarly, compare the case of the Scottish rebel William Wallace, who was hanged, drawn,

decapitations caused by some unforeseen maiming? It is already becoming clear that part of the cruel unintelligibility foregrounded in this passage arises precisely from the fact that the efficient causes of the various forms of human distress piled up in the gallery are not generally explained at all but, in being left open, are also left open to the worst imaginings and to dark surmise. Those wounded in body (line 389) might also conceivably have been subjects of murderous attack, in whatever context,[19] or even have been the victims of their own violence. As ever, the passage is reticent about causes, leaving gaps in the text in which fear can breed. Mad people (line 390) next to those wounded in body were commonly restrained lest they injure others or themselves,[20] and so again, by an association of ideas, self-injury may also have been connoted here, since madness and suicide were then often thought (as they still are today) to keep company.[21] Why some were armed on horseback (line 391) is equally mysterious. Presumably it was for some military encounter. That would be consistent, of course, with carnage of the sort hinted at at the start of the passage. Or was it, perhaps, for a joust? But jousts too were equivocal pastimes, being at best tolerated by the

---

quartered, and beheaded in London in 1305 and his limbs subsequently exhibited in various places in England and Scotland; W. F. Skene, ed., *Johannis de Fordun: Chronica Gestis Scotorum,* 2 vols. (Edinburgh: Edmonston and Douglas, 1871–2), 1:340. C. W. Bynum, *The Resurrection of the Body in Western Christianity, 200–1336* (New York: Columbia University Press, 1995), p. 324, notes the increase in the use of mutilation as a punishment for capital crimes in the late thirteenth century.

[19] Note, too, that Durandus said that those dying in a brawl or tumult were not to be buried in a cemetery (Davril and Thibodeau, *Rationale,* p. 62, lines 142–44). See also Barbara A. Hanawalt, "Violent Death in Fourteenth- and Early Fifteenth-Century England," *Comparative Studies in Society and History* 18 (1976): 297–320, who notes that in the data that she had examined, by far the commonest murder weapon was the knife (see especially ibid., appendix 4, p. 319); the commonest motives for murder were arguments, felonies, and acts of revenge (ibid., appendix 5, p. 320).

[20] As Bartholomeus Anglicus testifies in book 7, ch. 5, of his *De proprietatibus rerum; Bartholomæi Anglici de Genvinis Rervm Coelestivm, Terrestrivm et Inferarvm Proprietatibus, Libri XVIII* (Frankfurt, 1601), p. 283.

[21] And if so, the conjunction of wounding and madness may have intimated diabolic instigation; see M. MacDonald and T. R. Murphy, *Sleepless Souls: Suicide in Early Modern England* (Oxford: Clarendon Press, 1990), pp. 20–21. In the medieval period, a sin→madness→suicide trajectory was widely acknowledged. It often began in diabolic possession (this normally presumed a sinful disposition in the possessed person in the first place, since possession was something to which those in spiritual health were not prone). However, although sin and madness were commonly associated (as Penelope B. R. Doob, *Nebuchadnezzar's Children: Conventions of Madness in Middle English Literature* (New Haven and London: Yale University Press, 1974), pp. 49–53, has emphasized), the efficient causes of madness were thought to be various. Several are to be seen competing in Froissart's anatomy of the madness of Charles VI of France, for example (and see further on this below in n. 63).

church;[22] more usually, they drew ample church censure. Clerics were not even permitted to attend such spectacles where the danger of bloodshed was very real.[23] Thus if a jouster were to be killed, he would not be dying auspiciously in the church's view, neither might any cleric be at hand to administer the last rites. In the next line (line 392), in contrast to the martial world, whether real or stage-managed, the reader is now confronted by the death's head at the feast, and for the first time in the list there appears some hinted relation between an efficient cause and its effect—in this case, between eating and choking. Yet, not necessarily. It may be, alternatively, that these strangulated people were imagined by early readers as having been throttled by some other agency while in the course of doing something as domestic and routine as eating. Demons, for example, were fond of choking people,[24] but whether or not readers imagined demonic agency here—choking would certainly seem to have encouraged this option—the Christian discourse sometimes strove to contain unusual and unexpected death like this by viewing it as a justifiably merited end, one commensurate with, and diagnostic of, some spiritual malaise within the asphyxiated patient.[25] Thus, for

[22] On the attitude of the church to jousting, see Richard Barber and Juliet Baker, *Tournaments: Jousts, Chivalry and Pageants in the Middle Ages* (Woodbridge, Suffolk: Boydell, 1989), pp. 142–45. Also, John Beleth declared in his *Rationale divinorum officiorum* that if anyone dies jousting, without benefit of penance and priest, he should be buried "instar asini" ("like an ass"); Patrologia Latina 202, col. 159.

[23] Compare, for example, a legislation in the synodal statutes of 1279–83 for the diocese of Dublin in this respect: "Ab illicitis spectaculis se abstineant. & precipue torniamentis / Luctis / . & aliis vbi sanguinis effusio poterit formidari" ["Let them (i.e., clerics) abstain from spectacles, and especially from tournaments, contests and other events at which bloodshed is to be feared"] Dublin, Representative Church Body Library, Dublin Diocesan Records, D 6/1, fol. 27.

[24] The idea features a few times in the influential *Legenda aurea* of the thirteenth-century Dominican Jacobus de Voragine. See Th. Graesse, ed., *Legenda aurea vulgo historia lombardica dicta,* 2d ed. (Dresden and Leipzig: Impensis Libriae Arnoldianae, 1850), p. 222 (a demon waits to strangle a knight if he omits to say his daily Ave Maria); or p. 342 (one Carpasius, having blasphemed his pagan gods, is throttled by a demon). Choking while eating, whether by the devil's agency or not, might also be used to add further brushstrokes of horror to a moral *exemplum horrendum.* Compare again the *Legenda aurea*'s account of the death of King Herod. The sequence of events leading to his demise begins with him choking on an apple, next trying to kill himself out of frustration and being prevented, and finally dying five days later (Graesse, *Legenda aurea,* p. 66).

[25] Although a fifteenth-century witness, Thomas Gascoigne betrayed a similarly representative mentality when he gloated that Archbishop Thomas Arundel, who had been seized in the throat some days before his death, had received a visitation appropriate to one who had legislated to stop the mouths of almost all preachers in the realm for the sake of silencing a few heretics. See J. E. T. Rogers, ed., *Loci e libro veritatum* (Oxford: Clarendon Press, 1881), pp. 34–35.

example, to cite a related instance from 1244, when Enguerrand de Coucy suffered a bizarre death by drowning and simultaneous piercing with his own sword, the chronicler Matthew Paris was able to ascribe his end to his vicious character, correlating the two. The peculiar misadventure of de Coucy's death was read and rationalized by Paris as indicating the measure of the man.[26]

De Coucy's case neatly anticipates the next group in the gallery, the drowned (line 393), who in turn seem appropriately paired with their elemental binaries, people shriveled up in fire (line 394).[27] Possibly the fire/water dyad was abetted by recollection of the ordeals of fire and water that by the time of the poem's composition had been abandoned as juridical procedures in England but whose memory lingered on.[28] However, as we have by now come to expect of this text, no explanation is offered for these deaths by fire and water either. The reader has been left free to conjecture the circumstances. The drowning cases may have been the results of execution,[29] or deaths by misadventure, or by suicide, since death by drowning seems to have been one of suicide's better-recognized options.[30] How to arrange for the burial of a drowned person, then, could often pose difficulties, even when the actual reason for the drowning was known or could be safely guessed, and one famous case arbitrated by Pope Innocent III succeeded in finding its way into canon law. A young girl, fleeing from a group of men intent on her rape, fell from a bridge into the river below and was drowned. The anxiety of the

[26] H. R. Luard, ed., *Matthæi Parisiensis, Monachi Sancti Albani, Chronica Majora,* Rolls Series 57, 7 vols. (London: Longman, 1872–83), 4:360–61. Matthew Paris also chose to illustrate this bizarre scene. His verdict was not necessarily spiteful—though it would have been easy enough for anyone spitefully inclined to entertain thoughts of an enemy's death in similar circumstances in such terms—but belonged to an old tradition in which singular death was regarded as the just deserts of singular wickedness.

[27] The elemental binary may have suggested the pairing, but also the possible reminiscence of their pairing as forms of ordeal.

[28] R. Bartlett, *Trial by Fire and Water: The Medieval Judicial Ordeal* (Oxford: Clarendon Press, 1986), p. 94, notes that "many priests and prelates continued to countenance the practice and, indeed, did so well into the thirteenth century."

[29] See n. 17 above on execution by drowning.

[30] Compare the case from Bedfordshire in 1278 in MacDonald and Murphy, *Sleepless Souls,* p. 23. The *Liber poenitentialis* of Robert of Flamborough, composed between 1208 and 1215, puts suicide by drowning at the head of his list of methods of self-destruction; J. J. Francis Firth, ed., *Robert of Flamborough, Canon-Penitentiary of Saint-Victor at Paris, Liber Poenitentialis: A Critical Edition with Introduction and Notes,* Pontifical Institute of Mediæval Studies, Studies and Texts 18 (Toronto: Pontifical Institute of Mediæval Studies, 1971), p. 211, lines 30–44. His other listed forms of suicide were hanging, stabbing, and poisoning.

local clerics, in spite of their awareness of the circumstances of her death, is interesting to observe. After the body had been fished from the water, "dubitaverunt capellani eiusdem loci corpus tradere sepulturae" ("the chaplains of the same place hesitated to commit the body to burial").[31] They hesitated even though they knew that she had fled for an honest cause and had not actually thrown herself in. But as the pope implied, these were the key exonerating factors. Throwing herself in would have been suicide and an entirely different matter. In this girl's case, the canonical maxim would have applied that "Iustus . . . in quacumque hora moritur saluatur, presertim si dabat operam alicui licite rei" ("the just man may be saved whatever hour he dies in, especially if he was exerting himself about some legitimate business").[32] Nevertheless, had not her death caused problems for the local clerics, this case would never have come to light, let alone set precedents in canon law. Those devoured by flame may have suggested again deaths by chance, since fiery self-immolations do not feature in the way that hanging and drowning do as preferred methods of suicide. But another possible resonance here would have been that of the deliberate, judicial execution, and execution by burning was often reserved for heresy and its associated taints of sodomy and witchcraft.[33] Dead heretics, of course, were absolutely forbidden church burial. The burning of relapsed or impenitent heretics, which had become a widely accepted civil policy after 1224 with the decrees of Frederick II, had been adopted for the church by Pope Gregory IX in his constitution, *Excommunicamus et anathematisamus* of 1231. By the mid-thirteenth century, Pope Alexander IV declared anyone knowingly causing a heretic to be buried in consecrated ground excommunicate.[34] So while on the one hand the mention of people consumed in fire could have suggested that a fearful *mors improvisa* had befallen them,[35] on the other it may as likely have called to mind the supreme punishment for heresy.[36] Whichever way, unease and anxiety haunted holocaust death. And finally comes the last category of unfortunates in

[31] E. Friedberg and E. L. Richter, ed., *Corpus Iuris Canonici,* 2d ed., 2 vols. (Leipzig: Tauchnitz, 1879; rpt. Graz: Druk, 1955), 2: col. 553. Innocent III's arbitration was sent in a letter to the Archbishop of Tours.

[32] Davril and Thibodeau, *Rationale,* p. 62, lines 148–50.

[33] Pollock and Maitland, *English Law,* 2:549–50, 556–7.

[34] Finucane, "Sacred Corpse," p. 57.

[35] Again, whether their burning came as a result of malice, war, or accident is all the same: it was a *mors improvisa.*

[36] Pollock and Maitland, *English Law,* 2:549.

the gallery, women either dead, or raving, in childbed (lines 395–96).[37] There was some variety of church opinion about how the body of a woman dying in labor should be disposed of, for this too was a delicate matter. One view, expressed, for example, by the late-twelfth-century Paris theologian John Beleth, maintained that while the woman could not be buried in church, she could be legitimately buried outside it. The child must nevertheless be cut from her and buried outside the cemetery itself.[38] Alternative views were expressed by the thirteenth-century canonist William Durandus. He agreed that a woman so dying should not be set to rest within the church ("ne pauimentum ecclesie sanguine polluatur" ["lest the church pavement be defiled with blood"]), but should be buried outside in the cemetery, and he also agreed that her dead, unbaptized child should be removed from her womb and buried outside the cemetery. Yet Durandus noted that there were others who took a more lenient approach to this distressing human predicament: "qui dicunt quod partus debet una cum muliere in cimiterio sepeliri, eo quod pars uiscerum esse censetur" ("who say that the birth product must be buried in the cemetery with the woman, because it is considered to be a part of her viscera").[39]

As we take in *Sir Orfeo*'s gallery "wiþ-in þe wal" at a retrospective glance, a consistency of fear emerges, fear contoured as much by the current shibboleths of prevailing Christian ideology as by natural human instinct. The catalogue of casualties has concentrated together anxieties too familiar in the Christian society of late-thirteenth-century England to suggest that they have been assembled for anything other than deliberate reasons, while at the same time it has withheld any of the palliatives that contemporary Christian discourse had to offer for the alleviation of those anxieties. It has managed to do this by keeping obscure, for the most part, the exact nature of the efficient causes of the deaths and afflictions of those in the gallery. This results in their spiritual prognosis becoming hard to gauge. As we have seen, in the Christian discourse, even when their efficient causes were obvious, deaths like these were still experienced as highly problematic and their palliatives costly to come by. Their near intractability in this respect probed and

[37] This is the second and only other causal relation hinted at in the gallery. This time it is between the labor of childbirth and death/madness.

[38] Thus John Beleth in his *Rationale divinorum officiorum* (Patrologia Latina 202, cols 158–59).

[39] Davril and Thibodeau, *Rationale,* p. 62, lines 165–67.

helped to define the discourse's boundaries. But displaced from whatever consolations the rationalizing discourse could otherwise attempt to devise for them into *Sir Orfeo*'s romance narrative, the anxieties that they focused have been left utterly raw and unsalved. Therefore, once any possible solace of Christian intelligibility has been occluded (at least in any explicit form), their (calculated) legacy to the medieval reader would have been unmitigated fear. In the circumstances, readers could only rely on their personal Christian resources in trying to assuage that fear; the text of *Sir Orfeo* did nothing to help them toward whatever forms of Christian relief may have been available. And even if they persisted in their resort to the discourse of Christianity for consoling answers, even there they would not have found solutions to be effortless, but rather to be fraught with uncertainty.[40]

II. The Discourse of Astrology

However, some medieval readers of *Sir Orfeo* are likely to have had another formation also available to them, for it was not left solely to late-thirteenth-century Christianity, however much in the vanguard, to wrestle chaos into a meaningful shape. Astrology, which at this date was attracting fresh attention,[41] also existed as a parallel, indeed for many a competitive, discourse, and by its means a different set of explanations could be sought for life's calamities. At the time *Sir Orfeo* was written, the belief in the domination of earth by sky was widespread.[42] It can be seen percolating through other contemporary vernacular writings, and in their company the potential astrological resonance in lines 387–404 that will be illustrated here should seem less exceptional. *The Owl and the Nightingale,* for example, a poem that may not be far from *Sir Orfeo* both in time and place of composition,[43] evinces a notable interest in

[40] It could be argued that the withholding of any of the explicit Christian gestures of containment would have stimulated Christian readers to supply them, and that their withholding was, as it were, a gap or deficit in the text that readers could be expected to make good. But against this is the fact that those gestures were various and, as has been seen, for some, uncertain. Which should be made? No guidance is given, not to mention the (complicating) availability of the two alternative and competing discourses to be considered next.

[41] Thorndike, *History of Magic,* 2: *passim.*

[42] Ibid. Also, see J. D. North, ed., *Richard of Wallingford,* 2 vols. (Oxford: Clarendon Press, 1976), 2:84–85.

[43] The possibility of a date after the death of Henry III in 1272 is accepted by Neil Cartlidge, "The Date of *The Owl and the Nightingale,*" *MÆ* 65 (1996): 230–47; also, see

astrology, and out of this interest proceeds the Owl's litany of the assorted fates that she claims to be able to foretell. Indeed, their somber tone is reminiscent of the *Sir Orfeo* passage under consideration:

> "Ich wot of hunger, of hergonge,
> Ich wot ȝef men schule libbe longe,
> Ich wat ȝef wif luste hire make,
> Ich wat þar schal beo niþ & wrake,
> Ich wot hwo schal beon anhonge
> Oþer elles fulne deþ afonge.
> ȝef men habbeþ bataile inume
> Ich wat hwaþer schal beon ouerkume.
> Ich wat ȝif cwalm scal comen on orfe,
> An ȝif dor schul ligge astorue;
> Ich wot ȝef treon schule blowe,
> Ich wat ȝef cornes schule growe,
> Ich wot ȝef huses schule berne,
> Ich wot ȝef men schule orne oþer erne,
> Ich wot ȝef sea schal schipes drenche,
> Ich wot ȝef smiþes schal uuele clenche."[44]

So the contents of *Sir Orfeo*'s gallery could have invited an astrological understanding of their causality, and just as many of the gallery's human tragedies, as was seen, had a peculiar Christian resonance corresponding to whatever causality the reader chose to attribute to them, so too they would have had a peculiar astrological one for readers who had even the most rudimentary acquaintance with astrological discourse. The selection of the gallery's casualties could therefore once more be supposed to have been deliberate and calculated according to their exemplary value, this time of the activity of the two baleful planets of the zodiac, Mars and Saturn.[45] Those in the gallery would have been readily recognized by anyone acquainted with theories of planetary influence as Mars and Saturn's ill-starred children.

Alan J. Fletcher, "The Genesis of *The Owl and the Nightingale:* A New Hypothesis," *Chau R* 34 (1999): 1–17, where a data after 1275 is suggested, perhaps as late as ca. 1282.

[44] E. G. Stanley, ed., *The Owl and the Nightingale,* 2d ed. (Manchester: Manchester University Press, 1972), p. 83, lines 1191–1206. On the astrological resonances, see A. C. Cawley, "Astrology in 'The Owl and the Nightingale,'" *MLR* 46 (1951): 161–74.

[45] But whether deliberate or not, the point is that an astrologically informed reader could have discerned in them a Mars/Saturn causality.

Since the works of the second-century astrologer Ptolemy were a prime source of astrological lore in the thirteenth century, we might most conveniently consider lines 387–404 principally in Ptolemy's terms in our attempt to trace the lineaments of a putative medieval reader response that was astrologically informed.[46] Decapitation (line 391) and other mutilations (line 392) were to be put down to malign conjunctions of Mars, as were deaths by fire (line 398) and in childbed (line 400). Victims of Mars's planetary influence may likewise have been people wounded in body (line 393). Those prepared for some martial encounter or other (line 395) were self-evidently Mars's offspring.[47] Madness (line 394), as well as its associated propensity to suicide, was a condition that Mars was thought to bring about.[48] In Ptolemy's terms, there is one possible exception: death by strangulation (line 396) was attributable to an evil aspect of Jupiter.[49] But apart from this, the rest were Mars's handiwork, and in one instance—a salient one—Saturn's, death by drowning (line 397).[50]

The proximity of the discourses of Christianity and astrology in the late thirteenth century[51]—and for some important commentators, it should be stressed, their incommensurability—is reflected in the struggle that was taking place to reconcile them. For some, finding an accommodation between them had been a relatively easy matter, while for others it had been exceedingly difficult, if not downright impossible. Thus the theologian William of Auvergne (ca. 1180–1249) abhorred

[46] These were generally in the air in late-thirteenth-century England. His *Tetrabiblos* had been translated into Latin from Greek by 1138, and his ideas informed much of what later English writers believed (for example, Bartholomeus Anglicus); see L. Braswell, "Utilitarian and Scientific Prose," in A. S. G. Edwards, ed., *Middle English Prose: A Critical Guide to Major Authors and Genres* (New Brunswick, N.J.: Rutgers University Press, 1984), p. 339, and J. D. North, *Chaucer's Universe* (Oxford: Clarendon Press, 1988), p. 410.

[47] F. E. Robbins, ed., *Ptolemy Tetrabiblos* (London and Cambridge, Mass.: W. Heinemann and Harvard University Press, 1940; rpt. 1964), pp. 326–27 and 428–35 for all these.

[48] Robbins, *Tetrabiblos,* pp. 328–29 and 430–31. However, for evidence of the contemporary belief in the influence also of the moon on madness, see for example bk. 5, ch. 3, and bk. 8, ch. 30, of the *De proprietatibus rerum* of Bartholomeus Anglicus (*Bartholomœi Anglici de Genvinis Rervm Coelestivm,* pp. 125 and 415, respectively).

[49] Robbins, *Tetrabiblos,* pp. 428–29.

[50] Robbins, *Tetrabiblos,* pp. 326–27 and 432–33; at the head of the famous litany of Saturn's disastrous consequences in Chaucer's *Knight's Tale* (lines 2456–69) stands death by drowning.

[51] Astrology at many respectable Christian centers even earlier, as, for example, at Hereford Cathedral in the late twelfth century. See R. W. Hunt, "English Learning in the Late Twelfth Century," in *Essays in Medieval History* ed. R. W. Southern (London: Macmillan, 1968), pp. 106–28.

the astrological enthusiasms of his associates and censured Ptolemy's influence. William's criticisms, of course, testify to the strength of astrology's current vogue, and for all that astrology had eminent detractors like himself, it had eminent supporters too.[52] One such, William's more famous contemporary, the Dominican theologian Albertus Magnus (d. 1280), held the teachings of Ptolemy by contrast in high esteem.[53] Yet although Albertus believed that a reconciliation between the two systems *was* possible, the general debate continued unresolved over how compatible a belief in divine Providence and belief in the rule of the stars might be, especially when the question of human free will had also to be factored into the equation. Astrology might easily collapse into fatalism, and so earn Christianity's interdict.

However, even if we conceive a reader response to lines 387–404 that may have had more in common with an Albertus Magnus than a William of Auvergne, the salient point is this: the operation of these planets is not explicitly named inside the poem as the cause of the damage; it is only to be inferred, if at all, from the vantage point of an astrological discourse available outside the poem. Thus the discourse of astrology too has been disabled in the moment of its engagement, because even if the casualties invited certain readers to supply an astrological explanation, no such explanation is ostensibly registered within the text itself to endorse their interpretative choice. That is, readers had no ostensible help from the text in settling upon astrological causality; they were on their own again to make that connection, just as they were on their own if they tried to understand the gallery in terms of Christian discourse. Readers would have found no satisfactory closure any more from astrology than they would from Christianity. Moreover, such readers as were in touch with both discourses (anyone knowing some astrology would doubtless have known Christian theology) would necessarily have been confronted with an even greater surplus of possible explanations, and hence no one definitive explanation. Thus, in the moment that the range of interpretative options for some readers was becoming luxuriously

[52] J. D. North, ed., *Richard of Wallingford,* 3 vols. (Oxford: Clarendon Press, 1976), 2:84–85, emphasizes the general acceptability of astrology, its critics notwithstanding, during this period.

[53] For a survey of thirteenth-century responses to astrology, see G. W. Coopland, *Nicole Oresme and the Astrologers: A Study of His "Livre de Divinacions"* (Liverpool: University Press, 1952). See also L. Thorndike, *A History of Magic and Experimental Science during the First Thirteen Centuries of Our Era,* 8 vols. (New York and London: Macmillan, 1923–58), 2: *passim,* and for the views of William of Auvergne and Albertus Magnus, see, respectively, ibid., 2:369 and 582–83.

multiple, their access to settled knowledge was becoming proportionally more complicated; any chance of singular certainty was increasingly being put at risk by the prospect of plural possibility.

The *potential* astrological resonance of lines 387–404 seems all the clearer for being so largely consistent. In the main, it is Martian. Yet as I have emphasized, none of this is made explicit in the text itself. The astrological discourse has been disabled—one might say decapitated—just as the Christian one, by a somewhat different set of procedures, also was, and installed acephalous into fairyland. While the planets, especially Mars, might have been credited with the gallery's disasters, that was an inference left to the reader to make, just as the reader's own initiative would have had to struggle to supply any closure in Christian terms.

A third discourse remains for investigation, which, like Christianity but in contrast with astrology, *is* explicitly registered in the poem: this is the discourse of fairyland. If Christianity cannot easily reconcile the *mortes improvisae* of the gallery, and if astrology has no clear internal textual sanction by which their responsibility can be offloaded onto Mars and Saturn, may it be that causality can be explained in terms of the rules of fairyland?

III. The Discourse of Fairyland

A problem that arises immediately here is that, of the three discourses under review, fairyland proves the most elusive, although as will shortly be seen, it is not utterly beyond retrieval. Existing as it did chiefly at the oral and preliterate level, it was the least likely of the three to leave palpable traces. Indeed, Dorena Allen's explication of the gallery's "dead" and *taken,* the first to afford lines 387–404 any sustained critical attention, depended in the main on postmedieval folk analogues—unavoidably, she doubtless thought, given the intrinsically ephemeral nature of the folk culture that she was trying to access.[54] She believed nevertheless that her analogues, many of them of Gaelic and Breton origin, witnessed not just to the longevity in folklore of motifs also active within *Sir Orfeo,* but to a perennial human need to contain such unsettling aspects of life as *Sir Orfeo*'s "dead" and *taken* also epitomize.[55] The

[54] See Allen, "The Dead and the *Taken.*"

[55] Allen, "The Dead and the *Taken*"; indeed, several of her references date to classical antiquity (those on pp. 107–8, for example).

author of *Sir Orfeo,* Allen argued, had inherited an ancient narrative that had undergone an evolution. The classical fable of Orpheus's reclaiming of his dead wife, Eurydice, from Hades had been subsequently infiltrated, reinterpreted according to prevailing folk beliefs, which held that death might be no more than an illusion, a masking of what had in fact been a fairy abduction. Her analogues, she thought, were a testimony to folk attempts to transfigure and so alleviate the peculiar pathos of untimely death.

Whether that was a solace also extended to readers of *Sir Orfeo* is, however, a very different matter, and it is worth noting A. C. Spearing's historically alert reminder, itself a response to Allen's study, that the poet of *Sir Orfeo* was not a Gaelic or a Breton storyteller but an Englishman of the late thirteenth century who wrote not far from London.[56] Even so, analogues have their value, and since the time Allen wrote, another has come to light closer to the original circumstances of the composition of *Sir Orfeo* than any she was then able to adduce. The evidence of this new analogue is worth citing, for it establishes, more compellingly than any Gaelic or Breton analogue could, that closely contemporary with *Sir Orfeo* there actually existed a popular oral English discourse of fairyland. This evidence provides a basis for an analogical comparison, therefore, that lays a greater claim to our attention, since it has the advantage of immediate historical relevance and purchase.

In its discussion of the sin of sloth, the early-fourteenth-century preacher's handbook known as the *Fasciculus morum* contains the following passage:

> Set rogo quid dicendum est de talibus miseriis et supersticiosis qui de nocte dixerunt se videre reginas pulcherrimas et alias puellas tripudiantes cum domina Dyana choreas ducentes dea paganorum, que in nostro vulgari dicitur *elves?* Et credunt quod tales possunt tam homines quam mulieres in alias naturas transformare <et> secum ducere apud *eluenlond,* ubi iam, ut dicunt, manent illi athlete fortissimi, scilicet Onewyn et Wad et ceteri.[57]

[But, I ask, what is to be said about wretched and superstitious folk of this sort, who have claimed that at night they see very beautiful queens and other maidens dancing with the Lady Diana, goddess of the pagans, and leading ring

[56] Spearing, *Readings,* p. 71.

[57] S. Wenzel, ed., *Fasciculus Morum: A Fourteenth-Century Preacher's Handbook* (University Park: Pennsylvania State Press, 1989), p. 578, lines 61–7.

dances? In our language these beings are called elves. And folk believe that these creatures can transform both men and women into other shapes/natures and take them with them into elfland, where now, as they say, dwell those most mighty champions, that is, Onewyn and Wade and others.]

According to the *Fasciculus,* fairyland was a place into which men and women could be carried off. In it dwelt Onewyn and Wade, figures now relatively mysterious.[58] Its fabulous denizens could also change men and women into other shapes or natures. The fleeting, but unmistakeable, similarities between these motifs and ones used in *Sir Orfeo* are too obvious to need laboring here. What is of present interest is the passage's proof that yet another discourse currently existed by means of which some late-medieval English men and women, superstitious though they were in the *Fasciculus* author's view, might seek to explain certain aspects of their lives. This was the discourse of fairyland. The *Fasciculus* passage shows that it was confined not merely to some literary genre, though understandably, imaginative literature of the romance sort might be the first to register and transmit it: it was also at large in daily life. And it probably ranged between both ends of the social spectrum, from the relatively demotic that the *Fasciculus* author seems to have had in mind to the far more élite, even to the courtly.[59] What is also worth remarking in the *Fasciculus* passage, however, is a certain *difference* distinguishing its fairyland from that which *Sir Orfeo* evokes. I will return to this difference presently.

Allen's reading shed light on an important aspect of *Sir Orfeo*'s artistry: part of its transhistorical appeal is founded on the immemorial fears to which it gives an imaginative shape. But while *Sir Orfeo*'s appeal in this

[58] Of "Onewyn" I have discovered nothing, though perhaps on the strength of the association made here, s/he may have been a character from the lost Wade narratives. And on Wade, see further in the note following.

[59] At the élite level, compare the social tone of the context of Chaucer's two Wade allusions, one in *The Merchant's Tale* (line 1424 ["Wades boot"]) and the other in *Troilus and Criseyde* (line 614 [a "tale of Wade"]). Wade is alluded to as a character of romance (in company with Havelok and Horn) in the *Laud Troy Book:* "Off Hauelok, Horne, & of Wade;— / In Romaunces that of hem ben made / That gestoures often dos of hem gestes / At Mangeres and at grete ffestes"; J. Ernst Wülfing, ed., *The Laud Troy Book,* Early English Text Society, o. s. 121, 122 (London: Kegan Paul, Trench, Trübner and Co., 1902–3; rpt. as one volume, New York: Kraus, 1975), 1:1, lines 21–24. This extract also seems to imply a higher social level for the consumption of Wade narratives than that which the *Fasciculus* author had in mind.

respect may be legitimately dehistoricized—for dehistoricizing is the likely consequence of a reading largely dependent on noncontemporary analogues—it must also be historicized, as the passage from the *Fasciculus,* along with the two contemporary discourses surveyed earlier, has begun to make plain. Has the discourse of fairyland, then, been left intact, or has it, like the other two, also in some sense been *taken?* To be sure, the *Fasciculus* passage is brief, and what there is of it in which to descry contemporary ideas about fairyland is slender enough. Yet the signs are that something has happened to fairyland too. Its version in *Sir Orfeo* may not be quite that which the *Fasciculus* author described in one important respect. The fairy folk were able to carry people away into fairyland, said the *Fasciculus* author, and this they also did in *Sir Orfeo:* "Eche was þus in þis warld y-nome, / Wiþ fairi þider y-come" (lines 403–4). But according to the *Fasciculus,* they were also able to change men and women into other shapes or natures, and this was a power attributed to them prior to the detail that they could carry people off. In fact, the text may be read to imply that the shape changing was a condition of the abduction. In *Sir Orfeo,* however, the fairies' instrumentality in this regard is far less certain. Any ghastly transformation suffered by the people in the gallery happened first in the real world, not at the hands of the fairies. These, it seems, are to be credited only with spiriting them away, not with any transformation per se such as the *Fasciculus* author spoke of. The fairies of *Sir Orfeo* were collectors who merely followed their passion. This makes them even more alarming than if they had simply been presented as the efficient cause of disaster. Were causality attributable to them, it would render them intelligible within terms of the discourse of fairyland, as these are reconstructable from the *Fasciculus,* and therefore they would be less frightening. But it is not. True, the fairies were capable of murderous intervention, and such was their threat to Heurodis if she did not do as they had commanded her. But the question of their direct responsibility for chaos, at least as far as the gallery manifests it, is left wide open. There is no doubt that they were associated with it in some way—there is even a suggestion that they may have had a taste for it—but the text refuses to name them categorically as its instigators. With their instrumentality left in doubt, the fairies of *Sir Orfeo* are not a final explanation of chaos either. And while fairyland's intervention might offer an explanation of sorts for how the gallery came to be assembled in the first place, fairyland itself, as we understand it from the *Fasciculus,* is collected into the poem's album of discourses, one among several against which fairyland is similarly obliged to compete for any monopoly on explanation.

At the close of this survey, we may now be better placed to see not only that the stabilizing authority of the three discourses is problematized but that their very plurality has undermined any one definitive way of making sense of lines 387–404. Unless, that is, the reader consciously decided to choose between the options. But in helping the reader thus choose, the text offers little guidance. And so in the end, chaos is left as terrifyingly inscrutable as it ever was.

IV. The Flight from the Enchanters

The captured discourses in *Sir Orfeo* resonate incomplete, incapable of satisfactorily containing chaos in one totalizing explanation. A certain fascination subsists in being allowed to recognize them from without, as it were, in their gallery "wiþ-in þe wal," rather than from within, from the position of one who is subject to their authority in daily life and who lives unquestioningly inside their terms: once routinely familiar in their wonted everyday context, where they could hold sway with all the customary power of assumptions left unexamined, now transferred here they are displayed in an unwonted light as objects of scrutiny.[60] In their poetic re-cognition lurks a potential existential confusion too. As has been seen, the options available to late-thirteenth-century men and

[60] Displayed thus uncustomarily for scrutiny in an arena, they become objects made strange by contemplation. The effect here resembles what the Prague School of theatrical theory identified and enunciated in its first principle: essentially, the very fact of an object's appearance on stage (for "on stage" read "in the gallery" in *Sir Orfeo*) suppresses the object's practical function in favor of a symbolic or signifying role. As Karel Brušák observed, "while in real life the utilitarian function of an object is usually more important than its signification, on a theatrical set the signification is all important"; "Signs in the Chinese Theater," in Ladislaw Matejka and Irwin R. Titunik, eds., *Semiotics of Art: Prague School Contributions* (Cambridge, Mass.: MIT Press, 1976), pp. 59–73; see p. 62. Something similar might be said of the displayed discourses, disconnected as they are from routine practical application. The signification that combinatively they help to bear and that displaces their everyday function is chaos—that very thing against which ordinarily they stood as bulwarks. This estrangement of the familiar from itself could equally be conceived in terms of the culture of "play" with which the poem collaborates (and see further below on the poem as *performance*). As Don Handelman has noted, "play" culture is liable to "take apart the clock-works of reality, and question their organization, and indeed their very validity as human and as cultural constructs"; "Reflexivity in Festival and Other Cultural Events," in Mary Douglas, ed., *Essays in the Sociology of Perception* (London and Boston: Routledge and Kegan Paul, 1982), pp. 162–90; see p. 163.

women for making sense of some of the most intractable human predicaments have been allowed to multiply. In the wake of such multiplication, which explanatory discourse is to be preferred? *Sir Orfeo* offers no guidance. It seems reasonable to imagine that its early readers,[61] or to speak strictly, those who had prior acquaintance of the discourses that it has abducted, experienced a similar disorientation. After all, the late-thirteenth-century praxis of Christian, astrological, and fairy beliefs (though in literate culture, of course, most widely and preeminently that of the first) was vitally important, for these were beliefs according to which people actually shaped their lives. Consequently, the defamiliarization of these beliefs in the gallery would presumably have left a contemporary reader in a position not unlike that occupied today by anyone who finds cherished assumptions suddenly appearing less absolute than they had seemed before. In everyday life, the hegemony of the three discourses was protected in that each normally operated within its own exclusive province, its discreteness, and therefore its integrity, even being patroled by the striking of hostile, reactionary attitudes. Thus, for example, contemporary Christianity, which of the three discourses had the largest stake in organizing the culture enfolding *Sir Orfeo,* might often be heard reprobating astrology (for all that astrology had its share of Christian apologists in the late thirteenth century), just as it was quicker still to reprobate as a devilish phantasm any belief in fairyland.[62] In the gallery, however, whatever barriers may have been erected between the discourses elsewhere are removed, with the result that they freely associate, each becoming less absolute in the company of the other.

Bereft of any authoritative indication from the poem itself as to which to elect as an interpretative key, the mind of the reader is liable to return

[61] Here and throughout I have seemed to beg the question of the manner of the reception of the text by using the word "reader." "Reader," however, is to be understood as a mere convenience: it does not exclude other possibilities, and notably the active possibility of aural reception, the rule rather than the exception for popular literature during this period. See Joyce Coleman, *Public Reading and the Reading Public in Late Medieval England and France* (Cambridge: Cambridge University Press, 1996); Ruth Crosby, "Oral Delivery in the Middle Ages," *Speculum* 11 (1936): 88–110, is also still of value.

[62] Note that by the fourteenth century, astrology was coming more strongly under attack from the church; see Thorndike, *History of Magic and Experimental Science,* 2:949–50. And for an example of church reprobation of belief in fairyland, we need look no further than the trenchant *Fasciculus* author. For him, "Que omnia [non] sunt nisi fantasmata et a maligno spiritu illis demonstrata" ["All these things are nothing but phantasms and are shown to them by an evil spirit"], Wenzel, *Fasciculus Morum,* p. 578, lines 67–68.

defeated from its attempt to make steady sense of that mysterious realm embodied in the human casualties and ever promising to infringe unexpectedly on quotidian reality.[63] In addition, and as has been seen, in the terms in which that realm has been constructed in *Sir Orfeo,* it has been allowed to exceed the reach of the domesticating logic of either of the discourses. And beyond these, what other major paradigms of intelligibility would medieval readers have had at their disposal? In the last part of the poem, Orfeo—and the reader by proxy—flees from the enchanters. But it is not to the refuge of any "rational" discourse from whose resources chaos may be disciplined that they resort. The refuge awaiting Orfeo, rather, is dictated and invented by a trick of fiction: the narrative loop must be completed by returning him to the happily-ever-after. What refuge, alternatively, awaits the reader? I will later attempt to gauge it, but for the moment, suffice it to say that it cannot be so simple. Things may have come right for Orfeo inside the narrative, but the reader outside the narrative has been led to a frightening appreciation of how elemental chaos of its nature admits no clear motive or rationale. Perhaps the correlative of this, in the narrative's terms, is that fairyland may have been quitted but not dispatched; though out of sight for the time being, it still remains there. In any event, the aporia toward which the poem has allowed its readers to stray is not Orfeo's, and for them the anxieties provoked must be addressed differently.

While existential confusion, as noted earlier, may inhabit this aporia, perhaps also to be found there was the exhilaration of novelty, as belief systems formerly taken for granted were now tilted at an odd angle and readers discovered themselves empowered to choose, or even not to choose, between their relative claims. However, such value-free emancipation is the luxurious condition of the spectating connoisseur, and it resembles that of the person prepared to sever form from content, appreciating the one heedless of the other. An aesthetic capacity of this sort risks encouraging a certain moral vacuousness, and this was necessarily

[63] Defeated, that is, unless that mind can access the resources of its prior cultural formation for guidance. But as has been argued, *Sir Orfeo* problematizes that access. The demolition of certainty conducted in this part of the poem, of course, clears a space in which the ideology constructed in the latter part can stand unrivaled. Though admittedly later than *Sir Orfeo* by about a century, it is interesting to compare the competing attempts to explain the madness of Charles VI of France in the *Chroniques* of Jean Froissart. Froissart exposes a rich relativism, as different folk seize on different ways to explain the king's madness, always according to their inclination or bias. Their various explanations are summarized in Doob, *Nebuchadnezzar's Children,* pp. 45–49.

a perilous pathology in the culture in which the poem was produced.[64] Ultimately, a readerly refuge from this "black hole" opening up in morality would become imperative. If readers had strayed toward a fascinating and dangerous brink, finally the dominant *Weltanschauung* of late-thirteenth- and early-fourteenth-century England would ensure that they would recoil from the edge. Nevertheless, for a little while, it may be that, like the fairy folk, readers too were permitted to occupy a morally vacant space, becoming in turn detached connoisseurs, licensed to find intriguing and appalling the terms in which the reification of chaos had been held before their imaginations.[65] Thus the gallery in fairyland may be seen as a trope for a state where decisive interpretation was not possible, perhaps indeed where it may not even have mattered. As such it may be supposed to have had the potential to inspire a sort of interpretative hedonism that colluded to push monolithic answers and solutions, that is, authoritative meanings, into free fall.

What, exactly, was the refuge from this available to medieval readers who lived by master narratives that outlawed such free fall of meaning? For irrespective of the discursive relativism that the gallery may have exposed, it cannot, finally, cause everything thereafter to dissolve in a joyous Nietzschean indeterminacy, committing readers "to an endless free play, unconstrained by a sense of allegiance to anything beyond this freedom."[66] That may well have been a momentary aperçu, as has been argued, but if so, it was as a parcel of the giddy terror of chaos, not an emancipation embraced in its own right in the way the postmodern

[64] Here, in everyday life, people would normally operate according to, and certainly at least be conscious of, strongly enunciated moral codes that in many cases had been powerfully endorsed by an attribution to them of teleological significance. It is also probable that the majority of folk were too preoccupied with the routine business of living to have had much time for interrogating those codes or scrutinizing them in any sustained and systematic way. That was a prerequisite of the leisured classes, though even there the more dangerous speculations seem to have been conducted at a clerical level, and policed, moreover, by the ecclesiastical hierarchy. Nevertheless, *Sir Orfeo* has opened up a morally vacant space, and the degree of fascination and horror in readers accepting the invitation to occupy that space would have been proportional to the extent of their acculturation to the prevailing moral codes.

[65] Lucas, "An Interpretation," p. 6, shrewdly speaks of fairyland in this poem being "frightening, as well as fascinating." I would regard beauty and danger as being even more deeply recessed within the text: the reader seduced by fairyland's ostensible beauty is convicted of a dangerous moral vacuousness in the moment of seduction. This seduction confounds aesthetic response inextricably with questions of moral value.

[66] Charles Taylor, *Sources of the Self* (Cambridge, Mass.: Harvard University Press, 1989), p. 488. Compare Jacques Derrida, *Writing and Différance* (London: Routledge and Kegan Paul, 1978), p. 292.

might embrace it today. To read *Sir Orfeo* like that would be to read it anachronistically and against the grain of its informing culture. As a preliminary answer to the question just posed, we might consider first the proposition that a readerly refuge existed in the very ephemerality of the poem. It is conceivable that medieval readers could afford to take a short vacation from the security of the certitudes habitually enjoined upon them in their everyday lives precisely because, after all, their readerly detachment ultimately cushioned them from any seriously damaging implications of what they had appreciated: if they experienced any alarm from the interpretative disorientation that the poem purveyed, in the context of a (vernacular) work of literature whose probable immediate motive was (evanescent) recreation, it would doubtless have come as a thrill rather than as a threat.[67] At this date, durable literary *gravitas* meant to be taken lastingly to heart where it could influence the way people lived would doubtless either have come packaged in Latin or have been grounded in some other way on an authoritative Latin base.[68] Vernacular literary culture, by contrast, especially that represented by secular poetry, may have tended to inscribe its own transience in this respect, something not contradicted by the fact that the practice of secular poetry by the late thirteenth century had strong institutional roots.[69] So preliminary foundations of a readerly refuge could have been laid in the very insubstantiality of the vernacular at this date as a truth-bearing

[67] Compare the observation of Handelman, "Reflexivity," p. 172: "the active freedom of the self in festival is complementary to its restriction and incorporation in everyday life." *Sir Orfeo* could similarly be viewed as a "festival" text in this sense.

[68] While such authoritative information was available in the vernacular—compare the moral and spiritual instruction broadcast in vernacular preaching, for example—the vernacular in such contexts frequently legitimated itself by reference to an underwriting Latin *auctoritas.* Indeed, it may be the sheer weight of Latin's prestige as the standard language of clerical literary culture that contributed to the linguistic interference sometimes manifest in texts that, though probably delivered originally in English, came to be written up either in Latin or, even more tellingly, in a curious *mischsprache* of Latin and English (and on the ideological stakes of this phenomenon; see Alan J. Fletcher, "'Benedictus qui venit in nomine Domini': A Thirteenth-Century Sermon for Advent and the Macaronic Style in England," *Mediæval Studies* 56 [1994]: 217–45).

[69] The current general view among literary historians would doubtless state this more strongly. However, my suggestions below about the original auspices of *Sir Orfeo* necessarily call the view into question. Hence my use of the verb "tended" in the sentence above should be allowed full force in aiming to temper current orthodoxy (and compare Elizabeth Salter, *Fourteenth-Century English Poetry: Contexts and Readings* [Oxford: Clarendon Press, 1984], pp. 22–23, who noted that there is "no simple answer to the question of who read and wrote English poetry during the twelfth and thirteenth centuries," and that the choice of French over English cannot be safely predicted from "the nature of the patrons, the intended public, or the subject-matter").

medium: the beauty and danger at large in *Sir Orfeo* might be defused by trivializing them into the harmless pastime of a moment, one finished once the tale was told, the book put away, and the proper business of living resumed. But another, and possibly more reliable, refuge was also available to the reader.[70] It would take shape in a different, less negative set of terms, ones that also appropriately answered to the social milieu in which *Sir Orfeo* can reasonably be suspected as having originated; analysis of these terms will occupy the last part of this study.

Whatever refuge may have been available to readers in a self-marginalizing vernacular, then, it is, in addition, the performative culture predicating the poem that fights to make itself heard again above the meaninglessness of chaos. In that fight the harper, and through him the consolidating power of performative culture that his harping represents, becomes stability's champion. This proposition will be clarified later. First, let us consider the status of harping inside and outside the poem. Within the narrative, it is granted specifically to harping to retrieve stability and to be the instrument of a deliverance at once private and public.[71] That is, harping performs social normality for Orfeo, Heurodis, and their kingdom. To be sure, as has been seen, it is not necessarily the case that chaos has gone away for good—much less been routed—but for the time being, it is in abeyance, thanks to harping, and an exit has been opened once more into stability. No doubt the flight from the enchanters—whether that of Orfeo from the fairies or that of medieval readers from the somewhat different sort of disorienting magic worked by the text's existentially disturbing strategies—should be imagined as coming finally as a relief. Medieval readers may have been grateful for having found their toll gate into normality, even if it was one over which the sign "By Courtesy of Harping" was writ large and to which their attention had to be drawn as the price of admission. To the modern reader, conversely, it may seem, in view of the volatile forces that the earlier part of the poem managed to unleash that to

[70] While a refuge of sorts might be found by dismissing the existential threat of the poem on the grounds of the marginality of its vernacular, to do so might also entail depreciation of the "performative" refuge afforded by the poem that will be explained below.

[71] Lucas, "An Interpretation," p. 5, rightly considers the poem's concern with "private love and the public loyalty which is its corollary" to be in excess of anything it could have inherited in this respect from the Orpheus legend. The attitude of the fairy king to harping might be contrasted: for him, it seems that all that he appreciates in it is its aesthetic surface.

claim for harping so formidable a triumph in the face of them is almost bathetic.

And yet, was crediting this coup to harping really so preposterous? In medieval terms, perhaps not, though the medieval reader may also not have winked at the politics couched within the claim. The equation of harping with healthy civilization in *Sir Orfeo* cannot merely be regarded as a traditional piety inherited by its author from his predecessors in the romance genre. True, harps and harpers had long been celebrated there and in other literature too,[72] and the restorative power of harping would inevitably feature in any narrative descended from the Orpheus legend. But the terms in which the equation has been formulated in *Sir Orfeo* seem to be unique. The example of lines 387–404, which have shown how *Sir Orfeo,* refusing to limit itself to the world of self-referrential literary convention,[73] might reach out from this domain to touch the lived experience of its contemporary historical readers, suggests that the terms of the insistence on harping as the access to civil society might themselves be investigated to see whether they have exceeded literary convention, too. It may be that the twinned cure of private and public disorder that the performance of harping alone has been allowed to effect inside the narrative, a cure that inflates harping's salu-

[72] Examples of the celebration of harping in anterior romances are too numerous to catalogue. To cite but two: a performance is related in the *Tristan* of Thomas (ca. 1170), in which Iseut sings *lais* to harp accompaniment: "La dame chante dulcement, / La voix acorde a l'estrument; / Les mainz sunt beles, li lais bons, / Dulce la voix, e bas li tons" ["The lady [Iseut] sings sweetly, her voice in accord with the instrument. Her hands are beautiful, the *lais* are good, sweet is her voice and deep/soft her tone/music"], J. Bédier, ed., *Le Roman de Tristan par Thomas, poème du XIIe siècle,* Société des Anciens Textes Français, 2 vols (Paris: Firmin-Didot, 1902–5; rpt., 1964 and 1968), vol. 1, lines 843–46; and again in the *Roman de Horn* also of Thomas (ca. 1170), Horn sings *lais* to harp accompaniment: "E quant il out issi fait, si cummence a noter / Le lai dont or ains dis, de Baltof, haut e cler, / Si cum sunt cil bretun d'itiel fait costumier. / Apres en l'estrument fet les cordes suner, / Tut le lai lur ad fait, n'i vout rien retailler" ["And when he has done all this (i.e., played a harp prelude), he begins to play the aforesaid *lai* of Baltof, in a loud and clear voice, just as the Bretons are versed in such performances. Afterwards he made the strings of the instrument play exactly the same melody as he had just sung; he performed the whole *lai* for he wished to omit nothing"]; Mildred Pope, ed., *The Romance of Horn by Thomas,* 2 vols (Oxford: Blackwell, 1955 and 1964), 1:97, lines 2839–44. Outside the romances, one of the most important archetypes of the noble harper was, of course, King David, commonly to be identified in iconography by the harp that he bore.

[73] Another aspect of the timeliness of *Sir Orfeo* has been persuasively argued by Seth Lerer, "Artifice and Artistry in *Sir Orfeo,*" *Speculum* 60 (1985): 92–109; see pp. 98–101. He demonstrates how up-to-date the poem was in its references to the decorative and architectural arts of the period.

tary value beyond mere individual panacea into essential medication for a healthy body politic, is presented in such a way as to build another bridge between letters and life. The nature of this presentation may also have afforded the reader a second, more reliable, refuge.

Given the likely time and place of *Sir Orfeo*'s composition, its grand claim for harping could be regarded as indexed to the preeminent status to which a London harper at the turn of the century might aspire; equally, its claim necessarily implied a related esteem for the whole phenomenon of performative culture that harpers serviced. The elaborate Pentecost feast held by Edward I in London in 1306 in which harpers were egregious provides a convenient point of reference for their contemporary prestige and testifies to their central role in assisting Edward's objectification of a social harmony commensurate with his rule.[74] (After all, whatever else they were, feasts served as showcases of royal achievement.) In Edward's reign, however, harpers seem to have been especially favored among minstrels in the royal household where they were privy to the king himself, the prime mover of the political order.[75] Also—and the detail is noteworthy—when the queen was entertained with *miracula* ("miracle plays"?) at Lanercost Priory, Cumberland, in 1307, it was a harper, a certain James de Cowpen, who was one of their impresarios.[76]

This case aptly illustrates how harpers might be agents of contemporary performative culture in the most general sense; de Cowpen convened a performance that was not narrowly musical, though in it music had presumably a significant role to play. *Sir Orfeo* has been said to be about minstrelsy, and while this view is valid, it can be adjusted and deepened in two respects.[77] One is, of course, that *Sir Orfeo* is fundamen-

[74] See Constance Bullock-Davies, *Menestrellorum Multitudo: Minstrels at a Royal Feast* (Cardiff: University of Wales Press, 1978), pp. 27–28, for a statistical analysis of the composition of the minstrel classes.

[75] See ibid., pp. 10–11, for the role of the harper; also, John Southworth, *The Medieval English Minstrel* (Woodbridge, Suffolk: Boydell, 1989), pp. 87–100.

[76] He was also a King of Heralds; other references to him are catalogued (under Caupeny) in Constance Bullock-Davies, *Register of Royal and Baronial Domestic Minstrels, 1272–1327* (Woodbridge, Suffolk; and Dover, N.H.: Boydell, 1986), pp. 21–22. Cowpen is named as having performed the *miracula* with "Johanni de Cressy et aliis menestrallis"; the account of his payment is transcribed in Richard Rastall, "Minstrels and Minstrelsy in Household Account Books," in JoAnna Dutka, ed., *Records of Early English Drama: Proceedings of the First Colloquium* (Toronto: University of Toronto Press, 1979), pp. 3–25; see p. 7.

[77] Spearing, *Readings,* p. 79. *Sir Orfeo* is about minstrelsy in the wider sense that it is about *performance,* as will be explained further below.

tally and self-evidently about *harping.* It even implies its own performance to harp accompaniment,[78] whether in reality or as a fictional projection for its audience to imagine, and its royal hero is a harper.[79] Even if we choose to regard it as mere coincidence that harpers at this date appear to have been the most socially well positioned of all the minstrel classes in London (or, indeed, wherever the court assembled), the weight of their current status would still have borne unavoidably upon the contemporary reception of the poem. The value set on harping in *Sir Orfeo* should not be taken to imply that its author was himself a minstrel harper, but without question it illustrates how his poem happens for whatever reason to have collaborated staunchly with the professional interests of a particular minstrel caste that was culturally ascendant.[80] Whether the primary motive behind the poem was the furtherance of the harper's profession is unclear. That is not impossible—the poem patently subscribed to their professional mystique—but as already stated, another motive, less conspicuously self-interested, may have been at work: we need in addition to reckon with the broader and related issue of the socially performative power of secular vernacular poetry that the event of *Sir Orfeo* would have set free. However ephemeral the vernacular may have been, that ephemerality serving as one sort of refuge against apprehensions of existential chaos to which the text might have given rise, the sheer performativeness of the text in delivery, the text as an event, would have constituted a second, perhaps more reliable, refuge

[78] Bliss, *Sir Orfeo,* pp. 2–4, lines 1–24, and p. 50, lines 597–602.

[79] As Spearing, *Readings,* p. 79, has observed. (The tradition of harper-hero stories seems to have been characteristically British; see Christopher Page, The Owl and the Nightingale: *Musical Life and Ideas in France, 1100–1300* (London: Dent, 1989), pp. 229–30, n. 60.) The conflation of royalty with harping powerfully endorses the latter. But in addition, as the roles of king and performing harper-hero merge, so the actual performer of *Sir Orfeo* in reality (whether public reciter or private reader) could also through role assimilation have been brought into line with the fiction's value system: see further in the note following.

[80] Albert C. Baugh, "The Middle English Romance: Some Questions of Creation, Presentation, and Preservation," *Speculum* 42 (1967): 1–31; see pp. 9–14 for a good argument for minstrel "publication" of the original author's literary composition in the case of several romances. Wherever the reader (reading aloud, probably) was the "publisher," s/he might be conceived as acting in the minstrel's stead and hence to have embodied, by performative association, the value system fettled on minstrelsy. For a useful survey of medieval modes of "prelection" (a term borrowed from John of Salisbury to signify the reading of a text aloud to one or more listeners), see Coleman, *Public Reading.* Compare also Roger M. Walker, "Oral Delivery or Private Reading? A Contribution to the Debate on the Dissemination of Medieval Literature," *Forum for Modern Language Studies* 7 (1971): 36–42.

for the reader to shelter in. The performance of secular vernacular poetry evidently had an important, socially cohesive function to fulfil—this is implicit in the fact of its institutional tenacity—even if we are content to label that function somewhat superficially as "entertainment."

Before finally clarifying this question of *Sir Orfeo*'s performative value (and setting aside the question of any immediately self-interested motive on the part of its author), let us recall first the contemporary esteem in which harping was already widely held on account of its practical applications in real life, as a remedy for psychic distress, for example, and for supplying a range of social desiderata.[81] The narrative of *Sir Orfeo* does more than echo such esteem: it feeds it, incarnating it, as it were. The preexistent esteem for harping's salutary effects is given a local habitation and a name through the poem's narrative. And in a second, performative, stage, in the *event* in which the poem can alone exist, those effects are released back again into the society and historical reality of the reader. That is, the salutary effects imaged in the narrative take a tangible shape in the real world through performance. Early performances of *Sir Orfeo* could have taken various forms. They may have been in public, possibly in some circumstances to the sort of musical accompaniment to which the author seems to have been so alive, or in private—whatever, in fact, the full range of practical manifestations of "Romanz-reding on þe bok" could have been at that date.[82] Performance, then, as both narrated in the text and enacted in its reading, no matter what the exact modality of that reading, is the literary figure and literal actualization of contemporary esteem for harping. It is also the figure and actualization of the benefits that the performative culture served by harpers released into being: the performance of *Sir Orfeo* mimes palpably in the real world the salutary effects that are claimed for performance within the poem's narrative, and this is an important key to the second refuge from chaos prepared for the reader outside the text. This second, readerly refuge locates not in a discourse commonly encountered

[81] Evidence for therapeutic music in general is gathered in Madeleine P. Cosman, "Machaut's Medical Musical World," in Madeleine P. Cosman and Bruce Chandler, eds., *Machaut's World: Science and Art in the Fourteenth Century* (New York: New York Academy of Sciences, 1978), pp. 1–36.

[82] G. V. Smithers, ed., *Havelok* (Oxford: Clarendon Press, 1987), p. 64, line 2328. Coleman, *Public Reading*, pp. 84–85, summarizes the wide range of "prelectors," in addition to minstrels, to which sources witness. "Prelectors" included authors, priests, daughters of noblemen, and even the "wilde wymmen" mentioned in one of the Harley lyrics.

in verbal formulations, as were the (inadequate) discourses of Christianity, astrology, and even fairyland, but in an unverbalized, performative social practice, one especially characteristic of courtly culture at those moments when it sought to show itself off at its most optimistic and sanguine.[83] Performance, in such a society, makes a material difference to reality: it effects change. The moment of the reception of the poem would necessarily, after all, have been a tranquil, perhaps indeed convivial, one, a far remove from the upheavals catalogued in lines 387–404. The poem's performance hallowed the calm and ordered social moment in whose context alone its event could unfold and be received. Indeed, even the simplest imaginable context for the event of the poem—a private reading, unadorned with actual musical accompaniment—could have been understood as an enpowering enactment of socially therapeutic *musica* for this reason, that *musica,* in medieval terms, was thought to encompass *both* musical sounds *and* read or recited poetic words: because music and poetry share in common the measurement of sound in time, versification and musicianship were considered reciprocal.[84] Only performance, therefore, could close the circle, completing and actualizing for the reader through that performance a value system that the narrative had put in place as a refuge for its hero. So the benefits of performative culture were dealt in double measure in that their figure and agent, performance, was the point at which intra- and extratextual reality converged.

While self-evidently about harping, therefore, *Sir Orfeo* may also be said to have been about the socially transformative power of performance as opposed to that of a verbalized, "rational" discourse.[85] The event of the poem, even if experienced by its consumers no more strongly than as heart-warming entertainment, valorizes performance as a healing art, and in valorizing performance, *Sir Orfeo* has necessarily politicized it. Its

[83] And compare also Glending Olson, *Literature as Recreation in the Later Middle Ages* (Ithaca, N.Y.: Cornell University Press, 1982), who explicates the medieval medical theory that public reading was considered beneficial to the physical and mental health of listeners.

[84] See John Stevens, *Words and Music in the Middle Ages: Song, Narrative, Dance and Drama, 1050–1350* (Cambridge: Cambridge University Press, 1986), p. 377.

[85] Within the narrative, performance was both alluded to (performances of lays to the harp) and directly enacted (when Orfeo took out his harp and played, in private and in public). See respectively Bliss, *Sir Orfeo,* pp. 2–4, lines 1–24; pp. 24–25, lines 267–80; and pp. 37–38, lines 435–42.

political dimensions, in conclusion, are worth exploring, for they might be indicative of the cultural ambience in which the poem was fostered.

Any real-life performance of *Sir Orfeo* would have brought into being a shared performative community in which were implicated author, reciter, and audience (or author, book, and reader, if the medium of delivery consisted in private readership rather than in public presentation). Participants in this community inhabited an imaginative continuum where *musica* (in the medieval sense just defined), royalty, love and loyalty, sanity and civilization, could be synchronized as performable goods. The harmonious rapprochement of the intra- and extratextual performances of *Sir Orfeo,* therefore, builds another bridge between the world of fiction and contemporary reality, one all the more sturdy, paradoxical as it may seem, the more lighthearted was the context of the poem's actual social consumption. Whether or not the poem was primarily intended to further narrow professional interests, its performance would also have held a broader, holistic brief. Its performance would have put substance back into ceremony, proclaiming as a refuge for the reader the prospect of the self-presence of meaning within a social practice rather than within a verbalized discourse. *Sir Orfeo,* as Seth Lerer has pertinently noted, is a text full of (aristocratic and ceremonial) bright surfaces, especially its fairyland, which is presented as a kingdom of artifice "for the awe and delectation of the beholder."[86] But awe and delectation, the connoisseur's prerogatives, are finally empty unless, at the hands of the harper with his society-performing skill, they can be reunited with an undergirding morality that they ought, by rights, to predicate.[87] Similarly, the fairy king must be obliged to put content

[86] Lerer, "Artifice and Artistry," p. 93.

[87] So the text could be conceived as having attempted to salvage the self-presence of the sign, something it had earlier shown to be in peril, and therefore to stand relatively early in the tradition of late-medieval poets who demonstrated a central fear (as R. A. Shoaf, *Dante, Chaucer and the Currency of the Word: Money, Images, and Reference in Late Medieval Poetry* [Norman, Ok.: Pilgrim Books, 1983], p. 32, has argued), that the sign would become nonreferrential, a semiotic dead letter. The poem is touching in its reaffirmation of the possibility of self-presence in the face of the antithesis that it can be said to have invoked. *Sir Orfeo*'s community of performers has been given an object lesson in how it too might easily lose sight of moral substance. Robert W. Hanning, *The Individual in Twelfth-Century Romance* (New Haven, Conn.: Yale University Press, 1977), p. 108 and n. 4, has observed in certain romances the moral force of scenes that while having the veneer of a *locus amoenus,* nevertheless betray the application of the beauties of human craft as a disguise for latent danger. *Sir Orfeo* could be regarded as having connected with this topos, but if so, to have turned it to unique ends.

back into his words, honoring the substance that they signify: what he says, for the sake of the human and social happiness that is at stake, must not be allowed to become sundered from that to which it refers. So words can be mere glittering surfaces too, once they lose their purchase on reality.

The final testing of the steward, an episode that has caused some modern readers difficulty, can also be understood as the logical extension of this drive to marry *nomen* with *res*. Professed attitudes must be shown to connect with reality, and so the steward needs to be seen to mean what he has said. The test is a way of vesting his declared loyalty in flesh and blood; it makes loyalty really happen, at least as far as the world of the narrative is concerned. But the marriage of *nomen* and *res* is celebrated too in the real world of the reader when the performance of the poem is experienced as cordial entertainment. So the event of *Sir Orfeo* has articulated as a second refuge against chaos a politics of declarative performance in which moral substance has been reunited with the outward accidents of stately show,[88] and this is a reunion that it can only hope fully to enact by being performed itself.

In view of the performative power being claimed for it here, the event of *Sir Orfeo* would seem to fit well within that echelon of medieval society that we know from other historical evidence was habituated to moral pageantry and spectacle, where games of aristocratic display, as well as catering to awe and delectation, were contrived to advance messages thought conducive to the personal, and hence the communal, weal. Those games could also be contrived to play their messages into historical reality in a fashion approaching that argued here for *Sir Orfeo* on literary grounds.[89] Indeed, it may be surmised that the *miracula* staged by the harper-impresario James de Cowpen for Queen Margaret in 1307 served a similar double function in effecting delight and social consolidation, social changes even if in a minimal sense. Be that as it may, some performances provided a venue in which a more consequential political

[88] Logically, this argues sharp awareness in the poet of how empty systems of signification could sometimes be.

[89] No better examplar of such a culture is needed than the court of Edward I. The king's Arthurian theatricalizing of himself (and certain of his knights) as much for political, as for recreational, ends, at his wedding festivities on 10 September 1299 (Roger S. Loomis, "Edward I, Arthurian Enthusiast," *Speculum* 28 [1953]: 114–27; see especially pp. 118–19), is an excellent case in point.

consensus could be actualized, or sometimes in which a new or tendentious agenda could be smuggled in and normalized under a consensual, festive guise.[90]

This is the sort of performative culture to which *Sir Orfeo* can most appropriately be imagined as having belonged. An author so fluently conversant with current social practice as has been inferred here, someone so steeped in the (competing) discourses of his day,[91] and so deft at dressing them as subtexts within his poem, would necessarily have been culturally well connected and tutored. Hence his formation at least in some urban center, where a cosmopolitan pluralism might be expected to have prevailed, seems likely. This likelihood is consistent with the opinion that the poem's place of origin was London or the London region. Was the poem really a bourgeois product, as has usually been supposed? The question is worth posing again, for it has bearings on our understanding of the particular social level at which the interdependence between the social and the literary maintained here would have operated. Even were it possible to prove decisively that the Auchinleck manuscript was made for some wealthy, aspirant member of the middle classes, the circumstances of the poem's survival in such a context should not be permitted to foreclose this question of its ultimate origin.[92] But in any case, this view of the manuscript's auspices has recently been cast into doubt. Thorlac Turville-Petre has argued that, more probably, it was commissioned for some very rich secular household, perhaps one with historic crusading connections.[93] Such auspices would certainly

[90] Performances of the latter sort are well evidenced in Edward I's Arthurian games noted above. For further observations on the medieval practice of "imaginative activity which could transform received structures of value incrementally," see Franz H. Bäuml, "Varieties and Consequences of Medieval Literacy and Illiteracy," *Speculum* 55 (1980): 237–65; esp. pp. 256–59.

[91] At least the discourses of Christianity and fairyland, since these are explicit in the poem.

[92] This is the view of its origin held by Derek Pearsall, for example, in Derek Pearsall and I. C. Cunningham, *The Auchinleck Manuscript* (London: Scolar Press, 1979), p. viii.

[93] For a persuasive attempt to read the tastes to which the Auchinleck anthology has catered, see Thorlac Turville-Petre, *England the Nation: Language, Literature, and National Identity, 1290–1340* (Oxford: Clarendon Press, 1996), pp. 108–41; especially pp. 136–38. Further objections to the view of the bourgeois production of Auchinleck may be found in P. R. Coss, "Aspects of Cultural Diffusion in Medieval England," *Past and Present* 108 (1985): 35–79; see esp. pp. 40–41. Mercantile literary taste seems, if anything, to have out-Frenched the aristocracy in London at this date; see Anne F. Sutton, "Merchants, Music and Social Harmony: the London Puy and its French and London Contexts, circa 1300," *London Journal* 17 (1992): 1–17. *Sir Orfeo* squares uneasily with the

better agree with the poet's cultural literacy implied in this study, for such literacy feeds upon as much as it nurtures a mutual sophistication in its implied audience. In these circumstances, it seems to me that what Turville-Petre's research on historical grounds could be pressed into suggesting deserves also to be suggested on literary grounds, namely, that the original cultural epicenter of *Sir Orfeo* was, if not the court, then somewhere within the court's striking distance. Such a milieu, incidentally, would also help justify the present consideration of astrology as a possible component in the contemporary reader's formation, because astrological interests are evidenced at court from at least as early as the reign of Henry II.[94] And lest we cavil at the necessary corollary of this suggestion—the prospect of an aristocrat at this date enjoying literature in English, rather than French—a passing remark in another Auchinleck romance, *Of Arthour and of Merlin,* deserves to be accorded full counterbalancing weight. Its narrator declared: "Mani noble ich haue yseiȝe / þat no Freynsche couþe seye."[95] And for that reason the narrator of *Of Arthour and of Merlin* felt justified in telling his tale in English.

It is to be hoped that these comments will have complicated the understanding of the particular socioliterary dimensions that the event of *Sir Orfeo* took. Once its existence is reconceived as an event, the poem registers a degree of interactivity between the social and the literary that has seldom been conceded to it. In two different ways, then, the poem facilitated a flight from the enchanters that it had called into being. Its hero discovered one sort of refuge and its readers another. If Chaucer ever read the Auchinleck romances, as some have persuasively argued,[96]

---

literary activity of the mercantile London *puy,* as far as this can be gauged. The *puy* was modeled on a French institution and heavily indebted to French precedents in the way it was run and organized.

[94] See Hilary M. Carey, "Astrology at the English Court in the Later Middle Ages," in Patrick Curry, ed., *Astrology, Science and Society: Historical Essays* (Woodbridge, Suffolk; and Wolfeboro, N.H.: Boydell Press, 1987), pp. 41–56; esp. p. 41 and n. 1.

[95] O. D. Macrae-Gibson, ed., *Of Arthour and of Merlin,* Early English Text Society, o. s. 268 and 279 (Oxford: Oxford University Press, 1973–79), 1:5, lines 25–26. Even were this more a polemical than a neutral observation, it would amount to the same thing: it asserts that English is worthy of the aristocracy. And as Turville-Petre, *England the Nation,* p. 138, has observed, "It was all right to read romances in English" at that social level at that date. Note too a potential sympathy for English vernacular culture implicit in the anti-French claim of Edward I in 1295 that the French were plotting to wipe out the English language; see Michael Prestwich, *English Politics in the Thirteenth Century* (Basingstoke and London: Macmillan Education, 1990), p. 90.

[96] Three articles were contributed by Laura Hibbard Loomis: "Chaucer and the Auchinleck MS: 'Thopas' and 'Guy of Warwick,'" in *Essays and Studies in Honor of Carleton Brown* (New York: New York University Press; London: Oxford University Press, 1940),

then he would have found in *Sir Orfeo* not only a prompt-book for certain of his own motifs and ideas but also one in which his particular predilection for competing discourses had been anticipated, and perhaps anticipated by someone who, like himself, had moved within courtly precincts.[97]

---

pp. 111–28; "Chaucer and the Breton Lays of the Auchinleck Manuscript," *SP* 38 (1941): 14–33; and "The Auchinleck Manuscript and a Possible London Bookshop of 1330–1340," *PMLA* 57 (1942): 595–627. More recently, the case has been plausibly argued by Robert Cook, "Chaucer's Franklin's Tale and *Sir Orfeo*," *Neuphilologische Mitteilungen* 95 (1994): 333–36.

[97] I am indebted to the two anonymous readers of this article for their helpful criticism and comments.

St. Erkenwald and the Merciless Parliament

Frank Grady
University of Missouri–St. Louis

Critics have typically regarded the Middle English alliterative poem *St. Erkenwald* as an original and idiosyncratic vernacular contribution to the fourteenth-century theological debate about virtuous pagans. The poem is generally recognized as having been written somewhere in the long shadow cast by *Piers Plowman,* offering either a conservative corrective to Langland's unique and antisacramental account of the salvation of the pagan emperor Trajan, or further confirmation that Langland's liberalism on the matter of the righteous heathen represented the dominant trend in vernacular theological writing about the topic.[1] As such, the poem represents merely the latest version of the Gregory/Trajan legend, a story "notable for its flexible adaptability to the evolving patterns of medieval thought and culture" over the course of its 600-year circulation.[2] Gordon Whatley has described how various redactors revised this tale to serve disparate literary and philosophical ends, whether hagiographical, humanistic, scholastic, or "eclectic" (e.g., Lang-

I'm grateful to John Bowers, Elizabeth Fowler, E. Terrence Jones, and Jim Landman for essential intellectual and material support; I hope Jim Rhodes will not object to being identified as this essay's godfather.

[1] The essential survey of these opinions and the strongest statement of the conservative view is Gordon Whatley, "Heathens and Saints: *St. Erkenwald* in Its Legendary Context," *Speculum* 61 (1986): 330–63; for a response, see my "*Piers Plowman, St. Erkenwald,* and the Rule of Exceptional Salvations," *Yearbook of Langland Studies* 6 (1992): 63–88. Also germane are Whatley's "The Middle English *St. Erkenwald* in Its Liturgical Context," *Mediaevalia* 8 (1982): 277–306, and, for a survey of the versions of the Trajan legend that underlies the story of St. Erkenwald, his "The Uses of Hagiography: The Legend of Pope Gregory and the Emperor Trajan in the Middle Ages," *Viator* 15 (1984): 25–63.

[2] Whatley, "Uses of Hagiography," p. 26.

land and Wyclif).[3] In this essay I will argue that the legend's adaptability was exploited for specifically political ends as well, and that the theological interests of *St. Erkenwald* can be seen as part of a larger pattern of allusion and reference to contemporary texts and events. That is, I intend to expand the "textual environment" of *St. Erkenwald*[4] to include texts and documents concerned with the state of the law at the end of the 1380s—especially during and after the Merciless Parliament of 1388—and the relationship between the law and the royal prerogative. Viewing *St. Erkenwald* in the context of the events of 1388—perhaps "aftermath" would be a better word—renders several of the poem's peculiar and charming details newly intelligible, and also provides for the text a firmer place in the rapidly evolving literary and social history of Middle English alliterative poetry. Ultimately, I will argue, this recontextualizing of the poem demonstrates how it functions as a provincial but royalist response to the perceived aristocratic excesses of 1388 by offering an idealizing version of a London community in which popular sentiment, episcopal understanding, and royal-cum-divine will conform completely in their admiration for uncorrupted justice, and the uncorrupted judge who embodies it. In the end, the poem's account of the theological issue at stake in the question of the salvation of pagans makes an argument by analogy about royal power, pointing suggestively to an alignment of Ricardian authority with the divine *potentia* that authorizes exceptional salvations.[5] Miracles, it turns out, are sometimes politics by other means.

In arguing for a royalist *Erkenwald,* I am of course following the lead of Michael Bennett and John Bowers, who have recently described the ways in which the poetry of the Northwest Midlands—of greater Cheshire, as it were—might have benefited from a kind of indirect royal

[3] Ibid., pp. 26–27.

[4] I owe the phrase to Paul Strohm, who defines the concept in "The Textual Environment of Chaucer's 'Lak of Stedfastnesse,'" in his *Hochon's Arrow: The Social Imagination of Fourteenth-Century Texts* (Princeton, N.J.: Princeton University Press, 1992), p. 58. In fact, the environment Strohm describes for Chaucer's poem and the one offered here for *St. Erkenwald* are, if not identical, at least overlapping, though his interest in "a new syntax of personal relations" and forms of association, and various ideological responses to them, is broader than mine is here.

[5] Thus I depart from the conclusions drawn by Ruth Nissé in a fine recent essay on the poem's political context; in "'A Coroun Ful Riche': The Rule of History in *St. Erkenwald,*" *ELH* 65 (1998): 277–95, Shklar argues that the poem addresses "the ever-problematic relations between regal government and custom" and responds skeptically to Richard's absolutist excesses in the 1390s.

patronage stemming from Richard's increasing attention to the province over the last dozen years of his reign.[6] Bowers, in fact, argues that the author of *Pearl* was "steadily and specifically royalist, revealing a concern for the precise practice of kingship by his obsessive recourse to regalian themes and images."[7] The *Erkenwald*-poet, as I shall show, also takes up issues of regality, though unlike *Pearl* his poem mixes theological concerns with legal ones. In fact, *St. Erkenwald* offers a literary perspective on three volatile contemporary legal issues, each of which involved the monarch and each of which was the subject of particularly intense contention during and after the Merciless Parliament.

The first of these issues that I shall discuss is maintenance, and the general range of aristocratic intimidation and manipulation of the law that goes along with it, including the feeing and retaining of justices and the distribution of badges and liveries—wholesale distribution, according to the complaints. The second topic, and one that neatly captures the poem's attempt to mediate between secular and spiritual priorities, is sanctuary, a right honored more in the murderous breach than in the observance in the last quarter of the century. Finally, there is the complex issue of precedent, a topic always at issue in theological rationalizations of exceptional salvations and an acute concern in the Parliament, since clearly many of the actions taken by the lords appellant against Richard's partisans in 1388 were procedurally extralegal and legally unprecedented.

I

The representation of a righteous judge in a late-fourteenth-century text is itself something of a miracle, as other critics have noted, but in fact

[6] See Michael J. Bennett, "The Court of Richard II and the Promotion of Literature," in Barbara Hanawalt, ed., *Chaucer's England* (Minneapolis: University of Minnesota Press, 1992), pp. 3–20, and John Bowers, "*Pearl* in Its Royal Setting: Ricardian Poetry Revisited," *SAC* 17 (1995): 111–55. As Bowers notes (p. 115), Richard's large-scale Cheshire retaining was a phenomenon of the 1390s, though he had also done some recruiting during his self-imposed rustication in 1387. For the difficulties with this notion of Ricardian patronage, see Nigel Saul, *Richard II* (New Haven, Conn.: Yale University Press, 1997), pp. 360–64.

[7] Bowers, ibid., p. 113. Bowers confesses agnosticism about the *Pearl*-MS authorship question, though he does claim that *Erkenwald* shares the "political interests" of the other poems (p. 118). I agree, though I also think that the *Erkenwald*-poet was not the author of any of the others. On the controversy, see Larry D. Benson, "The Authorship of *St. Erkenwald*," *JEGP* 64 (1965): 393–405.

the *Erkenwald*-poet's estimate of what makes a judge righteous betrays anxieties slightly but significantly different from those traditionally expressed in contemporary moral writing and estates satire. Like Chaucer's portait of the Parson, in which are legible the malign traits of his evil twin who runs off to London to seek chantry work, the *Erkenwald*-poet's portrait of the virtuous judge implies the existence of its opposite and reveals to us the nature of those things that tend to corrupt justice. In the judge's own words,

> þe folke was felonse and fals and frowarde to reule,
> I hent harmes ful ofte to hold hom to riȝt.
> Bot for wothe ne wele ne wrathe ne drede
> Ne for maistrie ne for mede ne for no monnes aghe,
> I remewit neuer fro þe riȝt by reson myn awen
> For to dresse a wrange dome, no day of my lyue.
> Declynet neuer my consciens for couetise on erthe,
> In no gynful iugement no iapes to make
> Were a renke neuer so riche for reuerens sake.
> Ne for no monnes manas ne meschefe ne routhe
> Non gete me fro þe heghe gate to glent out of ryȝt,
> Als ferforthe as my faithe confourmyd my hert.
> þaghe had been my fader bone, I bede hym no wranges,
> Ne fals favour to my fader, þaghe felle hym be hongyt. (lines 231–44)[8]

The righteous judge is distinguished not only by his resistance to bribery and avarice but also by his indifference to aristocratic pressure, to the *manas* and *maistrie* of those who would try to influence or overawe the conscience of the justice, and of justice itself. Here the author of *St. Erkenwald* distinguishes himself from most of his contemporaries, who customarily point only to the venality and *covetise* of lawyers and judges in their satiric accounts of the subject.[9] In the ambiguous discretion of Chaucer's Man of Law, who often served as a justice of the assize; in

[8] All quotations from the poem are drawn from Clifford Peterson's edition of *St. Erkenwald* (Philadelphia: University of Pennsylvania Press, 1977), here pp. 78–79. Further citations will be made by line number in the text.

[9] The treatment of lawyers and justices in the estates satire tradition is discussed by Jill Mann, *Chaucer and Medieval Estates Satire* (Cambridge: Cambridge University Press, 1973), pp. 86–91, and by John A. Yunck, *The Lineage of Lady Meed: The Development of Mediaeval Venality Satire* (Notre Dame: University of Notre Dame Press, 1963), pp. 143–59. Mann remarks that "the tradition for lawyers is full but remarkably unified" (p. 86). Compare, e.g., Langland and Gower on the avarice of sergeants: "Thow myȝtest bettre

Gower's *Vox Clamantis* and *Mirour de l'Omme,* where "gold defies right and advances wrong";[10] in *Piers Plowman,* where Lady Meed winks and the lawyers come running to her side—everywhere what is decried is the corrosive influence of money on justice, the law, and the lawyers and judges responsible for its adminstration and application. The malignant effects are described in the conventional terms by Thomas Wimbledon in his famous 1388 sermon:

> ȝif a gret man plete wiþ a pore to haue owt þat he holdeþ, euerich officer schal be redy, al þat he may, and hiȝe þat þe riche man myȝt haue suche an ende as he desireþ. But ȝif a pore man plede wiþ a riche man, þan þer schal be so many delayes þat, þouȝ þe pore mannes riȝt be open to al þe comite, for pure faute of spendyng he shal be glad to cese.[11]

But while one can't deny that money and *maistrie* are related influences, they are not exactly the same thing.[12] In fact, if we turn from

---

meete myst on Maluerne hilles / Than gete a mom of hire mouþ til moneie be shewed" (*Piers Plowman,* ed. George Kane and E. Talbot Donaldson [London: Athlone, 1975], B.Prol.215–16); "Sergeants-at-law are deaf and dumb until they have received the gold which is pressed into their hands" ["Sergantz du loy sont sourd et mu / Avant que l'orr eiont resçu / Que l'en leur baille prest au main"] (*Mirour de l'Omme* 24,421–23, in *The Complete Works of John Gower,* ed. G. C. Macaulay [Oxford: Clarendon Press, 1899], 1:270; *Mirour de l'Omme,* trans. William Burton Wilson, rev. Nancy Wilson Van Bank [East Lansing, Mich.: Colleagues Press, 1992], p. 320.)

[10] "l'orr deffie / Le droit et met le tort avant"(*Mirour* 6227–28; Wilson trans., p. 87).

[11] Ione Kemp Knight, ed., *Wimbledon's Sermon "Redde Rationem Villicationis Tue": A Middle English Sermon of the Fourteenth Century,* Duquesne Studies, Philological Series 9 (Pittsburgh: Duquesne University Press, 1967), pp. 83–84.

[12] Though B. J. Whiting offers a relevant proverb—"lawe lieth muche in lordship"—he actually gets it from *Mum and the Sothsegger,* a poem composed later than *St. Erkenwald* and one clearly influenced by the increasing attention given in the last quarter of the century to legal leverage based on power rather than simply on wealth; *Proverbs, Sentences, and Proverbial Phrases from English Writings Mainly before 1500* (Cambridge, Mass.: Harvard University Press, 1968), L102, p. 321.

Before the Commons took up the issue in the 1380s (roughly speaking), complaints about how "might makes right" and thus perverts justice appeared in marginal texts like the 1381 letter of Jack Mylner preserved in *Knighton's Chronicle:* "if myȝt go before ryght, and wylle before skylle, þan is our mylne mys a dyȝt." See Henry Knighton, *Knighton's Chronicle, 1337–1396,* ed. and trans. G. H. Martin (Oxford: Clarendon Press, 1995), p. 222, where the letter of Jack Trewman offers the more conventional complaint: "No man may come trewþe to, but he syng si dedero. Speke spende and spede." Gower does refer briefly in the *Vox clamantis* to the overweening influence of *potentes* and *litera magnatis* on justices; see 6.271–78 (Macaulay ed., 4.237). The *Vox* was probably completed sometime soon after the 1381 uprising.

A poem from the reign of Edward II, preserved in the Auchinleck MS ("On the King's Breaking His Confirmation of Magna Charta"), makes a general observation in this vein:

poetic to parliamentary texts, we find a considerable body of literature devoted to making a conceptual separation between the corruption of justice caused by the power of money and that due to the power of influence, or rather, the influence of powerful persons. Such complaints are not entirely new in this era, and can easily be found in the reign of Edward I; but the early years of Edward III, when the king was often abroad, brought a special urgency to the issue.[13] So, for example, a Commons petition of 1340 called for the punishment of royal ministers and justices who took bribes, while six years later an ordinance promulgated by the king and his council before Edward left for his French campaign forbade the feeing and retaining of justices, demanding that they ignore "any writs and mandates from the king or others which might lead them to fail 'to do law and right'" and that they immediately report any such attempts to influence their decisions.[14]

In Richard's reign the petitions become more regular and more vehement, and complaints about the corruption of justice become linked with specific polemics against the related abuses of maintenance—essentially the partisan participation in lawsuits of individuals with no immediate interest in the case beyond some sort of sworn loyalty to one of the principals[15]—and the distribution of liveries and badges. The practice of widespread and indiscriminate retaining under the badge of the White Hart was to be one of the major complaints against Richard

"For miht is riht, the lond is laweless"; see T. Wright, *The Political Songs of England,* Camden Society 6 (London, 1839), p. 254. See also *Mandeville's Travels,* ed. M. C. Seymour (Oxford: Clarendon Press, 1967), p. 207.

[13] J. R. Maddicott, "Law and Lordship: Royal Justices as Retainers in Thirteenth- and Fourteenth-Century England," *Past and Present Supplement* 4 (1978): 14. See also Nigel Saul, "The Commons and the Abolition of Badges," *Parliamentary History* 9 (1990): 305.

[14] Maddicott, "Law and Lordship," pp. 40–43. The statute also provided for a salary increase, following the recommendations of 1340, though it was evidently not enough to secure freedom from corruption: in fact, in 1350 William Thorp, chief justice of the King's Bench, was prosecuted under the 1346 ordinance and, after his confession, was stripped of everything and sent to the Tower. However, though the statute was widely publicized, it was also largely ignored; even Thorp was released and restored to favor by March 1351. The 1346 statute was suspended in 1385 and declared null and void the next year during the Wonderful Parliament, one of the first successful attempts of the magnates to legislate their own influence during Richard's reign. See Maddicott, ibid., pp. 47–51, 66.

[15] For a modern definition of maintenance, see John A. Alford, Piers Plowman: *A Glossary of Legal Diction,* Piers Plowman Studies 5 (Woodbridge, Suffolk: D. S. Brewer, 1988), pp. 95–96. For a contemporary definition, see the one offered by the Commons in September 1388, printed in *The Westminster Chronicle, 1381–1394,* ed. and trans. L. C. Hector and Barbara F. Harvey (Oxford: Clarendon Press, 1982), pp. 359–59.

in the 1390s; the author of *Richard the Redeless* considered it one of his most egregious sins. But the first petition against retaining men for the purpose of maintaining quarrels appeared in 1377.[16] In 1380 and 1382 the Commons complained about the overly cozy relationship between justices and local lords in commissions of *oyer and terminer* and in the assize courts,[17] and in November 1384 it

> complained bitterly about the tyranny of certain locally powerful persons who, furnished with badges (taking various forms of embellishment) by lords of the realm and sheltered by their favour, and having in natural consequence an exaggerated conceit of themselves, unjustly oppressed and dismayed the poor and helpless of their neighborhoods, trying to overthrow laws passed and published for the common weal of the realm, and, in full reliance on their own smartness and the friendship of their lords, refusing to allow those laws to hold to their straight course.[18]

Here, the demand from the Commons for a statutory remedy was stonewalled by John of Gaunt, who found the accusations too vague and declared that "every lord was competent and well able to correct and punish his own dependants for such outrages,"[19] further boasting that were he to discover one of his retainers to be guilty of such offenses, he would bring such punishment "as would strike into the hearts of the rest a terror of committing similar misdeeds."[20] The Commons, evidently unimpressed by the deterrent powers of Gaunt's temper but very practically "hearing this as a statement that no remedy was going to be provided in this matter, were reduced to silence."[21]

Though the representatives in the Commons were individually un-

[16] Saul, "Abolition of Badges," p. 305.

[17] Maddicott, "Law and Lordship," p. 65; Alan Harding, "The Revolt against the Justices," in R. H. Hilton and T. H. Aston, eds., *The English Rising of 1381* (Cambridge: Cambridge University Press, 1984), p. 170.

[18] *West. Chron.*, pp. 81–83: "[isti] . . . graviter sunt conquesti super potentes homines in partibus dominantes, scilicet quomodo per dominos regni signis quasi ornamentis diversis prediti ac eorundem favore protecti et profecto ex hoc nimis elati pauperes et inopes in patria minus juste opprimunt ac confundunt legesque pro communi utilitate regni editas ac eciam promulgatas conantur evertere, ipsorum eciam subtilitatibus ac amicicia dominorum freti non permittunt eas suam rectitudinem tenere. . . ."

[19] *West. Chron.*, pp. 82–83: "quilibet dominus satis sufficiens est et potens suos ad se pertinentes pro talibus excessibus corrigere et punire."

[20] Ibid.: "[penam] quod ceteris at committenda similia timorem incuciet."

[21] Ibid: "hec audientes—quod nullum foret in hujusmodi datum remedium—tacuerunt."

likely to be entirely innocent of involvement in magnate retinues[22]—to be wearing the badge or the collar, as the case may be—they continued as a body to press the issue. Even in 1388, amid the tumult of the Merciless Parliament (itself, as we shall see, a masterpiece of maintenance), they offered a petition for relief from "the three or four within each county who are known as Second Kings" and "meistymours de querelles."[23] In the Cambridge Parliament of that year they tried again, calling for the abolition of all liveries and badges, the king's as well as the magnates'[24]—a move brilliantly exploited against the appellants by Richard, who said that he'd give up his if the lords would give up theirs. This offer "gave the utmost satisfaction to the commons," according to *The Westminster Chronicle;*[25] the lords, of course, demurred ("after launching a great deal of abuse and vituperation at the commons"[26]), and the issue was tabled for the time being, with Richard having gained an important victory in his post–Merciless Parliament public-relations campaign.[27]

By the first decade of the fifteenth century—in *Richard the Redeless* and a few years later in *Mum and the Sothsegger*—literary satires about the law regularly connect lawyerly venality with the abuses of maintenance and livery. *St. Erkenwald* stands at the very beginning of this trend, and although it displaces its remarks about aristocratic *maistrie* onto the litigious inhabitants of pre-Christian Troynovaunt, it also makes its virtuous judge particularly recognizable in fourteenth-century terms.

[22] Saul, "Abolition of Badges," pp. 304–5, 310–11.

[23] *Knighton's Chronicle,* pp. 444–45; "par .iij. oue par .iiij. en chescune conte appelez seconde royez" (p. 444). Knighton is the only chronicler to preserve this document, which he associates with the Merciless Parliament. It is undated, and Martin thinks it "a vivid reflection of popular discontent with the Appellants' conduct in the summer of 1388" (p. 442 n. 2).

[24] *West. Chron.,* pp. 356–57. Interestingly, the petition claims that the practice of distributing badges originated "puis le primer an del noble roy Edward tierce"—one more reminder of how the memory of 1327 lurked in the shadows throughout the events of 1388.

[25] Ibid.: "quod summe placuit communitati predicte."

[26] Ibid.: "set domini post multa convicia et verba probrosa illis de communitate prolata noluerunt consentire ad id quod eorum aviditas flagitabat."

[27] For Richard's rapprochement in the wake of his defeat, see below, and Strohm, "Textual Environment," pp. 63–65; Anthony Tuck, *Richard II and the English Nobility* (New York: St. Martin's Press, 1974), pp. 135–37; and R. L. Storey, "Liveries and Commissions of the Peace, 1388–90," in F. R. H. DuBoulay and Caroline M. Barron, eds., *The Reign of Richard II: Essays in Honour of May McKisack* (London: Archon, 1971), pp. 131–52.

Though the seventh-century Londoners who discover the miraculously preserved corpse mistake him for a king, because of the richness of his miraculously preserved clothes, he himself explains that his furred mantle of camelyn and golden girdle (along with his crown and scepter) were meant to celebrate his judicial achievements (lines 245–52):

> And for I was ryȝtwis and reken and redy of þe laghe
> Quen I deghed for dul denyed alle Troye.
> Alle menyd my dethe, þe more and þe lasse
> And þus to bounty my body þai buriet in golde,
> Cladden me for the curtest þat courte couthe þen holde,
> In mantel for þe mekest and monlokest on benche,
> Gurden me for þe gouernour and graythist of Troie,
> Furrid me for þe fynest of faithe me wytinne.

Conspicuous by its absence in these lines is the word "robed," a synonym for "cladden," "gurden," and "furrid" that would have made the judge instantly recognizable in fourteenth-century terms, since robes usually constituted part of the remuneration offered to a justice retained by the king (or a magnate, or a wealthy monastic establishment).[28] And the judge does essentially identify himself as a royal justice in contemporary diction: "I was of heire and of oyer in þe New Troie / In þe regne of the riche kynge þat rewlit vs þen, / the bolde Breton Ser Belyn" (lines

[28] Robes were a specific target of the 1346 ordinance (Maddicott, "Law and Lordship," p. 27); on their distribution (and their cash value), see E. W. Ives, *The Common Lawyers of Pre-Reformation England* (Cambridge: Cambridge University Press, 1983), pp. 305–6. For a contemporary record of the practice involving the Black Prince and Sir William Shareshull (at that time chief justice of the King's Bench), see *The Register of the Black Prince,* 4 vols. (London: Stationery Office, 1930–33), 4:229. I owe this reference to Carter Revard. The Register is an excellent source for episodes of this sort of transaction at midcentury, containing many instances of the Black Prince's retaining or rewarding justices and serjeants, e.g., 1:61, 135, 156; 2:268, 406; 4:168–69, 228, 264 (a grant of 20 marks yearly to Robert Thorp, king's justice, who is "retained to be one of the prince's council, and the prince wishes to give him a yearly reward for the labour and diligence which he must expend on the prince's business whenever a question of law arises"), 321.

The judge's robe is described as being "wyt menyuer furrit" (line 81). Langland depicts Covetise as accepting a "meneuer mantel" after his assault on Conscience and the "wit and wisdom of westmynstre hall" at B.20.129–39. In the 1460s, Sir John Fortescue would describe how a justice's robe "is edged with no other fur than minever, whereas the serjeant's is always furred with white lamb"; see Shelley Lockwood, ed. and trans., *On the Laws and Governance of England* (Cambridge: Cambridge University Press, 1997), p. 74.

211–13).[29] But what makes the judge unusual *qua* judge, in fact, is that his richly furred and embellished robe carries with it no satiric charge: rather than identifying him as an adherent of any one king or lord, his clothes show that he has earned the unusual (and in fourteenth-century terms, entirely fictional) distinction of having been literally robed and metaphorically retained by all the citizens of New Troy. Indeed, part of his popular appeal rests on his resistance to "monnes aghe" and "monnes manas," and the conceit of the poem is that such righteous dedication to the "laghe" has earned him not just popular but also divine sanction: "þe riche kynge of reson þat riȝt euer alowes / And loues al þe lawes lely þat longen to trouthe. . . . / He has lant me to last þat euer loues ryȝt best" (lines 267–68, 272).[30] The nameless judge participates (posthumously) in a characteristic fourteenth-century practice, but that practice—usually decried—is here purified rather than parodied. This passage is also the poem's first suggestion that a justice's two loyalties—to the law and to his king—are closely aligned, an implication to which I will return.

In fact, this connection of justice, judge, and king—adumbrated in the poem's initial error, when the city folk mistake the judge for a king—indicates again the way in which *St. Erkenwald* is particularly alive to contemporary debates and anxieties about the law. That is, we can say that the poem's Londoners make a very meaningful mistake when they first discover the body, if we acknowledge the resemblance between the misidentification of king and judge, on the one hand, and on the other, the identification of royal policy and true justice that is implied, for example, in Richard's actions at the Cambridge Parliament. For two years after the Merciless Parliament, Richard's efforts to restore his prestige and recoup the political power lost to the appellants were founded on an attempt to represent himself as the true patron of the law and the champion of justice for all. This was a savvy move overall, the

[29] Peterson sensibly amends MS line 211 ("an heire of anoye") to "of heire and of oyer," arguing that the poet means to indicate the judge's "having two posts and magnified competence"—that is, his having participated in both itinerant courts of eyre and the royal commissions of *oyer et terminer* that eventually replaced them in the latter half of the fourteenth century. See his note on pp. 106–7; and for the commissions of *oyer et terminer,* see Harding, "Revolt against the Justices," pp. 170–73, and Richard W. Kaeuper, "Law and Order in Fourteenth-Century England: The Evidence of Special Commissions of Oyer and Terminer," *Speculum* 54 (1979): 734–84.

[30] On the double sense of "alowes" in this sort of context—"commend" and "reward (with divine grace)"—see Whatley, "*Piers Plowman* B 12.277–94: Notes on Language, Text and Theology," *MP* 82 (1984): 1–12, esp. pp. 2–5.

medieval equivalent of modern poll-driven politics, since the one thing that the appellants could not plausibly lay claim to after the self-interested excesses of 1388 was respect for the law.

To discuss the poem's linking of regality and justice in this way is not, however, to make of *St. Erkenwald* simply an allegory of the events of its time. The poet, whenever he writes the phrase "riche kynge," is not making an inverted allusion to King Richard. But he is, I would argue, constantly drawing on contemporary thinking about the potential alignment (or elision) of royal will and royal justice. The same is true, as I shall argue at the end of this essay, of the poem's sacralization of the relationship between the king and the judge who serves him, its substitution of heavenly reward for the fees and robes of earthly remuneration.

Besides, there may be a more immediate allusion in the poem to contemporary events, and a more compelling connection between the poem and the Merciless Parliament. That body's treatment of Sir Robert Tresilian, chief justice of the King's Bench, mirrors provocatively the fate of the judge in the poem. Considered by the lords appellant to be one of the major malefactors in Richard's circle, Tresilian went into hiding, was condemned in absentia by the Parliament, and was then discovered nearby during the trial of Nicholas Brembre, the former mayor of London and another of Richard's adherents. *The Westminster Chronicle* tells us:

> But at this point the unexpected news arrived that Robert Tresilian was in the sanctuary of Westminster; and the lords speedily dropped everything else for the moment to hurry there, accompanied by a densely packed crowd: taking a mace, the duke of Gloucester forthwith arrested Robert Tresilian and shielded him from those who were making savage efforts to set upon him. . . . This, then, was the manner of Robert Tresilian's arrest on 19 February by the above-named lords, in whose fell clutches he was forcibly dragged from the sanctuary and taken to the Wool House outside. They were at pains to ask him whether the sanctuary of St. Peter, Westminster, gave immunity to a traitor against the king and the realm: he answered steadily that it did, since it was for such offenders in particular that the privilege had been conferred upon the church of Westminster. Supposing him to have made this assertion in order to save himself, the lords put no faith in what he said, but at once haled him away to face the whole parliament and to have recited to him how he had been three times called by proclamation and, because he did not appear, condemned by judgement of the parliament to be drawn and hanged as a traitor. His answer to this

was that the proceedings against him were founded in error and had no force and should accordingly be quashed; and this he wished to prove in accordance with his rights. But he was met by the swift retort that the action or judgement of the parliament was irrevocable, since it was by due process that it had pronounced against him as it had. Sentence was quickly passed on him, namely to be drawn and hanged, and he was at once hustled off to the Tower of London. On the same day he was drawn on a hurdle from the Tower through the city to the gallows at Tyburn and hanged out of hand; but no fear or shame or dread of death altered his refusal to admit that he had ever been a traitor.[31]

Evidently there was more than one story circulating at this time about a royal justice unexpectedly discovered in a venerable London church; and reading the story of *St. Erkenwald*'s pagan judge who was unearthed in St. Paul's in light of the story of Sir Robert Tresilian being found lurking in Westminster gives new resonance to some of the distinguish-

[31] *West. Chron.*, pp. 310–13: "Set tunc ex insperato innotuit illis quomodo Robertus Tresilyan erat in sanctuario Westm': mox predicti domini ceteris omissis pro tempore ad dictum sanctuarium cum multitudine glomerosa celeriter adierunt; at dux Glouc' accepta clava protinus dictum Robertum Tresilyan arrestavit et ipsum defendebat ab hiis qui in eum irruere crudeliter satagebant. . . . Sicque xix. die arestatum Robertum Tresilyan dicti domini de sanctaurio predicto violenter funestis manibus abstraxerunt et in domum lanarum extra sanctuarium adduxerunt, interrogantes eum sollicite an sanctuarium ecclesie Sancti Petri Westmon' regis et regni proditorem salvaret; quibus constanter dixit quod salvaret talem quia pro hujusmodi criminosis potissime fuit illa libertas ecclesie predicte concessa. Qui putantes ipsum in sui ipsius salvacionem hoc asseruisse ideo fidem suis dictis nequaquam dederunt set abhinc coram toto parliamento ipsum protinus perduxerunt, ubi fuit sibi recitatum quomodo fuerat trina proclamacione vocatus et quia non venit judicio parliamenti erat adjudicatus tanquam proditor trahi et suspendi. Quibus ipse dixit quod processus contra eum habitus erat erroneus et invalidus et per consequens annullandus; et hoc per jura sua vellet probare. Set confestim fuit contra eum replicatum quod factum sive judicium parliamenti manet irrevocabile quia per debitum processum fuit taliter contra eum pronunciatum. Unde confestim data sentencia super eum, scilicet trahi et suspendi, ilico ipsum rapuerunt ad Turrim London' et eodem die a Turri eadem per medium civitas usque Tybourne ad furcas super cratem erat tractus et indilate suspensus; qui nullo metu sive pudore seu mortis timore voluit fateri ipsum umquam proditorem fuisse."

Versions of this story are preserved in several places, even in Froissart (whose version is the most fanciful). Neither *Knighton's Chronicle* (pp. 498–99) nor the unique account (in more ways than one) of Thomas Favent (*Historia siue narracio et forma mirabilis Parliamenti . . .*, ed. May McKisack, *Camden Miscellany* 14 [London: Offices of the Royal Historical Society, 1926]) mentions any violation of sanctuary (more on which below), though each remarks that Tresilian was bearded and disguised in shabby clothes, the medieval equivalent of a fake nose and glasses. That the story was fairly widely circulated can be seen from a reference in the register of Henry Wakefield, Bishop of Worcester, and a record in the issue rolls of a payment of £10 to one William Forest, who allegedly discovered Tresilian; both instances are noted in Margaret Aston, *Thomas Arundel* (Oxford: Clarendon Press, 1967), p. 346 n. 4.

ing details of the poem.[32] In each case a large crowd takes part in an excited procession to see the man (or corpse) everyone has been talking about, while the duke of Gloucester's mace finds its match in *St. Erkenwald*'s description of "þe maire wyt mony maȝti men and macers"—that is, mace-bearers—"before hym" (line 143). In each instance there ensues a scene of public interrogation: on the one hand Bishop Erkenwald's inquiries into the judge's identity and the state of his soul, and on the other the lords' belligerent attack on Tresilian's efforts at self-preservation. In fact, both judges demonstrate surprising self-possession, Tresilian with his steady answers and the anonymous pagan in defense of his "wele-dede" and righteous acts, which ought to have earned him something better than being "dampnyd dulfully into þe depe lake" (line 302). And in each case judgment is immediate and irrevocable: Tresilian is haled away to the Tower, and then to Tyburn, while the pagan judge is released by Erkenwald's sacramental intervention "Fro bale . . . to blis" (line 340).[33]

[32] This allusion also provides a new *terminus a quo* for the poem's composition: February 19, 1388, the day of Tresilian's discovery and execution. The date traditionally associated with the poem is 1386, the year in which the Bishop of London, Robert Braybrooke, elevated the feast days of Erkenwald's Deposition and Translation to first-class status. Several early editors—Freidrich Knigge (1885), Sir Israel Gollancz (1922), and Henry Savage (1926)—argued that Braybrooke's proclamation was connected to and perhaps spurred the poem's composition. Peterson, who in general is skeptical about the occasional status of the poem, disputes this connection, pointing to similar attentions paid to Erkenwald in 1393, 1400, 1401 and 1407. Peterson himself settles on 1385–1410, in part because of his case for John Massey of Cotton as the poem's author (Peterson ed., pp. 11–15). My argument in this essay points to a much narrower range, say 1388–1392; see n. 86 below.

Though the action of *St. Erkenwald* is centered around St. Paul's, there is probably an oblique reference to Westminster in line 19 ("þat er was of Appolyn is now of Saynt Petre"). Gollancz notes in his edition of the poem (London: H. Milford, 1922, p. xv) a tradition, dating from at least the second quarter of the fifteenth century, that the church at Westminster had been first a church, then briefly a temple of Apollo, then a church again, dedicated to St. Peter; the story is told by John Flete, a monk of Westminster, in his *History of Westminster Abbey,* ed. J. Armitage Robinson (Cambridge: Cambridge University Press, 1909), pp. 33, 35, 76–77. In addition, the poem's references to the "New Werke" of the cathedral's reconstruction may refer obliquely to the rebuilding of the Westminster nave, as I will suggest presently.

[33] According to Favent (*Historia,* p. 18), Tresilian announced on the scaffold that he could not die while he wore any item of clothing; he was promptly stripped and discovered to be in possession of "certain magical devices and signs which were painted like heavenly characters" ("certa experimenta et certa signis depicta in eisdem ad modum caracterum celi"), along with the head of a demon and the names of many demons. These were promptly taken away, and he was hanged naked. The details—not only the connection between clothing and the preservation of life but also the necromantic writing—recall in a macabre way the poem's judge and the indecipherable, "roynyshe" writing on his sarcophagus.

Several more of *St. Erkenwald*'s details come into new focus in this context. For instance, the poem's peculiarly precise phrase "New Werke" (line 38), used to describe the putative rebuilding of St. Paul's during Erkenwald's time, has usually been assigned a metaphorical significance, in keeping with the emphasis on conversion in the opening lines of the poem: the Christian renovation of formerly pagan sacred sites. But the expression may be a topical reference as well: "novum opus," though doubtless a common phrase,[34] is the name used in the abbey accounts and the patent rolls to describe the rebuilding of the Westminster nave in the last quarter of the fourteenth century, the period of *St. Erkenwald*'s composition. This project was part of a larger building effort begun after a destructive fire in 1298, and was overseen by a special officer, the Warden of the New Work (*custos novis operi*). Begun in 1376, work on the nave languished for a decade for fiscal reasons, and then was spurred on by Richard's direct patronage in 1386, 1389, and throughout the 1390s in a series of grants, gifts, directives, and in his will. Despite his interest, at the time of his deposition the work was still more than a century away from completion; in fact, the task of dismantling the walls of the old Romanesque nave, begun in 1375/76, itself took about twelve years. Throughout the 1380s and 1390s, then, the west end of the church would have had a severe "under construction" look about it, much like the St. Paul's of the poem, for "Mony a mery mason was made þer to wyrke" (line 39).[35]

Gollancz and others noted long ago that the poem's repeated references to New Troy, as London was allegedly known in the judge's era, recall the claims made by Knighton and Walsingham that Nicholas Brembre had planned to rename contemporary London Petty Troy after setting himself up as its duke.[36] The echoes seem even stronger when we remember that Tresilian's discovery took place right in the middle

[34] As Peterson points out (pp. 36–37), the thirteenth-century reconstruction work done on St. Paul's was also known as the New Work.

[35] For the rebuilding of the nave and Richard's interest in it, see R. B. Rackham, "The Nave of Westminster," *Proceedings of the British Academy* 4 (1909–10): 33–96, esp. pp. 36–44; and Nigel Saul, "Richard II and Westminster Abbey," in John Blair and Brian Golding, eds., *The Cloister and the World: Essays in Medieval History in Honour of Barbara Harvey* (Oxford: Clarendon Press, 1996), pp. 196–218.

[36] Noted in *Knighton's Chronicle,* pp. 500–501; see also the *Historia vitae et regni Ricardi Secundi,* ed. George B. Stow Jr. (Philadelphia: University of Pennsylvania Press, 1977), p. 117 (this is the monk of Evesham's chronicle), and Thomas Walsingham's *Historia Anglicana,* ed. H. T. Riley, 2 vols., Rolls Series, vol. 28 (London: Longman, 1863–64), 2:174.

of the stalled parliamentary proceedings against Brembre.[37] To follow this thread to the end, in fact, we might also observe that the king of Troynovaunt, whom the judge claims to have served—"the bolde Breton Ser Belyn"—was involved in a lengthy and rancorous civil war with his younger brother, "Ser Berynge" (line 213), who had tried to claim the throne: a distant mirror of the political instability and civil/familial strife of 1387–88, involving uncles (Gloucester), nephews (Richard), and cousins (Bolingbroke). Belinus and Brennius, to give them the names that Geoffrey of Monmouth does, were the sons of Dunwallo Molmutius, who had during his reign established the Molmutine laws; Geoffrey says that Belinus, after defeating his rebellious brother, "confirmed the laws which his father had ordained, and commanded that even and steadfast justice should be done throughout the realm."[38] Those Molmutine laws included among other things the first law of sanctuary, which applied to the pagan temples of the era: "he ordained," Geoffrey writes, "that the temples of the gods and the cities should enjoy such privilege, as that in case any runaway or guilty man should take refuge therein, he should depart thence forgiven of his adversary."[39]

II

The law of sanctuary represents another intersection between the poem and the events surrounding its composition, and an especially fraught

[37] Another suggestive echo is the *Westminster Chronicle*'s claim that Brembre's great contrition on the way to his execution "moved almost all the bystanders to tears" (pp. 314–15: "Ejus revera contricio et devocio cunctos pene astantes ad lacrimas provocabant"), though Favent (*Historia,* p. 18) has Brembre himself weep when confronted by the son of his erstwhile antagonist John of Northampton. In the poem, of course, "all wepyd for woo þe wordes þat herden" (line 310) of the revivified judge.

[38] ". . . leges quas pater inuenerat confirmauit. Stabilemque iustitiam per regnum fieri precepit"; *The Historia regum Britanniae of Geoffrey of Monmouth,* ed. Acton Griscom (London: Longmans, Green, 1929), p. 281 (bk. 3, ch. 5); *Histories of the Kings of Britain,* trans. Sebastian Evans, rev. Charles W. Dunn (New York: E. P. Dutton, 1958), p. 50.

[39] "Statuit etiam . . . ut templa deorum & qui tantes [ciuitates] talem dignitatem haberent ut quicumque fugituus siue reus ad ea confugeret cum uenia coram inimico suo abiret" (Monmouth, *Historia,* p. 275 [bk. 2, ch. 17]; Dunn trans., p. 45). Geoffrey goes on to note that upon his death Dunwallo was buried "in the city of Trinovantum in the Temple of Concord, which he had built for the confirmation of his laws" ("in urbe trinouantum prope templum concordiae sepultus quod ipse ad confirmationem legum construxerat" [p. 276], a detail that also seems to have been in the *Erkenwald*-poet's mind.

Gollancz (p. xiii) felt that the *Erkenwald*-poet knew Geoffrey of Monmouth's *Historia* directly, while Savage in his edition (St. Erkenwald*, a Middle English Poem,* Yales Studies in English 72 [New Haven, Conn.: Yale University Press, 1926], pp. xxiv–xxviii) argued one. Certainly the pagan judge enjoys a kind of sanctuary prior to his discovery, and if it is in one sense the sanctuary of a pagan temple, it is nevertheless acknowledged and endorsed by the Christian God, who has been responsible for a thousand years or so of miraculous preservation.[40] Nor does the poem suggest that there will be some upper limit to the judge's stay. While in the fourteenth century parish churches could offer only forty days of sanctuary (after which the fugitive had to either surrender to the authorities or abjure the realm), the greater establishments—e.g., Westminster—could offer indefinite refuge.[41] *St. Erkenwald* presents a test case for this theory, as it were; though the judge has lain undisturbed for so long that he has "malte . . . out of [the] memorie" of the denizens of London, the fideistic Erkenwald assures his flock that God never forgets and has the situation well in hand (lines 163–66):

> Bot quen matyd is monnes myȝt and his mynde passyde,
> And al his resons are to-rent and redeles he stondes,
> þen lettes hit Hym ful litelle to louse wyt a fynger
> þat alle þe hondes vnder heuen halde myȝt neuer.

The judge himself specifically attributes his miraculous preservation to God (lines 265–72), and the poem thus implies that sanctuary is not just a statutory right but a divine one.

The nature of his "crime"—that he was, as he says, "ay a freke faitheles þat faylid þi laghes" (line 287)—seems to have made no difference either, though the questions of who deserved sanctuary, for what crimes, and for how long, were, to put it colloquially, hot-button issues around 1388. Exhibit A, of course, is the case of Tresilian himself; as *The Westminster Chronicle* describes it, he quite forcefully pleaded his rights after his capture, going so far as to claim that crimes of treason in particular were protected by the abbey's charters. The appellants concluded with typical prosecutorial acumen that he was speaking simply out of a desperate sense of self-preservation,[42] and sent him off to be

for Matthew Paris (either the *Chronica Majora* or the *Flores Historiarum*). Both chroniclers, however, describe the law of sanctuary as part of the Molmutine code.

[40] On the length of the judge's interment, scribally obscured in lines 205–10, see Peterson's note, p. 105.

[41] See J. H. Baker, *An Introduction to English Legal History,* 3d ed. (London: Butterworths, 1990), pp. 585–86.

[42] *West. Chron.,* p. 312: "putantes ipsum in sui ipsius salvacionem hoc asseruisse."

hanged, but this was not the end of the matter. Two months later, while the Parliament dragged on, Richard sponsored a formal review of the abbey's rights and privileges in which the abbey's representatives, armed with charters said to date back to the time of Edgar and Edward the Confessor, debated against Thomas Arundel, the chancellor (and archbishop of York since Alexander Neville's parliamentary condemnation and subsequent deposition), and William Wykeham, bishop of Winchester. An ironic spectacle ensued in which two bishops argued *against* the privilege of sanctuary. As Margaret Aston notes, to have done otherwise "would have been, in effect, to have condemned the judgement on Tresilian."[43] The Westminster chronicler, obviously an interested party, was not impressed—though he was evidently amused, observing that Wykeham "exposed himself to ridicule" in his final argument that according to the abbey's position the slayer of the king himself, even if he were to kill the king in the very sanctuary, should be protected.[44] The chronicler dismissed such a possibility as extremely remote, and then noted that the king took the side of the church and maintained that all those involved in extracting Tresilian from Westminster deserved excommunication.[45]

The possibility of bloodshed in the abbey's precincts was not just a theoretical issue in 1388; neither was excommunication. Ten years earlier, in August 1378, a spectacular and bloody breach of sanctuary during a high mass had left two men dead at the altar, one of them a sacristan who had tried to intervene in the pursuit of a fugitive. The abbey was closed to all religious services for four months, Parliament was forced to meet in Gloucester that November, and the chief offenders—Sir Alan Boxhull, constable of the Tower, and Sir Ralph Ferrers—received absolution from their sentence of excommunication only after paying fines of £200 each. The scandal was widely reported and led to the examination and confirmation of the abbey's privileges in the next parliament, as well as the production of a long tract on the abbey's rights, the *Objectiones et argumenta contra et pro privilegiis sanctuarii West-*

[43] Aston, *Thomas Arundel,* p. 347.

[44] *West. Chron.,* p. 324: "In hoc ultimo . . . fuit derisus."

[45] Ibid., pp. 326–27. According to the chronicler—who doggedly refuses to let the matter drop—on May 15 the duke of Gloucester and Sir John Cobham (evidently his accomplice in Tresilian's apprehension), spurred by troubled consciences, submitted themselves to the abbot of Westminster and promised to make satisfaction (pp. 332–33).

monasterii—one reason, doubtless, that the abbey's representatives were so well prepared to defend themselves in 1388.[46]

Richard played a relatively small role in 1378; he had been on the throne only thirteen months. But in 1388 his position was quite clear, and quite congenial to the Westminster chronicler: "How the noble king reveres and loves God's Church!" he writes. "How sympathetically and anxiously he exerts himself to champion her liberties and preserve them!"[47] And the king had another chance to demonstrate his sympathy a month later, when a clerk involved in a lawsuit over a benefice took refuge in Westminster. His pleas evidently ignored by Chancellor Arundel, the clerk—probably one William de Chesterton—sent a letter to Rome that was intercepted and found to contain some sort of state se-

[46] Two knights of the Black Prince, John Shackel and Robert Hawley (or Haule), had taken a Spanish nobleman prisoner at Najera in 1367; this Count de Denia left his son in England as a hostage while he tried to raise the ransom (something he never quite managed to do). When John of Gaunt, with his interests in the throne of Castile, demanded the prisoner's release in 1378, Hawley and Shackel refused and were committed to the Tower. They escaped and sought sanctuary in Westminster, where Hawley was slain. Evidently he was considered something of a martyr, and an inscription commemorating his death was engraved on the stone where he fell. The story is told by Walsingham (*Historia,* 1:375–79), the continuator of the *Eulogium historiarum . . .* (ed. F. S. Haydon, 3 vols., Rolls Series, vol. 9 [London: Longman, 1858–63], 3:342–46), the monk of Evesham (*Historia vitae,* ed. Stow, pp. 51–53, 55), and in the *Anonimalle Chronicle* (ed. V. H. Galbraith [Manchester: Manchester University Press, 1927], pp. 121–24). For modern accounts, see Arthur Penhryn Stanley, *Historical Memorials of Westminster Abbey,* 2 vols. (Philadelphia: G. W. Jacobs & Co., 1899), 2:152–54; J. Charles Cox, *The Sanctuaries and Sanctuary-Seekers of Mediaeval England* (London: George Allen & Sons, 1911), pp. 51–53; and May McKisack, *The Fourteenth Century* (Oxford: Clarendon Press, 1959), pp. 403–5. Edouard Perroy examines the case in the larger context of fourteenth-century military adventurism, and concludes that Shackel's ultimate compensation—500 marks' ransom and an annuity of 100 marks—was barely worth the risks involved. See his "Gras profits and rançons pendant la guerre de cent ans: L'affaire du comte de Denia," *Mélanges d'histoire du moyen âge dédies a la memoire de Louis Halphen* (Paris: Presses Universitaires de France, 1951), pp. 573–80.

For the *Objectiones* tract, see R. N. Swanson, *Church and Society in Late Medieval England* (Oxford: Blackwell, 1989), p. 156. One result of the parliamentary study of the issue was a statute that denied sanctuary in cases of fraudulent debt but did not affect the rights of felons.

[47] *West. Chron.,* pp. 326–27: "Ecce quomodo nobilis rex ecclesiam Dei veneratur et diligit! Quam affectuose et sollicite satagit ejus libertates defendere ac eciam conservare!" It is noteworthy that the *Anonimalle Chronicle* makes Richard the villain of the Hawley/Shackel story, for demanding their prisoner "par malveys conseil" and "saunz iugement ou resoun" (p. 121). It also includes the most detailed account of John Wyclif's appearance at the Gloucester Parliament, where he argued against the abbey's privileges.

On Richard's patronage of Westminster, see Saul, "Richard II and Westminster Abbey," and Barbara F. Harvey, "The Monks of Westminster and the University of Oxford," in DuBoulay and Barron, eds., *Reign of Richard II,* pp. 108–9.

crets (and some abuse of the chancellor). Once again the abbot was called in to defend the abbey's privileges; once again he was opposed by Arundel, aided this time by Sir Ralph Basset ("who never had a good word to say for the privileges of the Church"[48]), who argued that "it would be better that there should not be left one stone in the sanctuary standing upon another than that it should shelter traitors of this kind";[49] once again the king intervened on behalf of the abbey, asserting the sanctity of sanctuary and successfully deferring things until the next parliament.[50]

The Westminster Chronicle is understandably preoccupied with such incidents, as they represent specific attacks on the abbey's historical privileges. Indeed, the chronicler continues to report them: blood was spilled in St. Paul's when a fugitive was beaten and dragged out of sanctuary in September 1388,[51] and the whole Tresilian affair resurfaced in a 1392 entry about a felon named John Paule, who confessed, on his way to the scaffold, to having betrayed Tresilian and to having lured out of sanctuary at Westminster others who were later arrested and hanged.[52] Important for our purposes, though, is the way that Richard's position on this inflammatory issue—his willingness to see the privilege of sanctuary extended even to those judged (by some parties at least) traitors to king and country—corresponds to the *Erkenwald*-poet's essentially limitless conception of the protection offered to the pagan judge. The analogy between "a traitor to the king and the realm" and "a freke faitheles" to "þe riche kynge of reson" seems clear, as does the contrast between the partisan archbishop Arundel and the pious bishop Erkenwald, who exhibits humility toward God his "souerayn" (line 120) and tearful sympathy toward the entombed justice.

Indeed, the contrast between the egregious behavior of Arundel and

[48] *West. Chron.*, pp. 340–41: "qui numquam loquebatur bonum de ecclesiastica libertate."

[49] Ibid.: "dixit melius fore quod non staret lapis super lapidem in prefato loco quam sic tales proditores foveret." Basset is here adeptly (and from the chronicler's perspective, probably insufferably) paraphrasing Jesus' words about the Temple, e.g., Matthew 24:2—though the remark is a tantalizing one in terms of the destruction of temples with which *St. Erkenwald* begins.

[50] Chesterton was pardoned in July of 1389, when Arundel was no longer chancellor: see Aston, *Thomas Arundel*, p. 348 and n.

[51] *West. Chron.*, pp. 354–55. He also notes the fate of Richard Immworth, steward of the Marshalsea, who was dragged out of sanctuary in Westminster and executed by the rebels in 1381 (pp. 8–9).

[52] Ibid., pp. 496–99.

Wykeham (egregious to the chroniclers, anyway) and the sentimental and dutiful reaction of Erkenwald at the end of the poem further highlights the idealizing tendencies of the *Erkenwald*-poet. If, with the judge, the poet presents an example of juridical righteousness of a sort apparently unknown in Ricardian England, in *Erkenwald* he offers a similarly idealized account of episcopal behavior, a bishop who is politically unaffiliated (though capable of calming civil unrest—the "crye aboute a cors" [line 110]), devout, and humble—a "semely" (line 35) successor to St. Augustine. Moreover, he possesses a strong sense of his episcopal duty, both to strengthen the faith of the folk (it is in the name of "confirmynge þi Cristen faithe" that he petitions God to reveal the secret of the tomb [line 124]) and to do what is required for the newest addition to his flock, the pagan judge: he wishes the judge could be alive long enough to be baptized ("and not one grue lenger"! [line 319]) because "þen þof þou droppyd doun dede hit daungerede me lasse" (line 320). "Daungerede" clearly implies a sense of clerical responsibility toward the unbaptized, a responsibility that obtains no matter how anomalous the circumstances.[53] And *Erkenwald*'s impulse toward inclusiveness shows in even greater relief when we recognize, in the background, the exclusionary arguments of Arundel upon Tresilian. In its account of the relationship between bishop and judge, then, the poem reverses and reflects, through a glass rosily, the spectacle of spring 1388.

"Reflects" is perhaps not the best word here, however. Once again, I do not wish to claim that *St. Erkenwald* is some sort of roman à clef of the Merciless Parliament. The poem is not an oblique attempt to indict Arundel, nor an effort to somehow rehabilitate Tresilian, whom, frankly, nobody seems to have liked very much.[54] I do think, however, that the

[53] Cf. Peterson's note to this line (p. 112).

[54] Knighton, no friend of the rebels, notes the great severity with which Tresilian led the commissions sent out to punish the leaders of the 1381 uprising: "He went everywhere and did great slaughter, sparing none" (pp. 240–41). Evidently he was particularly keen to punish those who had during the rebellion targeted lawyers and justices (the murder of Sir John Cavendish had propelled Tresilian to the post of chief justice): "For anyone who appeared before him on that charge, whether justly or upon some accusation moved by hatred, was at once sentenced to death" (ibid.). Walsingham describes how Tresilian ran through three juries to secure convictions at St. Albans (*Chronicon Anglie,* ed. E. M. Thompson, Rolls Series, vol. 64 [London: Longman, 1874], pp. 322–24). See also Anthony Steel, *Richard II* (Cambridge: Cambridge University Press, 1941), p. 89, and Edward Foss, *The Judges of England,* 9 vols. (London: Longman, Brown, Green and Longmans, 1851), 4:102–3. Tresilian was probably the brains behind Richard's tendentious questions to the justices in the late summer of 1387; by rejecting the ordinances of the Wonderful Parliament and all but indicting the statutes' framers as trai-

poem's rehabilitation of its own judge is meant to evoke for its readers a recollection of the unfortunate chief justice and through him the aristocratic excesses of the Parliament—and through that the ways in which the poem is not only implicated in but takes a very definite position on contemporary political events. For although the poem is careful to represent Troynovaunt as a recognizable facsimile of the fourteenth-century metropolis—*viz.* the judge's robes and roles, the bishop's high mass, the mayor's mace-bearers, the crowds of guildsmen and apprentices flocking noisily to the tomb (lines 59–62)—the poem also makes a curious and tendentious omission in its rendering of events in Saxon London.

There are no aristocrats there, or rather, aristocrats play absolutely no role in the events of the poem. True, there is "mony a gay grete lorde" (line 134) present at the high mass Bishop Erkenwald says before visiting the corpse—"þe rekenest of þe reame repairen þider ofte" (line 135), says the poet of St. Paul's—and the poem does specify that "lordes" and "barones" accompany Erkenwald to the tomb, after showing the proper respect for the bishop ("þer plied to hym lordes" [line 138]). However, from that point on it is Erkenwald's show and the lords are absorbed into "þe pepulle" who stand quietly weeping on the fringes of the spooky scene. The players at this point are the bishop and the judge, who are defined not just by their relationship to one another but by their relationship to their kings, the "bolde Breton Ser Belyn" and "þe prince þat paradis weldes" (line 161). And the poem seems to elide the two, as, aided by Erkenwald and a suggestive echo, the judge passes from a retrospective allegiance to the former, "þe riche kynge þat rewlit vs þen," to the eternal worship of the latter, "þe riche kynge of reson þat

tors, the declarations made the confrontation of 1388 all the more inevitable. On the questions, see S. B. Chrimes, "Richard II's Questions to the Judges, 1387," *Law Quarterly Review* 72 (1956): 365–90; for Tresilian's likely role, see esp. pp. 372–74; Foss, *Judges,* 4:105; and Walsingham, *Historia,* 2:162. He was also the subject of numerous posthumous complaints, and although his attainder was overturned in Richard's Revenge Parliament in 1397, it was soon reinstated under Henry IV (Maddicott, *Law and Lordship,* p. 60; see also Saul, *Richard II,* p. 183). He seems, ultimately, to have been a fourteenth-century cross between the late Roy Cohn and Judge Roy Bean, and in the sixteenth century he would take pride of place in *The Mirror for Magistrates,* appearing as the very first if not the very worst example in that *de casibus* collection. The title of Tresilian's brief tragedy captures his reputation 150 years later: "The fall of Robert Tresilian chiefe Iustice of Englande, and other his felowes, for misconstruyng the lawes, and expounding them to serue the Princes affections"; *The Mirror for Magistrates,* ed. Lily B. Campbell (New York: Barnes and Noble, 1960), pp. 73–80.

ri3t euer alowes," explicitly approved and authorized by a populace whose tears flow like Erkenwald's, and who follow the mirthful and mournful procession at the end of the poem.

The poem stages at St. Paul's—a place with an important civic role, as opposed to the more national associations of Westminster—a utopian progress from mystery, "troubulle," and "ryngande noyce" to a state of perfect concord between urban and episcopal interests, an arrangement depicting what the right relations of judge, bishop, and king might look like without aristocratic interference. *St. Erkenwald* imaginatively repairs the damage done to the cozy and rewarding relationship that ought to exist among the seigneurial classes by pointedly excluding one of those groups from participation; the great lords who had caused so much trouble and spilt so much blood during the recent unpleasantness "At London in Englonde no3t fulle longe sythen," to quote the first line of the poem,[55] are in *St. Erkenwald* seen but not heard.[56] This anodyne gesture—in the alliterative poetry usually noted for its responsiveness to aristocratic tastes—perfectly inverts the situation of the Merciless Parliament, since there the lords spiritual had recused themselves from the proceedings rather than pass judgment in the capital cases involved.[57] In *St. Erkenwald,* by contrast, only the mediating presence of the bishop permits a happy resolution to the theological and historical mysteries of the tomb.

III

Oddly enough—paradoxically enough—that sort of anonymity is precisely what the lords appellant were looking for, at least at one point. On June 3, at the end of the parliament, the king was made to renew

[55] J. A. Burrow argues that the phrase "in Englonde" is not a redundancy but rather bespeaks the author's regional chauvinism by stressing the difference between the capital and the county palatine of Chester, the source of the poem's dialect; "*Saint Erkenwald* Line 1: 'At London in Englond,'" *N&Q,* n. s., 40 (1993): 22–23. The b-verse at first glance also suggests that recent London events are going to be the subject of the poem, before the almost immediate telescoping effect of line 2.

[56] Richard would himself do much the same thing when, in July of 1389, he appointed new commissions of the peace that contained absolutely no aristocrats—no lords, no knights, no squires (Storey, "Liveries and Commissions," p. 138). The experiment, presumably prompted by the desires if not the actual petitions of the Commons in the Cambridge Parliament of September 1388, lasted only sixteen months; nevertheless, it reflects the House of Commons's lack of confidence in the lords' ability to do justice in the realm in the aftermath of the Merciless Parliament, and Richard's cagey willingness to accomodate their anxieties.

[57] *West. Chron.,* 302–5; see also Aston, *Thomas Arundel,* pp. 345–46.

his coronation oath, and on the next day the lords presented another oath for all those present to approve and swear to. Some of it had to do with their own immunity from prosecution, of course, but one passage dealt specifically with the issue of precedent.

Also, that the appeals, pursuits, accusations, processes, judgements, and executions made and delivered in this present parliament shall be approved, confirmed, and established as a thing duly done for the weal and profit of the king our said lord and of all his realm . . . and that by imagination and interpretation or any other motion none of the same shall be reversed, infringed, or annulled in any manner: and if any makes pursuit to infringe, annul, or reverse any of the points abovesaid, such pursuit being of record, he shall be adjudged and have execution as a traitor and enemy of the king and of the realm: provided always that this acceptance, approval, confirmation, and establishment touching the assemblies, appeals, pursuits, accusations, processes, judgements, and executions abovesaid shall have and hold force and virtue only in these cases thus befallen and come to pass or declared and that they shall not be drawn in example or precedent in time to come, and that the said commission made at the last parliament shall not be drawn in example or precedent in time to come, but touching the matters abovesaid that they shall stand firmly for the time that is past inasmuch as they were so profitable to the king, support and maintenance of his crown, and salvation of all the realm, and done out of such great necessity; and although sundry points are declared for treason in this present parliament other than were declared by statute before, that no justice shall have power to deliver judgement of any other case of treason or in any other manner than he had before the beginning of this present parliament etc.[58]

[58] *West. Chron.*, 302–5: "Item que les appellez, pursuites, accusamentz, processez, juggementz et execucions faitz et renduz en ceste present parlement soient approvez, affermez et establiez come chose fait duement pur le bien et profit du roy nostre dit seignur et de tout soun roiaume . . . et qe par ymaginacioun et interpretacion ou autre mocion qeconqe nulle dycelles soient reversez, enfreintez ou annulez en ascune manere: et si ascun face pursuite denfreindre, anuller ou reverser ascuns des pointez suisditz, quele pursuite soit de record, soit ajugge et eit execucion come traitour et enemy du roy et du roiaume: porveu tote foithe qe ceste acceptacion, approve, affermance et establissement touchantz les assembles, appelles, pursuites, accusementz, processez, juggementz et execucions suisdit eiant et tiegnent force et vertue en cestes cases issintz eschuez et avenuz ou declarrez soulement et qils ne soient trietz en ensample nen consequencie en temps avener ne qe la dite commissioun fait au darrein parlement soit treite en ensample nen consequencie en temps avener, mes touchantz les matieres suisditz qils estoisent fermement pur temps qi passe est desicome ils estoient si profitables au roy, sustenance et meyntenance de sa corone et salvacion de tout le roiaume et faitz de si grant necessite; coment qe diverses pointz sont declarrez pur tresoun en ceste present parlement autres queux ne furent declarrez par estatut devant, qe nulle justice eit poair de rendre juggement dautre cas de tresoun nen autre manere qils navoient devant le comencement de ceste present parlement etc."

Now, it is one thing to try to prevent your legislative and judicial successes from being overturned—though in the long run this effort proved useless, as the judgments of the Merciless Parliament were repudiated in 1397, when two of the appellants, Gloucester and Arundel, lost their lives and a third, Warwick, was exiled.[59] It's one thing to try to consolidate your gains, and quite another to attempt in the same paragraph to deny that they ever occurred, and to prevent future generations—or more likely next year's parliament—from using your handiwork as "example or precedent."

Some caution is warranted here. "Precedent"—*consequencie* in the law French of the Parliament rolls—was not as developed a concept in fourteenth-century English law as it is now, or as it would be a century later under the Tudors, and a firm idea of "binding precedent" was still centuries away.[60] On the other hand, we have the contemporary example of Chaucer's Man of Law, who is distinguished by (among other things) his ready knowledge of cases going back to the time of William the Conqueror. In any case the will of the appellants in this oath seems perfectly explicit, and they would have had some reason to be anxious: not only did they understand the value of having precedent on their side but they also knew very well how flexible a strategy the recourse to precedent could be. From the beginning of the Wonderful Parliament in 1386 (the "last parliament" referred to in the oath) up through the events of 1388, they folded, spindled, mutilated—and sometimes invented—precedents in their pursuit of prosecutions that look transparently political, even from a late-twentieth-century perspective.

They first attempted to coerce Richard in 1386 by calling his attention to a (nonexistent) "ancient statute"[61] that required the king to call and attend parliament annually; when the king balked at this, they referred to another ancient statute, which "not long since, lamentably, had to be invoked," that provided for the deposition of a king judged derelict in his governance of the realm.[62] In the face of this explicit (if only fic-

[59] Richard, evidently preferring extortion to direct threats, encouraged similar legislation at the end of the 1397 parliament, according to which "all future peers were required to swear to maintain the Acts of the session before receiving livery of their temporalities or estates" (Saul, *Richard II,* p. 379).

[60] Baker, *English Legal History,* pp. 224–30. For an interesting discussion of how the appellants overcame written precedent through strategies of "orality," see Jesse M. Gellrich, *Discourse and Dominion in the Fourteenth Century* (Princeton, N.J.: Princeton University Press, 1995), pp. 171–83.

[61] *Knighton's Chronicle,* p. 356: "ex antiquo statuo."

[62] Ibid., pp. 360–61: "Habent enim antiquo statuo, et de facto non longe retroactis temporibus experienter (quod dolendum est habito)."

tionally statutory) recollection of the fate of his great-grandfather Edward II, Richard capitulated; parliament was held and his chancellor, Michael de la Pole, was impeached.

The Merciless Parliament was marked throughout by similar aristocratic inventiveness in the face of missing or unwelcome legal opinions. In the first place there is the questionable legality of the procedure itself, the thirty-nine articles of the appeal of treason against Richard's partisans made by the subsequently named lords appellant. The judges present in Parliament, led by the newly appointed chief justice, Sir Walter Clopton (himself a retainer of the duke of Gloucester[63]), observed on the one hand that the appeal was a procedure unknown to the civil law, and on the other hand that the Court of Chivalry, which did recognize appeals, had no jurisdiction over the charges made in the articles. Caught between two systems of law, the appellants invented their own, declaring simply that the high crimes in question could only be dealt with in parliament "by the law of parliament," which—whatever it actually meant—was superior to the law of any other court in the land.[64] Though this gesture has been accorded a prominent place in certain accounts of English constitutional theory,[65] it pretty clearly represents an arrogation of authority undertaken largely because it was possible—that is, because the appellants, in practice if not in theory, figured they could get away with it. And they did.

One more example will suffice. The case against Nicholas Brembre, the only one of the appellants' main targets to stand trial in person, stalled when a committee of twelve lords appointed to examine the evidence against him concluded that he had done nothing that merited the death penalty. Then a group of guild representatives put together to produce an indictment produced only another deadlock,[66] so the appellants had to turn to an ad hoc assembly of the mayor, aldermen, and

[63] Gellrich, *Discourse and Dominion,* p. 179.

[64] Tuck, *Richard II and the English Nobility,* pp. 121–22; Steel, *Richard II,* pp. 150–51; and T. F. Tout, *Chapters in the Administrative History of Mediaeval England,* vol. 3 (Manchester: Manchester University Press, 1928), pp. 431–33.

[65] See Tout, ibid., pp. 432–33, and the response by Steel, ibid., pp. 151–52. Kathryn Kerby-Fulton and Steven Justice suggest that the appellants' claim might not have been entirely spurious, and might have derived from the *Modus tenendi parliamentum,* a widely circulated if somewhat mysterious text describing the rights and procedures of Parliament. See Justice and Kerby-Fulton, "Reformist Intellectual Culture in the English and Irish Civil Service: The *Modus tenendi parliamentum* and Its Literary Relations," *Traditio* 53 (1998): 149–202 (esp. pp. 166–70).

[66] *West. Chron.,* pp. 311–15; Steel, *Richard II,* pp. 154–57; Tuck, *Richard II and the English Nobility,* p. 124.

recorder of London. This group admitted that Brembre was probably aware rather than ignorant of the treasons he had been accused of, and the recorder when pressed acknowledged that "anyone who, having knowledge of such matters, concealed instead of disclosing them, would be, and would deserve to be, punished by the loss of his life."[67] Case closed, said the appellants, and Brembre was hustled off to his execution.

Recalling the oath quoted above, it is clear that the appellants' lack of regard for precedent at the beginning of the Merciless Parliament was thus matched only by their fear of making precedent at its end, an irony that would be easier to appreciate had it not had such bloody consequences. And here, again, the events of 1386–88 intersect with the concerns of *St. Erkenwald,* for this fear of making precedent is characteristic of one of the poem's chief discourses, the theology of the salvation of virtuous pagans. The problem with exceptional salvations is that although they are, by their very nature, supposed to be unique, they somehow simultaneously encourage imitation and replication, often in vernacular texts beyond the reach of ecclesiastical regulation: the *Legenda aurea* account of Gregory and Trajan begets *Piers Plowman,* which begets *St. Erkenwald.* Moreover, though the story of the pagan judge ultimately follows a textual exemplar in the well-known Trajan story, that source text itself is riddled with doubts and anxieties about the legitimacy of its salvific project. The *Legenda aurea* states that, according to some versions of the tale, Pope Gregory was specifically enjoined by an angelic voice not to pray for any more damned souls, and was himself punished with a lifelong illness for having done so.[68]

Scholastic theology tends to exacerbate this problem, since the impulse to systematize the manifestations of the divine will tends to produce rules, rules that the theologians then have to ask us not to apply, or even to acknowledge: if I let you get a drink from the waters of eternal life, I'll have to let everybody get one. Thus Aquinas, discussing Trajan, has to finesse the question of precedent, lest the gates of heaven swing wide. On the topic of "Whether works of intercession profit those who are in hell," he writes:

[67] *West. Chron.,* pp. 314–15: "Pro certo ille qui scivit talia atque celavit et non detexit merito puniretur vite privacione etc."

[68] Jacobus da Voragine, *Legenda aurea,* ed. Th. Graesse (Leipzig, 1850), pp. 196–97; for a translation, see *The Golden Legend,* trans. William Granger Ryan, 2 vols. (Princeton, N.J.: Princeton University Press, 1993), 1:178–79. For the qualifications and uncertainties surrounding this episode, see Grady, "Rule of Exception Salvations," pp. 63–66.

Concerning the incident of Trajan it may be supposed with probability that he was recalled to life at the prayers of blessed Gregory, and thus obtained the grace whereby he received the pardon of his sins and in consequence was freed from punishment. The same applies to all those who were miraculously raised from the dead, many of whom were evidently idolators and damned. For we must say likewise of all such persons that they were consigned to hell, not finally, but as was actually due to their own merits according to justice, and that according to higher causes, in view of which it was foreseen that they would be recalled to life, they were to be disposed of otherwise.

Or we may say with some that Trajan's soul was not freed absolutely from the debt of eternal punishment, but that his punishment was suspended for a time, that is, until the judgment day. Nor does it follow that this is the general result of works of intercession, because things happen differently in accordance with the general law from that which is permitted in particular cases and by privilege. Even so the bounds of human affairs differ from those signs of the Divine power as Augustine says. (*De cura pro mort.* xvi)[69]

Don't use this case as a precedent, says Aquinas, for it's a unique situation—an injunction echoed in secular terms a century later by the appellants' oath. Once again, when the salvation of the pagan judge in *St. Erkenwald* is seen in the context of the events of 1388, that mystifying event—there is no source or analogue for it in any of the lives or legends of the historical Erkenwald—becomes newly intelligible, this time as both a broad joke and a pointed warning aimed at the appellants. They are misguided to think that they can prevent the recurrence of heretofore unprecedented events, because that would mean resisting "þe prouidens of þe prince þat paradis weldes" (line 161); and they are foolish to think that they have successfully buried true justice under the weight of their parliamentary manipulations, because that would run contrary to the will of "þe riche kynge of reson þat . . . loues al þe lawes lely þat longen to trouthe" (lines 267–68).

Moreover, the pagan justice in *St. Erkenwald* makes an implicit argument from precedent when he questions his own exclusion from the pardon granted during the harrowing of hell (lines 289–92):

[69] *Summa Theologica* III. suppl. q. 71 art. 5 ("Whether works of intercession profit those who are in hell?"), obj. 5 and resp. ob. 5, in *Opera Omnia* (Parma, 1854), 4:588–89; see also the similar remarks in Aquinas's *Commentary on the Sentences* I, dist. 43, q. 2 a. 2, obj. 5 and ad. 5, *Opera Omnia,* 6:351–52. For the translation, see *The Summa Theologica of St. Thomas Aquinas . . . Literally Translated by Fathers of the English Dominican Province* (London, 1913–42).

I was non of þe nommbre þat þou wyt noy boghtes,
Wyt þe blode of thi body vpon þe blo rode;
Quen þou herghedes helle-hole and hentes hom þeroute,
Þi loffynge oute of limbo, þou laftes me þer.

Though he acknowledges himslef a "paynym vnpreste" (line 285), he also implies that he and his London auditors share the common human taint of original sin (lines 294–97),

þe derke dethe þat dyȝt vs oure fader,
Adam oure alder þat ete of þat appulle
Þat mony a plyȝtles pepul has poysned for euer.
ȝe were entouchid wyt his tethe and toke in þe glotte.

The judge concedes that he lacked baptism ("fulloght in fonte wyt faitheful bileue, / And þat han we myste alle merciles, myselfe and my soule" [lines 299–300]), the "medecyn" that has cured Erkenwald and his contemporaries, but he nevertheless wonders why that omission ought to disqualify him, since he was otherwise so righteous (lines 301–4):[70]

Quat wan we wyt oure wele-dede þat wroghtyn ay riȝt,
Quen we are dampnyd dulfully into þe depe lake
And exilid fro þat soper so, þat solempne fest
Þer richely hit arne refetyd þat after right hungride?

The miraculous convergence that ensues—the bishop's sacramental tear falls on the corpse just as he recites the baptismal formula—indicates that, in one sense at least, the judge's case has merit. Upon further review, as it were, his righteousness is found to be sufficient for salvation.

Righteous heathen stories always extoll, explicitly or implicitly, the value of earthly activity, which in *St. Erkenwald* is specifically represented as juridical activity. Thus the poem celebrates that divine *potentia absoluta* that can bend to the point of breaking the laws of nature in order to reveal and reward the virtue inherent in devout adherence to

[70] Unspoken here is the even more troublesome fact that Adam and his fellow parolees also lacked the "medecyn" of baptism. Such a silence is perhaps a symptom of the way that the authorized and orthodox impulses behind the Harrowing—itself an extrabiblical episode—can inspire increasingly heterodox accounts of pagan salvations.

natural law. The king of heaven is not bound by precedents (though he may choose to observe them—hence the theologians' parallel concept of the *potentia ordinata*), and he may exercise his regality freely.[71] And so, the poem implies, ought it to be on earth: it is clear in the poem that doing justice well is closely associated with serving one's king well; by aligning his pagan judge with two kings, one earthly and one celestial, the *Erkenwald*-poet also links those monarchs—these "riche kynges"—to one another. The poet's recourse to the theology of exceptional salvations thus represents a hopeful attempt, after the disasters of 1388, to provide a theory for the rebuilding of Richard's battered regality.

Though the "royal absolutism" with which Richard has been associated by his detractors (both Lancastrian and modern) was largely a phenomenon of the 1390s, there was clearly a sense after 1386, among his allies at least, that his regality had been badly compromised in two successive parliaments. Certainly since the Wonderful Parliament, Richard had been worried about the status of the royal prerogative; at his departure from the Parliament, having been saddled with a continual council to oversee the government, he had protested that "he did not wish prejudice to come to him nor to his crown because of anything that had been done in this parliament, and that his prerogative and the liberties of his crown should be saved and guarded."[72] The judicial commissions that Richard put together in 1387 were entirely concerned with whether "that last Parliament held at Westminster was derogatory to the regality and prerogative of our lord the king,"[73] and the ten items prove that modern pollsters have nothing on their medieval counterparts when it comes to framing a question.

The appellants, too, were invested in preserving at least a rhetorical notion of the king's prerogative even as they worked to circumscribe it. In the thirty-nine articles of the appeal, de la Pole, de Vere, Tresilian, Brembre, and Neville are repeatedly accused of accroaching the royal power; this was a clear case of the pot calling the kettle *proditor,* since the appellants had themselves gone so far as to threaten the king with deposition at the end of 1387.[74] But though a thin disguise to their own

[71] The relevant distinctions and their deployment by fourteenth-century theologians are surveyed by Janet Coleman, Piers Plowman *and the Moderni* (Rome: Edizioni di storia e letteratura, 1981), esp. ch. 4.

[72] Chrimes, "Richard II's Questions," p. 376.

[73] Ibid.

[74] *West. Chron.,* pp. 218–19, 228–29.

ambitions, it was sufficient to give the odor of statutory due process to the proceedings—or at least to prevent any immediate outbursts of incredulity in the Parliament or in the chronicles.

Not that anyone was fooled by this rhetoric—least of all the *Erkenwald*-poet, who in depicting the salvation of the pagan judge was perhaps taking his cue from the one episode of the Merciless Parliament in which Richard exercised—or was permitted to exercise—the royal prerogative. Though Richard was unable to save the life, much less the soul, of his ally Tresilian, he did manage to aid the other judges implicated in the 1387 commissions. They too had been sentenced to death by the Parliament, but after the lords spiritual (and, according to Knighton, the queen[75]) pleaded for their lives, the king commuted their sentences to perpetual banishment to Ireland. Practically, this success was probably due to the appellants' lack of interest, since similar pleas for the life of Richard's tutor, Simon Burley, were vehemently resisted by the duke of Gloucester, who for some reason urgently desired Burley's execution (and ultimately secured it). Under the circumstances, however, even such a small victory must have been significant, and the way the gesture is described is significant, too: "[U]pon petition of the clergy and of others from among the lords temporal," writes the Westminster chronicler of the justices, "the king granted them their lives."[76] Ostensibly, at least, Richard himself used the power of his office to grant clemency.

Over the next several months Richard slowly rebuilt the prestige of that office and reclaimed his prerogative. By the fall of 1388 public dissatisfaction with the rule of the appellants had become considerable, as evidenced by the Commons petition on liveries and maintenance. In his own maneuverings around this issue, Richard tried to represent himself as the champion of law and order, a role closed to the appellants after the purges of the spring, and when he declared his majority at a meeting of the great council in May of 1389—dismissing most of the household officers he had been forced to accept a year earlier, including Archbishop

[75] *Knighton's Chronicle,* pp. 502–3.

[76] *West. Chron.,* pp. 316–17: "Set as peticionem clericorum aliorumque dominorum temporalium rex eis vitam concessit"; see also pp. 286–87 for a parallel account. Knighton, less interested overall than the Westminster chronicler in salvaging Richard's reputation at this point, writes that "the king, with the assent of the lords whom they had offended, granted them their lives" ("rex cum consensu dominorum in quos deliquerant condonauit eis vitam" [pp. 502–3]), capturing the likely role of the appellants in Richard's gesture.

Arundel—he also required the resignation of all the justices of the king's bench and the court of common pleas, reappointing them but also adding several new ones.[77] Later that summer Richard appointed new commissions of the peace for every shire, the first such general review in seven years.[78] In the Parliament of January 1390 he again presided over heated debate about liveries, promising to find some solution to the situation, and also agreed to a new statute regulating the dispensation of pardons for homicide, which the Commons had claimed were too easily given out.[79] According to Anthony Tuck, in the 1390 Parliament "the chancellor [then Wykeham, who had replaced Arundel] went out of his way in his opening speech to emphasize the king's desire to suppress lawlessness."[80]

It was in this environment, I would argue, that *St. Erkenwald* was conceived, as part of a concerted if not organized effort by his supporters and partisans (some of them anonymous, at least to us) to reimagine Richard's royal powers and prerogative.[81] The poet—perhaps a parliamentary clerk originally from the northwest, or a member of the retinue of a lord with Cheshire holdings in London for the Parliament—writes for an audience with some theological and political sophistication, able to appreciate (and recognize allusions to) the national significance of London affairs.[82] His focus on true justice and the rewards due to its exercise corresponds with the path Richard chose for the rehabilitation of his reputation, and at the same time alludes to the spectacle of the Merciless Parliament and the fate of justice—and justices—under its cruel auspices. And the poem's overt theological concerns link justice

[77] *West. Chron.,* pp. 390–93 (where this housecleaning is seen specifically as an anti-appellant move); *Knighton's Chronicle,* pp. 528–31; Tout, *Richard II and the English Nobility,* p. 455; Tuck, *Richard II,* pp. 134–37; Richard H. Jones, *The Royal Policy of Richard II* (New York: Barnes and Noble, 1968), pp. 64–66.

[78] Storey, "Liveries and Commissions," pp. 136–38, and see n. 56 above.

[79] Ibid., pp. 143–44.

[80] Tuck, *Richard II,* p. 148; see also Saul, *Richard II,* pp. 200–201, 262–64.

[81] Strohm, "Textual Environment," pp. 65–74, argues convincingly that "Lak of Stedfastnesse"—by one of Richard's non-anonymous partisans, Geoffrey Chaucer—was also part of this campaign, and its relatively conventional rhetoric ought to be understood as sharing the concerns of 1388–90. See also Don-John Dugas, "The Legitimization of Royal Power in Chaucer's *Man of Law's Tale,*" *MP* 95 (1997): 27–43.

[82] On the authorship of *St. Erkenwald,* see Peterson, pp. 15–23, and Benson, "Authorship." The connection between alliterative poetry and parliamentary records, and the readers and writers of both, is suggestively explored by Kathryn Kerby-Fulton and Steven Justice, "Langlandian Reading Circles and the Civil Service in London and Dublin, 1380–1427," *New Medieval Literatures* 1 (1998): 59–83.

and regality on earth with their heavenly counterparts, which puts contemporary events in a significantly larger perspective.[83]

Richard himself may have appreciated this larger perspective; as Bowers notes, and as Nigel Saul has demonstrated at length in his recent biography of the king, Richard paid increasing attention later in the reign to the sacred imagery of kingship and the cermonies designed to reinforce the analogy between earthly and divine rule.[84] In this regard it is worth noting that Richard also made a visit to the tomb of St. Erkenwald in St. Paul's in 1392; this event occurred at the end of the procession celebrating Richard's reconciliation with the city of London after his famous "quarrel" with the city, which was not only a pageant of incalculable splendor but also an event that put explicit emphasis on the sacral aspects of kingship. When the king and queen arrived at Eastcheap, according to *The Westminster Chronicle,* they were greeted by two boys dressed as angels who "descended from a lofty stucture" and placed "two gold crowns of great costliness" on Richard and Anne.[85] The author of *St. Erkenwald* would have appreciated—and perhaps witnessed?—such a gesture.[86]

The *Erkenwald*-poet was not the only writer to try to put the events of 1386–90 in some kind of perspective. Knighton, whose *Chronicle*

[83] It is even possible that the story of the poem was selected with Richard's predilections in mind; we know he was something of an antiquarian, and according to Nigel Saul he was also interested in the conversion of the heathen: "Exceptionally among English rulers, he was vigorous in sponsoring the conversion of unbelievers: on two occasions he was present when Jews were received into the faith in the chapel of his manor at King's Langley" (*Richard II,* pp. 448–49 and n.).

[84] See n. 6 above, and Saul, *Richard II,* pp. 339–57, on Richard's ceremonial style and its political meaning.

[85] *West. Chron.,* pp. 504–7: "ibi de quadam alta structura descenderunt quasi duo angeli in specie puerorum . . . ac in eorum manibus duas aureas coronas habentes magni valoris." For the quarrel, see Caroline M. Barron, "The Quarrel of Richard II with London 1392–97," in *The Reign of Richard II,* pp. 173–201; for the pageant, Gordon Kipling, "Richard II's 'Sumptuous Pageants' and the Idea of Civic Triumph," in David M. Bergeron, ed., *Pageantry in the Shakespearean Theatre* (Athens: University of Georgia Press, 1985), pp. 83–103. Though the procession is described by Walsingham, Knighton, and the Westminster chronicler, the detail of the visit to Erkenwald's tomb is found only in the Latin poem on the occasion by the Carmelite friar Richard of Maidstone, printed in T. Wright, ed., *Political Poems and Songs,* 2 vols., Rolls Series, vol. 30 (London: Longman, 1859–61), 1:282–300.

[86] Shklar, "Rule of History," pp. 279–80, argues that the *Erkenwald*-poet's critique of Ricardian royalist propaganda specifically recalls this 1392 procession; I tend to think that the poem had been completed by 1392, since by that time Richard had largely given up on his law-and-order campaign and had begun to enagage in the kind of behavior excoriated in the texts that describe his deposition—the quarrel with London being a prime example.

breaks off in 1396 and thus misses both Richard's revenge in 1397 and his deposition two years later, was no particular partisan of either party; though he may have used some appellant propaganda in preparing his account of the Merciless Parliament,[87] he also preserved the 1388 Commons petition about liveries and maintenance, a document clearly aimed at the great lords of the realm.[88] His point of view is perhaps visible in an anecdote he carefully places just after his account of Richard's declaration of independence of May 1389. For Knighton the king's reclamation of power clearly marks the end of some sort of chapter in the struggle between Crown and peers, and at first it seems to be an optimistic conclusion. "And there was none who sought to oppose the king's will, but all praised God that He had provided them with so wise a king to watch over them in future,"[89] he writes, capturing in one statement the most important theme of recent events, from the Ricardian perpsective: the status of the king's will, now evidently unopposed. But this sanguine remark is followed immediately by a rather monkish (or canonish) reminder of the sanguinary consequences of those same events. "In the month of July," says Knighton, "while the king was at Sheen, there gathered in his court a huge swarm of midges and flies, and coming together as it were in a battle they made a great slaughter of each other, so that the dead had to be swept up with brushes and shovels to clear the ground."[90] Shakespeare's duke of Gloucester, mindful of the divided state of the realm and the degraded regality of his king, would later lament, "As flies to wanton boys are we to the gods; / they kill us for their sport." Well, sometimes they do—and sometimes, unexpectedly, they (or He) offer a "riche restorment" to one who wears a crown and carries a scepter but "was kidde for no kynge" and "hades no londe of lege men" (lines 222, 224). Miracles—political miracles—do happen.

[87] *Knighton's Chronicle,* pp. xlvi–xlviii.

[88] See ibid., p. 7 and n. 25.

[89] Ibid., pp. 530–31: "et non erat quis, qui regis uoluntatem infringere conaretur. Set omnes Deum glorificauerunt qui sibi talem regem sapientem futurum prouidere curauit."

[90] Ibid., pp. 530–31: "Mense Iulii, dum rex esset apud Schene, conuenerunt in curia sua multe turme attomorum et muscarum, et in modum prelii congredientes fecerunt maximam stragem inuicem, adeo ut scopis et pertis mundarent locum de interfectis." See *West. Chron.,* pp. 400–401, which specifies the date of this event as July 3; Knighton, however, though he gives the same month, tells the story slightly out of order, before his account of the treaty of Leulingham (June 18, 1389), a transposition that the Westminster chronicler does not make.

The Lowly Paraf: Transmitting Manuscript Design in *The Canterbury Tales*

Joel Fredell
Southeastern Louisiana University

Modus legendi in dividendo constat . . . investigando dividimus quando ea quae occulta sunt reseramus. [The method of reading is founded upon division . . . by investigating we divide when we reveal those things which are hidden.]

—Hugh of St. Victor, *Didascalicon*

The symbol used as a paragraph or section mark in MSS. is frequently written in red in this MS., apparently in a haphazard manner. The frequent occurrence of it will not be subsequently noticed.

—Sanford Brown Meech, note in *The Book of Margery Kempe*

I HAVE DECIDED to champion the cause of a marginal figure, common throughout manuscripts of *The Canterbury Tales* yet commonly ignored. This figure is the paraf: ancestral graph of our modern symbol (¶) for a new paragraph, but distinct in the idiosyncracy of its uses in late medieval England. With their near relations the small initials, parafs crowd the margins of literary texts in positions that can seem at once obvious and mysterious. They flag points in the narrative considered important—shifts in episode or argument, dialogue, narratorial interjections, passages worthy of independent consideration and possibly recitation to an appreciative circle of listeners. Yet at other such points they do not appear. They have been ignored, I suspect, because, though they

Part of the research for this article was made possible by a stipend from the National Endowment for the Humanities, for whose support I am very grateful. I would also like to thank the British Library, Bodleian Library, Cambridge University Library, the National Library of Wales, and the Huntington Library and their staffs for invaluable help. Winthrop Wetherbee and Janice Coleman graciously offered to read and comment on an earlier draft of this article.

can appear in daunting numbers, they do not fit the strict consistency dictated by our rule-bound, post-Enlightenment notions of internal narrative divisions.

Such independence and selectivity for internal text dividers are precisely their value. These lowly decorations showed fifteenth-century readers how tales were structured and which elements were important in each tale, according to the producers of that manuscript—methods of reading we would do well to reveal. Some years ago A. J. Minnis argued convincingly that *divisio textus* was central to medieval literary interpretation;[1] more recently Mary Carruthers has described this technique as fundamental to storing knowledge in the "treasure-house" of memory.[2] The paraf and its partners flag these divisions that define structural units of text basic to the hermeneutics of reading in later medieval England. In manuscripts of *The Canterbury Tales,* these markers were used to set up two distinct methods for reading. Figures 1 and 2 provide a brief glimpse of the divisions in *The Franklin's Tale* from two "landmark" manuscripts, Cambridge University Dd.4.24 (Dd) and Oxford, Corpus Christi College 198 (Cp).[3] These parallel passages are taken from Dorigen's complaint, which raises the exemplary specters of women who killed themselves to protect their virtue (as Dorigen thinks she also must now do).

[1] A. J. Minnis, *Medieval Theory of Authorship: Scholastic Literary Attitudes in the Later Middle Ages* (London: Scolar Press, 1984), p. 118.

[2] Mary Carruthers, *The Book of Memory: A Study of Memory in Medieval Culture* (Cambridge: Cambridge University Press, 1990).

[3] Full citations and sigla for the ten "landmark manuscripts" of *The Canterbury Tales* are provided as part of the legend for the appended tables. The landmark manuscripts are defined in *The Text of the* Canterbury Tales, ed. John M. Manly and Edith Rickert, 8 vols. (Chicago: University of Chicago Press, 1940), 2:49–69. Among these manuscripts, the dense pattern appears in the key independent witnesses (Hg/El) and the earliest witnesses of families *a* (Ad^3) and *d* (Dd). Sparse pattern landmark manuscripts fall into families *b* (He) and *cd;* (Cp/La/Pw) Ha^4 exhibits its independence in both textual and decorative terms. I have included data for these ten manuscripts to reflect the traditions of textual scholarship on the *CT.* Eight of these (Hg/El/Dd/Gg/Ha^4/Cp/La/Pw) were used in Chaucer Society parallel-text and diplomatic editions. The ongoing Variorum Chaucer project has added two (Ad^3 and He) to that base. See also more recently Charles Owen, *The Manuscripts of the* Canterbury Tales (Cambridge: D. S. Brewer, 1991), passim. The massive Manley-Rickert edition (hereafter M-R) attempted to use the full corpus and thus ostensibly chose no base text; see Ralph Hanna III, *Pursuing History: Middle English Manuscripts and Their Texts* (Stanford, Calif.: Stanford University Press, 1996), pp. 132–34. However, the M-R text itself may come down to a revision of Skeat's *Student's Edition* of the *CT;* see Derek Pearsall, "Authorial Revision in Some Late Medieval Texts," in A. J. Minnis and Charlotte Brewer, eds., *Crux and Controversy in Middle English Textual Criticism* (Woodbridge, Suffolk; and Rochester, N.Y.: D. S. Brewer, 1992), pp. 39–40.

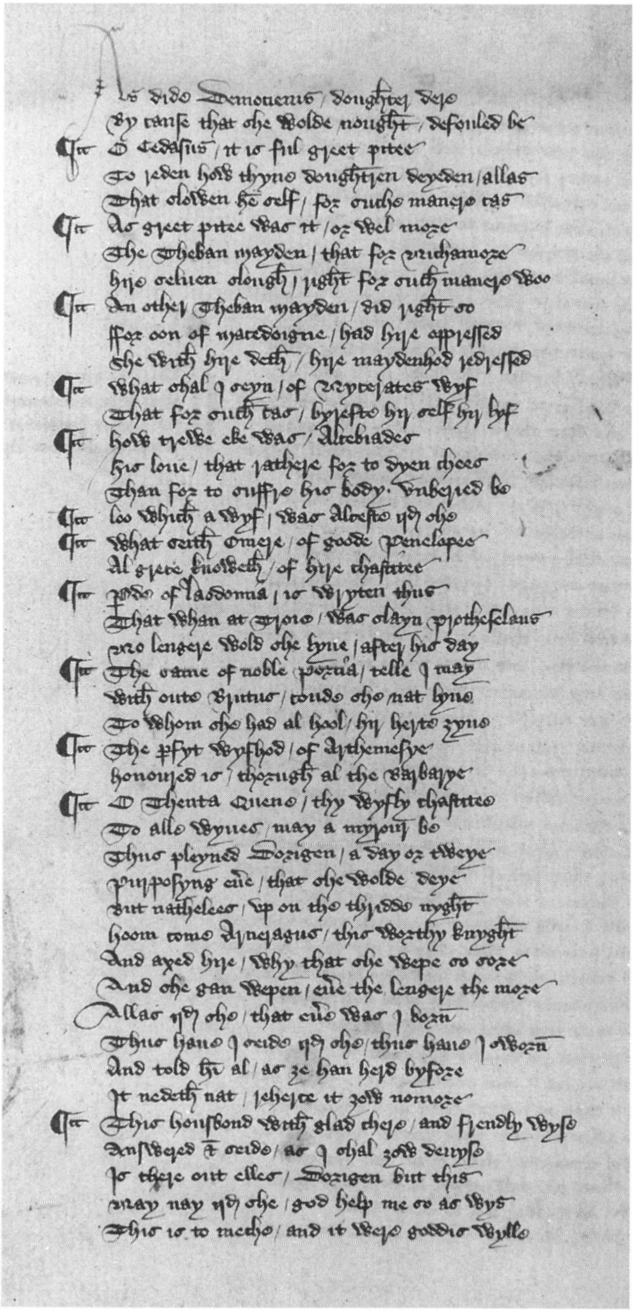

Figure 1: Oxford, Corpus Christi College MS 198, fol. 169r (*FranT* 1428–67). By permission of the President and Fellows of Corpus Christi College, Oxford.

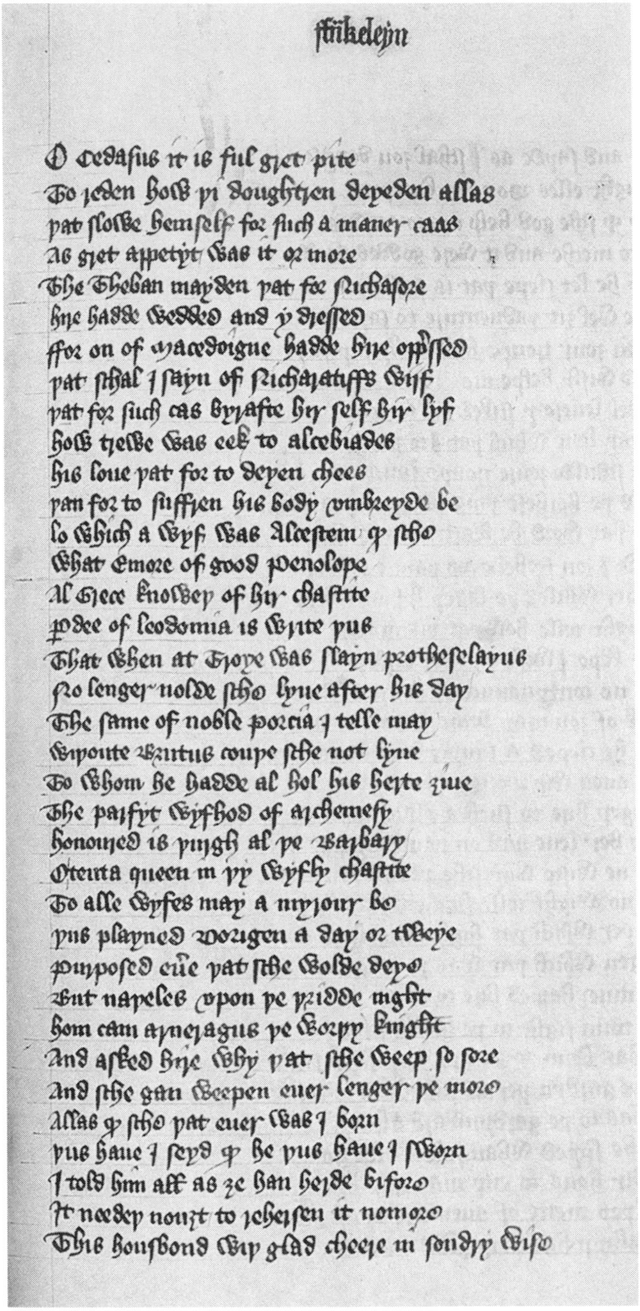

Figure 2: Cambridge University Library MS Dd. 4. 24, fol. 136v (*FranT* 1426–71). By permission of the Syndics of Cambridge University Library.

Quite simply, in Dd these exempla all are marked carefully with a paraf, whereas in Cp no such markers are used. Thus Dd insists on distinguishing each exemplum as a separate pearl of wisdom pulling toward the margins, regardless of narrative movement, for potential storage in that treasure-house of memory or reading out to a select audience. Cp preserves the purity of the text column and the narrative integrity of the speech as a whole, which contains these exemplars but is not overshadowed by them.

The energetic reader could check the facsimiles of the Hengwrt and Ellesmere manuscripts of *The Canterbury Tales* and discover that their divisions for this passage are virtually identical to those of Dd. The ambitious reader might go beyond these critical favorites to note, among the landmark manuscripts, that Cambridge Gg.4.27 and Additional 35286 also follow these divisions. Cp's restraint, on the other hand, is maintained in landmark manuscripts Lansdowne 851, Petworth, Helmingham, and to a lesser extent Harleian 7334. Not only classical exempla but also selected speeches, narrative intrusions, and other such jewels embedded in the narrative ground are flagged often in the first group, whereas the second group uses such divisions as a very occasional signpost at most. These opposed approaches to internal divisions typify broader strategies for the layout of vernacular books that competed in the literary marketplace throughout the fifteenth century and into the early printed editions of the sixteenth century.

From its earliest days as a reconstructed unity, *The Canterbury Tales* has been designed for two very different methods of reading, but no one has noticed this design. Ralph Hanna has mentioned briefly the thousands of internal divisions in Hengwrt and Ellesmere (the usual suspects) but has not extended his gaze to other witnesses.[4] Recent work on other Chaucer manuscripts, particularly *Troilus and Criseyde,* has begun to recognize marked-off lyrical insertions and annotations (using

[4] See Ralph Hanna III, "(The) Editing (of) the Ellesmere Text," in Martin Stevens and Daniel Woodward, eds., *The Ellesmere Chaucer: Essays in Interpretation* (San Marino, Calif.: Huntington Library, 1995), pp. 233–34, and his introduction to *The Ellesmere Manuscript of Chaucer's* Canterbury Tales: *A Working Facsimile* (Woodbridge, Suffolk: D. S. Brewer, 1989), pp. 11–14. My conclusions here, based on a larger sample and much narrower focus, differ from his observations in several respects; nonetheless, I am indebted to Hanna's pioneering example for inquiring into manuscript practices as complex mediations. Also see A. I. Doyle and M. B. Parkes's "Palaeographical Introduction" to The Canterbury Tales: *A Facsimile and Transcription of the Hengwrt Manuscript with Variants from the Ellesmere Manuscript,* ed. Paul G. Ruggiers, with intros. by Donald C. Baker, A. I. Doyle, and M. B. Parkes (Norman: University of Oklahoma Press, 1979), p. xxxix.

methods pioneered by Sylvia Huot) to analyze the response of readers.[5] The two patterns of division in the *Canterbury Tales* manuscripts, which I will call simply *dense* and *sparse,* are also reader responses, but those of the producers trying to assemble a unified single-author work out of the fragments available at Chaucer's death. In great detail, these responses define structures for Chaucer's narratives as well as the idiosyncratic concerns of each producer as an individual reader and annotator.

There is a growing awareness that production of vernacular literary manuscripts expanded rapidly in London after 1400, and at the heart of that expansion is the trinity of late-fourteenth-century, London-area poets: Chaucer, Gower, and Langland. The assertion of a humanist canon fueling that expansion founded the reputations, and consequently heavy manuscript production, of the three great frame-tale poems by each of the latter: *The Canterbury Tales* (hereafter *CT*), the *Confessio Amantis,* and *Piers Plowman.*[6] Although there is general agreement that text divisions and the creation of what the immortal team of Doyle and Parkes call the *ordinatio* in a manuscript are a crucial part of that process, parafs and minor initials have attracted little interest in Middle English manuscript studies, barely worth the notice of art historians as decoration or of editors as text dividers.[7] Professor Meech's dismissal of their place in his edition of *The Book of Margery Kempe* is notable only for its candor.[8]

[5] A special number of the *Huntington Library Quarterly,* 58.1 (1996), titled "Reading from the Margins: Textual Studies, Chaucer, and Medieval Literature," raises these issues, particularly in Ardis Butterfield's "Chaucer and French Manuscript Culture," pp. 49–80, and Julia Boffey's "Proverbial Chaucer and the Chaucer Canon," pp. 37–47. Also see Boffey's "Annotation in Some Manuscripts of *Troilus and Criseyde,*" *EMS* 5 (1995): 1–17; and Philipa Hardman, "Chaucer's Articulation of the Narrative in *Troilus:* The Manuscript Evidence," *ChauR* 30 (1995): 112–33. The influential studies by Sylvia Huot, anticipating much of this focus on lyric insertions in *Troilus,* are *From Song to Book: The Poetics of Writing in Old French Lyric and Lyrical Narrative Poetry* (Ithaca, N.Y.: Cornell University Press, 1987) and *The Romance of the Rose and Its Medieval Readers: Interpretation, Reception, Manuscript Transmission* (Cambridge: Cambridge University Press, 1993).

[6] A. S. G. Edwards and Derek Pearsall, "The Manuscripts of the Major English Poetic Texts," in Jeremy Griffiths and Derek Pearsall, eds., *Book-Production and Publishing in Britain, 1375–1475* (Cambridge: Cambridge University Press, 1989), pp. 257–78.

[7] A. I. Doyle and M. B. Parkes, "The Production of Copies of the *Canterbury Tales* and the *Confessio Amantis* in the Early Fifteenth Century," in M. B. Parkes and A. G. Watson, eds., *Medieval Scribes, Manuscripts, and Libraries: Essays Presented to N. R. Ker* (London: Scolar Press, 1978), pp. 163–210. Also see M. B. Parkes, "The Influence of the Concepts of *Ordinatio* and *Compilatio* on the Development of the Book," in J. J. G. Alexander and M. T. Gibson, eds., *Medieval Learning and Literature: Essays Presented to Richard William Hunt* (Oxford: Clarendon Press, 1976), pp. 115–41.

[8] Professor Meech gives up the paraf on p. 3 n. 3 of *The Book of Margery Kempe,* ed. S. B. Meech and H. E. Allen, Early English Text Society, no. 212 (London and New York: Oxford University Press, 1940).

More recently Derek Pearsall, in his introduction to the facsimile of the Douce 104 manuscript of *Piers Plowman,* did broach the topic but then threw up his hands at any attempt to find coherent patterns, a response students of that poem will recognize.[9] The importance of these divisions to *trecento* poetry has been acknowledged only recently;[10] despite some general recognition that *divisio scientiae* affects the narrative practice of *divisio textus* on a grander scale in Gower and Chaucer, analyzing this issue at the level of paragraphs seems to have been too much to face.[11] But I have soldiered on in the belief that these divisions play a crucial role in late-medieval interpretation of texts.[12]

Within Middle English manuscripts the paraf represents a long evolution, out of the oral rhythms of classical rhetoric adapted by Isidore of Seville and through the consciously textbound patterns of division laid out for the *lectio* of the scholastics and the poetics of Geoffrey of Vinsauf and Matthew of Vendôme.[13] This history is encapsulated in the graphic

[9] Piers Plowman: *A Facsimile of Bodleian Library, Oxford, MS Douce 104,* intro. Derek Pearsall, catalogue of illustrations by Kathleen Scott (Woodbridge, Suffolk; and Rochester, N.Y.: D. S. Brewer, 1992), pp. xxiii–xxv.

[10] See n. 44 and n. 47 below.

[11] See Rita Copeland, *Rhetoric, Hermeneutics, and Translation in the Middle Ages: Academic Traditions and Vernacular Texts* (Cambridge and New York: Cambridge University Press, 1991), pp. 207–20.

[12] Also see my discussion of division in some less examined manuscripts of the period in "Decorated Initials in the Lincoln Thornton Manuscript," *Studies in Bibliography* 47 (1994): 78–88; and "Reading the Dream Miniature in the *Confessio Amantis,*" *M&H* n.s. 22 (1995): 61–93.

[13] The only extended analyses of internal text division I have seen are by Roger Middleton and the team of Françoise Gasparri, Genevieve Hasenhohr, and Christine Ruby; both appear in *Les manuscripts de/The Manuscripts of Chrétien de Troyes,* ed. Keith Busby *et al.,* 2 vols. (Amsterdam and Atlanta: Editions Rodopi, 1993) 1:136–42, I:149–93. More broadly the history of the paraf (and other internal dividers) has been studied most fully for the period up to the thirteenth century, but almost entirely concentrated on the work of grammarians and scholastic commentators. Recent summaries can be found in Jean Chatillon, "Désarticulation et restructuration des texts à l'époque scolastique (XIe–XIIIe siècles)," in Roger Laufer, ed., *La notion de paragraphe* (Paris: Éditions du centre national de la recherche scientifique, 1985), pp. 23–40; Jean Vezin, "La division en paragraphes dans les manuscrits de la basse Antiquité du haut Moyen Age," in ibid., pp. 41–52; and Marc Arabyan, *Le paragraphe narratif: Étude typographique et linguistique de la ponctuation textuelle dans les récits classiques et modernes* (Paris: Harmattan, 1994), pp. 35–46. Older surveys by paleographers (which at least chart the development of the form of the paraf up through the fifteenth century) include Paul Lehman, *Erforschung des Mittelalters,* 4 vols. (Stuttgart: Anton Hiersemann, 1961), 4:9–11, 21, figs. 37–53; W. Weidmüller, "Paragraphzeichen," *Archiv für Geschichte des Buchwesens* (1966): cols. 469–84; Albano Sorbelli, "Dalla scrittura alla stampa: Il segno di paragrafo," in Raffaelo Morghen, ed., *Scritti di paleografia e diplomatica in onore di Vincenzo Federici* (Florence: L. S. Olschki, 1944), pp. 335–47. On the broader question of punctuation and sense units in the movement from oral to written, see the recent magisterial study by Malcolm Parkes, *Pause and Effect: An Introduction to the History of Punctuation in the West* (Berkeley: Univer-

form of what the French call the *pièd-de-mouche,* where the symbol "¶" functioned as an abbreviation for "caput" or its diminutive "capitulum" by attaching to the letter-form "c" one or two vertical descenders. This continuous association with "heads" of speech betrays the rhetorical roots of what became a marker for narrative episodes, embedded allusions, and other structural elements of written textuality. Small initials also play a role in this process, often creating a hierarchy of internal text dividers (i.e., breaks or points of emphasis within a tale, prologue, or link), beginning with parafs and going up the scale to initials several lines high and in some cases (though not in the *CT*) miniatures within the text column itself to indicate the relative importance of the division.[14]

To judge by modern editions of the *CT,* there is a general sense that these little markers should be an absent presence, as they are in modern paragraphing: indicated by a blank space when the editor happens to approve of a break within a tale or link, or normalized to modern practice and regularity without comment in critical editions.[15] This practice is one of the most substantial, yet unacknowledged, ways in which we have redesigned medieval texts to be very different from what their contemporaries would have read. In their efforts to make Chaucer accessible

---

sity of California Press, 1993); the brief discussion in Jean Vezin, "La ponctuation aux xiiie, xive, et xve siècle," in H. J. Martin and J. Vezin, eds., *Mise-en-page, mise-en-texte du livre manuscript* (Paris: Promodis, 1990), pp. 457–60; and the older survey by Walter Ong, "Historical Backgrounds of Elizabethan and Jacobean Punctuation Theory," *PMLA* 59 (1944): 349–54.

[14] For a review of decorative hierarchy in the design of late medieval manuscripts, see Sandra Hindman and James D. Farquhar, *Pen to Press: Illustrated Manuscripts and Printed Books in the First Century of Printing* (College Park: Art Dept., University of Maryland, 1977), pp. 63–72. On the use of miniatures as textual dividers in the *Confessio,* see Jeremy Griffiths, "*Confessio Amantis:* The Poem and Its Pictures," in A. J. Minnis, ed., *Gower's* Confessio Amantis*: Responses and Reassessments* (Cambridge: D. S. Brewer, 1983), pp. 163–78, and Fredell, "Dream Miniatures." On the probable use of miniatures as textual dividers in a *Troilus* MS (Cambridge, Corpus Christi College MS 61), see Hardman, "Chaucer's Articulation," p. 127.

[15] Divisions were handled much differently in the Chaucer Society transcripts of individual manuscripts of the *CT;* some of the initials and parafs are preserved and laid out on the page to replicate manuscript divisions. However, this partial fidelity seems to have sprung from a Victorian fascination with medieval visual effects, preserved as a quaint antiquity rather than as objects for serious study. No scholarship on these divisions beyond some art-historical description survive from the period. Both individual and parallel-text editions of the *CT* published by the Chaucer Society make an effort to include minor divisions in their proper place, but their accuracy is vastly lower here than in the matter of recording textual variants. I can say from personal experience that these transcripts are at best unreliable guides to general habits of division.

to modern readers, twentieth-century editors of the *CT* have regularly thrown out much of the apparatus vital to the manuscripts they rely on, particularly glosses and internal text dividers.[16] The two major sources these editors mine for their texts of the *CT,* the Hengwrt (Hg) and Ellesmere (El) manuscripts, have literally thousands of these dividers and substantial marginalia. Parafs in this dense pattern hover on the edges of the page with the commentary to flag passages perceived to have aphoristic wisdom—such as Dorigen's exempla—but also key dialogue, "authorial" interjections, references to *auctoritates,* pithy statements of opinion, and episodic shifts. Nonetheless, in both the prose and the decasyllabic couplet forms of the *CT,* modern editors indicate internal divisions by a blank indentation. This paragraphing is usually closest to the El divisions; but editors regularly accept El choices that fit modern paragraphing practice, ignore those that do not, and add without remark or justification other divisions the editors apparently prefer.[17] It is a pointed comment on our willing ignorance of the archaeology of the book that modern editors of the *CT* have been so dependent on El, yet so unwilling to sully their pages with the decoration and apparatus that lends El its particular authority as a deluxe edition and reappears in the printed edition of Wynkyn de Worde.[18] Less obvious is our ignorance of

[16] See the similar judgment on editorial practices for the *Vita Nuova* in the edition by Dino S. Cervigni and Edward Vasta (Notre Dame: University of Notre Dame Press, 1995), pp. 20–28, and the appendix proposing a new editorial system of parafs, pp. 304–25.

[17] Norman Blake, "Geoffrey Chaucer: Textual Transmission and Editing," in Minnis and Brewer, eds., *Crux and Controversy,* pp. 35–38, makes this point about the textual editing in *The Riverside Chaucer,* gen. ed. Larry D. Benson (Boston: Houghton Mifflin, 1987), used here for all citations for the *CT* as the standard edition it unquestionably has been from its first publication. Unless specific manuscript variants are noted, quotations and line numbering will follow the Riverside edition. Nonetheless, I must note one central concern here with that edition. Despite the assurance that Riverside editors at least reexamined textual variants in the *CT,* that new effort did not extend to textual divisions. A brief example should suffice. El, alone among the landmark MSS, places a logical enough division at *WBP* 393 with no break at *WBP* 395 (see table 3). Riverside places the break at line 395, a break for which there is no landmark manuscript witness, with no stated justification for its specific decision here or its general policy elsewhere. Apparently the editors simply follow F. N. Robinson, ed., *Works of Geoffrey Chaucer,* 2d ed. (Boston: Houghton Mifflin, 1957). Robinson himself suggests that in the pattern of textual arrangements "perhaps the only one of serious interest to the reader" is the order of the tales (p. 889). Any other matter of organization is apparently below the notice of the serious student willing to read the introduction to the textual notes, already a highly self-selected group among Chaucerians, I suspect.

[18] Exceptions to this tendency are Norman F. Blake, ed., The Canterbury Tales*; Edited from the Hengwrt Manuscript* (London: Arnold, 1980), and, of course, the diplomatic transcriptions coming out from the Canterbury Tales Project, under the direction of Blake

sparse patterns of division for the *CT,* which use minimal glossing and internal structuring of the tales. This is the competing tradition, absorbed by Caxton and, it could be argued, a more influential model for the modern construction of editions of the *CT* than El, most of whose features are known only to a small cadre of specialists.

At this point I fear that only that same cadre might be willing to read on, those who will brave the spectacle of textual editors brandishing their piles of collations or paleographers sorting out scribal hands among the masses of minims. I will confess here to tabulating all the text divisions for every tale in the ten landmark manuscripts. This confession may prompt little more than pity for the drudgery involved from colleagues who prefer to leave all such endeavors to a few specialists in each generation—or fear from the reader that I will document all this work below. Fear not: I will provide only limited evidence here. However, Chaucerians who do not know the *CT* in its early forms simply have not experienced the poem in all the glorious complexity of its mediating witnesses.[19] The early history of the *CT* is a particularly provocative topic because the first manuscript producers were assembling the poem as a unified text from fragments, *membra disiecta* floating around after the death of Chaucer.[20] So "construction" in this case has practical as well as theoretical meaning. Arranging the order of the tales is the most familiar problem associated with early constructions of the *CT* as a unit, but a more vital presentation issue for establishing the *CT* as a

---

and Peter Robinson. Thynne, it should be noted, uses blank indentations along with small initials and parafs to mark divisions.

[19] Pearsall, "Authorial Revision," p. 41, points out some problems in recent well-known critical arguments uninformed by textual complexities in the *CT.* Lee Patterson does grapple with the problem to defend his use of the El order as an interpretive tool in *Chaucer and the Subject of History* (Madison: University of Wisconsin Press, 1991), pp. 41–45. However, Patterson relies on the notion that Hg vs. El is the only question, the textual clash of titans, a common move that avoids the messy but substantial evidence from other early witnesses. In many respects a dutiful recognition of Hg before dismissing the irritatingly diverse textual evidence has become a Chaucerian security blanket rather than an informed critical position.

[20] An early pronouncement on this topic is Pamela Robinson's "The Booklet: A Self-Contained Unit in Composite Manuscripts," *Codocologica* 3 (1980): 46–69; she applies this idea to Chaucer in her introduction to *Manuscript Tanner 346: A Facsimile* (Norman, Okla.: Pilgrim Press, 1980). A fuller discussion for the *CT* followed in Charles A. Owen Jr., "The Alternative Reading of the *Canterbury Tales:* Chaucer's Text and the Early Manuscripts," *PMLA* 97 (1982): 237–50; refined more recently in Owens's *The Manuscripts of the* Canterbury Tales (Rochester, N.Y.: Boydell & Brewer, 1991). Also see the overview by Ralph Hanna III, "Booklets in Medieval Manuscripts: Further Considerations," in *Pursuing History,* pp. 21–47.

unified, monumental work is book design. Obvious factors that assert a work's importance are size and expensive programs of miniatures, but in this respect surviving *CT* manuscripts fall well below the contemporary standard set by John Gower's *Confessio Amantis* and John Lydgate's long poems into a realm more like that of *Piers Plowman.*[21] Given the still-undervalued literary stock of these poets in our day, and probably a hidden desire to save the unstable text of the *CT* from the editorial fate of *Piers,* the relative restraint and wide variations found in the design of *CT* manuscripts seem a bit embarrassing by comparison. Yet the more modest realm of internal text dividers provides an enormous font of information to make such comparisons at the original point of production for the canonical "father of English poetry."[22] I will argue that its minor decorations establish the primacy of Hengwrt in developing a distinctive method of reading the *CT* (which we now associate with Ellesmere), despite the uncertainties of its larger patterns of organization in the ordering of the tales. At the same time I hope to establish that a method of reading witnessed by Cp is at least as important in the history of the *CT,* dominating modern interpretation of each tale as an integrated narrative unit. Those concerned with the early cultural history of the *CT* may find the new body of data presented here broadly useful as an interpretive tool.

II. Dense and Sparse Patterns

The idea that there might be two different understandings of the *CT* among its earliest producers was first broached in a classic article by A. I. Doyle and M. B. Parkes:

> The *ordinatio* of the Ellesmere manuscript interprets the *Canterbury Tales* as a *compilatio* in that it emphasizes the roles of the tales as repositories of *auctori-*

[21] See Edwards and Pearsall, "Manuscripts," pp. 260–61.

[22] Similar patterns show up in Lydgate's long frame-tale poems in couplets. In the *Troy Book,* for instance, compare the sparse divisions of Cotton Augustus A.iv and Rawlinson C446 to the dense division and complex decorative hierarchy of Arundel 99 and Digby 232. These manuscripts share many other features of layout and probable London commercial provenance, as Doyle and Parkes observe ("Production," p. 201 and n.). In contrast, divisions in Gower's *Confessio* increased according to a kind of regular evolution over the fifteenth century in response to marginalia inserted into the text column: internal divisions marking "introductions" and other breaks created by these intrusions attempt to rationalize their presence within the Middle English narrative; one highly developed example is Morgan Library M 126.

tates—sententiae and aphorisms on different topics which are indicated by the marginal headings.

. . . .

In Corpus Christi Coll., MS 198 [our Cp] . . . is evidence of yet another attempt to interpret the unfinished work by imposing an *ordinatio* upon it. This interpretation emphasizes the *Canterbury Tales* as a sequence of stories on different topics.[23]

Doyle and Parkes use the term *ordinatio* to refer to some of the machinery of the *mise-en-page*—running titles, headings, colophons, illustrations, marginal glosses—as crucial elements organizing the poem. The distinction they point out is central to reading and understanding the *CT.* The El design presents the tales as a single-author vernacular encyclopedia, a category that could embrace poetic compilations like the *Roman de la Rose* of Jean de Meun or the *Tesoretto* of Brunetto Latini. This version of the *CT* can be understood in terms very similar to the *Confessio,* whose own frame tale, head verses, and marginal machinery arrange a vast array of exempla, pagan and Christian, into an encyclopedia organized by the familiar penitential branches of sin rather than the secular means of the alphabet or the quickly subverted social ordering of Chaucer's pilgrims.[24] The dense *mise-en-page* of El supports two sets of voices, those arising from the narrative itself in the text column, and those inhabiting the margins, with the parafs facilitating an exchange between the two camps.[25] The Cp design, however, presents the tales with virtually no such indexing, and virtually no commentary from the margins; the tales

[23] Doyle and Parkes, "Production," pp. 190 and 193, respectively. Also see the argument by Blake, *Textual Tradition,* p. 97, that the numbering system in Cp organizes the *CT* in book chapters rather than the structure of prologue-link.

[24] See A. J. Minnis, "John Gower, *Sapiens* in Ethics and Politics," *MÆ* 49 (1980): 207–29; also see his broader discussion in *Medieval Theories of Authorship* (London: Scolar Press, 1984), pp. 168–90.

[25] For a discussion of this interplay of voices in Gower's *Confessio,* see Derek Pearsall, "Gower's Latin in the *Confessio Amantis,*" in A. J. Minnis, ed., *Latin and Vernacular: Studies in Late-Medieval Texts and Manuscripts* (Cambridge and Wolfeboro, N.H.: D. S. Brewer, 1989), pp. 24–25; Winthrop Wetherbee, "Latin Structures and Vernacular Space: Gower, Chaucer, and the Boethian Tradition," in R. F. Yeager, ed., *Chaucer and Gower: Difference, Mutuality, Exchange* (Victoria: University of Victoria, 1991), pp. 7–35; and Siân Echard, "With Carmen's Help: Latin Authorities in the *Confessio Amantis,*" *SP* 95 (1998): 1–40.

speak for themselves with only a light structure of episodic pauses marked by occasional parafs in otherwise blank margins.

These distinctions are so fully supported by the use of internal text dividers, and so clearly developed in the landmark manuscripts, that they must represent opposed design traditions coexisting from the earliest days of the construction of the *CT.*[26] The Cp pattern occurs commonly in both Anglo-Norman and Middle English poetry, particularly in the flexible structure of narrative couplets, which do not have the inherent formal divisions of stanzaic poetry. For the sake of relative simplicity and the reader's patience I will concentrate here on tales in couplets, since Chaucer's rime-royal stanzaic and prose works represent distinct literary and decorative traditions.[27] Parafs in this sparse pattern within a tale primarily mark new episodes, the opening exposition of a long argument, or the head of some speech deemed crucial. This pattern is used in the secular Middle English poems of the Auchinleck manuscript from around 1330–40; in later vernacular saints' lives in couplets, such as the *South English Legendary* and the *Northern Homily Cycle* in the Vernon and Simeon manuscripts from around 1390; in most of the early London manuscripts of the *CT;* and in the romances of the later Lincoln and London Thornton manuscripts, to name just a few well-known

[26] Harleian 7334 (Ha[4]), a product of the same scribe (known to cognoscenti as "D") who gives us Cp, is closest to the sparse style but also has features that ally it with the El design. Scribe D was identified by Doyle and Parkes in "Production," pp. 174–82. The evidence that Scribe D was a professional regularly working in London on literary manuscripts is borne out by the list ("Production," p. 177) of manuscripts with his hand, to which recent study has added five more manuscripts; see the summary in Owens, *Manuscripts,* p. 1 n. The designs of Ha[4] and Cp thus cannot be judged simply the products of personal scribal habits or preferences, but like the *Confessio* MSS must reflect deliberate choices. The identification of Scribe D has been challenged by R. Vance Ramsey. An article that conveniently summarizes the challenge, early responses to this challenge, and Ramsey's counterresponse is the latter's "Paleography and Scribes of Shared Training," *SAC* 8 (1986): 107–44. There is no sign in print that Ramsey has gained any adherents in the years since his arguments were published.

[27] Both French and Italian traditions may be important here; one example of the latter is Boccaccio's *Teseida,* whose autograph manuscripts use a complex system of divisions marked by parafs at selected stanzas rather than the "all or none" pattern of markers at each stanza head one might expect (personal communication from William Coleman). Such dense patterns in Chaucer's stanzaic tales do occur, but need to be discussed fully in relation to continental literary traditions he clearly knew. Similarly, divisions in Chaucer's prose tales need explication in terms of the highly developed strategies found in devotional and scholastic prose treatises. Among Chaucer's other long poems in couplets, *The Book of the Duchess* has significant variations for its divisions in Tanner 346, Bodley 638, and Fairfax 16 (which also sprinkles *The House of Fame* heavily with notes).

points of reference.[28] These parafs map the narrative as parts of a linear progression, elements that must be understood in terms of the whole tale, and so are subordinated to the content and meaning of the larger narrative. A single passage or a small number of them may be emphasized, but they function as unifying interpretive touchstones for the narrative rather than independent windows onto a broader vista of literary authorities. The widely distributed romances of Alexander, for instance, use this tactic.[29] This tradition emphasizes the integrity of the individual tale, without the presence of extrinsic organizing agendas that highlight smaller chunks of narrative, or "intertextual" flags carried by marginal glosses. In effect, this kind of romance reading allows the rhythms to emerge out of the experience of the narrative with minimal direct mediation. The polyvocality and intertextual palimpsests still lodge in Chaucer's text, but they remain univocally contextualized; the voices resonate within the larger structures of the narrative, not in the learned cultural arena of the margins where the voices of commentators cluster.

The dense tradition appears to be most fully developed in Hg and El, but close parallels also exist in three other landmark manuscripts: Dd.4.24 (Dd), Gg.4.27 (Gg), and Additional 35286 (Ad^3).[30] This use of internal divisions corresponds more closely to texts found in lay devotional collections and academic texts where both prose and poetry are thick with scriptural allusions, proverbs, pagan *disticha,* and other such nuggets flagged for the reader as worthy of independent meditation and/or cross-referencing to authoritative sources. Manuscripts of *Piers* and the *Confessio* from the end of the fourteenth century already had appropriated this dense tradition before the first appearance of (surviving)

[28] I have deliberately chosen examples here that can be found in published facsimiles. See *The Auchinleck Manuscript: National Library of Scotland Advocates' MS. 19.2.1,* intro. Derek Pearsall and I. C. Cunningham (London: Scolar Press, 1977); *The Vernon Manuscript: A Facsimile of Bodleian Library, Oxford, MS. Eng. Poet. A.1,* intro. A. I. Doyle (Cambridge and Wolfeboro, N.H.: D. S. Brewer, 1987); *The Thornton Manuscript (Lincoln Cathedral Ms. 91),* intro. D. S. Brewer and A. E. B. Owen (London: Scolar Press, 1975); the Hengwrt facsimile cited above, n. 4; Daniel Woodward and Martin Stevens, eds., The Canterbury Tales: *The New Ellesmere Chaucer Monochromatic Facsimile of Huntington Library MS EL 26 C 9* (San Marino, Calif.: Huntington Library, 1997); and *Poetical Works: A Facsimile of Cambridge University Library MS. Gg4.27,* intro. M. B. Parkes and Richard Beadle (Norman, Okla.: Pilgrim Books, 1980).

[29] Fredell, "Decorated Initials," pp. 84–87.

[30] Other representatives of this tradition are Paris Anglais, Lichfield 2, Delamere, Selden, Harley 7333 (Fragment A only), Phillips 8136, and Rawlinson Poetry 141 (in *WBP, WBT,* and *SqT*).

manuscripts of the *CT.* Among the many examples I could mention here are the Cambridge Dd.1.17 manuscript of *Piers,* and the Fairfax manuscript of the *Confessio.*[31] Earlier I noted the similarities between El and deluxe MSS of the *Confessio* such as the Fairfax; indeed, the scribe now known to aficionados as "B" worked on a deluxe edition of the *Confessio* between his efforts on Hengwrt and Ellesmere.[32] However, I would like to add that the absence of a hierarchy of internal divisions is common to Hengwrt and the other examples of dense use among early *CT* MSS, and is in fact much closer to dense use in *Piers* MSS, a resemblance we might be more willing to consider now that scholars are trying to locate a Social Langland in London and Westminister circles intersecting those of Social Chaucer.[33]

In both forms of dense text division, hierarchical or horizontal, narrative and episodic shifts are mapped much more frequently, speech heads are flagged much more often, and the thick weave of allusions is bookmarked with great attention. Particularly in manuscripts such as the Hengwrt *CT* or the Cambridge Dd *Piers,* when no hierarchy of minor divisions is imposed, distinctions between narrative shifts, speech heads, and proverbs can disappear quickly. What results is an atomized text in which almost any moment could be read as a wisdom moment; any flagged lines could signal another aphoristic jewel embedded in the narrative ground, waiting to be extracted and polished for display by itself. This sapiential reading dictates the narrative rhythms horizontally, through the presence of marginal commentary that can extract moral wisdom from any worthy source—sacred, pagan, or local. The multiple voices of the narrative become a crucial point of entry (and exit) not only from tale to tale but within each tale. Similarly, the authenticating devices of academic texts taken over by vernacular poets—introductions, citations of source authors, and all the machinery that places the

[31] For a facsimile of a similar manuscript of *Piers* (Douce 104), see n. 9 above. No published facsimiles for manuscripts of the *Confessio* now exist.

[32] Doyle and Parkes, "Production," pp. 163–92; Doyle and Parkes also identify Scribe D's hand in this MS.

[33] See most recently Kathryn Kerby-Fulton and Steven Justice, "Langlandian Reading Circles and the Civil Service in London and Dublin, 1380–1427," *New Medieval Literatures* 1(1997): pp. 59–84; and Kerby-Fulton, "Langland and the Bibliographic Ego," in *Written Work: Langland, Labor, and Authorship,* ed. Steven Justice and Kathryn Kerby-Fulton (Philadelphia: University of Pennsylvania Press, 1997), pp. 110–22. On parallels between the layout of Hg and the Trinity College, Cambridge B.15.17 MS of *Piers* (B-text), see Doyle and Parkes, "Palaeographical Introduction," p. xxxiii.

text within the culture of the book—will be marked assiduously.[34] Yet these points of entry may also serve a public function beyond their index of closeted scholarly voices: such passages could be marked for reading aloud to a family or court circle of listeners, and glossed for that broader audience's edification.[35]

These dense and sparse patterns coincide with the other, better known features of manuscript *ordinatio* prompting the original distinctions by Doyle and Parkes. As the appended tables show, all of the landmark manuscripts announce the divisions between tales with major decorations, usually bar borders, and all respect the distinctions between prologue and tale (when both are present) with separate decorations setting off a section of text that constitutes an introduction. Hg and El always have the most divisions and minor initials, followed by Dd and Gg; Cp/La/Pw have far fewer in roughly equal numbers among themselves. Marginalia are common in the dense pattern (the first four MSS from the left in the tables), quite rare in the sparse pattern (the last three MSS from the left in the tables). Internal small initials are not unusual in the dense pattern, and virtually unknown in the sparse pattern, except to indicate what seems to be a new beginning (*WBP* 163, *CYT* 1012). Ha[4], with its relatively high proportion of initials and independent choices but relatively few divisions overall, does not fit easily in either camp.[36] For the other nine landmark manuscripts, nonetheless, these distinctions support clearly opposed reading design strategies: the thickly flagged text of the dense pattern follows the vernacular encyclopedia model found in decorated manuscripts of the *Confessio* and *Piers;* the lightly flagged text of the sparse pattern imitates the presentation of narrative poems in the Middle English romance tradition.

Although these general patterns occur with remarkable consistency in most early manuscripts, they still require several caveats. One complicating factor is that in *The Knight's Tale,* alone in the *CT,* the sheer

[34] On this assimilation, see A. J. Minnis, *Medieval Theory of Authorship,* 2d ed. (Philadelphia: University of Pensylvania Press, 1988), pp. 160–210. A recent theoretical assessment of this machinery, though with limited discussion of medieval practices, is Gérard Genette, *Paratexts: Thresholds of Interpretation,* trans. Jane E. Lewin (Cambridge and New York: Cambridge University Press, 1997).

[35] The best recent discussion of this widespread late-medieval practice is Joyce Coleman, *Public Reading and the Reading Public in Late Medieval England and France* (Cambridge and New York: Cambridge University Press, 1996).

[36] Ha[4] also appears to have different types of *ordinatio* for quires 1–11 and 20 vs. quires 12–19 and 21 onward; see Blake, *Textual Tradition,* p. 69.

numbers of divisions are closer to equivalent in all eight witnesses. Further complicating this evidence is that in Cp a second hand added most of the parafs in *The Knight's Tale* in a pattern roughly equivalent to the later witness Ad^3, a pattern that may have influenced the exceptional density for this tale in La/Pw.[37] Similarly, in Gg one hand marked paraf prompts for *The Knight's Tale* and Fragments 6–9 in the dense pattern, another marked paraf prompts in the dense pattern for Fragments 4–5, both hands marked *The Wife of Bath's Prologue* and *Tale,* and the remnant gets little attention. Dd has parafs added by at least two other hands; most of these mark marginal glosses in the scribe's hand.[38] These additions could be the equivalent of accreting layers of commentary, testimony to the arrival of other copies of the *CT* used for comparison and correction by a series of owners and/or the original team producing the manuscript.[39] I have been careful in my tables, therefore, to distinguish the dominant style of small initials, parafs, and decorating prompts in a manuscript from the additions of other hands. For similar reasons I have included in the tables a record of marginal glosses, since parafs may mark the text at points where there was a gloss in the exemplar or an earlier ancestor.[40] We may not be able to reconstruct the chronology of these additions, but we can separate out distinct layers. These internal

[37] This same hand adds parafs in Cp at *GP* 521, 542, 669, and 715, but does not appear again after *KnT.* Parafs in the second hand in Cp are now faded and often invisible on microfilm or in the M-R rotographs housed at the British Library. A third hand adds parafs at *WBP* 563 and at several lines of the *FranT.* I would like to thank Christine Butler, archivist for Corpus Christi College, Oxford, for her kind assistance in my examination of Cp.

[38] In Dd all parafs have a visible prompt except for marginalia; this level of decoration seems to be the product of two hands working together, using two different decorating prompts for parafs and two different styles of paraf. Prompt 1 (a flourished double virgule) is constant to the end of Frag. 1 of the *CT;* prompt 2 (a simple double virgule topped with a horizontal line in "pi" form) begins with the first paraf in the *MLT,* then predominates in the rest of the MS. Two forms of paraf occur intermingled throughout Dd (designated ¶ and ¶a in the tables) and are used with both prompts. The former predominates and always occurs to the left of the prompt, the latter always on top of the prompt. The former paraf is much more common; the latter (¶a) seems to be by a correcting and revising hand.

[39] Also see Doyle and Parkes, "Palaeographical Introduction," pp. xxxviii–xxxix, who note that Scribe B's attempt in Hg to mark specific stanza heads in rime royal tales with a double virgule is frustrated by the decorator's mechanical placement of parafs at every stanza head.

[40] My own observations suggest that such an association is rare, and that producers carefully distinguished parafs for text divisions from those for glosses in tales in couplets, though in prose works the paraf can function more like a footnote marker to associate the gloss with specific passages in the text. The glosses themselves are the subject of a forthcoming book by Stephen Partridge.

divisions thus serve as the record of an original reading process, of layers of variation on that process, and of the range of exemplars used in this continuous interaction with the physical manuscript.

III. Transmission

Still remaining is the question of how these patterns actually moved through what we now call the textual tradition of the *CT.* It is tempting to use the evidence to argue stemmatically: Cp would represent an original sparse version proximate or (that Shangri-la) identical to Chaucer's autograph original, Dd a later copy of an early form of the dense tradition expanded by Hg and improved by El; the divisions simply would build up from sparse to dense to denser through lost intermediaries in this line of reasoning. Of course, the stemmata could also be reversed, going from dense to sparse, since both patterns of division occur very early in the manuscript tradition. We have no idea how Chaucer's autograph for any of the tales might have looked, whether he indicated any system of divisions or glosses. Still, these data pose the question of what sort of divisions Chaucer would favor. Manuscripts of the *Confessio* and *Piers* with complex divisions and glossing circulated in the time Chaucer was writing the *CT.* If Chaucer meant to imitate the successful designs of these poems, then the dense tradition would be the likely authorial choice. However, we do not know the role Gower and Langland played in these divisions, either.[41] One problem is that any one of these manuscripts of the *CT* could represent an "original" tradition close to the urtext; the others could witness a movement away from this original to satisfy their own agendas or the integration of two or more traditions into a complex text hierarchy. Since there are reasons to believe that some tales circulated independently during the time Chaucer was writing others, Chaucer himself may have issued fair copies with a sparse pattern of division closer to the Middle English romance tradition for

[41] This topic simply has not been opened for *Piers;* as for the *Confessio,* older assumptions that Gower was personally involved in the production of early copies has been challenged, if not routed, by Peter Nicholson. See his "The Dedications of Gower's Confessio Amantis," *Mediaevalia* 10 (1988): 159–80, and "Poet and Scribe in the Manuscripts of Gower's *Confessio Amantis,*" in Derek Pearsall, ed., *Manuscripts and Texts: Editorial Problems in Later Middle English Literature* (Cambridge: D. S. Brewer, 1987), pp. 130–42.

such independent booklets, and another set in the dense sapiential pattern designed for a full-scale *Confessio*-like edition of the poem.[42]

The only tale for which hopeful evidence exists for a dense O-manuscript (Chaucer's original final copy, if one existed) is *The Knight's Tale* (table 1). Here, three marginal glosses, all in Latin, may be authorial by virtue of their presence in early manuscripts, dense and sparse: a quote from Statius that points indirectly to Boccaccio's *Teseida,* a quote from Boethius, and a gloss for the Bear constellation.[43] Similarly, the unique level of density for *The Knight's Tale* in Cp/La/Pw, and the presence of corrected divisions in Cp that parallel El/Ad[3] closely, suggest that this tale may have been conceived in a dense pattern allied to *trecento* vernacular poetry, particularly the *Teseida,* which established an authorially controlled and dense *mise-en-page* roughly equivalent to that of Gower's *Confessio.* Boccaccio wrote and arranged his own marginal *chiose* (glosses) and dense divisions marked by parafs, witnessed by a surviving autograph manuscript, and a copy of another autograph, of the *Teseida.*[44] There is evidence Chaucer used a glossed and densely divided *Teseida* as a source for *The Knight's Tale.*[45] We also know that an early version of *The Knight's Tale* circulated enough in courtly circles for it to be flaunted in the bibliographic credentials Chaucer presents in his introduction to *The*

[42] Chaucer's other poems in couplets (*The Book of the Duchess, The House of Fame,* and *The Legend of Good Women*) survive only in manuscripts with sparse divisions, suggesting that pieces from the *CT* circulating as independent poems did not incorporate the dense pattern. However, Thynne uses dense divisions throughout all three of these poems. These may come from a lost dense tradition, or may represent Thynne's generalizing the pattern from the *CT* to these poems. Also see n. 44 below.

[43] *Thebaid* 12.519–20 at *KnT* 859; *Consolation* 3.m12.52–55 at *KnT* 1164; "Ursus maior" at *KnT* 2058. See M-R 3:484–85, where they assert authorial status for the first two.

[44] The autograph MS of the *Teseida* (Aut. Laur.) is Florence, Bib. Laurenziana MS Acquisti Doni 325; the copy of an autograph (NO) is Naples, Bib. Oratoriana del Monumento Nazionale dei Gerolamini, MS Pil, X, 36. The *chiose* (glosses) include summaries, commentary, glosses, indexing marginalia, and other such humanist machinery, all written by Boccaccio. Translations of the *chiose* are available in *The Book of Theseus: Teseida delle nozze d'Emilia,* trans. Bernadette Marie McCoy (New York: Medieval Text Association, 1974). The dense parafs in these MSS have not yet been analyzed, but are the subject of a work in progress by William Coleman and Edvige Agostinelli (personal communication). The divisions at issue occur within stanzas of the *Teseida*—virtually all stanza heads have parafs in these MSS. I am grateful to William Coleman for bringing these manuscripts to my attention.

[45] See Piero Boitani, *Chaucer and Boccaccio* (Oxford: Society for the Study of Mediaeval Languages and Literature, 1977), pp. 113–16. However, William Coleman challenges this argument strongly in "Chaucer, the *Teseida,* and the Visconti Library at Pavia: A Hypothesis," *MÆ* 51 (1982): 97–99, and in "Chaucer's Manuscripts and Boccaccio's Commentaries on *Il Teseida,*" *Chaucer Newsletter* 9.2 (fall 1987): 1–6.

Legend of Good Women (F 420/G 408). Consequently, Chaucer may have developed a Boccaccian (or Gowerian) dense pattern for *The Knight's Tale* in a presentable, if not presentation, manuscript before the creation of the *CT,* a pattern that persisted into the surviving landmark manuscripts when copies of other tales were too "foul" for such attentions.

On the other hand, the paucity of these three possibly surviving glosses, and the relatively moderate density of divisions in Cp (in its original form)/Ha^4/La/Pw for *The Knight's Tale* do not constitute a very close parallel to the intense marginal commentary and divisions of the *Teseida* or the *Confessio.* The counterpoint of voices is still predominantly internal, contained within the column of Middle English narrative, as is the case with the rest of the tales. Other manuscripts of Chaucer's poetical works also have largely uninhabited margins; the most attention seems to come when a lyric voice bursts out of the narrative stream, as in the introduction to *The Legend of Good Women* or *Troilus and Criseyde.*[46] Looking back to the *trecento* once again, the closest analogy for this lyric bursting is Dante's *Vita Nuova,* a work where commentary and lyric poetry are self-consciously divided in terms discussed by the poet, but whose doubled literary voices stay (originally) within the bounds of the text column.[47] Significantly, it was Boccaccio who first tried to "free" the lyrics by copying the *Vita Nuova* himself with the commentaries removed to the margins, a *mise-en-page* he justified by declaring that the commentaries were *chiose,* not *teste* (text).[48] Chaucer's use of the lyric voice, however, is much more integrated with other voices in his narrative, rather than counterpoised with commentary. When an authorial voice does enter, it seems to be at least two steps removed from the double-barreled page of Boccaccio and Gower, and at least one step removed from Dante's single column of alternating authorial personae in the *Vita Nuova.*

[46] On these divisions in *Troilus,* see Boffey, Butterfield, and Hardman, n. 6 above; and Thomas C. Stillinger, *The Song of Troilus: Lyric Authority in the Medieval Book* (Philadelphia: University of Pennsylvania Press, 1992). In *LGW,* only the *balades* in the introduction attract a consistent flurry of internal divisions.

[47] The concordance in Cervigni and Vasta's edition notes forty-eight occurrences of the term *dividere* (in various forms) in the commentaries; on the importance of division for this work, see Steven Botterill, "'Però che la divisione non si fa se non per aprire la sentenzia de la cosa divisa' (*V.N.,* XIV, 13): The *Vita Nuova* as Commentary," in Vincent Molito, ed., *La gloriosa donna de la mente: A Commentary on the* Vita Nuova (Florence: Olschki, 1994), pp. 61–76.

[48] This declaration is contained in Boccaccio's own glosses, available in the edition of the *Vita Nuova* by Michele Barbi (Florence: Bemporad, 1932), pp. xvi–xvii.

Chaucer's personae are, of course, often comic or incapable of commenting effectively on a text in which they seem to have been trapped. This role could present a satire or other metacommentary on the commentary tradition, a strategy that asserts the role of the poet by deconstructing that of the Gowerian or Boccaccian critic/compiler: rather than take over the physical page with an assortment of learned voices, Chaucer the glossator gets stuck inside the funhouse of a narrative he should be able to control. These personae, and their distance from those of Gower, Boccaccio, and Dante in the matter of *divisio textus,* argue that Chaucer was not likely to have set up the *CT* in dense format. So do the signs that his early readers were looking for just such an authoritative presence in the handful of lines rather touchingly assigned to "Auctor," in tales with an uncertain tone where such a guiding voice may seem needed—notably the Merchant's.[49] Despite the fact that vernacular poets in England and Italy had gained control of the margins for autocommentary, there is little evidence that Chaucer valued that opportunity. Instead those blanks were open to a Lancastrian generation of compilers trying to align the *CT* with the designs of a vernacular sapiential literature.

What the evidence does support is that producers of the *CT* consulted multiple exemplars for parafs independent of their choice for a textual source, that they varied their practice from one fragment to another (probably based on the number and kind of exemplars available in booklet form for each fragment), and that they willingly added parafs and small initials as they saw fit from their own understanding of the text. Only when these patterns are set up comparatively can we begin to sort out important emphases: not the result of authorial intent but of reader response. In other words, we can identify when producers make independent and dependent choices for book designs in relation to what we can reconstruct of their exemplars. One result of earlier efforts to concentrate on design and supratextual machinery in *CT* manuscripts is that Hg comes off (familiarly) as the inferior sibling to El, despite Hg's apparent primogeniture by ten years. Another result is that El comes off (familiarly) as the pinnacle of appropriate organization and production decisions for the *CT:* earlier manuscripts at best only anticipate El's glories, later manuscripts only fall away. The evidence from minor text di-

[49] *MilT* 3611 (El/Dd/Ad^{3}); *MerT* 1783 (Hg/El/Dd/Gg/Ad^{3}/Ha^{4}), 1869 (Hg/El/Dd/Gg/Ad^{3}/Ha^{4}), 2057 (Hg/El/Ad^{3}), 2107 (El/Gg/Ad^{3}), 2125 (El/Gg).

visions complicates, if not contradicts, these truisms. Recent estimates put the production of El ten years after that of Hg, but there is no disputing that Hg was used as a model for this pervasive feature of El's famous *ordinatio.* Thomas Ross has called Hengwrt "an ugly little book," and even Doyle and Parkes deem it a "second-class" job;[50] though I have become quite fond of its look, I realize that a leap of faith is required to accept Hg as any kind of model for El's decoration. Ralph Hanna, at least, has made the leap, noticing that El follows the paraf placement of Hg with remarkable fidelity in the *Wife of Bath's Prologue* and *Tale,* though he does not pursue the apparent implications: the El team looked up the owner of Hg and borrowed it for its parafs, or Scribe B held onto Hg itself for ten years and followed it scrupulously for its parafs but not for its texts.[51] Either way, El looks astonishingly dependent on Hg for literally thousands of text divisions.

A third explanation would be that other exemplars with this kind of dense paraf use were floating around. Given the disjunction between parallels in text and parallels in division between Hg and El, we should be able to detach ourselves from the single-exemplar model of transmission, even within individual tales. Evidence of what textual editors still call "contamination" (the scholarly but inconvenient—for those stemmatically inclined—scribal habit of consulting other sources for readings) abound in the landmark manuscripts. If Scribe B did hang on to Hg or its prototype for El, the El team clearly used this exemplar for divisions, though, as I argue below, El also may have used sparse exemplars to develop its structure of small initials. Another parallel is Ad^3,

[50] See Doyle and Parkes, "Palaeographical Introduction," in *Hengwrt,* p. xxxix. Visitors to Hg—which is on permanent display at the National Library of Wales, Aberystwyth—will find a book "restored" by an undocumented cleaning in 1956, whose enthusiasm created a pristine velvet surface around the text columns and set off the distinctive Anglicana Formata script but robbed Hg of much of its history, once inscribed messily in those same borders; see Michael Pidd, Estelle Stubbs, and Claire E. Thomson, "The Hengwrt *Canterbury Tales:* Inadmissable Evidence?" in Norman Blake and Peter Robinson, eds., *The Canterbury Tales Project Occasional Papers, Volume II* (London: Office for Humanities Communication, 1997), p. 62.

[51] Hanna, intro., *Ellesmere Manuscript,* pp. 12–14. In a more recent discussion in "Ellesmere Text," pp. 233–34, Hanna falls back (appropriately for this scholarly venue celebrating El) on the familiar argument that El represents a vast increase in both numbers and intelligent placement of internal divisions for the *CT* manuscript tradition as a whole. Hanna does say that Hg "alone rivals El in efforts to divide the text; they are quite sporadic elsewhere" (p. 233). Since several later *CT* MSS survive with dense divisions rivaling those of Hg/El, as do the early printed editions of de Worde and Thynne, the survival of all these witnesses due to the direct influence of Hg/El alone seems to me a very unlikely history.

which contains a pattern of division and *mise-en-page* just as astonishingly close to El, but which uses different textual sources more closely aligned with Cp/La/Pw families. This parallel in presentation is attributed to some kind of access to El by the producers of Ad^3, though nothing like an identical scribe or decorative style connects the two.[52] Dd, well-known for its independent readings, also probably had access to dense exemplars; no obvious source for its consistent, if somewhat simplified, dense divisions survives, however. Gg adapts the El tale order but is "contaminated" by many corrections and independent readings, along with its patchy (probably unfinished) dense scheme of decorations.[53] By comparison Cp and the *cd* group of manuscripts seem to be substantially less edited, both in terms of text and division choices.

In short, producers who choose the dense pattern of division use the methods of a learned critic/compiler by interacting with the text and aligning it with multiple sources; producers who choose the sparse pattern seem more willing to let the text speak for itself. For all their astonishing parallels in division Hg/El/Ad^3 each have their own independent habits of emphasis. Scribe B and any other members of a production team for Hg may have started with exemplars whose paraf use was close to that of Dd, exemplars that already established the general emphases of the dense use of minor divisions and provoked Scribe Wytton's *nota*'s and Scribe B's further attention to women's issues. The reverse may also be true: Scribe Wytton may have had an exemplar whose text divisions were close to Hg/El, and selected the emphases he preferred. Whether or not it is an original baseline for the dense tradition, Dd functions as a useful comparison to indicate Hg's importance as an innovator and influence on El's textual hierarchy. Similarly, Cp provides a model for sparse *divisio textus,* whose principles would remain dominant throught the fifteenth century, even though points of structural emphasis may shift slightly.

IV. Reading the Patterns: Hg/El/Dd versus Cp/La

The two major patterns of internal division, dense and sparse, choose different elements of the narrative to emphasize. As I have mentioned,

[52] Most recently see Owens, *Manuscripts,* pp. 45–47.

[53] Parkes and Beadle, intro., *Poetical Works* (Gg facs.) 3:46–56; Owens, *Manuscripts,* pp. 23–24; M-R 1:176.

the sparse tradition consistently marks a few major episodic shifts and the heads of one or two critical speeches; the dense tradition marks wisdom passages, "authorial" interjections, references to *auctoritates,* pithy statements of opinion, changes in speakers in dialogues, shifts in episode, and shifts in the exposition of an argument. However, there is no mechanical consistency in flagging any of these points in the text. Though El marks speech heads more often than any other landmark manuscript, for instance, it does not come close to marking them all or even a constant type of speech. Internal divisions for these manuscripts are always the record of content-based selection, not rule-bound submission. These choices differ not only from one manuscript to another but from one tale to another. The data can be dizzying at first, especially among the sheer multitudes of dense divisions, but one key to this variation is genre. Different literary genres require different patterns of discovery to mark the distinctive forms sapiential reading can take. Speech heads for contrapuntal fabliau dialogue are treated differently than set-piece orations in romance; episodic shifts are similarly tied to the rhythms of their narrative types.

The most thoroughly flagged tales are those we might guess to be favorites for their syntheses of pagan mythology and medieval romance: *The Knight's Tale, The Squire's Tale,* and *The Franklin's Tale.* In these romances the gems that glitter most brightly are magical objects and pagan mythic insights. Occasional important speeches are marked, but the main fascinations beyond episodic shifts are the nuggets of magic and mythology—the magical gifts presented to Cambuskyan in *The Squire's Tale,* the necromantic illusions of the Clerk in *The Franklin's Tale,* the mythical temples in the amphitheater of *The Knight's Tale.* In the fabliaux, however, it is the dialogue that shines with the peculiar luster of moral inversion. In mixed-genre tales, these patterns tend to separate out according to the dominant narrative strategy of the moment, but the resulting structure uses densely flagged passages to establish a clear moral center.

An analysis of single tales across manuscripts, a rough cross-section of techniques for internal division, will serve to demonstrate the fundamentals of sparse and dense traditions. For the sake of brevity I will leave Gg, Ad^3, Ha^4, He, and Pw out of the discussion; their links with and departures from more regular avatars of dense and sparse should be evident, if not explicated, from the tables. Dramatic contrasts will still be apparent between the remaining witnesses in tales that provoke glossators medieval and modern. Right from the start, of course, one might suspect that any commonsense reader would come up with the same sorts of divisions noted in these manuscripts, since Chaucer's tales often provide overt verbal cues for narrative shifts. Such a shared view of narrative structure becomes less convincing if we consider, for instance, Dd's two-line initial at *MilT* 3406: "She sholde slepen in his arm al nyght." No other landmark manuscript marks this line in any way, let alone with the impact of a decorated initial—rare throughout Dd otherwise. This fascination with the sexual in Dd, also noticed by Ralph Hanna and Beverly Kennedy, plays out in all sorts of idiosyncratic divisions.[54]

For my purposes here, *The Miller's Tale* has the virtues of brevity and familiarity. This tale looms large in contemporary criticism because it provokes a "crisis of governance" in a tale-telling game whose social order breaks down very promptly, and it seems to reinvent the *CT* as a fabliau world in opposition to the romance of chivalric humanism painfully built by the Knight.[55]Yet the famous "mixed style" of the tale makes such oppositions less pervasive because learned elements—discussion of music and astrology; salvation history typology of floods, prophets, and *privitee;* the rhetorical *descriptio* techniques of the *poetria nova;* the fictions of empiricism used as an *apologia* by Chaucer the pilgrim—suffuse the burlesque of both *Prologue* and *Tale.* In the hands of Chaucer's first promoters, producers in Lancastrian England eager for a vernacular *sapiens,* many of these contradictory elements are simply passed over in dense and sparse structures that offer readings of the fabliau plot as moral exemplum.

Table 2 (in appendix 2) displays graphically the enormous difference in numbers between divisions for *The Miller's Tale* in Hg/El/Dd and in Cp/La. For convenience I have broken these divisions into categories in figure 3 (see appendix 1). Cp has no divisions in *MilP;* the "crisis in governance" and the knowing glosses of Robin and Geoffrey the pilgrim within the *Prologue*'s narrative are left to their own devices. La adds one paraf at the introduction for the Miller himself (*MilP* 3120). In Cp's *MilT* a total of six parafs appear. Of these six, four effectively map the plot macrostructure of the *Tale* in what I call shifts (a term that will cover shifts in plot, narrative exposition, and argumentative exposition).

[54] See discussion below and n. 65. Also see the observation by Doyle and Parkes that divisions in Hg can be "uneven in incidence and sometimes unexpected" ("Palaeographical Introduction," p. xxxix).

[55] Patterson, *Subject of History,* pp. 244–45.

The first paraf (line 3271) signals the shift from the opening exposition (three *descriptio* passages for Nicholas, John, and Alison, respectively, left unmarked after the initial for the first line of the tale) to the plot inaugurated by the *hende* courtship of Nicholas. The next paraf (line 3339) begins Absolon's secondary plot line after his own *descriptio* passage. The third (line 3397) returns us to Nicholas's plot to beguile John; the fifth (line 3601) heralds the final action arraying the three men around Alison's bed.[56] La's only additions to this elegant outline are to mark Absolon's description (line 3307) and his moment of entry into the first plot line (line 3657). Both manuscripts also flag one speech. Cp marks John's vow not to reveal Nicholas's prophecy (line 3508); La goes inside a speech by Absolon to point to his prophetic awareness of an itchy mouth (line 3682).[57] One intrusion of the narrator, given a paraf in both Cp and La, sounds like a wisdom moment: "Lo, which a greet thyng is affeccioun!" (line 3611). If this passage is marked out as a proverb despite the sarcasm that now seems to drip from it, it is the only one granted such status. It does, however, lend meaning to the isolated speeches flagged in Cp/La as well as the engine driving the double linear plot that these manuscripts outline. As such, this proverb becomes a touchstone for the exemplary power of the *Tale,* a single interpretation of events as products of the power of love, authorized by the manuscript producers to sum up the plot structure they articulate. Rhetorical devices and learned allusions are ignored in favor of straightforward fabliau actions whose meaning is articulated by a single world-weary proverb trading on a long sapiential literature that seizes on love as a universal organizing concept.

The approach to division in Hg/El/Dd is massive by comparison. The sparse tradition's simple outline of plot structure is lost among the spreading parafs in Hg/Dd. El sketches in a plot structure close to that

[56] A prompt for a decorator to insert a paraf occurs at Cp 3687, the opening of the first window scene. As I discussed above, parafs were added in a second hand to Cp in the *GP* and *KnT,* but this prompt is not in that second hand, and thus may represent an original indicator for a paraf missed by the first decorator.

[57] La is also alone in marking a speech by Alison at line 3709. All other witnesses mark *MilT* 3708, "Go fro the wyndow, Jakke fool." La's choice of the next line for a paraf may reflect a habit among Middle English producers to shift a division to the first line of a couplet, even if that division consequently is located away from the actual head of dialogue or logical shift; this habit shows up frequently in manuscripts of *CT,* the *Confessio,* and Lydgate's *Siege of Thebes* and *Troy Book.* I have noted similar habits in manuscripts of Brunetto Latini's *Il Tesoretto,* also in couplets (*settenari baciati,* in this case).

in Cp/La; two-line initials mark the major episodic shifts in El, but here emphasize the parallel roles of Nicholas and Absolon by separating out their plot lines.[58] Dd throws in only one two-line initial at line 3406, described above. Otherwise, the vast majority of dense divisions in all witnesses mark episodic shifts and heads of speech. Like Cp/La, these manuscripts pass over many sly and learned allusions without any sign of attention. All three manuscripts distribute episodic shifts fairly evenly across the *MilT* in the eighteen divisions they share, but clear emphases emerge in the shifts added by individual producers. Hg/El include nine more shifts not found in Dd, placing two in the scene where Nicholas prophecies the flood to John, and six in the window scenes at the end (lines 3419–600, 3708–823). The effects of concentrations are even more pronounced in the speech heads. The nine parafs whose placement Hg/El/Dd share are, with one exception, located in two scenes to the exclusion of all other speech in the *Tale:* the prophecy scene and the window scene that plays out Absolon's first kiss (lines 3687–746). The Hg/El additions thicken the marked dialogue heads in these two scenes, but also add dialogue heads through the second window scene, in which Absolon returns with the hot *kultour* (lines 3747–823). Hg/El thus include the dialogue between Absolon and Gervase as a link between the two window confrontations that melds the final action into one continuous scene. Within the *Tale,* then, two scenes become centers of attention, both of them focused on the tricks defining the parallel plot lines of John and Absolon's unrequited love.

Two passages marked in Hg/El/Dd strike me as wisdom moments: the narrator's interjection at line 3611, discussed above, and a speech by Nicholas at line 3298 when he boasts that a clerk has been wasting his time if he cannot beguile a carpenter.[59] The latter speech seems to play this role not because suitable passages are rare in this tale. Instead, this little speech by Nicholas pairs nicely with the narrator's comment on affection in the larger binary structure shaped by the parafs in the dense pattern. Although the divisions in Hg/El/Dd may seem to scatter across the *Tale,* in fact they concentrate attention on two pivotal points: Nicho-

[58] El outlines the Nicholas plot line (parallel to Cp) with two-line initials at lines 3271 and 3397; El outlines the Absolon plot line (parallel to La) with two-line initials at lines 3307 and 3657; El adds one independent two-line for the Absolon plot line at line 3681.

[59] Dd has a marginal indexing paraf at line 3611, but no text division paraf or initial.

las's beguiling Oswald through *scientia* with prophecy; and Alison's beguiling Absolon through *affeccioun* with her exhibition of a more carnal form of knowledge. This structure effectively imposes a single exemplary comparison on the *Tale:* Nicholas's trick on John is matched by Alison's trick on Absolon because these plot points emphasize the wanton methods of two successful adulterers playing with the forms of knowledge they control in a world deserving of another cleansing flood. Such a simplification of the *Tale* neatly pairs biblical and contemporary stories of a fallen world, where John gets to play a cuckolded Lucifer descending in a bathtub. Thus the wisdom of Cato on marrying similitude, for instance (line 3227), is left unacknowledged in favor of the pearls of cynicism on education and affection.

In *The Miller's Tale,* the production teams for Cp/La/Pw, manuscripts in the sparse tradition, completely ignored the mixed style that imports learned allusions into the ancient comic structure of machinations around a *senex amans.* Instead these manuscripts provide a clear guide to converging lines of plot and one wisdom moment loaded with the freight of worldly cynicism. Production teams for Hg/El/Dd, manuscripts in the dense tradition, also ignore the mixed style in that they do not use a battery of divisions and marginal glosses to mark out the wide array of allusions. For the dense manuscripts, the voices of the fabliau players within the roadside drama and the tale define meaning. In the Miller's *Prologue,* Hg/El/Dd signal the major shifts and speech heads up to line 3167, but leave the Miller's pithy statements on *privitee,* and Chaucer the pilgrim's on being true to his material, unmarked. The dense focus on the battle for narrative control does allow the "crisis in governance" to emerge in the *Prologue;* the reversals performed by the drunken Robin mirror the tropology of trickery in the tale. Still, these fabliau voices and centers of density in both *Prologue* and *Tale* do not admit any attention to the moral and epistemological complexities raised by the clever, knowledgeable voice that occupies Robin's *apologia* and his narrative persona.

Subtler versions of this moral dialectic abound in Hg/El/Dd. Parallel passages of dialogue are singled out for exemplary comparison in *The Franklin's Tale* and, moving to different ethical arenas, in the *Pardoner's* and *Physician's Tales.* However, there these dialogues are part of more intricate structures woven into acknowledged sapiential ideologies, best examined in a text whose manuscript history is particularly well documented now: *The Wife of Bath's Prologue* and *Tale.*[60] No other text in the *CT* raises such basic questions about voice, subjectivity, and the performativity of gender bound by explicit scholastic traditions of Jankyn's book.[61] Within these traditions there are important distinctions, however; in the *Prologue,* the bibilical words of Jesus and Solomon and St. Paul mingle with Jerome's rantings (as adapted by Walter Map), along with lists of women's proverbial failings in the Wife's own voice and the putative ("thou seist") indirect voice of a shadowy figure that seems to represent husbands one to three. The early manuscripts are quite attentive to these distinctions, and selective about the misogynist rhetoric they flag.

If we look at Cp first, once again a basic structural pattern and, in this case, a conservative idea of glossing stand out. Cp uses only one division in the tale itself, at the beginning of the hag's speech on gentilesse.[62] Further emphasis comes from marginal notes at this point and at the conclusion of the passage (line 1205).[63] In the *Prologue,* Cp charts three major shifts in the story of Alison's last two husbands, the only two for which any narrative chronology emerges (lines 453, 503, 563) and the Friar's interruption at the end (line 829).[64] As in the *Tale,* Cp flags one wisdom passage that may serve to sum up the message of Alison's prologue: "Stibourn I was as is a leonesse, / And of my tonge a verray janglеresse" (lines 637–638). Cp, however, does not invite us to consider who painted this lioness with any marginal flags at the many passages playing with male authority. La makes a few additions to this model, notably Alison's snappy line at 414 that "al is for to selle" and the hag's encomium on virtuous poverty (*WBT* 1180–1206).

Most striking, however, is Cp's dutiful recognition of the biblical passages Alison cites in the opening of her *Prologue* (lines 31, 35, 51, 111),

[60] See Peter Robinson, ed., *The Wife of Bath's Prologue on CD-ROM* (Cambridge and New York: Cambridge University Press, 1996), which transcribes all manuscript witnesses and includes extensive recent commentary on those witnesses.

[61] For a summary of these questions and an edition of the source texts, see Ralph Hanna III and Traugott Lawlor, eds., *Jankyn's Book of Wikked Wyves Volume 1: The Primary Texts* (Athens: University of Georgia Press, 1997).

[62] This division is not at the head of the speech itself (*WBT* 1106).

[63] For the text of this and other glosses, see M-R 3:496–502; see also Stephen Partridge's discussion in Robinson, ed., *Wife of Bath's Prologue on CD-ROM.*

[64] Cp is defective in the early section of the *Prologue,* but based on the evidence of La it is likely that Cp had divisions at two other major shifts at lines 163 and 193—the Pardoner's interruption.

though Scribe D inserts only brief glosses without any text dividers. This feature is striking precisely because no other landmark manuscript but the relatively late Pw bothers to recognize these passages at all.[65] El, which seems to become an all-consuming glossator in the Wife's *Prologue,* does gloss other allusions to *auctoritee* in the vicinity, but still does little to assert their importance with divisions. Cp glosses one other passage, which may reinforce the passage at *WBP* 637 (and Cp's conservative recognitions of biblical authority as an interpretive touchstone for Alison's *Prologue*): "Deceite, wepyng, spynnyng God hath yive / To wommen kyndely, whil that they may lyve" (*WBP* 401–2).

There seems to be a powerful disjunction between the Bible-sanctioned misogyny Cp annotates in the *Prologue* and the genteel meritocracy this manuscript emphasizes in the *Tale.* Across the entire *Tale,* Cp marks only the opening of the Hag's speech on gentility (line 1109) with a paraf and gloss, and a brief note for the passage on virtuous poverty (line 1179). La shifts these emphases slightly. Three passages are marked in La that qualify as wisdom moments: "Wynne whoso may, for al is for to selle," beginning at *WBP* 414; "Whoso that buyldeth his hous al of salwes," beginning at *WBP* 655; and a passage from Jankyn's book on wives entertaining their lovers next to the freshly murdered bodies of their husbands (*WBP* 765). Along with an added shift at line 379, these new emphases reveal La's sparse form of participation in the misogynist exempla that pervade Alison's *Prologue.* In the *Tale,* however, this attention disappears. To Cp's one paraf La adds only a paraf at the beginning of the passage on virtuous poverty and a note at its end. Nothing in the action of the tale is flagged. Again these closing meditations may serve the same interpretive purpose as do the opening biblical allusions for the *Prologue,* striking a suitably penitential theme in both cases: the biblical allusions cluster around the marriage theme of the *Prologue;* the meditations insist on the redemptive power of moral virtue in a case where male aristocratic privilege has led to outright rape. If we take these emphases in parallel across both *Prologue* and *Tale,* they propose a structure of vice and remedial virtue as applied to the Wife and to the hag.

This parallel comes up in more elaborate fashion for Hg. Although the sparse pattern witnesses remain close for Alison's *Prologue* and *Tale,*

[65] Hanna, "Ellesmere Text," p. 234, notes without discussion Cp's independence in glossing for *WBP.*

another rapid glance at table 3 reveals much wider variations among the dense pattern manuscripts, particularly up to *WBP* 453. For brevity and convenience I have sorted these differences in figures 4 and 5 (in appendix 1), and will avoid the temptation to discuss all these variations fully. Here we face something much more like individual response, though a core of common habits lies underneath. One critic has already taken up the question of Scribe Wytton's misogyny and "prurient interest in sexual relations," as evidenced by his peculiar glosses and notes in Dd's version of the Wife's *Prologue.*[66] Though the glosses in El can also be seen as misogynous, these two manuscripts select almost mutually exclusive passages for this purpose: ten passages in Dd are not glossed by anyone else in this group; forty-eight passages are glossed independently in El.[67] Hg has no glosses at all in the *Prologue* and only one note (at line 1109) in the *Tale.* Given the huge number of textual variants in the *Prologue* this variation may seem less surprising, and may be evidence that the *Prologue* circulated enough on its own that a particularly diverse choice of exemplars existed by the time they were gathered in for inclusion in productions of the full *CT.*

Still, certain habits we saw in these latter tales do carry over for the dense patterns of Hg/El/Dd. Dd's shifts elaborate on the Cp model to keep track of Alison's five husbands in the confusing narrative weave after *WBP* 453; the text itself is rewritten, possibly by Scribe Wytton, to provide a run-through of all five husbands.[68] Although this added

[66] Beverly Kennedy, "Contradictory Responses to the Wife of Bath as Evidenced by Fifteenth-Century Manuscript Variants," in Blake and Robinson, eds., *Canterbury Tales Project,* pp. 30–31. Two other articles by Kennedy take up similar issues: the most clear presentation is in "Cambridge MS. Dd.4.24: A Misogynous Scribal Revision of the Wife of Bath's Prologue?" *ChauR* 30 (1996): 343–58, and "The Variant Passages in the Wife of Bath's Prologue and the Textual Transmission of the *Canterbury Tales:* The Great Tradition Revisited," in Lesley Smith and Jane H. M. Taylor, eds., *Women, the Book, and the Worldly: Selected Proceedings of the St. Hilda's Conference, 1993, Vol. 2* (Cambridge and Rochester, N.Y.: D. S. Brewer, 1995), pp. 85–102. Together these articles build an argument that the passages from *WBP* found in El/Dd (five in Dd, four in El) but not in Hg/Ad³/Ha⁴/Cp/La/Pw/He (see textual notes for table 3) are misogynist scribal interpolations, probably from Scribe Wytton in Dd (see "Scribal Revision," p. 355). Although I see problems with this identification (how, for instance, did El get Dd materials?), I will note simply that Dd does not mark any of these variant passages with a text division or gloss beyond a brief note at line 608; El marks a division at line 575, provides two glosses for lines 609–12, and leaves the two later passages unmarked.

[67] See table 3 for citations. I include indexing marginalia and glosses to lines 609–12 (lines omitted from Hg/Ha⁴/Cp/La/Pw) in this count.

[68] *WBP* 480, 503, 525, 563, 587, 627. Kennedy, "Misogynous Scribal Revision," pp. 347–51, argues for Scribe Wytton's malign intentions here.

structure may seem merely helpful, Dd's absence of engagement with Alison's earlier life becomes more noticeable when it is again the man's journey that Dd follows through Alison's *Tale.* The knight's moves up through the "women's court" are charted, but not the hag's, Guinevere's, or any one else's passage through the plot.[69] Even the two speech heads Scribe Wytton chooses manage to underline this overriding concern with the man, since they both have the knight responding to the hag's demand to be married; the first begins "Allas and weylawey!" (*WBT* 1058), the second "My love? . . . nay, my dampnacioun!" (line 1067—marked only by Dd). Once again Scribe Wytton's reading of Alison seems not only misogynistic but fraught with personalized anger.

Hg expands all three categories of division from the lesser levels and particular obsessions of Dd, here instituting a hierarchy of one-line initials and parafs that diverges sharply from the *ordinatio* in its version of *The Miller's Tale.* In *The Wife of Bath's Prologue,* the small initials sketch out the same major shifts as Cp/La and El (in initials) did in *The Miller's Tale:* the interruptions of the Pardoner and Friar, and the point at line 453 that separates the dramatic scene with the shadowy "corporate" husband of lines 193–452 from the narrative of the last two husbands after line 453. Hg institutes a fuller recognition of important speech heads in the *Prologue,* and El adds its own small initials simply to expand Hg's dialogue structure. In the *Tale* El provides only one minor initial: at line 913, which details the knight's "wo" at being given the chance to save his life by finding out what women want. This single initial marks the knight's acceptance of his quest, shifting attention away from his rape (unmarked in Hg/El and unknown among the *Tale*'s analogues) to his more honorable and familiar role in an Arthurian romance.[70]

The parafs in Hg's *Prologue* and *Tale* for Alison are, however, structured more intricately. The twenty-one shifts in the *Prologue* are distributed fairly evenly across major sections with a minor concentration in her diatribe to the corporate stand-in for husbands one through three (*WBP* 235–378). These shifts mark the heads of several "thou seist" passages (lines 257, 308, 337, 362, 371); the selected "speeches" take form as a list of misogynist charges that will later be articulated fully in Jankyn's book. It is in this section (*WBP* 641–787) that an exceptional cluster of parafs gather to mark fourteen exemplary passages on the

[69] *WBT* 882, 983, 1023, 1043.

[70] For rape-free analogues, see the summary in *Riverside Chaucer,* pp. 872–73.

wickedness of women (see table 3). In Hg this antifeminine emphasis is offset slightly by four parafs at the opening remarks of Jesus and Solomon (lines 14, 17, 30, 35) and two more for Alison's arguments about the uses of "membres . . . of generacion" (lines 116, 134). Still, the interpretive weight of the decoration clearly lands at the misogynist end of the emphases and the concentration of sapiential maxims Jankyn's book wields as well, when Alison's opposition is expressed as physical violence rather than the engaged argument she deploys in the opening (and largely unmarked) review of patristic authority. In the hands of Hg's production team, the competition is not between *experience* and *auctoritee,* a binary of supposedly mutually exclusive terms Alison abandons in the early section when she takes up scholastic disputation herself; instead, Hg shifts the wisdom search to the last scene, where familiar gendered binaries of male/intellectual/rational versus female/physical/irrational define the conflict and its resolution.

This bias continues in the *Tale.* The three major dialogue scenes that encapsulate the knight's experience—in the hag's bower, in Guinevere's court, and in the bridal bedroom—all occur in spaces where women seem to control the language, and all receive some attention to carefully articulated speech heads and shifts (*WBT* 1000–22, 1037–69, 1086–249). However, the wisdom passages cluster in two distinct locations: for the hag's speech on meritocratic gentility and virtuous poverty (lines 1109–206) and for the derogatory list of "what women want" (lines 925–82). Again two passages are marked out by dense division and apparently set up as parallel or balancing statements. Two important differences separate this strategy from Hg's parallels in *The Miller's Tale.* Instead of dialogue, wisdom passages shape this parallel structure in the Wife's *Prologue* and *Tale.* As the words of patristic *auctoritas* are taken out of Alison's disputation and recognized only in the voices of Jankyn and his book, so the voices of women in the *Tale* are transformed into a misogynist list (which parallels the "thou seist" list imputed to the corporate husband in *WBP* 265–378) and a series of moral pearls quoted from secular authors. The disputes of Alison's *Prologue* return transformed in the magical hag's voice, but the issues are now generalized to "mankind" and shifted to the tenets of humanist wisdom from Seneca to Dante. Overall, where Dd latches on to the feminine in Alison's *Prologue* and *Tale,* however malevolently, Hg renders moot her gendered voice of opposition.

Before we leap to conclusions about Scribe B's sexual history (Scribe

Wytton seems a better candidate for such play, anyway), let me note that in *The Merchant's Tale* the long opening speech on the joys of marriage, now often understood as sarcasm on the Merchant's part, is very densely flagged in Hg at each allusion, and also given by far the most copious marginal glossing of any among the handful of passages in Hg that are glossed. Dd and El pay far less attention to the Merchant's marriage enconium. Dorigen's speech (fig. 2) is another example, but what is exceptional about Hg is how many examples like this there are that are not marked in Dd or developed further in El—the opening to *The Physician's Tale* is another case in point. Hg is interested to an exceptional degree in examining the moral character of women as it is established by the sapiential literary tradition, and will pass over other allusions to authorities to preserve that emphasis. These choices also point toward a larger method in the selective didacticism in Hengwrt. Throughout the manuscript, passages that can be understood to provide straightforward moral wisdom of all sorts are heavily flagged, even if the context leads us now to believe that a particular pronouncement is ironic or polyvocalic or dissonant in some current sense: the Merchant's enconium on marriage, mentioned above, is one example, but so also are the Pardoner's mini-sermon on deadly sins that opens his *Tale,* the Summoner's glossing of friars and his Senecan exemplum on the angry potentate, Chaunticleer's discussion of Macrobian dream theory, and the Nun's Priest's invocation of scholastic rhetorical theory at the moment of Chaunticleer's tragic fall. Yet other such passages are not marked, and seem to have been purposely ignored because they are more overtly intended to subvert the sapiential tradition. Such glaring omissions include not only Alison's opening allusions to biblical and patristic authorities but also the Pardoner's arguments about good sermons from evil intentions and the Nun's Priest's passage on predestination and free will, which drops the names of Augustine, Boethius, and Bishop Bradwardine in rapid succession. In other words, the Hengwrt team seems to have set up a structure of text divisions that separated what it considered wheat from chaff among the allusions.

By comparison, El's elaborations on Hg seem more mechanical than ideologically driven. In Alison's *Prologue,* El adds only one minor inital to the structure of major shifts Hg sets up (line 379, cf. Dd). El adds eleven parafs that further subdivide shifts in Alison's arguments, three newly marked wisdom passages, and five "indirect" speech heads to the four already noted in Hg.[71] El's single largest addition here is an extensive series of glosses up to the Pardoner's interruption (lines 1–163) and smaller clusters elsewhere.[72] One effect of this thoroughness is to disrupt Hg's shift to the marital battleground at the end of Alison's *Prologue,* and to present instead a more evenhanded documentation of the authorities and ideas Alison opposes when she is marshaling her arguments instead of her left hook. In the *Tale,* El marks six new wisdom passages; three of these further develop the emphases in the hag's pronouncements on *gentillesse.* However, El goes further in focusing attention on the hag's speech, substituting two-line capitals where there are parafs in Hg/Dd at the topic heads of *gentillesse* (line 1109), poverty (line 1177), age and authority (line 1207), and turpitude (line 1213).[73] These additions to the original concentration on *gentillesse* are accompanied by another host of marginal glosses not found in Hg. Here again El follows Hg but imposes a hierarchical logic on the hag's speeches as well as on the larger structure of the *Tale.* In El the exemplary parallels seem to be the old sapiential thinking of the *Prologue,* which ultimately relegates Alison and Jankyn to the fabliau world of a reverse-gendered *senex amans,* versus the "new man" vision of a meritocratic *gentillesse* that elides the whole question of gender conflict in a romance fantasy ending.

One last example will take advantage of the truncated state of *The Squire's Tale,* which still manages to provide its own distinct intersection with romance. *The Squire's Tale* is imbued with magic, like Alison's Breton *lai,* but placed in an exotic infidel setting and possessed of magical objects that attract glossing within the narrative itself by the admiring crowds at Cambyuskan's court. This glossing occurs in the odd context of a kind of learned rabble seething around a display of these objects and babbling contradictory information with little apparent regard for conventional authority (*SqT* 189–262); the narrator declares that they "maden skiles after hir fantasies, / Rehersynge of thise olde poetries" (*SqT* 205–6), a charge that could include much of vernacular literature's

[71] In the series of "thou seist" passages in *WBP* 265–378, El adds parafs at lines 265, 278, 285, 293, and 348.

[72] See table 3. These glosses have been seen as furthering misogynist ends by Hanna, "Ellesmere Text," pp. 234–35; and Kennedy, "Contradictory Responses," p. 33. For the argument that these glosses effectively support Alison's attack on male authority, see Susan Schibanoff, "The New Reader and Female Textuality in Two Early Commentaries on Chaucer," *SAC* 10 (1988): 71–108.

[73] Also at one earlier shift (line 983).

attempts to wrest new poetry out of old pagan wisdom in what the Squire sums up as "janglyng" (line 257). The exhibition itself smacks of idolatry and fetishization of what are to become, from the example of the ring at least, little more than plot facilitators. The ring's magical translation powers do seem to resolve the Squire's frequent (if not obsessive) resort to the inexpressibility topos, though the hints of incest in the promised tales of the Algarsif and Cambalo (lines 663–70) may explain the ultimate silence that falls in the end. Still, though *The Squire's Tale* is unfinished, it also attracts respectful glossing from both sparse and dense patterns.

In Cp, both glossing and episodic divisions are very light. In the long scene where the magic gifts are presented and exhibited, Cp glosses briefly only one mythological reference (Pegasus) and does not mark any divisions in a sequence with many shifts and numerous speech heads until Cambyuskan ends the scene by rising from the table (line 263). The beginning of supper is marked at line 297, the advent of sleep at the familiar division for part 2 at line 347, and the beginning of the scene between Canacee and the falcon at line 409. No speech heads are flagged, and the only passage that could function as a wisdom touchstone Cp locates at line 401, where the narrator declares the importance of getting to the "knotte" of the tale before the reader's desire cools. As this summary reveals, *The Squire's Tale* is remarkably short of plot; the action is defined by the aristocratic rhythms of eating and sleeping, despite the excitements of an Arabian ambassador entering with magical gifts. It is also short of single passages that could serve as interpretive touchstones: the learned chat surrounding the magic gifts render them opaque for any such purpose. La does add a division to mark a wisdom passage on the ring; this passage seems to function as an interpretive key for the one hopeful plot development in the dialogue between Canacee and the betrayed falcon, also marked by a division in La at line 447. Still, for these producers the *Tale* is an underdeveloped fragment from which little meaning can be wrestled beyond the disappointments of its narrative style. Its connections to sapiential literature are less acknowledged than its relationship to the slow aristocratic rhythms of romance; its truncated plot leaves the text shorn of structural illumination.

The dense manuscripts are much more attentive, but still apparently just as unaware of the critique of glossing embedded in the *Tale.* Once again the dense witnesses map the shifts in movement more minutely.

The simplest form, in Dd, notes introductory passages; major movements and speech by the ambassador, Canacee, and the falcon; and a sprinkling of wisdom passages on magic gifts and raptor proverbs (see figure 6 in appendix 1). Scribe Wytton thus does pick up on the humanist concerns of pagan science, the flow of pity in a genteel heart, and the natural attractions of greener grass. However, his lack of engagement with this material is palpable in the predictable choices (no idiosyncratic divisions here) and marginalia even less detailed than that of the minimalist Cp. The female point of view on betrayal in love simply does not seem to animate this scribe as much as male-centered conflict does. Hg/El, however, mine this fragment much more assiduously for its romance wisdom. Both the descriptions of the magic gifts and the debate are marked with great attention and, in the case of El, with a series of indexing marginalia to announce where their virtues are discussed. As if to validate the *Tale*'s authority as a repository for such jewels, Hg/El add brief Latin glosses for two Middle English incitements to solepcism, or at least self-absorption: Cambyuskan is glossed as the "center of the circle"; the falcon is described in terms of the Boethian analysis of self-gratification. Both Hg and El add a relatively thorough series of shifts consistently across the fragment. They diverge, however, in four shifts added by Hg alone and eight by El alone. Hg marks passages about the magic horse (lines 170, 199) and Canacee's herbal remedies (line 638) along with the stories of her brothers promised at the end of part 2. El only subdivides more fully the plot and rhetorical movements of the narrative, such as marking the moment at line 477 when the falcon comes out of her swoon before she starts her speech at line 479. El may point more overtly to the magical gifts with its indexing marginalia, but Hg is the more insistent on dividing out wisdom passages fully. Again El concentrates on mapping narrative shifts overall with a consistency that seems more mechanical than intellectually engaged.

We may now see the magical gifts and the learned glossolalia they provoke as a text in "the redemptive powers of culture" that the Squire fails, a romance Parliament of Pagans;[74] however, in both Hg and El, the parallel centers of concentration are the passages describing the gifts and the contested explications of these properties. Here the powers of humanist science redeem pagan magic, despite the Squire's clearly stated doubts, much in the way that Christian allegory redeemed pagan

[74] Patterson, *Subject of History,* p. 73.

love acts in Ovid's poetry. Here morality and culture become interchangeable terms or hermeneutic tools. Even magic is translatable, like Alison's hag, into language any new man can understand, rather than the jangling the Squire suggests; this kind of translation is precisly the purpose of sapiential reading.

Examples could be multiplied beyond all tolerance, but these three *Tales* should suffice to define the shared interests and the idiosyncracies of these five manuscripts. Cp concerns itself with major narrative shifts, at most a few brief and dutiful glosses with no connection to a literary/critical agenda, and a single wisdom passage that serves to comment on the whole of the tale. La's additions elaborate or slightly shift these emphases, but do not change the fundamental sparse preservation of the tale as an integrated unit explicable in its own terms. The trio of dense manuscripts, by contrast, atomize each tale into an intricate series of plot shifts and points of sapiential *gravitas.* Dd's version is the simplest, the most obviously engaged with a personal vision of wisdom, and the least consistent in structure. Passages that attract Scribe Wytton's substantial attention are moments of male sexual entrapment and female martyrdom. Hg presents a substantially more intricate pattern of subdivision and glossing. Beyond the sheer numerical increase is the attempt to create a discriminating choice of wisdom passages, and to establish a moral dialectic by establishing two centers of concentrated divisions within a tale. What we now see as Chaucer's irony, or polyvocality, or philosophical entanglements with Chartrian integuments, is constructed very differently by the Hg team. Those passages judged to have vital moral wisdom, whatever their narrative context might be, are flagged heavily with parafs and the occasional minor initial. Passages are left unflagged when they invoke authorities from biblical, patristic, and scholastic traditions, but are judged to be openly subversive or opposed to those traditions. Since these distinctions often occur within the same tale, the dense parafs become clear pointers toward the richest fields of wisdom, and are sometimes structured as single sources or exemplary pairs in tales now known for their resistance to interpretive closure. Hg's interpretive clusters of *gravitas* suggest a vision of poetry as intertextual moral fiction. This sophisticated method of reading of *The Canterbury Tales* was taken over with remarkable fidelity and thoroughness by the Ellesmere team. El's celebrated use of a hierarchy of decoration may elaborate Hg's model but it does not change it. For the most part, El simply uses small initials to establish a reassuring superstructure of episodes above the moments of dialogue and moral epiphany; its minor reworking of Hg's divisions does little more than further atomize the clusters of *gravitas* among some added parafs.

All these readings of the *CT* may seem to violate Chaucer's masterpiece, particularly its resistance to interpretive closure and its conscious play with the truth-claims of fiction. It is instructive to recall that the *CT* was first produced as a complete work in a conservative Lancastrian environment during Gower's dotage and the ascendancy of Lydgate and Hoccleve. Orthodox piety and vernacular poetry were expected to walk hand in hand, so we should not be surprised to see that both sparse and dense patterns discover a moral function in the tales they structure. The sparse pattern effectively preserves the individual voices of each tale and each pilgrim-narrator, thereby assuming a moral relativism, a democracy of fictions, within the *CT* as a whole. The dense tradition may seem to offer a comfortably postmodern reading of Chaucer, pulling apart the text like a body being drawn and quartered by a team of horses: a Bahktinian melée of performed identities, or a Lacanian *corps morcelé* of discovered independent voices within the text. However, though the horses (and voices) may pull in different directions, in the sapiential designs of the dense pattern they all are driven by the same whip of moral force and purpose. In Chaucer's case that drive comes from the literary piety of a Lancastrian humanism that would rewrite the *CT* as vernacular saints' lives and pagan exempla for aristocratic behavior.

In many respects the sparse pattern is closest to modern conceptions of the physical presence of the *CT*. This book design seems to have won the battle of public taste in the fifteenth century, if the evidence of surviving manuscripts and the authority of Caxton's editions are to be trusted. Take one look at *The Riverside Chaucer* and its spare, clean pages devoid of initials, glosses, or other features of Ellesmere's *mise-en-page;* you might think that a different, older vernacular tradition of reading narratives grips the imaginations of modern editors and book producers far more than Ellesmere ever could. I am not trying to suggest a new method of reading *The Canterbury Tales,* but am merely pointing out that opposing methods began at its very inception as a cultural artifact. And while I can already separate out the ten landmark manuscripts of *The Canterbury Tales* into opposing camps, each of these early production teams had its own peculiar emphases as part of an individual construction of *The Canterbury Tales,* and deserves its own detailed analysis as part of the kind of full codicological study granted Ellesmere for so long.

Appendix 1: Figures 3–6

Figure 3:

Cp dividers in *MilT,* sorted (with La unless noted)
Shifts: 3271, 3307, 3339, 3397, 3601, 3687 (prompt only).
Speech heads: 3508.
Wisdom: 3611.

La additions in *MilT,* sorted
Shifts: 3307, 3657, 3681, 3813.
Speech heads: 3709.
Wisdom: none.

Dd dividers in *MilT,* sorted (with Hg/El unless noted)
Shifts: 3199, 3221, 3233, 3271, 3288, 3307, 3312, 3364 (Dd only), 3397, 3423, 3434, 3448, 3487 (El/Dd), 3601, 3657, 3671, 3687, 3747, 3798, 3806 (El/Dd), 3816.
Speech heads: 3432, 3492, 3508, 3513, 3522, 3537, 3708, 3714, 3740.
Wisdom: 3298, 3611.

Hg/El additions in *MilT,* sorted
Shifts: 3496, 3643, 3723, 3727, 3730, 3744, 3772, 3824, 3840.
Speech heads: 3490, 3526, 3538, 3718, 3719, 3720, 3742, 3766, 3779, 3783, 3790, 3792 (window scenes, 3708–3823).
Wisdom: none.

Hg alone additions in *MilT,* sorted
Shifts: 3399, 3444, 3648.
Speech heads: 3368, 3804.
Wisdom: none.

El alone additions in *MilT,* sorted
Shifts: 3303, 3348, 3370, 3383, 3736, 3811.
Speech heads: 3501, 3638.
Shifts within speeches: 3465, 3547, 3563, 3583, 3589 (Nicholas's flood plan, 3538–3600).
Wisdom: none.

Marginalia

3382 "Vnde Ovidius Ictibus Agrestis" Hg/El/Ad^3/Dd/La
3417 "quia pro" (glossing "ffor for") Dd
3599 "mitte sapientem etc" Dd
3611 "Auctor" El/Ad^3/Dd
3734 "Nota Malum Quid" Hg/Dd

Figure 4:

Cp dividers in *ProWBT,* sorted
Shifts: 453, 503, 563 (\\¶b), 587.
Speech heads: 829.
Wisdom: 637.

La additions in *ProWBT,* sorted
Shifts: 163, 193, 379, 452.
Speech heads: none
Wisdom: 413, 655, 765.

Dd dividers in *ProWBT,* sorted
Shifts: 163, 353, 379 (3), 453, 480, 503, 525, 563, 587, 627.
Speech heads: 829, 840, 850 (all external—Friar/Summoner/Host).
Wisdom: none (see glosses).

Hg/El additions in *ProWBT,* sorted
Shifts: 115, 135, 169, 193, 224, 308, 379, 481, 543, 563 (¶/2), 587, 593, 627, 666, 711 (¶/2), 788, 803, 811.
Speech heads: 235, 257 ("thou seist"), 337 ("thou seist"), 362 ("thou seist"), 371 ("thou liknest"), 431, 833, 840, 844, 854, 856.
Wisdom: 17, 35, 184, 371, 647, 721, 724, 727, 733, 737, 740, 743, 747, 757, 762, 765, 769, 771.

Hg alone additions in *ProWBT,* sorted
Shifts: 59, 811.
Speech heads: none.
Wisdom: 14, 30.

El alone additions in *ProWBT,* sorted

Shifts: 77, 95, 105, 226, 265, 278, 285, 293, 303, 357, 393, 451, 469, 563, 575 (line omitted in other MSS), 659, 669, 673.

Speech heads: 265, 278, 285, 293, 348 (all "thou seist").

Wisdom: 323, 373, 655 (1), 657.

Marginalia:

See Partridge in Robinson, *The Wife of Bath's Prologue on CD-Rom;* Hanna and Lawlor, *Jankyn's Book,* pp. 84–87.

Figure 5:

Cp dividers in *WBT,* sorted

Shifts: none.

Speech heads: none.

Wisdom: 1109.

La additions in *WBT,* sorted

Shifts: none.

Speech heads: none.

Wisdom: 1177.

Dd dividers in *WBT,* sorted

Shifts: 882, 983, 1023, 1043.

Speech heads: 1058, 1067.

Wisdom: 1109, 1127.

Hg/El additions in *WBT,* sorted

Shifts: 882, 913, (1/2), 983 (¶/2), 1023, 1043, 1046, 1073, 1083, 1219, 1228.

Speech heads: 1005, 1009, 1013, 1014, 1037, 1058, 1062, 1098, 1104, 1105, 1106, 1236, 1238, 1239.

Wisdom: 925, 935, 945, 952, 961, 1109, 1125, 1139, 1177 (¶/2), 1207 (¶/2), 1213.

Hg alone additions in *WBT,* sorted

Shifts: none.

Speech heads: none.

Wisdom: none.

El alone additions in *WBT,* sorted
Shifts: 899 (added line), 919, 983 (2), 1031, 1250, 1257.
Speech heads: none.
Wisdom: 929, 931, 1109 (2), 1127, 1133, 1146, 1177 (2), 1191, 1207 (2), 1213 (2).

Marginalia:
See M-R 3. 502–3.

Figure 6:

Cp dividers in *SqT,* sorted
Shifts: 263, 297, 347,(Cp¶/La5bar), 409.
Speech heads: none.
Wisdom: 401 (//).

La additions in *SqT,* sorted
Shifts: 335.
Speech heads: 447.
Wisdom: 247.

Dd dividers in *SqT,* sorted (with Hg/El unless noted)
Shifts: 28, 76 (¶a), 89, 168 (¶a), 189 (Dd¶a/Hg¶/El2), 277 (Dd only), 297, 305, 335, 346 (Dd only), 393, 409, 423 (Dd/Hg only), 538, 632.
Speech heads: 110, 447, 499.
Wisdom: 132, 156, 225, 401, 479 (speech head, Dd/Hg only), 606 (Dd/Hg only).

Hg/El additions in *SqT,* sorted
Shifts: 58, 275, 283, 291, 312, 357, 376, 432, 472, 621, 651, 661, 671 (Hg3/El4).
Speech heads: 380, 447.
Wisdom: 137, 146, 212, 216, 228, 236, 243, 247, 253, 258.

Hg alone additions in *SqT,* sorted
Shifts: 663, 665.
Speech heads: none.
Wisdom: 170, 199, 638.

El alone additions in *SqT,* sorted
Shifts: 42, 73, 174, 340, 382, 477, 495, 574.
Speech heads: none.
Wisdom: none.

Marginalia
22 "centrum circuli" Hg/El
115 "Of the vertu of the steede of bras" El
132 "Of the vertu of the mirour" El
146 "Of the vertu of the ring" El
156 "Of the vertu of the swerd" El
207 "Pegasus" El/Dd/Cp/(La 206)
273 "Venus in Pisces" Cp
606 "Boece. . ." Cp/Dd
608 "reditu suo singula gaudent" Hg/(El 609)

Appendix 2: Tables

Legend
Hg = Hengwrt, i.e., National Library of Wales, MS Peniarth 392
El = Ellesmere, i.e., San Marino, Huntington Library MS El.26.C.9
Dd = Cambridge University Library, MS Dd.4.24
Gg = Cambridge University Library, MS Gg.4.27
Ad^3 = London, British Library, MS Additional 35286
Ha^4 = London, British Library, MS Harleian 7334
He = Helmingham, i.e., Princeton University Library, MS 100
Cp = Oxford, Corpus Christi College, MS 198
La = London, British Library, MS Lansdowne 851
Pw = Sussex, Petworth, Petworth House (Lord Leconfield) MS 7
¶ = paraf in the typical style of the manuscript, usually over or next to one of the decorating prompts listed below.
\\ = no paraf, but paraf decorating prompt indicated by two diagonal lines leaning either left or right (*virgula suspensiva*); most common prompt under finished parafs.
π = no paraf, but paraf decorating prompt indicated by two vertical lines topped by a horizontal—probably a modified double virgule, i.e., "*cc.*"
ω = paraf indicated by a small "w" with a tail curling above or on the

right of the letter form—probably an otiose or flourished double virgule; standard in Hg and Dd.

△ = two points in a horizontal line with a small "s" elevated between them as if the apex of a triangle, e.g., ".s.", possibly a positura ending a section; only found in Gg among manuscripts listed here.

n = marginal note, i.e., "nota," "nota bene," "verum est."

n¶ = marginal note flagged by a paraf on the left of the text.

i = indexing marginal gloss, i.e., "argumentum," "narrat," "exemplum," "auctor," name of character.

i¶ = indexing marginal gloss flagged by a paraf on the left of the text.

g = annotating marginal gloss, i.e., definitions, citations, relevant quotes, commentary.

g¶ = annotating marginal gloss flagged by a paraf on the left of the text.

☞ = manicula in the margin pointing to the line indicated.

5 = decorated initial whose size in ruled spaces for lines is indicated by the number, i.e., "5" indicates a 5-line initial, "1" indicates a 1-line initial, etc.

4bar = decorated initial with bar border whose size in ruled spaces for lines is indicated by the number.

- = no decoration at the line indicated.

0 = manuscript defective at the line indicated.

om = text omitted at the line indicated.

N.B. Interlinear glosses, scribal corrections (unless noted), and marginalia on topics not directly related to the text at hand (i.e., owners' family names, birthdays, love notes, rough drafts of business letters, doodles, pen trials, etc.) are not recorded in these tables.

Table 1
The Knight's Tale

Tale	Hg	El	Dd	Gg	Ad[3]	Ha	Cp	La	Pw	He
1.859	5	7bar	3	0	4	3	4bar	6bar	3bar	0
875	¶	¶	-	0	¶	-	-	-	-	0
893	4	4i¶	0[1]	0	3	4	-	¶	2	0
905	¶	¶	0	0	¶	-	-	-	-	0
912	-	¶	0	0	¶	-	¶a	-	-	0
915	¶	-	0	0	-	-	¶	¶	-	0
931	¶	¶	0	0	¶	-	¶	-	-	0
952	¶	¶	0	0	¶	-	1	¶	π	0
975	¶	3	0	Δ[2]	¶	2	1	¶	-	0
981	¶	¶	0	-	¶	-	¶a	-	-	0
985	¶	-	0	-	-	-	-	-	-	0
1001	¶	¶	0	-	¶	-	¶a	-	-	0
1005	¶	¶	0	-	¶	2	¶a	-	-	0
1013	-	-	0	i[3]	-	-	-	-	-	0
1014	-	-	0	i	-	-	-	-	-	0
1025	¶	-	0	-	-	-	1	¶	-	0
1033	¶	¶	0	\\	¶	-	¶a	-	-	0
1049	-	-	0	-	-	-	-	¶	¶	0
1052	-	-	0	-	-	-	-	-	-	0
1056	¶	-	0	-	-	-	-	¶	-	0
1061	-	-	0	i	-	-	-	-	-	0
1092	-	-	0	-	¶	-	¶a	¶	-	0
1093	-	¶	0	-	-	-	-	-	-	0
1101	-	-	0	-	¶	-	-	-	-	0
1112	¶	-	0	-	-	-	-	¶	-	0
1123	¶	¶	0	-	¶	-	¶a	-	-	0
1126	¶	¶	0	-	¶	-	¶a	-	-	0
1128	-	¶	0	-	¶	-	¶a	-	-	0
1129	¶	-	0	-	-	-	-	-	-	0
1145	-	-	0	-	-	-	¶a	-	-	0

[1] Dd 878–919 has mutilated edge, no decoration in margins remain. Dd missing 920–1170 entirely.

[2] Appears on right side of line, instead of left as usually.

[3] All indexing glossses boxed in *KnT* in Gg unless noted otherwise.

KnT	Hg	El	Dd	Gg	Ad[3]	Ha	Cp	La	Pw	He
1152	-	¶	0	-	¶	-	¶a	¶	-	0
1153	¶	-	0	-	-	-	-	-	-	0
1155	-	-	0	-	-	-	¶	-	-	0
1162	-	-	0	-	-	-	-	¶	-	0
1164	g	g¶	0	-	¶	-	g¶	g	g¶	0
1183	-	-	¶	-	-	-	-	-	-	0
1187	¶	3	¶	-	¶	-	¶a	¶	-	0
1209	-	-	-	-	¶	-	¶a	-	-	0
1219	¶	¶	-	\\	¶	2	¶a	-	-	0
1234	¶	-	-	-	-	-	¶	¶	-	0
1251	¶	¶	¶	-	¶	2	¶a	-	-	0
1255	¶	-	-	\\	-	2	-	-	-	0
1275	¶	¶	¶	\\	0	2	¶a	¶	-	0
1295	-	-	-		0		-	¶	-	0
1299	-	-	¶	-	0	-	-	-	-	0
1303	¶	¶	¶	\\	0	-	¶a	¶	-	0
1313	¶	¶	-	\\	0	-	¶	¶	-	0
1325	¶	-	¶	-	0	-	-	-	-	0
1334	¶	¶	-	\\	0	2	¶	¶	-	0
1337	¶	¶	¶	i	0	-	-	-	-	0
1347	¶	2	-	\\	0	-	¶	¶	¶	0
1355	¶	4bar	¶	-	0	2	i[4]	¶	¶	0
1361	¶	-	-	-	0	-	-	-	¶	0
1374	g	g¶	g¶[5]	-	0	-	-	-	-	0
1380	¶	¶	-	-	0	-	-	¶	-	0
1393	¶	¶	¶	\\	0	-	-	¶	-	0
1399	¶	¶	-	-	0	-	¶a	-	-	0
1417	¶	-	-	-	0	-	-	-	-	0
1429	¶	-	-	-	0	-	¶	-	-	0
1449	-	-	¶	-	0	-	-	-	-	0
1451	¶	2	-	π	0	2	¶	¶	¶	0
1459	¶	-	¶	-	0	-	-	-	-	0
1462	¶	¶	-	-	0	-	¶	¶	¶	0
1466	-	-	g¶	-	0	-	-	-	-	0
1472	g	g¶	g¶	-	0	-	-	-	-	0

[4] "incipit" in drypoint.

[5] Correction: *mania* for *manye.*

KnT	Hg	El	Dd	Gg	Ad[3]	Ha	Cp	La	Pw	He
1475	¶	¶	¶	\\	0	-	¶a	-	¶	0
1488	¶	¶	¶	π	0	-	¶	¶	¶	0
1490	-	-	n	-	0	-	-	-	-	0
1491	¶	2	i	-	0	2	¶a	-	-	0
1497	-	-	-	-	0	-	-	-	¶	0
1519	-	-	0	-	0	-	-	-	¶	0
1528	¶	¶	0	-	0	-	¶a	-	-	0
1540	¶	¶	0	\\	0	-	¶	¶	¶	0
1547	¶	g¶	0	-	0	-	-	-	-	0
1559	¶	-	0	-	0	-	-	-	¶	0
1563	¶	-	0	-	0	-	-	-	-	0
1574	¶	¶	0	-	0	-	-	¶	-	0
1577	-	-	0	-	0	-	-	-	¶	0
1596	¶	¶	0	-	0	-	¶a	¶	¶	0
1603	¶	-	0	-	0	-	-	-	-	0
1620	¶	¶	0	-	0	-	¶a	-	-	0
1623	¶	2	0	-	0	2	¶a	-	¶	0
1624	-	-	0	-	0	-	-	¶[6]	-	0
1628	¶	-	0	-	0	-	-	-	-	0
1637	¶	-	0	-	0	-	-	-	-	0
1648	-	-	0	-	0	2	-	-	-	0
1649	¶	¶	0	-	0	-	¶a	-	-	0
1661	-	¶	0	-	0	-	¶a	-	-	0
1663	¶	2	0	\\	0	2	¶a	-	¶	0
1673	¶	¶	0	\\	0	-	¶a	-	-	0
1683	¶	¶	0	-	0	2	¶a	-	-	0
1690	-	-	0	-	0	-	-	¶	-	0
1696	-	¶	0	-	0	-	¶a	-	-	0
1713	-	-	0	-	0	-	-	-	¶	0
1714	¶	¶	0	\\	0	-	¶	¶	-	0
1742	¶	¶	0	-	0	2	¶	¶	-	0
1748	¶	¶	0	-	0	-	¶a	-	-	0
1767	¶	-	0	-	0	-	-	-	-	0
1774	n¶	n¶	0	-	0	-	-	-	-	0
1785	¶	¶	0	-	0	-	¶	¶	-	0

[6] "O Cupid" in Hg/El, etc. reads "Occupide" in La, probably prompting the shift to 1628 for the ¶.

KnT	Hg	El	Dd	Gg	Ad^3	Ha	Cp	La	Pw	He
1791	¶	-	0	-	0	-	-	-	-	0
1799	¶	¶	0	-	0	-	¶	-	-	0
1808	-	-	-	-	0	¶	-	-	-	0
1829	¶	2	0	-	0	2	¶a	¶	-	0
1845	¶	2	0	-	0	2	¶	¶	¶	0
1870	¶	¶	0	-	0	-	¶a	-	-	0
1880	-	-	-	-	0	-	¶a	-	-	0
1881	4	4bar	0	i	0	2	-	-	-	0
1882	4	5	0	-	0	-	i	-	¶	0
1891	-	-	0	-	0	2	-	-	-	0
1893	¶	¶	0	πi	0	-	¶a	-	-	0
1895	-	¶	0	-	0	-	¶a	-	-	0
1904	-	-	-	i	-	-	-	-	-	0
1907	-	-	-	i		-	-	-	-	0
1912	-	-	-	i	-	-	-	-	-	0
1914	¶	¶	0	-	¶	-	¶a	-	-	0
1918	¶	¶	0	\\	¶	2	¶a	-	-	0
1943	-	-	-	-	¶	-	¶a	-	-	0
1947	¶	-	¶	\\	-	-	-	-	-	0
1951	-	-	-	-	-	-	-	-	¶	0
1953	-	-	¶	-	-	-	-	-	-	0
1955	¶	2	-	i	¶	-	¶a	-	-	0
1967	¶	¶	¶	-	¶	2	¶a	¶	¶	0
1969	-	-	-	i	-	-	-	-	-	0
1975	¶	¶	-	-	¶	-	¶a	-	¶	-
1985	-	¶g	g¶	-	-	-	-	-	-	-
1995	¶	¶	¶	-	¶	-	¶a	-	-	-
2005	¶	¶	-	\\	¶	-	¶a	-	-	-
2009	-	-	¶	-	-	-	-	-	-	-
2011	¶	¶	-	-	¶	-	¶a	-	-	-
2017	¶	¶	-	-	¶	om	¶a	-	-	om
2021	¶	¶	-	-	¶	-	¶a	-	-	-
2024	-	¶	-	-	¶	-	¶a	-	-	-
2027	¶	¶	¶	-	¶	-	¶a	-	-	-
2031	¶	¶	-	-	¶	-	¶a	-	-	-
2041	¶	2	¶	\\	¶	2	¶a	¶	-	-
2051	¶	2	¶	\\i	¶	2	¶a	¶	¶	-

KnT	Hg	El	Dd	Gg	Ad[3]	Ha	Cp	La	Pw	He
2056	-	-	-	-	-	-	¶a	-	-	-
2058	-	-	-	-	-	-	g¶	g	-	-
2059	n	g¶	g¶	-	-	-	-	-	-	-
2062	-	¶	-	-	¶	-	¶a	-	-	-
2065	¶	¶	-	-	¶	-	¶	¶	-	-
2069	¶	¶	-	-	¶	-	¶a	-	-	-
2073	-	-	-	-	¶	-	¶a	-	-	-
2075	¶	¶	-	-	¶	-	¶	¶	-	-
2083	-	-	-	-	¶	-	-	-	-	-
2089	¶	2	¶	\\	¶	-	¶a	-	¶	3
2093	-	-	-	-	-	-	¶	-	-	-
2095	¶	¶	¶	-	¶	2	¶a	-	-	-
2117	¶	¶	¶	-	¶	-	-	-	-	-
2128	¶	-	¶	-	-	2	-	-	-	-
2129	-	-	-	-	n¶	-	-	-	-	-
2155	¶	2	¶	-	¶	2	¶	¶	¶	3
2160	-	-	-	Δ	-	-	-	-	-	-
2187	¶	-	¶	-	-	-	-	¶	-	
2190	¶	¶	-	-	¶	-	-	-	-	-
2197	¶	¶	¶	-	¶	-	-	-	-	-
2209	¶	2	¶	π	¶	-	¶	¶	¶	3
2212	-	-	-	i	-	-	-	-	-	om
2221	¶	2g¶	3	\\	¶i¶	2	¶	¶	¶	-
2222	-	g¶	-	-	-	-	-	-	-	-
2230	-	-	-	-	¶	-	-	-	-	-
2242	-	-	n¶a	-	-	-	-	-	-	-
2251	¶	¶	-	-	¶	-	-	¶	-	-
2261	¶	¶	¶	\\	¶	-	-	¶	¶	-
2265	-	-	-	i	-	-	-	-	-	-
2271	¶	2	2	-	¶	2	¶a	-	¶	-
2275	-	-	-	i	-	-	-	-	-	-
2281	¶	¶	-	-	¶	-	-	-	-	-
2289	¶	¶	-	-	¶	-	-	-	-	-
2296	-	-	-	-	-	-	-	-	-	g[7]
2297	¶	2g¶	2	-	¶i¶	2	¶a	¶	¶	-
2331	¶	¶	¶	-	¶	2	¶[8]	-	-	-

[7] Glosses in He half-boxed by ascender on left connected to an underline.

KnT	Hg	El	Dd	Gg	Ad^{3}	Ha	Cp	La	Pw	He
2339	-	-	-	-	-	-	-	-	¶	-
2346	-	-	¶	-	-	-	-	-	-	-
2349	-	2g¶	-	-	¶	-	-	-	-	-
2350	-	g¶	-	-	-	-	-	-	-	-
2367	¶	2	¶	\\πi	¶	2	¶a	¶	-	3
2373	¶	2g¶	3	\\	¶i[9]	-	-	¶	¶	g
2374	-	g¶	-	-	-	-	-	-	-	-
2375	-	¶	-	-	-	-	-	-	-	-
2394	-	-	¶n¶a	-	-	-	-	-	-	-
2421	¶	2	¶	-	¶	2	-	¶	¶	-
2423	-	-	-	-	¶	-	-	-	-	-
2431	¶	-	¶	-	-	-	¶a	-	-	-
2435	¶	-	¶	-	-	-	-	-	-	-
2438	¶	¶	-	πi	¶	-	-	-	-	3
2439	-	-	-	-	-	-	-	-	-	g
2440	-	-	-	-	-	-	-	-	-	g
2441	-	-	-	-	-	-	-	-	-	g
2442	-	-	-	-	-	-	-	-	-	g
2447	-	-	n¶a	-	-	-	-	-	-	-
2453	¶	¶	¶	-	¶	-	-	-	-	-
2479	¶	¶	¶	-	-	-	¶	-	-	3
2483	¶	4bar	2	-	¶i¶	2	-	¶	-	-
2496	-	-	¶	-	-	-	-	-	-	-
2523	¶	2	¶	-	¶	-	¶a	-	-	-
2525	¶	-	-	-	-	-	-	-	-	-
2533	¶	¶	¶	Δ[10]	¶	-	-	-	-	-
2537	¶	¶	¶	-	¶	2	-	¶	-	-
2543	¶	¶	¶	-	¶	-	-	-	-	-
2548	-	-	-	-	-	-	¶a	-	-	-
2555	-	-	-	-	¶	-	-	-	-	om
2561	¶	2	¶	π	¶	2	¶a	-	-	-
2563	¶	-	-	-	-	-	-	-	-	-
2565	-	-	n¶a	-	-	-	-	-	-	3
2569	¶	¶	-	-	¶	-	¶a	-	-	-

[8] Unfinished paraf, no penwork flourishing.

[9] Different hand for indexing gloss here in Ad^{3}, beginning cut off at edge of margin.

[10] Far to left of text, outer margin.

KnT	Hg	El	Dd	Gg	Ad[3]	Ha	Cp	La	Pw	He
2577	¶	-	¶	-	¶	-	-	¶	-	-
2584	¶	¶	¶	-	¶	-	-	-	-	-
2587	-	-	-	-	-	2	-	-	-	-
2595	¶	¶	-	-	¶	-	¶a	¶	-	-
2599	¶	¶	¶	\\	¶	-	¶	-	-	-
2601	-	-	n¶a	-	-	-	-	-	-	-
2621	¶	¶	-	-	-	-	-	-	-	-
2623	-	-	¶	-	-	-	¶a	¶	-	-
2636	¶	¶	¶	-	¶	-	-	-	-	-
2652	¶	¶	¶	-	¶	-	-	-	-	-
2657	-	-	-	-	¶	-	-	-	-	-
2663	¶	2	¶	-	¶	-	¶	¶	-	3
2668	¶	¶	¶	-	¶	-	¶a	-	-	-
2671	¶	2	-	-	¶	-	-	¶	-	-
2676	¶	¶	-	-	¶	-	-	-	-	-
2689	-	n¶	-	-	n¶	-	-	-	-	-
2694	-	-	¶	-	-	-	-	-	-	-
2700	¶	¶	-	\\	¶	-	-	-	-	-
2705	¶	-	-	-	-	-	-	-	-	-
2707	-	-	-	-	¶	-	-	-	-	-
2711	¶	-	-	-	-	-	-	-	-	-
2719	-	-	¶	-	-	-	-	-	-	-
2731	¶	¶	¶	\\	-	2	-	-	-	-
2741	-	-	-	-	-	-	-	-	¶	3
2743	3	2	2	-	¶	2	¶	¶	-	-
2760	-	-	n¶a	-	-	-	-	-	-	-
2764	-	-	-	-	-	-	-	¶	-	-
2765	¶	¶	¶	-	¶n¶	2	¶	-	-	-
2771	-	-	n¶a	-	-	-	-	-	-	-
2783	¶	2	¶	¶	¶	\\	¶	-	-	-
2798	-	-	¶	-	-	-	-	-	-	-
2816	-	-	-	-	-	-	-	¶	-	3
2817	¶	2	¶	-	¶	2	-	-	-	-
2827	¶	¶	¶	-	¶	-	-	-	-	-
2837	¶	¶	¶	-	-	-	-	-	-	-
2843	¶g	2i¶	n¶ai¶a	-	¶i¶	2	-	-	-	-

KnT	Hg	El	Dd	Gg	Ad[3]	Ha	Cp	La	Pw	He
2844	-	-	-	-	n	-	-	-	-	-
2853	¶	2	¶	-	¶	2	-	¶	-	-
2865	-	-	-	-	-	-	-	-	-	g
2866	-	-	-	-	-	-	-	-	-	g
2868	-	-	¶	-	-	-	-	-	-	-
2882	-	¶	¶	-	¶	-	¶	¶	-	-
2899	-	-	-	\\	-	-	-	-	-	om
2905	-	-	¶	-	-	-	-	-	-	-
2913	¶	2	¶	-	¶	2	-	-	-	-
2919	-	-	¶	-	-	-	-	-	-	-
2925	-	-	¶	-	-	-	-	-	-	-
2947	-	-	-	-	¶	-	-	-	-	-
2963	-	-	-	-	¶	-	-	-	-	-
2967	¶	2	0	-	-	2	¶	¶	-	3
2981	¶	¶	0	-	-	-		-	-	-
2987	¶n	2	0	-	¶	2	-	¶	-	-
2988	-	-	-	-	n¶	-	-	-	-	-
3017	¶	2i¶	n¶a	-	¶i¶	2	\\	-	-	-
3021	¶	¶i¶	-	-	¶i¶	1	-	-	-	-
3027	0	¶	-	-	¶	2	-	-	-	-
3035	-	¶	¶	-	¶	-	-	-	-	-
3041	¶	-	¶	-	¶	2	-	-	-	-
3042	-	-	n[11]	-	-	-	-	-	-	-
3043	-	¶	-	-	¶	-	-	-	-	-
3057	¶	¶	-	-	¶	-	-	-	-	-
3067	¶	2	¶	-	¶	2	-	-	-	-
3075	¶	2	¶	0	¶	1	-	¶	-	-
3090	¶	¶	¶	0	¶	-	-	-	-	-
3097	-	¶	¶	0	¶	-	-	-	-	-

Textual notes:

Ad[3] omits 2681–82, 2934.

He omits 2012–17, 2044, 2165–66, 2212, 2501–2, 2549, 2655, 2787–92, 2815, 2899–2900, 2920.

[11] Dd nota abbreviation "w" with slashed extender.

Table 2
The Miller's Prologue and *Tale*

Prologue	Hg	El	Dd	Gg	Ad[3]	Ha	Cp	La	Pw	He
1.3109	4	6bar	4	5bar	3	3r	3	2	3	3
3114	¶	-	¶n[12]	-	-	-	-	-	-	-
3120	¶	¶	¶	-	¶	-	-	¶	-	-
3128	¶	-	-	-	-	-	-	-	-	-
3129	¶	-	-	-	-	-	-	-	-	-
3132	¶	¶	-	-	¶	-	-	-	-	-
3136	¶	¶	¶	-	¶	¶	-	-	-	-
3137	-	-	-	-	-	-	-	-	¶	-
3144	¶	¶	¶	-	-	2	-	-	-	-
3150	¶	¶	¶	-	¶	-	-	-	-	-
3163	-	-	n¶an[13]	-	-	-	-	-	-	-
3167	¶	¶	¶	-	¶	-	-	-	-	-
3179	-	-	-	-	¶	-	-	-	-	-

Tale	Hg	El	Dd	Gg	Ad[3]	Ha	Cp	La	Pw	He
1.3187	4	5bar	5	5bar	4	5bar	6bar	6bar	3bar	3
3199	¶	¶	¶	-	¶	-	-	-	-	-
3221	¶	¶	¶	-	¶	2	-	-	-	-
3233	¶	¶	¶n¶a	-	¶	1	-	-	-	-
3236	-	-	-	\\	-	-	-	-	-	-
3271	¶	2	¶	-	¶	1	¶	¶	-	-
3288	¶	¶	¶	-	¶	-	-	-	-	-
3298	¶	¶	¶	-	¶	-	-	-	-	-
3303	-	¶	n¶a	-	¶	2	-	-	-	-
3307	¶	2	¶	-	¶	-	-	¶	-	-
3312	¶	¶	¶	-	¶	2	-	-	-	-
3328	-	-	-	-	¶	-	-	-	-	-
3339	-	-	0[14]	-	¶	-	¶	¶	-	-

[12] "w" form to right of text with vertical extender to right minim, extender looped with two horizontal lines below the loop. Abbreviation for nota? Regular paraf to left of text.

[13] Second nota uses "w" form as at 3114.

[14] Dd 3319–45 folio mutilated, margin for decoration on left lost.

MilT	Hg	El	Dd	Gg	Ad3	Ha	Cp	La	Pw	He
3348	-	¶	-	-	¶	2	-	-	-	-
3361	-	-	-	-	-	1	-	-	-	-
3364	-	-	¶	-	-	-	-	-	-	-
3368	¶	-	-	-	-	-	-	-	-	-
3370	-	¶	-	-	¶	2	-	-	-	-
3380	-	-	-	-	-	-	-	g	-	-
3381	-	-	g¶a	-	-	-	-	-	-	-
3382	g\\	g¶	-	-	¶	-	-	-	-	-
3383	-	¶	-	-	¶	-	-	-	-	-
3385	-	-	¶	-	-	-	-	-	-	-
3391	-	-	-	-	-	2	-	-	-	-
3397	¶	2	¶	-	¶	-	¶	¶	-	-
3399	¶	-	-	-	-	¶	-	-	-	3
3406	-	-	2	-	-	-	-	-	-	-
3417	-	-	g¶	-	-	-	-	-	-	-
3419	-	-	-	-	¶	2	-	-	-	-
3422	-	-	-		-	1	-	-	-	-
3423	¶	¶	¶	-	¶	-	-	-	-	-
3431	-	-	-	-	¶	-	-	-	-	-
3432	-[15]	¶	-	-	-	-	-	-	-	-
3434	¶	¶	¶	-	¶	-	-	-	-	-
3439	-	¶	-	-	¶	-	-	-	-	-
3444	¶	-	-	-	-	-	-	-	-	-
3448	¶	¶	¶	-	-	-	-	-	-	-
3455	-	-	-	-	¶	¶	-	-	-	-
3465	-	¶	-	-	-	-	-	-	-	-
3487	-	¶	¶	-	-	-	-	-	-	-
3490	¶	¶	-	-	¶	-	-	-	-	-
3492	¶	¶	¶	-	¶	-	-	-	-	-
3496	¶	¶	-	-	¶	-	-	-	-	-
3501	-	¶	-	-	¶	-	-	-	-	-
3508	¶	¶	¶	-	¶	-	¶	¶	¶	-
3513	¶	2	¶	-	-	2	-	-	-	-
3522	¶	¶	¶	-	¶	-	-	-	-	-
3526	¶	¶	-	-	¶	-	-	-	-	-
3537	¶	¶	¶	-	¶	1	-	-	-	-

[15] Couplet at 3431–32 in reverse sequence in Hg, noticed and corrected in hand of scribe by ".b." and ".a." at head of lines.

MilT	Hg	El	Dd	Gg	Ad^{3}	Ha	Cp	La	Pw	He
3538	¶	¶	-	-	¶	-	-	-	-	-
3547	-	¶	-	-	¶	-	-	-	-	-
3563	-	¶	-	-	-	-	-	-	-	-
3583	-	¶	-	-	¶	-	-	-	-	-
3589	-	¶	-	-	-	-	-	-	-	-
3598	-	-	g¶	-	-	-	-	-	-	-
3601	¶	¶	¶	//	¶	2	¶	¶	¶	-
3607	-	-	-	-	¶	-	-	-	-	-
3611	¶	¶i¶	i¶	-	¶i¶	-	¶	¶	-	-
3633	-	-	-	-	-	-	-	-	¶	-
3638	-	¶	-	-	¶	-	-	-	-	-
3643	¶	¶	-	-	¶	-	-	-	-	-
3647	-	-	-	//	-	-	-	-	-	-
3648	¶	-	-	-	-	-	-	-	-	-
3657	¶	2	¶	-	-	2	-	¶	¶	3
3671	¶	¶	¶	-	¶	2	-	-	-	-
3675	-	-	-	-	¶	-	-	-	-	-
3681	-	-	-	-	-	-	-	¶	-	-
3687	¶	2	n¶	-	-	-	π[16]	-	-	-
3692	-	-	n¶b	-	-	-	-	-	-	-
3708	¶	¶	¶	-	-	¶n[17]	-	-	-	-
3709	-	-	-	-	-	-	-	¶	-	-
3714	¶	¶	¶	-	-	-	-	-	-	-
3718	¶	¶	-	-	-	-	-	-	-	-
3719	¶	¶	-	-	-	-	-	-	-	-
3720	¶	¶	-	-	-	-	-	-	-	-
3723	¶	¶	-	-	-	-	-	-	-	-
3727	¶	¶	-	-	-	-	-	-	-	-
3730	¶	¶	-	-	-	-	-	-	-	-
3734	nω	-	n¶	π	-	-	-	-	-	-
3736	-	¶	-	-	-	-	-	-	-	-
3740	¶	¶	¶	-	-	-	-	-	-	-
3742	¶	¶	-	-	-	-	-	-	-	-
3744	¶	¶	-	-	-	-	-	-	-	-
3747	¶	¶	¶	-	-	2	-	-	-	-

[16] Cp prompt in double virgule form without horizontal line or flourish; appears only in *MilT* and *Gam.*

[17] Note in Ha scribbled in informal hand.

MilT	Hg	El	Dd	Gg	Ad³	Ha	Cp	La	Pw	He
3766	¶	¶	-	-	-	-	-	-	-	-
3772	¶	¶	-	-	-	-	-	-	-	-
3779	¶	¶	-	-	¶	-	-	-	-	-
3783	¶	¶	-	-	-	-	-	-	-	-
3790	¶	¶	-	-	-	-	-	-	-	-
3792	¶	¶	-	-	-	-	-	-	-	-
3798	¶	¶	¶	-	-	-	-	-	-	-
3804	¶	-	-	-	-	-	-	-	-	-
3806	-	¶	¶	-	-	-	-	-	-	-
3811	-	¶	-	-	-	-	-	-	-	-
3813	-	-	-	-	-	-	-	¶	-	-
3816	¶	¶	¶	-	-	-	-	-	-	-
3824	¶	¶	-	-	-	-	-	-	-	-
3831	-	-	-	-	¶	-	-	-	-	-
3840	¶	¶	-	0	-	-	-	-	-	-

Textual notes:
Ad³ omits 3721–22.

Table 3
The Wife of Bath's Prologue

Prologue	Hg	El	Dd	Gg	Ad[3]	Ha[4]	Cp	La	Pw	He
3.1	4	4bar	4	0	3	3	2	3[18]	3	5
11	-	g¶	-	0	g¶	-	-	-	-	-
13	-	g¶	-	0	g¶	-	-	-	-	-
14	¶	-	-	0	-	-	-	-	-	-
17	¶	¶	-	0	-	-	-	-	-	-
23	-	g¶	-	0	g¶	-	-	-	-	-
28	-	g¶	-	0	g¶	-	-	-	-	-
30	¶	-	-	0	-	-	-	-	g¶	-
31	-	-	-	0	-	-	g¶	-	-	-
35	¶	¶	-	0	¶	-	-	-	-	-
36	-	-	-	0	-	-	g¶	-	g¶	-
46	-	g¶	-	0	¶g¶	-	-	-	-	-
49	-	-	-	-	g¶	-	-	-	-	-
50	-	g¶	-	0	-	-	-	-	-	-
51	-	-	-	0	g¶	-	g¶	-	g¶	-
52	-	g¶	-	0	-	-	-	-	-	-
54	-	g¶	-	0	-	-	-	-	-	-
55	-	g¶	-	0	g¶	-	-	-	-	0
56	-	g¶	-	0	-	-	-	-	-	0
57	-	g¶	-	0	g¶	-	-	-	-	0
58	-	-	-	-	g¶	-	-	-	-	0
59	¶	-	-	0	-	-	-	-	-	0
73	-	g¶	-	0	g¶	-	-	-	-	0
75	-	g¶	-	0	-	-	-	-	-	0
76	-	-	-	-	g¶	-	-	-	-	0
77	-	¶	-	-	-	-	-	-	-	0
81	-	g¶	-	-	g¶	-	-	-	-	0
86	-	-	-	-	g¶	-	-	-	-	0
87	-	g¶	-	-	-	-	-	-	-	0
95	-	¶	-	-	¶	-	-	-	-	0
103	-	g¶	-	-	-	-	-	-	-	0
105	-	¶g¶	-	-	¶	-	-	-	-	0

[18] Initial at head of spurious 4 lines before 3.1 in Cp.

ProWBT	Hg	El	Dd	Gg	Ad[3]	Ha[4]	Cp	La	Pw	He
111	-	-	-	-	-	-	g¶	-	g¶	0
113	-	-	n[19]	-	-	-	-	-	-	0
115	¶ω	¶i¶	-	-	¶	-	-	-	-	0
135	¶	¶	-	-	\\	-	-	-	-	-
144	-	-	-	-	¶	-	-	-	-	-
147	-	g¶	-	-	g¶	-	0	-	-	-
150	-	-	-	-	¶	-	-	-	-	-
155	-	g¶	-	-	g¶	-	0	-	-	-
156	-	-	-	-	-	-	-	g	-	-
157	-	-	-	-	-	-	0	-	g¶	-
158	-	g¶	-	-	g¶	-	0	-	-	-
160	-	g¶	-	-	g¶	-	0	-	-	-
161	-	-	-	-	¶	-	-	-	-	-
162	-	g¶	-	-	g¶	-	0	-	-	-
163	1	2g¶	¶[20]	π	¶g¶	¶	0	2	2	-
169	¶	¶	-	//	¶	-	0	-	-	-
182	-	-	g¶	-	-	-	0	-	-	-
183	-	-	n	-	-	-	0	-	-	-
184	¶	¶	-	//	¶	-	0	-	-	-
188	¶	¶	-	-	¶	-	0	-	-	-
193	1	2i¶	-	ω	i[21]	5bar	0	2	¶	3
194	-	-	-	ππ[22]	-	-	0	-	-	-
199	-	g¶	-	-	g¶	-	0	-	-	-
217	-	-	-	Δ	-	-	0	-	-	-
224	¶	¶	-	-	¶	-	-	-	-	-
226	-	¶	-	-	¶	-	-	-	-	-
228	-	-	n¶	-	-	-	-	-	-	-
235	¶	¶	-	-	¶	-	-	-	¶	-
257	¶	¶	-	-	¶	-	-	-	-	-
265	-	¶	-	-	¶	-	-	-	-	-
278	-	¶	-	-	¶	-	-	-	-	-
282	-	-	-	-	¶	-	-	-	-	-
285	-	¶	-	-	¶	-	-	-	-	-

[19] Dd nota abbreviation "w" with slashed extender.

[20] Dd returns to flourished "w" prompt here.

[21] Heading in Ad[3] text column between 192 and 193: "Biholde . . ."

[22] Gg ω at 193 and first π at 194 in different hand from predominant π; cf. "nota" at *ProWBT* 452.

ProWBT	Hg	El	Dd	Gg	Ad[3]	Ha[4]	Cp	La	Pw	He
293	-	¶	-	-	¶	-	-	-	-	-
303	-	¶g¶	-	-	¶g¶	-	-	-	-	-
308	¶	¶	-	-	¶	-	-	-	-	-
311	-	-	-	-	-	¶	-	-	-	-
323	-	¶	-	-	¶	¶	-	-	-	-
327	-	g¶	-	-	-	-	-	-	-	-
332	-	-	-	-	-	n¶	-	-	-	-
336	-	-	-	-	-	n¶	-	-	-	-
337	¶	¶	-	-	¶	-	-	-	-	-
341	-	g¶	-	-	-	-	-	-	-	-
342	-	-	-	-	g¶	-	-	-	-	-
346	-	-	-	-	g¶	-	-	-	-	-
348	-	¶	-	-	¶	-	-	-	-	-
353	-	-	¶	-	-	-	-	-	-	-
357	-	¶	-	-	¶	-	-	-	-	-
359	-	-	-	-	-	-	-	g	-	-
362	¶	¶g¶	-	-	¶g¶	-	-	-	-	-
369	-	-	-	-	g¶	-	-	-	-	-
370	-	-	-	-	g¶	-	-	-	-	-
371	¶	¶g¶	-	-	¶g¶	-	-	-	-	-
373	-	¶g¶	-	-	¶	-	-	-	-	-
376	-	g¶	-	-	g¶	-	-	-	-	-
379	¶	3g¶	3	-	¶	-	-	¶	¶	-
380	-	-	-	-	g¶	-	-	-	-	-
391	-	-	-	-	-	-	-	-	¶	-
393	-	¶	-	-	¶	-	-	-	-	-
401	-	-	-	-	-	-	-	g¶	g¶	-
402	-	-	-	-	-	-	g¶	-	-	-
413	-	-	-	-	-	-	-	¶	-	-
431	¶	¶	-	-	¶	-	-	-	-	-
451	-	¶	-	-	¶	-	-	-	-	-
452	-	-	-	πn[23]	-	-	-	¶	-	-
453	1	2i¶	¶	¶a	¶g¶	-	¶	1	¶	3
460	-	g¶	-	-	g¶g¶	-	-	-	-	-
466	-	-	☞	-	-	-	-	-	-	-
469	-	¶	-	-	-	-	-	-	-	-

[23] Different hand for both π and "nota" here in Gg; cf. *ProWBT* 182, 183.

ProWBT	Hg	El	Dd	Gg	Ad[3]	Ha[4]	Cp	La	Pw	He
480	-	-	¶	-	-	-	-	-	-	-
481	¶	¶	-	π	-	-	-	-	-	3
499	-	g¶	-	-	-	-	-	-	-	-
503	1	2i¶	¶	\\π	-	¶	¶	1	¶	3
505	-	g¶	-	-	-	-	-	-	-	-
509	-	-	n¶a	-	-	-	-	-	-	-
519	-	-	n¶a	-	-	-	-	-	-	-
525	¶	¶	¶	π	¶	-	-	-	¶	3
543	¶	¶	-	-	-	-	-	-	-	-
563	¶	2	¶	-	-	-	\\¶b	-	-	0
575	om	¶	-	-	¶[24]	om	om	om	om	0
577	-	-	-	-	¶	-	-	-	-	0
579	-	-	-	-	¶	-	-	-	-	0
582	-	-	-	-	¶	-	-	-	-	0
587	¶	¶	¶	-	¶	¶	-	-	-	0
593	¶	¶	-	-	¶	-	-	-	-	0
608	-	-	n¶a	-	-	om	-	-	-	0
609	om	g¶	-	-	-	om	om	om	om	0
610	om	g¶	-	-	-	om	om	om	om	0
627	¶	¶	¶	-	¶	-	-	-	-	0
637	-	-	-	-	-	-	¶	-	-	-
643	-	g¶	-	-	g¶	-	-	-	-	-
647	¶	¶	-	-	¶	-	-	-	-	-
655	-	1	n¶a	n[25]	¶n¶	¶	n	¶n	n¶	-
657	-	¶g¶	-	-	¶g¶	-	-	-	-	-
659	-	¶	-	-	-	-	-	-	¶	-
666	¶	¶	-	-	-	-	-	-	-	-
669	-	¶	-	-	-	-	-	-	-	-
673	-	¶	-	-	-	-	-	-	-	-
678	-	-	i[26]	-	-	-	-	-	-	-
692	-	g¶	-	-	g¶	-	-	-	-	-
702	-	g¶	-	-	g¶	-	-	-	-	-
705	-	g¶	-	-	g[27]	-	-	-	-	-
711	¶	2	-	-	¶	-	-	-	-	-

[24] Ad[3] 575–87 inserted out of place.

[25] Same hand as predominant "π"?

[26] Dd 678 gloss in later hand, 671–87 bracketed.

[27] Possible paraf in Ad[3] cut off at edge of folio.

ProWBT	Hg	El	Dd	Gg	Ad³	Ha⁴	Cp	La	Pw	He
721	¶	¶	-	-	¶	-	-	-	-	-
724	¶	¶	-	-	¶	-	-	-	-	-
727	¶	¶	-	-	¶	-	-	-	-	-
733	¶	¶g¶	-	-	¶g¶	-	-	-	-	-
737	¶	¶	-	-	¶g¶	-	-	-	-	-
740	¶	¶	-	-	¶	-	-	-	-	-
743	¶	¶	-	-	¶	-	-	-	-	-
747	¶	¶	-	-	¶	-	-	-	-	-
757	¶	¶	-	-	¶	-	-	-	¶	-
762	¶	¶	-	-	¶	-	-	-	-	-
765	¶	¶	-	-	¶	-	-	¶	-	-
769	¶	¶	-	-	¶	-	-	-	-	-
771	¶	¶	-	-	¶	-	-	-	g¶	-
774	-	-	-	-	-	-	g¶	-	g¶	-
780	-	-	n¶a	-	-	-	-	-	-	-
785	-	g¶	-	-	g[28]	-	-	-	-	-
788	¶	¶	-	-	¶	-	-	-	-	-
803	¶	¶	-	-	¶	-	-	-	-	-
811	¶	-	-	-	-	-	-	-	-	-
829	1	4	¶i¶a	¶a	¶	¶i¶	3	2	2bari¶	3
832	-	-	i¶a	-	-	-	-	-	-	-
833	¶	¶	g¶a	-	¶	-	-	-	-	-
840	¶	¶	¶	-	¶	-	-	-	-	-
844	¶	¶	-	-	¶	-	-	-	-	-
849	-	-	-	-	¶	-	-	-	-	-
850	¶	¶	¶	-	-	-	-	-	-	-
854	¶	¶	-	-	¶	-	-	-	-	-
856	¶	¶	-	-	¶	-	0[29]	-	-	-

Textual notes:

No divisions or glosses in Dd 44a–f.

El omits 44a–f.

Ad³ omits 44a–f, 619–26, 717–20.

Hg/Ha⁴/Cp/La/Pw omit 44a–f, 575–84, 609–12, 619–26, 717–20.

Ha⁴ omits 605–8.

[28] Possible paraf in Ad³ cut off at edge of folio.

[29] Cp 855–59 mutilated.

Table 4
The Wife of Bath's Tale

Tale	Hg	El	Dd	Gg	Ad[3]	Ha	Cp	La	Pw	He
3.857	4	4bar	6	m13bar	3	6bar	bar[30]	7bar	2	4
882	¶	¶	¶	-	¶	-	0	-	-	-
899	om	¶	-	-	¶	-	-	-	-	-
905	-	-	-	-	-	-	-	-	¶	-
913	1	2	-	-	¶	-	-	-	-	-
919	-	¶	-	-	-	-	-	-	-	-
920	-	-	n¶a	-	-	-	-	-	-	-
925	¶	¶	-	-	¶	-	-	-	-	-
929	-	¶	-	-	¶	-	-	-	-	-
930	-	g¶	-	-	-	-	-	-	-	-
931	-	¶	-	-	¶	-	-	-	-	-
935	¶	¶	-	-	¶	-	-	-	-	-
945	¶	¶	-	-	¶	-	-	-	-	-
951	-	-	☞	-		-	-	-	-	-
952	¶	¶	-	-	¶	-	-	-	-	-
961	¶	¶	-	-	¶	-	-	-	-	-
970	-	-	n¶a	-	-	-	-	-	-	-
975	-	-	g[31]	-	-	-	-	-	-	-
980	-	-	n¶a	-	-	-	-	-	-	-
983	¶	2	¶	-	¶	¶	-	-	¶	-
1005	¶	¶	-	-	¶	-	-	-	-	-
1009	¶	¶	-	-	¶	-	-	-	-	-
1013	¶	¶	-	-	¶	-	-	-	-	-
1014	¶	¶	-	-	¶	-	-	-	-	-
1023	¶	¶	¶	-	¶	-	-	-	-	-
1031	-	¶	-	-	¶	-	-	-	-	-
1034	-	-	-	¶	-	-	-	-	-	-
1037	¶	¶	g[32]	n	¶	¶	-	-	-	-
1043	¶	¶	¶	-	¶	-	-	-	-	-
1046	¶	¶	-	-	¶	-	-	-	-	-

[30] Remnant bar on mutilated page, no surviving initial in Cp here.

[31] Dd gloss in later hand crossed out at 970, repeated at 975.

[32] Dd gloss in later hand at 1037, 1037–39 bracketed.

WBT	Hg	El	Dd	Gg	Ad^3	Ha	Cp	La	Pw	He
1053	-	-	-	-	¶	-	-	-	-	-
1058	¶	¶	¶	-	-	-	-	-	-	-
1062	¶	¶	-	-	-	-	-	-	-	-
1067	-	-	¶	-	¶	-	-	-	-	-
1073	¶	¶	-	-	¶	¶	-	-	-	-
1083	¶	¶	-	-	¶	-	-	-	-	-
1098	¶	¶	-	-	¶	-	-	-	-	-
1104	¶	¶	-	-	¶	-	-	-	-	-
1105	¶	¶	-	-	¶	-	-	-	-	-
1106	¶	¶	-	-	¶	-	-	-	-	-
1109	¶n¶	2i¶	¶n¶a	-	i¶	-	¶n¶	-	¶n¶	-
1112	-	-	g¶a	-	¶	-	-	-	-	-
1115	-	-	n¶a[33]	-	-	-	-	-	-	-
1125	¶	¶	-	-	¶	-	-	-	-	-
1127	-	¶	-	-	¶	-	-	-	-	-
1129	-	-	-	-	¶	-	-	-	-	-
1133	-	¶	-	-	¶	-	-	-	-	-
1139	¶	¶	i¶a	-	-	-	-	-	-	-
1140	-	-	n	-	-	-	-	-	-	-
1146	-	¶i¶	-	-	¶	-	-	-	-	-
1153	-	-	-	-	¶	-	-	-	-	-
1165	¶	¶	-	-	¶	-	-	-	-	-
1170	-	-	n¶an[34]	-	-	-	-	-	-	-
1177	¶	2i¶	¶n¶a	-	¶i¶	-	-	¶	-	-
1179	-	-	-	-	-	-	n	-	n¶	-
1182	-	g¶	-	-	g¶	-	-	-	-	-
1183	-	g¶	-	-	-	-	-	-	-	-
1186	-	g¶	-	-	g¶	-	-	-	-	-
1191	-	¶	-	-	-	-	-	-	-	-
1193	-	g¶	n[35]	-	g¶	-	-	-	-	-
1195	-	g¶	-	-	g¶	-	-	-	-	-
1196	-	g¶	-	-	-	-	-	-	-	-
1200	-	-	-	-	¶	-	-	-	-	-
1201	-	-	n¶a	-	-	-	-	-	-	-

[33] Dd lines 1113–15 bracketed.

[34] Dd nota in "w" form with slashed ascender.

[35] Dd nota in "w" form with slashed ascender, 1193–94 bracketed, note in later hand.

WBT	Hg	El	Dd	Gg	Ad³	Ha	Cp	La	Pw	He
1203	-	g¶	-	-	-	-	-	-	-	-
1205	-	-	-	-	-	-	-	n¶	-	-
1207	¶	2i¶	-	-	¶i¶	-	-	-	-	-
1208	-	-	-	-	-	-	-	-	n¶	-
1213	¶	2i¶	-	π	¶i¶	-	-	-	-	-
1219	¶	¶	-	-	¶	-	-	-	-	-
1228	¶	¶	-	-	¶	-	-	-	-	-
1236	¶	¶	n[36]	-	¶	-	-	-	-	-
1237	-	-	-	-	¶	-	-	-	-	-
1238	¶	¶	-	-	¶	-	-	-	-	-
1239	¶	¶	-	-	¶	-	-	-	-	-
1250	-	¶	-	-	¶	-	-	-	-	-
1257	-	¶	-	-	¶	-	-	-	-	-

Textual notes:
Ad³ omits 890.

[36] Dd nota in "w" form with slashed ascender.

Table 5
The Squire's Tale

Introduction	Hg	El	Dd	Gg	Ad^{3}	Ha	Cp	La[37]	Pw	He
5.1	om	¶	-	0	¶	¶	om	om	om[38]	om
4	om	¶	-	0	¶	¶	om	om	om	om

Tale	Hg	El	Dd	Gg	Ad^{3}	Ha^{4}	Cp	La	Pw	He
5.9	4	4bar	4	bar[39]	3	5bar	6bar	7bar	3bar	3
22	g¶	g¶	-	0	-	-	-	-	-	-
28	¶	¶	¶	0	¶	-	-	-	-	-
42	-	¶	-	0	¶	-	-	-	-	-
58	¶	¶	-	0	¶	-	-	-	-	-
73	-	¶	-	-	¶	-	-	-	-	-
76	¶	¶	¶a	-	-	-	-	-	-	-
89	¶	¶	¶	-	¶	-	-	-	-	-
95	-	-	-	-	-	i	-	-	-	-
110	¶	¶	¶	-	¶	ω[40]	-	-	-	-
115	-	i¶	-	-	i¶	-	-	-	-	-
132	¶	¶i¶	¶	π	¶i¶	ω	-	-	-	-
137	¶	¶	-	-	-	-	-	-	-	-
146	¶	¶i¶	-	-	¶i¶	ω	-	-	-	-
156	¶	¶	¶i¶	-	¶	ω	-	¶	-	-
168	-	¶	¶a	-	-	-	-	¶	-	-
170	¶	-	-	-	-	-	-	-	-	-
174	-	¶	-	-	-	-	-	-	-	-
189	¶	2	¶a	π	¶	-	-	-	-	-
199	¶	-	-	-	-	-	-	-	-	-
206	-	-		-	-	-	-	g	g¶	-
207	-	g¶	g¶a	-	g¶	-	g¶	-	-	-
212	¶	¶	-	-	¶	-	-	-	-	-
216	¶	¶	-	-	¶	-	-	-	-	-
225	¶	¶	¶	-	¶	-	-	-	-	-

[37] La has 8 spurious lines linking *SqT/ProWBT,* manicula pointing to first line of spurious link.

[38] Lines V.1–4 in Pw used as part of Franklin's Prologue.

[39] Folio mutilated at this point in Gg; no initial visible.

[40] Ha^{4} "ω" form with extender start in SqT, and coexist with a few completed parafs.

SqT	Hg	El	Dd	Gg	Ad[3]	Ha[4]	Cp	La	Pw	He
228	¶	¶	-	-	¶	-	-	-	-	-
236	¶	¶	-	-	¶	-	-	¶	-	-
243	¶	¶	-	-	-	-	-	-	-	-
247	¶	¶	-	-	¶	-	-	-	¶	-
253	¶	¶	-	-	¶	-	-	-	-	-
258	¶	¶	-	-	-	-	-	-	-	-
263	¶	2	¶	-	-	2	¶	-	-	-
273	-	-	-	-	-	-	g¶	-	-	-
275	¶	¶	-	-	¶	-	-	-	-	-
277	-	-	¶	-	-	-	-	-	-	-
283	¶	¶	-	-	-	-	-	-	-	-
291	¶	¶	-	-	¶	-	-	-	-	-
297	¶	¶	¶	-	¶	-	¶	-	¶	-
305	¶	¶	¶	-	¶	-	-	-	-	-
312	¶	¶	-	-	¶	-	-	-	-	-
335	¶	¶	¶	-	¶	-	-	-	¶	-
340	-	¶	-	-	¶	-	-	-	-	-
346	-	-	i¶	-	-	-	-	-	-	-
347	-	-	-	3	2	2	¶	5bar	2	3
357	¶	¶	-	-	¶	-	-	-	-	-
376	¶	¶	-	-	¶	-	-	-	-	-
380	¶	¶	-	-	¶	-	-	-	-	-
382	-	¶	-	-	¶	-	-	-	-	-
393	¶	¶	¶	-	¶	-	-	-	-	-
401	¶	¶	¶	-	¶	ω	\\	-	¶	-
409	¶	2	¶	π	¶	-	¶	-	¶	-
423	¶	-	¶	-	-	-	-	-	-	-
432	¶	¶	-	-	¶	-	-	-	-	-
447	¶	¶	-	π	¶	ω	-	¶	¶	-
472	¶	¶	-	-	¶	-	-	-	-	-
477	-	¶	-	-	-	-	-	-	-	-
479	¶	-	¶	-	om	-	-	-	¶	-
495	-	¶	-	-	¶	-	-	-	-	-
499	¶	¶	¶	π	¶	ω	-	-	-	-
538	¶	¶	¶	-	-	-	-	-	-	-
574	¶	¶	-	-	-	-	-	-	-	-

SqT	Hg	El	Dd	Gg	Ad[3]	Ha[4]	Cp	La	Pw	He
575	-	-	-	-	-	-	¶	-	¶	-
606	¶	-	¶g¶a	-	-	-	-	-	-	-
607	-	-	-	-	-	-	g¶	-	¶g¶	-
608	g¶	-	-	-	-	-	-	-	-	-
609	-	g¶	-	-	¶g¶	-	-	-	-	-
621	¶	¶	-	-	¶	0	-	-	-	-
632	¶	¶	¶	-	¶	0	-	-	-	-
638	¶	-	-	-	-	0	-	-	-	-
651	¶	¶	-	-	¶	0	-	-	-	-
661	¶	¶	-	-	¶	0	-	-	-	-
663	¶	-	-	-	-	0	-	-	-	-
667	¶	-	-	-	-	0	-	-	-	-
671	3[41]	4	om	-	-	0	-	om	g	-
672	-	-	om	-	-	0	-	om	π	-

Textual notes:
Dd omits 69–72.
La omits 414, 617–672, 673–708.
Ad[3] omits 479.

[41] Corner of folio torn in Hg, part of capital visible at 671.

The *Prive Scilence* of Thomas Hoccleve

Sarah Tolmie
University of Waterloo

Now, if þat ye graunten by your patente
To your seruauntes a yeerly guerdoun,
Crist scheelde þat your wil or your entente
Be sette to maken a restriccioun
Of paiment; for þat condicioun
Exileþ þe peples beneuolence,
And kyndeleþ hate vndir priue scilence. (lines 4789–95)[1]

So WROTE THOMAS HOCCLEVE, Privy Seal clerk, in his *Regement of Princes,* circa 1411. People seem to have long missed the final pun. Such concise and deliberate poetic usage is not what we have come to expect from Hoccleve, often portrayed as a poet who fails to control both self and utterance; the threatening political posture runs counter to a recent consensus that sees the poet as entirely, if not always successfully, subordinated to his Lancastrian masters, chiefly to Prince Henry, to whom the *Regement* is dedicated.[2] This essay proposes, instead, to study

[1] Citations throughout are to Frederick J. Furnivall, ed., *Hoccleve's Works: III.* The Regement of Princes *and Fourteen Minor Poems,* Early English Text Society [hereafter EETS], e.s., vol. 72 (London, 1897) and will hereafter be made in the text. I would like to thank Derek Pearsall, James Simpson, Scott-Morgan Straker, C. David Benson, Mary-Jo Arn, and the *SAC* readers for valuable comments on this paper.

[2] This political position is summarized in Derek Pearsall, "Hoccleve's *Regement of Princes:* The Poetics of Royal Self-Representation," *Speculum* 69 (1994): 386–410. He relies in part on Larry Scanlon, "The King's Two Voices: Narrative and Power in Hoccleve's *Regement of Princes,*" in Lee Patterson, ed., *Literary Practice and Social Change in Britain, 1380–1530* (Berkeley: University of California Press, 1990), pp. 216–47. The poet's status as subordinated subject likewise governs Anthony J. Hasler, "Hoccleve's Unregimented Body," *Paragraph* 13 (1990): 164–83. Hoccleve is a Lancastrian subject in Paul Strohm's *England's Empty Throne: Usurpation and the Language of Legitimation, 1399–1422* (New Haven, CT: Yale University Press, 1998). The growing number of objectors to these views include Ethan Knapp, "Bureaucratic Identity and the Construction of the Self in Hoccleve's *Formulary* and *La male regle,*" *Speculum* 74 (1999): 357–76;

the Hoccleve who wrote the foregoing stanza: a technician at the top of his poetic craft, and the resentful member of an emergent administrative class that was in possession of restricted information. This Hoccleve is neither an inept Chaucerian nor a royalist stooge, but a poet with a very nice line in innuendo: a potential blackmailer.

The passage has several typically Hocclevean features and I will comment on them briefly by way of introduction, in order to set out generally the kind of poet I believe Hoccleve to be, before turning to the specificities of my argument. Firstly, the pun on *privy seal* (*prive scilence,* line 4795), a place where documents are constructed, is anticipated by the word *patente* (line 4789), one of the most common forms of royal document that passed through the hands of Privy Seal clerks, thereby suggesting obliquely the stream of information to which such clerks have access.[3] Additionally, it was the kind of document required for presentation at the Exchequer to claim payment for an annuity, such as Hoccleve's own, which was in arrears at the time of writing.[4] He alludes to this process of payment in his conversation with the old man in the prologue, mentioning his "long seruise" and the fact that he is to be "guerdoned" with an annual "duetee" in the Exchequer (lines 818–24). The above passage, while it is couched in both universal and hypothetical terms, is therefore both topical and personal.[5] Henry IV imprudently

Judith Ferster, *Fictions of Advice: The Politics of Counsel in Late Medieval England* (Philadelphia: University of Pennsylvania Press, 1996), pp. 146–47; James Simpson, "Nobody's Man: Thomas Hoccleve's *Regement of Princes,*" in Julia Boffey and Pamela King, eds., Westfield *London and Europe in the Later Middle Ages,* Publications in Medieval Studies, vol. 9 (London: Centre for Medieval and Renaissance Studies, Queen Mary and Westfield College, University of London, 1995), pp. 149–80; Charles Blyth, "Thomas Hoccleve's Other Master," *Mediaevalia* 16 (1993): 349–59. Ethan Knapp has also recently addressed Hoccleve's various strategies of resistance to Chaucer in "Eulogies and Usurpations: Hoccleve and Chaucer Revisited," *SAC* 21 (1999): 247–73.

[3] For an overview of this office, see A. L. Brown, "The Privy Seal Clerks in the Early Fifteenth Century," in D. A. Bullough and R. L. Storey, eds., *The Study of Medieval Records: Essays in Honour of Kathleen Major* (Oxford: Clarendon Press, 1971), pp. 260–81. For Hoccleve's place there, see A. Compton Reeves, "Thomas Hoccleve, Bureaucrat," *Medievalia et Humanistica,* n. s., 5 (1974): 201–14, and "The World of Thomas Hoccleve," *FCS* 2 (1979): 187–201; Malcolm Richardson, "Hoccleve in his Social Context," *ChauR* 20 (1985–86): 313–22.

[4] Hoccleve refers to the difficulties he has in procuring payment with his own *patente* at Exchequer; the old man suggests having it made over to the prince's hanaper instead (lines 1877–80).

[5] The other great debate in Hoccleve studies concerns the autobiographical nature of his work, a topic defined and brought to a conclusion in J. A. Burrow, "The Poet as Petitioner," *SAC* 3 (1981): 61–75; "Autobiographical Poetry in the Middle Ages: The

granted more annuities than could be paid (this passage occurs in the body of the *Regement* text under the rubric of prudence); Hoccleve's was one of them. It is also highly critical, even rebellious, referring to "hate" being fostered in royal servants. The potential force of this criticism—I, Hoccleve, hate you for unjustly depriving me of my annuity, granted by a legal instrument—is dissipated by its conditional mode ("if þat ye graunten"), its punning or double language, and its studiously impersonal status as a general exemplary statement within a *speculum principis.*

This hypothetical construction, a primary feature of Hoccleve's style, can also be looked on as the natural condition of specular language, addressed as the genre usually was, to a future, not a present, ruler. The conditional "if þat ye graunten" has, in this respect, prospective force: when you are king, Prince Henry, avoid the imprudence of your father, which has caused such dangerous sentiment in his present subject. Hoccleve can thus deploy his own anger effectively in a pointed exemplum, offering himself, in effect, as a historical object: a case study from the present of Henry IV's reign, soon to be superseded—and implicitly recuperated—by the future reign of Henry V. I point this out as a "Lancastrian" feature of the text, conceding the justice of the general opinion that Hoccleve was trying to gain the notice of this new dynasty, and also that he was prepared to exploit an existing rift between father and son. I suggest only that the means he employed were neither servile nor subordinate, but conspiratorial, as I hope will become clear over the course of my argument. It remains true, however, that the hope of future recuperation in the face of past disaster is endemic to the *speculum principis,* and the tendency of such commissions to straddle a dynastic divide (frequently being designated for heirs) makes them apt to this kind of political commentary: it is frequently an oedipal genre.

It is easy to assume that if the powers of poet and prince are in dia-

---

Case of Thomas Hoccleve," *Proceedings of the British Academy* 68 (1982): 389–412; "Hoccleve's *Series:* Experience and Books," *Fifteenth-Century Studies: Recent Essays,* ed. Robert F. Yeager (Hamden: Archon Books, 1984), pp. 259–73. Burrow has satisfactorily formulated the position that his work is both conventional and autobiographical, reflecting real experience in a literary mode that was used not only for the creation of textual personae but also for the understanding of the medieval Christian self. I therefore refer to the Hoccleve persona in the *Regement* variously as a persona, a narrator, and as Hoccleve. The discussion of Kathryn Kerby-Fulton, "Langland and the Bibliographic Ego," in Stephen Justice and Kathryn Kerby-Fulton eds., (*Written Work: Langland, Labor and Authorship* Philadelphia: University of Pennsylvania Press, 1997), pp. 67–143, is also a useful overview of the issues surrounding authorial voice.

logue, the royal one is inevitably primary; the complex mirroring structures critics have identified between poet and patron, Hoccleve and Henry, in the *Regement,* have generally assumed that the poet and subject seeks to mirror the superior reality of the prince. Hoccleve, however, is the writer—a status of which he is very conscious—which puts him, arguably, at the advantage in his text-world. His work generally presents a world in which he, the author, is superbly present; he performs the invisible or naturalistic functions of the author (e.g., omniscient narration, framing devices), he intrudes as a character, and as is significantly indicated in the present passage by the words *priue scilence,* he is also available in his own texts as a brooding absence, a negative figure for the godlike will of the author who cannot be contained in the language he writes. In the face of this writerly artillery, any Lancastrian can only be a cipher in the text, and one, moreover, created by the author. If Hoccleve leaves a space for prospective amelioration, suggesting a hypothetical future in which he will get his money and Prince Henry will get the crown, his is the governing desire. Further, the advice that he offers so amply to the prince in the body of the *Regement* is regularly punctuated by the "if that you. . ." hypothetical formula: the prince's regal power exists in the text conditionally and he is held in abeyance, mirroring Hoccleve's unfulfilled status. The relationship between Hoccleve and Henry cannot be explained as one of simple lack and plenitude: the prince is textually constrained as Hoccleve is professionally and financially. The recipient of an advice text cannot, at least within the text's terms, answer back.

A final preoccupation of Hoccleve is revealed in our passage, one that very much governs the language of the *Regement.* This is the contrast between word, particularly the written word, and intention. Their potential difference, and potential coincidence, is emphasized in the rhyme *patente/entente* (written document/intention). Likewise, the distance between what is *patente,* open, written, and in the public domain, and what is *priue* or secret, hidden in the realm of wordless emotions like hate or benevolence, is metrically highlighted, located as they are on two opposite ends of a short string of alliteration (*patente-paiement-peples-priue*). The materiality of text and the immateriality of will is a prevailing theme of Hoccleve's writing; the interrelationships between these two fields, and the dangers and liberties created by the gap between them, are major poetic topics in all his longer works. The boundaries of language are very much his territory. This tends to bring him out of the realm of Chaucerian concerns in which he is usually considered, and into proximity with a poet like Langland, who displays a similar conflation of interests in satire, metaphysics, and language.[6] Hoccleve's intense interest in Lollards, for instance, is often taken strictly as an attempt to represent himself as politically and religiously orthodox, as topical commentary on a current issue. This it certainly is, but it is also an area of metaphysical speculation that evidently fascinated him as a poet, revealing an ambivalence similar to that of Langland toward hermits: heretics like Oldcastle or John Badby are paradoxes of identity, characters in whom inside and outside, signifier and signified, refuse to coalesce.[7] He condemns them, but feels an anxious kinship with them; this is nowhere better revealed than in the *Complaint,*[8] a meditation upon essence and accidence, that topic which became so widely associated with Lollards and the problem of transubstantiation. In this poem, Hoccleve subjects his self to an analogous kind of interrogation and ends up defending (in orthodox fashion) the supremacy and unknowability of essence. The poet's inner character and sanity cannot be judged by any external sign, up to and including his words. Needless to say, this complicates his poetics, and reveals a general tendency in his work for metaphysical speculation to converge on issues of language.

Like Langland again, I contend, Hoccleve veers between the material and immaterial, concrete and abstract, personal and public, resisting any final resolution. He is a poet literally weighed down with immaterial *thoghte*—"Thought leyd on me full many an hevy loode" (line 42)[9]—

[6] Chaucer's interest in metaphysics and language, in how things come to be and how they are communicated, revolves around issues of narration, where Hoccleve's concern signification. The distinction between the material and the immaterial and the boundaries of representation that Chaucer sketches briefly in the fart joke of *The Summoner's Tale* are matters of obsessive concern to Hoccleve. He is so fascinated with the problems of the sign that he can rarely sustain a narrative. The same is to some degree true of Langland.

[7] He addresses Oldcastle directly in a short poem, printed in Frederick J. Furnivall and I. Gollancz, eds., *Hoccleve's Works: The Minor Poems,* EETS, e. s., vols. 61 and 73 (London: Oxford University Press, 1970), pp. 8–25, and Badby is featured in the *Regement.* The Oldcastle poem has recently received extensive treatment by Ruth Nissé, "'Our Fadres Olde and Modres': Gender, Heresy and Hoccleve's Literary Politics," *SAC* 21 (1999): 275–99.

[8] See *Minor Poems,* pp. 95–110.

[9] Compare his similar line "My schip is wel ny with dispeir y-fraght" (line 858), a metaphorical admixture of abstract and concrete. This line is Hocclevean, also, in its reliance on the image of a vessel, particularly one filled with something immaterial—a characteristic device, and one I take to have hermeneutic and metaphysical application, such vessels being images either of the word (as in Canace's empty box discussed below)

and in whom immaterial, untraceable thoughts breed in *priue scilence* as the result of the physical privation of his unpaid annity. His inability to get paid is a personal ill, a widespread social problem, and an offense against the universal category of prudence. This view bucks a general trend that sees Hoccleve's more extended utterances, at least—the *Regement,* the *Series*—as palliative processes.[10] There is much to recommend Hoccleve as one of the first exponents of the talking cure, but to insist that by the end of any given work he succeeds in pulling himself together, reassembling the fractured personality that critics have remarked on with varying levels of alarm, is to nullify his poetic project in large part. This is because much of the import of his work is carried not in what he is saying, but in his perception of what cannot be said, or of what cannot be contained in words. Dissent may be expressed in silence, as several instances in the *Regement* make clear (the painful quietness of the Privy Seal clerks at their task of writing, or the silent resistance of John Badby), but *benevolence* (goodwill), an important word in the *Regement,* is likewise a trust beyond language, which guarantees the authenticity of human verbal communication. It is, as I hope the rest of this article will demonstrate, the ineffable gold standard that underlies the consensual production and exchange of truth.

Arguments *a silentio*

In his extended prologue, Hoccleve describes the physically demanding task of the writer, picturing the workers in the Privy Seal (lines 988–94):

> A writer mot thre thynges to hym knytte,
> And in tho may be no disseverance;
> Mynde, ee, and hand, non may fro othir flitte,
> But in hem mot be joint continuance.
> The mynde al hoole with-outen variance

or of the self (as here), or both. The line also makes personal the motif of the ship of state in a typical conflation of the personal and public.

[10] These include Burrow, "Autobiographical Poetry," who mentions a "talking cure"; Hasler, "Hoccleve's Unregimented Body," who proposes a Lacanian resolution; and the proposal of a Boethian consolation in David Lawton, "Dullness and the Fifteenth Century," *ELH* 54 (1987): 761–99.

> On þe ee and hande awayte moot alway,
> And þei two eek on hym; it is no nay.

He explains that while other workers may talk and sing, the clerks must rigidly hold their faculties together in silence, performing a job that causes them various kinds of physical suffering (lines 1016–22):

> Wrytng also deth grete annoyes thre,
> Of which ful fewe folkes taken heede
> Sauf we oure self; and these, lo, they be:
> Stomak is on, whom stowping out of dreede
> Annoyeth soore; and to our bakkes, neede
> Mot it be greuous; and the thrid, our yen,
> Vp-on þe whyte mochel sorwe dryen.

This is a mutinous picture. It is a remarkable image of powerful silence—*trauaillous stilnesse*—and repression, keeping *our songe and wordes in* while recording and interpreting other people's utterances. The image of bodily affliction is typical of Hoccleve's reliance on the physical self and on the relations of material body to language:[11] here we see the copying clerks made literally sick on a surfeit of the king's words. This description considers the operation of the mental faculties, the invisible wits, and of the physical body: the whole man is constrained. Notice also how painful it is to Hoccleve to have all his faculties thus concentrated; here, perhaps uniquely in the poem, we have a unified personality, and it is disastrous. The self, he suggests, is less of a burden when strung out into the multiple voices he uses throughout the rest of the work. It may also be more authentic in such a condition. Consider the mimetic task in which the Privy Seal clerks are engaged: they are directing their discrete wills to follow or co-produce the royal will embodied in the warrants issued by their office. Their bodies are inhabited by an alien volition; the quiet horror of the scene reveals personalities superficially held together, but hollow, possessed. Such people are regulated, but are even more radically incomplete than the various disembodied or partially fleshed out personae Hoccleve produces elsewhere. This is

[11] In his lines to the old man "mekely yow beseche I of pardoun / Me submittyng vnto correccioun" (lines 755–56), for instance, although the posture is conventional, he suggests the identity of the Hoccleve narrator as a body of text, liable to textual correction.

definitely an image of the self operating under the law, in the realm of the symbolic governed by paternal prohibition and the constraints of language (there is little doubt that the clerks themselves are being written by the texts they are copying), but against the Lacanian position advanced by Anthony Hasler, I do not see this moment as one of satisfactorily formulated subjection. On the contrary, it is agonizing and untenable. It is the failure of this paradigm of writing that has driven Hoccleve into attempting the overarching poetic writing, the *Regement,* that contains and itself subordinates this description. This authoritarian conception of textual production haunts the *Regement,* as his career in the Privy Seal and the kind of writing it entails, I believe, haunts the entire work of Hoccleve.

John Burrow, in discussing Hoccleve's "poetics of address," comments on the profound effect the petitionary forms that Hoccleve encountered at work had on his poetry. He describes likewise the bureaucratic culture in which he existed, one that relied on patronage and "which takes the law-abiding modern reader deep into an unfamiliar world of chicanery and influence."[12] Hoccleve describes working in the Privy Seal as damaging, as above, and as frustrating, especially in the passage that elicited Burrow's remark about "influence" (lines 1499–512):

> But if a wyght haue any cause to sue
> To vs, som lordes man schal vndertake
> To sue it out; & þat þat is vs due
> For oure labour, hym deyneþ vs nat take;
> He seiþ, his lord to þanke vs wole he make;
> It touchiþ him, it is a man of his;
> Where þe reuers of þat, god wot, sooþ is.
>
> His letter he takiþ, and forþ goþ his way,
> And byddeþ vs to dowten vs no thyng,
> His lord schal þanken vs an oþer day;
> And if we han to sue to þe kyng,
> His lord may þere haue al his askyng;
> We schal be sped, as fer as þat oure bille
> Wol specifie þe effecte of oure wylle.

[12] Burrow, "Autobiographical Poetry," p. 406. This theme is developed in detail in Knapp, "Bureaucratic Identity."

This situation can safely be described as chicanery: the lord's man makes off with the clerks' fee by hoodwinking the gullible stranger, and the powerless clerks are left without redress. More generally, however, the world of bureaucracy and patronage in which Hoccleve operates is anything but unfamiliar to the modern academic, a fact that renders intelligible much of the hostility that Hoccleve's relatively naked petitionary devices have sustained in this community. *The Regement of Princes,* seen in this light, is the equivalent of a versified job application: a specimen book akin to the formulary Hoccleve compiled for use in the Privy Seal.[13] The poetic work includes passages or motifs of dream vision, low-register comic dialogue, penitential lyric, social commentary, high-style didacticism, psychomachia, translation. However, Hoccleve also complains about something else in this passage. The couplet "We schal be sped, as fer as þat oure bille, / Wol specifie þe effecte of oure wylle" (lines 1511–12) contains a Hocclevean doubling: he comments on the irony of the immediate situation, citing a hypothetical future *bille* or petition of the clerks that will not gain the promised support of the putative lord, and he refers simultaneously to the chronic distance that obtains in the lives of the clerks, that between *oure bille,* the letters they write, and *our wylle.* He draws attention, again, to the dehumanized status of the clerks. The lord's man, in fifteenth-century terms, is no more guilty than a twentieth-century academic plotting to make the department pay for personal photocopying, so alienated are these clerks from their labor.

The systematic indirection and fragmentation of Hoccleve's poetic style may also have its roots in the Privy Seal culture. The business of Privy Seal was the drafting of writs, responses to previous petitions made to the king or the continual council, concerning such items as land grants, annuities, or letters of pardon.[14] Some writs were ends in themselves, but most were warrants to obtain action in greater (and slower) departments, the Chancery or the Exchequer. That is to say, they were requests to make a request, a species of institutional indirection that very much anticipates Hoccleve's poetics: the staging of his practical request within the tradition of the melancholic narrator, within a Boethian framework, via the conversation with the old man, and so on. Hoccleve was employed in the fifteenth-century version of Dickens's

[13] This comparison is pursued in Knapp, "Bureaucratic Identity."

[14] This is discussed in Brown, "Privy Seal Clerks," and the office is also described briefly in E. F. Jacob, *The Fifteenth Century, 1399–1485,* Oxford History of England (Oxford: Clarendon Press, 1961), p. 426.

Circumlocution Office (almost literally, since the function of the smaller and more flexible office of Privy Seal was to "talk around" the older and greater offices with their established institutional forms), and it is not surprising that his personal writing should reproduce its tendency toward stepped or tiered communication.

Hoccleve's daily life in the office would also have been crowded with fragmented, disembodied voices, those of the written petitions originally submitted and those of the particular and often minute responses contained in the writs clerks were expected to draft. These would have dealt with a hodgepodge of matters great and small, and the clerks might not always be apprised of both sides of the conversation, as it were, copying out a petition on its way to the king and council one minute, and a writ, itself a response to a possibly unknown previous communication, the next. The copying clerk would be merely a conduit for these voices, interfering editorially only in the matter of institutional or generic form. Hoccleve's occasionally jarring method of partially resolved generic impersonation, the creation of fleeting demi-characters from many genres whose voices are temporarily coextensive with the author's, may well owe something to this manner of receiving and processing information. Incidentally but very importantly, I would add that his exposure to this world of jumbled, particular, and fragmentary volition means that it was impossible for him to have gained the kind of grand, unified, Kantorowiczian impression of the eternal royal body or transcendental will that is required to ground any Lacanian argument about the *Regement.* Hoccleve's practical experience would have led him to understand the royal power as a disconnected series of filaments radiating outward from the court, as something more reactive than creative, as local and temporal. Even the documents that he dealt with—signet letters, diplomatic documents, military orders—were of a markedly less fossilized mode than those of Chancery or Exchequer, making it unlikely that he particularly identified the crown as the timeless giver and maintainer of forms. Given that the throne had been forcibly seized in his lifetime, while Chancery and Exchequer formulae changed little, he may even be forgiven for trying to get a transient prince on his side to move the mountain of the bureaucratic machinery. Kantorowicz's doctrine of the king's two bodies, which is synthetic and ahistorical, has had an invidious effect on scholarship that persists in regarding it as historical. It is not, being on the contrary a masterly synthesis of nearly a thousand years of culture, one that cannot ever be perfectly reproduced in a single historical moment. It is true, however, that Hoccleve's life in the Privy Seal would have contributed to an understanding of royal power as being dialogic, produced from a process of question and answer, being located neither in the person of the king nor the person of the subject, but being created at some movable point of convergence external to both of them. He himself, as the clerk, a third party who made these transactions manifest in text, was definitely located at one of these points. He was, in this respect, a man who made the invisible visible, a transubstantiator, an institutional identity he also transformed into a poetic one.[15]

He refers to writing as *laboure* and *trauaile,* and prefaces his discussion of the clerkly work of writing with mention of two other social tasks: warfare (describing campaigners in the French wars [lines 869–924]) and agriculture (lines 974–80). He claims that his back is worn out *at instance of writyng, his Werreyour* (line 986)—equating textual production with the high-status action of making war, a move of class satire and appropriation he makes several times in his writing (another important one is made in his reference to himself as knight-bureaucrat jousting in lists at the Exchequer, which will be discussed below).[16] He reconfigures the traditional tripartite division of society into those who fight, those who work, and those who write. Those who pray, the clergy, are elided, which suggests structurally that governmental clerks have usurped their place, becoming, in effect, the high priests of the bureaucratic state. This simple but radical formula explains much of Hoccleve's self-understanding, I think, but the situation is, typically, more complex than this. The task of writing can be seen to subsume the other two divisions of society as well. Hoccleve, insofar as he is identifiable with his professional vocation of writing, is a warrior. This is, of course, only a partial and metaphorical identification, satirically identifying distance from as well as proximity to the chivalric ideal. However, even real warriors, especially aged warriors like the veterans of the French wars, are

[15] The idea of poetic transubstantiation, as it develops in this essay, is indebted to Eugene Vance, "Chrétien's Yvain and the Ideologies of Change and Exchange," in *Mervelous Signals: Poetics and Sign Theory in the Middle Ages* (Lincoln: University of Nebraska Press, 1986), pp. 111–51. It is also relevant to Hoccleve's views of Lollards, a topic I am pursuing elsewhere.

[16] This moves Hoccleve once more into the realm of Langland, at least as interpreted by Ralph Hanna III, "'Meddling with Makings' and Will's Work," in A. J. Minnis, ed., *Late-Medieval Religious Texts and Their Transmission: Essays in Honour of I. A. Doyle* (Woodbridge: D. S. Brewer, 1994), pp. 85–94, and "Will's Work," in Justice and Kerby-Fulton, eds., *Written Work,* pp. 23–66.

not thriving in the current culture, becoming poor and neglected. Likewise, Hoccleve describes the physical exhaustion caused by writing, identifying it in this way as a species of heavy work, a productive and penitential form of manual labor.[17] From his brief and passing references to the plight of the laboring classes throughout the *Regement,* it is evident that prospects in this estate are not encouraging either, and his identification with it is similarly partial. Hoccleve is making a double point here: first, that the triordinal thesis is wearing thin, and the traditional divisions are no longer serving the population at large; and second, that his role fits none of them anyway. He is, as James Simpson has pointed out, nobody's man.[18] He falls through the cracks between the existing estate discourses, and is reduced to penciling in provisionally, by dint of these transient and unsatisfactory impersonations, the negative space that must be occupied by the new man, the civil servant.

Beggar, Broker, Bawd

The Regement of Princes displays a seemingly disproportionate amount of prologue, a fact that could be interpreted uncharitably as a sign of Hoccleve's lack of poetic control. Far from being a failure of *mesure,* however, the proliferating front matter is deliberately deployed. In a poem of 5,464 lines, more than a third of the text (2,163 lines) is devoted to prefatory material: first, a short inverted dream motif that opens the poem, in which the sleepless Hoccleve, hardly knowing if he's waking or sleeping, stumbles out of London's Chester's inn; next, his extended conversation with an enigmatic old man whom he meets while wandering in a field at the edge of town; and finally a short proem or direct address to his intended patron, Prince Henry. After all this, he presents a motley collection of maxims and exempla translated from advice texts: the *Secreta secretorum,* Aegidius Romanus's *De regimine principum,* and Jacobus de Cessolis's *De ludo scaccarium.* The multiple prologues, far from being digressive, serve a series of interrelated functions. First, it is here that Hoccleve establishes the story of his missing annuity, and his resulting need for patronage. Scholars have generally taken this position of rhetorical supplication literally, seeing the *Regement* as a begging poem, a

[17] He refers to his writing as *manuel labour* in the *Male Regle* 364 (in *Minor Poems,* pp. 25–39).

[18] Simpson, "Nobody's Man," follows Hoccleve's cue in his choice of title, citing the poet's designation of one Nemo, the clerks' friend and patron (lines 1485–91).

degenerated piece of language for hire like an advertisement, removed from the motiveless realm of pure art. Such a perspective fails to consider this bid for patronage as a strategy of poetic initiation, a way around the common problem medieval poets experienced, that of generating a reason for written utterance. Hoccleve appeals to the authority of need in producing his poem, and, as he himself quotes from the extensive body of Aristotelian and Thomist debate about this topic, "Neede haþ no law." Furthermore, by dwelling on the process and circumstances of its writing, the *Regement* self-referentially incorporates a meditation on its own process of becoming, giving it a kind of poetic immanence or circularity familiar to the postmodern reader. Third, the prologues function as a series of dress rehearsals for an important reception: the reception of the advice text by Prince Henry. The byplay of the Hoccleve narrator and the aged man is an extended and enacted meditation on the purposes, motives, and strategies of giving and receiving advice. While the production and trade of advice is shown to have redeeming features for both maker and patron, it is also evident that the essentially commercial relationship so established is based on mutual self-interest. Crucial to these transactions is the multifaceted figure of the old man.

John Burrow has remarked that the old man of the prologue is not very convincing as a character, comparing him adversely to the old man in Chaucer's *Pardoner's Tale.*[19] On balance, I think this is true. He does not seem to hang together. Everything he utters is conventional, but the graver problem is the bewildering number of conventions that might be brought to bear on him and his speech and function. He is caught in the Hocclevean dilemma of indefinability: he is not a monk, a knight, a peasant, a merchant, or an artisan. He claims a riotous and wealthy past, and lives a poor and sketchy present. He can be defined loosely by his poverty and his proximity to a house of Carmelite friars, possibly, as some kind of self-made mendicant, but evidently not the member of an order. Is he an urban hermit? A lay brother? He corresponds to no existing social category. Similarly, if we turn to the generic and textual realm, his discursive position could be occupied by a variety of voices: the didactic paternal advisor, the confessor, the voice of age, the speaker of penitential lyric, the Boethian consoler, the fool. He could even be the hermit of romance, that curious figure who addresses the protagonist from some marginal place, possesses both social acumen and other-

[19] Burrow, "Autobiographical Poetry," p. 402.

worldliness, and whose role it is to give directions. Closer to home, he is at least in part the voice of Hoccleve's own past, the narrator of the *Male Regle* redux. He becomes thus a figure for a failed poetics: had Hoccleve continued in the relatively simple complaint mode of the *Male Regle,* he would have ended up destitute. The much more ambitious gambit of the *Regement* is authorized jointly by his recommendation, and by his failure: he metaphorically passes the torch.

Finally, though, the most important precursor of the old man, I suggest, is Chaucer's Pandarus, the go-between. Just as Pandarus is the amatory broker between Troilus and Criseyde, the old man is the specular broker of the exchange between Hoccleve and Prince Henry. They share a portentous and often specious style, and use common *sententiae.*[20] Their motives are similarly obscure. Their self-identifications to their respective disconsolate protagonists in their first encounters are equally unrevealing: "A! who is þer?" (line 134), asks the distraught Hoccleve when he meets the old man, to which the latter replies unhelpfully, "I . . . am heere" (line 135), just as Pandarus closes his initial expostulation to the suffering Troilus with "Wostow naught wel that it am I, Pandare?"[21] The phatic content of either utterance suggests the mysterious status of these agents of exchange, assimilators who cannot themselves be assimilated, either in a romance plot or in public life. The old man calls attention to his own role as the go-between of *speculum* author and prince by mentioning the success of *he þat flatter can, or be a baude* (line 547).

The old man does this, as one might expect, indirectly. He works in his line about the activities of bawds in the context of a discussion of excessive display in dress, one couched in a universal and authoritative voice, a voice indeed, of bland exemplarity that Hoccleve will employ later within the body of the *Regement.* This remark is made as an aside in the midst of what is apparently a digression. How, then, can we deter-

[20] All Chaucer citations are from Larry D. Benson, gen. ed., *The Riverside Chaucer,* 3d ed. (Boston: Houghton Mifflin, 1987). Compare the old man's "Wo be to hym þat list to ben allone! / ffor if he falle, helpe ne haþ he none / To ryse" (*Regement* 204–5) to Pandarus's "The wise seith, 'Wo hym that is allone / For, and he falle, he hath non helpe to ryse'" (*TC* 2.694–95). Likewise, Pandarus cries out, "Awake," to Troilus in their initial interview, just as the old man does to Hoccleve. Pandarus's description of the fragmentary state of Troilus as "he that departed is in everi place / [and who] Is nowhere hol" (*TC* 1.960–61) could be a description of the Hoccleve narrator. Chaucer's Pandarus offers a model of specious and unavailing Boethian consolation in an amatory context that Hoccleve reconfigures into a political one. This transition implies that the relationship between poet and prince is, structurally, an erotic one, formed of mutual desire.

[21] *TC* 1.588.

mine that his line has self-referential force? Finally, only by proximity (i.e., the old man himself says it) and by an appreciation of the old man's structural position (as a man with no other identifiable trade, and as a character literally interposed between the Hoccleve persona and the Henry persona who appears in the proem). This could be an isolated instance of willful misreading but for the continuous problem of determining referents throughout the entire prologue. The impression the reader gets of floating, disembodied voices making unattributable and often politically hot utterances—of individual sentences, words, or phrases that seem topical and frequently menacing randomly occurring in innocuous dialogue—cannot easily be dispelled. Upon meeting the old man, Hoccleve admits that he's somehow misplaced, and possibly multiplied, himself, explaining that "here and þer I my selven sought" (line 763)—*selven* can be either accusative or plural. In this topsy-turvy world we see the wakeful narrator as a kind of somnambulist; the old man comes up to the wandering Hoccleve in a field in broad daylight and cries "scleepys þou, man? Awake!" (line 131). Hoccleve reinforces this confusion by using a staple of his poetic style, the double entendre. He refers to both meanings of the word *mette* (dreamed, encountered) while apologizing to the old man for his initial reception of him: "I wot wel, first when þat I with yow mette / I was ful made, and spak ful rudely, / þogh I nat slepte, yit my spirit mette / fful angry dremes" (lines 757–60). This is a classic instance of *rime riche,* or homonym rhyme, used regularly by Machaut and occasionally by Chaucer.[22] This form of rhyme, with its implied hermeneutic lesson—namely, that it is only in the judgment of the reader that the distinction between the two identical written words lies—and its lyric compression, is guaranteed to appeal to a poet who relies in crucial instances on puns and the implied hermeneutic activity of their decipherment.

Identifies shift: the old man himself sometimes appears as a figure of authority, a precursor of Hoccleve's patron Henry. The old man's impersonation of Henry shows in his regal phraseology, in which he relies on images of governance: the narrator must not "wilfully rebelle and dissobeye" (line 190), exhibit "mysruled conceyt" (line 195) or be "obstinat," but "execute" his teaching (line 215), and the Hoccleve persona appeals to him in terms that recall his modesty topos in addressing the

[22] See *TC* 1.17–18: "the hooly blisful martir for to seke / That them hath holpen, whanne that they were seeke."

prince: "mekely yow beseche I of pardoun / Me submittyng vn-to correccioun" (lines 755–56). The old man takes a high moral line on the execution of the heretic John Badby, condemning him as the devil's servant by the "outward token resonable" that he denied the host, mirroring the personal decision of the young Henry at the actual burning (line 320). At the same time, Hoccleve denies the man's real power to help him, telling him directly, "In þe liþe not redresse my nuysance. . . . / It moste be a greter man of myght / þan þat þou art, þat sholde me releve" (lines 172–77). His pseudoclerical authority is ultimately not convincing either, as even after their extended conversation Hoccleve cannot be talked round to Boethian fatalism, and seeks another patron. The Hoccleve persona sums up the old man's curious multiplicity, telling him, "Ye ben not he whom þat I wende han founde" (line 772). Finally, the old man himself admits his status as the poet's creation, retorting with his parting words: "And such as þat I am, sone, I am thyn" (line 1992).

Threats

The old man offers to the Hoccleve narrator advice that would be appropriate for a crowned prince—"if þou go feerless, / Al solytarie, & counsel lakke, & rede . . . / þou likly art to bere a dotyd heed" (lines 197–200). This rather unexceptionable advice is reproduced inside the body of the *Regement* text in the section on counsel, addressed to Henry in *propria persona.* The old man, however, also produces an alarming series of utterances guaranteed to be unpalatable to a Lancastrian dynast, but which would be better addressed to one than to the hapless Hoccleve. Several occur in the prologue's otherwise odd discursus on the importance of proper clothing. Here John of Gaunt, a man known for his conspicuous display and royal pretensions, is cited as an example of personal modesty (lines 512–20). In the same passage great lords are held to blame because their men *Vsurpe swiche a lordly apparaille* (line 441) and this subversion of good order is to be *putte in exyl,* or *in exyl perpetual,* and *bannyshe*[*d*] (lines 460, 523, 539). Gaunt himself was unofficially banished; his son Henry Bolingbroke was exiled for a decade, and returned prematurely to usurp the throne. This section also contains the subversive open-ended question, supposedly a propos of excessively long sleeves that might encumber a retinue: *What is a lord withouten his meynees / I putte cas, þat his foos hym assaile / Sodenly in þe stret* (lines 463–65). There were several occasions in the life of John of Gaunt in which he might well have been attacked in the street: whose palace of the Savoy in London was burned during the 1381 uprising? The retinues of both Thomas, duke of Clarence, and John, duke of Bedford, were accused of brawling and public disorder in London on different occasions.[23] In a more direct vein, later in the advice section, *seruice unquyte*—unrewarded service, which Hoccleve is factually suffering—and *murdre* and *desheritaunce,* both of which the reigning Lancastrian king likely practiced on Richard II, are linked together as sins that will provoke vengeance (lines 4177–79). Such unsettling examples might be multiplied indefinitely.

These unattributable threatening utterances exist in a textual atmosphere of continual punning and references to writing, to learned and literate people and to disputed control of text. The poet deliberately calls attention to his oblique and riddling language in a set piece of decipherment in which the narrator claims that he has more tow on his distaff than the old man knows about (line 1226)—a heraldic reference to the female being the distaff side of a genealogy, meaning that he's married—to which the old man replies, when the talk gets round to wives some time later, "A, sone! I haue espied, and now se / þis is the tow þat þou spoke of ryght now" (line 1457). Emphasis is placed on the superior interpretative power of the literate: "Lettred folk han gretter discrecioun, / And bet conceyue konne a mannes saw" (lines 155–56), says the old man. He asks the Hoccleve persona when he meets him, "Art þou oght lettred?" (line 150), and when he hears that he is, replies punningly, "þan hope I, by seint Gyle / þat god to þe þi wit schal reconcyle" (lines 151–520)—referring potentially to St. Aegidius, invoked by Chaucer in *The House of Fame,* to Aegidius Romanus, author of *De Regimine Principum* ("Gyles of the Regement of Prynces"), which Hoccleve will claim subsequently to translate, and, I suspect, to *seint gyle,* reverent deception, a strategy of learned, oblique, perhaps even godlike writing that the poet continuously employs.

Language itself, when properly employed, is at best a reverent deception to Hoccleve. At worst, it is an impious one, polluting trust and the channels of communication. Lords and princes, in contrast to the interpretative facility of the learned, are constantly beguiled by flattering words; they make the mistake of attending to the words them-

[23] The chronicle sources for these urban conflicts are reviewed in Scott-Morgan Straker, "Ethics, Militarism and Gender: John Lydgate's *Troy Book* as a Political Lesson for Henry V" (Ph. D. diss., Cambridge University 1998), p. 235.

selves, to the semantic field, and not to their relations with whatever wordless intentions and assumptions might lie behind them, that is, to their performative field. This is a failure induced by the politics of court life, one reproduced mimetically in the genre of the *speculum principis,* itself perforce as much an act of flattery as an act of genuine instruction. The sequence of prologues appended to the *Regement* is an attempt to circumvent the problem by presenting dramatically—wordlessly, as it were, by means of structural juxtaposition like a dumb show—that language exists in a performed context. This is a supralinguistic trick he performs again at the beginning of the *Series,* in the *Complaint* and *Dialogue.*

Hoccleve provides a hermeneutic tour de force in his direct address to Henry in the proem, revealing the dangerous skill of clerks (lines 2109–21):

> And al be it that in that place square
> Of the lystes, I mane the eschekere,
> A man may lerne to be wise and ware,
> I, that haue auentured many a yere,
> My witte there-in is but littil the nere,
> Save that somwhat I knowe a kynges draught;
> Of other draughtes, lerned haue I naught.

Hoccleve has previously described himself as a warrior of writing; this time he is in *lystes* as a writer. The *escheker* or chessboard described by de Cessolis's book on the game of chess, one of the *speculum* texts he will be translating, has become the Exchequer. From this chessboard Hoccleve has learned the king's draw, or the king's move, meaning the royal behavior that his specular source conveys. Revealing wheels within wheels, Hoccleve adds a second meaning: what has he spent his whole life doing but working at the *kinges draught*—the king's writing? It is to this, the contents of the documents he copies in the office, many of which were sensitive, as much as to the royal movements on the hypothetical chessboard of de Cessolis, that Hoccleve refers. As a clerk, he is in possession of restricted information. He points to this fact using a rhetoric of decipherment, continuing to add yet a third meaning to *draught:* "To your hyeness, thynke it not to longe, / Though in that draught I somwhat wade depe" (lines 2143–44). We are moving away here from the humble scenario of a begging poem and toward a poetics of extortion. Even if we choose to consider the *kynges draught* as the form, not the content, of the letters Hoccleve drafts in the king's name in Privy Seal, Hoccleve is still pointing to his own identity as the transcriber of the royal words, the man who substantiates the royal will. It is, in fact, not the king who gives manifest form to words that are publicly and legally royal, but the clerk. He wades deep in the current of the king's words; indeed, he draws them down from inchoateness, the minutiae of transient negotiation, into the concrete reality of legal text.

The apogee of threat in the text, however, is the Lollard John Badby, who poses quite a different problem. If the clerkly Hoccleve dangerously converges with the king, Badby diverges. He dies silently resisting royal and ecclesiastical authority, his purposes unknowable, and even his divine judgement after death unclear: "If he inward hadde any repentaunce, / þat wote he, þat of no þing haþ doutaunce" (lines 321–22). The old man, in his guise as upholder of orthodoxy, and Prince Henry jointly condemn him, but fail to control him. He is preserved in the text as a frighteningly powerful, subversive interpreter, a man who "museþ forþer þanne his wyt may strecche" (line 282), a producer of unspoken, unchartable, and unstoppable speculation. He embodies the most potentially disorderly and reversing aspect of the kind of silent, suffering, unrevealing will that is also exhibited by the repressed figures of the clerks laboring in the Privy Seal office or encapsulated in the phrase *priue scilence,* used to describe their state of mind. As such, his death and exorcism may be a relief even to the mutinous poet—the killing off of a monstrous double—but there is no doubt that their projects of invisible criticism and pure denial are related, as is perceived by the old man; he compares Hoccleve's excessive *thoghte* to the heretic's, characterizing both as despair (line 279), an uncreative and unregenerate state.

Badby, one might well argue, is effectively controlled by being executed, as the copying clerks are kept quiet as wage slaves. A persuasive argument has recently been put forward that sees Badby's theatrical burning as an event whose staging had a double effect: one, that a declared enemy of the church, a heretic, was destroyed and his subverting power extinguished and dramatically appropriated, and two, that this process itself was hijacked by the Lancastrian state, in the persons of Henry IV and Prince Henry and their several interventions in the affair, to further transform the negative energy of the Lollard into political and representational capital.[24] This Lancastrian event, however, cannot control Badby's possibilities in Hoccleve's text. In the supremely writerly *Regement,* Badby appears as the fullest logical extension of the melancholic narrator, the man whose utterances and silences neither the state nor the socialized self can constrain. He could be taken as a figure for the unconscious, or for the Kristevan imaginary, except that he participates in language. He may be one of the earliest figures for the radical artist. Instead of being a sign in which signifier and signified do not correspond, an outside with no inside, gesturing toward the traumatic lack of a legitimate king at the sacral centre of the master social text, the dangerous silence of the heretic in Hoccleve's text is a pure configuration of the gap between word and thing. His silence is a form of inverse narration. He illustrates the fact that meaning cannot be entirely controlled, inhabiting that destabilizing remainder that will always overflow any authority's attempt to assign fixed values. In Hoccleve's version, the silent Badby is another partially resolved simulacrum of the author; he anticipates the dumb show performed before Claudius in *Hamlet,* or the performance of the mime Fancioulle before the tyrannical prince in Baudelaire's *Une morte heroique,* a hermeneutic assault on the principle of hegemonic interpretation.[25]

Money and Meaning: Nonmimetic Poetics

We now come to the final salient factor of the poem for the purposes of my overall argument. This is the omnipresence of money metaphors; they form an insistent descant well suited to a clever begging poem. I believe, however, that these money references—and more significantly, the references to absence of money—have a meaning crucially connected to Hoccleve's poetic project. The text contains a series of references to empty purses and treasure chests, to void spaces that are supposed to contain objects of value for trade. The following are some important

[24] This is a loose summary of Strohm's extended argument about Lollards in *Empty Throne,* pp. 32–63. A similar argument is contained in the earlier work of Peter McNiven, *Heresy and Politics in the Reign of Henry IV: The Burning of John Badby* (Woodbridge: Boydell Press, 1987).

[25] In short, this is an example of Derrida's *dissémination.* Baudelairean light can be shed on Hoccleve with less anachronism than one might imagine; compare the useful article by Nathaniel Wing, "Poets, Mimes and Counterfeit Coins: On Power and Discourse in Baudelaire's Prose Poetry," *Paragraph* 3 (1990): 1–18. Both poets are fundamentally concerned with failures of genre.

examples, and in each case the emptiness is curiously creative, prone to change its state and take on other metaphors. The first is the old man showing the narrator his empty bag (lines 676–93):

> And in my purs so gret sommes be,
> þat þere nys countour in al cristente
> Which þat hem can at any noumbre sette;
> þat schaltow see, my purs I wole unschete.
>
> . . . .
>
> Here seest þow noght þat man may handil or touche;
> þe feend, men seyn, may hoppen in a pouche
> Whan þat no croys þere-inne may a-pere;
> And by my purs, þe same I may seye here.
>
> O wher is now al the wantoun moneye. . . .
> That I was maister of, and gouernour,
> Whan I knewe nat what pouert was to sey?
> Now is pouert þe glas and þe merour
> In which I se my god, my sauyour.
> Or poverte cam, wiste I nat what god was;
> But now I know, and se hym in þis glas.

Notice the carefully paradoxical language; the attribution of a mysterious, uncountable, expansive power to the nothingness inside the purse; the quick reference to the devil being able to operate there, much as he is able to operate in the equally mysterious and infinite mind of John Badby. Chiefly, observe that the empty purse, a hollow or void space, becomes a mirror. This is a deft reference to the *speculum* genre and a quotation of Paul in 1 Corinthians 13:12: "[B]ut now we see as through a glass, darkly; now I know in part, but then shall I know, even as also I am known." The St. Paul paraphrase refers to a realm of secret and hidden knowledge that can now only be expressed or apprehended partially. It also refers, apocalyptically, to the end of time and the end of the obfuscations of the material. The old man's statement, that is, while being a conventional remark about social life, remains imbricated in the larger metaphysical and soteriological questions that surround any discussion of the state of material poverty.

There are several other occasions in which the poet refers jokingly to the infinite divisibility of nothing. He says to the prince in the proem (lines 2031–37):

> Though that my livelode and possessioun
> Be skant, I riche am of benevolence;
> To you therof kan I be no nygoun:
> Goode hauve I none, by whiche your excellence
> May plesid be, & for myne impotence
> Stoppeth the way to do as I were holde,
> I write as he þat your goode lyfe fayne wolde.

He sets up a deliberate contrast between his material lack and his immaterial liberality: he is not a niggard of benevolence, and he can contribute will (*I . . . wolde*) toward the prince's moral life. To the old man in the prologue he exclaims: "Wisseth me how to gete a golden salue; / And what I haue, I wele it with yow halue" (lines 1245–46). The old man will give him immaterial knowledge, and in return will receive half of Hoccleve's missing or prospective assets, as the Hoccleve persona is evidently not in a position to give anything else away. Half of nothing is still nothing. Or is it?

Later in the poem we find an empty purse that has a strange transforming power: "So have I plukked at my purse strynges / And made hem often for to gape & gane" (lines 4369–70). Here we have Hoccleve playing his purse; its emptiness is literally instrumental to him. The instance of fiscal emptiness that has most troubled critics, however, is the story of John of Canace that occurs in the main body of the advice text.[26] John has two married daughters on whom he spends all his money. They are flattering to him until the funds run out, whereupon they spurn him. John borrows ten thousand pounds from a merchant and arranges that his family will see him unpacking it out of a chest and counting it. He returns the money to the merchant, and moves in with his daughters, who are suddenly reconciled to him again in the hopes of

[26] The best discussion of this episode, to which this consideration is to some extent a reply, is contained in Strohm's section on "The Amnesiac Text" (*Empty Throne,* pp. 196–214), in which he also reviews the other contexts of the story. It is also addressed in Larry Scanlon, *Narrative, Authority, and Power: The Medieval Exemplum and the Chaucerian Tradition,* Cambridge Studies in Medieval Literature, vol. 20 (Cambridge: Cambridge University Press, 1994), pp. 320–22.

inheriting his loot. He leaves them his locked strongbox in his will, and they keep him in comfort for the rest of his life. When he dies, they get hold of the keys (lines 4348–54):

> They opnede þe chist, & founde riȝt nought
> But a passyngly greet sergeantes mace,
> In which ther gaily made was and I-wrought
> This same scripture: "I, Iohn of Canace,
> Make swiche testament here in þis place;
> Who berith charge of othir men, & is
> Of hem despised, slayn be he with this."

Various interpretations of the inscription on the mace are possible. What is significant for me about the words is not their content, but their location, emerging as they do from emptiness, symbolizing the poet's power to create meaning apparently *ex nihilo*. It is this emptiness that allowed John of Canace to command the respect of his daughters. Nothingness is his treasure. Consistently throughout the text physical money is described as worthless; truly valuable objects are described as absent or void. True peace is empty: "she stryveth nat; of discord hath she lak; / She voyde and empty is of cruelte" (lines 5052–53). Chaucer, for instance, is gone: "Allas! my worthi maister honorable, / This landes verray tresor and richesse" (lines 2080–81). Being placed carefully in the text by means of the famous author portrait,[27] the ultimate dumb show, he is located beyond language; his material remains are textual, but otherwise he has dissolved into the realm of pure intention. Hoccleve is keen to show himself, of course, to be just as absent as Chaucer. In an oedipal contest of negative capability, Hoccleve reveals himself to be a network of absences (broke, dull, mad, silent, unable to constitute himself in an existing estate), a more various species of immaterial presence than Chaucer's, if not as majestically unified. Finally, of course, Hoccleve's professed lack of money enables the whole poem in the first place.

A poet, it seems, can create something from nothing. One could, at this point, wrap up with a facile conclusion: Hoccleve is pointing continuously to his fizzing, effervescent poetic power. He is placing it

[27] This is mentioned briefly in Pearsall, "Royal Self-Representation" and at greater length in David R. Carlson, "Thomas Hoccleve and the Chaucer Portrait," *Huntington Library Quarterly* 54 (1991): 283–300.

within a money metaphor because he is offering it for sale to his royal patron. This is too easy; it cannot accommodate the genuine threat of the poem, its refusals of subordination. Nor can such an explanation cope with the plangency and authenticity of the empty places in the text; these gaping holes in language are too easily overwritten by such a reading. After all, would you buy an item of goods that was only half there? With these empty purses and locked boxes and the presiding broker of the old man, something is definitely for sale here, but the product is nothing so concrete as the text itself, the poetic artifact of *The Regement of Princes*—or even anything as unproblematic as the poet's signifying ability, if we take the poem as a brochure for his overall poetic talents. I think what is for sale is the poet's will: this is the paradoxical anti-matter that fills the empty purses—impervious, untouchable, potentially annihilating, a force of pure critical intention. This would be valuable, indeed priceless, as it is the only thing that could restore real corrective force to the advice to princes genre, hopelessly corrupt and corrupting as the *Regement* reveals it to be, a prey both to the instability of language and the machinations of courtiership. Flattery, feigning, and double meaning are shown to be endemic to language; these devices are used by the poet even as he is inveighing against them. Intention, as we learn from the episode of Canace's box, cannot be coincident with representation; the inside and outside are never the same. Immaterial things alone are integral. After all, we see John assaying the coins he borrows from the merchant, on the assumption that some will be defective. The ones in the empty box can never be flawed, just as the emperor's new clothes cannot be lost or torn.

It will not surprise anyone at this point to learn that I read Canace, also, as a figure of the author. He produces the empty box, the word, which is not full of its own intrinsic meaning but which is, on the contrary, empty inside; its meaning must be imposed on it from the outside.[28] He demonstrates mastery of this hermeneutic fact, orchestrating the external interpretation of the box by his family. In doing so advanta-

[28] Hoccleve himself sets up a hermeneutic interpretation for the Canace episode in his lines in the prologue, referring to the *Secreta secretorum,* one of the texts he is translating: Aristotle "His Epistles to Alisaundre sent / Whos sentence is wel bet than gold in cofre, / And more holsumer grounded to trewe entente" (lines 2029–31). The value of the *sentence* first exceeds gold—suggesting a commensurate materiality, two things that might be exchanged for one another in some proportion—and then dissolves into an immaterial *entente.* This process revolves around the image of the coffer, which somehow becomes the locus of this transformation: a coffer containing gold giving way to one

geously to himself, he also demonstrates the superiority of his hermeneutic paradigm: where his daughters' desire for gold is a desire for guaranteed meaning in language (each word a box full of something naturally valuable), the wise old man John realizes that meaning is actually produced by substitution and exchange. This is what I mean by "nonmimetic poetics" in the title of this section. Unlike Paul Strohm, that is, I do not see the gap Hoccleve is discussing here as a fundamentally tragic one, as representing the irrecoverable Lacanian *objet petit a,* or as gesturing unconsciously toward the disturbing lack at the heart of the kingdom, the lack of a legitimate king. I think, in contrast, that Hoccleve has to a large extent moved past realist poetics. He might be called a nominalist, or he might be hailed as the first postmodern poet. He retains the acute suspicion of text that is the legacy of medieval realism, the feeling that the letter kills and the spirit gives life, but finally, I think, he is a writer who is not made fearful by the arbitrary sign, but enabled by it. If actual, physical gold in this *exemplum* is a sign of a fatal cupidity just as it is in *The Pardoner's Tale,* the absent or imaginary gold that latterly fills the chest is its redeemed opposite, the gold standard of trust that must animate filial bonds. John of Canace is the clearest impersonation in the main text of the poet as transubstantiator: the man who makes the visible invisible (transforming the gold into nothingness) and the invisible visible (transforming his daughters' greed into his own sustenance). In so doing he re-creates social order. He is the double of the Privy Seal clerk in the prologue, the man making the invisible wills of rulers and petitioners apparent in his documents, with his implicit power of dissolving them again. The two of them conflate into a picture of literacy, or more exactly, of the metaphysical act of writing, which is always an act of imperfect copying—the will of the writer consenting to, and thereby creating, the meanings of the words he writes. This copying is not imperfect in the sense of being a lesser version of an ideal form (e.g., the transient human record of the divine word, or a restricted usage like a single subsection of an authoritative dictionary definition), but not-perfect, assuming that there is no ultimate form. The writer is choosing a currently available, consensually determined meaning for each word from a teeming range of hypotheti-

---

containing a book, the "secrets of secrets," itself giving way to a chest full of intention. In line 301 of the *Dialogue* (*Minor Poems,* p. 120), Hoccleve uses an explicit image of the mind as a chest filled with immaterial volition: "þat purpos caste out of thy myndes cheste."

cal possibilities. This places every writer in the dizzying position of de facto creator of meaning, an identity that Hoccleve relishes in his ludic moments, but it also places writers—and everyone else who uses language—in a position of great responsibility. If, in all our acts of communication, we are copying texts without an original, then, as any Privy Seal clerk knew, we are always in danger of descending into incomprehensibility.

Benevolence

Hoccleve privileges writers, poetic or practical, as the supreme handlers of language; they have the most intense and arduous engagement with it, being literally its warriors. A person who is concentrating mind, eye, and hand in the task of writing is at a nodal point, inventing the words of his language by investing them with his will—impersonating, or embodying, his culture. He does not, however, deny others their integral connection with language, which is the common property of the polity; throughout his work he discusses the semiotic activities of readers, princes, advisors, beggars, heretics, courtiers, clerics, crowds, coiners, prostitutes. Everyone communicates, and it is equally important for everyone to invest in the general, wordless social trust that must lie behind language. This trust is the unspeakable precondition for all verbal exchange, and in the *Regement* Hoccleve usually calls it *benevolence.*[29]

In his later *Dialogue,* he expressly discusses the need for trust as a guarantor of verbal communication (lines 330–36):

> Who so nat leeueth what þat a man seith,
> Is signe þat he trustith him but lyte.
> A verray freend yeueth credence & feith

[29] This section was much aided by a brief argument at the end of Jill Mann's "Price and Value in *Sir Gawain and The Green Knight,*" *Essays in Criticism* 36, no. 4 (1986): 294–318. She suggested that the *Gawain*-poet, by dint of an unstated or posited relation between two exchanges, reveals the way in which the exchange of a wordless or willed *trawþe* (truth or trust) must precede any other kind of trade transaction. She explained that the *Gawain*-poet, in constructing the exchange of winnings game, describes the usual form of a commercial exchange but changes its engine, producing a hypothetical exchange that is not governed by need but by honorable agreement. The result is a purely formal exchange that illustrates the power of culture to transform objects and to confirm social relationships. This exchange of trust, she claimed, "lies behind the exchange of blows, controlling and determining its outcome by an invisible power" (p. 311).

Vn-to his freend what so he speke & wryte.
ffrendshipes lawe nat worth wer a myte,
If þat untrust vn-to it wer annexid;
Vntrust hath many a wight ful sore vexed.[30]

In stressing the aspect of faith necessary to human friendship, the element of wholly undemonstrable intentionality required in order for relationships to function or words to be understood, Hoccleve echoes St. Augustine:

Tell me, I ask you, with what eyes do you see your friend's will toward you? For, no will can be seen with bodily eyes. Or, indeed, do you also see in your mind that which is taking place in the mind of another? But, if you do not see it, how do you, on your part, requite his loving kindness, if you do not believe what you cannot see?

Or, perhaps you will say that you see the will of another through his deeds? Then you will see acts and hear words, but of your friend's will you will believe that which cannot be seen or heard. The will is not a color or a figure that may be impressed upon the eyes; nor is it a sound or a formula that may strike upon the ears; nor indeed is it yours to be felt by the affection of your heart. . . .

Lo, verily you believe in a heart that is not yours, and you place faith where you do not focus the glance of either your body or your mind. You discern your friend's countenance by means of your body; you discern your faith by means of your mind; but your friend's faith is not appreciated by you, unless there is in you a reciprocating faith, by which you may believe that which you do not see in him.[31]

Such social faith underlies interpersonal interaction ("what þat a man seith"), textual interpretation (such as the act required of the reader of Hoccleve's poem), and ultimately, as the *Complaint* and *Dialogue* jointly illustrate, even the constitution of the individual personality itself. In a typical hermeneutic fusion of self and text, Hoccleve devotes the first two parts of the *Series* to proving that a person and a book (and even other forms of material signs like coins) are subject to the same tasks of social reading: the recovered poet feels sane, he acts and writes sanely,

[30] *Minor Poems,* p. 122; Hoccleve uses the significant word *trust* again in line 469: "But of your trust to me ward, be ye scant" (*Minor Poems,* p. 126).

[31] Augustine, *On Faith in Things Unseen,* trans. Roy Joseph Deferrari and Mary Francis McDonald, in *Writings of Saint Augustine,* Fathers of the Church: A New Translation (New York: CIMA Publishing Co., 1947), 2:452–53.

but he needs the belief of his textually constructed friend, a hypostasis of the reader, in order to be fully reconstituted. Hoccleve's thoroughgoing volitionism is arguably the key to his outbursts of volubility; moments of seeming excess like his descants on the theme of flattery are a kind of textual *auto-da-fé* in which he struggles to convey the purity of his will by sheer proliferation of language (*Regement* 1912–46, 3039–101, 4439–64, 5251–85). The repetition, multiplication, density, or platitude of such passages conveys the intransigence of his textual medium, the hopelessness of relying on the intrinsic lucidity of the words themselves; like many passages in Langland, the language outruns itself and forces the reader to acknowledge the gap of meaning that his or her will is continually bridging via the act of reading. The intangible intentions of author and reader must reciprocate in the defining human act of *comunyng,* the only means of determining anything (*Complaint* 217; *Dialogue* 470).

As St. Augustine had definitively pointed out, volition defies representation. We must all assume it to be there, in order for anything in the human world to have meaning. Hoccleve, nonetheless, manages to contain it in language by encapsulating it in Canace's box and in the old man's empty purse: these are proffers of *benevolence* extended to the characters within the text, to the readers, and to Prince Henry, the prospective patron. These empty vessels constructed out of words highlight the immaterial contribution our wills must make to all acts of verbal communication. They reflect also, in a limited and ludic way, a traditional scholastic tenet: the impossibility of true nothingness.[32] Canace's box is symbolic of the word "nothing," for which we have a conceptual category; it cannot be empty, for it contains space or potentiality, a place for something to be. In the face of the hermeneutic instability of Hoccleve's text-world, this is perhaps a reassuring glimpse of Thomist metaphysics, a series of ineradicable, although immaterial, categories.[33] Indeed, the images of emptiness on which Hoccleve relies are perhaps not surprising, given that truth or trust—like other omnipresent, intangible, but necessary items, like air—is part of a scholastic category in which value must be inferred negatively, by measuring the consequences of its hypothetical loss.[34]

[32] See Peter Kreeft, ed., *A Summa of the* Summa (San Francisco: Ignatius Press, 1990), pp. 192–94.

[33] Hoccleve shows signs of exposure to scholastic learning: pervasive antinomialism and a tendency to make faintly goliardic jokes on topics like nothingness or infinity.

[34] Mann, "Price and Value," p. 311.

Hoccleve repeats throughout the text of the *Regement,* via various personae, two things. His words are useless, inert matter. The multiplication of words is dangerous: it is flattery in courtiers, rashness in kings; it causes physical degeneration among the Privy Seal clerks. Human communication is made real only by the combination of text and *benevolence,* good will. The old man who gives so much sententious advice is *wele-willed,* and the Hoccleve narrator uses both words to describe his intentions toward the prince. Chaucer is praised for his ability to write English verse, to manipulate textual material, but also for the *fructuous entendement* (line 1963) that animated it and that invites a matching investment from the reader.

Several strands discussed here are knit into one in Hoccleve's envoy sending the poem off to Prince Henry. The lines contain a veiled reference to secret knowledge and to his clerkly role at Privy Seal (*I am so priue unto thy sentence,* ostensibly apostrophizing the poem but very applicable to his relationship with Henry) and they insist that the actual words of the poem are inadequate for its purpose, emphasizing compensating *benevolence.* Finally, they provide the last glimpse of the governing money-metaphor, in a pun on *cheerte,* which has connotations both of affection (being *cher,* or dear) and costliness or value (being expensive because of scarcity, OF *chierté*).[35] The words of a well-intentioned critic, he claims, are rare and hence doubly precious. I give the poet the last word (lines 5448–55):

> Bot o thyng wote I wele: go where thou go,
> I am so prive [un]to thy sentence,
> Thou hast, and art, and wolt ben euermo
> To his hyeness, of suche benevolence
> Though thou not do to hym due reuerence
> In wordes, thy cheerte not is the lesse.
> And yf lust be, to his magnificence
> Do by thy rede: his welthe it shal witnesse!

[35] *Chierte* is a word Hoccleve places in his punning register, evidently being aware of its etymological sense: see also "the fervent chiertee / That this worthy clerk ay to this kyng bere / Trustyng his welthe durable to be" (lines 2045–47), in which the word is likewise used in conjunction with *welthe.*

Commentary and Comedic Reception: Dante and the Subject of Reading in *The Parliament of Fowls*

Daniel Pinti
Niagara University

NO ONE DOUBTS that one of the sources for Chaucer's *Parliament of Fowls* is Dante's *Comedy.* When Chaucer creates the famously bifurcated gate that opens into the *locus amoenus* leading to Venus's temple, he does so by directly invoking the inscription above the gate of hell that inaugurates Dante's journey through the underworld in canto 3 of the *Inferno,* translating Dante's thrice-inscribed "Per me si va" as "Thorgh me men gon."[1] Chaucer's *Parliament,* however, is ostentatiously a poem of many sources; thus an essay that, oddly enough, focuses on not only just one of these sources but indeed perhaps one of the least of them requires some explanation at the outset.[2] Considerable scholarly authority weighs against such an essay: Howard Schless claims that "Dante's contribution is not sufficiently extensive to have any fundamental effect on the poem as a whole," a claim quoted recently and ap-

The research for this article was in part supported by a 1997 Summer Research Award from the College of Arts and Sciences, New Mexico State University. An earlier version of this argument was presented at the International Congress on Medieval Studies, Western Michigan University, May 7, 1998. I am grateful to David Wallace for suggesting a number of improvements to this essay.

[1] Text and translations from Dante are taken from *The Divine Comedy,* ed. and trans. Charles Singleton, 3 vols. (Princeton, N.J.: Princeton University Press, 1970–77). All citations of Chaucer are from Larry D. Benson, gen. ed., *The Riverside Chaucer,* 3d ed. (Boston: Houghton Mifflin, 1987). Subsequent citations will be made in the text.

[2] Among these sources, of course, are Boccaccio's *Teseida,* Cicero's *Somnium Scipionis* as preserved in Macrobius's commentary on that work, Alain de Lille's *De planctu naturae,* and Ovid's *Fasti.* For a thorough, recent discussion of the source material, see the chapter on the *Parliament* in A. J. Minnis, with V. J. Scattergood and J. J. Smith, *The Shorter Poems,* Oxford Guides to Chaucer (Oxford: Oxford University Press, 1995).

provingly by A. J. Minnis, who "share[s] Schless's opinion."[3] Minnis also notes Dorothy Everett's comment that with regard to the *Parliament,* it is Dante's repeated "Per me si va" that "perhaps more than anything else . . . constitutes [Chaucer's] 'debt' to the Italian poet."[4] All three scholars are right, of course—right, that is, in terms of the economics of source study that works on metaphors of "contribution" and "debt," and asks questions about what Chaucer "owes" to Dante, or what Dante ultimately "owned," in the *Parliament.* I propose, however, to exchange this critical model for a different one, one of "intertextuality," and submit that there is good historical reason for doing so.[5] At least twelve different commentaries or sets of glosses, covering all or part of the *Comedy,* were composed between 1322 and 1375—that is, by the time of Chaucer's journeys to Italy in 1373 and 1378.[6] These early Dante commentaries provide, I believe, a heretofore untapped resource for understanding Chaucer's reading of, and responses to, a distinctively fourteenth-century Dante.

Some of the commentaries in question (like those of the poet's youn-

[3] Howard Schless, *Chaucer and Dante: A Revaluation* (Norman, Okla.: Pilgrim Books, 1984), p. 89, and Minnis, ibid., p. 289.

[4] Dorothy Everett, *Essays on Middle English Literature,* ed. Patricia Kean (Oxford: Oxford University Press, 1955), p. 143; quoted in Minnis, ibid., p. 289.

[5] I do not mean to suggest that such an approach is entirely new in studies of the *Parliament,* much less in Chaucer studies more generally. It should be noted, though, that "intertextuality" can mean many things, including de facto source study. Minnis himself describes the *Parliament* as "an intricate case of Chaucerian intertextuality" (ibid., p. 265).

[6] These early commentaries include those of Jacopo Alighieri (1322), Graziolo de' Bambaglioli (1324), Jacopo della Lana (1324–28), Guido da Pisa (1333), the "Ottimo Commentatore," now thought to be the Florentine notary Andrea Lancia (1329), and Pietro Alighieri (first version, 1340), along with the anonymous Italian glosses known as the *Chiose Selmiane* (1337) and the Latin glosses known as the *Anonimo Lombardo* (1322–25) and the *Chiose Ambrosiane* (1355). These commentaries circulated throughout the century and influenced later commentators writing closer to Chaucer's time, such as Boccaccio (1373) and Benvenuto da Imola (1380), both of whom I'll have occasion to mention below. The order of composition of the earliest commentaries, and the ways in which earlier commentators influenced later ones, are much debated; I am following dates given by Paola Rigo, "Commenti danteschi," *Dizionario critico della letteratura italiana,* vol. 2 (Turin: UTET, 1986), pp. 6–22, and cited in Deborah Parker, *Commentary and Ideology: Dante in the Renaissance* (Durham, N.C.: Duke University Press, 1993), p. 29. For information on the early commentaries, see, in addition to the works cited above, the appropriate articles in Umberto Bosco, ed., *Enciclopedia Dantesca,* 6 vols. (Rome: Istituto dell'Enciclopedia Italiana, 1970–78). Bibliographical information on editions of these commentaries will be included below. On Chaucer's Italian journeys, see Derek Pearsall, *The Life of Geoffrey Chaucer: A Critical Biography* (Oxford: Blackwell, 1992), pp. 102–9, and the works cited in n. 17 below.

gest son, Jacopo Alighieri; the so-called Ottimo Commentatore; and Boccaccio) are written in Italian, while others (the most important being the commentaries of Guido da Pisa; Dante's second son, Pietro; and the monumental work of Benvenuto da Imola) are in Latin. Jacopo della Lana's important Italian commentary has the distinction of being the earliest to cover the entire *Comedy.* Judging from the surviving manuscripts, Lana's also seems to have been the most widely circulated of the Trecento commentaries, extant in more than eighty manuscripts, at least twenty-five of which survive from the fourteenth century; indeed, it served as a primary source for many of the later commentators.[7] The first of the three recensions of the Ottimo Commento, for example, reproduces from Lana the entirety of his glosses on *Purgatorio* 1–6, most of the prologues to individual cantos, and virtually all of his commentary on *Paradiso,* leading one recent critic to claim that it is not too much to call Lana's commentary "la pietra angolare su cui l'Ottimo commentatore costruí la sua opera (the cornerstone on which the Ottimo commentator constructed his work)."[8] Lana's commentary, of course, was hardly the only one to be appropriated by other, later interpreters, yet despite their criss-crossing influences and sometimes confusing chronology, it would be misleading to suggest that the commentaries show a critical consensus about the meaning of Dante's poem in the fourteenth century that contrasts utterly with the critical variety of the twentieth. Although in this essay I will be looking for and describing certain predominant hermeneutic strands in the commentaries, it is nonetheless important to remember that each commentary has its origin in a particular time and place. Fourteenth-century commentaries seem to have been produced in Venice, Milan, Pisa, Florence, and Naples (to offer only a partial list) by commentators who quite clearly by century's end recognized themselves and their audiences to be a good deal further removed from the cultural world of the Italy of Dante's exile than, say, the poet's son Jacopo would have been in 1322 Verona. Consequently, each commentary, when taken as a whole, can be seen to reflect the particularities

[7] Steven Botterill, in *Dante and the Mystical Tradition* (Cambridge: Cambridge University Press, 1994), p. 131, gives this number of Lana manuscripts.

[8] Giuliana De Medici, "Le Fonti dell'Ottimo Commento alla *Divina Commedia,*" *Italia medioevale e umanistica* 26 (1983): 71–123; the quotation is from p. 75. Given the wide circulation of Lana in Italian, its translation into Latin, and the numerous surviving manuscripts of the first recension of L'Ottimo, it seems that of all the commentaries Lana's would have been the most likely one for Chaucer to have encountered, although of course that does not preclude the possibility of contact with other commentaries as well.

of its distinctive cultural context, and will often vary greatly from others in terms of its governing assumptions about Dante and his poem as well as its interpretation of specific passages and personages.[9]

The point here is simply that the *Comedy* was already in the fourteenth century, not unlike today, a poem that existed within an intricate and contestive dialogue of commentary that worked not only to explicate the poem but, as Deborah Parker has pointed out, to authorize it as well—that is, to construct the poem's authoritative place by means of the process of explicating it.[10] What I am interested in is the ways in which Chaucer's clear marking of the gate scene in *The Parliament of Fowls* as "Dantean" opens the poem into that web of commentary and allows Chaucer's poem to refract those textual negotiations. From an intertextual perspective, words become, in Julia Kristeva's phrase, "mediator[s], linking structural models to cultural (historical) environment," and so "each word (text) is an intersection of words (texts) where at least one other word (text) can be read," and the word thus functions as "a set of ambivalent elements."[11] In terms more specific to this argument, by thinking intertextually we can better recognize how Chaucer, when he appropriates "Dante's" words in his poem, is necessarily not only "citing" a source but also linking his text to a larger "cultural . . . environment" that included the many other words with which Dante's

[9] For an excellent overview in English of the early Dante commentaries, see Steven Botterill, "The Trecento Commentaries on Dante's *Commedia*," forthcoming in *The Cambridge History of Medieval Literary Criticism.* I wish to thank Professor Botterill for graciously allowing me to read a typescript version of his article. Deborah Parker, in *Commentary,* examines some of the ways in which particular civic and political contexts could impinge on the works of various Renaissance commentators. To cite briefly but one significant example of the kind of variation I have in mind, Pietro Alighieri considers his father's work to be that of a theologian and poet, while Guido da Pisa, in exalting contrast, reads him as a "prophetic visionary." See David Wallace's discussion in A. J. Minnis and A. B. Scott, with David Wallace, *Medieval Literary Theory and Criticism, c. 1100–1375, The Commentary Tradition,* rev. ed. (Oxford: Clarendon Press), p. 451.

[10] See Parker, *Commentary,* p. 31: "Trecento commentators tend to speak of the *Comedy* as fixed, as a polestar by which to chart the position of contemporary culture and thought. But their defensive critical practice often belies this concept of a timeless, authoritative, universal Dante. Such a contradiction shows the force of their desire—their wish to *make* the poem authoritative" (emphasis added).

[11] Julia Kristeva, *Desire in Language: A Semiotic Approach to Literature and Art,* ed. Leon S. Roudiez, trans. Thomas Cora, Alice Jardine, and Leon S. Roudiez (New York: Columbia University Press, 1980), p. 66. Qtd. in Allen J. Frantzen, "Writing the Unreadable Beowulf: 'Writan' and 'Forwritan,' the Pen and the Sword," *Exemplaria* 3 (1991): 327–57, on pp. 331–32.

intersect: the material and intellectual environment of learned commentary.[12] Moreover, in Allen Frantzen's words, "Intertextual analysis stresses both the doubling and the negating effect of the transformation of texts . . . and examines the poem's meditation on writing."[13] This is exactly what I plan to do: to examine Chaucer's writing "on" his gate as a kind of meditation on writing, and therefore on reading, specifically on reading and writing Dante in the fourteenth century.[14]

As Minnis has rightly pointed out, "There is remarkable critical consensus on [the *Parliament*'s] lack of explicit answers, though wide variation in how the significance of this is perceived," and one might infer an attempt here to contribute directly to the many finely nuanced arguments on "antithesis" or "indeterminacy" in *The Parliament of Fowls*

[12] By focusing on this particular Dantean "environment," I do not mean to deny the importance of others. That is to say, while my interest is learned Dante commentary and what that body of work can suggest about Chaucer's reading of Dante, other texts mediated Dante to Chaucer as well, most notably many of the works of Boccaccio. Although this subject is not the primary focus of his book, David Wallace, in *Chaucer and the Early Writings of Boccaccio* (Cambridge: D. S. Brewer, 1985), does perceptively demonstrate some of the common ground between Chaucer's and Boccaccio's respective poetic reworkings of Dante. Regarding *The House of Fame,* for example, Wallace writes, "Chaucer follows Boccaccio in attempting to accommodate the influence of Dante within a French-derived, dream poem format. And he follows Boccaccio in producing a poem [like Boccaccio's *Amorosa Visione*] that has traditionally been taken to express a crisis in his development" (p. 6). As undeniably important as such poetic intersections are—and to be sure, more work needs to be done on Chaucer's reading of Dante through a Boccaccian lens—I think my exclusive focus on the learned commentaries to be warranted, first because of their own imposing intricacy (both individually and collectively), and second because their explicit efforts to explicate and authorize Dante's poem raise questions of readerly authority that cannot be fully investigated in the same way in other sorts of early appropriations and mediations of the *Comedy.*

[13] Frantzen, "Writing," p. 332.

[14] As John Fyler concisely states, "The *Parliament* explicitly raises the question of what it means to be a *reader* instead of a lover" (emphasis added). See *Chaucer and Ovid* (New Haven, Conn.: Yale University Press, 1979), p. 83. On the intersections among reading, writing and commentary in medieval literature, see John Dagenais, *The Ethics of Reading in Manuscript Culture: Glossing the "Libro de Buen Amor"* (Princeton, N.J.: Princeton University Press, 1994). Since I am fundamentally interested in Chaucer as an occasional translator (in the broadest sense) of Dante, my work has also been informed by the recent scholarship on medieval translation and on Chaucer as a translator. See Rita Copeland, *Rhetoric, Hermeneutics, and Translation in the Middle Ages: Academic Traditions and Vernacular Texts* (Cambridge: Cambridge University Press, 1991); David Wallace, "Chaucer's 'Ambages,'" *American Notes and Queries* 23 (1984): 1–4; Leonard Koff, "'Awak!': Chaucer Translates Bird Song," in Roger Ellis and René Tixier, eds., *The Medieval Translator* 5 (Brepols, 1996): 390–418; Paul Beekman Taylor, "Chaucer's Strategies of Translation," *Chaucer Yearbook* 4 (1997): 1–19. Taylor argues, I think correctly, that "Chaucer's translations are intertextual links of time, place and linguistic order" (p. 17).

made by David Aers, Michael R. Kelley, Larry Sklute, and others.[15] The inference, perhaps, would not be inaccurate, although with an important qualification. I am less interested in the ways the *Parliament* represents, or ends in, indeterminacy or undecidability than I am in the way the "reading scene" at the gate suggests something about Chaucer's *interrogation* of the *nature* of indeterminacy, specifically his exploration of its paradoxically constitutive role in the construction of poetic *auctoritas.*[16] The complex set of intertexts for this investigation is the opening passage of *Inferno* 3—ironically, perhaps the most seemingly determinate texts in the history of literature—in its medieval textual environment: the commentary tradition encompassing, penetrating, and in some sense sustaining Dante's poem. After examining this body of commentary and then suggesting a new reading of the gate scene in the *Parliament* in light of what the commentaries can tell us, I want to offer some tentative suggestions for the way in which this approach to Chaucer's reading of Dante can lead us to reconceptualize Chaucerian/Dantean intertextuality, specifically by viewing the very literary history of the *Comedy* in the Trecento as, in medieval terms, fundamentally "comedic."[17]

[15] Minnis, *Shorter Poems,* p. 215. See also David Aers, "The *Parliament of Fowls:* Authority, the Knower and the Known," *ChauR* 16 (1981): 1–17; Larry M. Sklute, "The Inconclusive Form of the *Parliament of Fowls,*" *ChauR* 16 (1981): 119–28; Thomas Reed, *Middle English Debate Poetry and the Aesthetics of Irresolution* (Columbia: University of Missouri Press, 1990); and Michael R. Kelley, "Antithesis as the Principle of Design in the *Parlement of Foules,*" *ChauR* 14 (1979): 61–73. Other important interpretations of the theme and poetics of the *Parliament* include J. A. W. Bennett, The Parlement of Foules: *An Interpretation* (Oxford: Oxford University Press, 1957); chapters on the poem in Robert R. Edwards, *The Dream of Chaucer: Representation and Reflection in the Early Narratives* (Durham, N.C.: Duke University Press, 1989), Lisa J. Kiser, *Truth and Textuality in Chaucer's Poetry* (Hanover, N.H.: University Press of New England, 1991), and A. C. Spearing, *Medieval Dream-Poetry* (Cambridge: Cambridge University Press, 1976); and articles by H. Marshall Leicester Jr., "The Harmony of Chaucer's *Parlement:* A Dissonant Voice," *ChauR* 9 (1974): 15–34, James Dean, "Artistic Conclusiveness in Chaucer's *Parliament of Fowls,*" *ChauR* 21 (1986): 16–25, Kurt Olsson, "Poetic Invention and Chaucer's *Parlement of Foules,*" *MP* 87 (1989): 13–35, Russell A. Peck, "Love, Politics and Plot in the *Parlement of Foules,*" *ChauR* 24 (1990): 290–305, and Craig E. Bertolet, "'My wit is sharp; I love no taryinge': Urban Poetry and the *Parlement of Foules,*" *SP* 93 (1996): 365–89.

[16] In this respect I share an interest with Aers, who also discusses "Chaucer's concerns with the *processes* by which authority is constructed" ("Authority," p. 1).

[17] As with virtually every topic in Chaucer studies, the scholarship on Chaucer and fourteenth-century Italian literature is considerable and growing. See, for wide-ranging studies, the articles in Piero Boitani, ed., *Chaucer and the Italian Trecento* (Cambridge: Cambridge University Press, 1983); Howard Schless, "Transformations: Chaucer's Use of Italian," in Derek Brewer, ed., *Geoffrey Chaucer: The Writer and His Background,* 2d ed.

I.

The first step toward understanding Chaucer's reading and representation of Dante's text in the context of Trecento Dante commentary is to ask, What in *Inferno* 3.1–12 gives rise to heremeneutic anxiety in the commentaries?[18] What aspects of Dante's poem here elicit comment and complication? One could argue for three governing hermeneutic threads in the responses of the Trecento commentators to Dante's hell-gate inscription.[19] What these different strands of interpretation collectively share is their insistent attention to the textuality of the inscription in several different ways. First, there is a certain limited amount of attention paid to the rhetorical strategy of *anaphora* itself, the repetition of "Per me si va" on which Chaucer seems to have focused. In perhaps the Trecento's most widely circulating and influential commentary, Jacopo della Lana remarks:

> Questo modo di parlare che recita più volte una parola è ditto dalli rettorici *parlare effettivo,* in lo quale mostra l'affezione dal dicitore essere molta. E però replica Dante qui *per me* tre volte, a mostrare come aveva grande affezione di fare suo viaggio.

> [This mode of speech where one repeats a word several times is called by the rhetoricians "affective speech," in which one shows the emotion of the speaker

(Cambridge: D. S. Brewer, 1990), pp. 184–223 (along with Schless's book, cited in n. 3 above); and, most recently, David Wallace, *Chaucerian Polity: Absolutist Lineages and Associational Forms in England and Italy* (Stanford, Calif.: Stanford University Press, 1997). Recent book-length studies specifically of Chaucer's relationship to Dante include R. A. Shoaf, *Chaucer, Dante and the Currency of the Word* (Norman, Okla.: Pilgrim Books, 1983); Karla Taylor, *Chaucer Reads "The Divine Comedy"* (Stanford, Calif.: Stanford University Press, 1989); Richard Neuse, *Chaucer's Dante* (Berkeley: University of California Press, 1991); and Ann W. Astell, *Chaucer and the Universe of Learning* (Ithaca, N.Y.: Cornell University Press, 1996).

[18] There are other arguable allusions to the *Comedy* in the *Parliament.* These are noted by D. S. Brewer in his edition, *The Parlement of Foulys* (London: Thomas Nelson and Sons, 1960), pp. 45–46. Most recently, Janet Smarr has asserted that *Inferno* 5 is part of a "confluence of interacting sources" in the *Parliament;* see "The *Parlement of Foules* and *Inferno* 5," *ChauR* 33 (1998): 113–22, esp. p. 114. Because my primary interest is the moment in which Chaucer is quoting Dante and not those points at which he may or may not be alluding to him, I have left these out of my consideration.

[19] In developing my understanding of commentary on *Inferno* 3, I have been helped by the fine discussion of the canto by Maria Picchio Simonelli, *Inferno III,* Lectura Dantis Americana (Philadelphia: University of Pennsylvania Press, 1993).

to be great. Therefore, Dante here repeats "Per me" three times, to show how he had great emotion when going on his journey.][20]

Lana's comment highlights the artificiality of the gate, its "constructedness" as a text; moreover, his comment suggests just how easily conflated are the poet and his poem. That God himself presumably wrote these verses, if we are to believe Dante's prophetic claims, or that the gate itself seems to be given a voice by these lines, does not seem to have entered Lana's mind at this point.[21] For Lana, the inscription somehow voices *Dante's* "affezione." The gate in a real sense is *about* Dante—it says something about the author as much as it says something about hell. And it does so precisely because, as a text, it is a rhetorical construct more than a divine proclamation, and a text that is more pointedly a part of a larger text. The comment also implicitly compares the poem and the journey—the lines show that Dante "aveva grande affezione di fare suo viaggio"—in a way that Dante himself will often play upon, as for example in *Inferno* 16–17 and the comparison he invites between his poem and his descent on Geryon, and in *Purgatorio* 1.1–6.[22] This hermeneutic turn is particularly intriguing in view of the Chaucer-persona's reaction to the gate in the *Parliament.* Whether or not the gate's inscription is "about" him is a real question for the dreamer, provoking a moment of intense anxiety and confusion.[23] Both reactions, Lana's and the dreamer's, are products of meditations on texts and their rhetoricity, the former from the angle of the writer, the latter from that of the reader. In other words, Lana looks at the inscription as a means to convey a personal reaction, whereas Chaucer looks at his as a means to provoke one. This is not to say, of course, that the dreamer's reaction in the *Parliament* is not very much like the pilgrim Dante's in *Inferno.* Dante, too, is temporarily stymied when he encounters the text on the gate. Unlike Chaucer's dreamer, though, Dante at least partially articu-

[20] Jacopo della Lana, *"Commedia" di Dante Allaghieri col Commento di Jacopo della Lana bolognese,* ed. Luciano Scarabelli, 3 vols. (Bologna: Regia, 1866–67), 1:127. The translation is my own. I am grateful to David Wallace for suggesting the alternative translation for "come aveva grande affezione di far suo viaggio": "he looked forward to his journey with great anticipation."

[21] On Dante's prophetic claims and narrative technique, see Teodolinda Barolini, *The Undivine "Comedy": Detheologizing Dante* (Princeton, N.J.: Princeton University Press, 1992), esp. pp. 3–20.

[22] See ibid., pp. 58–72.

[23] As Thomas Reed describes it, "The narrator's most overt, if not most consequential, dilemma involves deciding whether or not to pass through the mysterious and paradoxical gate" (*Debate Poetry,* p. 305).

lates his response: "Maestro," he tells his guide, "il senso lor m'è duro" (3.12). But if "duro" here connotes both "hard to accept" as well as "hard to understand," Chaucer clearly casts his reaction toward the latter sense, paradoxically dramatizing confusion by eliminating a degree of ambiguity.

I shall have more to say about the dreamer's reaction to the gate's inscription below, but before considering it further, it is best to look at the two other main subjects taken up in the Trecento commentaries on Dante's gate. In line with this formal interest in the inscription's textuality is the commentators' attention to its allusions to and reliance on other texts. Notable in the commentary is the degree of intertextual ambivalence registered in response to Dante's lines themselves, intertexts drawn from both classical and biblical sources. Pietro Alighieri, the poet's son and author of a midcentury commentary surviving in three different versions (first version, 1340), simultaneously connects the scene to *Aeneid* 6.126–27 ("facilis descensus Averno: / Noctes atque dies patet atri janua Ditis" ["easy is the descent to Avernus: night and day the door of gloomy Dis stands open"])—which some scholars, notably Derek Brewer, see as another possible source for Chaucer's gate—and Matthew 7:13 ("Intrate per angustam portam: quia lata porta et spatiosa via est quae ducit ad perditionem" ["Enter by the narrow gate; for the gate is wide and the way is wide that leads to perdition"]).[24] Boccaccio cites the lines from Matthew as well, while Guido da Pisa, one of the earliest commentators writing in Latin, hears not only Virgil and the gospel but also echoes of Ovid and Statius (*Metamorphoses* X.13; *Thebaid* I.96): "Et Statius, primo *Theybaidos:* 'Trenaree limen perit irremeabile porte [she sought Taenarus's gate, the gate of no return].' Ovidius etiam, ubi loquitur de descensu Orpehi ad inferos, sic ait in X° libro *Metamorphoseos:* 'Ad Stigia Trenarea ausus est descendere porta [He dared descend through Taenarus's dark gate / To Hades]."[25] As a conse-

[24] See Brewer's edition of the *Parliament,* p. 46, n. 2. For Pietro's comments, see Pietro Alighieri, *Il Commentarium all' "Inferno,"* ed. Roberto della Vedova and Maria Teresa Silvotti (Florence: Olschki, 1978), pp. 76–77. The translation from the *Aeneid* is from the Loeb Classics edition, trans. H. Rushton Fairclough, 2 vols. (Cambridge, Mass.: Harvard University Press, 1935).

[25] See Giovanni Boccaccio, *Esposizioni sopra la "Comedia" di Dante,* in Giorgio Padoan, ed., *Tutte le opere di Giovanni Boccaccio,* vol. 6 (Verona: Mondadori, 1965), 1.160: "Avendo adunque riguardo a parte delle parole scritte sopra la porta, la quale l'autor discrive, e alla ampieza di quella e similemente all'averla senza alcun serrame trovata, possiam comprendere quella essere la via della morte, con ciò sia cosa che il nostro Signore dica nell'*Evangelio: Intrate per augustam portam, quia lata et spatiosa via est que ducit ad perditionem, e multi sunt qui intrant per eam*": e così per questa via il peccato ne mena a dannazione

quence, it is important that for Dante's learned readers—among whom we would surely number Chaucer—Dante's gate is a kind of palimpsest through which one can read other texts.[26] Moreover, Dante's characterization of hell as a "città" prompts intertextual authorization and debate among the commentators. The commentary of Benvenuto da Imola cites both Augustine and Aristotle as intertexts and suggests Dante may be mistaken in his choice of words:

Per me si va nella città dolente, idest infernalem, plenam poena et dolore sed contra; nam secundum Augustinum in libro de civitate Dei et Philosophum primo Politicorum *nihil aliud est civitas quam multitudo civium ad bene vivendum ordinata;* ista autem est multitudo civium ad semper male vivendum ordinata.

[. . . that is, the infernal city, full of punishment and pain. But one can dispute this, for according to Augustine in the *City of God,* and the Philosopher in the first book of the *Politics,* "a city is nothing but a multitude of citizens ordered so as to live for the good." This is, however, a multitude of citizens ordered so as to live always dedicated to evil.][27]

One response to this explication of Dante's allusions is to see the commentators "stress[ing] Dante's syncretism."[28] It seems just as possible, though, from the other direction, to read the commentaries here as fragmenting the text, or rather, unraveling Dante's syncretized textual whole into disparate parts that, once made discrete, bear no single, necessary relationship to one another. Once Pietro Alighieri, for instance, suggests that Dante's inscription is modeled on both *Aeneid* 6.126–27 *and* Matthew 7:13, the inscription on Dante's gate, in its own way, is shown to be hardly less bifurcated than Chaucer's.

Third, there is the primary doctrinal issue that Dante's gate seems to

eterna." Also, Guido da Pisa, *Expositiones et Glose super Comediam Dantis,* ed. Vincenzo Cioffari (Albany, N.Y.: SUNY Press, 1974), pp. 56–57. The translations of Statius and Ovid are from Statius, *Thebaid,* trans. A. D. Melville (Oxford: Oxford University Press, 1995), and Ovid, *Metamorphoses,* trans. A. D. Melville (Oxford: Oxford University Press, 1987), respectively.

[26] In such a manuscript context, I think, the limitations of the adamantly positivist approach to Chaucer/Dante source study of the kind employed by Schless in *Chaucer and Dante* become readily apparent.

[27] Benvenuto da Imola, *Benvenuti de Rambaldis de Imola comentum super Dantis Aldigherij Comoediam,* ed. J. P. Lacaita, 5 vols. (Florence: Barbèra, 1887). Cited and translated in Simonelli, *Inferno III,* p. 14.

[28] Simonelli, ibid., p. 13.

raise for the Trecento commentators. Doctrinal debate about the *Comedy* was from the start not uncommon, with commentators taking very different views of Dante as prophet. For example, as noted above, Pietro Alighieri sees his father's works as that of "'a glorious theologian, philosopher, and poet' rather than (as in Guido's account) of a prophetic visionary."[29] In more extreme cases, the poem was forbidden to be in the possession of Florentine Dominicans, and even openly denounced as an instrument of the devil.[30] Less dramatically, a recurrent topic of commentary on the gate is sparked by Dante's "Dinanzi a me non fuor cose create / se non etterne, e io etterno duro" ["Before me nothing was created if not eternal, and eternal I endure"] (lines 7–8), lines which, as Maria Picchio Simonelli says, "posed a serious interpretive problem for all the commentators."[31] Specifically, a debate ensues over the appropriateness and meaning of "etterno." Graziolo de' Bambaglioli, commenting in 1324, insists that hell could not have existed "nisi post ruinam Luciferi" (line 18), and thus is not rightly called "eternal," while Boccaccio suggests that Dante is speaking "impropriamente," but with "licenzia poetica."[32] Similarly, Guido da Pisa has it that the gate means:

> ante me nihil fuit, nisi Deus qui est eternus . . . et ego etiam post meam creationem duro in eternum. Ubi nota quod eternum accipitur pro sempiterno, quia eternum est illiud quod caret principio et fine; et secundum hoc nihil fuit, nisi Deus.
>
> [before me there was nothing, except God, who is eternal . . . and I furthermore endure eternally after my creation. Note that "eternum" is to be understood for "sempiterno," because "eternum" is that which lacks both a beginning and an end, and according to this there was nothing, except God.][33]

At this point it is necessary to note that the amount of medieval ink spilled over a deceptively simple declarative statement on the gate suggests two things: first, the desire to construct Dantean *auctoritas* in the face of what could be viewed as a doctrinal infelicity; and second, that

[29] See n. 9 above.

[30] Minnis and Scott, *Medieval Literary Theory,* p. 445.

[31] Simonelli, *Inferno III,* p. 15.

[32] Ibid., pp. 15–16. See also Boccaccio, *Esposizioni,* 1.140. Simonelli also cites the commentator known as the Anonimo Fiorentino (1400), who claims that "here with poetic license [Dante] uses 'eternal' instead of 'perpetual'" (p. 16).

[33] See Guido da Pisa, *Expositiones,* pp. 56–57. The translation is my own.

what Chaucer calls his gate's "pleyn sentence" (line 126) is not and cannot be "pleyn" in and of itself. The verses are not written as "pleyn" but read as such, ironically complicating their "sentence" in the process. The possibility of a double meaning for "pleyn" here—both "clear" or "open" and "full" or "complete"—adds to the richness of the inscription in relation to glossing. The full ("pleyn") meaning of a line is made clear ("pleyn") by exegesis that, as the glosses surrounding *Inferno* 3.1–12 demonstrate, reacts to the text itself as if it were inevitably incomplete and equivocal.[34] These comments again dramatize anxiety about the textuality and rhetoricity of Dante's gate. It is clearly Dante's gate (part of a particular fiction) and Dante's poetic misstep (if such it is deemed to be by the commentator in question). Here the gate's comment on its own originary moment ("Fecemi la divina potestate, / La somma sapïënza e 'l primo amore"), at a kind of originary moment in the journey, prompts commentary on its textual origin, on Dante's choice of words and theological ideas that, even as they are explicated for the purpose of safeguarding *auctoritas,* inevitably call its ultimate authorization into question. One might note in passing that such candid and inquisitive discussion of theological issues in the context of a vernacular poem resonates suggestively with what Nicholas Watson has described recently as "an impressively innovative tradition" of vernacular theology in England developing over the years 1340–1410, a tradition that, before Archbishop Arundel's Constitutions of 1409 and their effective attempt "to curtail all sorts of theological thinking and writing in the vernacular," found expression in works ranging from *The Cloud of Unknowing* to *Piers Plowman.*[35] One finds in the early Dante commentaries theological exegesis articulated by and for an often lay readership, and done so frequently (albeit not exclusively) in the vernacular about a vernacular poem. Chaucer's propensity for raising and playing with (without offering determinate answers to) many of the key questions surrounding theology, authority, and the status of the vernacular in late-fourteenth-

[34] I am grateful to Professor Frank Grady for calling my attention to this possible play on the word.

[35] Nicholas Watson, "Censorship and Cultural Change in Late-Medieval England: Vernacular Theology, the Oxford Translation Debate, and Arundel's Constitutions of 1409," *Speculum* 70.4 (1995): 822–64; the quotations are found on pp. 823 and 826. Watson himself remarks that his research "may have implications . . . for the study of secular literature" as well as religious writing (p. 824), and he points out emphatically that Chaucer's *Canterbury Tales* should be seen as the product of a "pre-Arundelian" world that allowed for lay, vernacular debate on questions of theology (p. 858).

century England at least finds an analogue in the interests and anxieties of Dante's medieval interpreters.[36]

I would like to add one final example from the early commentaries, one that also relates to the anxiety generated by potential theological problems in Dante's poem. Perhaps the most pointed acknowledgment of the predicaments presented to the commentators by Dante's invocation of the idea of "eternal" creation and punishment is found in the Latin commentary known as the Anonimo Lombardo (1322–25). On line 9 ("Lasciate ogni speranza, voi ch'intrate" ["Abandon every hope, you who enter"]) the commentator explains:

> Quia in inferno nulla est redemptio hic posset fieri questio de Traiano, qui fuit tanto tempore in inferno, et tamen postea ad preces Gregorij exivit. Hanc questionem insolutam dimitto, ut alii habeant aliquid dicere.
>
> [Because in hell no one is redeemed, here might be raised the question of Trajan, who was in hell for so long a time but nevertheless afterwards left on account of the prayers of Gregory. I put forth this unsolved question so that others may have something to say.][37]

Such a comment is not only one of the more adroit rhetorical moves any commentator makes on this passage; it also serves as a touchstone for the degree to which commentary fosters indeterminacy in its very efforts to eliminate it, specifically by, to paraphrase Rita Copeland, achieving difference, and it suggests the degree to which Dante's text—traditional assumptions notwithstanding—could and did function as a more "open" text in the Middle Ages than we might at first suspect.[38] This

[36] For more extensive consideration of similar issues surrounding Dante's reception, but with a focus on fifteenth-century England, see David Wallace's article "Dante in Somerset: Ghosts, Historiography, Periodization," *New Medieval Literatures* 3 (1999). My thanks to Professor Wallace for sending me a copy of his article in typescript.

[37] Anonimo Lombardo, *Anonymous Latin Commentary on Dante's "Commedia": Reconstructed Text,* ed. Vincenzo Cioffari (Spoleto: Centro Italiano di studi sull'alto Medioevo, 1989), p. 34. The translation is my own.

[38] Rita Copeland writes, "Latin commentary substitutes itself for the text in question, inserting itself into the *auctoritas* of that text, hence appropriating that authority, and to varying degrees performing in lieu of text. The dynamic effect of exegesis is to achieve a certain difference with the source" (*Rhetoric,* p. 103). On the degree to which Dante's text was an "open" one for medieval readers, it is worth noting David Wallace's remark that "Judging [Dante's] poem to be too open and accessible for its own good, [learned writers] attempted to keep the illiterate at bay by 'classicizing' the text behind a high wall of Latin commentary" (Minnis and Scott, *Medieval Literary Theory,* p. 439). Wallace may be using the word "open" somewhat differently from the way I am, but the point

question of openness throws new light on some of the work that has been done thus far on the Chaucer/Dante relationship, work that not only has not taken commentaries into account but, much more questionably, has tacitly assumed that Dante's status as an authority was a given—that Dante's claims for the truth value of his poetry were beyond debate, indeed that Dante himself was largely beyond debate, before Chaucer got to him. In this reading, Chaucer, with characteristic skepticism, looks askance at Dante's claims themselves and inevitably adopts some kind of parodic stand vis-à-vis Dante. Moreover, the degree to which Dante is aware of, anxious about, and even possibly skeptical himself of his own truth claims is only rarely taken into account in Chaucer/Dante criticism.[39] While I certainly agree that Chaucer's poetry displays a good deal of suspicion about the ultimate truth value of poetry, I would argue that in his appropriations of Dante he is not exactly parodying his Italian predecessor or trying to topple some poetic monolith, but rather entering a complex and ongoing debate over the very issues the *Comedy* and its commentators raise. In any case, as we see in this particular debate over the gate's claims, commentary produces more commentary—indeed, the Anonimo Lombardo invites it—and enough commentary gives rise to *auctoritas* if not interpretive certainty. For Trecento commentators, the inscription on Dante's gate is itself a kind of comment that glosses both hell and its poet—his feelings, his reading, his thinking.

II.

At this point it might be useful to recall the entire scene at the gate in *The Parliament of Fowls.* Chaucer begins, we might note, by writing "gret

remains the same: learned explication of Dante's poem worked to stave off (some) interpretation(s) even as it (paradoxically) promoted more of it.

[39] Scholarly opinion on this aspect of Dante's poetics ranges from Barolini's arguments in *The Undivine Comedy* (cited above) to John Kleiner's recent discussion of Dante's interest in error and imperfection in *Mismapping the Underworld: Daring and Error in Dante's "Comedy"* (Stanford, Calif.: Stanford University Press, 1994) to, in the most extreme instance, Jeremy Tambling's deconstructionist Dante described in his *Dante and Difference: Writing in the "Commedia"* (Cambridge: Cambridge University Press, 1988). Ann Astell, in *Chaucer and the Universe of Learning,* has recently articulated another version of the "open" Chaucer versus the "closed" Dante: "A philosophical poet like Dante, Chaucer can chart a curriculum and provide an occasion for learning, but he, much more so than Dante, entrusts the completion of his work to his audience and, ultimately, to the mercy of God" (p. 226).

difference" (line 125) into the gate itself, suggesting not only how his gate, like Dante's, functions as a gloss on what lies beyond it but also how such glossing is inevitably multivoiced—at least doubled (lines 120–47):

This forseyde Affrican me hente anon
And forth with hym unto a gate broughte,
Ryght of a park walled with grene ston;
And over the gate, with lettres large iwroughte,
There were vers iwriten, as me thoughte,
On eyther half, of ful gret difference,
Of which I shal yow seyn the pleyn sentence:

"Thorgh me men gon into that blysful place
Of hertes hele and dedly woundes cure;
Thorgh me men gon unto the welle of grace,
There grene and lusty May shal evere endure.
This is the wey to al good aventure.
Be glad, thow redere, and thy sorwe of-caste;
Al open am I—passe in, and sped thee faste!"

"Thorgh me men gon," than spak that other side,
"Unto the mortal strokes of the spere
Of which Disdayn and Daunger is the gyde,
Ther nevere tre shal fruyt ne leves bere.
This strem yow ledeth to the sorweful were
There as the fish in prysoun is al drye;
Th'eschewing is only the remedye!"

These vers of gold and blak iwriten were,
Of whiche I gan astoned to beholde.
For with that oon encresede ay my fere
And with that other gan myn herte bolde;
That oon me hette, that other dide me colde;
No wit hadde I, for errour, for to chese
To entre or flen, or me to save or lese.

The rhyme of "difference"/"pleyn sentence" (lines 125–26) only underscores how deeply Chaucer is engaged in the problem: clarification begets complication. Once the inscription proper begins, one irony is that the gate itself first describes what it guards as a place of healing and wholeness.[40] When Chaucer's and Dante's lines are paralleled, Dante's "città dolente" is now a place not of suffering but "Of . . . dedly woundes cure" (line 128); Dante's eternal pain is now Chaucer's "welle of grace" where May springs eternal (line 130). Closing the first stanza of the inscription, Chaucer, like Dante, gives the gate an injunction, but one that foregrounds the readerliness of the scene: "Be glad, thow redere, and thy sorwe of-caste; / Al open am I—passe in, and sped thee faste!" (lines 132–33). Two additions here have counterparts in the Trecento commentaries. First, although Dante never explicitly mentions the gate's being open, the commentators often make this "openness" explicit through citation of other gates (as those from Pietro Alighieri mentioned above) or simply by writing it rather casually into their commentaries: in Jacopo Alighieri's commentary (1322) the gate is clearly "sanza serrame," as it is for the Ottimo Commento (1333).[41] Boccaccio in particular makes much of the gate's "ampieza" and its being "senza alcune serrame." Moreover, Chaucer's verses are addressed explicitly to "thow redere"—Dante's are not, rather to "voi ch'intrate"—and thus they overtly make the subject of the verses not only their message but their interpreter as well. The couplet linking the reader here with the "openness" of the gate suggests at once that any/every reader can and should conclude the verses are addressed to him, and thus makes Affrycan's dismissive insistence later that "this writyng nys nothyng ment bi the" (line 158) all the more surprising. A further irony: Chaucer writes the gate's openness explicitly on its "good half," while Dante's other readers invoke openness to connect the gate directly to the way "ad perditionem."

[40] As should be clear by now, that I see some irony involved in Chaucer's Dantean gate does not mean that I agree wholeheartedly with readings such as the following: "[I]t is Chaucer's distance from the moral seriousness of Dante . . . which must impress us: if he borrows the motif of the poet led by an august guide to an awesomely inscribed gate from the *Inferno* . . . he borrows nothing of its original significance"; Elizabeth Salter, *Fourteenth-Century English Poetry: Contexts and Readings* (Oxford: Clarendon Press, 1983), p. 129.

[41] Jacopo writes, "In questo cominciamento del capitolo il prencipio dell'intrare ne' vizî si significa, trovandosi sanza serrame una porta, sopra la quale le proposte parole si contengono"; see Jacopo Alighieri, *Chiose all'"Inferno,"* ed. Saverio Bellomo (Padua: Antenore, 1990). The Ottimo Commentatore echoes the earlier gloss: "Cominciasi a significare il principio dell'entrare ne' vizii, trovando una porta senza serrame, sopra la quale sonoscritti il primi nove versi"; see *L'Ottimo Commento della "Divina Commedia" di un contemporaneo di Dante,* ed. Alessandro Torri, 3 vols. (Pisa: Capurro, 1827–29), vol. 1, p. 25.

Like the inscription on Dante's hell gate, Chaucer verses "On eyther half" of the gate (lines 125) collectively function as a gloss on what lies beyond the gate itself, as a way into both the place and the experience that the gloss itself borders. The gloss, however, only complicates matters; in fact, as the dreamer tells us: "No wit hadde I, for errour, for to chese / To entre or flen, or me to save or lese" (lines 146–47). This gloss promotes rather than staves off "errour," uncertainty about meaning introduced by the labyrinthine nature of medieval textuality and reading.[42] The dreamer's "errour," his confusion, contained within himself, is finally glossed by the dreamer's face: as Affrycan directly tells him, "It stondeth writen in thy face, / Thyn errour, though thow telle it not to me" (lines 155–56). His face's "gloss" reveals the confusion promoted by the gate's gloss.

If, as I have tried to argue, Chaucer's gate not only invokes Dante's poetry but evokes Dante commentary, then the gate scene in the *Parliament* resonates in new ways with other key dramatic and thematic elements in the poem: specifically, the use of the *Somnium Scipionis* before the dreamer gets to the gate, and the problem of choosing as it is played out in the avian parliament itself.[43] On the subject of the former, it is intriguing that Cicero's book is introduced with little if any attention paid to its commentary—that is, to the context in which it survived in the Middle Ages.[44] "Affrican" appears to the dreamer and says only these lines before his speech that comes after they have passed through the gate (lines 109–12):

> But thus seyde he: "Thow hast the so wel born
> In lokynge of myn olde bok totorn,
> Of which Macrobye roughte nat a lyte,
> That sumdel of thy labour wolde I quyte."

[42] On the labyrinth and medieval literature, with reference to Dante as well as to Chaucer's *House of Fame,* see Penelope Reed Doob, *The Idea of the Labyrinth from Classical Antiquity through the Middle Ages* (Ithaca, N.Y.: Cornell University Press, 1990).

[43] Although her emphasis and conclusions differ from mine, Roberta Payne recognizes the importance of the "theme of choice" in both Chaucer's and Dante's gate inscriptions, in *The Influence of Dante on Medieval English Dream Visions* (New York: Peter Lang, 1989), p. 111–12.

[44] See the notes to *The Riverside Chaucer,* p. 995. Charles Muscatine there writes that "Chaucer had probably read the combined Dream and Commentary, but in [lines] 36–84 he summarizes only the Dream." For background on Macrobius and an English translation, see William Harris Stahl, ed. and trans., *Commentary on the Dream of Scipio by Macrobius* (New York: Columbia University Press, 1952).

Interestingly, the subject of the book claims it as his own, and the commentator—responsible, in fact, for the survival of the book—is mentioned, albeit via litotes, as a devotee of the book implicitly comparable with Chaucer himself. Chaucer, like Cicero's commentator—like Dante, for that matter—cares deeply about his books as sources. Instead of having a commentator talk about a book, Chaucer has a "book" talking about its commentator, "reading" the commentator's intentions and affections in a way not unlike the way in which the commentators read Dante's intentions and affections on the gates of hell. While David Aers argues that "Chaucer deletes the incarnate agents through whose contingent projects and practices the human world becomes known," here at least it would seem that Chaucer writes the agent (i.e., Macrobius) explicitly into his fictions—his own and Macrobius's.[45]

The question of choice is also raised here at the gate, and of course echoed later in the debate portion of the poem. During the introduction to the debate proper and the initial speeches of Nature and the royal tersel, "chese" and "choys" appear no fewer than eight times in eight stanzas, and of course the ultimate resolution of the poem's drama is suspended when the formel eagle asks Nature "respit for to avise me, / And after that to have my choys al fre" (lines 648–49).[46] Kathryn Lynch, in a complex discussion of medieval theories of free will and determinism in relation to the *Parliament,* recognizes that the dreamer's hesitation after reading the inscription "suggestively anticipates the formel's deferral of choice," and she then links the dreamer's predicament to that of "Buridan's ass":[47] "In its most widely known form, the problem of Buridan's ass presents a donkey suffering from extreme hunger, positioned equidistant from two identical bales of hay (in some versions, from a bale of hay on one side and a container of water on the other). Unable to decide which to approach, the beast perishes without availing itself of the nourishment that it desperately needs."[48] Lynch, after tracing versions of the example from Aristotle through Aquinas and John

[45] Aers, "Authority," p. 2.

[46] Thomas Reed, *Middle English Debate Poetry,* p. 294, describes the *Parliament* as "a work variously about not knowing and not deciding." Interestingly, the word "chese" seems to largely disappear from the debate until its end, in Nature's discussion with the formel; in other words, explicit choice is largely if not only at issue for the royal birds.

[47] See Kathryn L. Lynch, "The *Parliament of Fowls* and Late Medieval Voluntarism. Parts I and II," *ChauR* 25.1 (1990): 1–16, and 25.2 (1990): 85–95. The preceding quotation is found on p. 7.

[48] Ibid., p. 8.

Duns Scotus, concludes that the dreamer's paralysis at the gate "demonstrate[s] a failure of self-determination," making him "a parodic example of indifferent choice in the tradition of Buridan's ass."[49] What Lynch underestimates, I believe, is the import of "errour" (line 146) in the scene and its connection to reading. The temporary "failure" to act is ultimately about confusing (because seemingly self-contradictory) texts on the gate which gloss what lies beyond it, statements made from a rhetorically authoritative point of view that seem at first irreconcilable. In other words, operating as a conscientious reader of authorities, of other readers who produce readings designed to guide or determine actions, the dreamer is perplexed, until yet another authority makes the decision for him, resolving the issue in terms of audience ("this writyng nys nothyng ment bi the" [line 158]). In relation to Dante, what Chaucer recognizes is the one overriding irony in the authoritative "gloss" on hell that is Dante's gate: that its reader, in the actions of the poem, despite its ominous directive to (presumably) all who enter, should not and does not lose "ogni speranza" (line 9). In one sense, Virgil could have made the same statement to the pilgrim Dante that Affrican makes to Geoffrey—"this writyng nys nothyng ment bi the."

III.

As I mentioned above, and as my reading of the gate scene in the *Parliament* is meant to imply, Chaucer's use of Dante, when viewed in the light of the Trecento commentary tradition, at once stages and interrogates a kind of "comedic" literary history: that is, a mode of literary historiography within which the medieval genre of comedy is perceptibly at play. This proposition raises the question, obviously, of what exactly is meant by "comedy" in the Middle Ages—more specifically, how the genre was understood by Dante himself and in the Trecento at large. Turning to this question, one finds not one simple answer, but rather two trends of thought, clearly distinct but, I wish to argue, ultimately complementary in the case of the *Comedy*'s reception.[50] Chaucer, I believe, recognized

[49] Ibid., p. 11.

[50] For succinct overviews of medieval comedy, see the two articles by Paul G. Ruggiers, "A Vocabulary for Chaucerian Comedy: A Preliminary Sketch," in *Medieval Studies in Honor of Lillian Herlands Hornstein,* ed. Jess B. Bessinger, Jr. and Robert R. Raymo (New York: New York University Press, 1976), pp. 193–225; and "Some Theoretical Considerations of Comedy in the Middle Ages," in *Versions of Medieval Comedy,* ed. Paul G. Ruggiers (Norman: University of Oklahoma Press, 1977), pp. 1–17.

this complementarity, and in doing so understood that nothing could be more "comedic," in the sense that I shall go on to delineate, than the consolidation of these two views by means of his reading and representation of Dantean poetry. Chaucer, in short, read the *Comedy* as a comedy and read its reception as comedic as well, and his use of Dante demonstrates his efforts to question and illustrate, if I may, the "comedification" of the *Comedy.*[51]

The first of the two broad views of comedy is widely known today and found throughout the Trecento, not least pertinently for my purposes in the brief *commentarium* on the *Comedy* that is the *Epistle to Cangrande.*[52] It is really a twofold definition in itself, based at once upon style and structure. A "comedy" is a "rustic song," etymologized from *comos* ("village") and *oda* ("song"), and appropriate as a label for Dante's *Comedy* because of the work's vernacular status. Moreover, "comedy" is a genre that begins in misery and ends in happiness. As the *Epistle* puts it, "comedy begins with sundry adverse conditions, but ends happily, as appears from the comedies of Terence."[53] The *Epistle*'s author explains that "if we consider the subject-matter, at the beginning [the poem] is horrible and foul, as being *Hell;* but at the close it is happy, desirable, and pleasing, as being *Paradise.*"[54] As Howard H. Schless characterizes this definition of comedy (referring to the *Epistle* and taking Dante's authorship of it for granted), "For Dante . . . comedy is the movement from disaccord to accord, from the discordant shrieks of individual sinners in Hell to the harmonic expression of the choirs of Heaven."[55] Very often, and quite

[51] Although this essay deals only with the *Parliament* directly, I should clarify that I consider this conception of the Chaucer/Dante literary relationship to be illuminating and valid for reading other Dantean moments in Chaucer—which is not to say that Chaucer always poetically responds to or represents the "comedic" mode of literary reception in the same way. I discuss other Chaucerian uses of Dante and other facets of this process in my book in progress, *Chaucer, Dante, and the "Comedy" of Literary History.*

[52] See Judson B. Allen, "Commentary as Criticism: Formal Cause, Discursive Form, and the Late Medieval Accessus," in J. Ijsewijn and E. Kessler, eds., *Acta Conventus Neolatini Lovaniensis* (Munich: Wilhelm Fink Verlag, 1973), pp. 29–48 (see p. 30). For a discussion of medieval theories of comedy and tragedy specifically with regard to Dante, see H. A. Kelly, *Tragedy and Comedy from Dante to Pseudo-Dante,* University of California Publications in Modern Philology,vol. 121 (Berkeley and Los Angeles: University of California Press, 1989). Quotations from the *Epistle to Cangrande* are from *Dantis Alagherii Epistolae,* ed. P. Toynbee and C. Hardie, 2d ed. (Oxford: Oxford University Press, 1966), as reprinted in Minnis and Scott, *Medieval Literary Theory.*

[53] Minnis and Scott, ibid., p. 461.

[54] Ibid.

[55] Howard H. Schless, "Dante: Comedy and Conversion," in Paul G. Ruggiers, ed., *Versions of Medieval Comedy* (Norman: University of Oklahoma Press, 1977), pp. 135–49. The quotation is from p. 136.

predictably, this explanation is contrasted with a common definition of "tragedy," a story that begins in prosperity and ends in misery: as the *Epistle* states, "tragedy at the beginning is admirable and placid, but at the end or issue is foul and horrible."[56] Among the Trecento Dante commentaries, such a definition of "comedy" is found in Guido da Pisa, Pietro Alighieri, and Boccaccio, its frequent appearance being read as duplication by some scholars and used as evidence of an early date for the *Epistle,* for the commentators' use of the document, and, ultimately, for Dante's authorship of the *Epistle* itself.[57] Such conclusions are far from definitive, but nonetheless, it is impossible to deny that many readers of Dante's poem interpreted its genre partly—but not, it must be stressed, exclusively—in terms of this definition. I am interested, however, in the implications of this way of reading the genre's structure, and of this theorization of comedy as (merely) the opposite of tragedy. The former genre, in this definition, is a de facto paradigm of fulfillment, of a movement from lack to sufficiency, from (if one will forgive the cliché) chaos to order. "Comedy" enacts, in other words, a process of stabilization and conservation; perhaps counterintuitively to our sensibility, it is driven by the desire for stability. By means of the iteration of this definition, some *grammatici* thus make a hermeneutic choice that effectively performs the genre's declared function by balancing the disruptive tragic paradigm, at once creating and stabilizing a generic dichotomy—comedy becomes tragedy's generic antidote, in a sense incomprehensible and even unnecessary without the preexistence of tragedy. Comedy accomplishes tragedy's generic redemption.

It is worth pausing briefly to consider, before moving to the second theoretical definition of "comedy" in the Middle Ages, the two times Dante uses the word "comedìa" in the *Comedy* itself, the first at *Inferno* 16.128:

[56] Minnis and Scott, *Medieval Literary Theory,* p. 461. The Chaucerian version of the tragedy/comedy dichotomy, of course, comes from the Knight in his response to the Monk's series of tragedies. The "contrarie," as the Knight puts it, to the movement of tragedy, "is joye and greet solas, / As whan a man hath been in povre estaat, / And clymbeth up and wexeth fortunat, / And there abideth in prosperitee. / Swich thyng is gladsom, as it thynketh me" (NPP 2774–78).

[57] For the broad outlines of the debate surrounding the *Epistle*'s authorship, see Francesco Mazzoni, "L'Epistola a Cangrande," in *Atti della Accademia Nazionale dei Lincei. Classe di Scienze morali, storiche e filologiche,* ser. 8, 10 (1955): 157–98; and Luis Jenaro-MacLennan, *The Trecento Commentaries on the "Divina Commedia" and the Epistle to Cangrande* (Oxford: Clarendon Press, 1974). Both authors favor Dante's authorship for the epistle. A very different conclusion is reached by Henry Ansgar Kelly and Zygmunt Barański, respectively; I discuss their view below.

Sempre a quel ver c'ha faccia di menzogna
 de' l'uom chiuder le labbra fin ch'el puote,
 però che sanza colpa fa vergogna;
ma qui tacer nol posso; e per le note
 di questa comedìa, lettor, ti giuro,
 s'elle non sien di lunga grazia vòte,
ch'i' vidi per quell' aere grosso e scuro
 venir notando una figura in suso,
 maravigliosa ad ogne cor sicuro.

To that truth which has the face of a lie a man should always close his lips so far as he can, for through no fault of his it brings reproach; but here I cannot be silent; and, reader, I swear to you by the notes of this Comedy—so may they not fail of lasting favor—that I saw, through that thick and murky air, come swimming upwards a figure amazing to every steadfast heart. (16.124–32)

A few cantos later, beginning at *Inferno* 21.2, Dante writes:

Così di ponte in ponte, altro parlando
 che la mia comedìa cantar non cura,
 venimmo; e tenavamo 'l colmo, quando
restammo per veder l'altra fessura
 di Malebolge e li altri pianti vani;
 e vidila mirabilmente oscura.

Thus from bridge to bridge we came along, talking of things of which my Comedy is not concerned to sing, and we had reached the summit, when we stopped to see the next cleft of Malebolge and the next vain lamentations: and I saw it strangely dark. (21.1–6)

As Teodolinda Barolini has persuasively argued, both of these passages function as part of the ongoing redefinition of the genre of comedy that the *Comedy* itself is meant to accomplish, a redefinition that eventually makes this *comedìa* a *tëodia* and links the genre inextricably with the truth.[58] The earlier passage obviously characterizes this comedy as a "truth which has the face of a lie," while the later lines invoke the genre in "a clause that functions as a subliminal garnerer of verisimilitude: the verses give life to the text by casually insisting on a life outside the text,

[58] See Barolini, *The Undivine Comedy,* p. 59. The term *tëodia,* which Singleton translates as "divine song," is coined by Dante in *Paradiso* 25.73, in reference to Psalm 9 [10].

an independent reality that the text does not choose to reveal to us."[59] A kind of "life outside the text" is also invoked, of course, alongside the earlier mention of "comedìa"—Dante hopes for remembrance. Each passage creates for the reader—the first by direct address and the evocation of literary history, the second by the intimation of secrecy—a space distinctly inviting readerly inference but a space outside of which the reader must ultimately remain. The Ottimo Commento seems in his own way cognizant of these effects when remarking on *Inferno* 16.128: "Consider here, reader, that the Author swears by the verses of this Comedy, where two things are to be observed: one is the name of this book, which the Author himself places here, and the other, which the Author desires, is that his work be welcome among the people for a long time."[60] The reader is directed to note, in effect, a kind of originary moment of literary historiography—the naming of the book—that the reader at once observes and enacts in the very process of reading. As these examples from the *Comedy* suggest, Dante uses the word "comedìa" at moments that markedly call attention to and complicate the reader's involvement in his poem. It is thus hardly surprising to find a rather more complex theorization of the genre also current at the time. The "woe to weal" conception of comedy is, by the standards of the fourteenth century, a rather conservative, not to say retrograde, view; this second definition was less widely cited, less readily clear, therefore more challenging, and quite likely held in considerably higher regard by Dante himself.

In a recent article that should be of great interest to anyone looking seriously at the intersection of Chaucer and Dante, Zygmunt Barański rejects the attribution of the *Epistle to Cangrande* to Dante partly on the

[59] Barolini, ibid., p. 81. See also pp. 59–60, and Barolini, *Dante's Poets: Textuality and Truth in the "Comedy"* (Princeton, N.J.: Princeton University Press, 1984), pp. 269–86.

[60] "Considera qui, lettore, che l'Autore fa suo giuro per li versi di questa Commedia, ove sono da notare due cose: l'una, il nome di questo libro, lo quale qui l'Autore medesimo impone; l'altra, che l'Autore desidera, che questa sua opera sia gradita infra le genti per lungo tempo" (1.307). It is not uncommon for the commentators to simply use the mention of "comedìa" as an opportunity to reiterate, usually in abbreviated form, their definitions. For instance, here is Guido da Pisa commenting on *Inferno* 16: "Volens hic autor revelare que vidit, et timens ne propter novum inauditum sibi veridice crederetur, iurat cuilibet qui istam legerit Comediam, quod si ipsa Comedia non possit longa gratia vacuari, quod vera sunt illa que hic se vidisse confirmat. Comedia autem est iste liber. Quid vero sit comedia, et quot sunt genera poetarum, in prologo superius est expressum" (p. 304). With regard to *Inferno* 21.2, Guido (p. 404) offers a twofold definition of comedy, etymological ("villanus cantus") and structural ("incipit a miseria et finit in felicitatem").

grounds of the *Epistle*'s rather backward-looking and simplistic idea of what constitutes the genre of "comedy." Clarifying the work of Henry Ansgar Kelly, who argues, based on his survey of medieval thinking on the *genera dicendi,* that "comedy [in Dante's mind] is a form of writing that is unrestricted in subject matter and can take in the whole of humanity, and it also has a wide stylistic range," Barański suggests that "The 'comic' seems to touch on every subject and style: to stand for literature in its entirety. Comedy was thus the only genre for a medieval writer intent on dealing with the wealth of 'ciò che per l'universo si squaderna' (*Par.* 33.87)."[61] This view is much closer than is the *Epistle*'s, Barański points out, to that articulated in book 2 of Dante's (assuredly) own *De vulgari eloquentia:*

Deinde in hiis que dicenda occurrunt debemus discretione potiri, utrum tragice, sive comice, sive elegiace sint canenda. Per tragediam superiorem stilum inducimus, per comediam inferiorem, per elegiam stilum intelligimus miserorum. Si tragice canenda videntur, tunc assumendum est vulgare illustre, et per consequens cantionem ligare. Si vero comice, tunc quandoque mediocre quandoque humile vulgare sumatur: et huius discretionem in quarto huius reservamus ostendere. Si autem elegiace, solum humile oportet nos sumere.

[Then, when dealing with the various subjects that are suitable for poetry, we must know how to choose whether to treat them in tragic, comic, or elegiac style. By "tragic" I mean the higher style, by "comic" the lower, and by "elegiac" that of the unhappy. If it seems appropriate to use the tragic style, then the illustrious vernacular must be employed, and so you will need to bind together a *canzone.* If, on the other hand, the comic style is called for, then sometimes the middle level of the vernacular can be used, and sometimes the lowly; and I shall explain the distinction in Book Four. If, though, you are writing elegy, you must only use the lowly.][62]

In Barański's reading, this passage shows Dante's comparatively early attempt to construct "a single system [out of] the two major rhetorical

[61] See Kelly, *Tragedy and Comedy,* 121:9, and Zygmunt Barański, "*Comedìa:* Notes on Dante, The Epistle to Cangrande, and Medieval Comedy," *Lectura Dantis* 8 (1991): 29–55. The quotations are found on p. 9 and p. 37. As Barański puts it, "The gulf between the *Commedia*'s view of comedy and that propounded by the Epistle to Cangrande is fathomless" (p. 38).

[62] Text and translation from Steven Botterill, ed. and trans., *De vulgari eloquentia* (Cambridge: Cambridge University Press, 1996), pp. 56–59.

traditions through which literature was defined in the Middle Ages: namely, the tripartite division of 'styles' and the binary opposition between tragedy and comedy."[63] What the *Comedy* does is carry the direction set in Dante's Latin treatise further, showing emphatically (despite the discomfort of some Trecento exegetes) that "comedy" could include any and potentially all of the literary styles, or, as Jacopo Alighieri has it, was the genre "under which generally and universally all things are treated, and thence the title of this present book proceeds."[64] This view underwrites the metaliterary poetics of the *Comedy* itself, informing Dante's efforts in the poem to encompass all styles and subjects, to compose a kind of poetic encyclopedia that shows how, as Giuseppe Mazzotta lyrically puts it, "the poetic imagination is the faculty empowered to resurrect and glue together the fragments of a broken world."[65] We find ourselves back to the theoretical theme of redemption again, although now in terms not of structure but of content. The *Comedy* as a comedy, able to treat "tutte le cose," is characterized by not merely stylistic and topical variety or complexity, but indeed by completeness, an inclusiveness that mirrors, that at once reproduces and comments on, the universe itself.[66]

We have, then, on the one hand, a view of comedy that is more or less linear and somewhat restrictive set alongside a view that is collective or cumulative and so unrestricted that one can almost call it grandiose. Both views, however, hinge on ideas of completion and fulfillment. Both

[63] Barański, "Notes," pp. 33–34.

[64] See Jacopo Alighieri, *Chiose,* p. 86: "sotto il quale generalmente e universalmente si tratta de tutte le cose, e quindi il titol del presente volume procede."

[65] Giuseppe Mazzotta, *Dante's Vision and the Circle of Knowledge* (Princeton, N.J.: Princeton University Press, 1993), p. 14.

[66] It is interesting to note a different and rare definition of "comedy" found in the Latin translation of Jacopo della Lana's commentary on Dante made by Alberigo da Rosciate in 1350: "De isto inferno et eius penis pulcerime et venuste tractat auctor iste venerabilis in ista prima parte que *Infernus* appelatur, et mirabiliter et bene, conformans penas quibuslibet pecatis in forma poeticha que appelatur chomedia, quia ab antiquo tractata fuit a rusticis et ex solitu [*lege* sonitu] fistularum; unde postea apparuerunt chomedi, idest socij, gui pariter recitabant comedias, hoc est magnalia que occurebant, unus videlicet cantando, aliter [*lege* alter] succinendo et respondendo, ut notatur in glosa ff. *de Edil. edito. 1. cum eisdem,* et *Ad l. Aquil 1. proinde* § finali, et in prohemio Tragediarum succinte per commentatorem. Et isti chomedi adhuc sunt in usu nostro: apparent enim maxime in partibus Lombardie aliqui cantatores qui magnorum dominorum in rithimis cantant gesta, unus proponendo, alius respondendo." Cited in Kelly, *Tragedy and Comedy,* p. 32–33, n. 36. Kelly comments on the "alternating" style described here, and it is intriguing, even if unrelated to my discussion, that here again "comedy" is envisioned as a joint effort of a sort, a participative genre that needs accompaniment to work.

see comedy as a genre capable of unifying that which has been divided. Ironically enough, though, the tradition of learned Dantean reception and commentary, the *Comedy*'s Trecento literary history, testifies to the ultimate insufficiency and even untenability of either view in relation to the *Comedy* itself. Charting "comedy" as a genre that moves from unhappiness to happiness obviously begs far more questions than it answers when juxtaposed with a work as complex as the *Comedy.* At the same time, claiming "comedy" as a genre that in itself encompasses all styles and subjects seems to suggest that the poem should always already incorporate its own explication in a way utterly belied by the recurring efforts to explicate it by means of supplemental commentary. What the Trecento commentaries collectively signify by their very existence is the somewhat paradoxical fact that when a "comedy" takes the form of the *Comedy,* the genre can be constituted only by the commentaries themselves, by the writing of responsive texts that delineate the amalgamation of styles and subjects inherent in the text and spell out, in fragmented and heterogeneous form, the text's divisions, structures, movements, and ends.[67]

Dante commentaries in the Trecento, then, at once legitimate or authorize the *Comedy* as a comedy and, to an extent, participate in the genre of comedy themselves, insofar as they are works that, in Deborah Parker's words, "eschew the univocal," incorporating "a wide range of discourses . . . deriving from different professional, institutional, oral, popular, religious, philosophical, and social influences."[68] I would extend this point by emphasizing their attempts to supplement and stabilize meaning, making the (implicitly lacking) text whole or complete, leading the unglossed text from its "adverse conditions" to the "happy state" of glossed meaning. Commentary on the *Comedy* enacts the "comedic" nature of literary history in two ways. First, the gloss supplements and, in a sense, fulfills the text, bringing the text closer to its fullness of meanings, making potential meanings actual. Insufficient language is made sufficient, even redeemed, by the complementary gloss.[69] More-

[67] This is not to say that Dante had this understanding of it himself. The point here is that this is an observation allowable by the commentative treatment of the *Comedy* more so than by the *Comedy* alone.

[68] Parker, *Commentary and Ideology,* p. 46.

[69] John Dagenais, focusing on Juan Ruiz's *Libro de buen amor,* has articulated this situation eloquently in his book *The Ethics of Reading in Manuscript Culture* (Princeton, N.J.: Princeton University Press, 1994), p. 6. His comments are worth quoting at length: "Jerome and Augustine had wrestled with these issues [of the fallen state of language]

over, and no less significantly, the commentaries' array of styles, subject matters, areas of interest, and solutions to interpretive cruces link the commentaries themselves to the genre of comedy, imagined as an all-encompassing genre that could appropriate for itself the widest possible discursive range, and thereby effectively write the early literary historiography of the *Comedy* in a comedic mode.

On a superficial level the connection between the genre of comedy and discursive multiplicity is immediately evident in Chaucer's works. The diversity of Chaucerian comedy, or, more precisely, of comic narrative in Chaucer's works ranges from the scatological satire of *The Summoner's Tale* to the sophisticated comedy of rhetoric of *The Nun's Priest's Tale* to the comic versions/visions of learning in *The House of Fame.* My purpose, therefore, is not to reduce Chaucerian comedy to the subject of literary history or the genre (however variegated) of commentary, particularly given that my interest is less "Chaucerian comedy" per se than the ways in which Chaucer's appropriations of Dante rehearse and interrogate a fundamentally (medieval) comedic mode of literary reception. On these grounds, however, it is worth considering the one and only time Chaucer uses the word "comedy" in his writings. In the famous stanza near the end of *Troilus and Criseyde* Chaucer bids farewell to his "litel bok" (5.1786–92):

> Go, litel bok, go, litel myn tragedye,
> Ther God thi makere yet, er that he dye,
> So sende myght to make in som comedye!
> But litel book, no makyng thow n'envie,
> But subgit be to alle poesye;
> And kis the steppes where as thow seest pace
> Virgile, Ovide, Omer, Lucan, and Stace.

a millennium before [Juan Ruiz]. This fallen world was man's condition and his fault. But the fallen status of man, his world, and his language was not the endpoint of interpretation, any more than it was the limit of human existence or of human aspiration. The fallen state was, in fact, the happy beginning of salvation. . . . For men and women who were neither mystics nor saints, that salvation had to be worked out through the fallen signs of God's creation, and these included the imprecise, error-prone signs of human language. . . . [T]he very 'indeterminate areas' in the text are invitations to 'glossing' the text. I extend this observation to argue that, along with other paradoxes that lie at the very heart of the *Libro,* the larger or more numerous the places of indeterminacy and impasse, the larger the saving gloss."

While Alfred David is doubtless right to say that the "sheer variety of Chaucerian comedy seems to defy . . . efforts [to systematically define it]," much can be gleaned from this sole use of the word itself.[70] It is intriguing that "comedye" appears in a stanza so self-consciously focused on the subject of literary history. As Karla Taylor puts it, "Chaucer explicitly links his poem to a tradition that will help preserve it from the silence of oblivion."[71] The *Troilus* is being released here to the world of books and readers, located in that world in terms of an axis of "makyng" and "poesye" so commonplace in medieval literary theory.[72] The "tragedye," however humbly, is linked with the "poesye" of the great authors of antiquity, while the hoped-for "comedye" seems at first glance something for a mere "maker"—Chaucer aspires "to make in som comedye," and the *Troilus* is not to envy any (such) "makying." But is the dichotomy between "making" and "poetry" really so clear here? Two subtleties in the stanza need to be recognized. On the one hand, the "making" of comedy seems to be ultimately empowered by God, implicitly aggrandizing the genre even as the genre of tragedy is explicitly humbled ("litel," "subgit"). Moreover, by invoking God as the "Firste Moevere" (*KnT* 2987), so to speak, of comedy, near the end of a poem that is strewn with Dantean quotations and allusions, the stanza points us to the *Comedy* and prompts a consideration of the *Comedy*'s, and of comedy's, place and role in literary history. Dante's *Comedy* is, among much else of course, the Christian fulfillment of what Virgil calls "l'alta mia tragedìa," the *Aeneid* (*Inferno* 20.113). In Chaucer, the farewell to the present book seemingly cannot be performed without invoking some (redemptive) future book—indeed, the stanza looks to the future book even before the instructions to the "tragedye" are complete. Consequently, the *auctoritas* implicitly claimed for the *Troilus* by associating it with valorized "poesye" and the poetic *auctores* of the classical world is qualified. Here "comedye" is once again the corrective for tragedy, and more than that, it is literally written into it in such a way so as to insinuate the impossibility of ever really completing the latter without the former. Comedy, in short, writes the boundaries of authoritative "tragedye," delimiting it precisely by opening it up to the promise of the new.

[70] Alfred David, "Chaucerian Comedy and Criseyde," in Mary Salu, ed., *Essays on Troilus and Criseyde* (Cambridge: D. S. Brewer, 1979), p. 92.

[71] Taylor, *Chaucer Reads,* p. 187.

[72] On this subject, see the important article by Glending Olson, "Making and Poetry in the Age of Chaucer," *Comparative Literature* 31 (1979): 272–90.

This promise of the new—of renewal through glossing, interpretation, meta-narrative, imitation, learned (and not-so-learned) debate—links the genre of comedy and the practice of commentary. In the case of the *Comedy* itself, so insistent on its own *novitas* in so many ways, it opens the poem to the construction of authority, of "the new author." I believe that Chaucer's experience of the *Comedy* of Trecento literary history was thus a matter of not simply reading a vernacular *auctor,* or a vernacular poet claiming unprecedented *auctoritas,* but of seeing vernacular authority "in the makyng," as it were—not only the potential of the vernacular to claim *auctoritas* but also the necessity of subsequent readers to write that *auctoritas,* to write the *Comedy* into the comedic mode of literary history. In Chaucer's work the comedic nature of the reception and representation of Dante manifests itself in the interrogation of the reading moment and the reading subject in *The Parliament of Fowls,* through a carefully structured exploration of the relationship between authorship as both a self-construction and the construction of other readers. In short, what Chaucer's poem reflects are the ways in which the writing of Dantean literary reception is a polyvocalic and multigeneric process in its own right, one that at once complements and constitutes Dante's *Comedy* in the fourteenth century.

In *The Parliament of Fowls,* Chaucer's repeated "'Thorgh me men gon'" functions as a motto not only for the nature of gateways but also for the workings of commentaries, and the contradictory nature of Chaucer's gate, its "doubleness" of language, embodies the contradictory effect of commentary. Medieval commentary assumes the task of providing access to meaning, of serving as a kind of gate through to the hidden truth of the text. At the same time, of course, it is imposing, even intimidating, often self-contradictory; it can often conceal as much as it reveals, obscure as much as it illuminates.[73] Medieval readers approached authorized meaning through the gate of commentary, not sure if the gate

[73] The conception of the true meaning of poetry as something hidden beneath a concealing surface (typically, though not always, a veil), and revealed by an interpreter or an interpretive gloss, is of course widespread in medieval thinking about reading and interpretation, from Augustine to Boccaccio. For an analysis of Dante's use of the figure, interestingly in relation to a different gate scene and one where the pilgrim's paralysis is at issue, see John Freccero, "Medusa: The Letter and the Spirit," in Rachel Jacoff, ed., *Dante: The Poetics of Conversion* (Cambridge, Mass.: Harvard University Press, 1986), pp. 119–35. As Freccero has it, the Medusa in *Inferno* 9 and the "petrification" she threatens are "interpretive as well as a moral threat[s]" (p. 121). What I am claiming here is in a sense Chaucer's reversal of that model: the *integumentum* forestalling (temporarily) access to truth is the gloss itself.

itself might not have a paralyzing effect in its promotion of doubt, confusion, and perplexity. More specifically, the *Comedy* commentaries claim to provide ways into Dante's poem and, given the claims the poem itself makes, Dante's visionary experience. But that very commentary, itself a record of readerly experience, threatens to become so multivoiced, so potentially productive of "errour," that it effectively becomes its own text needing clarification.[74] And yet, as John Dagenais succinctly reminds us, "Incoherence is a powerful force in the medieval textual world," and it is this often incoherent multivocality that, at least partly, is responsible for *auctoritas.*[75] We might conclude by recalling that Chaucer's gate scene ends with Affrycan promising to "shew mater of to wryte" (line 168) to the dreamer, at which point, in a gesture reminiscent of Dante's Virgil, Chaucer tells us "myn hand in his he tok anon" (line 169), dramatizing something seemingly built into the processes of authorization intrinsic to medieval textuality and at work specifically in *The Parliament of Fowls* itself. The subject of reading results in a particular kind of reading subject, so that, not infrequently, confusion and authority go hand in hand.

[74] Here it is worth recalling the comments of Robert Edwards: "Chaucer's pressing need, evidenced by the indeterminacy of the earlier narrative poems, is for a pragmatic middle term on which to ground poetry as a form of knowledge" (*Dream,* p. 125). For a similar (though not identical) claim for Dante, see Mazzotta, *Dante's Vision.* Edwards goes on to say that by the *Parliament,* Chaucer "has realized in a fundamental way how poetry is part of the world it represents and thus that its claims, though always problematic, have real authority" (p. 146). I would add the chronologically obvious but crucially important clarification that Chaucer is interested in grounding *poetry in manuscript culture* as a form of knowledge, and thus in examining the intersections of poetry, materiality, and critical practice.

[75] Dagenais, *Ethics,* p. 16. Compare Leicester's comments: "Though each individual act of explication was presented as the expression of a common and God-given truth, the multiplication of these interpretations inevitably began to reveal disagreements and contradictions. It began to become apparent that the sense of unity could only be safely maintained as long as it remained *latent,* as long as nobody tried to spell it out too thoroughly" ("Harmony," p. 19).

The Case of the Variable Source: Alan of Lille's *De planctu Naturae*, Jean de Meun's *Roman de la Rose*, and Chaucer's *Parlement of Foules*

Theresa Tinkle
University of Michigan

Which who will read set forth so as it ought,
Go seek he out that *Alane* where he may be sought.
—Edmund Spenser, *Fairie Queene*

GEOFFREY CHAUCER DECLINES to describe the goddess Nature in his *Parlement of Foules,* referring curious readers to her portrait in Alan of Lille's *De planctu Naturae* (*Plaint of Nature*):

> And right as Aleyn, in the Pleynt of Kynde,
> Devyseth Nature of aray and face,
> In swich aray men myghte hire there fynde.[1]

Contemporary literary critics obligingly take Chaucer at his word and do what he refused to do: specify how "Aleyn devyseth Nature." This converts Chaucer's nonportrait into an interpretable image and Alan's text into its self-evident supplement. Thus hastening to fill the descriptive lacuna, critics neglect to read it. "Right as Aleyn devyseth" raises certain questions, chief among them: In which version of the text? Critics of medieval literature conventionally repress this question and rarely acknowledge the substantial difference between modern standard edi-

I extend grateful thanks to Andy Kelly, and the anonymous reader of this article for *SAC,* each of whom offered generous criticisms that led to considerable improvements in this essay. I am fortunate to have met such excellent readers.

[1] Lines 316–18 in Larry D. Benson, gen. ed., *The Riverside Chaucer,* 3d ed. (Boston: Houghton Mifflin, 1987). I cite this edition unless otherwise noted.

tions and medieval manuscripts. (Editors of standard editions tend to foster the convenient illusion of textual stability.) Even where the possibility of manuscript variation is granted, the source text remains serenely immutable, a stable Verbal Icon unaffected by revolutions in editorial and critical theory.[2] This hoary critical tradition fails to grasp the most elementary fact about *De planctu:* it is subject to significant, even dramatic, variation in medieval manuscripts. Indeed, manuscript variations make *De planctu* unusually opaque precisely where Chaucer cites a seemingly transparent source.

We imagine the medieval *De planctu* to have a single, fixed form chiefly because our modern editions give it one.[3] All our editions and translations present *De planctu* as a prosimetrum beginning with meter, ending with prose, and containing a total of nine meters interspersed with nine proses.[4] This version of *De planctu* begins with the narrator's poetical lament over men's betrayal of natural sexuality (that is, the Roman Church's heterosexual norms). Nature arrives and preaches to the

[2] The most thorough and cogent analysis of Alan as source remains J. A. W. Bennett, *The Parlement of Foules: An Interpretation* (Oxford: Clarendon Press, 1957); Bennett's assumptions about the transparent fixity of the source text are especially clear on pp. 27, 50–51, 108, 124–32, 139–40, 153. See also Bennett, "Some Second Thoughts on *The Parlement of Foules,*" in *Chaucerian Problems and Perspectives: Essays Presented to Paul E. Beichner,* ed. Edward Vasta and Zacharias P. Thundy (Notre Dame and London: University of Notre Dame Press, 1979), pp. 132–46. Alan still appears as an invariable source in Sylvia Huot's meticulously researched and thoughtful study of textual variation, *The "Romance of the Rose" and Its Medieval Readers: Interpretation, Reception, Manuscript Transmission* (Cambridge: Cambridge University Press, 1993), pp. 106–15. Similar assumptions about textual invariability allow a modern translation to replace the medieval text for some scholars: thus Jack B. Oruch, "Nature's Limitations and the *Demande d'Amour* of Chaucer's *Parlement,*" *ChauR* 18 (1983–84): 29–30; Kathleen Hewitt, "'Ther it was First': Dream Poetics in the *Parliament of Fowls,*" *ChauR* 24 (1989–90): 25–27; and Ordelle G. Hill and Gardiner Stillwell, "A Conduct Book for Richard II," *PQ* 73 (1994): 317–28. Needless to say, Chaucer's sources are not unique in literary history; similar assumptions inform Spenser criticism, as in Edwin Greenlaw's comments on Alan in the Variorum ed. of *The Faerie Queene, Books Six and Seven,* ed. J. G. McManaway, D. E. Mason, B. Stirling, pp. 396–98. (Baltimore: The Johns Hopkins University Press, 1938).

[3] Another issue here is a division between hermeneutics and textual scholarship, which allows critics to ignore manuscript evidence and the construction of the edition: see D.C. Greetham's astute comments in "The Resistance to Philology," in *The Margins of the Text,* ed. D.C. Greetham (Ann Arbor: University of Michigan Press, 1997), pp. 9–24.

[4] The editions are J. P. Migne, ed., *Patrologia Latina,* vol. 210; Thomas Wright, *Anglo-Latin Satirical Poets and Epigrammatists of the Twelfth Century, Rerum Britannicarum Medii Aevi Scriptores,* no. 59 (London, 1872; rpt. Millwood, NY: Kraus, 1964), pp. 429–522; and Nikolaus M. Häring, "Alan of Lille, *De planctu Naturae,*" *Studi medievali* 3.19 (1978): 797–879. The translations are by Douglas M. Moffat, *The Complaint of Nature* (1908; rpt. Hamden, Conn.: Shoe String Press, 1972), and James J. Sheridan, *The Plaint of Nature* (Toronto: Pontifical Institute of Mediaeval Studies, 1980). I cite Häring's edition (by prose or meter and line) and Sheridan's translation (by page) throughout.

converted, instructing him in the philosophical bases of heterosexuality. She cannot restore natural order, and the text ends with a prose section recounting the excommunication of those unnatural humans who embrace extramarital partners, nonreproductive sexual activity, innovation in sexual positions, or passion in sexual relations.

This summation accurately represents the work's form in the majority of surviving manuscripts, but other versions exist. In a number of manuscripts *De planctu* ends with a final meter, its modern title *Vix nodosum* derived from the first line, "Vix nodosum ualeo nodum denodare" ("I can scarcely untie the knotty knot").[5] This meter takes the sexual instruction of *De planctu* in interestingly vulgar new directions. Additionally, one fourteenth-century manuscript attributes to Alan a prose prologue that lucidly summarizes the plot and announces his moral focus.[6] The prose prologue and final meter create two quite different works of *De planctu,* yet the texts have passed almost unremarked in studies of *De planctu* or its influence, all of which remain devoted to the familiar, received text.[7] This is unfortunate, for the prologue and meter provide excellent evidence of the work's historical potential for diverse, even conflicting meanings. Such variation obviously affects intertextuality. Chaucer does not cite a transcendent text but a work that lives only in the material forms that shape its specific meanings.[8] We cannot fully

[5] Nikolaus M. Häring, ed. (with trans. by J. J. Sheridan), "The Poem *Vix nodosum* by Alan of Lille," *Medioevo: Rivista de storia della filosofia medievale* 3 (1978): 165–85.

[6] Françoise Hudry, "Prologus Alani *De Planctu Nature,*" *Archives d'histoire doctrinale et littéraire du moyen age* 55 (1988): 169–85.

[7] Neil Cartlidge offers a rare interpretive comment on the meter, comparing it with *The Owl and the Nightingale: Medieval Marriage: Literary Approaches, 1100–1300* (Woodbridge: D. S. Brewer, 1997), p. 191. Savvy literary critics have long registered a keen awareness of the significant linguistic variations between Migne's and Wright's editions, based as they are on different medieval witnesses, though even these critics do not question the fixed modern form. Foremost among Alan's savvy critics stands Winthrop Wetherbee: see *Platonism and Poetry in the Twelfth Century: The Literary Influence of the School of Chartres* (Princeton: Princeton University Press, 1972), pp. 188–211, esp. p. 188 note 3. Wetherbee does not, so far as I can tell, later question the seemingly fixed form of Alan's work: compare, e.g., his "Latin Structure and Vernacular Space: Gower, Chaucer and the Boethian Tradition," in R. F. Yeager, ed., *Chaucer and Gower: Difference, Mutuality, Exchange* (Victoria: English Literary Studies, University of Victoria, 1991), pp. 13–15. I too overlook the textual scholarship on Alan in my *Medieval Venuses and Cupids: Sexuality, Hermeneutics, and English Poetry* (Stanford: Stanford University Press, 1996), pp. 22–26, as does Alexandre Leupin in his *Barbarolexis: Medieval Writing and Sexuality,* trans. Kate M. Cooper (Cambridge, Mass.: Harvard University Press, 1989), pp. 59–78. In our neglect of these versions, we exemplify the unfortunate division between textual scholarship and hermeneutics mentioned above, n. 4.

[8] Robert R. Edwards takes a similar position, adroitly considering manuscript traditions for a source and Chaucerian adaptation in "Source, Context, and Cultural Translation in the *Franklin's Tale,*" *MP* 94 (1996): 146–53.

understand medieval writers' treatment of their sources without reference to manuscript traditions and variance.

Just as material books mediate Chaucer's understanding of Alan, so too do other writers. Chaucer's descriptive lacuna obviously responds both to Alan, who patiently catalogues interminable graphic details, and to Jean de Meun, who eagerly itemizes his reasons for not similarly describing Nature in *Le Roman de la Rose.* Literary critics traditionally line these citations up in a neat patrilineal sequence in which each writer passes a poetic seed directly to his successor, as if in some perfect Platonic communion that allows them to dispense with material texts.[9] This model represses the womb of textual life: the material textual condition that nourishes multiple and variant versions. By contrast, recent textual scholarship compels us to revalue those lettered wombs, obliging us to acknowledge the long-neglected "illegitimate" *De planctu* variations as well as the more familiar received text.[10] As we shall find, the prose prologue and final meter of *De planctu* illuminate the work's internal complexities, and the light thus shed can help us perceive how Alan invites the very different appropriations of Jean de Meun and Chaucer.

[9] E.g., Oruch, "Nature's Limitations," pp. 29–34; Helen Cooney, "The *Parlement of Foules:* A Theodicy of Love," *ChauR* 32 (1997–98): 339–76.

[10] My position here is indebted to a number of recent studies and collections, among which I find the following especially stimulating and admirable: Michael Camille, *Image on the Edge: The Margins of Medieval Art* (Cambridge, Mass.: Harvard University Press, 1992); Greetham, ed., *The Margins of the Text;* Ralph Hanna III, *Pursuing History: Middle English Manuscripts and Their Texts* (Stanford, Calif.: Stanford University Press, 1996); Huot, *The "Romance of the Rose" and its Medieval Readers;* Seth Lerer, *Chaucer and His Readers: Imagining the Author in Late-Medieval England* (Princeton, N.J.: Princeton University Press, 1993); Seth Lerer, ed., *Reading from the Margins: Textual Studies, Chaucer, and Medieval Literature* (San Marino, Calif.: Huntington Library, 1996); Tim William Machan, *Textual Criticism and Middle English Texts* (Charlottesville and London: University Press of Virginia, 1994); Leah S. Marcus, *Unediting the Renaissance: Shakespeare, Marlowe, Milton* (London and New York: Routledge, 1996); Jerome J. McGann, *The Textual Condition* (Princeton, N.J.: Princeton University Press, 1991); Stephen G. Nichols and Siegfried Wenzel, eds., *The Whole Book: Cultural Perspectives on the Medieval Miscellany* (Ann Arbor: University of Michigan Press, 1996); Martin Stevens and Daniel Woodward, eds., *The Ellesmere Chaucer: Essays in Interpretation* (San Marino, Calif.: Huntington Library; Tokyo: Yushodo Co., 1997); Evelyn B. Tribble, *Margins and Marginality: The Printed Page in Early Modern England* (Charlottesville and London: University Press of Virginia, 1993). My debt to all these scholars is obvious in my definition of the textual issues and in my methodology; perhaps more tellingly, my interest in the topic owes much to their invigorating work. I would like particularly to thank the participants and respondents of the conference on the *Iconic Page in Manuscript, Print, and Digital Culture* (Ann Arbor: University of Michigan Press, 1998), which I coorganized and coedited with George Bornstein, for a splendidly collegial exchange of ideas about (to me new) directions in textual studies.

This essay, then, begins with materialist textuality and progresses to materialist intertextuality.[11]

I. *Vix nodosum*

Let us begin by considering the most dramatic variation of the *De planctu* we know: the meter *Vix nodosum.* Versions of this poem appear in 27 manuscripts, including 4 manuscripts from the thirteenth century, 6 from the fourteenth century, 16 from the fifteenth century, and 1 from the seventeenth century. Manuscripts present the meter variously in relation to *De planctu:* the meter may precede *De planctu,* follow it (as a conclusion or with varying degrees of separation), or appear as an independent work.[12] Attributions to Alan have not been contested recently (perhaps less a sign of consensus than of inattention). There is some foundation for the attribution in manuscripts; more persuasive evidence is the fact that the poem exhibits stylistic excesses characteristic of Alan.[13] The meter assesses the relative merits of virgins and married women as lovers. It concludes that men should rank virgins above mar-

[11] James I. Wimsatt comments persuasively on the benefits source scholars can derive from theories of intertextuality: "Theories of Intertextuality and Chaucer's Sources and Analogues," *Mediaevalia* 15 (1993 for 1989): 231–39. We can derive still more benefits from materialist intertextuality, and so David Lorenzo Boyd argues in "Compilation as Commentary: Controlling Chaucer's *Parliament of Fowls,*" *South Atlantic Quarterly* 91.4 (1992): 945–64. Boyd insists on an intertext's power to disambiguate meaning, and he develops a "notion of contextual determinism" (p. 947), a notion I profoundly resist. Michael Riffaterre theorizes a comparable but to me more persuasive approach to intertextuality: for a lucid assessment of his and other prominent theories, see Thais E. Morgan, "Is There an Intertext in This Text?: Literary and Interdisciplinary Approaches to Intertextuality," *American Journal of Semiotics* 3 (1985): 1–40. Brenda R. Silver engagingly proposes that we consider adaptation as editorializing, an idea that complements intertextual studies by similarly calling attention to the "politics of adaptation"; "Whose Room of Orlando's Own? The Politics of Adaptation," in *Margins of the Text,* ed. Greetham, pp. 57–81.

[12] See Häring's bibliographic description, "*Vix nodosum,*" pp. 171–77.

[13] Marie-Thérèse d'Alverny reviews the then-available manuscript evidence and inclines to regard the meter as one of Alan's youthful works, partly on the basis of its style, in *Textes Inédits/Alain de Lille,* Études de philosophie médiévale 52 (Paris: J. Vrin, 1965), pp. 42–44; as do Häring, "*Vix nodosum,*" p. 165, and Sheridan, *Plaint of Nature,* pp. 29–30. Their consensus would place *Vix nodosum* early in Alan's career. I suspect this conclusion is partly based on the notion that a medieval author begins (as Ovid did) with frivolous and erotic pieces and then moves on (as Ovid did) to more serious philosophical and religious works. Although I do not find this model compelling, I do not aim to resolve the relation of *Vix nodosum* to *De planctu* here; I am seeking not authorial intention but the implications of manuscript versions for intertextuality.

ried women—not because virginity is sanctified but because virgins offer men greater sexual pleasure.

Whether or not Alan meant the meter to be part of *De planctu* must remain an open question. Bits in *Vix nodosum* (a phrase, a usage, an image) resemble bits in *De planctu.* The parallels between these texts show that Alan reworked passages for different contexts over some period of time, but present evidence does not allow us to establish which passages are the original, which revisions.[14] *Vix nodosum* could be a partial early draft of *De planctu,* its conclusion in some (not necessarily final) version of the work, or a closely related independent work. We cannot recover Alan's intention, but as Nikolaus M. Häring points out, "It is obvious [from the manuscript presentations] that at least some Mediaeval scribes or librarians considered the poem to be part of the *De planctu nature.*"[15] A version of the meter is attached to *De planctu* in one of the "oldest and best texts" of the work (MS Seo de Urgel, Archivio Capitular 2055, written about 1230). The meter also appears in later manuscripts closely related to the "best text" family.[16] These manuscript presentations make *Vix nodosum* crucial to intratextuality (the relation among works by the same author) as well as intertextuality.

That we have overlooked the meter rather than studying it testifies to the power exerted even now by the early print editions that established our received text. Although authoritative manuscripts connect *Vix nodosum* and *De planctu,* they have been separated throughout their print history. *Vix nodosum* was first printed ca. 1475, *De planctu* in 1494. The Cistercian Prior Charles de Visch's 1654 edition of Alan's writing includes *De planctu* but not *Vix nodosum.* De Visch referred to two manuscripts of *De planctu;* one was missing the beginning and end, and neither contained the meter.[17] Because the poem was not included in the de Visch edition, it was effectively severed from the tradition of the received text. J. P. Migne incorporated de Visch's work into the *Patrologia*

[14] Derek Pearsall argues that we should distinguish authorial versions or revisions when possible; "Theory and Practice in Middle English Editing," *Text* 7 (1994): 107–26. We need also to respect the theoretical and methodological issues involved in assessing evidence of revision (see Hanna, *Pursuing History,* pp. 159–73), but a full analysis is beyond the scope of this essay.

[15] Häring, ed., "*Vix nodosum,*" p. 172.

[16] MSS Angers 544 (thirteenth century), Cambridge Univ. 1350 (fourteenth century), and Vat. Chigi 1.5.182 (thirteenth century), as per Häring, ed., "*Vix nodosum,*" pp. 172–77, and "*De planctu Naturae,*" p. 801.

[17] For bibliographic discussion, see Häring, "*De planctu Naturae,*" pp. 802–3.

Latina edition (1855); Thomas Wright (1872) apparently drew on Migne and two other manuscripts.[18] The received text thus grants an exaggerated scholarly importance to a few (late) manuscripts, which in the form of the received text continue to dominate literary criticism, source study, and the like. Only with Häring's *De planctu Naturae* (1978) do we get an edition based on a considered selection of manuscripts, but he too edits the received work. In short, the prosimetrum has remained fixed in its earliest print form, which neither follows one of the earliest and best texts nor represents the fullest historical version of the work.[19] Häring attempts to improve our understanding of the work by editing *Vix nodosum* (1978) as a parallel text to the received *De planctu,* but critics have failed to take his perspicacious hint.

The received texts of Chaucer reveal a telling contrary tendency. From the first decades of Chaucer reception, compilers and editors eagerly expanded the canon, and his works are now presented in the fullest possible form, often with passages from minority witnesses intercalated into other versions. Sometimes only parallel versions will suffice to capture his shifting nuances. The *Parlement*'s closing "roundel" (lines 680–92) exemplifies the Chaucerian tendency. Although the earliest manuscript evidence for this text dates ca. 1440, critics, desiring to incorporate every last fragment of Chaucer's art, accept it unquestioningly as part of the poem.[20] We have better manuscript authority for *Vix nodosum* as the close of *De planctu!* Surely we have sufficient cause to accept the meter as an alternative, historically significant conclusion to *De planctu.*

It is a sensational conclusion. *Vix nodosum* opens as *De planctu* does, with the narrator's description of Venerean disorders: Venus's witchcraft denatures and transforms men so that Bacchus grows sober, Mars peaceful. The language echoes *De planctu* meter 1 (detailing monstrous vener-

[18] It is not entirely clear what Wright's three base texts are, but Häring conjectures credibly that "M" is Migne, and the other two are MSS London, BL Cott. Cleop. B.6 (fifteenth century) and London, BL Add. 24361 (fifteenth century), "*De planctu Naturae,*" p. 804. Neither of these MSS contains *Vix nodosum.*

[19] The standard edition of *De planctu* suffices admirably for many critical purposes, but critics need to recognize its historical limitations, particularly for source and intertextual studies. As Hanna argues with compelling thoughtfulness, the study of historical documents and textual variation allows us to be more precise in defining the uses and interest of different kinds of editions, such as parallel texts (*Pursuing History,* pp. 63–82).

[20] Hanna discerningly analyzes the manuscript evidence, in *Pursuing History,* pp. 182, 185–90. The five variant passages in *The Wife of Bath's Prologue* present a similar situation, which I discuss in "The Wife of Bath's Textual/Sexual Lives," in *Iconic Page,* pp. 59–63.

ean transformations) and meter 5 (describing how love transforms the shapes of all mankind). *Vix nodosum* then offers an oxymoronic definition of love—"Dulce malum amor est et dulcor amarus" (line 21)—that further recalls meter 5 "Dulce malum, mala dulcedo, sibi dulcor amarus" [5.7]. When *Vix nodosum* concludes *De planctu,* such echoes emphasize the work's repetitious quality and give it the aesthetic closure of a reversion to the monstrous Venus who denatures men. The meter's depiction of sexual love similarly recalls the *De planctu* account of Hymen and Antigenius (prose 5): each contrasts fruitful and barren (adulterous) love, nobility and commonness, silvery fountains and drought, glades and wastelands, sweet joy and bitter regrets. The meter recalls other language and imagery from *De Planctu:* unhappy is the man who forges on a married anvil, who sows his seed in barren sand; the love of matrons is positive, that of maidens superlative. The numerous parallels suggest that Alan recurs to material over some period of time, with different contexts shaping the ideas anew.[21] As a consequence, *Vix nodosum* and *De planctu* read as "echo chambers" of each other even when presented as separate works.[22]

After outlining Venus's oxymoronic effects, the narrator takes up the question of whether a man should prefer virgins or matrons as sexual partners. He answers by detailing their respective erotic values. The narrator's attitude resembles Alan's pastoral position in *Liber poenitentialis* (as described by James A. Brundage): "it was a lesser offense . . . for a man to have illicit sex with a beautiful woman than with an ugly one—the greater the temptation, the less the offense."[23] Here the argument favors loving virgins, who are, it seems, inevitably beautiful. Maidens bloom freshly and sweetly; they are private, unspoiled fountains of delight. Married women are withered and threshed flowers, public wells, parched land, worn paths, spoiled goods. A woman's deflowering is precious. Deflowered, a woman becomes wanton, nurtures an insatiable sexual appetite, and grows avaricious. Matronly love is shameless, mad, criminal, homicidal: adulterous feminine sexuality brings men to emasculation and beheading. (Given that virgins are so precious and women so quick to decline, the meter could be seen as recommending a series

[21] Sheridan, *Plaint of Nature,* p. 30, cites other parallels.

[22] I adapt this idea of intratextuality from Roland Barthes, *Roland Barthes,* trans. Richard Howard (New York: Hill and Wang, 1977), p. 74.

[23] James A. Brundage, *Law, Sex, and Christian Society in Medieval Europe* (Chicago: University of Chicago Press, 1987), p. 350.

of one-night stands.[24]) As the meter develops, painfully pleasurable love transforms into either painful love or pleasurable. The narrator effects this transformation by reminding man that he can more clearly perceive light and dark, good and evil, when they are juxtaposed. Consequently, he replaces oxymorons with contraries, untying the knotty knot, as it were, and amending Venus's confusion of terms.

The meter envisions a virgin as delightful because unable to refuse her lover's prayers or to expect anything in return for her love. In this, she conforms to nature. The risky married woman acts independently of nature and lovers' pleas, responding to her own hunger. She causes men to lose control, first of their bodies, then of their (nether)purses, and finally of their lives. In other words, independent feminine desire overwhelms men and is unnatural (that is, disruptive of masculine order). The short version of the work does not mention the most explicit of these dangers, in effect minimizing the threat of feminine sexuality.[25] The longer version concludes by recommending the love of virgins, whose dependent pliancy defers masculine sexual perils. Throughout this assessment of women's erotic value, the narrator's misogyny competes with his enthusiasm for sexual love. His conflicted attitude toward masculine desire qualifies Nature's lessons in *De planctu,* for he makes it painfully obvious that desire for women is ambivalent, fraught with dangers, problematic—not a simple remedy for masculine vice.

Although his sexual instruction differs from Nature's, this narrative persona binds *Vix nodosum* closely to *De planctu.* Both narrators sympathize with an aristocratic ideology of sexual love (e.g., meter 1, toward the end of prose 4). Both follow amatory conventions, represent aristocratic love as innately superior, and naturalize a particular class code of heterosexual relations.[26] *De planctu* and *Vix nodosum* alike present the narrator as at once a courtly sensualist and a moralist burdened with one idea. *De planctu* opens with him rejecting male homosexuality and longing for fruitful feminine kisses:

[24] Henry Ansgar Kelly suggested this implication to me (private correspondence dated December 12, 1997).

[25] Häring notes ("*Vix nodosum,*" p. 171) that the meter survives in complete (148 lines) and shortened (98 lines) versions; the latter omits the final section, which vividly elaborates the dangers of adultery (lawlessness, castration, and murder).

[26] Toril Moi perceptively analyzes the class implications of a similar construction; "Desire in Language: Andreas Capellanus and the Controversy of Courtly Love," in *Medieval Literature: Criticism, Ideology, and History,* ed. David Aers (New York: St. Martin's Press, 1986), pp. 15–20.

> Virginis in labiis cur basia tanta quiescunt,
> Cum reditus in eis sumere nemo uelit?
> Que michi pressa semel mellirent oscula succo,
> Que mellita darent mellis in ore fauum. (m1.43–46)

Why do so many kisses lie fallow on maidens' lips while no one wishes to harvest a crop from them? If these kisses were but once planted on me, they would grow honey-sweet with moisture, and grown honey-sweet, they would form a honeycomb in my mouth. (pp. 70–71)

Between meter 1 and his awakening, Nature muzzles this desire. It revives in *Vix nodosum:*

> Melius uel mellius nil hoc est amore, . . .
> Dicius uel dulcius nil hoc est dulcore.
> Primos flores uirginis, prima rudimenta,
> Ver primum decerpere prima sub iuuenta
> Veneris preludia sunt delectamenta. . . (lines 74, 76–79)

. . . nothing is better or more honey-sweet than this love; . . . nothing is more precious, more sweet than this sweetness. To gather up a virgin's first blooms, her firstlings, her first Spring, in the first flower of one's youth—these are the preludes, the delights of love. . . (trans. Sheridan, pp. 168–69)

Where *Vix nodosum* concludes *De planctu,* this irrepressible narrator unifies the work in unexpected ways. His reappearance returns us to the beginning, and his final advice about sexual love can be read as proof that he grasps Nature's basic lesson and is eager to help men forge without economic, social, or physical risk. His lesson addresses new issues, and his pragmaticism about sexual love provocatively replaces Nature's despair over the human condition. His scene-stealing Ovidian performance demonstrates that a little masculine forethought may avert some romantic and sexual problems.

Whereas Nature defines acceptable love by choice of gender (the opposite) and sexual position (man active and on top), the *Magister amoris* remembers less rudimentary criteria: the age and marital status of the woman. Beyond selecting the correct gender and position, beyond aptly inserting tab A into slot B, the lover must now distinguish between the love (*amor*) of virgins and other women's desire (*luxuria*). While Nature adheres to monastic ideology and treats sexual reproduction as a rational labor exclusive of sensual pleasure,[27] the narrator remains interested in the youthful, courtly pleasures and dangers of sexuality. He views sexuality as an expression of love and concentrates on enhancing erotic pleasure. Procreation may result but is not his declared goal. The narrator and Nature embody what Winthrop Wetherbee perceives as a "dislocation" in *De planctu* between courtly tradition and conventional Latin *auctoritas*.[28] Though never absolute, this discursive split becomes most apparent when the narrator's interests take precedence in *Vix nodosum.* As his concerns become less tangential, more authoritative, they compete more equally with Nature's ascetic teachings about sexuality.

Nature's and the narrator's diverse perspectives on sexuality link *De planctu* to a heterogeneous intertextual network. That network advances not a single sexual code but conflicting values associated with sensual desire and love, and the authority of a position depends on its context.[29] Both Nature and the narrator are authoritative within the self-limiting contexts of their chosen discourses. Yet the multiplication of individual perspectives and authoritative traditions demonstrates that no one discourse defines sexuality for all cultural contexts. Placed side by side, Nature and the narrator reveal each other's inadequacies. If Nature seems in retrospect unaware of the social contexts of eroticism, the narrator seems ignorant of philosophical and academic contexts. The two figures manifest the tenuous cultural connections between their discourses.

Whether presented as the conclusion of *De planctu* or as a separate meter, *Vix nodosum* enlarges its potential for meaning. As a conclusion, *Vix nodosum* intriguingly revises *De planctu* by adding instructions on love to Nature's interest in sexual positions, and by recognizing that masculine desire for women will not automatically remedy all sexual vice or correct all social ills. *Vix nodosum* reopens *De planctu* by addressing central issues from the narrator's hitherto marginal perspective. Alterna-

[27] As per my *Medieval Venuses and Cupids,* pp. 23–24.

[28] Wetherbee, "Latin Structure and Vernacular Space," p. 15.

[29] The following studies forcefully demonstrate the diversity of contemporary and later attitudes about sexuality: John T. Noonan Jr., *Contraception: A History of Its Treatment by the Catholic Theologians and Canonists,* enlarged ed. (Cambridge, Mass.: Harvard Univ. Press, 1986), pp. 143–300; Brundage, *Law, Sex, and Christian Society,* pp. 176–324; John W. Baldwin, "Five Discourses on Desire: Sexuality and Gender in Northern France around 1200," *Speculum* 66 (1991): 797–819; and my *Medieval Venuses and Cupids,* pp. 42–99.

tively, *De planctu* revises *Vix nodosum* by minimizing love and by simplifying the problem of masculine desire. For those readers who know it, *Vix nodosum* reinforces discursive conflicts in *De planctu:* the contest between Nature's asceticism and the narrator's interest in love; the competition among academic, courtly, and monastic conceptions of sexuality; and the struggle between an idea of women as pliantly phallocentric and a notion of women as aggressive man-traps. *Vix nodosum* emphasizes the conflicts inherent in Alan's broad spectrum of intertexts—and thereby discloses the perspectives and values struggling for supremacy in his culture.

Modern readers, coming upon *Vix nodosum* some centuries after it was severed from *De planctu,* will find it a shocking conclusion and may welcome these conflicts as evidence that these are two separate works, joined by mistaken scribal action rather than by authorial intention. This response owes something to the power of the received text, which functions to make any other version seem inauthentic. The response also testifies to a bias in favor of a unified *De planctu* and against this "new" appendage. Current rumors of the work's decorous unity are greatly exaggerated, however, and earlier criticism offers an instructive counter tendency. J. Huizinga, for instance, judges *De planctu* so disunified that he supposes Alan wrote the meters independently and clumsily incorporated them into a prose treatise.[30] G. Raynaud de Lage describes *De planctu's* artistry as "gauche," its progress "déconcertante."[31] C. S. Lewis grudgingly recommends the work because it has the winning virtue of being far shorter than *Anticlaudianus.*[32] Such disparagement encourages later critics to recuperate the work's "inner unity" while respecting its "surface diversity."[33] Still later critics take unity for granted.

We need not remain bound to the rock of this essentially New Criti-

[30] An attractive hypothesis, though Huizinga does not go quite far enough. He notices discrepancies between verse and prose but passes over discontinuities in the prose: *Über die Verknüpfung des Poetischen mit dem Theologischen bei Alanus de Insulis,* Mededeelingen der Kgl. Akad. van Weetenschappen, Afdeeling Letterkunde 74, ser. B, no. 6 (Amsterdam, 1932), pp. 16–18.

[31] *Alain de Lille, Poète du XIIe siècle* (Montreal: Institut d'Études Médiévales; Paris: J. Vrin, 1951), pp. 43–44.

[32] *The Allegory of Love: A Study in Medieval Tradition* (1936; rpt. Oxford and New York: Oxford University Press, 1990), pp. 105–9.

[33] Quoting Richard Hamilton Green's influential essay, "Alan of Lille's *De Planctu Naturae,*" *Speculum* 31 (1956): 649. George D. Economou similarly emphasizes Alan's harmonious integration of Nature's several aspects: *The Goddess Nature in Medieval Literature* (Cambridge, Mass.: Harvard University Press, 1972), pp. 72–97.

cal aesthetic. As Huizinga noted, the prose and metrical sections of *De planctu* do not always mesh; neither is the prose itself wholly consistent. Alan advances in fits and starts, seemingly heedless of confusion in his wake. Vital narrative events recur from one section of *De planctu* to another, with Alan not simply repeating but effectively rewriting the event and its meaning. His internal variations make the text resistant to a notion of stable, fixed meaning—even without the complication of *Vix nodosum.* In order to appreciate *Vix nodosum* as a variant conclusion, we need to attend closely to the pattern of the whole, including the pattern of internal variation.

Two explanations of a parenthesis-like flaw in Nature's tunic exemplify Alan's tendency toward variation. First, humans put off the sluggishness of sensuality and, seeking to penetrate divine mysteries with reason as charioteer, tore the garment:

In huius uestis parte primaria homo, *sensualitatis deponens segniciem, directa ratiocinationis aurigatione,* celi penetrabat archana. (pr1.232–34; emphasis added)

On the first section of this garment, man, divesting himself of the indolence of self-indulgence [*sensualitatis*], tried to run a straight course through the secrets of the heavens with reason as charioteer. (p. 98)

In other words, men chose reason over sensuality. The problem is that reason alone may not grasp the mysteries of faith.[34] The second explanation of the tear rewrites Boethius's satire of philosophical sects into the context of the sexual vices that prostitute Nature. Here Alan indicates that the tear results from sensual men violently stripping Nature of her garments. This explanation leads the narrator to wonder how man's spark of reason was extinguished, how he became so intoxicated by sensuality that he assaulted natural law:

. . . que irrationabilis ratio, que indiscreta discretio, que indirecta directio, ita in homine *obdormire rationis coegit scintillulam ut homo, leteo sensualitatis poculo debriatus,* in tuis legibus apostata fieret, uerum etiam tuas leges illegitime debellaret? (pr4.175–78; emphasis added)

[34] G. R. Evans valuably elucidates Alan's treatment of reason in relation to theology, in *Alan of Lille: The Frontiers of Theology in the Later Twelfth Century* (Cambridge: Cambridge University Press, 1983), pp. 41–61.

> . . . what unreasonable reason, what indiscreet discretion, what indirect direction forced man's little spark of reason to become so inactive that, intoxicated by a deadly draught of sensuality [*sensualitatis*], he not only became an apostate from your laws, but even made unlawful assaults on them? (p. 143)

Now the tear results from sensuality prevailing over reason. Alan's conflicting explanations of the tear perplex its meaning and make the essential human error a riddle. He leaves the garment torn between rival interpretations.

Alan's tendency to rework his ideas is evident throughout *De planctu.* The narrator's question about reason's failure opens further hermeneutic difficulties (or pleasures, depending on the reader's sensibilities). Nature refuses to use plain or vulgar words in her response, preferring to gild immodesty so as to render vice beautiful—that is, not offensive:

> In sequenti tamen tractatu, ne locutionis cacephaton lectorum offendat auditum uel in ore uirginali locum collocet turpitudo, predictis uiciorum monstris euphonia orationis uolo pallium elargiri. (pr4.192–95)

> In the following disquisition, however, it is my intention to contribute a mantle of fair-sounding words to the above-mentioned monsters of vice to prevent a poor quality of diction from offending the ears of readers or anything foul finding a place on a maiden's lips. (p. 144)

Nature leads us to expect that "the following disquisition" will be a gilded survey of vice. Instead, she supplies a lengthy mythic account of divine generative order. The narrator intervenes with a request to hear about desire (*cupido*), and Nature once again promises to let this topic be "refined by the sublimity of the writer's pen" (p. 148) ["stili tamen altitudine castigata" (pr4.276)]. To this end, she describes an oxymoronic love (*amor*): "Love is peace joined to hatred, loyalty to treachery" (p. 149) ["Pax odio fraudique fides" (m5.1)]. Here she finally does beautify vice by representing it in mythic scenes. After the meter, she applauds her "artistic exposition" (p. 154) ["ex hoc mee doctrine artificio" (pr5.1)].

Nature's idea of poetic gilding is coherent—until she turns about-face and reinterprets this "histrionic discourse" as mere "jests and jokes," "trivial crude pieces" adapted to the narrator's childish "naivete" (p. 155) ["Predicta igitur theatralis oratio, ioculatoriis euagata lasciuiis, tue puerilitati pro ferculo propinatur. Nunc stilus, paululum ad pueriles tue infantie fescenninas digressus" (pr5.17–19)].[35] In other words, she surrounds the meter with praise for its ornate sublimity and then dismisses it for puerile crudity. She begins by advocating an elevated style for ugly subjects, proceeds to exemplify that style in relation to divine creation, finally describes *amor* with poetic rectitude, and ends by reversing herself about what constitutes her high style. Her exposition renders her theory increasingly imprecise, even impenetrable.[36]

Alan also repeats and varies his description of Nature, who arrives before the narrator three times. She first appears walking toward him (prose 1), her eroticized body a collection of tender swells and luscious fragrances, with lips that ask for kisses, arms that call for embraces, and garments that catalogue sensuous, creaturely life. She resembles nothing so much as a sturgeon or shad offering its body for man's delectation. For her second arrival (prose 2), she acquires a male charioteer and chariot, wherein she occupies herself by drawing images of mutable life. Her presence now stimulates joyous sensuousness in the goddess Juno and the nymphs of shore and sea, recalls the earth to vernal benedictions, and stuns the narrator so that his eyes shun her. Her third approach turns her into her own charioteer (prose 3.2–4), but her arrival strikes the narrator into a mental stupor that precludes close description. At this point Nature becomes a monstrous apparition and punishing mother as well as an erotic object. As her appearance is diverse, so too are her positions. A dualist, she despises the material world, yet she also defends its innate dignity and worth. At one point, she describes how she retired from earth's tumult in order to dwell in a celestial palace of meditation; at another point, she laments that human vice forces her to inhabit the brothels of this world. Alan shapes her from such diverse and sometimes conflicting discourses as amatory poetry, Platonic philosophy, and anti-Cathar sermons. Inconsistencies and contradictions often arise as she shifts from one discourse to another.

Vix nodosum compounds the effects of these discursive and narrative

[35] Sheridan's "historic" altered to "histrionic." Jan Ziolkowski proposes that the trivial, crude pieces are the elegiacs of meter 5, *Alan of Lille's Grammar of Sex: The Meaning of Grammar to a Twelfth Century Intellectual* (Cambridge, Mass.: Medieval Academy of America, 1985), p. 26. This is an excellent explanation, though it does not account for Nature's reversal in prose 5.

[36] Winthrop Wetherbee comments eruditely on Nature's ambiguous view of poetic allegory, in "The Function of Poetry in the 'De planctu Naturae' of Alain de Lille," *Traditio* 25 (1969): 101–10.

variations. Neither version of *De planctu* presents Nature as a fixed, stable figure, yet her particular instabilities vary. Each version sets her and thus her sexual pedagogy in a slightly different intertextual matrix; each emphasizes a slightly different set of cultural conflicts. One version of the work gives her values supremacy; the other replaces her with a *Magister amoris.* The variant conclusion retrospectively transforms the work and Nature with it—much as variations within the work continually challenge and alter interpretations. As separate works, *Vix nodosum* and *De planctu* comment similarly on each other, though separating the texts softens the narrator's answer to Nature's defeatist conclusions.

Vix nodosum paradoxically coheres with *De planctu* by continuing its established pattern of internal variation. The progress of *De planctu* is essentially accretive, the organization loose; it easily accepts another meter or prose. The final meter resembles the rest of the prosimetrum in its nonchalant attachment to the "whole" and in its variations on prior passages. *Vix nodosum* and *De planctu* therefore disclose how significantly Alan subjects his ideas and language to revision, and how unsettled those ideas actually are. Alan's texts evidence ongoing, dynamic reworking rather than a single, definitive revision. Since each version of *De planctu* manifests conflicting sexual codes rather than one dominant code, later writers can cite it for vastly different ideas about sexuality, ranging from the narrator's interest in erotic pleasure to Nature's concept of generation. Inconsistencies in *De planctu* and its versions lead to a variable reception. Any two writers (say, Jean de Meun and Chaucer) may well know the work in different versions, and they may focus on quite different passages on sexuality.

II. A Hypothesis about Jean de Meun

Parallels between *Vix nodosum* and Jean de Meun's *Roman de la Rose* are provocative and merit close study (certainly closer than is possible here). Much as Alan confronts Nature's *auctoritas* with the narrator's art of safe sex, so too does Jean follow Nature's confession with a bawdy *ars amatoria,* a guide to seduction without harm to men. The two *Magistri amoris* adopt similarly conflicted tones, each wavering ludically between clerical-misogynist and conventional amatory attitudes toward women. Both conclusions replace Nature's reproductive agenda with the masculine concerns of love, erotic pleasure, and physical and social security. Both represent masculine amatory concerns as slighting or ignoring the rigorous ascetic rule (which should come as no surprise in a culture that accepts prostitution as a remedy for masculine sexual tension[37]). The enduring conflict between Nature and the lover discloses an ongoing competition between the Roman Church and nobility over the power to regulate sexual love. A century (or two) does not erase that cultural tension.

Some of Jean's specific language and imagery may further imply a knowledge of *Vix nodosum.* The meter represents virginal sexuality with imagery of fresh flowers, dew, clear springs, a path not yet beaten—all of which recur in Jean's paradise of love. And Jean contrasts, as Alan does in *Vix nodosum,* the deception and mercantilism of experienced women with virginal simplicity, the well-trodden path with the private fountain. Jean's final bawdiness matches Alan's vulgarity in *Vix nodosum,* though Jean complicates the effect by uniting sexual and religious connotations. Jean thereby points his bawdiness toward more expansive, more ambiguous intertextual relations and cultural contexts.

Alan's narrator discusses the value of contraries: just as men know good from evil, light from dark, so too they may discriminate between maidens and matrons. These maxims serve to usher in his *ars amatoria.* Jean's narrator similarly comments—just before he assails the aperture—that we should try everything so as to know good from evil, for "things go by contraries; one is the gloss of the other" ("Ainsinc va des contraires choses: / Les unes sont des autres gloses").[38] In each case, the commonplace idea of contraries becomes the remarkable ground of sexual knowledge.

None of the parallels between Jean's *Roman de la Rose* and Alan's meter is conclusive alone, but together they encourage us to speculate that Jean read *Vix nodosum* either as part of *De planctu* or as a separate text. Perhaps Jean alienates Nature from the masculine business of love, casting a humorous retrospective eye at her, in imitation of Alan rather than in parody. Jean certainly revises *De planctu* very much as Alan does in *Vix nodosum,* and with similar implications for Nature's sexual model.

[37] See the splendid studies by Leah L. Otis, *Prostitution in Medieval Society: The History of an Urban Institution in Languedoc* (Chicago: Chicago University Press, 1985), and Jacques Rossiaud, *Medieval Prostitution,* trans. Lydia G. Cochrane (Oxford: Basil Blackwell, 1988).

[38] *The Romance of the Rose,* trans. Charles Dahlberg (Hanover and London: University Press of New England, 1971), p. 351; *Le Roman de la Rose,* ed. Ernest Langlois, Société des anciens textes français, 5 vols. (Paris: Champion, 1914–24), 5:21573–74. Further citations are to these editions and will be made parenthetically in the text.

The possibility that Jean borrows from *Vix nodosum* invites us to reassess long-settled assumptions about the relations between the two writers. In other words, *Vix nodosum* invites us to challenge the last few centuries of literary history—all of the scholarship based on the received version of *De planctu*—and to raise new questions about how Jean appropriated Alan's work.

Although Jean seems at points closer to Alan than we would imagine without the evidence of *Vix nodosum,* Jean detaches Nature from twelfth-century discourses and locates her in his own cultural contexts. That is, he turns *De planctu* into an intertext. Most obviously, Jean replaces Alan's descriptive and discursive multiplicity with a self-consciously superior absence of description. Jean writes:

> Bien la vous vousisse descrire,
> Mais mes sens n'i pourrait soufire.
> Mes sens! Qu'ai je dit? c'est du meins.
> Non ferait veir nus sens humains,
> Ne par voiz vive ne par notes;
> E fust Platons ou Aristotes,
> Algus, Euclidès, Tholomees,
> Qui tant ont or granz renomees
> D'aveir esté bon escrivain,
> Leur engin seraient si vain,
> S'il osaient la chose emprendre,
> Qu'il ne la pourraient entendre;
> . . . non pas trestuit li maistre
> Que Nature fist onques naistre;
> Car, or seit que bien entendissent
> Sa beauté toute, e tuit vousissent
> A tel pourtraiture muser,
> Ainz pourraient leur mains user
> Que si trés grant beauté pourtraire.
> Nus fors Deus ne le pourrait faire.
> E pour ce que, se je poïsse,
> Volentiers au meins l'entendisse;
> Veire escrite la vous eüsse,
> Se je poïsse e je seüsse;
> Je meïsmes i ai musé
> Tant que tout mon sen i usai,
> Come fos e outrecuidiez,

Cent tanz plus que vous ne cuidiez;
Car trop fis grant presompcion,
Quant onques mis m'entencion
A si trés haute euvre achever. (4:16165–76, 16203–21)

I would willingly describe her to you, but my sense is not equal to it. My sense! What have I said? That's the least one could say. No human sense would show her, either vocally or in writing. Even if it were Plato or Aristotle, Algus, Euclid, or Ptolemy, who now have such great reputations for having been good writers, their wits would be so useless, if they dared undertake the task, that they could not do so. . . . Not all the masters that Nature ever caused to be born could do so, for supposing that they grasped the whole of her beauty and that they all wanted to waste their time in such a representation, they could sooner wear out their hands than represent such very great beauty. No one except God could do so. Therefore I would willingly at least have tried if I had been able; indeed I would have described her to you if I could have and had known how; I have even wasted my time over it until, like a presumptuous fool, I have used up all of my sense, a hundred times more than you suspect. I made too great a presumption when I ever set my intent on achieving so very high a task. (pp. 273–74)

The narrator signals the range of discourses that shape Nature by naming those who have failed adequately to represent her: Plato, Aristotle, Algus, Euclid, Ptolemy, Pygmalion, Parrasius, Apelles, Miro, Polycletus, Zeuxis, Cicero. By implication, Alan's attempt to imitate such *auctores* exposes his artistic arrogance; his copiously detailed descriptions of Nature now appear implausible.

With this dense network of classical and other authorities, Jean links Nature (and his poem) to a universal and transhistorical intertextual culture. Far from authorizing a specific concept of Nature, this makes her a variable subject of bookish profusion. So she is in *De planctu,* but with a difference. For Alan everything is written in the book of divine archetypes, and the artist imperfectly copies a world that defectively reproduces those archetypes. Still, his Nature speaks as if in "archetypal words that had been preconceived ideally" (p. 116) ["quasi archetipa uerba idealiter preconcepta" (pr3.12–13)]. Surrounded by deceptive images of truth, the narrator glimpses the shadows of a divine order. Jean replaces Alan's symbolic portraits with contradictory human representations of Nature. For Jean, "everything is written elsewhere in a book" (p. 303)

["Tout est ailleurs escrit en livre" (4:18252)], but the writing is only human. Nature herself becomes unrepresentable, beyond human capacity:

> Pour ce n'est dreiz que conte face
> Ne de son cors ne de sa face,
> Qui tant est avenant e bele
> Que fleur de lis en mai nouvele,
> Rose seur rain, ne neif seur branche
> N'est si vermeille ne si blanche.
> Si devraie je comparer,
> Quant je l'os a riens comparer,
> Puis que sa beauté ne son pris
> Ne peut estre d'ome compris. (4:16239–48)

It is therefore right that I make no tale either about her body or her face, so pleasing and beautiful that no lily at the beginning of May, no rose on its twig nor snow on a branch is so red nor so white. Thus should I pay homage when I dare compare her to anything, since her beauty and worth cannot be understood by men. (p. 275)

The absence of description indicates that Nature exceeds human comprehension; the divine order cannot be inscribed by human pens. The narrator refuses to claim knowledge—however limited or qualified—of a universal natural order. He calls upon the *auctores* not in order to assert some truth about Nature but in order to point up the dubious multiplicity of human truths.[39] As a consequence, Nature speaks as just one of many characters; the natural order does not reveal a divine plan to humanity or guide humans toward spiritual truth.

Jean's overpopulated descriptive lacuna thoroughly revises Alan's variability, not only the artistic surface but also the intertextual matrix. Alan's extraordinary Platonic and grammatical discourses depend on contemporary intellectual contexts, and connect his work to a vast web of twelfth-century and earlier intertexts. The passages of richest intertextual complexity become least accessible to later readers. Most obviously, both grammar and Platonism soon become inapposite to the topic

[39] Eva Martin persuasively argues that the pervasive multiplicity of the poem allows Jean to eschew responsibility for it: "Away from Self-Authorship: Multiplying the 'Author' in Jean de Meun's *Roman de la Rose,*" *MP* 96 (1998): 1–15.

of sexual reproduction.[40] Hence Jean deploys his own discursive contexts for sexual love, including classical myth, Ovidian and Virgilian poetry, Aristotelian science, religious devotion, and Latin commentary. Helping readers to organize so encyclopedic an array, Sylvia Huot insightfully characterizes Jean's poem as a "mixture of authoritative citations, worthy philosophy, and lascivious doctrines."[41] This intertextual matrix raises questions about the relative authority of so many competing perspectives on passionate love. The hermeneutic questions Jean raises are answered variously in the poem's reception, as readers condense, clarify, appropriate, and re-invent the work to suit their own agendas.[42] Conflicts within the work initiate a diverse reception, much as they do with Alan's work.

The historical meanings of each work are clearly far more complex than can be recovered from received versions alone. *Vix nodosum* calls attention to the diverse implications of *De planctu,* to the meanings essentially lost to literary history since 1654, and therefore prompts exciting revisions in our understanding of the relations between Alan's and Jean's works. Most notably, *Vix nodosum* greatly complicates the possibilities for Jean's dependence on and independence from Alan. *Vix nodosum* should also affect our study of how both *De planctu* and *Le Roman de la Rose* are received in the later Middle Ages. Alan's bawdy meter might well, for instance, prompt scholars to investigate anew that most famous debate about Jean's and Alan's intertextual relations, the Quarrel of the Rose.

III. A Prose Prologue to *De planctu*

One fourteenth-century manuscript has an epilogue linking *Vix nodosum* to *De planctu* and reading the work as an argument "contra prelatum

[40] Marcia L. Colish's magisterial study asserts that the discipline of grammar loses its preeminence after the twelfth century. She divides the Middle Ages into chronological periods in which an emphasis on rhetoric gives way to an emphasis on grammar (seventh to twelfth century); grammar is then replaced by logic. See *The Mirror of Language: A Study in the Medieval Theory of Knowledge,* rev. ed. (Lincoln and London: University of Nebraska Press, 1983), pp. 63–64, 109. Interestingly, John A. Alford establishes with great erudition that grammatical metaphors persist despite the discipline's relative decline; "The Grammatical Metaphor: A Survey of Its Use in the Middle Ages," *Speculum* 57 (1982): 728–60. Twelfth-century Platonism is neither one coherent philosophy nor identical with later Platonism. Winthrop Wetherbee offers a cogent overview of Alan's immediate context; "Philosophy, Cosmology, and the Twelfth-Century Renaissance," in *A History of Twelfth-Century Western Philosophy,* ed. Peter Dronke (Cambridge: Cambridge University Press, 1988), pp. 21–53.

[41] Huot, *The "Romance of the Rose" and Its Medieval Readers,* p. 22.

[42] Huot's book (ibid.) meticulously, brilliantly explores this process.

sodomitam."[43] This comment recognizes that *Vix nodosum* follows *De planctu* both in rejecting sodomitical love and in offering sexual instruction about what should replace it. By explicitly directing this interpretation, the epilogue clarifies the connection between the antique literary work and contemporary cultural values. The lines function as a valuable intertext: they designate how the work participates in known cultural discourses, how its diverse potential for meaning is focused, how its meaning is simplified for a particular manuscript audience.

We discover this process at work in a more substantial addition to *De planctu,* a unique prose prologue transcribed by Françoise Hudry in 1988. This prologue is preserved in MS Cambridge St. John's College 115, dated to the second half of the fourteenth century.[44] The text falls some leafs after *De planctu* (sans *Vix nodosum*) in the book, which makes it look more like an afterword than a prologue. This presentation suggests that the works are separated in the exemplar(s). The supplemental text ends with an explicit identifying it as the "prologus Alani de Planctu Nature" (p. 185). This prologue aptly and thoughtfully introduces or comments on *De planctu* by abstracting a chronological plot from the discontinuous, achronological prosimetrum. Beginning with remarks on the divine creation of man, a singularly virtuous and rational being designed to serve as a soldier under Nature's laws, the text proceeds to recount his departure from proper self-regulation and his prostitution in the service of Iocus (Cupid's bastard brother). Such human error debases Nature, forcing her into the public streets, and the golden age of chastity gives way to the rusty iron of strange voluptuous practices. The very heavens weep and grow dim, yet man refuses to leave his monstrous spear-games ("monstruosis hastiludiis," p. 184). Like *De planctu,* the prologue conflates the most basic Christian plot, the human fall from virtue, with the classical myth of a lost golden age. This plot serves to order the work for the reader. As the prologue concludes, Alan, unable any longer to conceal the universal evil, utters his tearful verses:

[43] MS Oxford Bodleian Digby 166; the full "Epilogium fratris Walteri de Burgo" is published by d'Alverny, *Alain de Lille,* p. 43. Some French manuscripts include a similar colophon to *De Planctu:* "Pereat sodomita prophanus," quoted by Hudry, "Prologus Alani," p. 181.

[44] This manuscript is closely related to the "best text" family of *De planctu* (see Häring, "*De planctu Naturae,*" p. 801, for textual classification). Hudry describes, discusses, and edits the "Prologus Alani *De planctu Nature,*" pp. 169–85; he offers a particularly rich analysis of how the manuscript context emphasizes themes in *De planctu* (pp. 169–79). I cite the prologue by page number; the trans. is my own.

"In lacrimas"—that is, "To tears"—the first words of *De planctu* meter 1. Thus the prose prologue is linked to the work's familiar metrical opening.

Hudry contends this prologue was written by Alan but suppressed because it too explicitly engaged an unmentionable historical situation. Hudry locates the text's historical explicitness primarily in the prologue's last sentence:

> Quapropter autor iste Alanus, dolore tactus intrinseco nec ultra valens crimina celare tam enormia, hiis flebilibus versibus taliter est conquestus: "In lacrimas," etc. (p. 185)

> [Wherefore this author Alan, touched with inner grief and not having the strength longer to conceal so extravagant misdeeds, has complained with these tearful verses, so: "To tears," etc.]

This attribution leads us into the living presence of the author, whose emotions authorize his verse, and affirms that the work perfectly realizes his intention. The sentence suggestively authenticates Alan's persona in meter 1. Sensitive to these effects, Hudry reads this sentence as candid autobiography and ascribes Alan's personal grief to the habitual sodomy and horrific crimes of Roger de Pont, archbishop of York and antagonist of Thomas Becket. According to this analysis, Alan's work compares with John of Salisbury's lurid account of York's homosexuality and cold-blooded crimes: in short, Alan wrote *De planctu* to condemn the English clergy, astray and without discipline under York's leadership. This too-apparent historical application kept the work with its prologue from being circulated. The censorship continued for about a century, which ingeniously explains why we can discover no comment on *De planctu* in that time.[45]

Although Hudry speculates engagingly, the attribution to Alan and the reference to a particular twelfth-century figure seem unlikely. The prologue is actually quite general, concerned with *humana natura* (human nature, p. 182) and vaguely unnatural sexuality rather than with a deviant ecclesiastic's sodomy. Nothing besides the last sentence (quoted

[45] Hudry concludes: "L'oubli dans lequel est tombé le prologue en prose au *De Planctu Nature* pourrait être signe d'une désapprobation, d'une censure qui frappèrent l'auteur et son ouvrage, pour avoir poussé un cri d'alarme trop ardent devant l'affaiblissement spirituel et le désordre moral de l'Église de son temps" (p. 182).

above) implies a specific historical-biographical context, and we need not read that sentence as Alan's self-disclosure statement. The language is in fact improbable for twelfth-century autobiography. The title *auctor* (author) belongs to dead writers from an authoritative past: hence Walter Map remarked that he could not be an *auctor* because he was still alive,[46] and when Adelard of Bath published something new he attributed it to someone else.[47] As A. J. Minnis compellingly demonstrates, an emphasis on individual human *auctores* and their moral intentions develops through the thirteenth and fourteenth centuries.[48] A later scribe or compiler would be far more likely to bestow the title than Alan to claim it.

The attribution to an *auctor* suggestively authorizes *De planctu:* in the fourteenth-century manuscript context, *auctor* recalls the language of scholasticism, thereby creating intertextual relations between the prosimetrum and a broad range of scholastic and other works by *auctores.* The manuscript reinforces the effect of this attribution, for it presents Alan as foremost among its *auctores*—Walter Map, Richard de Bury, and Seneca.[49] The manuscript design, like the last sentence of the prologue, argues for Alan's artistic integrity, his status, his fully realized moral intention, and his importance to the compilation. This idea of Alan's *auctoritas* is hardly his own.

Nor does the rest of the prologue facilitate the attribution to Alan. The whole is more academic than poetic in its insistence on a comprehensible and orderly plot. In fact, it somewhat resembles a later scholastic prologue that supplies the author's moral intention and clarifies his narrative structure.[50] By contrast, Alan's prose prologue to *Anticlaudianus* offers an intriguing apologia for his art; it does nothing so mundane as elucidate the work's plot, summarize its argument, or put his intentions in a thimble.[51] Alan could conceivably have written most of the *De planctu* prose prologue in a fit of literary sobriety. Still, the prologue

[46] Qtd. in A. J. Minnis, *Medieval Theory of Authorship: Scholastic Literary Attitudes in the Later Middle Ages,* 2d ed. (Philadelphia: University of Pennsylvania Press, 1988), p. 11.

[47] Qtd. by Jacques Le Goff, *Intellectuals in the Middle Ages,* trans. Teresa Lavender Fagan (Cambridge, Mass. and Oxford, UK: Blackwell, 1993), p. 55.

[48] Minnis, *Medieval Theory of Authorship,* pp. 73–117.

[49] Hudry describes the striking first leaf of *De planctu,* which stresses its importance in the manuscript ("Prologus Alani," p. 169).

[50] Minnis characterizes this type of prologue: *Medieval Theory of Authorship,* pp. 15–39, 85–112.

[51] Contra Hudry, who discerns a resemblance to the double prologues of *Anticlaudianus,* "Prologus Alani," pp. 173–74.

seems more likely, particularly in its close, the work of someone following after him, influenced by scholastic ways of reading and solicitous to represent this text so as to reveal its narrative order, establish its author's status and individuality, and define his artistic intentions. In sum, the attribution to Alan is better read as an authorizing device than as an autobiographical statement of fact.

Although certainty about authorship eludes us, as it so often does with medieval works, the manuscript admits of no doubt: it confidently attributes the prologue to Alan and presents it as an authorial supplement to *De planctu.* The prologue therefore has secure contextual authority. Far from merely resuming *De planctu* in Alan's usual vein, however, the prologue consolidates the prosimetrum, supplants it, and edits it for a new value system. The prologue's plot summary condenses Alan's unwieldy, digressive prosimetrum, displacing it for the sake of the continuous, unified narrative of the Fall.[52] The prologue similarly presents a unified Nature, the sign of an unerring hierarchical order that does not permit variation or semiotic confusion. All of her shifting appearances and roles are contracted into that of the distressed widow. In the end, Alan's grief identifies him with her, and he speaks as if in her archetypal words.

Much as the prologue edits the work by clarifying its plot and consolidating Nature's (Alan's) meaning, so too it greatly simplifies *De planctu's* arcane metaphorical instruction about sexual relations. Instead of Alan's veiled but nonetheless detailed inquiries into sexual positions, his guarded examination of the many ways lovers might join their various body parts, the prologue merely defines natural sexuality as generative and vaguely cautions its readers about the dangers of sensual indulgence. Chaucer comments comparably in *The Parson's Tale* (lines 575–76), making sure that penitential instruction does not give anyone new ideas about sexual positions or the like. Such generality is a common pastoral strategy from Alan's time to Chaucer's: the cleric must not speak explicitly lest he encourage lay sexual experimentation.[53] (Clerical celibacy is apparently no impediment to the acquisition of expert knowledge about sexuality.) The prologue's vagueness about natural sexuality anticipates an audience unable or unwilling to process Alan's arcanely titillating

[52] Hudry similarly remarks that the prologue amends the work's disunity; "Prologus Alani," p. 174.

[53] Noonan comments on Alan, *Contraception,* p. 271.

survey of sexual innovation. Finally, the prologue condenses Alan's inaccessible philosophy, transforming his tricky Platonic cosmos into a commonplace of hierarchical microcosm and macrocosm.

In style, the prologue emphasizes Alan's interest in classical myth, evident throughout the prosimetrum. This aspect of *De planctu* suits the manuscript context particularly well: the fourteenth-century "classicizing friars" popularized myth, and it is fashionable in the latter part of the century.[54] The prologue retains this feature of Alan's high style while creating points of ready access: the story of a fall from virtue, the definition of natural sexuality, the ideal of hierarchical order. The prose prologue thus combines the high style of the *auctores* with hermeneutic spoon-feeding.

This text offers what many readers desire: a reliable key to Alan's meaning. Everything is written to express his (homophobic) grief over human sin. The work can support this as well as any number of other simplified meanings, much as the Bible, in its diversity, can support diverse religious doctrines. Readers can certainly have an easier time of it with *De planctu* if they limit its focus, repress its inconsistencies and contradictions, and simplify its arcane discourses. Alan's specialized academic discourses are not self-evident and need editing in each new historical context. Still, the effort to make *De planctu* accessible in precisely these ways distances this prologue from Alan's literary methods. When Alan reworks material, he tends not to make things more simple or more cohesive. His own revisionary accretions nonetheless make the second prologue eminently believable, and the prosimetrum accepts this as easily as it does *Vix nodosum.* The vital point for intertextual study is that the manuscript presents the prose prologue as Alan's own creation, his own summary of *De planctu.* Hence Alan himself authorizes its coherent Nature and her easy doctrine of sexual reproduction. That the prologue seems tailored to a fourteenth-century academic audience would raise no protesting murmurs at the time, for the wearer does not complain of a good fit. Taken together, the prologue and Jean de Meun's *Roman de la Rose* suggest the diversity of medieval responses to *De planctu.* The variable text generates a heterogeneous reception.

[54] The friars are insightfully studied by Beryl Smalley, *English Friars and Antiquity in the Early Fourteenth Century* (Oxford: Basil Blackwell, 1960), and Judson Boyce Allen,

IV. Chaucer and the Sentence of Plesaunce[55]

Chaucer refers to Alan's "Pleynt of Kynde" as if to an invariable authority. Just as Alan described Nature, so must Chaucer's reader imagine her: "And right as Aleyn, in the Pleynt of Kynde, / Devyseth Nature of aray and face, / In swich aray men myghte hire there fynde" (*PF* 316–18). Finding Nature in Alan's text apparently involves no difficulty, so description is unnecessary. We might recall Jean de Meun's proud refusal to describe Nature, his insistence that humans cannot comprehend or adequately represent her; Jean implicitly comments on Alan, who presumed to discover in nature the revelations of divine truth. Rejecting Jean's argument, Chaucer returns to Alan's text as to the site of authoritative description; he grants Alan the status of *auctor.* What is written elsewhere becomes fixed, its meaning closed.[56] These lines imply that Nature is conceptually as well as iconographically static in Alan's prosimetrum and in the *Parlement.* As we have seen, however, Alan's Nature evidences considerable variation, and there is no single original to "fynde" in the way Chaucer directs us to do. His citation does not (and cannot) guide the reader to a particular descriptive passage; instead, it serves to give the goddess an ancient origin. By citing Alan (and such other *auctores* as Cicero and Macrobius) in this way, Chaucer links the *Parlement* to esteemed, erudite literary traditions, suggesting a paternal Latin lineage for his vernacular poem. The lessons of Nature that follow seem to have been drawn from the same antique source as her "aray." In short, Chaucer cites Alan in order to present Nature's teaching as if it were long accepted and authoritative. Thus she can command the birds to "tak hed of my sentence," as if to do so were to participate in an unchanging natural order (line 383).

With this and numerous other passages, Chaucer devises "a concep-

---

The Friar as Critic: Literary Attitudes in the Later Middle Ages (Nashville: Vanderbilt Univ. Press, 1971).

[55] I discuss *Parlement of Foules* from a complementary perspective, focused on Venus and Cupid, in my *Medieval Venuses and Cupids,* pp. 166–77, 198, 201. As Roland Barthes puts it, "I do not strive to put my present expression in the service of my previous truth" (*Roland Barthes,* p. 56).

[56] This implication depends on an idea specifically of Latin literature, as demonstrated by Tim William Machan, "Editing, Orality, and Late Middle English Texts," in *Vox Intexta: Orality and Textuality in the Middle Ages,* ed. A. N. Doan and Carol Braun Pasternack (Madison: University of Wisconsin Press, 1991), pp. 230–36.

tion of culturally significant authority, an authority that demands textual correctness."[57] Correctness equates with invariability: Chaucer treats Alan's text as if it were always and everywhere the same. Although books are actually subject to deterioration and written in scripts that become increasingly difficult to read—Cicero's text is "write with lettres olde" (line 19) in an "olde bok totorn" (line 110)—verbal texts seem to transcend their material condition. Manuscripts and early print editions reinforce the impression that the passage advances a self-evident meaning about an invariable source. There is no manuscript tradition of annotation, and the unmarked pages assert that the citation refers straightforwardly to Alan's transcendent text.[58] The dearth of annotation implies the absence of difficulty: the naked text promises an immediate apprehension of uncomplicated meaning. Modern editions of Chaucer similarly inculcate the belief that a source is invariable, its meaning notoriously lucid and accessible. Manuscripts of Alan's work obviously correct this tendency and help us to recognize that Chaucer idealizes his source, removing it from material history and repressing its internal complexities.[59] In short, he appropriates *De planctu* and Nature for his own purposes.[60]

Like the Cambridge prose prologue, Chaucer's lines advance a way of

[57] Hanna, *Pursuing History,* p. 175. David Aers views Chaucer in this poem as thoroughly subversive of established authority: "The *Parliament of Fowls:* Authority, The Knower and the Known," *ChauR* 16 (1981–82): 1–17. I find his analysis compelling; our conclusions differ because we have very different ideas about medieval *auctoritas.*

[58] I base this conclusion on facsimiles of the following: MSS Bodley Fairfax 16, Bodley Tanner 346, Bodley 638, Cambridge GG.4.27, William Thynne's *Works of Geoffrey Chaucer* (1532). I have also consulted the Chaucer Society texts. *A Parallel-Text Edition of Chaucer's Minor Poems,* ed. Frederick J. Furnivall (London: N. Trubner; rpt. New York and London: Johnson Reprint, 1967), includes MSS Cambridge Univ. Lib. Gg.4.27, Trinity Coll. Cambridge R.3.1, Harl. 7333 (Shirley's MS), LVII St. John's Coll. Oxford, Cambridge Univ. Lib. Ff.i.6, and Caxton's edition of 1477–78. *A Supplementary Parallel-Text Edition of Chaucer's Minor Poems,* ed. Frederick J. Furnivall (London: N. Trubner; rpt. New York and London: Johnson Reprint, 1967), encompasses MSS Bodley Tanner 346, Bodley Digby 81, Bodley Arch. Seld. B.14, Bodley Fairfax 16, Bodley 638, and the Marquis of Bath's Longleat 258. *Odd Texts of Chaucer's Minor Poems,* ed. Frederick J. Furnivall (London: N. Trubner; rpt. New York and London: Johnson Reprint, 1967), adds MS Pepys 2006. For bibliographic discussion of the MSS, see Eleanor Prescott Hammond, "On the Text of Chaucer's *Parlement of Foules,*" *Decennial Publications of the University of Chicago,* 1st ser., vol. 7 (1903): 3–25.

[59] Chaucer's appropriation is so thorough, in fact, that the *Parlement* does not so much as hint at any particular version of *De planctu.*

[60] Rita Copeland's splendidly erudite work on translation as "cultural appropriation" influences my conception of Chaucer's relation to Alan and Latin *auctoritas: Rhetoric, Hermeneutics, and Translation in the Middle Ages: Academic Traditions and Vernacular Texts* (Cambridge: Cambridge University Press, 1991).

reading Alan that unifies his work while affirming his status as a moral *auctor.* It might be tempting to imagine that Chaucer derives his idea of *De planctu* directly from the prose prologue, but the similarities are common to much of fourteenth-century English literature: a classicizing style, an interest in conjoining classical and medieval *auctores,* and a developing regard for conceptual unity (often expressed as the "sentence" of a work). These characteristics suggest not a particular influence but rather joint participation in a shared literary culture. Despite their very general similarities, the prose prologue and the *Parlement* advance quite different interpretations of Nature: the grieving widow of the former concerns herself with sexual generation, while Chaucer's Nature cares primarily to preserve social hierarchy and sexual pleasure. Both portrayals are authorized by reference to Alan, but each work notably revises his idea of natural sexuality. As it turns out, Chaucer's Nature does not develop a single ideal sexual code or resolve disputes by appealing to an ostensibly unchanging divine order. Instead, she continually revises her decrees in response to the ongoing process of mating.

Chaucer's Nature appears an aristocratic heroine, a "noble goddesse" and "noble emperesse" in her arborial hall (lines 303, 319). Chaucer recalls her philosophical contexts, alluding to both Boethius's and Alan's hymns to divine love (lines 379–85):

> Nature, the vicaire of the almyghty Lord,
> That hot, cold, hevy, lyght, moyst, and dreye
> Hath knyt by evene noumbres of acord,
> In esy voys began to speke and seye,
> "Foules, tak hed of my sentence, I preye,
> And for youre ese, in fortheryng of youre nede,
> As faste as I may speke, I wol yow speede."

By presenting Nature as the force that unites the cosmos, Chaucer heightens her authority to pronounce on sexual love. As vicar of God, she intends first of all to hasten the birds' "ese"—their pleasure. Pleasure becomes an acceptable goal, a way of participating in the "acord" of divine order. Nature accordingly recognizes that the birds have come to choose mates "as I prike yow with plesaunce" (line 389); she explicitly accepts sensual impulse and the anticipation of pleasure as the basis for mating. So prompted, the birds should follow her rule (lines 400–404):

> ". . . by ordre shul ye chese,
> After youre kynde, everich as yow lyketh,
> And, as youre hap is, shul ye wynne or lese.
> But which of yow that love most entriketh,
> God sende hym hire that sorest for hym syketh!"

She is at first concerned to preserve a hierarchical order in mating: the selection process begins with the most worthy male's choice. Hence the very cosmos seems to legitimate class privilege and superiority, the unquestionable rights of royalty and gentility. Besides hierarchical order and the prick of sensual desire, love governs the mating process. Her initial "sentence," then, stresses that an emotional and passionate bond is not only proper but necessary between mates. The love of mates mirrors the love that binds the elements in "evene noumbres of acord."

We might recall the asceticism of *De planctu* and specifically Nature's decree that physical generation should be a rational labor devoid of sensual pleasure. While she permits sexual activity directed toward procreation, she perceives sensual pleasure as evil. (The narrator of *Vix nodosum* obviously offers a different point of view.) Nature's conception of sexuality is dominant in the twelfth century, but it does not pass without challenge then or in later ages. As John Noonan demonstrates, later theologians conceive a "rehabilitation of pleasure as a positive value."[61] Most notably, Thomas Aquinas denies the notion that sexual pleasure is in itself evil; indeed, he argues that God designed pleasure as an inducement to the sexual act.[62] The narrator of *Vix nodosum* would agree, as would some characters in *Le Roman de la Rose;* the idea does not wait for Aquinas but does gain validity from his analysis. This is not to say that Aquinas's belief is universally accepted or even dominant in the later period. The older conception of pleasure as evil remains vital and competes with new ideas.[63] Still, sexual pleasure can increasingly be viewed as a positive aspect of marriage relations, implicated in the emotional bond between spouses.[64]

[61] Noonan, *Contraception,* p. 293.

[62] Noonan offers cogent discussion; see *Contraception,* pp. 292–95.

[63] For instance, legal thought continues to be based on the assumption that sex is evil and pleasure not an acceptable goal: see Brundage, *Law, Sex, and Christian Society,* pp. 487–550.

[64] Henry Ansgar Kelly perceptively establishes these late-medieval tendencies in Chaucer's works: *Love and Marriage in the Age of Chaucer* (Ithaca: Cornell University Press, 1975).

Chaucer's Nature is far closer to Aquinas (and Jean de Meun) than to Alan's goddess. Not only does she view "plesaunce" as an incentive for mating, but she also positively values sexual pleasure and love—without reference to generation. Modern scholars typically fail to appreciate Nature's literal meaning, primarily because they assume a rigorous sexual code persisted unchanged from the time of Augustine of Hippo to that of Martin Luther. They accordingly expect Alan's Nature and Chaucer's to advance the same sexual code (that is, the rule of sex for procreation).[65] Recent scholarship in the history of sexuality should allow us to correct this misapprehension,[66] and more accurately to value the meaning and implications of Nature's "sentence."

Chaucer could owe some of his emphasis on pleasure and love to Alan's Ovidian narrator and to *Vix nodosum* (though closer influences exist), but he did not borrow it from Alan's Nature anymore than he learned details about the Trojan war from Lollius. Still, by invoking Alan, Chaucer can make Nature seem what she is not: an unvarying feature of the cosmos. As she declares, "This is oure usage alwey, fro yer to yeere" (line 411). In short, Chaucer cites Alan in order to attribute new ideas to an old *auctor.*

As she develops her initial "sentence," Nature comments in passing that masculine success or failure comes by "hap": "as youre hap is, shul ye wynne or lese" (line 402). With this aside, she reverses the usual Ovidian amatory fiction, which holds that masculine success derives from skill in the chase (or from gifts, especially gold). Her offhand com-

[65] This is a long-standing misdirection in Chaucer studies, usually expressed as an opposition between Venus (sterile, lascivious) and Nature (generative). Representative positions include Bennett, *Parlement of Foules,* pp. 94–95, 109–11; Bernard F. Huppé and D. W. Robertson Jr., *Fruyt and Chaf: Studies in Chaucer's Allegories* (Princeton, N.J.: Princeton University Press, 1963), pp. 101–48; Rhoda Hurwitt Selvin, "Shades of Love in the *Parlement of Foules,*" *Studia Neophilologica* 37 (1965): 146–60; Michael R. Kelley, "Antithesis as the Principle of Design in the *Parlement of Foules,*" *ChauR* 14 (1979–80): 67; Donald R. Howard, *Chaucer: His Life, His Works, His World* (New York: Dutton, 1987), pp. 310, 316; Craig E. Bertolet, "'My wit is sharp; I love no taryinge': Urban Poetry and the *Parlement of Foules,*" *SP* 93 (1996): 376–89; and Janet Smarr, "The *Parlement of Foules* and *Inferno* 5," *ChauR* 33 (1998–99): 113–22.

[66] I am indebted to the insights and evidence offered by the following: Kelly, *Love and Marriage;* John Boswell, *Christianity, Social Tolerance, and Homosexuality: Gay People in Western Europe from the Beginning of the Christian Era to the Fourteenth Century* (Chicago: University of Chicago Press, 1980); Noonan, *Contraception;* Brundage, *Law, Sex, and Christian Society;* Peter Brown, *The Body and Society: Men, Women, and Sexual Renunciation in Early Christianity* (New York: Columbia University Press, 1988); David F. Greenberg, *The Construction of Homosexuality* (Chicago: Univ. of Chicago Press, 1988); Pierre J. Payer, *The Bridling of Desire: Views of Sex in the Later Middle Ages* (Toronto: University of Toronto Press, 1993).

ment implicitly deflates masculine pretensions about the mating process even as she affirms the masculine right to select a partner. Masculine privilege is further challenged as Nature gradually makes feminine choice the sine qua non of mating. She begins by placing a condition on masculine selection: "in this condicioun, / Mot be the choys of everich that is heere, / That *she agre to his eleccioun,* / Whoso he be that shulde be hire feere" (lines 407–10; emphasis added). Nature qualifies the masculine power of selection by requiring feminine consent. In this she differs significantly from Alan's Nature, who glorifies feminine passivity and sexual receptivity. In *Vix nodosum* as throughout *De planctu,* a man has only to choose a woman to possess her. Desire for women can be seen as the remedy for masculine (homosexual) vice because women are always available and receptive to masculine advances. Women become dangerous only when sexually aggressive: when they make independent choices about sexual partners and conditions; when they fail to preserve an exclusive bond with a dominant man. Alan takes feminine agreement to sex for granted; feminine choice leads only to disorder. He requires marriage for sexual legitimacy, but he is not concerned with the social process of mating. By contrast, Chaucer focuses on the process of establishing a union based on mutual accord: a marriage bond. Feminine consent is necessary to this alliance—in part because mutual consent can, without further ado, establish a valid, legal marriage.[67]

In the *Parlement,* Nature's initial rule utterly fails, for the selection of mates proves more complicated than she anticipates. Several males desire the same female, and the "worthiest" among them cannot arouse his beloved to desire him. Instead of resolving the issues by invoking a dominant discourse, Nature turns the work of interpreting and implementing her rule over to the birds. Natural sexuality becomes a subject of debate rather than, as it is for Alan, a feature of divine order (albeit an order that appears contradictory and ever-changing). The birds enlarge on a number of possible criteria for mating (rank, knightly worth, love, fidelity, feminine election) but fail to reach consensus. It is worth noting that they do not mention procreation as a justification or incentive for mating. They debate the nature of love, which appears profoundly factional,[68] far from the unifying force originally represented by

[67] For Chaucer's cultural contexts and treatments of marriage, see Kelly, *Love and Marriage,* pp. 163–242; and see also Brundage on the legal issues of consent, *Law, Sex, and Christian Society,* pp. 235, 238, 243, 250, 275, 288, 352, 354, 376, 436–37, 484, 564.

[68] Bertolet offers an astute analysis of this theme: "'My wit is sharp,'" pp. 365–89.

Nature. Nature's second rule—the verdict of all the birds—thus produces social controversy but no definitive standard to guide feminine consent or produce mutual accord.

Nature tries once again to provide a rule for mating (lines 620–23; emphasis added):

> ". . . fynally, this is my conclusioun,
> That *she hireself shal han hir eleccioun*
> Of whom hire lest; whoso be wroth or blythe,
> Hym that she cheest, he shal hire han as swithe."

Her initial "sentence," requiring that the female "agre to his eleccioun," has transformed into "she hireself shal han hir eleccioun." The male retains the right of possession ("he shal hire han"), but the female gains the power to bestow herself. Nature reminds the formel that love and mutual accord are the basis for mating (lines 624–28; emphasis added):

> "For sith it may not here discussed be
> *Who loveth hire best,* as seyde the tercelet,
> Thanne wol I don hire this favour, that she
> *Shal han right hym on whom hire herte is set,*
> *And he hire that his herte hath on hire knet. . . .*"

Nature's "conclusioun" enlarges on the principle of harmonious accord that she represents. Here the lovers appear perfectly balanced: the inclination of "hire herte" is matched by that of "his herte," and the rhyme *set/knet* suggests the reciprocity and harmony of their union. Nature then recommends the royal tercel as most eligible bachelor, "Which I have wrought so wel to my plesaunce / That to yow hit oughte to been a suffisaunce" (lines 636–37). The rhyme *plesaunce/suffisaunce* emphasizes the sufficiency of pleasure as an incentive to mating—and this principle is offered, significantly, as the counsel of Reason. Nature's "sentence" thus consistently represents "plesaunce" as the basis for the mutual accord of love.

The formel chooses first to seek advice, though she does not characterize what that means or what wise counselor could untie the knot that has defeated so many. While the legitimate feminine activity has changed from consent to choice—from compliance to resistance and independence—we are no closer to explicating the enigma of feminine desire. The conclusion does not resolve this enigma. Nature "gives" mates to every other fowl present, and they end the day in "blisse and joye" (line 669), fulfilling her initial promise of sensual pleasure. Yet the central question of the final sequence remains open: What do females most desire? Chaucer does not reduce feminine desire to Venus's flaming arrow or bags of gold, the usual Ovidian answers to that question. The formel exemplifies the possibility that females can defer sensual desire and pleasure—that females are not, in fact, always sexually available. At the same time, the nonprogress of the central courtship exposes masculine limitations: males cannot always exercise the "natural" right of dominance or make an independent "eleccioun."

Nature's imperative is clearly the accord of mating, and not, as it was for Alan's Nature, the endless cycle of generation. Hence Chaucer dwells on the problems of coordinating masculine and feminine "eleccioun." As vicar of God, Nature is responsible to "knyt [the elements] by evene noumbres of acord" (line 381), and to do the same with her creatures. She mediates among competing interests in order to promote enduring bonds of love, passion, and pleasure. Chaucer thus interprets anew the idea of nature as the bond of love between creatures and creator. As the *Parlement* unfolds, the birds' disputes and Nature's developing "sentence" suggest the challenges of mating in this context, when something other than the alliance of property (or countries) is at stake.

The poem offers several other "sentences" and promises of pleasure that intriguingly augment Nature's perspective. First, the narrator introduces Cicero's "Dream of Scipioun": "Of his sentence I wol yow seyn the greete" (line 35). The "Dream" and commentary emerge with a unified meaning, easily summarized by Scipio: all humans, being immortal, will ultimately discover "blysse" (lines 73–84). This pagan promise of universal salvation distinguishes between those who work for the common profit (who pass after death directly into bliss), and those who violate the law or indulge in sensual pleasure (whose entry into bliss is delayed). For Scipio, "sentence" guides political action; "blysse" is discovered only in the afterlife. The narrator next proceeds to the "pleyn sentence" (line 126) of the verses over the gate to the earthly paradise, which recount the conventional extremes of sexual love: bliss and sorrow, grace and *daunger,* cure and wounds. "Sentence" now refers to the amatory union of contraries, and "blysse" is decidedly sexual and emotional. These first two "sentences" establish a range of meanings and discursive contexts for "blysse." The semantic range expands in Nature's "sentence," which repeatedly identifies sexual "blysse" with orderly mating and the bonds of passionate love. Chaucer's diverse "sentences" delineate a wide array of spiritual, affective, and sexual pleasures. No single "sentence" is presented as dominant, and none excludes the others. The poem renders the bliss of love as essentially ambiguous, associated with pagan reward, courtly sentiment, mutual accord, and sensual satisfaction. Through these ambiguities, Chaucer explores the "possibilities inherent in love itself" and "the wide range of love's manifold experience."[69]

Chaucer's "sentences" invite reflection on the connections and disconnections among authoritative accounts of sexual love. Like a medieval encyclopedist, he accumulates explanations without needing to settle on a single dominant account or to resolve contradictions among the *auctores.*[70] The wide assortment of intertexts incorporated into the *Parlement* similarly emphasizes diversity: besides *De planctu* and Macrobius's commentary on Cicero, Chaucer draws on Boccaccio's *Teseida,* love visions, demandes d'amour, faculty psychology, and parliamentary debate.[71] His "encyclopaedic taste," as Dorothy Bethurum remarks, accepts "inconsistencies and loose connections."[72] The poem accordingly invites readers to exercise their hermeneutic ingenuity and erudition.[73] In sum, the *Parlement* lends itself to diverse acts of reception, encompassing the full range of its own sentences, and then some. Textual variance—most notably in this case, the presence or absence of the roundel—only heightens this potential.

V. Sexuality and Textuality

Our survey has encompassed intriguing developments in the history of sexuality. Alan's Nature rationalizes sexual activity with an ascetic rule

[69] Wolfgang Clemen's felicitous expression: *Chaucer's Early Poetry,* trans. C. A. M. Sym (London: Methuen, 1963), pp. 139, 147.

[70] Modern readers unfamiliar with this genre may find further detail helpful, see, e.g., my *Medieval Venuses and Cupids,* pp. 42–99.

[71] Kurt Olsson usefully analyzes how Chaucer makes new science from these many old books: "Poetic Invention and Chaucer's *Parlement of Foules,*" *MP* 87 (1989): 13–35.

[72] Dorothy Bethurum, "The Center of the *Parlement of Foules,*" in *Essays in Honor of Walter Clyde Curry,* Vanderbilt Studies in the Humanities (Nashville: Vanderbilt University Press, 1954), p. 49.

[73] Modern critics have brilliantly engaged the challenge, and the following stand out: Robert Worth Frank Jr., "Structure and Meaning in the *Parlement of Foules,*" *PMLA* 71 (1956): 530–39; Clemen, *Chaucer's Early Poetry,* pp. 122–69; Henry M. Leicester Jr., "The Harmony of Chaucer's *Parlement:* A Dissonant Voice," *ChauR* 9 (1974–75): 15–34; and Aers, "Authority, the Knower and the Known."

of procreation; at the same time, his Platonic context reveals the disappointing inadequacy of all reproduction (not just sexual) in comparison with eternal archetypes. His narrator, particularly in *Vix nodosum,* reveals to us the tensions that can arise between such philosophical concerns and masculine amatory interests. Jean questions our capacity to comprehend Nature, while his lover (like Alan's *Magister amoris*) minimizes the procreative rule. The prose prologue advances an unexceptional pastoral lesson in place of Alan's stimulating graphic details; it affirms the dominant procreative rule. Finally, Chaucer's Nature advances a late-medieval recuperation of pleasure, depicts passionate love as mirroring divine order, and expresses a firm regard for feminine choice. In the *Parlement* as in *Le Roman de la Rose,* love is not held captive to austere theology or to rigorous conceptions of sexual pleasure. The works studied here help us to appreciate that a wide range of ideas about sexuality has currency in any age: hence each text advances varied, even contradictory perspectives on sexuality. As well, these works reveal that ideas about sexuality change dramatically over the course of a few centuries. They discover not a cohesive, linear reception of *De planctu* but continuous, radical reinterpretations of natural sexuality.

Vix nodosum and the prose prologue help to illuminate the complexities of *De planctu* that initiate this varied reception. What they reveal may well shock us, accustomed as we are to the received text. It is perhaps good to be startled out of complacence and reminded once again of the vast difference between medieval textual variance and the modern textual condition. *Vix nodosum* in particular invites us to reassess our understanding of Alan's poetic career, and to recognize the multiplicity of his attitudes toward sexuality, all too often now reduced to homophobia. The meter also demands that we reexamine our assumptions about *De planctu's* medieval reception, for our favorite canonical writers may well refer to different versions of the text. In all these ways, *Vix nodosum* suggests the tremendous revisionary potential of materialist textual scholarship—and perhaps even the value of uniting textual scholarship and theoretically informed hermeneutics.

The recovery of the variable historical work is very like the repossession, in psychoanalysis, of the events behind the long self-deceptions of memory. Materialist intertextuality both reclaims the historically variable work and helps account for later writers' distorting memories of it. Each reaction to *De planctu,* beginning with Alan's own *Vix nodosum* as its manuscript conclusion, brings to light the intellectual and ideological investments of particular literary cultures. Together they reveal how *De planctu* is subject to "cultural appropriation,"[74] repeatedly rewritten to bring out that potential for meaning that answers current interests. Alan's *Vix nodosum,* Jean de Meun's *Roman de la Rose,* the prose prologue, and Chaucer's *Parlement of Foules* all interpret Nature anew, binding her to new cultural contexts and altering her sexual instruction. Each revision signals a partial, highly selective appropriation of Nature and of Alan's diverse, contradictory ideas about sexuality. Some part of *De planctu* echoes in each work; the echoes are never pure, never heard single and entire, yet they reverberate with the richly variant, erratic, and discontinuous life of the intertext.

[74] Copeland's apt phrase, in *Rhetoric, Hermeneutics, and Translation.*

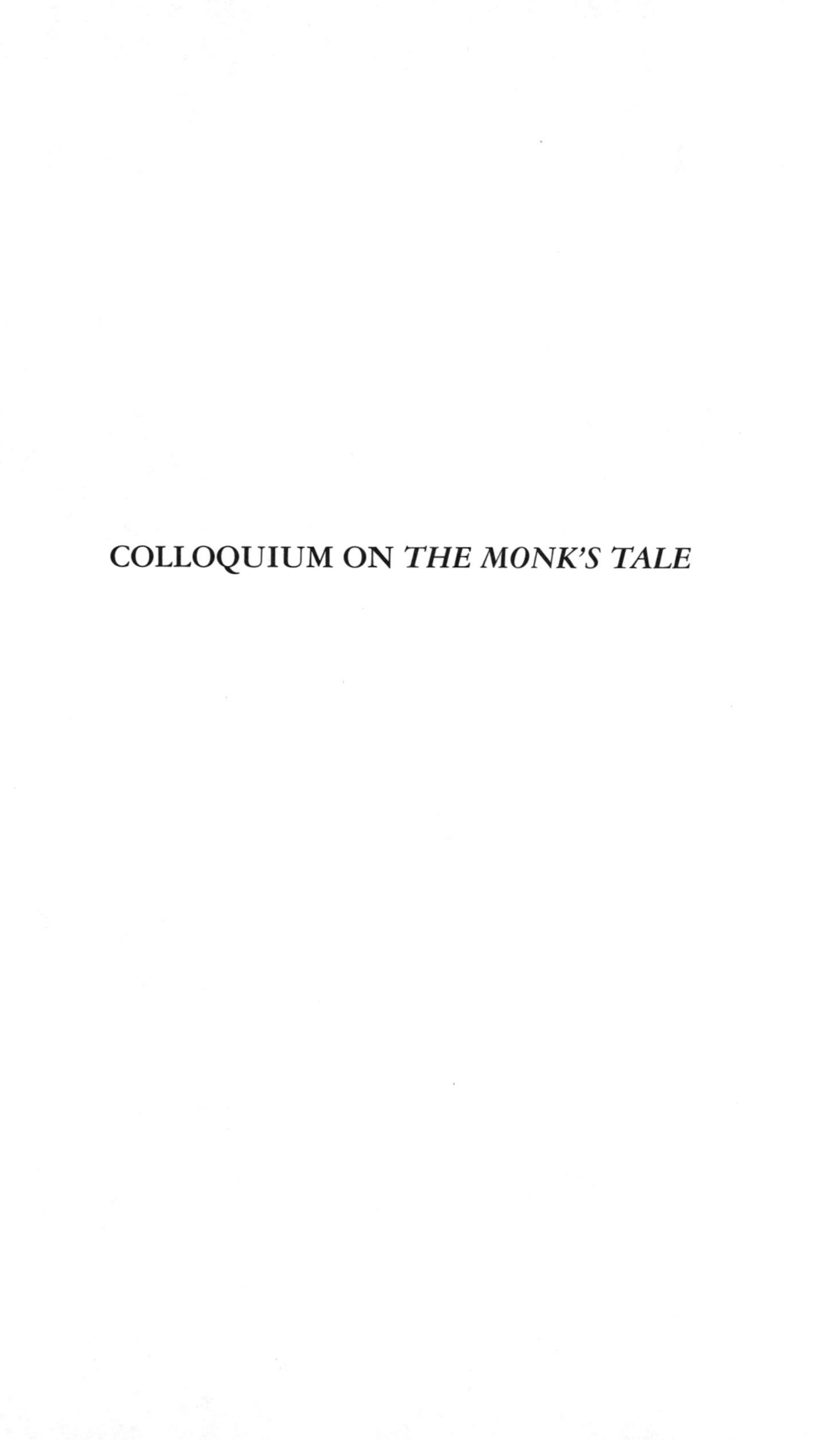

COLLOQUIUM ON *THE MONK'S TALE*

Colloquium on *The Monk's Tale**

"My lord, the Monk"

Stephen Knight
Cardiff University

TRUISTICALLY, *THE GENERAL PROLOGUE'S* description of a pilgrim will suggest some key feature of that pilgrim's *Tale.* That this is obscure in some cases (the Physician, the Merchant) and oblique in others (the Clerk, the Franklin) does not destroy that notional connection, dear to expositors.

The Monk has appeared as one of the obscure cases, the thrust of his *Tale* seeming to have little relation to what's usually described as the ironic and character-revealing motifs of the *General Prologue* description—gluttony, hunting, and, perhaps, sexuality. In spite of some hermeneutic gymnastics to link some of these features with the series of stoic tragedies of the *Tale,*[1] in the Monk's case the notion of a *General Prologue–Tale* link has seemed little more productive than in the zero case of the Nun's Priest.

This view, however, rests on a double misreading. First, the actual dynamic link between *The General Prologue* and a given *Tale* is in most cases concealed: an Agatha Christie–like distraction maneuver leads readers to overlook at first what will turn out to be the mainspring of the *Tale*—the Wife's underlying feminist seriousness; the Franklin's conservative *arrivisme;* the self-indulgence of the Prioress's sentimental-

**Editor's note:* This colloquium is based on a panel at the Eleventh Congress of the New Chaucer Society, July 17–20, Paris in 1998. Each of the panelists has prepared longer versions of his or her remarks. Helen Cooper and L. O. Aranye Fradenburg, both of whom were in the audience and spoke during the question period, have prepared responses.

[1] See, for example, Jane Dick Zatta, "Chaucer's Monk: *A Mighty Hunter before the Lord,*" *ChauR* 29 (1994): 111–33.

ity. So we should be looking in the *General Prologue*'s description of the Monk for a relatively concealed motif of tale generation, not the obvious red herring.

Second source of misreading: The key motif of the *General Prologue–Tale* link may well be visible only in the context of contemporary sociocultural assumptions about this pilgrim's proper role and his/her misfit to that structure, late-fourteenth-century knee-jerks called up by a briefly electric verbal probe: the Summoner's autodiabolism (his complexion is the cue); the Knight's class assumption of moral authorization (suggested by compulsive board-beginning); the Reeve's self-gratifying evaluationism (cf. the hairdo); the Maniciple's malign self-protection (hidden in the secrets of his books).

Careful attention is needed to both the language representing the Monk—especially in the mouths of other pilgrims—and the contemporary sociocultural expectations of a monk against the personal claims of *this* monk. Such careful attention will reveal that the actual focal concern of the *General Prologue* description and the *Tale* is lordship.

Language tells all: the Host addresses the Monk at once as "My lord, the Monk" (*MkP* 1924), just as he called him "sir Monk" after *The Knight's Tale* (*MilP* 3117). The motif repeats: "my lord," "maister," "governour," and in the conclusion of the headlink "my lord" again (*MkP* 1929, 1938, 1940, 1963). These are the only social terms used of the Monk by that broad-spectrum social critic the Host; and even the Host's sexualization of the monk figure is itself directed in a lordly direction by its stresses on "every mighty man" and "heires" (*MkP* 1951, 1957): an inheritance-focused extension of the Monk's procreative power.

It is noticeable that this "lordship" motif is not shared by the Knight, who interrupts the Monk and calls him merely "good sire" (*ProNPT* 2767). Then the Host falls into characteristically hierarchical line, addressing the Monk as "daun Piers" (line 2792), "daun" being a correct professional term for a notionally learned dominus from a monastery.

Where does this idea of "lordship" come from? It is well enough known in *The General Prologue* that the Monk belongs in the "religious" estate group, just as the Knight belongs to and heads that of the feudal family. Whereas the lordly estate was filled with those who held land and defended it, the religious estate was meant to be filled with those who prayed, who lived in the spiritual land. The interests of the Monk so lusciously detailed in *The General Prologue* and taken by so many critics to be personal interests are in fact signs of estate false consciousness:

in dress, food, and recreation, the Monk is a bogus knight. His estate false consciousness is the underlying *General Prologue* motif, and *The Monk's Tale* realizes that—to the predictable annoyance of the Knight, a true lord.

The idea of a monk's false claim to lordship was not at all unknown in the period, and has been noticed by some good readers of the text, though none of them made much of their observation. R. E. Kaske saw the challenge of the Monk to the Knight only in terms of horsemanship.[2] Donald Howard commented that the Monk "plays the aristocrat with his horses and hounds and fine clothes, [and] he must have yearnings to be a nobleman," a little later commenting that "the Monk has the air and manner of a powerful noble but is no more than a 'keeper of the cell.'"[3] Jill Mann, after a full representation of the "stereotypical" motifs of monastic corruption, gluttony, pride, and sexuality, notes the use of the "lord" idea in *The General Prologue;* she also gives a couple of very interesting French analogues: "L'Ordre de Bel Ayse" criticizes monks for pretending to be a "prodom"; the other is a fuller treatment of the same theme from Gilles li Musis, who employs the term "preudhomme," Mann suggests, "ironically."[4]

These comments, convergent though they are with the idea of false lordship, are by no means as socially sharp as Chaucer's, nor indeed as the comment from *The Simonie* (also noted by Mann), when the text says: "And thise abbotes and priours don ayein here rihtes / Hii riden wid hauk and hound, and contrefeten knihtes."[5] Chaucer and other satirists are not the only ones to record serious conflict between monastic social presumptions and traditional order. It is well known that in St. Albans and Bury St. Edmund's Benedictine monasteries were made objects of attack in the events of 1381, and hostility to monastic claims to lordship is a central feature of the medieval outlaw texts, which occupy culturally something of the same terrain as the political rebels of that year. While Eustace of Boulogne was a renegade monk himself, both Hereward and

[2] R. E. Kaske, "The Knight's Interruption of the *Monk's Tale,*" *ELH* 24 (1957): 249–68.

[3] Donald Howard, *The Idea of the* Canterbury Tales (Berkeley: University of California Press, 1976), pp. 280 and 281.

[4] Jill Mann, *Chaucer and Medieval Estates Satire* (Cambridge: Cambridge University Press, 1973), p. 35.

[5] Qtd. from Thomas Wright, ed., *Political Songs of England,* 2d ed., ed. Peter Cross (Cambridge: Cambridge University Press, 1997), p. 329, lines 121–22; see Mann, *Medieval Estates Satire,* p. 34.

Fulk saw monastic intrusion into secular politics as a major problem—one of the reasons for their own loss of lordship—and took violent reactive action in response. Closer to the time in question, in *Gamelyn* we hear how the hero and his faithful steward took pleasure in attending to the tonsures of prior and abbot with large heavy clubs and how, as a result of that direct response to estate false consciousness among monks, the aspirants changed their style of travel: "Thidere thei come ridinge joly with swaynes, / And home ayein thei were ladde in cartes and waynes."[6]

In "Robin Hood and the Monk," Little John, like Chaucer's Knight, put an end to the activities of a monk, but not by polite interruption or even concussion—he simply cut off his head. That monk had merely fingered Robin Hood to the Sheriff and caused his possible execution. A closer parallel to claims of false lordship is in *The Gest of Robin Hood,* where Robin and the outlaws frustrate the attempt of the abbot of York, clearly identified as a Benedictine monk, to seize by malfeasance the lands of—of course—a knight.

In the context of this awareness of false lordship claims coming from monks, as well as the underlying theme of estate false consciousness in the *General Prologue* description and also the verbal patterns of the Host's words to the Monk, it is easy to see how the themes of *The Monk's Tale* are themselves a projection of lordship fantasies in the Monk, and in that a sufficient cause for the Knight's dissatisfaction, which has therefore a sociopolitical rather than a literary or moral basis.

It has been often observed that the Monk's tragic tales are not devout, moral, or notably Christian in their morality; they are just about great people, whose greatness is as much savored as their sudden and much-empathized-with fall. It has also been noted that the Monk's first idea is to tell about a king who was at least a saint, but his attention wanders onto less holy figures, people who are lordly in only the secular sense.

I do not think it has been noted, however, that in the first few tales the issue of social status is strongly stressed. The introductory stanza is about those who fall from "heigh degree" (*MkT* 1992), and that focal phrase recurs. Lucifer is not so much a fallen angel as a disgraced baron: an man of "heigh degree" (line 2002). Adam is represented as having something like feudal lordship in Eden, before his mislordly "mysgover-

[6] See *Robin Hood and Other Outlaw Tales,* ed. S. Knight and T. Ohlgren (Kalamazoo: Western Michigan University Press, 1997), p. 208, lines 523–24.

naunce" (line 2012) causes his own loss of "heigh degree" (line 2011). Samson's "noblesse" (line 2018) is a main feature (the word "noble" recurs at lines 2023, 2052, and 2075) and the bitterness of his fall is that he becomes treated like a laboring churl, only to bring vengeance on these overweening lords (lines 2083–86).

The next three stories have a somewhat reduced stress on social status and its loss, though the idea of "laude and heigh renoun" is there for Hercules (line 2096), "estaat" for Nebuchadnezzar (line 2169), and "hye estaat" for Balthazar (line 2188). The following lives, however, seem to show clearly reduced social anxiety; there is a more purely literary treatment that itself seems to mesh with the reference to "my maister Petrak" (line 2325), the rather finer poetry of the Zenobia sequence, and indeed the reference to Dante in the sad case of Hugelino (line 2461).

It is of course common in *The Canterbury Tales* for a tale teller to be fairly closely characterized in the opening of a *Tale,* and for the *Tale* then to drift toward the less personal voice of the overall narrator, that of Chaucer, who has collected this library of genres and their appropriate narrators. The notion of assumed and nervously held lordship and high degree is in the later stages of *The Monk's Tale* set aside for the not unrelated but certainly not so clearly focused prince-admiring tone of the *Tale*'s development. The process is also seen when the Franklin's uncertain rhetoric is set aside for a development about gender and authority, both male and professional, or when the Wife's domestic dramas, as her *Tale* moves on, are replaced with matters of wider social and ethical gravity and poetic value. Yet a *Tale*'s closure reprivileges the character figured in the verbal texture of *The General Prologue:* and here the irruption of the Knight reminds us, and the Monk, of the inappropriate nature of his assumed lordship. That claim by the Monk, and its inevitable rejection by a true lord, is as evident in the language and substructure of *The General Prologue,* headlink, and *Tale* as it is in the contextual materials that help locate this monk as, indeed, an arriviste fish out of his proper ecclesiastical water.

It is interesting to note that, seen as a conflict over projected status, *The Monk's Tale* stands vis-à-vis that other narrative based on monastic projection, *The Shipman's Tale,* as the Knight's does to the Miller's; and in both fabliaux the wife is complicit with her end, where the higher mode deals in falls caused only by fate.

That curious parallel—or homological interrogation—aside, to see *The Monk's Tale* as a projection of estate false consciousness is to see the cultural politics embodied in the fateful fables, especially and directly in the first of them, as the teller is initially and consciously characterized; and to see the *Tale* as forwarding the Monk's claims to false lordship is to see clearly just why and how it is that the Knight is interpellated as the Monk's antagonist. Daun Piers, that knightly kind of monk, is as much an estate transgressor as the ladylike Prioress, and the often-noted barely Christian character of his tales indicates that he, like her, is not aware of the role inherent to the estate in which they are located, however much they might like to be elsewhere.

The Monk's Tale

Terry Jones
St. Edmund Hall, Oxford

I'M ONE OF THAT growing band of awkward customers who don't think that *The Monk's Tale* is a complete and utter disaster. I think it hits its target right on the nose. I simply do not buy the idea that Chaucer realized he'd made a mistake in embarking on this series of "tedious and repetitive tragedies" and so has the Knight cut them short.[1] Authors don't do that sort of thing. If a writer thinks he's produced something that stinks, he doesn't get his other characters to criticize it—he simply doesn't publish it.

The fact that many modern readers have been so ready to agree with the objections to *The Monk's Tale* voiced by the Knight and the Host might be a good indicator that we are missing something—an essential perspective on the *Tale* and what Chaucer is doing in it.

The Monk's Tale Is a Reply to *The Knight's Tale*

At the end of *The Knight's Tale,* Chaucer has the Host turn to the Monk and say: "Now telleth ye, sir Monk, if that ye konne, / Somewhat to quite with the Knyghtes tale" (*MilP* 3118–19). Either you have to believe that Chaucer wrote things for no reason or you have to agree that he has deliberately set up the Monk to somehow "quit" (that is "repay" or "match") *The Knight's Tale.* Of course the drunken Miller interrupts and quits *The Knight's Tale* in his own way, but when the Monk does finally get around to telling *his* tale, the Knight appears to get rather agitated by it, and cuts him short. This in itself suggests that the Monk has indeed "quit" the Knight in some manner—and the Knight doesn't like it one bit!

[1] R. M. Lumiansky, *Of Sondry Folk: The Dramatic Principle in the* Canterbury Tales (Austin: University of Texas Press, 1955), p. 103.

The main problem, as I see it, is that most readers are convinced that the Knight is a "parfit gentil knight"—beyond criticism—and they therefore assume that his *Tale* is a noble and philosophical story that somehow probably also represents Chaucer's own point of view. This means that when the Knight breaks his own self-imposed promise—"I wol nat letten eek noon of this route; / Lat every felawe telle his tale aboute" (*KnT* 889–90)—and interrupts the Monk, most modern readers assume he does so because, like them, he finds *The Monk's Tale* boring. Of course, a lot of modern readers also find *The Knight's Tale* boring, so that's a bit of a problem in itself.

Various critics have also pointed out from time to time that *The Knight's Tale* has serious shortcomings as a philosophical statement.[2] But, for some reason, people seem to be more prepared to believe that such shortcomings are Chaucer's rather than to question their deeply held belief that the Knight is, indeed, a "parfit gentil knyght."

The Knight and *The Monk's Tale*

Since the Monk is quitting the Knight, we can't understand what *The Monk's Tale* is getting at unless we understand what *The Knight's Tale* is about—although actually it's easier to say what *The Knight's Tale* isn't about. In the first place it is not a work of deep philosophy. The Knight himself admits that he has no interest in the metaphysical. When Arcite dies, the Knight comments (*KnT* 2809–15):

> His spirit chaunged hous and wente ther,
> As I cam nevere, I kan nat tellen wher.
> Therfore I stynte; I nam no divinistre;
> Of soules fynde I nat in this registre,
> Ne me ne list thilke opinions to telle
> Of hem, though that they writen wher they dwelle.
> Arcite is coold, ther Mars his soule gye!

What's this the Knight is saying? "I am no 'theologian.' I don't find anything about souls written in my 'register' (presumably a military

[2] See, for example, Dale Underwood, "The First of the *Canterbury Tales,*" *ELH* 26 (1959): 455; Elizabeth Salter, *Chaucer: The Knight's Tale and the Clerk's Tale,* Studies in English Literature, no. 5 (London: Edward Arnold, 1962), p. 34.

"registre" including only the living). And what's more, I don't like hearing the opinions of others (presumably theologians and the like) who write about where the souls of the dead dwell." Hardly an intellectually curious mind at work! If there is any philosophy here, it's the down-to-earth philosophy of a practical soldier.

When Theseus delivers his great speech (the "First Mover" speech), the Boethian argument "does not lead to a spiritual vision but merely to the tyrant's plea, 'To maken vertu of necessittee.'"[3] In fact, *The Knight's Tale* itself is profoundly un-Boethian. Both the Knight and his hero Theseus come to the conclusion that the only ultimate good that human beings can aspire to is to die in the flower of their manhood, when they are most sure of their good name: "And certeinly a man hath moost honour / To dyen in his excellence and flour, / Whan he is siker of his goode name" (lines 3047–49). Of course, honor and fame are the things that most concern Chaucer's Knight, who has "ful ofte tyme . . . the bord bigonne / Aboven alle nacions in Pruce" (*GP* 52–53). But can one imagine anything further from what Boethius actually taught: "[I]f you really consider the infinite space of eternity, have you any reason to rejoice in the long life of your own name? . . . However long a time fame last, if it is thought of in the context of boundless eternity, it is clearly seen to be, not small, but nothing at all" (2.pr7.95–102). Theseus fails to make the crucial Boethian distinction between Fortune and Providence. He consistently twists Boethius's thought and imagery or gives us only half the picture in order to support the concept of the authoritarian state—the kind of states that were then tightening their grip in northern Italy with the aid of the mercenary free companies under soldiers of fortune like Hawkwood.

The Knight's image of the "registre" is drawn from the military reality of his day, and, indeed, *The Knight's Tale* itself is shot through with the imagery of the free companies and of their employers—the "tirauntz of Lumbardye" (*LGWP* F374). In the temple of Mars, which Theseus has built for the tournament, the Knight describes the statue of Mars in a very curious way. He says it is standing on a "carte" and at its feet is a wolf with red eyes eating a man (*KnT* 2041–48). Of course the "carte" might just mean a war-chariot, but a literal "cart" or *carroccio* was also an important part of the iconography of north Italian warfare. Geoffrey

[3] Richard Neuse, "The Knight—The First Mover in Chaucer's Human Comedy," *UTQ* 31 (1962): 305.

Trease describes the great *carroccio* of Padua as "that curious symbolic object which served the Italian states as a standard and as something more. It has been described as a sacred war-chariot. More correctly, it was a flat rectangular cart or dray, brightly painted and carrying not only the civic banner but an altar at which Mass could be celebrated. It was usually hauled by oxen. In the heat of the conflict it afforded a convenient platform from which trumpeters could transmit orders to the various commanders. Combining as it did the sentimental associations of the regimental colours with the practical importance of a battle headquarters, the *carroccio* was always stoutly defended."[4]

This association with the *carroccio* is supported by the other detail mentioned above, "A wolf ther stood biforn hym at his feet / With eyen rede, and of a man he eet" (lines 2047–48). Modern scholars follow Skeat in concluding that Chaucer was here pictorializing the derivation of the word Mars (*Mauors*) offered by Albricus Philosophus as *mares uorans* ("devouring males"). But Chaucer would have seen with his own eyes a much more relevant image when he visited the court of the despot Bernabò Visconti in 1378, for a dragon eating a man was the emblem of the Visconti family. Of course, it was in Bernabò's court that Chaucer negotiated with the most famous of all condottieri, the Englishman Sir John Hawkwood. So at the same time that he became familiar with the Visconti coat of arms, Chaucer must have been assessing the man who, more than any other, epitomized the new breed of professional soldier: the self-made military commander who had worked his way up through the ranks to achieve a position of power and—dare I say it—respectability, and yet who (since he was no aristocrat) represented the death-knell of a dying social order and with it chivalry itself.

The Knight identifies the behavior of his hero Theseus with another famous north Italian despot: the usurper Doge of Pisa, Giovanni dell' Agnello. The chronicler Matteo Villani tells us: "Never was a ruler more odious or overbearing. . . . [I]n the palace, he placed himself at the window where the people could see him, as if he were some sacred relic—swathed in a cloth of gold, and leaning on cloth of gold cushions."[5] For the Knight, however, such behavior is only to be expected of a ruler—in fact, he clearly admires it (lines 2528–31):

[4] Geoffrey Trease, *The Condottieri* (London, 1970), p. 120.
[5] Cited in ibid., p. 73.

Duc Theseus was at a wyndow set,
Arrayed right as he were a god in trone.
The people preesseth thiderward ful soone
Hym for to seen, and doon heigh reverence.

The Knight depicts Theseus as a typical Italian despot,[6] whose own whim is the only justification for his actions, and the Knight sees nothing wrong in that.

Theseus also has "many of the characteristics of the Renaissance machiavel," as Richard Neuse put it some time ago.[7] For example, when Theseus finally orders Palamon and Emelye to marry (and note that it is an order, not an invitation!), he does it not for any noble reasons or to carry out Arcite's deathbed wish but for purely political ends: to gain total domination of Thebes through the marriage and thus finish off what he had started at the beginning of the poem, when his triumph is interrupted by the weeping women.

The Knight's values, as they appear in his *Tale,* are a little hard to reconcile with the traditional image of him as the chivalrous aristocrat who has dedicated his life to fighting for Christianity. There is no dissonance, however, once you accept him as a military professional who has spent his life in the pay of despots and tyrants and whoever else will pay him—Christian or heathen; someone whose record in the service of his own king and country is not thought worth mentioning.[8]

This image of the Knight as a self-made, nonaristocratic, professional soldier who has made his way up through the ranks (like Sir John Hawkwood) also explains why the *Tale* he tells fails to retain the courtly love

[6] David Wallace, in his excellent discussion of Chaucerian polity, feels it is inaccurate to characterize Theseus as a tyrant, citing as his reason the way Theseus concedes to the demands of the weeping women at his homecoming. Although Theseus's behavior at this point does indeed appear altruistic, by the end of the *Tale* we have found out that his real motive for acquiescing to their petition is because it fits with his long-term strategy: the domination of Thebes. See David Wallace, *Chaucerian Polity: Absolutist Lineages and Associational Forms in England and Italy* (Stanford, Calif.: Stanford University Press, 1997), pp. 104–27.

[7] Neuse, "The Knight," p. 307.

[8] It can be argued that his service to Edward III is covered by the line "Ful worthy was he in his lordes werre." The "lordes" has been taken as the King of England or God. On the other hand "lordes" could be plural and refer to the war of his various lords. In any case it hardly explains why the most important triumphs of English chivlary such as Crécy (1346), Calais (1347), Poitiers (1356), and Najera (1367) should have been rushed over in a single line.

elements that permeate Boccaccio's *Teseida.* As David Wallace puts it: "Although the Knight's Tale is ostensibly a love story, it contains little of the poetry we might expect from a courtly poet of love."[9]

Perhaps the most outrageous example of this de-romanticizing of Boccaccio is the reaction of Palamon and Arcite to the sight of Emily. In Boccaccio, the two prisoners fall in love with Emily and then spend their hours comforting each other and trying their best to help their friendship through their mutual affliction. In Chaucer's Knight's version of the story, the moment Palamon and Arcite set eyes on Emily they fall to squabbling and insulting each other like a couple of ill-bred louts. The Knight unwittingly strips out the courtly voice and the romantic idealism and inserts a matter-of-fact realism that smacks of personal experience.

David Wallace tells us that Petrarch turned religion into a "tool for tyranny" both in the speeches he wrote for the Visconti and in his version of Boccaccio's Griselda story.[10] I wonder if Chaucer is also nodding toward Petrarch, who employed his talents in the service and support of despots like Bernabò Visconti, when he has his Knight turn Boethian philosophy into a tool for tyranny.

The question of tyranny—or what made the rightful ruler—was a burning political issue in Chaucer's day. Contrary to popular belief, kingship in the Middle Ages was not characterized by the concept of divine right nor even by absolute power. The king might be appointed by God but he was not above the law. It was precisely for trying to put himself above the law that Richard II was arraigned in the articles of deposition of 1399. On his travels to Italy, Chaucer would have been exposed to the argument that a rightful ruler should rule in the interests of his people, and that once he started to act solely in his own interests he became a tyrant and forfeited his right to rule. This is the concept of kingship we glimpse through Chaucer's pages.[11]

Although Richard stands accused by the chroniclers, it is Archbishop Arundel who—seven years after Chaucer's death—was defending fascism. Haranguing the Lollard William Thorpe, the Archbishop claimed that St. Paul "commanded all subjects to obey their sovereigns, even if they were vicious tyrants. If a ruler commanded a subject to do wrong,

[9] Wallace, *Chaucerian Polity,* p. 105.

[10] Ibid., pp. 262, 270, 285.

[11] For an excellent discussion of this point, see Margaret Schlauch, "Chaucer's Doctrine of Kings and Tyrants," *Speculum* 20 (1945): 133–56.

the ruler was to blame; the subject deserved praise for his obedience."[12] An argument which, I am sure, would have lifted a few hearts at Nuremburg. It is also the political philosophy that the Knight promotes in his *Tale.*

The Knight's Tale is not Chaucer's failed attempt at a courtly poem embodying the Boethian outlook. Why on earth should we imagine that Chaucer—the great translator of the *Consolatione*—might have been incapable of reproducing Boethius's ideas coherently? *The Knight's Tale* is a complex production that examines one of the most burning issues of the day: the nature of depotism and the men who serve it.

The Monk's Tale "Quits" *The Knight's Tale*

The Host asks the Monk to "quit" the Knight's *Tale,* and that is exactly what the Monk does. The Knight concluded that the only happiness human beings can hope to achieve is to win glory and fame and to die when they are at the height of their powers. The conduct he recommends is unquestioning obedience to our lords and masters. The Monk replies by telling the stories of those who have placed their trust in worldly fame and power, and who have been brought low by Fortune's wheel. His "tragedies" embody the Boethian idea that human happiness cannot be found in wealth, power, or fame, and that those who seek to find it in these things will be disappointed. Of course, the Monk doesn't get the chance to develop the positive side of Boethius's argument because the Knight interrupts him.[13]

But the Monk also has a more mischievous agenda going. He not only refuses the Knight's philosophical outlook, he brings the examples right home to the very despots the Knight has himself served under; and what is more, he lays the blame for their downfall at the door of men like the Knight.

The Modern Instances Should Go at the End

Donald K. Fry noted that it is probably the tragedy of Peter of Cyprus that provokes the Knight's interruption, for Peter is the warlord whom

[12] Peter McNiven, *Heresy and Politics in the Reign of Henry IV: The Burning of John Badby* (Woodbridge, Suffolk; Wolfeboro, N.H.: Boydell Press, 1987), p. 107.

[13] For a view of *The Monk's Tale* as Boethian, see Douglas L. Lepley, "The Monk's Boethian Tale," *ChauR* 12 (1978): 162; for the *Tale* as philosophically inadequate, see Don-

the Knight has followed into battle on at least three occasions: "The tragedies by themselves would be upsetting to the Knight, however philosophical he was, and the reference to the tragic fall of his former liege lord would bring the application to his own life to a crucial point."[14] But why, Fry asks, is there then such a long gap between the Monk's narration of the downfall of Peter of Cyprus and the Knight's outburst, some eight more tragedies and 368 lines? Fry's solution is that the Modern Instances really belong at the end. I am sure Fry is absolutely right. Common sense would put them there. Chronological order would put them there. Manuscripts (including Hengwrt and Ellesmere) put them there. In fact, Ralph Hanna argues that Hengwrt's placement of the Modern Instances at the end is evidence of its fidelity of Chaucer's text.[15]

One argument, that the line about Fortune covering "hire brighte face with a clowde" must come at the end because Harry Bailey refers to it a few lines later, assumes that Chaucer felt his audience would be incapable of retaining something said eighty-eight lines earlier. I cannot see anything to justify this. The other argument, that the Monk's reflections on the nature of tragedy provided a conclusion to the *Tale,* is a nonstarter, since it ignores the fact that the Knight interrupts the *Tale:* "Heere stynteth the Knyght the Monk of his tale" reads the headlink. The Knight couldn't have "stinted" the Monk of his *Tale* or said "goode sire, namoore of this!" if the Monk had already neatly brought his *Tale* to a conclusion with a peroration.

The Modern Instances and the Knight

The Modern Instances are all examples of the kind of rulers in whose service the Knight has spent his life. In fact, two of them are acknowledged former warlords of his. Peter of Cyprus is the very man in whose service he fought at the seige of Alexandria and at Lyeys and at Satalye. About the same time that Chaucer must have been writing *The Monk's Tale,* the French crusader and counselor of Charles V, Philippe de Mé-

ald R. Howard, *The Idea of the* Canterbury Tales (Berkeley: University of California Press, 1976), pp. 280–81.

[14] Donald K. Fry, "The Ending of the *Monk's Tale,*" *JEGP* 71 (1972): 366.

[15] See Ralph Hanna III, *Pursuing History: Middle English Manuscripts and Their Texts* (Stanford, Calif.: Stanford University Press, 1996), p. 151.

zières, attributed Peter of Cyprus's downfall to the jealously that Peter's native Cypriot knights (his "owene liges") felt toward the foreign knights and mercenaries in Peter's service.[16]

The Monk is saying the same thing: Peter, he says, did a lot of harm to many a heathen, for which his "owene liges hadde envie." Now, "envie" could here mean "jealousy" or it could mean "harm." So it could be a play on words: Peter did a lot of harm to a lot of heathens but he also did harm his own knights. And they slew him because of his "chivalrie," that is, because of his military activities or because of his large entourage of knights. According to the historian Peter Edbury, Peter of Cyprus was squandering his county's wealth in his pursuit of "chivalry": "The wars, and also Peter's costly diplomatic perambulations in western Europe, had strained the resources of his island kingdom. . . . As early as 1366 the king's counsellors had shown concern at the cost to the crown of the military expeditions. . . . Both crown and vassals were in a dilemma: the cost of the war was too great for the island's resources, yet expenditure on mercenaries and the other pre-requisites of warfare had to be maintained."[17]

The knights who killed the king were all men of old, noble families with distinguished records of service, and although their chroniclers tend to record the murder as a breakdown in personal relationships, Peter Edbury argues that the real reasons were legal and political. An ordinance issued the same day as the murder declares, among other things, that "the king is not to declare war, nor make peace, nor recruit more than a hundred men-at-arms without the vassals' agreement." Their dissatisfaction with the current military situation forced the loyal lieges to try to curb regal policy. And yet, even as they tried to do this by constitutional means, there were those who knew they would have to go further: "They no doubt feared that if they attempted to impose restraints of this type, Peter would strike back at them later. But it may be that there was a further reason why constitutional restraints would not serve. For them to work, the king would have to be isolated. But in 1369, however united in their opposition the Cypriot nobility might be, Peter could look elsewhere—in particular to the foreign knights he had

[16] N. Jorga, *Philippe de Mézières, 1327–1405, et la croisade au XIVe siècle* (Paris, 1896), p. 386, n. 5.

[17] Peter Edbury, "The Murder of King Peter I of Cyprus (1359–1369)," *Journal of Medieval History* 6 (1980): 228–29.

brought into the island—for assistance and support."[18] In other words, the foreigners, like Chaucer's Knight, in Peter's service, had upset the balance of power between king and nobility. As mercenaries were wont to do, they had begun to lend their support to a tyranny.

When the Monk attributes the death of Peter of Cyprus to the justifiable action of his "owene lieges" against the alien knights who were bleeding his country to death, he is looking directly at Chaucer's Knight (*MkT* 2393–96):

> Ful many an hethen wroghtestow ful wo,
> Of which thyne owene liges hadde envie,
> And for no thyng but for thy chivalrie
> They in thy bed han slayn thee by the morwe.

The Monk also attributes the murder of the King of Spain, Pedro the Cruel, to a mercenary—in fact the most famous mercenary of them all: Bernard Du Guesclin. He doesn't refer to Betrand by name but by his coat of arms: "The feeld of snow, with th'egle of blak therinne, / Caught with the lymrod coloured as the gleede, / He brew this cursednesse and al this synne" (lines 2383–85). Such a reference also demonstrates how familiar with these foreign mercenaries and events Chaucer could assume his audience to be. It seems fair to assume that they would have been equally aware of the unspoken background to Peter of Cyprus's demise. All these events must have been eagerly talked over and discussed from court to tavern.

The Monk is also "quitting" *The Knight's Tale* when he refers to the downfall of Bernabò Visconti, the man whom the Knight identifies with Mars, the god of war. Bernabò represented for Chaucer's contemporaries the essential modern tyrant; he was also for many years the chief employer of Sir John Hawkwood. While I do not suggest that Chaucer's Knight is supposed to be Hawkwood, I have no doubt that Chaucer's personal contact with the great English mercenary captain informs his portrait of the Knight, and that Chaucer's contemporaries would have readily identified Hawkwood and his type both in the portrait and in the Lombardian landscape of his tale telling. The Modern Instances quit *The Knight's Tale* on both a philosophical and personal level. No wonder the Knight cannot hold himself back from interrupting the Monk.

[18] Ibid., p. 230.

The Knight's Character

What the Knight actually says when he interrupts the Monk is most revealing. He says: he doesn't like hearing about the downfall of the rich and famous; he prefers stories about poor men who have worked their way up to Fame and Fortune and then stay there. What's this? This hardly sounds like the taste of an aristocrat! What noble man worth his salt would want to hear stories about poor men rising to wealth and power? That would be more the taste of a Jack Straw or a Wat Tyler—or of a self-made man like Sir John Hawkwood—a man who had risen from a taylor's boy to become a captain and general. What's more, if the Knight had been imbued with a single ounce of Boethian thought he would have known that "to climb up and wax fortunate" is not a sound basis for human happiness.

Conclusion

If the Knight is seen as the traditional "parfit gentil knyght"—an uncritical portrait of an aristocratic Christian warrior whom Chaucer genuinely admires—then *The Knight's Tale* is a disaster as a piece of storytelling, and so is *The Monk's Tale.* If, on the other hand, the portrait of the Knight is the portrait of one of the new-style military commanders, like Sir John Hawkwood, then *The Knight's Tale* becomes a more interesting poem altogether—treating as it does with the nature of tyranny and of its servants, whether military servants like Hawkwood or literary servants like Petrarch.

The Monk's Tale is a politically informed and mischievous attack on everything the Knight and his career and his *Tale* have stood for.

The Monk's Tragical "Seint Edward"

Ann W. Astell
Purdue University

FOR MY PART in this colloquium, I would like to focus on just one of the many unanswered questions concerning *The Monk's Tale:* the mention of the "lyf of Seint Edward."[1] Why does the Monk offer first to tell "a tale, or two, or three," then to say "the lyf of Seint Edward," and finally to replace or to preface that legend with the telling of "tragedies" (*MkP* 1968–71)? This is the only place in Chaucer's works where Edward is named. The name appears somewhat awkwardly as a rhyme word at the end of a line, and the choice of that saint, rather than any other, is deliberate. The rapidity with which the Monk backs off, announcing in the next line, "Or ellis, first, tragedies wol I telle" (line 1971), points to a certain rhetorical anxiety about reciting Edward's legend and raises questions about the relationship between Edward's "lyf" and the tragedies of once prosperous people ("popes, emperours, or kynges") who are "yfallen out of heigh degree" (line 1976). The forcible cutting short of the Monk's tale collection, with the consequence that the life of St. Edward is never literally told, makes the mention of it all the more suggestive.

Chaucerians have, however, paid little attention to the allusion to St. Edward. His "lyf," after all, is not the tale the Monk tells. Indeed, it is sometimes remarked that the Monk's failure to tell a saint's life—the kind of story that would, after all, be proper to him as a religious—registers yet another Chaucerian criticism of his worldliness. Andy Kelly insists similarly that the saint's legend is a comedic "upbeat genre" that stands by definition against tragedy, the Monk's genre of choice. Still others (Terry Jones among them) are inclined to regard the

[1] All quotations from Chaucer's works are from Larry D. Benson, gen. ed., *The Riverside Chaucer,* 3d ed. (Boston: Houghton Mifflin, 1987). Further citations are made parenthetically in the text.

mention of St. Edward as a passing, incidental, Chaucerian "compliment" to King Richard II.

Susan Cavanaugh notes in *The Riverside Chaucer* that "Seint Edward" is "probably Edward the Confessor (c. 1004–66), King of England," to whom "Richard II had a special devotion" (p. 929). The note correctly points us in the direction of Richard, whose "special devotion" to the Confessor amounted to a virtual identification with him. As Dillian Gordon observes, the Confessor "died on 5 January, the eve of Richard II's birthday" and Richard consciously endeavored to make his life a continuation of St. Edward's.[2]

Chaucerians need to think more seriously about the rhetorical force of an allusion to one of the king's patron saints at the heading of an unfinished *tale de casibus virorum illustrium* that includes "modern instances" of deposed and murdered rulers. Without wanting to deny in any way that "Seint Edward" refers to Edward the Confessor, I follow Roger Ellis and David Wallace in insisting that "Seint Edward" is also purposely ambiguous, in order to evoke at the same time the memory of Edward II, Richard's deposed and murdered great-grandfather, whose cause for canonization as a martyr Richard ardently supported and whose style of "governance" Richard consciously imitated, with disastrous consequences.[3]

I would argue that the mention of "Seint Edward," like references to Saint Kenelm and "King Richard" in *The Nun's Priest's Tale,* serves to key in a sustained, three-part political allegory that begins with Chaucer's *Tale of Melibee* and ends with the fable of Chauntecleer.[4] The mention of the untold "lyf of Seint Edward" is, in rhetorical terms, an *occultatio,* as well as a *praecisio,* that awakens the suspicion of veiled meaning. It helps to gloss the emphatic, ironic reference to the body—"corpus" (*MkP* 1906), "brawnes" (line 1941), "bones" (line 1941)—and to the Monk's lack of spirit and spirituality ("thou art not lyk a penant or a goost" [line

[2] Dillian Gordon, *Making and Meaning: The Wilton Diptych* (London: National Gallery Publications, 1993), p. 54. I expand on Richard II's devotion to the Confessor in chapter 4 of my *Political Allegory in Late-Medieval England* (Ithaca, N.Y.: Cornell University Press, 1998).

[3] See Roger Ellis, *Patterns of Religious Narrative in the* Canterbury Tales (Totowa, N.J.: Barnes and Noble, 1986), p. 198, n. 1; David Wallace, *Chaucerian Polity: Absolutist Lineages and Associational Forms in England and Italy* (Stanford, Calif.: Stanford University Press, 1997), p. 331.

[4] For a full development of this argument, see ch. 4 of my *Political Allegory in Late-Medieval England.* For the colloquium, I drew upon this work, which was at that time yet unpublished. I echo it now with the kind permission of Cornell University Press.

1934]) in the *Prologue* as indications that the carnal letter of his *Tale* veils an allegory. Chaucer, in other words, supplies the spiritual meaning that the Monk's person and *Tale* lack.

The assignment to the Monk of the *Tale*—whether considered literally as a collection of *de casibus* tragedies or allegorically as a Richardian life of St. Edward—becomes all the more important and appropriate when we remember how central the cult of Edward the Confessor was to the monks of Westminster Abbey, where Richard II was eventually entombed, and when we recall that the body of Edward II was entrusted to the keeping of the monks of the abbey of St. Peter in Gloucester. A body believed to be Edward's was buried there with "great pomp and circumstance on 20 December 1327," and the abbot and convent erected a magnificent tomb to the martyr, which, according to Cuttino and Lyman, "in time attracted so many pilgrims that the abbey could be transformed into the imposing cathedral it is today."[5]

Richard himself ensured the proper observances of Edward II's anniversaries at St. Peter's Abbey.[6] As early as 1385, the year of Barnabò Visconti's murder, Richard wrote to Pope Urban VI to further Edward II's cause for canonization,[7] and in 1390 he traveled to Gloucester to consult with the bishops assembled at the abbey about dispatching to the pope testimony about miracles attributed to Edward's intercession.[8] In 1395 such a "Book of Miracles" was sent to Pope Boniface IX.[9] According to Caroline Barron, "The Exchequer records bear witness to the considerable sums which Richard spent in pursuing the canonisation at the Papal Curia."[10]

Anthony Goodman is no doubt right when he declares that "Richard II regarded Edward II as a saint."[11] Richard's devotion to Edward had also a political dimension, however. Anthony Tuck voices the consensus of English historians when he points to a conscious, early decision on

[5] G. P. Cuttino and T. W. Lyman, "Where is Edward II?" *Speculum* 53 (1978): 525.

[6] Anthony Tuck, *Richard II and the English Nobility* (London: Edward Arnold, 1973), p. 71.

[7] Edouard Perroy, ed., *The Diplomatic Correspondence of Richard II,* Camden Third Series, vol. 48 (London: Royal Historical Society, 1993), letter no. 95, p. 62.

[8] *The Westminster Chronicle, 1381–1394,* ed. and trans. L. C. Hector and Barbara F. Harvey (Oxford: Clarendon Press, 1982), p. 437.

[9] Tuck, *Richard II and the English Nobility,* p. 103; Anthony Steele, *Richard II* (Cambridge: Cambridge University Press, 1962), p. 122.

[10] Caroline Barron, "Richard II," in Gordon, *Making and Meaning,* p. 18.

[11] Anthony Goodman, *The Loyal Conspiracy: The Lords Appellant under Richard II* (London: Routledge and Kegan Paul, 1971), p. 25.

Richard's part to adopt his great-grandfather's "methods of government and . . . rhetoric of political argument": "Richard's attitude to kingship in its governmental aspect bears many marks of reflection upon the reign of Edward II—his use of the chamber, its close connection with the secret seal, and his realization of the ability and administrative potential of the clerks of the chapel royal."[12] Like Edward II, Richard was repeatedly accused by his enemies of listening to bad advisors and of showing favoritism.

The association of Richard II with Edward II gained explicit expression in 1386, when the "Wonderful Parliament," citing a statute of 1310, threatened Richard by asserting its right to depose an unruly king.[13] In response, in 1387 Richard posed to Robert Tresilian and other justices a series of constitutional questions, including the proper punishment for the traitors who had recalled "that statute . . . whereby King Edward [II], son of King Edward and great-grandfather of the present king, was in time past adjudged in parliament."[14]

As Wallace suggests, Richard defended himself and his philosophy of government by enshrining the memory of Edward II as a saint and martyr.[15] Given Richard's own subsequent deposition and murder, his devotion to Edward II and his choice of him as a model seem a sadly self-fulfilling prophecy. Indeed, Richard must have been conscious early in his reign that his fate might well be a "martyrdom" like Edward's, should he insist, in theory and practice, on the royal prerogative of the king as God's anointed. His experience of the Parliaments of 1386 and 1388 confirmed him in this belief, as did the reports of assassinations abroad.

The Westminster Chronicle curiously links such a report with Richard's concern for Edward's canonization. Marginal notes on the same page record mention both of the king's "special letter to the pope" in 1385 and of the supposed murder of Barnabò Visconti, lord of Milan, in that same year: "Barnabò died in prison, but the manner of his death, whether by cold steel, by starvation, or by poison, is not known."[16] The coincidence of the notations suggests an association of Edward II, Bar-

[12] Tuck, *Richard II and the English Nobility,* p. 71.
[13] Goodman, *Loyal Conspiracy,* p. 103.
[14] *Westminster Chronicle,* p. 201.
[15] Wallace, *Chaucerian Polity,* p. 331.
[16] *Westminster Chronicle,* p. 159.

nabò, and Richard himself in the mind of the chronicler, who was himself a monk.

Chaucer's *Monk's Tale* also tells the story of the murder in prison "Off Melan grete Barnabo Viscounte" (*MkT* 2399) at the hands of his nephew and son-in-law. Like the monk of Westminster, Chaucer's Monk declares himself ignorant about why and how Barnabò was slain (line 2406). The brief, one-stanza "tragedie" of Barnabò appears in third position in a grouping of four so-called Modern Instances of lordly misfortune: those of Peter of Spain (d. 1369), Peter of Cyprus (d. 1369), Barnabò Visconti (d. 1385), and Ugolino of Pisa (d. 1289). As Susan Cavanaugh notes in *The Riverside Chaucer,* "Like the two Peters, Barnabò was a figure of special interest to Chaucer and the English court. His niece, Violanta, married Chaucer's first patron, Lionel, duke of Clarence; his daughter Caterina had been offered in marriage to Richard II; and his daughter Donnina married the English condottiere, Sir John Hawkwood" (p. 933).

All four of the Monk's recent examples were murdered. Unlike most of the other unfortunates whose downfall the Monk relates, their deaths apparently do not result from their own pride and tyrannical acts, but rather from the envy and ambition of their enemies. The Monk compares Peter of Spain, who was betrayed by his own brother, to the virtuous Roland, betrayed by Ganelon (*MkT* 2387–90). Similarly, he declares that the crusader-king, Peter of Cyprus, was killed by his lieges "for no thyng but for [his] chivalrie" (line 2395). Barnabò's murder, too, is described as an impious act committed by his "double allye" (line 2403). Finally, Ugolino's death by starvation, and that of his innocent children, results from the "fals suggestioun" raised against him by an ambitious prelate, "Roger, which that bisshop was of Pize" (lines 2416–17). The imagery of Ugolino's story contrasts the impiety of the bishop, Ugolino's spiritual father, with the piety of Ugolino's children, who offer their starving father their own flesh to eat. Unlike Dante's account, to which Chaucer explicitly refers, the Monk's tale of Ugolino assiduously avoids imputing cannibalism to him.

All four stories are "pitous" (line 2377) both in their affecting woefulness and in their evocation of pious victims and impious murderers. The first three are unusually brief. They thus focus attention on the murders and their cruelty, rather than on the tyrannical acts that may have provoked them. The fourth account, that of Ugolino, amplifies the guilt of others while suppressing Ugolino's own. The "modern instances" are, in short, told in a way that reflects Richard's parallel attempt to canonize Edward II as a martyr. Edward's greatest claim to sanctity, after all, was his death in prison at the hands of political assassins. As Wallace has remarked, the "modern instances" in Chaucer's *Monk's Tale* make it "a book of grim *Realpolitik* to put beside the book of 'miracles' ascribed to a deposed king of England."[17]

In fifteen manuscripts of *The Canterbury Tales,* including the authoritative Ellesmere manuscript, these four tragedies appear in final position in *The Monk's Tale,* whereas in twenty-nine manuscripts they appear between the tragedies of Cenobia and Nero. Donald K. Fry has argued convincingly that the final position reflects Chaucer's own revision of *The Monk's Tale* and offers a double motivation for the Knight's interruption. Not only is the Knight, as a member of the ruling estate, understandably ill at ease to hear of the "sodeyn fal" of lords who had been "in greet welthe and ese" (*NPP* 2772–73); he had a personal, historical connection with Peter of Cyprus, having fought under his command at Alexandria, Ayas, and Attalia.[18]

Like Terry Jones and Stephen Knight, I regard *The Monk's Tale* as a response to *The Knight's Tale* and as a dramatic expression of personal antagonism between the two pilgrims as members of rival estates. Behind the figure of the ill-at-ease Knight, however, I see a higher-ranking noble, King Richard himself, whose state most closely matched that of the "popes, emperours, or kynges" in the Monk's tragic-tale collection. The Knight's interruption of the Monk would have prompted Chaucer's audience to complete what the Monk had begun, to supply other "modern instances" in addition to the Monk's four, to remember Edward II, and to wonder about the fate of Richard II.

Judith Ferster has taught us that the 1352 Statute of Treasons explicitly prohibited not only "making war on the king, aiding his enemies, counterfeiting the currency, and killing high government officials" but also imagining "the death of our lord the king, or our lady his consort, or of their eldest son and heir."[19] Since such an act of the imagination was adjudged treasonous, a court poet like Chaucer who foresaw the possibility of the king's deposition, who sought to criticize his unwise

[17] Wallace, *Chaucerian Polity,* p. 331.

[18] Donald K. Fry, "The Ending of the *Monk's Tale,*" *JEGP* 71 (1972): 355–68.

[19] Judith Ferster, *Fictions of Advice: The Literature and Politics of Counsel in Late Medieval England* (Philadelphia: University of Pennsylvania Press, 1996), p. 33.

actions, and who wished to warn him about the possible consequences of his folly, virtually had to use indirect means. In Ferster's words, "if one could not safely imagine the death of one's own king, one might turn to imagining the death of someone else's."[20] *The Monk's Tale* is a collection of such imaginings.

Like Boethius, who likens himself in the *Consolation of Philosophy* to Seneca, Chaucer images himself in *The Monk's Tale* as a latter-day "Seneca the wise"—who endangers himself in the very act of instructing his king, Nero: "For he fro vices wolde hym ay chastise / Discreetly, as by word and nat by dede" (*MkT* 2515, 2505–6). Employing exempla and allegory, and thus using a "discreet" approach "by word," Chaucer endeavors similarly to teach Richard II. The comic (because happily ending) tale of Nebuchadnezzar makes it clear that even a proud king can repent, regain his wit, and experience God's "myght and grace" (line 2182). The tragedy of Balthasar "provides an instance of a son who fails to learn from his father's example of conversion and humility": "He by his fader koude noght be war, / For proud he was of herte and of array" (lines 2185–86). Richard II learned many lessons from his "fader," Edward II, but (as Chaucer suggests) they were the wrong ones. He too "koude by his fader noght be war."

Edward II was deposed and assassinated, and Richard II consciously chose him, alongside St. Edward the Confessor, as his model in statecraft and sanctity. Against this historical background, it is not surprising that the life of a saint and the tragedies of kings are not unrelated topics for Chaucer's Monk.[21] The relationship between them has, however, been too little recognized by Chaucerians, and it has, I believe, enormous significance not only for how we read *The Monk's Tale* but also for our understanding of Chaucer as a Ricardian poet. Chaucer was ready to convey a political allegory through the persona of a Monk, the archetypal representative of scriptural exegesis, and he was prepared to address Richard himself in this occult way, holding up a warning mirror to the king's own "lyf."

[20] Ibid., p. 38.

[21] For an instructive reminder that "monks routinely buried their noble patrons," see Constance Brittain Bouchard, *Strong of Body, Brave and Noble: Chivalry and Society in Medieval France* (Ithaca, N.Y.: Cornell University Press, 1998), pp. 159–71, esp. p. 165.

The Evolution of *The Monk's Tale:* Tragical to Farcical

Henry Angsar Kelly
University of California, Los Angeles

I FIND *THE MONK'S TALE* extraordinarily important for two reasons: it constitutes Chaucer's resurrection of the genre of tragedy, and it shows him revising and rearranging his material in more detail than anywhere else in *The Canterbury Tales* or his other works.

Before I turn to these subjects, let me address a question that I was originally asked to consider in this symposium: whether the Monk or his *Tale* engenders a tragic view of life, as opposed to the Christian comic view. My initial response is that this is a modern query begging several questions that I do not grant. It supposes that the ancients agreed on a fatalistic idea of tragedy; and that this is "our" idea of tragedy; and that tragedy in this sense is negated by the Christian doctrine of salvation (though it would seem to fit pretty well with the idea of predestined damnation!). Rather than imposing our views of "the tragic" upon Chaucer, let us first inquire into Chaucer's own ideas of tragedy and then, following the generally accepted working hypothesis that he wrote the tragedies first and only later assigned them to the Monk,[1] ask what his motivations were in making the assignment and what effect it had on the character of the Monk.

I. Chaucer's Discovery of Tragedy

Chaucer's series of minibiographies in its original form (following the above hypothesis) was not only the English author's first experiment in

[1] See, for instance, Manly and Rickert, speaking of the finished appearance of the Croesus tragedy: "This is a definite proof that MkT was not originally composed for CT and is one of the numerous instances of Chaucer's use of older material with little or no adaptation to its new use"; John M. Manly and Edith Rickert, eds., *The Text of* The Canterbury Tales, 8 vols. (Chicago: University of Chicago Press, 1940), 2:410.

writing tragedy, it was the first attempt at writing tragedies by any author in any European vernacular since Latin stopped being a vernacular. For even though Dante in *De vulgari eloquentia* classified his love lyrics as tragedies (according to his peculiar definition of tragedy: a work that dealt with the highest kind of subject and used the best form and diction), this was a retrofitting: he did not write them as tragedies. He also retrofitted the poems of his colleagues and contemporaries as tragedies.[2]

Chaucer performed a similar retrofitting on the case-histories of Boccaccio's *De casibus virorum illustrium.* Because of a widespread and longstanding assumption that Chaucer got the idea of writing tragedies from the Italian author's Latin prose exempla, I cannot stress this point too much. Boccaccio did not call his cautionary tales *tragedies,* and he did not consider them to be tragedies—and neither did anyone else apart from Chaucer, until Lydgate got the idea from Chaucer and did a systematic conversion of the entire *De casibus* into a series of tragedies.[3]

Boccaccio considered tragedy, like comedy, to be a form practiced by the ancients, consisting exclusively of the dialogue of characters and exemplified by Seneca (and, for comedy, Terence and Plautus). Chaucer, in contrast, considered tragedy to be a narrative genre that was not limited to past eras. He got his idea of tragedy from Fortune's characterization in Boethius: tragedies are tearful histories of happy kingdoms overthrown by unexpected misfortunes. He was also indirectly influenced by the definition of William of Conches, taken over by Nicholas Trevet, who characterized tragedy as a writing or poem of great iniquities beginning in prosperity and ending in adversity. But Chaucer was directly exposed to a Boethianized version of this definition, which he found in his glossed copy of the *Consolation* and translated verbatim. This modified definition eliminated the idea, deriving from Isidore of Seville, that tragedy dealt exclusively with wicked protagonists, and thus opened it to everyone—not only those who deserved to come to grief but also blameless persons who suffered disasters, like Boethius himself.

I should note here that Alastair Minnis contests my notion that Chaucer obtained his gloss on tragedy from his own lightly glossed Latin text

[2] For details, see my *Tragedy and Comedy from Dante to Pseudo-Dante* (Berkeley: University of California Press, 1989), pp. 2–4, and *Ideas and Forms of Tragedy from Aristotle to the Middle Ages* (Cambridge: Cambridge University Press, 1993), pp. 144–48.

[3] For Boccaccio, Chaucer, and Lydgate, see my *Chaucerian Tragedy* (Cambridge: D. S. Brewer, 1997).

of Boethius.[4] Rather, Minnis believes that Chaucer took the gloss directly from Trevet's full commentary and modified it by leaving out the "great iniquities" (*de magnis iniquitatibus*). He therefore believes that the compiler of the manuscript that John Croucher later gave to Cambridge University Library (now CUL Ii.3.21),[5] acting independently of Chaucer, made the identical selection from Trevet and the identical excision from it. Minnis writes this off as mere coincidence, as he does with a couple of other agreements of Chaucer and Croucher against Trevet. He must also consider it coincidental that Chaucer and the Croucher compiler made the identical selection of dozens of other excerpts from Trevet—unless, of course, Chaucer himself were the glossator who prepared his own copy text. I reject this latter idea as unlikely because, in my view, Chaucer was not enough of a Latinist to have performed the task. Minnis clearly thinks more highly of Chaucer's linguistic accomplishments than I do, but he does not discuss this possibility. The coincidental theory is not impossible, of course, especially since the Croucher apparatus is much fuller than Chaucer's limited selection of glosses. But it would seem preferable to fall back to Skeat's sensible view that the Latin portion of the Croucher text was a copy of Chaucer's own glossed text.

If so, we must try to explain how it came to pass that Chaucer in various places draws on parts of Trevet's commentary that are not in Croucher. One answer is indicated by Skeat (who, however, did not know about Trevet): he postulated that the Croucher manuscript was an *abridged* copy of Chaucer's copy text. In other words, the text that Chaucer used may have had more Trevet glosses in it than the Croucher scribe recorded. A second possibility is that, in addition to using his own glossed copy text, Chaucer consulted Trevet's full commentary and translated some glosses from it directly. A third possibility is that a collaborator—say, his learned friend Strode—provided Chaucer with extra

[4] See, mostly recently, A. J. Minnis, "Chaucer's Commentator: Nicholas Trevet and Boece," in his *Chaucer's Boece and the Medieval Tradition of Boethius* (Cambridge: D. S. Brewer, 1993), pp. 83–166, esp. pp. 87–89, 108, 124–25, and 134 n. 246. For my latest discussion, see *Chaucerian Tragedy,* pp. 52–57.

[5] Edmund Taite Silk, "Cambridge MS Ii.3.21 and the Relation of Chaucer's Boethius to Trevet and Jean de Meung" (Yale diss., 1930; available from UMI). Silk edits the first half of the manuscript, which contains the glossed Latin text of Boethius, with each meter or prose followed by Chaucer's translation, in appendix A, pp. 62–551(!). The gloss on tragedy in book 2 prose 2 is on p. 142 (fol. 37), and Chaucer's translation on p. 146 (fol. 38).

glosses later on (and in fact a collaborator of this sort may have produced his copy text in the first place). A fourth possibility is some combination of these three. The "bottom line" would remain the same: Chaucer had most of his glosses ready at hand in his copy text, placed there by the unknown glossator who prepared it, who drew mainly on Trevet, and who decriminalized the definition of tragedy.

If there was no tradition of "*De casibus* tragedy" for Chaucer to be influenced by, he must have arrived on his own at the conclusion that Boccaccio's series was a collection of tragedies; and Boccaccio's unintended example undoubtedly inspired him to create his own series of tragedies, to which he gave the same title, *De casibus virorum illustrium,* a rubric found in both major families of manuscripts of *The Monk's Tale.* In other words, Chaucer did not get the idea of writing tragedies from Boccaccio, but he got the idea of writing a *series* of tragedies from him. Chaucer, then, not only resurrected tragedy but also invented *De casibus* tragedy.

II. The Evolution of *The Monk's Tale*

When did Chaucer first encounter Boccaccio's work (which he seems to have thought was by Petrarch)? He could hardly have seen it on his first trip to Italy, for he was back in England by the end of April 1373, and it was only around 1373 that Boccaccio published the first version of the *De casibus.*[6] If, then, we assume that Chaucer did not see it until he was on his second trip, in 1378, we can hypothesize that he composed the bulk of his minitragedies in the early 1380s, while writing or after finishing the *Boece,* and before he set about writing his grand tragedy, *Troilus and Criseyde.*

He opened his series of tragedies by versifying his glossator's definition of tragedy and warning all men against sudden misfortunes, teaching the lessons of proper caution to prevent preventable misfortune (not trusting in blind Prosperity) and resignation when misfortune is not preventable (when Fortune decides to flee, there's no stopping her). He ended the series, after the tragedy of Croesus, by versifying Fortune's remark about the fall of happy kingdoms—here, kingdoms that are

[6] Vittorio Zaccaria, "Le due redazioni del *De casibus,*" *Studi sul Boccaccio* 10 (1977–78): 1–26. He basically finished the work by 1356, but held it back, making some modifications in 1370 or so but not releasing it until a few years later.

"proud," to rhyme with "cloud"—and repeating the warning against trusting in good fortune.

We see, then, that just as Chaucer's glossator kept him from limiting tragedy to wicked protagonists, Chaucer kept himself from adopting Boccaccio's program of trying to reform wicked princes by describing the judgments of God on historical figures. However, Chaucer must have intended his series as seriously as Boccaccio did his, and he must have added to it the same spirit even after finishing the *Troilus,* for the tragedy of Barnabò, who died in December of 1385, could only have been written in 1386 or later. The other Modern Instances were probably written together with it, and perhaps simply added at the end, for the time being, after the Croesus tragedy, where they appear in some manuscripts, including Ellesmere. Or, as Ralph Hanna suggests, they "may have been on loose sheets inserted into the archetype diversely by various scribes."[7]

When scouting around for material to give to the pilgrims he was creating for *The Canterbury Tales,* Chaucer would naturally have had his tragedies at the ready, but he does not seem to have assigned them to the Monk until late. He may first have intended the Monk to tell the story of January and May in retaliation against the Wife of Bath for her story of the lecherous monk Daun John.[8] The decision to give the tragedies to the Monk may also have come after Chaucer gave the story of Chanticleer to the Nuns' Priest,[9] and after having the Host characterize the Nuns' Priest in the Epilogue as a brawny treadfowl. The usual view is that Chaucer canceled this epilogue when he worked the same ideas into the Host's bantering exchange with the Monk in the *Prologue* to the tragedies.

We can doubtless be assured that Chaucer's original serious attitude toward the tragedies, which we postulated above, had now changed,

[7] Ralph Hanna III, "Textual Notes," in Larry D. Benson, gen. ed., *Riverside Chaucer* (Boston: Houghton Mifflin, 1987), p. 1132.

[8] The idea of the Monk as original teller of *The Merchant's Tale* is favored by Manly (1928) and Garbaty (1969–70); see Derek Pearsall, *The Canterbury Tales* (London: Allen & Unwin), 1985, p. 338 n.6. It is considered possible/probable by Robert A. Pratt, who says that *The Merchant's Tale* "was perhaps originally written for the Monk as a rejoinder to the (Shipman's) Tale originally written for the Wife of Bath, probably preceded by the first 450 lines of her Prologue"; see Pratt, ed., *The Tales of Canterbury* (Boston: Houghton Mifflin, 1974), p. 343.

[9] I place the apostrophe *after* the *s* in "Nuns"—thus making it "the Nuns' Priest" rather than "the Nun's Priest"—since I consider him to be a priest not just for the Prioress but also for the other nuns of the convent.

judging by the tone of mockery that Chaucer has the Host showing toward the Monk. A similar change of attitude can be seen in the Host himself. We must remember that he had earlier named the Monk as the pilgrim best able to match the Knight's noble *Tale,* whereas in the present encounter coarse jesting replaces his previous posture of respect. We can also discern objective changes in Chaucer's characterization of the Monk. His new look is still in keeping with the original report of him as a manly man, though he is now portrayed, admittedly through the eyes of the Host, as able to be a father as well as an abbot. But to justify the Monk as teller of the tragedies, Chaucer was forced to make him more receptive to reading than he had shown him to be originally. He converts the Monk from a bibliophobe to a solemn bibliophile, a collector, we presume, of saints' lives as well as tragedies. In addition to the seventeen tragedies that he manages to recount, he has at least another eighty-three in his cell, and he has clearly pored over them carefully without driving himself "wood" with boredom.

But we are not to think that this last-minute addiction to the rare genre of tragedy, newly excavated by Chaucer, colors the Monk's whole outlook. After all, the Monk's first suggestion is that he tell the life of St. Edward, and the *vita sancti* is a much more upbeat genre than tragedy, even when it is a question of martyrs (like St. Edward the Martyr) rather than confessors (like St. Edward the Confessor). Moreover, the Monk's avocation as a hunter and his distinctively "flashy" harness bells are retained from *The General Prologue.*

Therefore, to return to the question referred to above, about whether the Monk has "a tragic view of life," now that we have qualified it in terms of Chaucer's view of tragedy, my response is, no.

III. The Upshot of the Tragedies

There is a more detailed reaction to *The Monk's Tale* than to any other *Tale* in the whole of *The Canterbury Tales.* Chaucer's original idea was to have the Host interrupt the Monk. But then he changed his mind and wrote in a new interrupter, the Knight. And if Chaucer had ever deliberately placed the Modern Instances at the end of the series, he now moved them into the interior in order to have the Croesus tragedy last, for the Host's new comments are a direct take-off from the last stanza, which deals with Croesus. When Chaucer has the Monk in his Prologue apologize for not telling his tragedies in chronological order, he is probably referring primarily to the intrusion of the four recent protagonists into the midst of the victims of ancient misfortunes.

In the first version of the Epilogue to *The Monk's Tale*—to which we can supply the rubric "Heere stynteth the Hoste the Monk of his tale"—the Host's reason for interrupting the Monk was similar to his reason for interrupting Chaucer's *Tale of Thopas:* the tale teller was not doing a good job. Specifically, the Monk's stories were boring. But the Knight's reason for interrupting is quite different; it is not because the tragedies have not held his attention, but rather because they have fulfilled their goal too well and have made him depressed. He prefers, at least in the context of travel entertainment, the pattern of comedy—that is, the unfunny medieval kind of comedy—with misfortune at the beginning and good fortune at the end. That is the way the Knight's own *Tale* works.

Then the Host weighs in with his original opinion, and he adds another reason: it does no good to cry over spilt milk. This, of course, is to deny the Monk's premise: seeing others' spilt milk may help us keep our own milk unspilt. But then the Host affirms that he too could appreciate tragedies if they were better told. In point of fact, the Host is moved by the tragic story of Virginia, though most modern readers do not find it well reported. However, what the Host wants now from the Monk is humor, which he is unwilling to supply.

We deduced above that Chaucer had come to see his experiment in writing brief tragedies in a less solemn light than he presumably began with. Perhaps it was because he had come to agree with the Host that they were badly told, and he may also have agreed that it was a good idea at times to leaven heaviness with mirth. One of the most striking things that he did in transforming Boccaccio's *Filostrato* into the tragedy of *Troilus and Criseyde* was to add a hefty dose of humor in the person of Pandarus. On the other hand, he may have thought that comedy did not require laughter to be mingled with the rejoicing that eventually ends the action. At any rate, for whatever reason or set of reasons, he removed the pervasive humor from Boccaccio's *Teseida* in transforming it into *Palamon and Emily* (the early version of *The Knight's Tale*), which he would have considered a comedy. As for *The Monk's Tale,* Chaucer kept the original tragedies as they were, but sandwiched them between a humorous prologue and humorous epilogue and capped the lot with a humorous beast-fable, *The Nuns' Priest's Tale.* Perhaps, then, it is not too far-fetched to look upon the story of Chanticleer, Partlet, and Daun Russell as corresponding to the satyr play that traditionally ended trilogies of tragedies in ancient Greece. This would be a way of reconciling the seriousness of the tragedies, which Chaucer reinstated with the Knight's rationale for stopping them, with the farcical aftermath.

They Had Their World as in Their Time: The Monk's "Little Narratives"

Richard Neuse
University of Rhode Island

[Julian Schnabel's paintings of the female Christ and the black St. Francis] exhibit careful attention to cultural history while interrogating—politically and ethically—the traditional representations of heroic sacrifice. . . . It is not simply a matter of at last dignifying suffering women and poor blacks, but of decentering classical patriarchy in some of its most moving moments. . . . The doubleness and ambivalence of postmodern pastiche—simultaneously set in and against cultural history—regularly tilts toward social criticism. The politics here is neither neoconservative nor revolutionary, but nearer to anarchistic.
—Vincent Leitch, *Postmodernism—Local Effects, Global Flows*

LIKE BOCCACCIO'S *De casibus virorum illustrium,* from which it takes its (sub)title, *The Monk's Tale* is a somewhat disconcerting mixture of a kind of world chronicle and literary fiction. In his *Prologue,* the Monk leaves it an open question whether his primary concern is with his *Tale* as fiction—in this case, tragedy, which he, in a manner of speaking, is the first to introduce into English literature[1]—or with history. He begins with a definition (of sorts) of tragedy and follows that with an apologia for his ignorance of history in case he "by ordre telle nat thise thynges, / Be it of popes, emperours, or kynges" (*MkP* 1985–86). Commentators have usually taken this profession of ignorance at face value, partly because of their unsympathetic view of the Monk as, in Renate Haas's phrase, a "sham humanist,"[2] and partly because there are indeed manifest violations of chronological order in the arrangement of the *Tale*'s tragedies. Two further possibilities in this connection have not

[1] See Renate Haas, "Chaucer's *Monk's Tale:* An Ingenious Criticism of Early Humanist Conceptions of Tragedy," *Humanistica Loviniensa* 36 (1987): 44–70. In all probability, Chaucer "was the first to experiment with tragedy in the vernacular" (p. 44).
[2] Ibid., p. 67.

been raised, so far as I am aware. The first is that the apologia is a mere humility formula not meant literally, such as we get a number of times at the beginning of tales.[3] The second possibility, for which I shall argue here, is that the Monk deliberately violates chronological order as part of his agenda of breaking with the "grand narratives" of biblical-Christian history writing framed by Creation, Incarnation, and Apocalypse.

What I am proposing, in other words, is that the Monk is not to be seen as a frivolous character or a fraud but as a serious-minded humanist with a bent toward postmodernism[4] *avant la lettre.* His *Tale,* I suggest, is one in which the distinction between literary fiction and history is tacitly elided and traditional ideas of historiography are subverted in a number of ways. It might be objected that to apply the term *postmodernism* to a fourteenth-century text is an anachronism, but as used by Lyotard and others, *postmodernism* stands precisely for "anachronism" in a literal sense: a break with the idea of time and history as one thing after another, a diachronic series or progression. Instead, postmodernism posits a historiography of unique and hence discontinuous events, involving a doubling of time, that of the past and that of the present of representation/narration.

The Monk's Tale has some of the appearance of a traditional world chronicle, but the tragedies in terms of which it is presented quickly put the lie to any such appearance. It begins with the fall (*casus*) of Lucifer, followed by that of Adam, and takes the reader all the way to present times. Yet even if the so-called Modern Instances are placed at the end of the *Tale* (as they are in some MSS), there is, as already observed, no real chronological order in the arrangement of the *casus,* and these display such a variety of frequently contradictory historical paradigms as to undermine any notion of a coherent historiographic perspective or intent. The façade of a universal history dissolves, and *The Monk's Tale*

[3] A familiar example is the Franklin's elaborate apologia for his "rude speche" (lines 716–28). There are also "Chaucer's" notorious apologias, as when he asks forgiveness for not setting "folk in hir degree" in *The General Prologue* (lines 743–46).

[4] I am avoiding the use of quotation marks, but will just be drawing on a couple of notions of postmodern theory and make no pretense at claiming any more than these for the Monk's intellectual stance. My principal sources here are Jean-Francois Lyotard, *The Postmodern Condition,* trans. G. Bennington and B. Massumi (Manchester: Manchester University Press, 1984); *The Lyotard Reader,* ed. Andrew Benjamin (Oxford: Basil Blackwell, 1989); Bill Readings, *Introducing Lyotard: Art & Politics* (London and New York: Routledge, 1991); and *Postmodernism Across the Ages: Essays for a Postmodernity That Wasn't Born Yesterday,* ed. Bill Readings and Bennet Schaber (Syracuse: Syracuse University Press, 1993).

reveals itself as a series of "little narratives," Lyotard's well-known phrase for what he regards as the only viable form of history writing: narratives that in their respect for the irreducible diversity of the world's cultures refuse subordination to an overarching or dominant metahistorical paradigm.

The view of *The Monk's Tale* as postmodernist fits rather well with his earlier unabashed defense of his way of life—of which the reader gets only snippets in *The General Prologue*—in which he bluntly tells "Chaucer" of his indifference to the old monastic rules and aligns himself with a "newe world" no longer bound by various traditional preconceptions. In this world the figures of the past, like the founding fathers of monasticism, no longer command automatic authority and indeed may fade into a kind of obsolescence. Such, at any rate, appears to be the sense of our pilgrim: "This ilke Monk leet olde thynges pace, / And *heeld after the newe world the space*" (lines 175–76; emphasis added). Accordingly, when a little later in the same conversation he poses the question "How shal the world be served?" (line 187), we must assume that he has a very different understanding of "the world" from that of his predecessors and more orthodox contemporaries. The point of difference appears most clearly, perhaps, if we juxtapose the Monk's question with the church's traditional "How shall the world be saved?" To serve the world means that it is a kind of master to whom human beings are obligated, or that it is constituted as a collective enterprise that depends on people's active concern and participation. In either case, human beings are an integral part of the world, whereas in the perspective of the church they ultimately do not belong to a world that needs to be saved. The world of Christian eschatology, furthermore, being "fallen," is essentially unitary and homogeneous (however flawed), whereas the Monk's is historically conditioned and always shared with others, whether a group, community, or society. At times, indeed, it looks as though "the world" has become altogether subjective, a character's private domain, as when the Wife of Bath recalls with a sense of triumph "That I have had my world as in my tyme" (*WBP* 473). But of all the pilgrims to Canterbury, the Wife most assuredly incarnates the spirit of fellowship, the Chaucerian term that to my mind comes closest to the idea of an originary sharing of the world.[5]

[5] The phrase is taken from Jean-Luc Nancy, *The Inoperative Community,* ed. Peter Connor, trans. Peter Connor et al. (Minneapolis and Oxford: University of Minnesota Press,

At times the Monk's tragedies feature protagonists whose hubris leads them to the belief that they can impose themselves on the world in absolute terms. Such seems to be the case with Hercules setting up the limits of his—or Trophee's?—(idea of the) world: "At bothe the worldes endes, seith Trophee, / In stide of boundes he a pileer sette" (*MkT* 2117–18). And it may apply to the protagonists of the first two tragedies, Lucifer and Adam, starkly solitary figures who appear to have no others to share the world with but are nonetheless cast down by a mysterious Other that may also prove to be the Self. As an angel not vulnerable to Fortune, the Monk acknowledges, Lucifer is not really an appropriate beginning for his tragedies, and his seemingly unmotivated "fall" looks like a descent into a psychic duality (lines 2002–6):

> From heigh degree yet fel he for his synne
> Doun into helle, where he yet is inne.
> O Lucifer, brightest of angels alle,
> Now artow Sathanas, that mayst nat twynne
> Out of miserie, in which that thou art falle.

Adam, created by "Goddes owene fynger" (line 2008) rather than "bigeten of mannes sperme unclene" (line 2009), has a similar fall. He "welte al paradys savynge o tree. / Hadde never worldly man so heigh degree" (lines 2010–11). But then, because of an unspecified "mysgovernaunce," he "Was dryven out of hys hye prosperitee / To labour, and to helle, and to meschaunce" (lines 2012–14).

The first two *casus* might well lead the reader to expect that the Christian master narrative will in fact dominate *The Monk's Tale:* a mankind always already fallen, the human psyche marked from the outset by a conflicted duality. And this expectation might be reinforced by the Monk's opening statement that he is dealing with tragedy, defined as "a certeyn storie, / . . . Of hym that stood in greet properitee, / And is yfallen out of heigh degree / Into myserie, and endeth wrecchedly" (*MkP* 1973–77). However, it is precisely the idea of a tragic fiction that allows the Monk to focus on a particular figure in isolation from any larger historical context and without reference to any presumed telos of history. His narrative, furthermore, treats each figure with an empathy that

1991), p. 103. I am indebted to Nancy's illuminating discussion of the shared world (Heidegger's *Mitwelt*).

in true postmodernist fashion confronts the reader with the question, By what criteria shall we judge past historical agents and events?

Contrary to what has at times been argued, then, the Monk's resort to tragedy does not imply a fixed narrative pattern. To be sure, there is the recurrent fall (*casus*) of the central characters, and the Monk stresses his concern with them from the start: "I wol *biwaille* in manere of tragedie / The harm of hem that stoode in heigh degree" (*MkT* 1991–92). Even disregarding the fact that, as I have already indicated, the causes, nature, and consequences of that fall vary widely from one story to another, it would be a mistake to regard the Monk's introductory formula as definitive for each of the stories, since they range in tone and manner from elegiac or tragic to ironic and satiric, the satire frequently being aimed at the chief metanarrative of the Monk's time. The intrusion of Fortune into the story of Lucifer, indeed, serves notice from the outset that the Monk intends to undermine any suggestion of such a narrative. Aside from being at odds with a providential view of history (pace Boethius), Fortune serves the Monk as the great indeterminacy principle in his historical discourse, capable of standing for any number of explanatory schemes or none at all. At times, for example, Fortune seems to be identified with the will of the populace, as in "Nero," where she decides she no longer wants to "cherice" the emperor's pride (line 2520), whereupon the people rise up against him because of his wickedness (lines 2535 ff.). In this same scene there is a kind of Boethian joke when Fortune, communing with herself, twice swears "By God!" (lines 2522, 2525), suggesting a category contamination that actually is to be found much earlier, in "Balthasar." There, in the final stanza, the Monk credits Fortune with taking away a man's kingdom and wealth when she decides to forsake him, and in doing so tacitly identifies her with the God of Daniel *and* with a totally amoral international power-politics: when Belshazzar is slain, "Darius occupieth his degree, / Though he therto hadde neither right ne lawe" (lines 2237–38).

With her wildly contradictory and contaminating identifications—at times Fortune even appears to act in accord with the moral law—this slippery figure seems a perfect emblem of the Monk's brief narratives. As a forever elusive force (or set of forces) in human affairs, it protects the narrative from being absorbed into a pre- or early-modern metanarrative. And as a personified narrative agent it thwarts ambitious characters like Samson, Caesar, Alexander, and Croesus in their drive to arrange the world in accordance with their ideas or desires. Here, then,

Fortune functions as the supreme force guarding against the establishment of a single "world order" and preserving multiplicity and singularity.

This last point may be unconnected with another of Fortune's roles as "the return of the repressed." In the story of Adam's fall, Eve is conspicuously absent, which may imply that he is to be held responsible for something that by misogynist tradition she is usually blamed for. It may also foreshadow, however, a scandal of (male) historiography, namely, its refusal to grant women historical agency. This routine repression, a frequent target of Boccaccio's satire in *De casibus virorum illustrium* and *De mulieribus claris,* may be seen as the cause of the text at various times turning in on itself in the form of a seductive, fickle, and malicious figure as the prime mover of the narrative.

The two stories following "Lucifer" and "Adam" illustrate the point with emphatic irony, dealing as they do with the hypermasculine heroes Samson and Hercules. Both of these men rely on their physical prowess to realize their ambitions—one to be as "almyghty" as God in his world (see lines 2023 and 2052, as well as line 2017: "to God Almyghty consecrat"), the other to rid the world of monsters and in so doing presumably make it safe for Greek civilization.

For all their manliness, both are eventually done in by their respective "lemmans," a term possibly appropriate to Dalida, but scarcely to Dianira, Hercules' (second) wife. In any case, neither "lemman" is accorded more than a strictly subordinate role in the story. Beyond being named, Dalida has no identity except to demonstrate Samson's inability to keep a secret from his "wyves" (a point reiterated three times), and she is reduced to a generic wife in the *Tale*'s concluding "moral," "That no men telle hir conseil til hir wyves" (line 2092). At first glance, Dianira fares somewhat better than Dalida when the Monk alleges disagreement among "thise clerkes" regarding Dianira's culpability for the death of Hercules. "[S]omme clerkes," he says, "hire excusen / By oon that highte Nessus" (lines 2127–28), and he chivalrously sides with them: "Be as be may, I wol hire noght accusen" (line 2129). However, it is soon evident that Dianira as an agent in the story is not the issue; she is, rather, a mere cypher in the Monk's elaborate ironic joke whereby a legend is treated as sober history over the details of which historians ("clerkes") engage in controversy (one reason, presumably, for its obvious pairing with "Sampson"). Having thus repressed Dianira's agency in Hercules' death—we are given no hint of her motives or feelings; in other words, she doesn't really count—the Monk is suddenly confronted by a woman truly dangerous to mankind (lines 2139–42):

> Ful wys is he that kan hymselven knowe!
> Beth war, for whan that Fortune list to glose,
> Thanne wayteth she her man to overthrowe
> By swich a wey as he wolde leest suppose.

The Monk *may* even be startled by his own narrative here. However, though like Sampson and Hercules he is "a manly man," there are signs that he is quite aware of the "gender issue" in the narration of history. One of the signs is the story of Zenobia, an apparent interloper among the famous men featured in his tales. (There are several such interlopers among Boccaccio's *viri illustres;* for reasons I won't discuss here, there are no reverse interlopers among his famous women.) An obvious reason for Zenobia's inclusion is that she subverts traditional gender stereotypes by the fact that she equals or beats men at every game they might care to mention: sexual (Augustinian) puritanism; hunting and killing lions, leopards, bears (as opposed to the Monk's "prikying and . . . huntyng for the hare" [*GP* 191]); command of "sondry tongues," despite her dedication to hunting(!); book learning; devotion to virtue; prowess in military matters. This last feature finally leads to her downfall, however. By insisting on challenging the male establishment in the form of the Roman empire, she at length meets defeat at the hands of the emperor Aurelian. The conclusion is especially dispiriting, because the one figure who appeared destined to bridge the gender divide is reduced, by Rome and all it stands for, to the marginal status of—a woman! And to make matters even worse, by way of syntactic-pronominal (con)fusion, Zenobia is identified with Fortune, so that it looks as though an eternally masculinist Rome has won out over its last female nemesis (lines 2367–74; italics mine):

> Allas, Fortune! *She that whilom was*
> *Dredeful to kunges and to emperoures,*
> Now gaureth al the peple on hire, allas!
> And she that helmed was in starke stoures
> And wan by force townes stronge and toures,

Shal on hir heed now were a vitremyte;
And she that bar the ceptre ful of floures
Shal bere a distaf, hire cost for to quyte.

This triumph is of course illusory. Even the Roman empire is, after all, not the whole world, as its radically diminished and altered status in Chaucer's lifetime would make all too evident.

There is, finally, another female figure, at the very end of *The Monk's Tale* (in the usual ordering of the tales, at least), who is endowed with agency. I am referring to Phania, Croesus's daughter, who expounds her father's dream and in so doing recalls the prophet Daniel's role in "Nabugadonosor" and "Balthasar." By implication she also assumes the mantle of Danielic authority in a paradoxical way, to be sure, but one perfectly suited to what would seem to be the Monk's outlook. Croesus's dream of being on a tree where Juniper washes him and Phoebus brings him a towel to dry him with, Phania interprets in a thoroughly demythologizing way, as signifying that he will be hanged on a gallows where snow and rain will wash him and the sun will dry him. Here, then, is a final unexpected turn in the Monk's polymorphous brief narratives: a woman debunking men's pretensions to supernatural assistance and authority.

The Monk's little narratives, then, do more than subvert the grand narrative of Christian history. They also effectively cancel the grand narrative of fourteenth-century European society with its hierarchy of social classes and its subordination of women at every level. And in this respect they anticipate what is accomplished by *The Canterbury Tales* as a whole, whose pilgrimage-cum-tale-telling subtends an ideal of fellowship, as my earlier comments about the Wife of Bath suggest, in which all participate as equals.[6] As with the Monk's stories, none of the pilgrim's *Tales* is designed to dominate the others, no matter what the Host's idea of a tale-telling *contest!* Instead, the game gives voice, at least potentially, to *all* members of the pilgrimage and allows each an equal attention, without any prejudgment with respect to social, literary, or other considerations.

The Monk's Tale may continue to occupy the despised margins of *The*

[6] This fellowship would correspond to the liminal community that the Turners posit as the creation of pilgrimage. See Victor and Edith Turner, *Image and Pilgrimage in Christian Culture: Anthropological Perspectives* (New York: Columbia University Press, 1978).

Canterbury Tales as an "experiment" that didn't quite come off. For all that, however, it seems to me rather more central to the poetics of *The Canterbury Tales* than its deferred, interrupted, and so apparently marginal status might lead one to expect. As a series of tales, it already mirrors the larger poem; but more important, it is the tales' postmodern refusal of a thematic unity, as I have argued,[7] that parallels them to the other pilgrims' *Tales* on the road to Canterbury. Though the framework of *The Canterbury Tales* suggests that the poem as a whole is structured by the master trope of pilgrimage, there has yet to appear a convincing demonstration of this or any other trope as the principle that organizes the individual *Tales* in a thematic (or other) progression. Obviously this is not to deny all kinds of intertextual links among the *Tales*—any more than among the Monk's little narratives—but equally obviously these never signify the erasure of differences. To the contrary, the intertextual links always serve to underscore points of opposition, of divergence in ideological or other perspective. In short, each of the Canterbury *Tales* remains a unique event unassimilable to the others, in what might be called Chaucer's postmodernist epic.

[7] And has recently been argued again in a fine article by Emily Jensen, "'Winkers' and 'Janglers': Teller/Listener/Reader Response in *The Monk's Tale,* the Link, and *The Nun's Priest's Tale,*" *ChauR* 32 (1997): 183–95. Of course Jensen does not use the label "postmodern" in reference to *The Monk's Tale.*

RESPONSES

Responding to the Monk

Helen Cooper
University College, Oxford

If *The Monk's Tale* has been thought to be devoid of critical interest, the five papers collected here should show the error of that assumption. Between them they offer a remarkable range of lines of access to the *Tale:* the social or socialist, in Stephen Knight's analysis of false class consciousness; the reflection of history, in Terry Jones's calling on the Monk as evidence for his attack on the mercenary Knight; the political, as Ann Astell extends the *Tale*'s concern with history from the sources of its narratives to its possible target, whom she identifies as Richard II himself; the generic, as H. A. Kelly reminds us of the revolutionary significance of Chaucer's calling the narratives "tragedies"; the postmodern, as Richard Neuse connects the methods of narration with a decentering of an apparently dominant patriarchal structure.

What is refreshing about all of them is the extent to which the old agendas have been rethought or replaced. Inward-looking questions about Chaucerian irony or the psychology of the teller are superseded by considerations of larger contexts; and the possibility of its being a deliberately bad tale is decisively scotched by Terry Jones in his first paragraph. As he says, authors don't do that sort of thing. When Chaucer wants to write bad verse, he writes *Sir Thopas,* a virtuoso performance in the truly awful, assigned to himself, that is matched by little beside Shakespeare's "Pyramus and Thisbe."

So what is Chaucer doing? Five different answers are offered here, and they can't all be right: which is to say that although each of them shows how its own approach can be valid, some of them contradict each other in ways that cannot be reconciled. If the aptly named Stephen Knight is right that the Knight is a "true lord" who puts down the Monk's false claims, Terry Jones cannot also be right that the Knight is an upstart parvenu whose tenuous social and moral position the Monk is out to reveal. (One can imagine a work in which both characters would be arguing against the other; but since such issues never get any explicit mention whatsoever in the text as it stands, that work is not *The Canterbury Tales* as Chaucer wrote it.) Uncertainties about the evolution of the text (early or late composition? the "modern instances" in the middle or at the end?) allow critics to select the hypothesis that suits their own argument, and use their argument to bolster the hypothesis. The reference to *Palamon and Arcite* in the *Prologue* to *The Legend of Good Women* indicates that *The Knight's Tale* had an existence before the Knight was ever invented (so inviting a complication of Jones's indictment of its teller); by contrast, there is no *direct* evidence for what H. A. Kelly describes the "generally accepted working hypothesis" that the series of tragedies preexisted the Monk. Arguments to that effect were based on the inclusion of the falls of men who died in 1385–86, and who seem, in view of the way their stories float around the manuscripts, to have been added as an afterthought, so pushing the bulk of the *Tale* back earlier. The further reasoning behind the hypothesis lay in the belief that *The Monk's Tale* was bad poetry; it therefore had to be excused as an immature work that Chaucer outgrew, and which, rather than discarding, he gave to an inadequate pilgrim. This forum challenges such assessments at their root by taking *The Monk's Tale* seriously.

The contributors differ, however, in the degree of dependence they assume for the *Tale* on the larger framework of *The Canterbury Tales.* For Jones and Knight, the Monk and the Knight are inseparable. For Neuse, the discontinuity of the tragedies epitomizes the resistance offered by the whole *Canterbury Tales* to the grand narrative of Christian history. For Astell, they belong to the storytelling series only contingently: their primary context is in contemporary politics, and their placing in the *Tales* links them in with other texts that similarly look to the historical world beyond the fiction. For Kelly, the Monk is decidedly subordinate to Chaucer, and the tragedies should be regarded in the longer story of literary and generic history. One wonders, however, how the series of tragedies would have looked as an independent work without the storytelling framework. Chaucer wrote one other single-topic story collection, *The Legend of Good Women,* but there he gave himself space to develop each history; *The Monk's Tale* reads like a male version of the

Legend in fast-forward, with the wheel of Fortune revolving at maximum speed.

The Monk's Tale was taken seriously enough in the fifteenth century to be twice copied independently of the pilgrimage frame, but both manuscripts provide an alternative context for it by placing it alongside Lydgate's *Fall of Princes.* Lydgate was himself, of course, a monk, and he was just as conscious of following in Chaucer's footsteps when he turned to *de casibus* tragedy as when he wrote himself into his supplement to *The Canterbury Tales* to offer his own alternative Monk's Tale, the *Siege* (or more properly, as James Simpson has recently shown, the *Destruction*) *of Thebes.*[1] This recounts the events leading up to the queens' plea to Theseus at the opening of *The Knight's Tale.* Like the *Fall of Princes,* it is a story of unmitigated disaster; and it might therefore be thought to correct what is often seen as the Knight's excessive optimism. But the point of *The Knight's Tale* is rather that it recognizes that the world contains both joy and misery, that Palamon's marriage can happen alongside, or even because of, Arcite's death. It is the most comprehensive tale of any in the Canterbury sequence, with none of the metaphysical simplification of *The Monk's Tale.* Even its Boethianism is deeply and consciously problematic, just as Chaucer subjected the *Consolation of Philosophy* to critical inquiry in *Troilus and Criseyde.* The metaphysic that the Monk offers more or less corresponds to the prisoner's view that everything is the fault of Fortune (only without even his concern over the resulting absence of Providence); and that cannot be enough.

The idea of Fortune was, however, compelling, as its treatment elsewhere shows. Lydgate's *Fall* was widely read, in manuscript and in several printed editions, and universally admired until the mid-sixteenth century, when it was displaced by the runaway success of its Tudor imitation, the *Mirror for Magistrates.* It is in that work that numerous Elizabethan plays were grounded—dramatic tragedies, at last, as Kelly indicates: plays that include Shakespeare's *Richard III, Richard II,* and *King Lear.* The literary afterlife of *The Monk's Tale* therefore confirms that something about it mattered very much indeed. That "something" cer-

[1] See *Lydgate's* Fall of Princes, ed. Henry Bergen, Early English Text Society, e.s. 121–24 (London: Oxford University Press, 1924–27), Prologue 246–52, for Chaucer's "ful pitous tragedies" lamenting "the fall of pryncis"; and James Simpson, "'Dysemol daies and fatal houres': Lydgate's *Destruction of Thebes* and Chaucer's *Knight's Tale,*" in *The Long Fifteenth Century: Essays for Douglas Gray,* ed. Helen Cooper and Sally Mapstone (Oxford: Clarendon Press, 1996), pp. 15–33.

tainly included the political, but the very comprehensiveness of its scope—Adam to the 1380s—makes any particular topical reading, such as Ann Astell and Terry Jones would both see, difficult to prove. The 1559 title page of the *Mirror for Magistrates* announced that it was a volume "wherein may be seen by example of other, with howe greuous plages vices are punished: and howe frayle and vnstable worldly prosperitie is founde, even of those, whom Fortune seemeth most highly to fauour." By that time, Richard II himself had become the subject of one of the tragic narratives. His appearance there might be taken as endorsing Ann Astell's argument, based on that fascinating and undercommented mention of St. Edward, that the work was designed as a comment on the king; but equally, the fact that Richard fell endorses the scattershot effect of the work, that this is what can happen to anybody and everybody in high office. The strong potential of both the *Melibee* and *The Monk's Tale* for political reference further endorses their seriousness. The fact that their sources were largely intended as all-purpose statements of political advice makes a topical application possible, even likely, but very hard to nail down (and I am not convinced that the saint's name alone would be sufficient as a reminder that Richard was hoping for the canonization of his great-grandfather, or cue any specific thoughts on the two kings' manner of government). Chaucer was prepared to offer political advice very directly to the king when he wished, as in *Lack of Steadfastness,* but he never mentions Richard as a possible reader of *The Canterbury Tales,* however appropriate these tales might be for royal consumption. The mention of St. Edward could, alternatively and perhaps more accessibly, function as a reminder of the different possibilities inherent within the office of kingship. There were two saints of that name, both pre-Conquest kings with late medieval cults, and both were exemplars of kings who put their trust in God rather than Fortune. Edward the Confessor, by far the dominant one and no doubt the one Chaucer has in mind, had also effectively functioned as the patron saint of England for some time before Richard II took up his cult.[2] He might indeed get a mention from Chaucer in order to underline the potential contemporary political relevance of the alternative tale the Monk tells; or because Chaucer was reflecting current royal fashions in

[2] For details of both saints, see David Hugh Farmer, *The Oxford Dictionary of Saints* (Oxford: Clarendon Press, 1998), pp. 123–25.

devotion, or wanted his ambitious Monk to be anxious to do so; or because, while a monk might be expected to tell a saint's life, *this* monk would never dream of telling the life of any saint who was less than a king.

The Monk is often castigated for his predilection for tales of downfall over the Christian morality contained in saints' lives, and his lack of a religious view of life is seen as Chaucerian satire. Daun John Lydgate's pagan epic is a reminder of how much else might be taken into account. One could of course argue that the *Destruction of Thebes* (and indeed the *Fall of Princes*) proves the accuracy of Chaucer's satire: real monks were just like his fictional one. On the other hand, it was largely through the monastic foundations that learning had been kept alive and furthered, and Lydgate's project—and therefore potentially also Chaucer's Monk's project—could be represented as the work of a "serious-minded humanist," as Neuse suggests (with or without the penchant for postmodernism), in a positive sense rather than with the negative, antispiritual implication that Ann Astell would perceive. The *Fall* was after all commissioned by Humphrey, duke of Gloucester, whose gift of books to the University of Oxford is commemorated in the name of the manuscripts room of the Bodleian Library.

The point of Chaucer's pilgrims, however—or at least, part of their point—is that they are not real historical individuals, but variations on types; and those types are familiar from estates satires. Whatever the Monk who tells the tragedies may be, the Monk of *The General Prologue* is not a humanist. He has more in common with Sir Bertilak than St. Benedict, being fond of hunting, good food, and fine clothes, and with views about monastic vows that are both decisively expressed and forward-looking ("newe world"—why have not the North American New Historicists yet seized on that, as a prophetic phrasing for the individual freedom to get ahead?). He is, as R. E. Kaske noted over four decades ago, living the life of a country gentleman (Stephen Knight is too dismissive when he says that Kaske was only talking about horses). If one takes the spoilsport attitude to Terry Jones's wonderfully energetic views on the Knight,[3] and regards him as one of the few unsati-

[3] A forum on the Monk is not the place to embark on an extensive argument about the Knight, but Chaucer's single-minded emphasis on the Knight as Crusader would seem to rule out any equation with Hawkwood, Bertrand du Guesclin (who was widely proposed as a Tenth Worthy), or anyone whose military career was conducted within

rized pilgrims—one of four ideal portraits, representing the three estates of fighting, prayer, and labor, with the Clerk added in for teaching and learning—then the Knight has all the humility of manner and devotion of life to God that the Monk so signally lacks, he being out to advance himself in the world both in office and in lifestyle. A similar perception of the Monk underlies Stephen Knight's paper on false class consciousness. Class and estate, however, are not strictly comparable, and what Marx or Lukacs would have made of the application of the idea of class consciousness, true or false, to a *monk* is hard to imagine; there is, I take it, more than a little mischievous irony on Knight's part in inviting us to try. Estates literature required monks to be poor, chaste, obedient, stable, and all the rest of it. But monks did not belong to the ranks of the poor; you had to be very well off, or very well patronized, if you were to enter a religious order. For every professed monk, there were at least a couple of dozen lower-ranking workers attached to the monastery who had not taken monastic vows, and could not have done so even had they wished. The monastic orders owned vast swathes of England, and their interests were in many respects to be identified with the landed aristocracy even more than with the landed gentry. Prelates and most abbots, of the kind the Monk would like to be (*GP* 167, 204), sat with the lords in Parliament, not with the knights of the shires in the Commons. If class consciousness is an issue in the *Tales,* then the concern of a monk with those at the top of Fortune's wheel may be more right than estates literature would ever allow. The quite obsessive interest in them shown by this particular monk, with his ambitions for climbing up the ecclesiastical hierarchy, would follow naturally: he would like nothing better than to be in a position high enough to fall from.

Astell, Jones, and Knight are all concerned with placing the Monk historically. Richard Neuse makes him a postmodernist, even if a "historically conditioned" postmodernist. He is entirely right to see in Chaucer attitudes and techniques for which technical terms have only

---

Christian Western Europe. I would find Jones's argument that the Knight feels personally threatened by the Monk's account of Peter of Cyprus much more persuasive if Peter were ever mentioned in connection with him; the link seems to be much too obscure to be picked up without a much clearer cue being offered. The argument that Peter's followers' "envie" of his "chivalrie" means that they were jealous of his "alien knights" also seems implausible: the sense of the verse links "chivalrie" with his success against the heathens, indicating that it was his military prowess that scared them, not his choice of followers.

recently been invented, just as the Wife of Bath (and all her sect) can be analyzed in terms drawn from feminist theory; modernism and postmodernism have provided the concepts and the vocabulary for analyzing many of Chaucer's poetic practices. Neuse's paper invites the most radical rethinking of the Monk, not because of his placing him against the postmodern rather than the medieval world, but because of the way he applies those perceptions. His insistence that the Monk's narratives "refuse subordination to an overarching or dominant metahistorical paradigm" is immensely attractive—this is the Chaucer we all want to have—but it seems to me quite peculiarly difficult to argue in the case of this particular *Tale,* with its relentless assignment to Fortune (varied randomly, but without any real sense of difference, to women and God) of every conceivable historical fall. I am not sure either that the few appearances by women such as Delilah or Deianira in the *Tales,* or even the dominant part played by the female personification of Fortune, represent "the return of the repressed"; or if they do, it is only to confirm male anxieties and encourage an even more rigorous control over women, who bring about the downfall of great men whether they are literal or allegorical (and the two are not always very clearly distinguished). I have argued elsewhere that *The Monk's Tale* is an example of the kind of story collection that Chaucer is precisely *not* writing in *The Canterbury Tales* at large: that the generic variety of those tales allows for his telling what he intends as the best romance or fabliau or miracle of the Virgin, and even, in *The Monk's Tale,* the best collection of stories of a single genre, as most story collections were.[4] Such collections, of beast fables or saints' lives or sermon exempla, were far more familiar than the wide-ranging heteroglossia of the whole *Canterbury Tales.* The Monk's mini-narratives are generically different from any of the other *Tales* in the Canterbury series; but their generic similarity to each other is relentlessly stressed, so that the fall at the hands of Fortune can appear as an imposition on material that is often resistant to such shaping, rather than a pattern seeming to emerge naturally from the content. Even the manner of the storytelling represses any alternative views. All the other *Tales,* except for the Parson's, contain a high proportion of direct speech from the characters: disagreement is built into the fabric of the narra-

[4] See *The Structure of the* Canterbury Tales (Athens: University of Georgia Press, 1984), pp. 8–55, and *Oxford Guides to Chaucer:* The Canterbury Tales, 2d ed. (Oxford: Clarendon Press, 1996), pp. 328–37.

tive. Daniel's speech on God's purposes briefly offers an alternative to Fortune; Hugelyn's infant son offers a momentary reminder of the utter lack of justice in the *Tale*'s paradigm. But those are almost the only voices apart from the Monk's own, and he never pauses to acknowledge what they are saying. The one other significant direct speech, and the last in the *Tale,* is from Croesus's daughter, and that merely ventriloquizes Fortune. The dialogic energy that informs the other *Tales* is here stripped out.

The five papers here offer a different kind of dialogics, of tale against context. There are other things to be said about its context too (the debate with Dante implied by the inclusion of the story of Ugolino is not covered here, for instance),[5] and there is still no full account of its poetics, a much more interesting topic than one might guess from the general silence. H. A. Kelly is the only participant to record the question he was asked to address: Does the Monk, or his *Tale,* engender a tragic view of life? It is a question that is distinctly anachronistic, insofar as it gives a weighting to the idea of tragedy and the tragic that is almost entirely post-Romantic. It does, however, point to two important qualities of *The Canterbury Tales.* First is that Chaucer is the first writer in English of whom a question about genre could be asked. One of the oddities of the *Tales* is the overt generic label attached to almost all of the stories in the links, in a process that first introduces into English the idea of genre as the key both to writing and to hermeneutics: a process more extraordinary even than the resurrection, or introduction, of the idea of tragedy. Second, it insists that genre is not enough. Other *Tales* have been stopped because they are displeasing in some other way; only this one is attacked because the vision imposed by its *de casibus* model is inadequate.

The Knight's Tale, which the Monk's in some sense "quites,"[6] or fails to

[5] For contrasting views, see Piero Boitani, "The *Monk's Tale:* Dante and Boccaccio," *Medium Ævum* 45 (1976): 50–69; David Wallace, "Dante in English," *The Cambridge Companion to Dante,* ed. Rachel Jacoff (Cambridge: Cambridge University Press, 1993), pp. 237–58 (237–8); Richard Neuse, *Chaucer's Dante: Allegory and Epic Theater in the* Canterbury Tales (Berkeley and Los Angeles: University of California Press, 1991), pp. 151–53; and Helen Cooper, "The Four Last Things in Dante and Chaucer: Ugolino in the House of Rumour," *New Medieval Literatures* 3 (1999): 39–66.

[6] I agree with Kelly and the sources he cites that Chaucer may have originally intended the Monk to tell the story of January and May in requital of *The Knight's Tale;* it is in many respects a closer parody than *The Miller's Tale,* and it seems likely once to have had an ecclesiastical narrator. The fact that he has the Knight interrupt the Monk

quite, is by far the most wide-ranging of all the Canterbury sequence, and it doubles a "tragedy" (Arcite's) with a "comedy" (Palamon's)—a doubling that caught Shakespeare's attention when he dramatized the tale as *The Two Noble Kinsmen.* Terry Jones is entirely right that it is deeply problematic, but I would locate the origins of the problems not in the Knight's inadequacy but in Chaucer's comprehensiveness. He gives it to the Knight, not for satirical reasons, but because it can set the standard for the *Tales* that follow; perhaps even with a final judgment of the contest in mind, in which the rank-conscious Harry Bailey will choose the top man as winner. It is therefore the very capaciousness of *The Knight's Tale,* its refusal to impose answers, that gives the Knight the right to interrupt the Monk. To say that is not to return *The Monk's Tale* solely to its fictional context, or to deny it any further influence from, or in, its real historical world. On the contrary, the effect of challenging the premises of the *The Monk's Tale* is a reminder that a determinist view of human misery is not enough: that the processes of historical event and social change require active participation and recognition regardless of one's apparent helplessness. Chaucer's ethic is the Christian ethic of individual responsibility; the Monk's is not. *The Monk's Tale,* that story collection of subjugation to capricious and overwhelming Fortune, is, if anything, too seductive, as its afterlife was to prove. The Knight, who interrupts, and the Nuns' Priest, who is instructed by the Host to follow on with something better, are two of the most intelligent people on the pilgrimage—or, to put it another way, they are the pilgrims into whose mouths Chaucer puts his most intelligent *Tales.* Both stories overflow their notional generic frames, and encompass something of the range of the whole Canterbury sequence, to insist that a single or simple view of the world or of history, of the Fall of Man or Richard II, is not enough. A single view of *The Monk's Tale* is similarly not enough; and this forum has given us plenty to think about.

---

does, however, indicate that he kept in mind some antagonistic connection between them even after assigning a different tale to the Monk and placing its telling much later.

Return to *The Monk's Tale*

L. O. Aranye Fradenburg
University of California, Santa Barbara

PRESENTED FOR A plenary panel at the New Chaucer Society conference in Paris in 1998, the papers to which this discussion responds share a common goal: rescuing *The Monk's Tale* from its critics. Terry Jones is "one of that growing band of awkward customers who don't think that *The Monk's Tale* is a complete and utter disaster"; instead, to him it provides "an essential perspective," offering "a politically informed . . . attack on everything the Knight and his career and his *Tale* have stood for." For Ann Astell, the Monk's allusion to "the lyf of Seint Edward" and the relationships suggested thereby between Edward II and Richard II, hagiography and "the tragedies of kings," are "of enormous significance not only for how we read *The Monk's Tale* but also for our understanding of Chaucer as a Ricardian poet." No longer a failure that Chaucer, for various and murky reasons, determines to use anyway, *The Monk's Tale* is now invaluable to interpretation of *The Canterbury Tales* and its historical referents.

Enormous significance and essential perspective are linked to *important* histories, just as they are in "the tragedies of kings": the life-and-death matters of Ricardian and Henrician high-end politics [for example, "The whole question of tyranny . . . was a burning political issue in Chaucer's day" (Jones)]. The meaningfulness of *The Monk's Tale* is secured by its reference to great historical matters and vice versa. Is this desire for enormous significance discordant with the anti-elitist politics expressed by so many of theses papers?

For Stephen Knight, "the themes of *The Monk's Tale* . . . are themselves a projection of lordship fantasies in the Monk." The Knight interrupts the Monk's tale telling because he wants to expose the Monk as a "bogus knight" who inappropriately desires aristocratic styles of power/enjoyment—this despite the fact that monks were often from aristocratic families. To argue his case, Knight invokes the Marxist notion of false consciousness. The Monk not only misrecognizes his social conditions but deliberately tries to arrogate others. There is no concept here of any social status being a matter of performativity; there are bogus knights, and there are real ones, who, *because* they are real, recognize misrecognition in the bogus ones. The Monk's false claim is rejected, inevitably, "by a true lord."

The Monk's interruption by the Knight (and the Host) turns into a drama of (mis)recognition that enables its assimilation to the "conflict between monastic social presumptions and traditional order" ongoing in the later fourteenth century and acted out in the rebellion of 1381. Stephen Knight puts *The Monk's Tale* in the big picture by analyzing its analysis of class consciousness; but he appeals to and, as authorial voice, seems almost to inhabit ideals of true knighthood and traditional order which themselves require scrutiny. Can the signifier be this powerful?

Steven Knight's formulation that "the Knight's dissatisfaction" has "a sociopolitical rather than a literary or moral basis" takes us back to the Marxist problematic of the relations between "substructure" and "superstructure." Most other papers in this collection likewise find allegories of the fourteenth-century socius in *The Monk's Tale.* But despite their tendency to "read for" history, these papers, including Knight's, all indicate the importance of the politics of literary form in the *Tale.*

H. A. Kelly wants to discover Chaucer's motive for assigning the tragedies to the Monk and the effect of this decision on the Monk's "character." Kelly finds nothing particularly "realpolitik" in *The Monk's Tale;* the tragedies are *tragedies,* so-called by Chaucer and therefore among the first texts to be so-named in the later Middle Ages. Kelly aestheticizes the political matter of tragedy. But his paper argues that forms have histories, or at least beginnings. He gives historical significance the form of formal innovation, extending the panel's themes of return and resuscitation by taking us back to the topic of literary creativity: "Chaucer . . . not only resurrected tragedy but also invented *de casibus* tragedy." Categories of innovation and invention are also important, in reverse, in Kelly's reading of the Monk's tragedies. As the Monk himself explains, for tragic misfortune "ther nas no remedye." Action, virtuous or otherwise, is no longer relevant. In this Chaucer was inspired, Kelly argues, by glosses on the *Consolation of Philosophy* that "decriminalized the definition of tragedy." Tragedy is about the fact that bad things can happen to all people, good or bad. Moreover, Kelly's conclusion takes meaning and its vicissitudes back to the level of his own critical project: he indicates his interest in "reconciling the seriousness of the tragedies . . . with [their] farcical aftermath."

Kelly's paper produces significance by reading the *The Monk's Tale* as emptying tragedy of a certain kind of moral significance, the kind that seeks for "fatal flaws." In a sense, Stephen Knight performs a similar action by assigning to the Knight the role of social critic: the Monk's discourse is emptied of significance, just as the Knight is emptied of significance by the Monk in Jones's paper. What might the connection be between the strong formal markings, the marking of the issue of form (including its historicity), found by Kelly in the *Tale* and the social/political/economic critiques (and therefore rhetorics) found in the *Tale* by our other critics? Does the errancy of the figures cut by meaning and agency in this group of papers comment in turn on the question of form, and, if so, how? How do the figures of farcicality and seriousness—one can't help but think of *The Eighteenth Brumaire*—illuminate the relation between form and historicity? There is a certain either/or structure at work in these readings of the Monk's and Knight's interventions: most analyze one or the other, but not both. But why does *The Monk's Tale* end with a Knight who finds that the Monk's tragedies are just too much and a tavern-keeper who finds they're just not enough for him? How is the question of estate to be correlated with this apparent difference in critical response? And with the figure of critical response itself?

Richard Neuse's Monk is a "serious-minded humanist with a bent toward postmodernism *avant la lettre,*" where postmodernism "stands" for anachronism in a literal sense: "a break with the idea of time and history as one thing after another, a diachronic series or progression." The Monk means to break with "the 'grand narratives' of biblical-Christian history writing." Again, the *Tale*'s break with meaning is just how the poem means to be. But a notion of history as, so to speak, just one damn thing after another is not necessarily a notion of a "series" or "progression." For Neuse, *The Monk's Tale* is instead a series of Lyotardian "little narratives" that respect "the irreducible diversity of the world's cultures." The Monk's tales are not so much meaningless as they are "respectful," presumably humble ("little" rather than "grand"), and fascinated with diversity rather than with historical repetition. But how is

Neuse's reading to account for the *Tale*'s formal repetitions and interest in the laws of genre?

Neuse's assimilation of "one thing after another" to "series" or "progression" marks for us the absent presence of the just-one-damn-thing-after-another plot in critical consideration of *The Monk's Tale.* This prompts us to ask whether and how Neuse will recover the Monk's meaning. Respect for diversity is an ethics; the Monk's performance illustrates both the respect for particular figures "in isolation from any larger historical context and without reference to any presumed telos of history" (again, these are not quite the same) and the vision of a world "always shared with others."

Finally, for Neuse, the Monk's "little narratives" also "cancel the grand narrative of fourteenth-century European society with its hierarchy of social classes and its subordination of women at every level. And in this respect they anticipate what is accomplished by *The Canterbury Tales* as a whole, . . . an ideal of fellowship . . . in which all participate as equals." Fellowship and equality are not, however, necessarily implied by the concepts of diversity and particularity; indeed, there can be considerable tension between them, as is suggested by the history of commentary on *caritas* and its role in governance, as well as contemporary democratic theory. How can a "unique event unassimilable to . . . others" (each of the Canterbury *Tales*) join in equality *as such* without the intervention of concepts of measure and identity? Neuse is of course not alone in invoking difference and indeterminacy as a means of revivifying the group, even of returning "to the idea of an originary sharing of the world." Invoking indeterminacy as the route to recovery of meaning, difference as a route to fellowship, are knowledge-practices common to, perhaps even constitutive of, current literary and cultural studies, which too often privilege the "specific" without analyzing its dialectical relation to the "general"—that is, how each concept constructs the other in any given discourse.

Thus, new critical discourse on *The Monk's Tale* represents it as "more central to the poetics of *The Canterbury Tales* than its 'marginal' status might lead one to expect" (Neuse). But why it is now important to see *The Monk's Tale,* in particular, in this way? To put it another way, why is *The Monk's Tale* now beginning to bear the burden of the recovery of centrality in marginality? Could we say that there is something about the *Tale* that permits or invites this charge? The most obvious answer would be that these critics want, like Neuse's Monk, to hold "after the newe world the space," and *The Monk's Tale* hasn't in recent years had the kind of critical attention given to *The Knight's Tale,* etc. But it is far too easy to dismiss such wishes as "mere" trendiness (as if trendiness were something "mere," and changing styles of reading not, in fact, history). Moreover, these papers especially remind us that the privilege and protection accorded to difference in today's academy may indeed be telling us that difference matters to our desire, and not simply on the score of our putative aversion to it. These papers remind us that the project of recovery and return—of the critical moment ("now") that desires return—is a life-and-death matter. It seems that reading is an encounter with absences(s)—no news now. But why does that resonate, for these papers, so strongly with *The Monk's Tale?*

We build verbal and material artifacts around absence, pointing to what isn't there, to its ways of not being there, to the ways it forms our forms. We struggle against the mortality of the artifact and its maker—against the mortality of our "works," and therefore of ourselves—and insofar as the activity of forming brings out this mortality, we are ambivalent about form, about the signifier as such, and the extent to which form forms what "meaning" and "history" are, or at least how they behave. These papers tend to separate the literary from the political/historical, for example, but *at the same time* to suggest rich possibilities for thinking about the power of form: Neuse's attention to "narrative"; Jones's belief that Monkish satire of the Knight can illuminate the very structure of *The Canterbury Tales;* Astell's interest in the relations between tragedy and saint's life.

It is through the question of form that I propose we view the topic and practice of return in this group of papers. A thinking of form—and its historical iteration in genre (genre being the Monk's self-stated concern in telling his little narratives)—is both what these papers don't fully take on and what they provoke us to undertake. Form brings out our death and our deadliness, and thus, on top of everything else, reminds us that in desiring to form, we are trying to approach ground zero. The ethics of difference is a sign of our *enjoyment* of difference, limit, otherness. This is the enjoyment offered by *The Monk's Tale.* We could go so far as to say that *The Monk's Tale* points this out; but the most important point for our purposes is that we have found this enjoyment unbearable (the Knight) or hard to enjoy (the Host), precisely in order to rescue ourselves from its intensity. The panel whose thinking we have been accompanying has begun to show us what this enjoyment might mean. In doing so, it gives voice in and to the end of the "Deleuzian century," to the question of the ethics *of* the thinking, and desiring, of difference—which still means the ethics of *making*—that preoccupies us today.

REVIEWS

CHRISTOPHER ALLMAND, ed. *The New Cambridge Medieval History: Volume VII c. 1415–c. 1500.* Cambridge: Cambridge University Press, 1998. Pp. xxi, 1048; 24 plates. $95.00.

Professor Allmand has assembled an excellent team of scholars and produced a major, meticulous, and often analytically provocative survey of fifteenth-century Europe, one that offers literary scholars a powerful set of historical questions and models and a vast range of information about a period increasingly occupying center stage in medieval literary inquiry. Given so much differentiated national detail yet such recurrent attention to parallel structures—monarchical, representational, educational, artistic, and the conditions and negotiations behind the formation of European states—this volume is also a timely statement about the complex unity of Europe, since interactive and analogous forces and concerns can be seen working across its varied cultures. The work's structure follows the pattern of J. R. Lander's admirable history of later fifteenth-century England (*Government and Community: England, 1450–1509* [Cambridge, Mass.: Harvard University Press, 1980]): chapters on themes and pan-European institutions come first ("Politics: Theory and Practice," "Religious Belief and Practice," "The European Nobility," "Rural Europe," etc.), followed by chapters on the political history of individual states or areas. The emphases throughout, however, are on wide-ranging issues; the growth of monarchical and courtly claims and authority, the expansion of literacy and education, and the power of the mercantile class are some of the recurrent topics that inform all of the chapters. And the chapters all proceed via rigorous structural analyses, whether of the variety of and various impetus behind specific institutions, such as representational institutions in Europe (in a particularly helpful chapter by Wim Blockmans), or of various dynastic crises or complexities of state formation that seized most of the European nations, such as the mysterious failure of Scotland to produce a nationalist propaganda, discussed in a canny chapter by Jenny Wormald. The permeable boundaries of Europe, often in view, are directly treated very well: the "Byzantine" East receives a particularly fine discussion in Anthony Bryer's chapter; the Latin East is valuably surveyed by Anthony

Luttrell; and there are useful surprises in both. Given that Europe is now at a juncture of reconsidering state formation and larger cultural identities, the comparative approach of this excellent volume seizes the opportunity to set forth the elements behind the emergence of these entities with great accuracy and enormous scope and energy.

English literary scholars may find less immediately directive work; the chapter on "Lancastrian England," by Edward Powell, is a good one, but the discussion features political culture at the very top—the Lancastrians rather than Lancastrian England—providing clarity about the way claimants to the crown might imagine or force their options rather than other cultural elements with which literary scholars are concerned. Malcolm Vale's chapter on France at the end of the Hundred Years' War is very helpful and stimulating; but his chapter on "Manuscripts and Books," while perfectly sound, does not offer grounds for new research or any of the sustained scrutiny of particulars that makes codicology and book production so vital a field at present in medieval European literary studies. Both gaps are, however, easily compensated by current specialized work, some listed in the bibliographies here; others, in English literary scholarship especially, are not listed but are readily findable (e.g., the work of Seth Lerer, Kathleen Scott, Paul Strohm, and Ralph Hanna III, to name only four among many currently producing exciting work in these areas).

More important for medieval literary scholarship generally, however, is the broad impetus this history provides to consider patterns and interactions in Europe as a whole, at a crucial juncture of cultural transition to the modern state, marked by tension between "Europe" as a notion of religious unity and as a notion of a region dominated by secular authorities. Especially relevant for literary study are those chapters featuring the question of cultural or social self-image, such as the emergence of "humanist" fascination with classical literature, which, in a provocative chapter, Robert Black argues was intellectually insubstantial but significant as a new stylistic and ideological marker of aristocracy and nobility. (Black's definition of "intellectual history" as excluding such social meaning seems, however, unnecessarily narrow.) Jean-Philippe Genet's opening comments on various aspects of political theory and practice, Allmand's pan-European consideration of "war," and the numerous other comparatist chapters are very enlightening indeed, if occasionally fragmented in style.

A replacement volume in a venerable series provokes some reflection on what has changed in the interim. Naturally, the analytical rigor in tracing the range of topics or layers of import in broad issues or specific nations or areas sharply contrasts with the "old" Cambridge history of the fifteenth century. Published amid great difficulties in 1936, that volume announced its overarching historical narrative, and its emphasis *on* narrative, in its subtitle, "The Close of the Middle Ages." In the *New Cambridge Medieval History Volume VII,* narrative often appears as one calculated stylistic and analytical tool among others, as in Antony Black's breathless (and unfootnoted) political narrative of the councils of Pisa and Constance, followed by his trenchant analyses of the ideologies, and then the wider cultural implications, of the Conciliar Movement. Between the "old" and new *Histories,* Marxism, as a increasingly sophisticated but then increasingly denounced historical method in the academy, came and went; it loomed perhaps just long enough to dispel narrative impressionism of the old-fashioned kind. Marxism never overtly appears in either history, but just as in the "old" *History* it informed K. B. McFarlane's chapter on the "bastard feudalism" of England or the editors' epilogue describing "the enfranchisement of capitalism" amid "the last stage of feudal monarchy," so it and the decades of rebuttals to it generated the conditions of structural rather than narrative historical study so dominant in the new one.

Even when treating single events at length, analysis here dominates over narrative. The "old" *History* has room in W. T. Waugh's chapter on the councils of Constance and Pisa for mentioning the "hosts of craftsmen, pedlars, minstrels, and prostitutes" glomming around the Council of Constance (p. 3), and for reflecting on how well the civic magistrates organized the food supply for the attendants. Black's parallel account in the *New* rigorously isolates a "political" narrative of the Council from such matters as these urban hangers-on or civic food-supply. But of course there is now Barrie Dobson's whole chapter on "Urban Europe" in the new *History.* Nothing on prostitutes appears in Dobson, but there is a much more analytically comprehensive view of urban social structure than such anecdotal glimpses as Waugh indulges in. On certain matters, to be sure, the "old" *History* of 1936 had more analytical ambition; in the prominent location of the conclusion, its editor suggested the logic of the increasing European persecution of the Jews in the fifteenth century (a feature, it was argued, not of "the expiring unity of Christendom" but "of a new exclusive force—nationality," since their alien status was perceived more in "racial" and cultural terms than religious ones [p. 805]). The new *History* has a bit more to say about Jews in various scattered passages but never attempts to explain so broadly their persecution.

In some ways literary scholars may need encouragement to relinquish historical strategies and views that resemble those of the "old" *History* more than of the *New:* McFarlane's analysis of fifteenth-century England, for example, has in its broad claims long outlived its value in literary studies. But if I (as a literary scholar) felt reeducated by so rigorous a treatment of multiple historical strands and so wide a cultural scope as are displayed here, in other elements, and not just on codicology or Lancastrian legitimacy, I imagined that most English literary scholars, and probably many historians, would notice some suppressions, especially of the agents who constituted some of the losing figures in history. Women are not discussed in any detail except in John Klassen's chapter on Hus; and while that chapter is thorough and trenchant on Hus and his larger political setting and impact, the women granted some authority by Hus tend to disappear as individual agents, even as grammatical subjects:

> Women responded [to Hus's call for their equality]. Female patrons placed reformers into parishes; women preached and wrote tracts. . . . However, their gains were short. After 1421, Czech men reverted to the principle of masculine privilege, and the body politic remained an arena reserved for males. (p. 376)

What happened to the women? The rigorous focus of analytical history, and of course the imperatives of editors' word-counts, requires heavy losses; but given the *History*'s general lack of close attention to women's circumstances and struggles in a century noted for their emergence into some literary and intellectual culture, or indeed its lack of attention to the oppressions of many other groups, their smooth disappearance from grammatical agency in the concluding sentence, like their total disappearance from "the body politic," is troubling.

Overall this is not a history inclined to find or analyze much barbarism in European history. A useful exception is the brief explanation for the emergence of witchhunting in Francis Rapp's rapid but valuable chapter on "Religious Belief and Practice," where it is argued that such persecutions appeared as peasant culture was put under new pressures by increasing religious strictures. But heretics have only fleeting mention. Ethnic rivalry gets some attention, but the heat of events and of individual passions is deep-cooled by impersonal constructions and abstract language in the presentation of this and other topics. Felipe Fernández-Armesto's chapter on "Exploration and Discovery" is unforgettably vivid in its evocation of individual explorers, some unsavory, but never dwells on the victims.

At any rate, this is a vitally up-to-date and very well produced introduction to a complex period of European history that will open up the interest of that century for those who may still dismiss it. I found only one typo (the wrong font on p. 756), and was disappointed by only one plate (13, where the embossed scene is difficult to see). Rather than simply "reference," this is recommended *reading* for all medieval and Renaissance scholars, for it will provoke much consideration both of academically divided "periods" and their disciplinary separation. Indeed, its publication is an event of great importance in European historiography and an opportunity to contemplate Europe's history and developments as a whole, even at a moment when several comprehensive histories of Europe have already charted new ways of imagining so vast, destructive, and productive a culture.

ANDREW GALLOWAY
Cornell University

BARBARA K. ALTMANN. *The Love Debate Poems of Christine de Pizan:* Le Livre du debat de deux amans, Le Livre des Trois jugemens, Le Livre du Dit de Poissy. Gainesville: University of Florida Press, 1998. Pp. 294; 4 color plates. $49.95.

In this exemplary edition Barbara K. Altmann offers us the three debate poems by Christine de Pizan, composed between 1400 and 1403 and last edited by Maurice Roy in the late nineteenth century. Roy based his edition on manuscript Paris, BNF 835, while Altmann chose London, British Library, Harley 4431, the presentation copy prepared by Christine de Pizan herself for queen Isabeau de Bavière. As has become clear in recent years, this manuscript provides superior readings for many of Christine's texts.

Altmann has done a superb job not only in considering the codicological and philological questions her texts raise but also in providing a stimulating and thorough discussion of the genre of the love debate and its place in Christine's thought on women and the conventions of courtly love.

The long introduction (eighty-three pages) provides a good overview of Christine's works in general and then focuses on Christine's attitude toward courtly love, which she "simultaneously [engages] and [dismisses]" (p. 5). With this insightful remark Altmann has put her finger on the central achievement of these texts: while ostensibly forming part of an established literary tradition, represented especially well by Guillaume de Machaut, they at the same time undermine it by questioning and reorienting its very premises.

Altmann begins with very helpful synopses of the poems and then goes on to examine the genres that fed into the love debate poems, the *jeu-parti* and especially the *dit,* characterized, according to Jacqueline Cerquiglini, by "discontinuity," by the presence of the writer within the text and by his or her identity as a "writer-clerk" (p. 13). Altmann highlights this discontinuity particularly for the *Dit de Poissy,* where a long and detailed description of women's life in a religious community (the Dominican abbey of Poissy, home to many royal ladies, as well as Christine's daughter) is juxtaposed with a debate between a mournful lady and a squire. The result of this juxtaposition is, as Altmann demonstrates convincingly, an indictment of courtly love as hollow and unhappy (p. 14). Further, the fact that no actual judgment is rendered (unlike in the debate poems by Guillaume de Machaut) shifts the dynamic away from the actual debate—which in the *Poissy* focuses on who is more unhappy in love—to the relationship between the writer and the patron. In fact, all three poems defer the actual pronouncing of the sentence to the extratextual patron.

In one of the most interesting sections of the introduction, Altmann examines the relationship of the three poems to each other; she suggests that "One simple and mildly provocative formula might be to say that *Deux amans* treats love from a theoretical viewpoint, *Trois jugemens* from a practical viewpoint, and *Poissy* from a comparative perspective of contemplative versus courtly life" (p. 24). After considering this "dynamic of transtextuality" in detail, Altmann concludes that what we find here is a "debate among debates" (p. 28), debates that are in addition subtly undermined by women's voices and that therefore do not promote the very subject matter they speak of. Altmann's excellent analysis will be indispensable reading for any further discussions on the topic of courtly love.

In a section on "Orality, Reading, and Writing," Altmann takes a new look at modes of presentation and representation. I especially appreciated her discussion of the manuscript initials and illustrations as aids to textual interpretation. The four beautiful color plates that adorn the volume show one illustration from Brussels, Royal Library Albert 1er, B.R.11034, and three from Harley 4431. In a judicious editorial strategy, Altmann decided to add the manuscript's paragraph marks to the edited text.

The exemplary section on philology and codicology offers a good introduction to Christine's use of Middle French, as well as an analysis of the versification and the miniatures; it also explains the establishment of the text. The notes provide a wealth of information, including (in note 138) an incisive observation on the indiscriminate use of illustrations made by authors of some modern medieval picture books.

The texts themselves are preceded by short introductions that add yet more new material to the discussion of the love debates. Each text is followed by a list of variants. Extensive notes explain difficult expressions and mythological allusions, analyze particularities of the versification, and give extremely detailed information on the manuscripts (in addition to finding more specific remarks on the variants, we learn where letters were crossed out and replaced, what the catch words were, etc.). The glossary of difficult Middle French words is very helpful, as is the up-to-date bibliography.

The texts themselves are a pleasure to read. They draw the reader into fascinating but ultimately fruitless discussions on whether a lady whose lover is a prisoner of the Turks after the battle at Nicopolis in 1396 suffers more than a squire whose lady has rejected him (*Poissy*); whether love brings more suffering (the position of a slightly older knight) or joy (the view of a young squire)—incidentally, neither of the debaters pays any attention to a lady who pronounces love a barely adequate pastime and mocks the so-called martyrs of love (*Deux amans*); or, finally, who is right in three cases of rather involved love relationships, complicated by jealous husbands, faithless lovers, and changeable ladies (*Trois jugemens*). In all these debates Christine's presence as an observer, scribe, and potential judge is one of the most intriguing aspects.

Altmann's excellent volume now allows scholars to read these intriguing texts in a reliable critical edition. It will undoubtedly contribute to discussions on many issues of late medieval literature: Christine de Pizan's feminism *avant la lettre;* the intense criticism and ultimate demise of the tradition of courtly love; the importance of the material manuscript for textual interpretation; the presence and significance of historical events in fictional texts; and the growing intrusion of writerly figures into their own texts.

RENATE BLUMENFELD-KOSINSKI
University of Pittsburgh

ANN W. ASTELL. *Political Allegory in Late Medieval England.* Ithaca and London: Cornell University Press, 1999. Pp. xi, 218. $35.00.

In her most recent book, Ann W. Astell reproaches many scholars' frequent neglect of political allegory in medieval literature. Responding to scholars who prefer moral and philosophical allegory, Astell wishes to restore political allegory as an element consciously integrated with poetic matters by the author and eminently relevant to his contemporary audience. To recognize and decode these allegories, however, Astell deploys her methodology in a way that many medievalists might find troubling.

Rejecting the long-held assumption that *inventio* nearly disappeared after Christians appropriated classical rhetoric, Astell reconsiders invention as medieval authors' gathering their *materia* before building their work. She concludes that the poem's materiality (and, by extension, the means of invention) "included the poem's literal subject, its intended allegories, and its anticipated audience—the total discovery of which then directed the poet's decisions concerning arrangement and style" (p. 25). Astell then presents allegorical readings of six texts spanning roughly a century, from the 1381 Uprising to the Battle of Tewksbury; her book becomes a key unlocking the "recognizable codes and procedures" the authors used to transform the "pressing issues of the day" into "artful and rhetorical" political allegory (p. 42). She convenes a host of literary genres and tropes capable of carrying the unspoken message—dream-vision, parable, personification, wordplay, coded messages, Latin expressions, exempla, and even rhetoric itself—providing many fresh topical connections between the texts and concurrent political events. But rather than reading these topical connections as part of the cultural context informing and shaping the texts, Astell pursues the authorial intention behind the political allegory.

Beginning her examination with John Ball's letters and *Piers Plowman,* Astell not only locates the political allegory embedded in the rebellious priest's letters but also speculates on how he allegorically interpreted *Piers.* By tying Ball's exhortations to the popular sermon exemplum "Sayings of the Four Philosophers" and Langland's poem, Astell finds purposely hidden intertextual relationships buried among the letters, the "Sayings," and *Piers Plowman.* Moreover, she argues, Langland provides a potent model for allegorical reading and writing. According to Astell, where Langland does not mention certain things, Ball considered the unspoken politically dangerous and, accordingly, supplied them himself; Ball then used his interpretation to justify his action and to exhort others to rebellion, thereby illustrating the rhetorical efficacy of political allegory.

In her next chapter, "Gower's Arion and 'Cithero,'" Astell locates several veiled references to contemporary events, including an unusual dolphin sighting that explains Gower's reference to Arion. Based on the date of the dolphin's appearance, Astell argues that Gower presented the *Confessio Amantis* to both Richard II and Henry of Derby around 1393. She confronts directly the question of multiple versions of the *Confessio* by arguing that Gower did not revise his "bok for King Richardes sake" until the Lancastrian usurpation, when its political allegory no longer obtained. By arguing for concurrent and multiple audiences, she astutely recognizes the interpretive levels available—and frequently found—in Gower.

Her fourth chapter, "Chaucer's Ricardian Allegories," begins by revisiting the allegorical occasion for *The Legend of Good Women* and the topical issue of Queen Anne as intercessor. Astell's reading derives from the similarities and differences between Chaucer's poem and Richard's highly charged court. Because these narrative arguments repeatedly shift perspectives—Cupid represents not only Richard but also Arundel, the lord appellant responsible for executing some of Richard's closest confidants—they aptly illustrate how the reader must "bridge a gap between and among several different (and apparently mutually exclusive) levels of meaning" (p. 97). In her *Canterbury Tales* section, after briefly describing *The Tale of Melibee*'s political allegory, Astell uses topical references to demonstrate that *The Monk's Tale* provides the wise counsel missing in *Melibee.* For *The Nun's Priest's Tale,* she argues that references to St. Kenalm connect to Richard II and produce a "multi-layered allegory," warning Richard against bad counsel and flattery.

In "Penitential Politics in *Sir Gawain and the Green Knight:* Richard II, Richard of Arundel, and Robert de Vere," Astell demonstrates "a pattern of systematic allusions" providing narrative parallels between the poem and scenes in the chronicles. She not only finds ingenious connections between depictions of Arundel and the Green Knight's decapitation but also discloses an interesting "pattern of heraldic reference" in Bertilak's hunts whereby the hart equals Richard II, the boar de Vere, the fox Gloucester (p. 128). Based on these topical decodings, she speculates that *Sir Gawain* appears between 1397 and 1400 and therefore imaginatively restores Richard (deposed in 1399) as "a latter-day Arthur, who pursues a penitent's path [and] welcomes reconciliation with his enemies" (p. 137). The poem thus becomes a belated and failed attempt to reestablish moral and political order, beginning with the king.

Astell's final chapter, "Joan of Arc, Margaret of Anjou, and Malory's Guenevere at the Stake," weaves the Yorkist and Lancastrian struggles for the throne into the Arthurian and Jehannine legacy, revealing how the changing valence of Joan of Arc during the fifteenth century and the threat posed by Margaret of Anjou inflect Malory's presentation of Guenevere. Moreover, Astell demonstrates that Malory adopts the role of the Arthurian prophet, Merlin, to show that Camelot prefigured the reign of Edward IV, a reading that supports Yorkist interpretations of *Morte Darthur.* Astell provides ample reason for continuing to examine topical references in Malory.

All in all, Astell continues to restore the hermenuetics of political allegory and provides medievalists with a fresh list of topical references for these texts. That said, I must state my reservations with the methodology behind Astell's project. Despite her nuanced introduction discussing the period's "shared theory of allegorical composition," her readings claim to privilege the "principles of formalism" (p. 162), while simultaneously ignoring critical problems with locating and relying on authorial intention. Although she credits her authors with creative indirection, she repeatedly insists that uncovering topical clues reveals authorial intent. For example, regarding *The Monk's Tale,* she hastily claims "Chaucer's original plan was to interrupt this logical and chronological sequence by inserting the 'Modern Instances' after Cenobia's tragedy"

(p. 108). More understandably but no less problematically, she becomes so concerned with demonstrating a topical connection that she misconstrues the text, ignoring important textual clues that render the passage more complex and intriguing than she allows. Admittedly, Astell offers the occasional reminder that her author was not "creating a new story that corresponded exactly to the [referenced] events" (p. 150), but to say that they unequivocally represent the author's intention defies much of the recent, hard-won theoretical sophistication in medieval studies. Bearing this caveat in mind, scholars can expect Astell's book to illuminate numerous patterns of association and topical clues hitherto overlooked in these richly laden texts.

CANDACE BARRINGTON
Iona College

ANNE CLARK BARTLETT, with THOMAS H. BESTUL, JANET GOEBEL, and WILLIAM F. POLLARD, eds. *Vox Mystica: Essays on Medieval Mysticism in Honor of Professor Valerie M. Lagorio.* Cambridge: D. S. Brewer, 1995. Pp. xiv, 235. $81.00.

This collection is divided into four main sections. In the first, "Methods," Rosemary Drage Hale writes on sensory perception and memory in works by medieval German mystics; John Hirsh examines the literary treatment of encounters with the supernatural in three Middle English romances, *Sir Gawain and the Green Knight, Havelok,* and *Lay le Freine;* Alexandra Barratt provides a critical survey of editions, translations, and versions of Julian of Norwich's *Revelations;* and Frank Tobin discusses the possible influence of Augustine's theory of visions on Mechtild of Magdeburg's *Das fließende Licht der Gottheit.* In the second section, "Practices," Ritamary Bradley argues that the monastic Latin *vita* of Beatrice of Nazareth is an unreliable witness to the nature of her spirituality, imposing an essentially antifeminist stereotype of the "holy woman" not substantiated by Beatrice's own writing; Robert Boenig examines the relationship of Augustine's *jubilus* to Rolle's *canor;* Edwin L. Conner suggests Aelred of Rievaulx's *De spirituali amicitia* as a source of the *Cloud of Unknowing;* Beverly Boyd finds "a strain of mysticism" expressed through the translated prayers in Chaucer's works; Elizabeth Psakis

Armstrong cogently compares the ideal of "womenly men" in Thomas à Kempis with that of "manly women" in Teresa of Avila; and Mary E. Giles draws parallels between the "ecstatic theatre" of Sor María of Santo Domingo—a fifteenth-century Spanish mystic whose ecstasies sometimes involved dramatic performance—and the "holy theatre" of Jerzy Grotowski and some other modern directors. In the third section, "Communities," Anne Clark Bartlett explores interestingly the complications of spiritual friendship between the sexes in late medieval England; Ann M. Hutchison narrates the misadventures of three English Brigittine nuns in Elizabeth's reign; and Gertrud Jaron Lewis discusses the place of music and dancing in the fourteenth-century German Dominican "Sister-Books." In the fourth section, "Texts," Margot King translates three letters on Christ as lover from Mechthild of Hackeborn's *Book of Special Grace,* bk. 4, ch. 59; Stephen E. Hayes edits for the first time "Of Three Workings in Man's Soul," a short Middle English prose meditation on the Annunciation; and James Hogg offers a detailed study of the Middle Low German version of St. Birgitta's *Revelationes* published in Lübeck in 1496, an adaptation designed for readers less concerned with mysticism than with practical guidance on leading the Christian life.

Unlike most *Festschriften,* this collection works as a coherent whole, firmly focused on medieval European mysticism; the only exception, Hutchison's study of the Elizabethan "Catholic underground," provides a relevant, and at times moving, postscript to the medieval material. Certain themes recur in more than one article: the influence of Augustine of Hippo on later mystical writings, the place of spiritual friendship in the religious life, and the nature and (at times) subversion of medieval gender stereotypes. The majority of the articles are substantial, interesting, and useful, and some are of notably high quality; it would be invidious to list names, but (to take a single example) Barratt's unpretentious and workmanlike survey of the tradition of Julian's *Revelations* should be required reading for anyone approaching the study of Julian for the first time. As a whole, the collection does credit to its dedicatee, and will be of interest to anyone working in the area of medieval mysticism.

It does not, however, escape some of the faults of the broader (and steadily growing) category of publications to which it belongs, the rapidly produced themed anthology whose compilation depends on personal connections as well as shared academic interests. The combination of time pressures and an unwillingness to lean too heavily on contributors inevitably works against effective quality control. In some of the articles, firmer editorial intervention on dubious argument (e.g., the identification of prayer with mysticism, p. 103) and careless writing would have been fairer to both contributor and readers; a few passages have been allowed to stand that would hardly be acceptable in an undergraduate essay, and even some of the stronger contributors argue less than rigorously, using terminology loosely, drawing questionable parallels, or claiming direct links between works on insufficient evidence. The articles do not follow a consistent format throughout; Psakis Armstrong's piece uses quite different bibliographical conventions from the rest, and King's translation is not accompanied by a reference to its source text. More of a problem is the inconsistent policy on translation of quotations: sometimes both text and translation are provided, sometimes translation only, sometimes text only. This means that at one extreme, readers are left to struggle unsupported with the baffling claim (p. 9) that Mechthild of Magdeburg sees "Sin" as the guardian of the senses (the Middle High German original has not *sunde* but *schult,* which like MnE "guilt" can mean not only wrongdoing but the acknowledgment of wrongdoing); at the other, they will not be able to make full use of James Hogg's groundbreaking research in primary sources unless they have a thorough grounding not just in Latin but in Middle Low German. There is also a remarkably high level of errors and misprints for a work with no fewer than four editors, and produced by a reputable academic publisher. The Latin of p. 7, n. 11 (to take perhaps the worst example), is so scrambled as to be barely comprehensible, and there are numerous individual typographical and spelling errors: e.g., "Amerkanistik," "anheleare," "Auguntine," "auten," "Bridgittine," "crie de coeur," "exhuberance," "experiernce," "exultation" (for "exaltation"), "hebdomidal," "hexachoard," "laud" (for "laude"), "libidonously," "naivite," "les neige d'antan," "Penquin," "phenomona," "referrent," "Symthe" (for "Smythe"), "weening" (for "weaning") . . .

But there is much that is profitable in this *Festschrift,* and a few small pleasures, not least the account in Giles's article of the unorthodox approach to pastoral care of Sor María's confessor, "who insisted on spending nights in her cell, even atop her bed, in order, he explained, to protect her from her infirmities and the insidious attacks of the Devil" (p. 124).

BELLA MILLETT
University of Southampton

LAWRENCE BESSERMAN. *Chaucer's Biblical Poetics.* Norman: University of Oklahoma Press, 1995. Pp. xi, 338. $39.95 cloth, $17.95 paper.

As long as "folk digne of reverence" such as Brewer, Fisher, and Pearsall remain as firmly on their pillars as did those famous chaps in Chaucer's elaborate Palace of Beryl, "that shoon ful brighter than a glas" (*HF* 1289), the task of recent critics might seem to be largely one of reference. Nevertheless, for several decades Chaucerians steeped in medieval culture and possessing individually a considerable knowledge of the Bible have sought out Chaucer's biblical references with the enthusiasm of closet inquisitors. They would be unsurprised by Besserman's main contention: that there exists an obsessive relationship between Chaucer and the Bible.

When it seems that the last drop has been drained from "the well of English undefiled," with such eloquent results that even our colleagues who may be "liberal, humanist atheists" have been forced to pay attention, here is Besserman, cogent, lively, verbose, pedantic, and rhetorical, telling us first of all of the ingenious ways in which God's word was impressed upon the lettered and the unlettered in the fourteenth century and then demonstrating the various devices whereby the Bible was absorbed and regurgitated in Chaucer's text. As Besserman reminds us, Chaucer was writing at a time when the Bible was presumed to be the absolute authority on questions of human endeavor, both religious and secular. Bibles in pocket-book form were popular and circulated widely. Whole quires were ripped stealthily from chained Bibles in churches.

In *Chaucer and the Bible* (1988) Besserman provided a bibliographical survey and a review essay on the study of Chaucer's uses of the Bible and an index of the pervasive biblical diction, imagery, and themes in Chaucer's works. In the preface to his latest work, Besserman makes clear at the beginning his central argument: that "Chaucer's biblically suffused poetry reflects his response both to long-standing medieval truisms about the preeminence of biblical authority and to the late medieval and specifically English problematization of those truisms." He adds that "Chaucer's innovative uses of the Bible and the concomitant delight that he evinces in his poetic responses to the 'literariness' of biblical narratives are aspects of his art that have not been generally acknowledged or adequately explored" (p. 3).

While one might not agree with this contention, one may nevertheless appreciate Besserman's contribution to the discussion of Chaucer's shaping of late-medieval biblical poetics. Besserman states that "thinking about Chaucer's biblically suffused writing in relation to that of his European and English contemporaries highlights the importance of biblical poetics as a common if hitherto undervalued element in various domains of Ricardian culture" (p. 4). He examines Chaucer's appropriation of the Bible for secular purposes under various headings: "The Bible and Late Medieval Literary Culture," "The Bible as Book, Metaphor, and Model for Secular Literature," "Biblical Translation, Quotation, and Paraphrase," "Partial or Oblique Quotations and Allusions." Some examples in the last section might be defined by Chauncey Wood as "quarks," in that they "can explain sometimes what might otherwise not make much sense."

The remaining chapters discuss "Biblical Glossing and Poetic Meaning," and "'Figura' and the Making of Vernacular Poetry," where Besserman discusses Chaucer's placing of "figura" in two ways: by using explicit biblical or exegetical motifs and, secondly, by examining the figural interpretations of characters and motifs proposed by critics. This survey focuses on "four of Chaucer's early dream visions, the *Book of the Duchess,* the *House of Fame,* the *Parliament of Fowls,* and the *Legend of Good Women*[,] and on two of the Canterbury Tales, the *Nun's Priest's Tale* and the *Pardoner's Tale.*" In his conclusion, Besserman considers Chaucer's biblical poetics in relation to the early tradition that saw Chaucer as the "Father of English Poetry," looking forward to the Reformation, and as the "Father of Modern Standard English" (p. 6).

While some of us might claim that as a result of Besserman's concentration on "biblically suffused poetry" in Chaucer, we are in danger of losing the secular perspective of Chaucer's work, we must admire Besserman's ingenuity. He suggests that Dryden's remark on *The Canterbury Tales* as being "God's plenty" may have implied that Dryden and his contemporaries saw an affinity between Chaucer's poetry and the Bible, "an affinity similar to that which was familiar to generations of previous readers." Besserman adds that "it was an affinity that had been subtly implied by Chaucer himself" (p. 206). And even in the contemporary view—the Variorum edition of Chaucer's works currently in progress, with "its gilt-edged pages and its Bible-like layout of bits of Chaucer's text overwhelmed by commentary and variants"—testifies to a sacralization of Chaucer's poetry . . . that Chaucer himself was sometimes bold enough to hint at" (p. 207).

Besserman further claims that the medieval Christian author might think of his own written word in some sort of relation of propinquity to the revealed word of God or to some kind of inspired writing found in the Bible. He suggests that "as a Christian author active in England at the end of the fourteenth century Chaucer might well have thought of his works in precisely this audacious way" (p. 207).

How Chaucer thought of his work is a subject on which there are many views. Besserman, however, feels confident that Chaucer was searching for "a biblically inspired and biblically modeled vernacular literary solution to the fragmented and fractious flood of biblical translation and interpretation in which his Christian community was adrift" (p. 207). The author is responding, so Besserman maintains, to "a problem that had bedeviled Christian culture from the time of Augustine: the problem of the mutual translatability of secular and biblical poetics" (p. 209).

Besserman argues persuasively that in common with the poetry of Dante, Petrarch, and Boccaccio Chaucer's poetry was shaped by what he perceived to be "the affinities between biblical and secular poetry and biblical and secular poetics" (p. 17). The vernacular biblical paraphrases and translations that were a prominent feature of Chaucer's cultural milieu and the artistry of the biblically centered works by his Ricardian contemporaries were inspired by the religious milieu of fourteenth-century theologians and secular drama and reflect "the unprecedented authorial freedom and affective intensity" that may be seen in some of the "biblically suffused" writing of the time (p. 23).

As will be realized, this work is for the specialist. Apart from Chaucer's works, the beginning student should, I suggest, read good critical biographies by scholars such as those I have already named. What misconceptions might arise if this book were made a primary text for beginners in Chaucer, I cannot imagine.

Beryl Rowland
York University and University of Victoria

Kathleen Biddick. *The Shock of Medievalism.* Durham and London: Duke University Press, 1998. Pp. 304. $49.95 cloth, $17.95 paper.

The Shock of Medievalism means to explore how "trauma (then and now) affect[s] the ways in which medievalists connect the past to the present and to the future" (p. 16). It also means to shock, and some of its readers will likely feel perplexed about the relation between the book's stated wish to work through trauma and its investment in provocation. But the book's power to perplex results, at least in part, from the way it replays trauma in the structure and procedures of its arguments: a bold point is made, but its working-through is delayed. Presentation of evidence and reasoning often arrives too late to reassure the reader that Biddick's aim is demonstration rather than denunciation. She claims, for example, that in *The Dream of John Ball* William Morris "misrecognized the work of mourning as melancholy for work. That misrecognition persists even today among such strong new historicist readings of the uprising as Steven Justice's" (p. 39). Careful discussion of this criticism of Justice doesn't arrive, however, for four pages. Neither the essayistic ambience of the chapters nor the very wide range of topics they address—from "Gothic Ornament" in the nineteenth-century (chapter 1) to humanist/colonialist knowledge-production in virtual reality (chapter 3)—do much to dispel the impression that Biddick's authoritativeness may be more a matter of temper than pains taken. Rather than being good reasons not to read this book, however, these are reasons to read it twice.

Because Biddick's book seems to be a particularly challenging instance of the medievalist syndrome it also analyzes, and because her refusal to settle keeps questions open that might otherwise prefer to close over, this book should be read by positivists, New Historicists, and theorists alike. Positivists may not be interested in Biddick's theoretical arguments, but if they are interested in historicizing their own technique—which would seem logical—they will find much in this book to think about. The book also includes fascinating specifics and the fascination with specifics that has been so inspirational for New Historicism. At many moments one feels, happily, the touch of Biddick's training as an historian: Why was *Past and Present* so thick with discussion of Robin Hood? (p. 64 ff.) Why did Geertz's essay on the Balinese cockfight, "Deep Play," find its way to medieval studies in the early nineties, in essays by Gabrielle Spiegel and Allan Frantzen (p. 85 ff.): That is, why *then,* so many years after its first publication in 1973? And why in the name of interdisciplinarity, without analysis of the history of its reception by anthropologists? *The Shock of Medievalism* can be at its most satisfying when it takes to historical narration—for example, the sketches of William Stubbs's appointment as Regius Professor of Modern

History in 1866, or of the founding of the Early English Text Society, or the history of the notion of "life as information" in the mid-twentieth century (pp. 5 ff., 93 ff., 196 ff.)

The Shock of Medievalism should not, then, be dismissed as deficient in historical interest. It's not that Biddick's historiography is beyond question. Her account leaves out complications like the activism of John Kemble, editor of the Anglo-Saxon laws, or the Grimm brothers, expelled from their university by the duke of Hanover for subversive activities. Morris's commodification of Gothic ornament needs to be read in the context of his socialism, just as the pastoralism of *Past and Present* needs to be understood in the context of the journal's attempts to revise valorizations of urban life as "motor of history" and/or to dispel myths of rural idiocy. Does a leftist agenda for change, when yoked to a certain atavism, simply lose its credibility? After all, medievalism pops up all over the political map of the nineteenth century, and at its most contradictory moments. But if Biddick's handling of the political functions of archaism is less nuanced than it might be, if she treats with a certain single-mindedness the complications she herself brings to light, nonetheless by these very lights her rich, innovative assemblage of moments and movements in medieval studies decisively disturbs what we thought we knew.

Biddick's textual readings, moreover, are often brilliantly interesting. Not everyone will find it easy to follow Biddick's study of the nineteenth-century figure of the "hand" and its works all the way to the "case of the mistaken hands" in Steven Justice's *Writing and Rebellion.* But if some of us will pause at the idea of Justice's melancholic introjection of the hand of scribal handicraft (pp. 43–44), there is no question that Justice's project is one of recovery of the lost; nor is there any question that his valorization of paleography—of skill and touch, of the handwritten, of holding a manuscript in the hand—has a passional quality well worth addressing. Should we prefer not to address it as Biddick does, we are certainly challenged to address it somehow. By the time we have noted Morris's concern that no one dare "touch" a Gothic monument except to preserve it from weather, Wilde's description of Morris as "the greatest handicraftsman we have had in England since the fourteenth century," and the role of the "hand of God" in 1381, a compelling network of signifiers indeed takes shape before us. The nineteenth century's passion *for* technique (of which philology is not the least instance) could quite reasonably have taken the form of "elite male sorrow over the radical disembodiment attending industrialization" (p. 13).

This brings us to the heart of Biddick's project: to decipher the relations between academic and popular medievalism. Philology's passion for technique is read by Biddick as a melancholic refiguration of the loss incurred when medievalism made itself academic by projecting its enjoyment onto a putatively degraded popular medievalism. Following Eric Santner's *Stranded Objects,* Biddick attributes a similar structure to the twentieth-century "diasporan scientists" whose "failed mourning" and "externalization of lost objects [was] . . . a source of the fascination of simulation technologies" (pp. 196–97). This formulation doesn't take the fullest possible measure of Lacan's (and Freud's) point that the unconscious is *always-already* structured by the signifier—meaning, and not just in effect, that the subject is always-already technologized. But the intrication of desire and technicity certainly clarifies the point of a book about inquisitorial techniques of visioning witches (chapter 2) and *Star Trek: The Next Generation* (chapter 3). It also clarifies what's at stake in Biddick's account of cyberspatial visioning. Her insistence on the *embodied* status of the image, as against the overinvestment in its virtuality in information-technology discourse, is a very important intervention (and one that demonstrates the usefulness of medievalist perspectives to the theorizing of contemporary culture).

Finally, the intrication of desire and technicity clarifies the once-and-future status of the Middle Ages in popular culture today as scene both of technological deprivation/innocence, and of technology's noblest forms of sophistication (Jedi skill with light-sabres) (p. 84). On this score, Biddick cogently brings together (without conflating) what Umberto Eco sets apart in *Travels in Hyperreality* (precisely, philology and popular medievalism). Writes Biddick, "What better material [than the Middle Ages] for a dream frame for popular culture, a truly relative past that can be read as either the present or the future?" (p. 84). This plasticity, paradoxically, enables the production of the impasse at which medievalism loves to arrive. Recent discussions of how we might make use of, but also correct, our students' medievalist enthusiasms (the Society for Creative Anachronism is typically instanced, to the accompaniment of fond, rueful eye-rolling) are sufficiently stereotyped to suggest that their purpose is to reinforce the divide they lament. In this way the split between passion and scholarly integrity—and the enjoyment of correction—can be reiterated indefinitely. Anyone who has sat through such a discussion might have reason to welcome Biddick's rereading of the academic/popular divide, since it promises to get us past the impasse that has structured our discipline at least since the early nineteenth century, when the translations, redactions, garlands, and curious collections of medieval poetry favored in the eighteenth century came to seem technically inadequate to the sublime project of nationalizing history.

Admittedly—and perhaps predictably, since I'm a medievalist if not altogether a melancholiac—I was disappointed by the book's failure to develop techniques that would produce "openness to futurity rather than negative processes of expulsion" (p. 4). This is, of course, partly because the book has so much ground to break. Though a number of medievalists have been hard at work on the concept of alterity, we still don't know much about how to avoid driving wedges between knowledge and desire. Biddick does nuance the alterity of the past by noting its melancholic resurgence as technique/technology. But, while her yoking together of what historiography has previously kept asunder will be productively imitable, on the whole she produces something more in the nature of a lexicon than a method: *bringing together* or *joining* ("My allegorical reading joins the social fears of 'unreliable components,' African-American females, with the technical fears of 'unreliable components' in the logical, statistical world of machine reproduction" [p. 199]); *echoing* ("[t]he arrival of Azeem on the shores of southern England uncannily echoes the arrival of Gibreel Farishta on the beach below Battle Hill, as told by Salman Rushdie [*Satanic Verses*])"; *embedding* ("[e]mbedded in the 'oppressed past' of Gothic Revival ornament is a traumatic allegory of critical theory in medieval studies today"); *genealogy* ("The genealogy of artificial life as a simulation technology is a complicated one" [p. 195]); above all, *haunting* ("In postcolonial times, the historic womb work of enslaved African females haunts . . . an unrepresentable counterimage of the fetus").

But what form does this historical haunting take? How do we know it's a haunting (uncanny revenance, return of the repressed death wish) rather than an echo (attenuation by means of iteration) or a Benjaminian irruption (the lost signifier finds its explosive moment of articulation centuries later)? How do these different forms of resurgence behave libidinally, rhetorically, historically? Does resurgence happen, and intervene historically, only when the signifiers of the past are reread in the present? The significance of these questions for Biddick's aims (and ours) becomes clearer in the face of statements like the following (Biddick's paraphrase of Hortense Spillers): the colonial order "represents for its African and indigenous peoples a scene of *actual* mutilation, dismemberment, and exile" (p. 193). How then are we to understand the historical agency of the signifier, including its power to violate, actually or otherwise? If there is a difference between "*actual*" and rhetorical mutilation, what are the implications for, say, the rhetorical "autocannibalism" of William Morris's medievalism (p. 41)? Is it not so serious after all?

Analogies between the *nachtraglichkeit* of trauma and the belatedness of historical process have been proposed before. What interests me here is that the difficulty of answering the very questions necessary for a post-historicist medievalism may itself be a reflex of the complex temporality of the signifier on which *nachtraglichkeit* depends. The suspensions of meaning associated with this temporality are, however, edifying in their own way, as Biddick's writing suggests. What she does not, or cannot, make explicit sometimes emerges as a consequence of the excellent way she can be inexplicit, the way her multiglossolalia can open gaps in her certitudes and turn repetition into an engine of ambiguity.

At times Biddick understands her reading practice as verging on violence: "History writing disfigures since it can never leave a record in the same condition it finds it. A critical history writing reflects on its own disfigurement in the act of disfiguration" (p. 187). We need to know whether and how this kind of disfiguration differs from "*actual* mutilation," or from "the structure of violence that made Orientalism historically possible" (p. 90). When does a writing that disfigures turn into a disfigured writing? Does *critical* writing accomplish this reversal through the process of reflection? What exactly does this improve? And if history writing is imagined as disfiguring a "patient" record, a record whose power to shape the ways it is (dis)figured seems limited at best, how has the concept of alterity been altered?

When Biddick imagines Bede conversing with a Chicana theorist about multilingualism, she has him *blushing* at the thought of his potential duplicity/complicity in the language wars of his day (p. 83 ff.). This scene of shame and shaming is also one in which the past is patient with respect to an active present. Despite the appearance of dialogue, and despite the interest taken by the Chicana theorist in Bede's situation, Biddick clearly imagines that he has far more to learn from the Chicana theorist than vice-versa. Where enlightenment is concerned, Bede's out of the picture, and frankly, in such a formulation, so is the Middle Ages.

How does it help to ease up on the "hard-edged alterity of the Middle Ages" (p. 4) if the Middle Ages nonetheless needs to know its place and approach the present with proper humility? We need to do more than identify resemblances between the problematics of the past and those of the present; we need to develop reading practices that recognize how the signifiers of the past still inform and produce the present. If *The Shock of Medievalism* does not take us as far along this road as we might have hoped, it prepares us well for this work, by allowing us to see that, for the mode of enjoyment known as medieval studies, not only loss but aggressivity is required; and as a consequence we will know better how to rethink our obsolescence, by realizing how the past itself figures in the ways we disfigure it.

L. O. ARANYE FRADENBURG
University of Santa Barbara

LILLIAN M. BISSON. *Chaucer and the Late Medieval World.* New York: St. Martin's Press, 1998. Pp. 304. $45.00.

This introduction to Chaucer and his world had its genesis in two institutes on Chaucer for secondary-school teachers sponsored by the National Endowment for the Humanities (NEH). In her preface Lillian Bisson calls these experiences "exhausting" and "exhilarating" (p. ix), two states that will be recognized by many: a successful NEH institute is a Platonic ideal of intellectual fellowship. The materials in *Chaucer and the Late Medieval World* make clear the wide learning, alert curiosity, and tireless dedication that Bisson put into her institutes. If the book cannot equal their achievement, that is only to be expected. As with so many of the best moments in pedagogy, you had to be there.

Bisson's study is really about *The Canterbury Tales* and the late medieval world. Although *Troilus and Criseyde, The House of Fame, The Parliament of Foules,* and *The Legend of Good Women* are mentioned, they are not discussed in any detail and are not referred to at all in the concluding section. Moreover, the late medieval world is more prominent than Chaucer's poetry (not to mention other English and Continental poetry, which is hardly mentioned at all), and even it does not come first. Bisson explains that each chapter "is essentially funnel shaped, starting from a discussion of the topic in its seminal phrase, usually the early Christian period" (pp. ix–x). The result of this approach is strongly chronological and has the effect of making Chaucer the representative of progressive historical forces that have culminated in our own time, almost a Whig view of the poet.

Bisson's aim is more to provide a "rich cultural context for approaching *The Canterbury Tales*" (p. ix) than to analyze its many literary achievements. Even when she talks about Chaucer's poetry rather than his times, her emphasis is less on its art than on its ideas: "the societal contexts Chaucer is exploring" and "the major issues that underlie his work" (p. ix). Bisson's Chaucer does not so much tell stories as ask questions ("How can society best be governed?" or "What is the value of human love?" [p. viii]), and she assumes his primary purpose is to instruct rather than to delight: "This book's governing conviction, however, is that Chaucer used his poetry—for both himself and for his audience—as a way of trying to make sense of and to bring order to the confusing, conflicted world in which he lived" (p. x).

Chaucer and the Late Medieval World is written in a clear, lively style (without the condescension found in so many introductory works) and has an impressive bibliography of secondary works with only a few obvious omissions (such as Eamon Duffy's *The Stripping of the Altars,* which may not have yet appeared during the original research). Without many primary materials (except for Chaucer), the bibliography functions as a kind of guide to scholarship on Medieval Cultural Literacy.

The book is divided into eleven chapters under five sections. The first section is "The Poet and His World." Chapter 1, entitled "Double Vision: The Gothic Mind's Eye," is a rapid survey of the shared official beliefs of the Middle Ages. Yet, as the phrase "double vision" suggests, Bisson is not content with a harmonious view of the period. She stresses instead binary oppositions, such as those between the early and the late Middle Ages or between human and divine values. Bisson also sees progress behind these dualities, as "long-established certainties" yield to "new realities" (p. 22). Here as throughout, it is sometimes suggested that Chaucer's greatest achievement is the degree to which he anticipates modern concerns and values (see p. 142). Chapter 2 locates duality in Chaucer himself: the man of affairs in contrast to the poet. Chaucer's literary career is seen to have culminated in *The Canterbury Tales,* a work in which the medieval balance between spiritual and earthly is said to be firmly tipped toward the latter (p. 45).

The second section is on religion. The title of chapter 3, "The Church in Turmoil: The Hierarchy and Heresy," reads a little like a tabloid headline (when was the church not in turmoil?), but it also contains much information on subjects modern students (and sometimes their teachers) are often ignorant about, including an efficient account of the development of medieval penance (p. 60). As is her habit throughout, Bisson tends to concentrate on the pilgrims rather than their tales. Thus she lists different views of the Pardoner's sexuality (p. 62), including those of the author of this review, but says little about the Pardoner's extraordinary exemplum of the three revelers and death, perhaps Chaucer's most successful moral tale. Chapter 4, on the regular clergy, provides more useful information, such as the history of monks and friars. Here as elsewhere Bisson works hard to be evenhanded in representing the variety of critical views on an issue (the range of her citations is wide), though very naturally her own position comes through, sometimes indirectly and sometimes more explicitly: "But the readings that see the Prioress's spiritual immaturity reflected in the tale's superficial religiosity strike me as convincing" (p. 93). We again note Bisson's emphasis on pilgrims and on the meaning rather than the art of a tale. Chapter 5 contrasts official and popular Christianity. Although Bisson offers a useful account of medieval religious practice, she believes that Chaucer's heart is elsewhere, "on the changing, conflictive, problematic world of everyday life" (p. 119).

The next two sections and the conclusion deal with that world. Section 3 is on class and conflict: chapter 6 deals with the aristocracy, chapter 7 with the poor, and chapter 8 with trade and the money economy. Each chapter contains useful summaries of current scholarship on these topics, noting development from the early to the late Middle Ages: "we must trace the broad outlines of chivalry's development from the tenth to the fourteenth centuries" (p. 124). Emphasis remains on pilgrims (the Knight rather than *The Knight's Tale*) and on the values expressed in *The Shipman's Tale* rather than on its art (pp. 183–87).

Section 4 is on gender and sexuality. Chapter 9 treats women and records some of debates that have made this one of the most fruitful topics of recent criticism. Bisson's observation that it is hard to determine "how Chaucer fares on the feminist litmus test" (p. 208) humorously reveals her own modernist perspective. Extreme positions tend to be discounted (Elaine Hansen, on the one side, and Robertson, on the other), though her own views may seem insufficiently nuanced to some, such as her claim that the Wife of Bath grows into "an independent self" (p. 213) almost beyond Chaucer's control. Chapter 10 on love, marriage, and sexuality displays a somewhat complacent assumption that contemporary values are normative, with its talk of "personal growth" (p. 240). To conclude that poets like Chaucer played an "increasingly insistent role in the cultural dialogue that ultimately yielded a much more affirmative view of love and marriage's role in securing human happiness" seems overly optimistic in the face of that reality that marriage in *The Canterbury Tales* is almost always nasty, brutal, or short. The conclusion, "A Zone of Freedom: Carnival as the Emblem of an Age," also perhaps too easily assumes that Chaucer endorses the Miller's physicality and the Wife of Bath's sexuality.

Chaucer and the Late Medieval World may sometimes rely too much on our modern world and assumptions, but its emphasis on everyday and even transgressive contexts makes it a worthy successor (and corrective) to Robertson's more pious *Chaucer's London.* Bisson's book is not a serious study of Chaucer's poetry, but it is a clearly written, heavily researched introductory guide for those who want to know what is now being written about Chaucer and his times. Although addressed to new and beginning readers, experienced Chaucerians may also benefit from it.

C. DAVID BENSON
University of Connecticut

CHRISTOPHER CANNON. *The Making of Chaucer's English: A Study of Words.* Cambridge Studies in Medieval Literature, vol. 39. Gen. ed. Alastair Minnis. Cambridge: Cambridge University Press, 1998. Pp. xiii, 435. $69.95.

This book comes in two distinct halves, introducing its argument in part 1 ("The Study of Words") and the lexical evidence for it in part 2 ("Words Studies"). Part 2 is "an index of all of Chaucer's vocabulary that can be historicized (that is, generally, excluding proper nouns) according to the system of Larry Benson's *Glossarial Concordance to the Riverside Chaucer*" (p. 5). It gives, for each headword, the number of "the particular subheading in the *MED* where the *first recorded use* of the headword appears" (p. 228); the etymology; the date and text in which the headword first appears in the written record; the text in which it first occurs in Chaucer; and the number of times the word is used by Chaucer "in the texts concorded in Volume I of Benson's *Glossarial Index*" (p. 234). It is an index, not a glossary or a concordance: neither meanings nor variant spellings are given, since what matters for the purposes of this book is only that a word is used, not what it means or how it is spelled (thus the only form found for the thousand-odd occurrences of the possessive plural of the personal pronoun is that of the headword, *here*). This is an economical system, allowing much information to be packed into a small space. To take a straightforward example: the entry "**mortification n.** b *ML & OF* Chaucer *PARS T* 1" tells us that Chaucer is the first-recorded user in English of the noun *mortification;* that he uses it once only, in *The Parson's Tale;* and that the sense in which he uses it is *MED*'s sense b (correctly 1b, but spot checks did not reveal any other such errors).

Part 1 questions the standard view of Chaucer's crucial place in the development of English—the view that sees him both as the great improver and refiner of the language ("the father of English") and as the model for future writers ("the father of English poetry"). It demonstrates, on the contrary, that Chaucer's linguistic practices, far from being novel (as generally assumed), were entirely traditional. He is usually credited with having been not only a great borrower of words from French and Latin with which to enrich the language but also the *first* great borrower. Cannon, however, shows otherwise: that borrowing was standard practice throughout the Middle English period (especially in the century and a half *before* Chaucer, from 1200 to 1350); that Chaucer's own new borrowings are outnumbered three to one by his use of words borrowed from Romance languages by his predecessors; that borrowing, at first an aspect of translation, became habitual for Middle English writers even without the pressure of translation; and that linguistic novelty was so much the norm in Middle English that Chaucer's new word-formations (such as *mayster-hunte* in *The Book of the Duchess*) are as traditional in this respect as are his new borrowings. All of this is shown with force and clarity.

Another of the long-held beliefs attacked here is that Chaucer's English went on developing throughout his writing career in parallel with his artistry. Cannon argues that this is not so: that Chaucer's English was static; that the *rate* of new usages, though it varies from work to work and from poetry to prose, remains more or less the same throughout. This is true equally of new borrowings (like *superstitious*), of "derived words" (newly formed compounds like *convertible*), of "reserved words" (Old English words not used earlier in his writings, such as *ded* ["death"] and *minnen* ["remember"] in the Envoy to Scogan), and of nonce-words (words used by Chaucer once only, or in only one of his works (*gnof* in the Miller's *Tale, octogamie* in the Wife of Bath's, *pirie* in the Merchant's, etc.).

Having dealt in the early chapters with individual words, Cannon proceeds to widen the focus to consider words in their contexts. He shows how Chaucer handles and moves between both English and European traditions, consciously blurring the two (*Thopas* is an "English" romance, but romance is a European form; *Melibee* is a "European" translation, but religious prose has strong English roots); and how he moves easily between high and low styles (he can make English laureate; he can write plain English in a high style; he uses the *Canterbury Tales* pilgrims to demonstrate everything the vernacular is capable of). The argument is that Chaucer's high and low styles are traditional *in themselves;* that what is new is how Chaucer marks the difference between them; and that there is in fact no difference "in degree or kind of linguistic invention" between Chaucer and his contemporaries (p. 178). The analyses here (of the invocation to Cipris in *The House of Fame* 509–28; of the comments on Petrarch in the Clerk's *Prologue* 26–33; and of the conclusion to *Troilus and Criseyde,* 5.1783–92) are finely detailed; what is less convincingly demonstrated is the claim that although Chaucer's contemporaries were doing the same kinds of thing as he was, he has received all the credit for linguistic inventiveness simply because he's a better poet.

The final chapter of part 1, "The Myth of Origin and the Making of Chaucer's English" (effectively the book's conclusion), argues that Chaucer's originality was retrospectively constructed by his admirers: first by his immediate successors and imitators, who claimed him as their master (just as he, at the end of *Troilus,* had claimed Virgil, Ovid, Homer, and the rest as *his* masters); later by sixteenth- and seventeenth-century writers who, although linguistic change had made imitation impossible, nevertheless claimed him as their forefather; finally by the historical lexicographers of the *OED,* whose method (choosing quotations as far as possible only from the *best* authors) constructs the very myth of Chaucer's "presumptive originality" that it is claiming to test (p. 199). Cannon shows here how the editors' a priori opinion of Chaucer as one of the founding fathers of modern English predisposed them to choose quotations from *his* works even when earlier ones were available (pp. 201–6); thus Chaucer frequently appears in the *OED* as the earliest-recorded user of a given word even when he was not; thus his patriarchal position is (falsely) confirmed.

This last point is nicely made, but other parts of the argument are more doubtful. Why did Hoccleve, Lydgate, and others name Chaucer as their master rather than Virgil or Ovid (pp. 185–87), unless it was because they *had* been influenced by Chaucer? Their repetition of Chaucer's aureate words (such as *enluminen*) in their tributes to him (pp. 213–17) seems to me positive evidence of his influence on their language (and hence on the future of English), not of some (false) myth about it. Derrida may claim that "the idea of writing . . . is meaningful for us only in terms of an origin" (p. 180), but who says that all that Derrida writes is true? The book strikes me finally as perverse (in spite of the excellence of the opening chapters and the exhaustive research that has gone into the compiling of part 2). If what you really want to write is "a general history of . . . the 'rise of English as a literary language,'" paying due attention to the importance of "the early Middle English writing that preceded Chaucer" (pp. 218–19)—a very valuable project, surely?—isn't it self-defeating to write instead (merely because it will sell better) a book on the *un*importance of Chaucer to the history of the language? Let's hope that, having done the second of these things (against both his inclination and his better judgment, it seems), Cannon will now go back to do the first.

T. L. Burton
University of Adelaide

W. A. Davenport. *Chaucer and His English Contemporaries: Prologue and Tale in the* Canterbury Tales. New York: St. Martin's Press, 1998. Pp. x, 245. $55.00 cloth, $19.95 paper.

With the publication of William Davenport's latest book, Chaucer studies has achieved an appropriate symmetry in book titles containing the words "English" and "French." Davenport's study of the domestic context of *The Canterbury Tales* is less ambitious than James Wimsatt's review of Chaucer's French lyric influences in *Chaucer and His French Contemporaries* (1991). Its intended audience is also different: *Chaucer and His English Contemporaries* is geared toward beginning readers of Middle English (most textual quotations have glosses) and beginning researchers in Chaucer studies (its engagement with other criticism is kept at an appropriately limited level). Nonetheless, it provides a nuanced analysis of the specifically English artistic environment of *The Canterbury Tales,* and it successfully suggests the generic complexities and innovations of Chaucer's last great work. Similar in tone and method to his earlier book on Chaucer, *Chaucer: Complaint and Narrative* (1988), Davenport's latest book is a readable and thoughtful study. It can be recommended as a useful resource for any course situating *The Canterbury Tales* with contemporary English literature.

There are seven chapters: a brief introduction, a summarizing conclusion, and five middle chapters: "Prologues," "Tales," "Romances," "Chaucer, Gower, and the *Gawain*-Poet," and "Forms of Narrative." The subjects of the second two chapters establish the basic areas of analysis. Chapter 2 provides a good review of the literary notion of a prologue in Chaucer's day, and it challenges some received ideas about how Chaucer's own prologues work. Drawing from the rhetorical tradition of text division (from Cicero to Isidore, Geoffrey of Vinsauf, and John of Garland) as well as from the analysis of Gottfried von Strassburg's *Tristan,* Davenport identifies the traits of "composite prologues" (p. 16) and their "overlapping strategies" (p. 18): they both introduce the work to come and insinuate the speaker into the reader's confidence. Davenport then analyzes the prologues to Gower's *Confessio Amantis* and Langland's *Piers Plowman* as unique examples of composite prologues in order to modify the familiar generic characterization of Chaucer's *General Prologue* as an estates satire. Counterintuitively, but convincingly, Davenport argues that "comparison with Gower and Langland suggests that Chaucer is deliberately avoiding the provision of a formal prologue" (p. 28)—but also that *The General Prologue* introduces a prefatory statement of "purpose, content, and quality" (p. 35) by means of its uniquely unprologue-like framing narrative. This line of analysis, along with the analyses of the several prologues within *The Canterbury Tales,* is the most insightful and useful part of the book.

The analysis of "Tales" in the third chapter is similarly challenging but somewhat less successful. Again with reference to a series of contextualizing literary sources (Cicero, Thomas of Salisbury, the *Book of the Knight of La Tour-Landry,* the *Cursor Mundi,* Mannyng's *Handlyng Synne*), Davenport seeks to establish the idea of a "tale" as fundamentally exemplary. He provides an extended consideration of several Canterbury tales with exempla (the Summoner's, the Nun's Priest's, the Wife of Bath's, and the Monk's *Tales*) and of several tales as exempla (the Physician's, Manciple's, and Pardoner's *Tales*). The importance of understanding exemplary narratives is unarguable, and the observations of how Chaucer "plays with preaching styles" (p. 66) are well presented. But to move from these examples to the assertion of "the basic idea of a 'tale' as exemplifying a moral" (p. 66) is a bit of a leap. Gower's use of exempla provides an instructive comparison, but the reduction of all "tales" to forms of exempla—and in the case of fabliaux, they are reclassified as "cherles tale[s]" (p. 74), which is a type of negative or antiexempla—simply seems too narrow. The later part of the chapter reads the tales back through the lens of *The Parson's Tale,* a strategy that certainly provides the moral foundations for the "satirical exposure of vice and folly" (p. 83) but that also introduces a host of unconsidered problems—such as how readers might be expected to carry off such a retrospective assessment in the first place.

Despite these objections, the chapter on "Tales" is thought-provoking and its general conclusions are sound. A similar judgment can be rendered on the remaining chapters. In chapter 4, Davenport analyzes Chaucer's engagement with romance. (It is worth noting that in Davenport's scheme, a "romance" is implicitly not a "tale," a distinction that can be confusing.) Here he summarizes several romances from Thomas Chester (*Arthour and Merlin, Lybeaus Desconsus, Sir Launfal*) and others (*Havelok, Gamelyn, Sir Degrevant*). The summaries of the romances are just that; but they provide the necessary background for understanding the kind of romance writing that was contemporary with Chaucer. The comparison to the romance elements in Chaucer's narratives (the Knight's, Franklin's, Clerk's, and Squire's *Tales*) leads to the basic conclusion that "Chaucer does not complete a single, 'straight' romance . . . but he cannot leave romance alone" (p. 132).

A similar combination of the obvious with the insightful is achieved in chapter 6. In the analysis of "Forms of Narrative," the comparisons to other writers are at times perfunctory, but this unevenness is compensated for by the directness and clarity of the conclusions. Davenport divides the individual Canterbury tales into two groups: "well-made narratives," which are complete and well-balanced stories such as *The Knight's Tale* and *The Second Nun's Tale,* and "wayward narratives," which are "eccentric" stories (p. 189) that tend to stray from balance in structure and thematic content, such as *The Physician's Tale* and *The Manciple's Tale.* Again, this simple rubric proves quite productive of insight.

By comparison, the analyses of chapter 5 are less compelling, largely because they need more room. The reading of Chaucer along with the *Gawain*-poet in particular is simply too short to do justice to either. The comparison of Chaucer's *Man of Law's Tale* to the romance *Emaré* and to Gower's version in the *Confessio Amantis* is successful primarily for the good evidence it provides for a standard reading of the *Tale.* And the comparison of *The Tale of Florent* to *The Wife of Bath's Tale* and *The Weddyng of Sir Gawain and Dame Ragnell* is perhaps too teasing; the bon mot that concludes this section left me wanting to hear more.

Indeed, there are many such moments in this book that make the reader want more, and the truly quotable observations, which are everywhere in the text, are even more prevalent in the concluding chapter. Occasionally Davenport's easy manner gets the best of him. But throughout the book, Davenport's analysis repays close reading with elegant formulations and observations. As the author states early on (p. 5), history and theory (or at least the self-conscious kinds) are not treated in this study. Although these exclusions lead to the occasional impasse or naive statement (e.g., p. 75: "Chaucer seems to claim, in the case of *The Miller's Tale,* that laughter unifies all classes"), the decision to forgo nonliterary concerns is perhaps understandable in light of the book's intended audience. It would be worthwhile to compare and contrast Davenport's critical uses of exemplarity with those of Larry Scanlon, for example, or his analyses of Chaucerian romance with those of Susan Crane; but these are exercises necessarily left to the more advanced reader. As it stands, *Chaucer and His English Contemporaries* is an accessible elementary study of several key literary topics that were of great importance to Chaucer and his fellow poets.

MATTHEW GIANCARLO
Yale University

MARILYNN DESMOND, ed. *Christine de Pizan and the Categories of Difference.* Medieval Cultures, vol. 14. Minneapolis and London: University of Minnesota Press, 1998. Pp. xix, 287. $57.95 cloth, $22.95 paper.

The twelve essays comprising this important collection, like the 1995 Binghamton University conference engendering them, attest to the recent "boom" in Christine studies, not only in the domains of literary history and women's writing but also in those of patronage and dissemination, law and social issues, and medieval medicine. This volume also gratifyingly introduces several newcomers: not only younger scholars but also those well established in other fields.

The editor's introduction intriguingly conjoins Christine's unique talent for textual and symbolic hybridization (an aspect keenly analyzed among Christine and her contemporaries by Kevin Brownlee in 1989 in *A New History of French Literature,* though uncited here) with Donna Haraway's modern-day cyborg, doubling as an attempt to unify the various strands represented in the volume. This hybrid image segues neatly into the first of the volume's three main divisions, entitled "The Belly of the Monster." In "Christine and the Art of Warfare," Christine's way of dealing with the monster of war is masterfully discussed by the venerable pioneer of Christine de Pizan scholarship, and particular expert on the *Fais d'Armes,* Charity Willard. Another plenary address from the conference, Roberta Krueger's "Christine's Anxious Lessons: Gender, Morality and the Social Order from the *Enseignemens* to the *Avision,*" deftly marshals much current scholarship together with her own insights to extend our perceptions of Christine's notion of pedagogy well beyond Astrik Gabriel's classic 1955 study, while situating Christine within the (otherwise male) tradition of medieval conduct manuals for women. Diane Wolfthal brings an art historian's expertise to examining the dark specter of rape as represented in Christine's works both visually and textually. Mary Anne Case applies legal ethics and actual decisions to less violent but equally self-defense–oriented aspects of the *Cité des dames*'s pragmatic feminism in "Christine de Pizan and the Authority of Experience."

Part 2, entitled "Situated Knowledges," begins with Thelma Fenster's "'Perdre son latin': Christine de Pizan and Vernacular Humanism," which explores her ideas of gender, politics, and language as applied to her translations of Latin works. Benjamin Semple, in "The Critique of

Knowledge as Power: The Limits of Philosophy and Theology in Christine de Pizan," elucidates her critique of theological and philosophical knowledge in the *Cité* and, later, the *Avision,* comparing them to Aristotle's *Metaphysics* and Jean Gerson's *Montaigne de contemplacion.* An effective visual component to this section is ably supplied by Mary Weitzel Gibbons's "*The Bath of the Muses* and Visual Allegory in the *Chemin de long estude,*" marred only by (minor) errors in translation (pp. 138–39). Christine's opinions on a less sibylline realm of knowledge, gynecology, benefit from Monica Green's elegant analysis in "'Traittié tout de mençonges': The *Secrés des dames,* 'Trotula,' and Attitudes toward Women's Medicine in Fourteenth- and Early-Fifteenth-Century France," of why the *Cité des Dames* excludes the legendary female doctor Trotula (another hybrid: part person, part book) from its pantheon: a paradox Green rightly parallels with Christine's near-omission of Heloise.

"Engendering Authorship" titles part 3, primarily devoted to publishing and patrons except for the first essay, Judith Kellogg's "Transforming Ovid: The Metamorphosis of Female Authority," a comprehensive treatment of Christine's reworking of Ovid, perhaps more appropriate to part 1 (the beast of male mythographical authority) or part 2 (exegesis as a path to knowledge). More to the point of this section, Deborah McGrady's "What is a Patron? Benefactors and Authorship in Harley 4431, Christine de Pizan's Collected Works," deploys an astoundingly mature command of material, ranging from Christinian codicology to Foucault's theories, in arguing that the poet controlled her patrons rather than vice versa. In "The Reconstruction of an Author in Print: Christine de Pizan in the Fifteenth and Sixteenth Centuries," Cynthia Brown carries Christine's posterity a major step further into the complex arena of early printed editions, many of which invariably involved "translations"—more properly, reconstitutions—of her work, even those remaining in French. Brown clarifies these developments via an authoritative schema. Finally, Michel-André Bossy, in "Arms and the Bride: Christine de Pizan's Military Treatise as a Wedding Gift for Margaret of Anjou," expertly reveals the extent of the author's prestige fifteen years after her death, since this particular manuscript (BL Royal 15.E.VI) containing a copy of the *Fais d'armes,* the only copy naming her as its author, was a gift to the queen from no less than John Talbot. Bossy's article also provides the omega to Willard's alpha in returning to the *Fais d'armes,* if in another light.

The strongest articles appear to be those by Case, Brown, Fenster, and

Green. These, and doubtless others this reviewer is now too limited to appreciate fully, will become classics in their respective areas. Regardless of perspective, each contributor manages to demonstrate Christine's distinct authorial voice as marginalized by her gender yet privileged by her own self-determinism. If she is not always as radical as modern feminists would like, she nonetheless enlightens us as to how a single woman could survive respectably in her time, and even ours.

The editor has carefully cross-referenced the essays to each other at pertinent moments throughout. A reasonably accurate cumulative bibliography and useful (proper-name) index complete the volume.

However, a final word, a caveat, seems necessary. That only twelve articles are herein contained out of the seventy papers, many by major international specialists in Christine de Pizan, presented at the Binghamton conference—the "small proportion of that dialogue" to which the preface alludes—might lead one to question why. Neither the panicky, unappealing title—scrambling, like the introduction, to impose trendy cohesiveness where little exists due to decimation—nor the prefatory remarks furnish a real explanation. For those involved in both enterprises, the conference was a labor of love, generating lively discussion and true cultivation of "difference"; by contrast, this volume emerged out of needless dismay and hurt, even for some of those included, though benefiting those journals and volumes that later welcomed the withdrawn and rejected articles. The abundant world of Christine studies should not exact its namesake's capacity for suffering from its diverse participants.

NADIA MARGOLIS
Leverett, Massachusetts

JODY ENDERS. *The Medieval Theater of Cruelty: Rhetoric, Memory, Violence.* Ithaca, N.Y.: Cornell University Press, 1999. Pp. viii, 268. $45.00.

Jody Enders is an unabashed foundationalist. She is after the Ur narratives of Western civilization (p. 232). She goes looking for them at her ground zero: rhetoric. These latest efforts bring her deeper than in her first book, *Rhetoric and the Origins of Drama* (1992). They probe frames of mind and the sorts of abstract scenes played out on a classical *theatrum* or stage. What she finds there is a far cry from the uplifting stories of progress that once typified the search for foundations. In the spirit of our times, she tracks with fierce intent a disturbing side of our culture. Enders's argument runs like this: Rhetoric's work on the mind is coercive; it is expressed dramatically and sticks violently. The so-called civilizing process that rhetoric enables is anything but civil. People are wont to discount this understanding because to do otherwise would sap their most basic assumptions about social behavior.

This is a very tricky picture to grasp, and Enders grapples with it by concentrating on many kinds of public actions that may well substantiate such mental happenings. She ranges ambitiously over legal trials, schoolroom exercises, mystery plays and urban rituals in classical and premodern Europe, cutting back and forth between her two favorite sources: Latin rhetoric, and French and English drama. The story Enders ends up telling is a conventional one of origins, yet flipped over to show its underside. Like Artaud, her *compagnon de route,* her work packs iconoclastic punch.

The Medieval Theater of Cruelty is organized according to three principal categories of rhetoric: invention, memory, *actio* or delivery. Chapter 1 takes on torture as a way into rhetorical *inventio.* It develops the premise that there is a "similarity between finding the truth in a tortured victim's body and finding a rhetorical proof in one's own mind through the dramatic procedures of invention" (p. 30). Both quests are relentless; and their troubling quality suggests why their connection has been left unprobed. Enders does not flinch at the task. She goes right to the psychomachia in classical and medieval rhetorical treatises such as Geoffrey of Vinsauf's *Poetria Nova.* Here, as in the *Rhetorica ad Herennium,* she confronts a primal scene of a mind at war with itself. It captures for her the outbursts of violence inherent to invention.

Further on, she tests the philological evidence in vernacular texts for signs of such violence. The terms *la question* or *quaestio,* for example, which can mean "torture" or simply "legal investigation," highlights the violent fuse running through what are rhetorical, legal, and scholastic techniques. Enders consistently explores points of origin by analogy. Christ's suffering is like the torture of Roman convicts; it is like the ordeal of legal interrogation; and once we take into account the full sweep of this chapter, the final analogy reads: Christ's passion resembles the mind tormenting itself in the act of inventing something new and good. The gamble of Enders's arguments lies in just these analogies. Ultimately, she is more interested in the conceptual parallels between classical rhetoric and the texts of learned Christian dramatists than in the specifics of any individual cases.

Chapter 2 inquires into the violence of memory. The centerpiece is Cicero and Quintilian's legend of Simonides, which describes a man who identifies victims of a collapsed building by visualizing where they sat before the accident. Remembering involves putting maimed corpses back together. The legend incorporates all the elements that are crucial to Enders's thinking on memory: an architecture implying a rhetorical structure, the embodied images within it, the force needed to restore them. She begins by investigating the architectural tropes of crypt and womb. The *Life of Saint Erkenwald,* with its scene of discovering an encrypted body, represents a mnemonic. So too the *quem quaeritis* fragment that relates the search for Christ's body missing from the tomb. The trope of the womb accentuates instead the generative verve of violence. Remembering is also a kind of birthing; its convulsive, painful circumstances ensure that the images created will endure. In the *de memoria artificiali* of Thomas Bradwardine, Enders zeroes in on how memorizing involves inflicting harm. The images to be retained—in this case the signs of the Zodiac—are beaten into the mind. They take hold because they hurt.

In chapter 3, the category of rhetorical delivery leads Enders to performances of religious drama. The theater of her title involves at last the sound and sweat of players in action. Studying these body languages means reckoning with the physical experience of violence. Enders looks first to the audience as witness to figure out how spectating becomes active involvement, how it changes into complicity in the suffering performed. She surveys the special effects of the medieval stage: the secret sponges soaked in red liquids, the doughy breasts to be lopped off, the instruments of torture. Throughout, she takes care to distinguish between the realistic enactment of pain, close calls or accidental pain, and episodes of deliberately inflicted pain (p. 200). Her care draws attention to the charged overlap: cruelty that was represented was also felt.

Her analysis culminates with an apparent case of onstage execution in Tournai in 1549: an actor playing Judith in a biblical drama sticks to her part and beheads Holofernes, acted by a convicted murderer. Here the theory of theatrical catharsis is a cover, and the effort to inculcate civility, a desperate act. Whether this gruesome confusion of roles and real life happened in Tournai or not, Enders uses it to advance one stark thesis: The perennial term of culture is violence, in all its damaging and creative vigor. A true Nietzschean, she stands by a universal aesthetics of cruelty (p. 232).

The Medieval Theater of Cruelty exhibits the postmodern eagerness to undo ideals that have proved dear to our culture. At what cost do they continue to be maintained? By investigating this question, it takes its place in a line-up of shrewd, finely argued inquiries. I am thinking of Gordon Teskey's *Allegory and Violence* (1996) and Regina M. Schwartz's *The Curse of Cain: The Violent Legacy of Monotheism* (1997). All three books agree that some of the most prestigious premodern cultural forms—arts of language, the Bible, and high literary genres—are rooted in a negative value: in fact, violence energizes their ongoing influence.

Judging from this company, Enders's passion for foundations stands out—especially her resolve to exploit the corollary case, what I would call "continuity through violence." Her writing style reinforces it. This book is full of phrases that forge a chain linking contemporary critics with their predecessors centuries back: "long before a de Lorde, a Kristeva, or a Kubiak . . . medieval drama had . . ." (p. 118); "long before Stanislavski . . . classical and medieval theorists had . . ." (p. 154); "from Aristotle to Lucian of Samosata to Marivaux to the current American reality-based crime shows . . ." (p. 185). Even at the level of sentence structure, Enders asserts continuity systematically. By dint of repetition, the rat-a-tat rhythms of her prose, the argument starts to look irresistible. At times, however, it is overstated. Her drive to establish "continuity through violence" is so headstrong that it blunts the details of medieval drama, Kubiak, or Marivaux. I missed these particulars.

Her selection of evidence from religious drama highlights for me the problem of overstatement. Repeated in every chapter is an analysis of scourging scenes. Enders claims that "bloodshed is the highpoint of the spectacle" (p. 212); these scenes mark the predictable climax of her argument, again and again. Certainly they are crucial to it; but they serve overtime without contributing additional decisive pieces to Enders's continuum of violence.

These repeated analyses also point up my one reservation about this book. Christ's scourging emerged out of and was represented continuously in a matrix of religious culture. Further, it was an event that evokes the ritual of sacrifice. In mystery plays, this was the defining ritual. Enders uses religion as a descriptive label, but never as a criterion for interpretation. Her commentary on these scenes hits this limit. Enders anticipated this; she fends off the criticism that she has chosen to "decontextualize them. . .divorc[ing] them from the religiosity that inspired such a genre" (p. 6). Still, her work would have been enriched by some consideration of the legitimizing model of sacrifice, however modest.

The Medieval Theater of Cruelty is a hard, provocative read in the best sense. It risks large strokes of an argument that explains our fascination with pain in the world. It delivers wonderfully. I count on Enders to show us why the groundwork of intellectual history still matters today.

HELEN SOLTERER
Duke University

LOUISE FRADENBURG and CARLA FRECCERO, eds., with the assistance of Kathy Lavezzo. *Premodern Sexualities.* New York and London: Routledge, 1996. Pp. xxiv, 276. $70.00 cloth, $19.95 paper.

One of the most exciting and productive movements in recent medieval and early modern scholarship has been a historicist rethinking of culture in relation to queer sexuality. Louise Fradenburg and Carla Freccero's collection of essays, *Premodern Sexualities,* takes an important place in this emerging field of study. Originating as a special issue of *GLQ* (1:4 [1995]), the collection appears here in expanded form, with seven new essays and with the original introduction and five essays, at times significantly revised and expanded.

Fradenburg and Freccero's "Preface" and "Introduction: Caxton, Foucault, and the Pleasures of History" constitute the volume's strongest contribution. Defining the "chief purpose" of *Premodern Sexualities* as "help[ing] us think further about what we mean when we say that sex has a history and that we need to know more about it" (p. vii), they emphasize especially the ways in which queer theory has pointed us toward a recognition of the active *pleasure* we might take in doing historical work (p. viii):

> We do not . . . pursue the history of sexuality just because we must; we study it because we know that what we must or ought to do is intimately related to

> what we want to do. And we want history; the joy of finding counterparts in the past, for example, problematic though it may be, is not simply to be dismissed as anachronism. . . . History . . . is an erogenous zone, and knowing this helps us understand sexuality itself a lot better. It might also help us better understand the kinds of ethical structures at stake in historical thinking. For example, the argument that modern desires and perspectives can and must be set aside if we are to read the past properly is itself revealing, for it suggests that historical knowledge is often founded on the renunciation, the *ascesis,* of "self."

Fradenburg and Freccero consider how history might be done otherwise—and not just by "traditional" historians but also by those working with models indebted to queer theory, especially the first volume of Michel Foucault's *History of Sexuality.* Following a dominant understanding of Foucault, many have insisted on a clear line of demarcation between an era of modern sexuality and a time "before sexuality," when sexual "acts, rather than identities, are targeted for cultural attention" (p. xx). Fradenburg and Freccero call for a fuller analysis of whether such a distinction best characterizes the difference between "modern" and "premodern" sexualities. More radically, they interrogate the dependence of *both* traditional and queer historicism on an "alteritism" that makes the past essentially different from the present. Calling attention to the otherness of different times, places, and cultures, such alteritism treats the recognition of similarities or continuities as a "transhistorical" imposition of ourselves on others. Fradenburg and Freccero insist, however, that forging common cause with the past might be not an imposition of self on other but an identification, charged with "dangers and pleasures," that is also potentially a "subversive reinscription" of our understanding of *both* past and present (p. xviii).

The essays collected in *Premodern Sexualities* address the issues raised by this introduction with varying degrees of success. Most disappointing in the collection as a whole is the failure—despite the bringing together of essays by scholars of both the early modern and the medieval—to consider questions regarding the traditional division between the two periods. Fradenburg and Freccero themselves ask, "To what extent are current histories of sexuality participating in discourses of 'enlightenment'—of which the notion of the Renaissance is itself an instance—that have sought . . . to distinguish a darker, blinded, 'other' past from a more clear-sighted and splendid present?" (p. xx). But the individual essays do not consider how it might be different to think a "medieval premodern," constructed wholly outside modernity, and an "early modern premodern," placed in some relation of continuity to modernity even as it is distinguished from it.

The first section of *Premodern Sexualities,* "The Erotics of Conquest," is its most uneven and least satisfying. Here, Jonathan Goldberg's "The History That Will Be" most fully addresses the sorts of issues raised by Fradenburg and Freccero's introduction. Goldberg considers two interrelated questions: 1) how to theorize cultural history and the history of sexuality without falling back into the foundational heteronormativity of Lévi-Strauss's anthropology or of psychoanalysis (for Goldberg, unsurprisingly, the answer here lies with a turn to Foucault); and 2) how, in the "imbrication of colonialism with sexuality" (p. 11), an "assumption" tying "historical reproduction . . . to heteronormativity" (p. 5) is at work. Goldberg examines "narratives of the European invasion of the Americas" (p. 3) to argue that historical thinking should be opened more fully to contingency, "the multiple and conflicting openings towards a future" (p. 15). José Piedra's "In Search of the Black Stud" also considers intercultural contacts, focusing on the intersections among race, gender, and sexuality more fully than do the other essays in the volume. But Piedra attempts to cover so much ground (eight or nine centuries), and he does so with such universalizing and stereotyping force (for instance, "It is no surprise that the act of verbal and genital self-assertion unifies blacks, women, and gays" [p. 28]), and with such frequent inaccuracies (identifying Moses, Mohammed, and Christ all as "Messiahs" [p. 27]), that the essay's value is questionable.

The two remaining essays in part 1—María M. Carrion's "The Queen's Two Bawdies: *El burlador de Sevilla* and the Teasing of Historicity" and Richard Corum's "Henry's Desires"—present readings of texts that will be of greatest interest to specialists. Treating the seventeenth-century Don Juan play *El burlador de Sevilla,* Carrion reflects on how the "formation of new masculine identities" intersects with "the formation of new national and political identities" (p. 46). Corum's essay takes up Shakespeare's *Henry V,* arguing that the play dramatizes Henry's self-willed movement from a "penile" and "sodomitical" position antithetical to royal and national power, to a "phallic" and "homosocial" one necessary for effective rule. Corum notes, however, that the very move to repress sodomy expresses "sodomitical libido" (p. 88), and he calls on readers, critics, and producers of the play to grasp its "irresponsible" excess and turn it against a hegemonic homosociality (p. 90).

The three essays gathered in the book's second section, "Medicine and Law," share not only a focus on disciplinary knowledges but also an emphasis on the centrality of *gender* to medieval and early modern sexualities. Thus Ruth Mazo Karras and David Lorenzo Boyd, in their discussion (much expanded over the original treatment in *GLQ*) of a fourteenth-century London legal document concerning the male transvestite prostitute "John Rykener calling [himself] Eleanor" (p. 111), argue that "Sodomy was only one of the manifestations of a more important issue subtending the denunciation of male homosexual contact in medieval culture: gender transgression and conflation" (p. 106). Although gender *is* integral to medieval concerns about sexual transgression, I wonder why it is necessary here to see gender as somehow *more* crucial than sexuality. Lorraine Daston and Katharine Park, in "The Hermaphrodite and the Orders of Nature: Sexual Ambiguity in Early Modern France," consider how differing medical traditions come together in a remarkable late-sixteenth- and early-seventeenth-century efflorescence of interest in hermaphrodites, in which the gender double- or middleness of hermaphroditism becomes "strongly associated with sexual ambiguity and thence with the otherwise unrelated phenomena of sexual metamorphosis, transvestism, and sodomy" (p. 118). Stepping back from their materials, Daston and Park also consider the need to historicize the very categories—sex/gender, nature/culture—that tend, unquestioned, to structure historical work. Karma Lochrie's "Don't Ask, Don't Tell: Murderous Plots and Medieval Secrets" is one of the most ambitious pieces in *Premodern Sexualities,* drawing connections between the recent controversy over American military policies on homosexuality and medieval discourses of female sexuality. (The argument of Lochrie's essay as originally published in *GLQ* is here considerably elaborated.) In a comparative analysis that "preserve[s] historical difference and continuity without foreclosing either" (p. 139), Lochrie examines the complex and contradictory ways in which both medieval gender and late twentieth-century regimes of sexuality form "part of secrecy's plot and its historical span" (p. 149).

The two essays that constitute the third section of *Premodern Sexualities,* "Sexuality and Sanctity," consider particular texts in order to raise questions about the significance of sexuality in medieval religious contexts. Kathy Lavezzo, in "Sobs and Sighs between Women: The Homoerotics of Compassion in *The Book of Margery Kempe,*" reads Kempe's devotion as participating in "a powerful and disruptive form of female homoerotic bonding" (p. 176), modeled on the Virgin Mary's compassion. That "the female homoeroticism produced at the site of female lamentation constitutes a disruptive act in which the proper turns improper, and the pious strays into the perverse" is not, however, a *necessary* conclusion. Though Lavezzo sees Kempe's version of the afterlife as suggesting an "alternate female community," visions of such a community of "holy maidens and virgins" might of course serve hegemonic as well as "disruptive" ends (p. 191). Simon Gaunt's "Straight Minds/'Queer' Wishes in Old French Hagiography: *La Vie de Sainte Euphrosine*" considers the complicated circulation of desire (and secrecy) in the Old French life of a transvestite saint, arguing that the text does not so much "curb" as "enhance" the "'risk' of homosexuality," while at the same time "forc[ing] us . . . to question what is meant by the categories 'man' and 'woman'" (p. 166). More generally, Gaunt is concerned to argue that vernacular hagiography is "central to European culture, and to the construction of sexuality therein" (p. 156) and to "point out that a hetero/homo dialectic, similar though not identical to that which . . . structures and regulates modern Western societies, manifests itself in medieval culture" (p. 157).

Premodern Sexualities closes with a strong group of essays on "Rhetoric and Poetics." Patricia Parker's "Virile Style" traces a gendered rhetorical tradition from classical Rome into the sixteenth century (though without considering medieval mediations of the Renaissance return to the classics). A "nervosus" (sinewy) style was explicitly seen as masculine and adopted as an ideal in such disciplines as scientific writing. But as Parker also shows, writing itself was often feminized, and writers like Montaigne who embraced a "virile" style might also find themselves implicated in "lax and feminized" (p. 211) speech. Elizabeth Pittenger's "Explicit Ink" turns to Alain de Lille's *Complaint of Nature,* a text receiving much current queer attention, and proposes that, despite its explicit antisodomitical argument, the *Complaint* implicates itself in the sodomitical—depending upon tropes of language, poetry, and writing that it codes as perverse, and constructing a scene of instruction haunted by "the specter of pederastic pedagogy" (p. 229). Pittenger ultimately argues that "the eradication of excess that characterizes not only the campaign against sodomy waged through and around Alanus's *Complaint,* but also the broader attacks launched in the name of protecting the proper way from the threat of heresy," must in part operate by an erasure of the "material and physical manifestations" of "scribal labor" in order to construct the "laws of proper reading" as transcendent and metaphysical (pp. 237–38). Bruce W. Holsinger closes the volume with a complex and satisfying discussion of Dante, "Sodomy and Resurrection: The Homoerotic Subject of the *Divine Comedy*." Arguing that a queer medievalism should attend to "medieval categories for identity and desire" (p. 245), Holsinger considers "not . . . *sexual identities* as stable and unchanging, but rather . . . *homoerotic subject positions* as historically contingent, fleeting, unstable, produced at certain moments, by certain texts, and through specific cultural practices" (p. 245). More particularly, Holsinger considers both Dante and "the reading subject fashioned by the same male homosocial sphere of pedagogy, poetics, and paternity that produced Dante and his writings" (p. 246) as "subject[s] of homoerotic desire" (p. 246).

Fradenburg and Freccero's collection thus brings a widely varied group of essays to our attention. If some of these are disappointing, others are extraordinarily rich. And the book as a whole, framed as it is by the editors' theoretically challenging introduction, is sure to shape in important ways future queer work in the Middle Ages and early modernity.

STEVEN F. KRUGER
University of Alberta

ALLEN J. FRANTZEN. *Before the Closet: Same-Sex Love from* Beowulf *to* Angels in America. Chicago and London: University of Chicago Press, 1998. Pp. x, 369. Illustrations. $35.

Before the Closet is a straightforwardly polemical book that seeks to argue a specific way of understanding same-sex love in England, primarily in the early Middle Ages, by using an intriguing range of contemporary art (theater, dance, opera) as interpretive foils. Frantzen sets four objectives for the book: to examine categories of same-sex relations in Anglo-Saxon England; to explore what he sees as "fundamental similarities" between the experience of individuals in Anglo-Saxon England and in the contemporary world of Europe and North America; to argue that the evidence from Anglo-Saxon England is "straightforward" rather than "queer"; and to argue that the early Middle Ages lacked an identity as "sexual subject." Frantzen reads a range of texts from Anglo-Saxon England, from the celebrated (*Beowulf,* the *Wanderer, Wife's Lament*) to the virtually unknown (the complex texts of the Anglo-Saxon Penitentials). And in subsequent chapters he also considers (though in less detail) texts from the twelfth and fourteenth centuries as well as work by the antiquarian John Bale, before moving on to *Angels in America.* Frantzen is a recognized authority on the early medieval penitential (a handbook of penances designed for pastoral care), and his presentation of the material from the English and Anglo-Latin penitentials offers readers a rich opportunity to encounter the sexual schemata of these penitentials in terms of the tariffs of penances they assess for sexual transgressions.

Throughout the book, Frantzen reads his texts through the figure of the "shadow," a metaphor that is made to bear considerable interpretive freight (see esp. pp. 13–15). In constructing the "shadow" as the interpretive frame for these texts, Frantzen writes in explicit opposition to queer theory and theorists to counter (in his view) their emphases on genital sex, liberation, and promiscuity with his own emphasis on same-sex love and legitimation. In pursuing such a goal, he must develop a hermeneutic different from queer strategies used to deconstruct heteronormativity. Frantzen is fully aware of the rhetorical risks that he takes in pursuing such a strategy. The questions that readers of the book must answer for themselves is whether the figure of the "shadow" and the punning label "straightforward" perform more than a rhetorical function in directing the reader's attention to same-sex love in the early Middle Ages. Frantzen is explicit about the difficulties and potentials of the "shadow" as his controlling figure: "Shadows cannot exist on their own, but nothing can be seen without them. Durable, adaptable, inescapable, they *define*" (p. 14; his emphasis). Yet it is a hard figure to settle for, not only because of the often unhappy connotations of shadows but also because (to take metaphor at its word) the length and depth of a shadow depend on the angle and strength of the light trained on the object that casts it. Frantzen's scholarship certainly can cast a bright light on the objects of his attention, but he does not always give directions for angling the light.

"Straightforward" is often a tendentious term in the book. Its range includes "unveiled," "clear," "direct," "not needing interpretation." The latter meaning, particularly when applied to the "straightforward" value of the penitential material, is curiously positivist, and this tactical use is surprising, given the impassioned critique of that very archival positivism he makes in *Desire for Origins* (1990; see esp. pp. 103–5). Yet this critical position is necessary to his argument, even inevitable, given his vociferous rejection of current queer theory throughout the book. The penitentials in their enumerations of sexual (and other) transgressions would appear to offer a grounding for same-sex acts and a point of origin centuries before the "invention" of sodomy (see pp. 112 and 134). His claim that these penitentials "reflect" what people were doing sexually in Anglo-Saxon England is a way of grounding his interpretive strategies applied to more broadly literary texts (p. 145). The model of "reflection" is a problematic assumption, as Frantzen certainly knows, that flies in the face of the body of historicist interpretation of the last twenty years that has made "representation" its watchword. However, while Frantzen locates penitentials outside a hermeneutics, effectively as a ground and point of origin, the hermeneutic reading of individual texts he does offer is intensely political and personal. The moment of positivism is thereby balanced by a criticism that uses the different experiences of straight and gay audiences when viewing trouser roles in the opera, most particularly *Der Rosenkavalier,* or in a different manipulation of conventions, Mark Morris's *Dido and Aeneas* or *The Hard Nut.* Frantzen argues that audiences—straight and gay—hope to see confirmation of their desires. On this basis, art will appear straight to straight people and gay to gay people (p. 65). His readings, from the desire to see same-sex love, and from the politics of legitimation, decline queering texts in favor of "the rhetoric of straightforwardness" (p. 66).

Frantzen gives a number of readings of the Old English (and later) materials he covers in his book. His reading are always informed and sensitive to nuance, but often they are coyly multiple, allowing him to have a queer reading and deny it at the same time. For example, in his reading of the Wanderer's dream of the act of homage to his lord, Frantzen deromanticizes it deliberately (by envisioning the likelihood of vermin on the Wanderer) while maintaining of "clyppe ond cysse" that "the gesture must be allowed an erotic, even sexual aura, if only for a moment; it is a kiss, after all, and a clasp" (p. 99). "Only for a moment" must then direct us to Frantzen's notion of shadow, but it raises an unanswered question: Whose light is trained on the object to produce the shadow and from what angle? How long is the shadow, and how do we readers (whatever our sexual orientation) learn to produce one accurately? And accuracy is an issue for the book. Disagreeing with Boswell about the meaning of Alcuin's erotic language in his letters, Frantzen cites Stephen Jaeger approvingly for pointing out that erotic language in such correspondence was permitted "to the exact degree" that it was not sexual. The language in Alcuin's letters, it would appear, is not straightforward. Yet such an interpretive maneuver would seem to be called for when reading the bed shared by Custance and Hermengyld in *The Man of Law's Tale.* The two holy women in this tale may share the bed to the exact degree that it is not sexual. But here Frantzen both affirms and denies the sexuality of the passage: "Chaucer made . . . nothing sexual of it, in any case. Nor should we. But we should not forget that it *is* same-sex love" (pp. 261–62; his emphasis). Further in the paragraph he suggests (on the basis of the source history of Hermengyld's name) that "for us, the name faintly masculinizes her and deepens the same-sex shadow of the love she and Custance share" (p. 262).

The positivism of the reading of the penitential evidence juxtaposed with Frantzen's deeply personal account of his coming to an understanding of his own sexual orientation work to affirm his belief in "fundamental similarities" between the experience of individuals in Anglo-Saxon England and in the contemporary world. This is why it is necessary for the penitential evidence to be beyond interpretation: "The sexual histories of farm boys of my era could, with some changes, be sexual histories of boys in Anglo-Saxon England" (p. 296). The penitentials, with all their complex tariffs on various forms of sensual pleasure, evoke in this book a time, before the closet, that offered acknowledgment, if only in punishment. It is impossible not to respond to the passion of Frantzen's argument and readings; the question that remains, however, is whether the book gives away more than its argument is permitted to achieve.

I note some difficulties with translation that, though infrequent, can occasionally be misleading in an argument that depends on not interpreting the evidence. The most significant of these occurs in the penitential evidence. In word choice, Frantzen translates *hæman* (in its various inflections) as "fornicate" when the word is the neutral "copulate." (The word "fornicate" in OE is *forlicgan.*) In so doing, he is silently transferring the language of the Latin penitentials to the Old English versions. Similarly he translates the gloss "hi beoþ hnesclice swa forlegene" as "they are as soft as the adulteress," when the word *forlegene* simply means "fornicators" (plural, not singular). In context, the regendering is significant, since his translation in this instance ascribes the gendering found in Theodore 1.2.6 where it is not clear in the OE "Supplement."

On occasion he will also specify a meaning where is it not so clear in the Old English: he renders the header "Be þam men þe ungedafenlice hæmð, þæt is wið nytenum, oððe hine mid geonglingum besmiteð, oððe wæpnedman wið oðerne" as "Concerning those who fornicate unlawfully, that is with animals, or one who soils himself with young ones, or a male who has intercourse with another male." The Old English actually says, "Concerning the man who copulates indecently, that is with animals, or pollutes himself with young ones, or [concerning] the man [who pollutes himself] with another [man]." The specific polluting act is not mentioned in the header or text proper. Since the text is clearly distributing "besmiteð" (soils, pollutes) over the two phrases, inserting "has intercourse with" here overreads the Old English evidence. There are instances where the translation alters the grammar of a passage. His modern English rendition of *Genesis A* 2408–18 misunderstands two genitive plurals and transforms sinners into sins, i.e., actors into acts: *synnigra cyrm* is (mis)translated "outcry of sin" and *ealogalra gylp* as "an ale-foolish boast" when the poem is referring to the noise of sinners and the boast of people drunk on ale. Similarly the translation of the section of *Genesis A* describing the Sodomites' destruction (lines 2581–82) mistakes object for subject; the correct reading should be: "pride and drunkenness advanced in them to such a degree that they became too greedy for wicked deeds." (Two lines further, *dugeða* should be translated "prosperity" not "retainers.")

KATHERINE O'BRIEN O'KEEFFE
University of Notre Dame

PAUL FREEDMAN. *Images of the Medieval Peasant. Figurae:* Reading Medieval Culture Series. Stanford, Calif.: Stanford University Press, 1999. Pp. xvi, 459. $65.00 cloth, $22.95 paper.

Static and phatic is the normal concept of the image of the medieval peasant, inarticulately stuck in the hierarchical mud, capable of the occasional gesture devout or resistant, but essentially the flat and featureless feet of the human social body.

By titling his book in the plural—*Images,* not *Image*—Paul Freedman implies from the start there is more than that reductive account, and the rich detail of this full and scholarly book justifies the claim. Freedman (well named to liberate his servile topic from ignorance) is well known as a historian of medieval Catalonia, but he has researched much more widely here, looking in some detail at late medieval German materials, as well as English, French, and Hungarian sources and a wide range of Latin authors, both familiar and recondite, who transmit concepts and expectations of peasantry.

The inherent methodological problem of a project like this, with masses of material gathered over twenty years, is how to sort it for writing up. It would have been straightforward to move by areas and periods, and that might have made a useful handbook, comparing the geohistorically varying images of peasantry and contextualizing the differences. Freedman has chosen to sort his material in a more difficult theme-focused way, more likely to highlight the ideas and issues that consider, define, and to a substantial degree both validate and interrogate the concept and state of medieval peasantry.

The first three parts of the book set out broad categories with regard to peasantry: "Peasant Labour and a Hierarchical Society" considers how the peasant was seen to fit into a downward-organized social structure; "The Origins of Inequality" explores ways in which the evident imbalance of power was explained away; and "Unfavorable Images of Peasants" describes varied explanations of why the low deserved their position.

These three parts of substantial length range over all the material that Freedman has gathered, but parts 4 and 5 are more historically focused: he first considers "Peasant Agency, Peasant Humanity," where most of the empowered and positive images of the peasant are late medieval, and then his final section, "The Revolt against Servitude," delineates events and especially concepts involved in the major peasant revolts, all from after 1350.

In his final pages Freedman notes that the Black Death was a watershed; after it authority was more easily delegitimized, the problem of servility more acute and harder to elide via ideas of duty, sin, or salvation. In fact Freedman may well have been better advised to divide all his material into pre- and post-1350, so considerable are the differences he reports, especially in Germany and England. This would have enabled him to historicize more fully matters that are somewhat underconsidered, such as the differing media and audiences of the texts discussed or the varying types of social organization that coexisted with and perhaps in part generated the changing views of peasantry.

Closer as it is to New Historicism than either traditional history of ideas or literary thematics, the strongest features of Freedman's book are the isolation of complex and potentially reversible foci, such as what he calls "the idea of mutuality" that lies behind the Three Orders concept, and that, in terms of the peasants getting a share of the mutual profits, was always potentially a problem. An older historicism might have used the term *dialectical,* and similarly, while Freedman recognizes the varied ways in which the prospect of heaven can lessen the burden of labor, like New Historicists he prefers to call these formations discursive rather than ideological, and so tends to separate them from their physical impact.

More positively Freedman, like other North American post-Foucauldians, offers a wealth of fascinating detail: the varied nature of the Catalan and Hungarian revolts, for example, or the multiple ways in which Ham's misbehavior to his father was deployed as a source for ethnic and social explanations. The latter is one of the few instances where Freedman follows through a formation into more modern politics, as he debates the impact of anti-Hamitism in the American South—an interesting approach he does not use elsewhere, even though such treatment is invited by issues like the idea of the Norman Yoke in England or the wider relation between neo-Protestantism and peasant self-recognition.

To literary scholars this book will tend to have a general interest, though some interesting specific points are made: Freedman is firm that John Gower is the most severe commentator of all on peasants as beasts, and many texts support his view that peasants were often metonymically identified with the earth and dung of their environment. But issues of literary relevance rarely appear followed up as thoroughly as might be useful: how and why, for example, did the plow mutate from the context of Cain's evil to an Abel-like sanctity? Was there any link between the Carolingian explanation that peasants were of cowardly origin and the beast-men who appear in French romance?

Literary scholars may well also want to test—and often confirm—Freedman's ideas against readily available material not discussed here much, if at all, such as "The Song of the Husbandman," "Pierce the Plowman's Crede," "How the Plowman Learned his Paternoster," the "Jack Upland" poems, the "King and Subject" texts, and especially the important, if not large, number of English songs and proverbs that can be taken, with some caution, to represent the self-concepts of the peasantry.

It would be unduly demanding to expect a scholar to survey a large field and also produce highly focused analyses in most of the areas it touches. Freedman's book has the energy and scope of a wide-ranging survey—though there might well have been more on the Jacquerie—and it makes available a bulk of primary and secondary sources on the medieval conceptions and manifestations of peasantry. The bibliography is of great value, but it is a pity that the index is, for a book of this size and density, distinctly hypermetropic. But if that means that people have to plow steadily through the book, rather than seek the indulgence of a quick quote, that will appropriately prove a silent immobile labor with its own future reward.

STEPHEN KNIGHT
Cardiff University

DOLORES WARWICK FRESE and KATHERINE O'BRIEN O'KEEFFE, eds. *The Book and the Body.* Notre Dame and London: University of Notre Dame Press, 1997. Pp. xviii, 169, including 9 black-and-white illustrations. $24.95.

Here is a compact, well-introduced book of four essays by eminent medievalists on a topic of general contemporary interest. The essays constituted the 1995 Ward-Phillips Lectures in English at the University of Notre Dame. The contributors show how absorbing are the possibilities in bodies as books, books as bodies.

In the first essay, "Reading with Attitude, Remembering the Book," Mary Carruthers returns to an earlier interest in memory. Since her topic entails rehearsal of the fundamentals of medieval memory theory, the essay functions in part as a valuable condensation of these materials. At the same time it provides a fine backbone for the present volume (how oddly self-conscious the habitual bodily metaphors suddenly become in the context of a book on *Body*). Carruthers takes the opportunity to argue that the medieval process of memorizing, a process of etching loci, routes and likenesses in the mind, was envisaged not as studiously tranquil but as emotionally charged and even violent: as incision, mental vexation, harsh militaristic training. Converging in the Latin *pungo, punctus,* are the "'wounding' of page (in punctuation) and the wounding of memory (in 'compunctio cordis')" (p. 2).

Carruthers develops the interconnections with practiced agility. We are put in mind of the harsh invasiveness of the act of writing on and erasing from parchment, but we are also put in mind of the cultivated "violence" with which the mind (it was recommended) memorizes and recalls or obliterates from memory. By the expression "Reading with Attitude" in her title, she alludes to the crucial dynamic role of a person's attitude (*intentio,* or "gut reaction" [p. 10]) that reinforces the laying down and retrieval of a memory. The surprise in store for us here is that "gut reaction" was precisely what was commended in the words of John Cassian, who wrote that to be memorized effectively, knowledge must be *inviscerata,* "felt in your guts" (pp. 15–16). Conversely the expulsion (even excretion) of unwanted memories might be as traumatic as the attempt to erase script from a porous parchment.

This essay opens *The Book and the Body* with powerful élan, but Michael Camille is guilty of no anticlimax in his ensuing discussion of "The Book as Flesh and Fetish in Richard de Bury's *Philobiblon.*" Arguing suggestively that whereas the modern library is a site designed for "purely mental" experience, in the medieval library books had immense tactile presence and were physically engaged with (pp. 40–41), Camille characteristically goes on to catch his medieval topic in the challenging cross-lights of modern theory, especially psychoanalysis. De Bury, rampant book collector though he was, is found to show a curious distance from the physical objects of his desire. Camille hypothesizes that books must be the *fetishized* object of de Bury's desire—hence his treatise is an "occluded expression of personal possession in which the fetish object is hidden rather than revealed in language" (p. 46). The hypothesis makes cogent sense of de Bury's revulsion from such potential defilers of books as the runny nose, grimy fingernail, or straw bookmark. Although Camille sometimes makes lurid play with what to others may seem unexceptional (does the learned bishop's desire to have books read to him at mealtime really "sublimate the need for physical contact with the flesh through rhythmic pulsations on the ear [p. 43]"?), this essay's account of the book/body interface in *Philobiblon* is invigoratingly probing. In particular Camille memorably identifies an elision of maternality from de Bury's discourse on the propagation of books by transcription. Such "avoidance," the essay persuasively maintains, "lies at the heart of his attitude to books" (pp. 53–54).

The third essay is Seth Lerer's "The Courtly Body and Late Medieval Literary Culture." In itself an interesting discussion of courtly Tudor writing by Hawes and his imitator Humphrey Wellys, it implies a somewhat elusive definition of the body. Lerer's nomencalture slides disconcertingly (to me) between "the courtly body" and "the courtly self" (e.g., pp. 84, 90–91), as well as "the courtly identity." The distinctions beg clarification. Yet the essay regains a sharp focus when it addresses the use of the female *blazon* in Hawes and Wellys. It suggests that the same fragmentation of the woman into parts that characterizes this trope (pp. 87–88, 94) can also be seen as a significant structuring (or should one say destructuring) device in Wellys's centos, which use extracted or dismembered chunks of lines and stanzas from Chaucer, Lydgate, and Hawes.

Fragmentation is also a concern of the final essay, Carolyn Dinshaw's "Getting Medieval: *Pulp Fiction,* Gawain, Foucault." Reverting to an argument aired in her 1994 *diacritics* article on *Sir Gawain,* she finds Gawain embroiled in prospective acts of homosexuality, adumbrated by the kisses of the "exchange" game. The poem both raises the homosexual possibility and then closes it down, she suggests—and in Tarantino's *Pulp Fiction* a similar "straightening" effort can be discerned. Dinshaw is particularly stimulating on the "identity confusion" suffered by Gawain as the bedroom scenes temporarily "feminize" him (pp. 130–32). Just as the bodies of the quarry hunted by Bertilak are broken up, she argues, Gawain the lady's quarry seems on the brink of losing his unified identity as if by "corporeal disaggregation" (p. 134). Although the slippage here from reading other kinds of fragmentation in Gawain's psyche to reading fragmentation of his "knightly body" is questionable, it helps Dinshaw to forge another bold connection—with Foucault and his "politics of disaggregation" in *The History of Sexuality.*

The Book and the Body is a strong collection. In short space it achieves much more than many a thick volume of academic essays. Its coherence of aim and achievement should give it a significant role in underpinning the still burgeoning interest in both body and book in the Middle Ages.

Alcuin Blamires
Goldsmiths College, University of London

WARREN GINSBERG. *Dante's Aesthetics of Being.* Ann Arbor: University of Michigan Press, 1999. Pp. ix, 175. $42.50.

This absorbing study seeks to recuperate the aesthetic as a useful category in the critical and historical study of medieval literature. To do so, it must wrest the aesthetic from the embrace of three suitors: first, the New Critical celebration of poetic form per se; second, the Robertsonian celebration of order and serene hierarchy per se; and third, the more suspicious New Historical and/or psychoanalytic disenchantments of the aesthetic as a mystification of the really Real. Ginsberg is well aware of medieval uses of the aesthetic (with the three estates, for instance) as a "placatory ideology of political identity" (p. 3), and indeed astutely explains how Aquinas's intellectual and Suger's quasi-mystical treatments of the order, harmony, and proportions of beauty work to limit its fundamentally sensual and earthly dimensions, and thus its potential social power. The danger Aquinas and Suger sought to foreclose is the subject of this book: that vernacular "love poetry [would] sit down at the same table as metaphysics" (p. 3), as indeed happens in Dante's efforts to join love and knowledge in poetry that speaks at once to the senses and to the mind.

Rather than demystifying aesthetic discourses to ferret out what they might hide, Ginsberg sympathetically unfolds the scholastic psychology of perception, imagination, and intellection to show how Dante uses it to underwrite his vernacular poetry of analogy. In the *Vita Nuova,* the aesthetic is a form of knowledge between sensory experience and intellectual abstraction. In the *Commedia,* it is more than epistemology; it is an essentially poetic and analogic discourse of being in which divine love expresses itself in terms appropriate to the unique human condition, midway between animals and angels. It is also essentially vernacular: Ginsberg correlates Dante's developing poetic vision, traced through the signature modes of the *stil novo* and the *tenzone,* with his growing use of the aesthetic as an arena of cultural contestation in which he challenged and reformed Latin authority and learning, not only of scholastic psychology and theology but also of the literary tradition defined by Ovid and Virgil.

The introduction defines the aesthetic as a form of knowledge mediating between sensation and the intellect by means of analogy. Originating in the scholastic synthesis of neo-Platonism and Aristotelian metaphysics with Christian theology, it was taken over by the vernacular stilnovist poets, who used analogy as the philosophers did: to claim the universal (rather than particular) beauty of their ladies, and to make analogies (for instance) between direct angelic intellection and a lover's immediate desire to obey his lady. In this first stage of cultural contestation, analogy enabled poets like Guinizelli and Cavalcanti to appropriate the disciplines of Latin learning—the liberal arts, philosophy, and theology—for vernacular love poetry. This is the basis for Dante's vast expansion in the scope of aesthetics in the *Commedia,* where it becomes not just epistemology, but a mode of existence itself.

The long second chapter anchors the *Vita Nuova* in a detailed treatment of scholastic perception, pneumatology, and the process of intellection. The explications are not easy reading—the material is formidably abstract—but they are as clear an account as I have encountered. The background is crucial to aesthetics because it conceives of knowledge as based in a series of likenesses—analogies—by which the outside world is made available to the rational soul. It is also the stuff from which the *Vita Nuova*—a book of analogies—is made. Tracing Dante's ascent and descent through the hierarchies of knowing, this chapter precisely lays out how the work conceives Beatrice as the being in which the physical and the transcendent are assimilated as analogies of one another. It also shows precisely why Dante parts ways with Cavalcanti. In the central *canzone* "Donne, ch'avete intelletto d'amore" ("Ladies, who have understanding of love"), Dante's understanding of Beatrice as the principle of aesthetic knowledge who embodies transcendental beauty breaks decisively with Cavalcanti's phenomenology of love, which (as in "Donna me prega") finally blocks any similitude between perfect beauty (an idea) and any individual woman.

The last three chapters treat parallel regions of the *Commedia* to show how Dante revises his own earlier as well as other Italian poetry, Ovid, and Virgil into a new, radically embodied transcendent aesthetics that revises his very being. Chapter 3 begins from Dante's answer to Bonagiunta da Lucca in *Purgatorio* 24.52–54, usually taken as a programmatic definition of the *stil novo.* Ginsberg shows that it revises the aesthetics of the *stil novo* both stylistically and in transforming it into a discourse of being: it equates Dante's "identity as a poet with his existence as a human being" (p. 78), who "goes signifying" the analogies of Love's dictation within. In an unusual conjunction, these three lines ("a concentrated treatise on the cognitive conditions of literary representation *per se,*" p. 95), glossing and extending the *stil novo,* are set next to the *tenzone*—a poetic exchange of insults—with Forese Donati; the searching intertextual analysis here shows first how saturated the passage is with the competitive discord of the *tenzone,* and then how all the formerly competing voices are knotted together in a new, harmonious poetic mode that reorders and subsumes literary history. Coterminous with stylistic revision, a new aesthetics enables Dante to grasp the shade of his friend and competitor as both individual human and intelligible species.

This passage becomes a key point of reference in grasping the nature of souls in all three realms of the afterlife (paradisal souls are pure form; infernal souls pure matter without animating form) and in the aesthetics appropriate to each. Chapter 4 extends Dante's new poetic being to his meeting with his ancestor Cacciaguida, the progenitor of his physical and linguistic identity (*Paradiso* 15). Cacciaguida, who resembles Anchises inclining toward Aeneas in the underworld, greets Dante with Latin cast into Italian *terza rima;* in praising the Trinity, he also breathes out the love that inspires Dante's poetry. As the exemplar of all the father figures in the poem, especially Brunetto Latini and Virgil, Cacciaguida is the "fons et origo" of Dante's style. The intertextual analysis here implicates not only Forese and his *tenzone* with Dante but also Brunetto (through revisionary parallels linking him to both Forese and Cacciaguida), as well as the competition between Latin and vernacular, for Virgil and Statius are shown to be the authors of the antagonisms that produced the *tenzone.* Through Cacciaguida, Dante transforms all the *tenzoni* that have gone into making him as a poet into a new poetry that instead speaks the language of a metaphysical love.

Chapters 3 and 4 concern primarily the quarrels within the vernacular that are subsumed into Dante's new poetic; chapter 5 takes on Dante's competition with the Latin tradition of Ovid and Virgil, figured in the transubstantial metamorphoses of the thieves in *Inferno* 24–25. Dante's opponent here is not so much Ovid himself as medieval allegorized interpretations of Ovid, which were incapable of sustaining the depth of unbecoming signified by their exchange of being. Ginsberg skillfully brings out the full horror of the souls' exchanges and of their wholly unnatural materiality (which he insists is fully literal), and shows how both crime and punishment speak to the issue of justice. But his signal contribution here is to show how Dante's competition with Ovid is simultaneously a revision of both the *stil novo* and the *tenzone*—his defining modes of vernacular poetic activity prior to the *Commedia.* Through detailed persuasive analysis Ginsberg shows how the cantos of the thieves are also a palinode of Dante's last *canzone,* "Amor, da che convien pur ch'io doglia" ("Love, since after all I am forced to grieve"), a poem that takes to a bitter extreme the stilnovist trope of the dissolution of the lover's soul. The most disenchanted contemporary critic could not match Dante's pitiless self-critique here. Although *stil novo* and *tenzone* have usually been treated as opposites, Ginsberg shows how Dante brings them together three times in the *Commedia* to suggest that "whenever contentious sonnets or amatory 'canzoni' present themselves as the reified objects of their own narcissism, they become Ovid's offspring" (p. 158). In order to construct Dante's new aesthetics, they must instead become "stepchildren of Virgil" by taking on the structure and depth of allegory, in which the solidity of literal experience is not wiped out by later events, but is instead subsumed and fulfilled. Thus competition with Virgil results in Dante's stylistic reauthoring as well as Statius's conversion, and also is fulfilled as well as subsumed by Cacciaguida's Virgilian exemplar.

Dante's Aesthetics of Being continues the welcome trend toward knitting together poetry and other forms of knowledge—science and philosophy as well as the theological poetics that has dominated American Dante scholarship since Charles Singleton. As a study of Dante's poetic development, it is an excellent example of a deeply learned, exquisitely sensitive intertextuality in which every formal echo has ethical reverberations. In explaining Dante's poetic endeavors in the very metaphysical terms that the stilnovists had raided for their love poetry, Ginsberg also contributes to the equally welcome scholarship that traces both the influx of scientific learning and discourses into the European vernaculars in the later Middle Ages, and the resulting discursive transformations.

Translating Italian into English is not straightforward; nonetheless, Chaucerians will profit, at least by analogy, from Ginsberg's treatment of both science and literary tradition in Dante's poetry. Chaucer too was seen as a difficult poet, drawing on scientific discourses with as yet scanty attestation in English; and he constructed his place in literary history from most of the same classical poets. We should regard this study as an invitation to explore the same momentous cultural changes in English vernacular poetry, not only Chaucer's but also that of other writers.

Karla Taylor
University of Michigan

RICHARD FIRTH GREEN. *A Crisis of Truth: Literature and Law in Ricardian England.* Philadelphia: University of Pennsylvania Press, 1999. Pp. xvi, 496. $62.50.

Richard Firth Green has written a wildly learned and massive study, a kind of mature superdissertation that will leave other scholars toiling in his wake. The reviewer's task is like that of the cartographers in the Borges story: the only accurate way to map such a book would be to reproduce it in full. For it is full of detail—wonderful detail—and the detail becomes the point, to the extent that Green has had the sense to let its proliferation overgrow the neater borders of the merely very ambitious book he first set out to write. Readers will encounter, and surely enjoy, Green's deep familiarity with legal record and handbook over four centuries, his use of literary and legal texts together, his command of historical semantics, intellectual history and theology, his excursions into anthropology and ethnography, even the Nigerian novels that put in frequent appearances of inspired eccentricity. It would be impossible not to profit from such a book, and dishonest not to register my first reactions as gratitude and pleasure.

One of the pleasures is to watch Green's design grow visibly more complex. The original project, to which the title still testifies, is orderly: to take "truth," which Green calls "arguably the archetypal keyword in English" (p. 4), and investigate its several senses and shifts of meaning that crystallize, he says, in the fourteenth century. Green shows how the legal and ethical meanings of the word occur first, and only much later come the theological and intellectual senses. Playing through the shifts in meaning is the "dislocation caused by a powerful centralized authority employing a highly literate bureaucracy to enforce a common law still profoundly local and oral in its structural assumptions" (p. 124), "the way in which an increasing willingness to trust writing generated a corresponding crisis of authority, both intellectual and political" (p. 123). While recognizing that the movement begins clearly in the reign of Henry II, Green still wants to claim the reign of Richard II—which does happen to have all these texts foregrounding "truth"—as marking the point of no return, the moment at which the bureaucratic prevails in English polity and culture. Green would therefore wish to postdate a shift from communal memory to written record that Michael Clanchy has ascribed to an earlier period. This is because Green himself emerges as a powerful partisan and advocate of older ways of doing things, of local, oral traditions and subcultures against the brutality of a rootless regime of the written: "If the king's law might one day learn to frame workable solutions, in Chaucer's day it was plainly making the situation progressively worse" (p. 163).

But if this is the core of the book, the need to document the argument itself ensures that the Ricardian period cannot altogether remain the focus (as Green cheerfully and candidly admits in his preface). The original floorplan is much extended before the book properly starts, and the range of documentation goes from late Anglo-Saxon well into the fifteenth century, with as much attention devoted to the first half of the fourteenth century as to the second. Chapter 2 documents "Trothplight" and chapter 3 "The Folklaw," close-reading a wealth of documentary evidence with depth and sensitivity. Already the reciprocal use of literary and legal is paying extraordinary dividends. "Ordeals offered neither so daunting a challenge nor such unequivocal results as romance and ballad imply," writes Green (p. 107), while also demonstrating that literary play on equivocal oaths is no mere folkloric device but "a reflection of actual judicial practice" (p. 115). The magnificent chapter 5, "Folvilles' Law," as well as discussing contemporary attitudes to lovedays from the thirteenth century on, opens with "The Outlaw's Song of Trailbaston" from Harley 2253, deals with marginalized outlaw bands in literature and life, and, by showing that a documentary mentality destroys "trouthe," swells into an examination of the Peasants' Revolt as carnivalizing "antijudicial uproar" (p. 199).

By this stage it would seem that Green has intuited that nothing in the history or textuality of later Middle English is irrelevant to his book, and from here on he contributes some useful discussion on almost all the major topics of recent scholarship, such as notions of treason and Richard II's kingship (chapter 6), or Lollardy and literacy (chapter 7). He concludes with two more literary chapters. Chapter 8, "Rash Promise," asks what the law would have said about Dorigen, and explores the opposition between the intentionalism of canon law and the contractual formalism of civil law. Green argues that honor is demonstrated by being prepared to keep one's word, especially in the case of a promise one is not legally obliged to keep, and his argument, which unexpectedly and cleverly aligns *The Franklin's Tale* and *Sir Gawain and the Green Knight,* identifies the Abraham and Isaac story as a presiding archetype. Less satisfactorily, the last chapter, "Bargains with God," takes on the three other poems of Cotton Nero A. x and contrasts them with *Piers Plowman* in a suggestive but much too abbreviated argument about Langland's rejection of Anselmian soteriology and support for traditional covenantal theology, privileging baptism, the original contract, over penance. This chapter works in part against the earlier dating, shifting some of the focus of cultural change back into the twelfth century while fully documenting the endurance of older covenantal attitudes in Grosseteste and Langland.

And this is still not the end, amid increasing signs that ending it is not what this author most wants to do: there follows a four-page epilogue that introduces the scientific meaning of "truth" and Robert Boyle in the final paragraph, and after even that an appendix on the Nigerian novel, brought back in a kind of Pythonesque reprise. This is a book that stops, if at all, under protest. It works so well because for the most part it is persuasive that its range is valid. And, with its occasional faults and frequent magnificence of example and insight, it is a book to live with rather than read and set aside: it demands rereading, and the sort of disagreement with it that will follow from extended meditation.

When rereading, however, readers would do well to photocopy page 9 and keep it in hand as a key to the whole work. It is here that Green takes a hugely important step, conflating the thirteen *MED* senses of *treuth* into "four main areas of meaning" and assigning to each of these a different spelling of the word. This makes for great cogency in Green's exposition, which in any case separates the senses along the lines of his chronological argument, but it runs the risk of leaving an impression that we are in fact looking at four separate words. My major reservation after two readings of this book is that I want to go back and substitute a single uniform spelling for all four main senses: I want to feel the conflict that occurs at the lexical level itself, the extraordinary burden on one word over centuries undergoing cultural contestation and semantic change.

DAVID LAWTON
Washington University, St. Louis

LAURA L. HOWES. *Chaucer's Gardens and the Language of Convention.* Gainesville, Fla.: University Press of Florida, 1997. Pp. xi, 142. $39.95.

"This pleasant tale is like a little copse!" The critic is John Keats, remarking upon the pseudo-Chaucerian "The Floure and the Leafe." The impulse to equate poetic texts with the groves and gardens they contain is an old and enduring one; there may or may not be an hors-texte, but there are plenty of hortus-texts. A critic treating the Chaucerian garden might be tempted to metaphorize and textualize the concrete thing beyond recognition, but this is a temptation thoroughly resisted by Laura L. Howes in *Chaucer's Gardens and the Language of Convention.* Her topic is the literal gardens that appear in Chaucer's poetry; she discusses ten of them.

I am reminded of the line from Keats not because it's the kind of thing Howes might say, but rather because it's the kind of thing I want to say about her book. This pleasant monograph is, in its own way, like a little garden. It *is* little, at 109 pages of text. It is also, like a good medieval garden, extraordinarily well bounded: the focus is on a selection of Chaucer's gardens, and, though the argument certainly points to large areas for further exploration, it remains (as it were) within the walls of the garden looking out. In an age of Big Books, the modesty and clarity of Howes's project make for refreshing reading. And there are other garden pleasures as well. The writing is lucid and elegant; there are interesting insights and smart formulations; there is an air of unhurried contemplation. One feels throughout the book that one is *seeing* the gardens, the "pleasaunces," in Chaucer's life—the real and textual gardens he visited as well as those he created. Six illustrations showing gardens from illuminated manuscripts help make the book an appealing object. (At $39.95, it will of course be charged more frequently to library cards than to Visa cards.)

After a good, clear introduction, the first chapter, "Gardens Chaucer Knew," takes the reader on a brief, informative tour through pleasing spots in (among other locales) the *Roman de la Rose,* the Song of Songs, and real life. The organization of this chapter could be clearer. The literary gardens, discussed first, are divided into families, but the families tend to blur into each other. This must be partly mimetic; as Howes writes, "we may understand the confluence of various garden *topoi* as inevitable" (p. 21). The second part of the chapter presents the findings of "garden historians," and gives an impression of what actual medieval gardens must have been like. Again, it's hard to find a driving argument; the chapter feels like a stroll.

If the first chapter is content to wander through Chaucer's garden contexts, the remaining three argue clear, well-reasoned positions about the gardens Chaucer created. In chapter 2, Howes suggests that the gardens of *The Book of the Duchess* and *The House of Fame* stand for literary convention: when the narrators of the dream visions enter their respective dream gardens, they submit themselves to poetic tradition. The result is a gain in narrative coherence, but also a poor fit between narrator and tradition that opens up a critique of the latter. Chapter 3 treats the gardens in *Troilus and Criseyde.* Boccaccio's *Filostrato* features only one garden setting; Chaucer keeps this one and adds four more. The gardens here stand for another kind of convention: courtly love as a set of ideals and a mode of lyric utterance. Howes ends by suggesting an ambivalence toward convention, as both necessary and limiting. The fourth and final chapter treats three gardens from *The Canterbury Tales,* those that appear in the *Tales* of the Knight, the Merchant, and the Franklin. Here gardens are associated especially with women, and the conventions in question are purely social. Once again there is ambivalence; the book is unified by the claim that, throughout his career, "Chaucer both demonstrates the power of conventions to control individual action and provides examples of resistance to that power" (p. 109).

A conclusion, commenting on the meaning of the trajectory described here (from "literary convention" to "courtly convention" and then to "social conventions" [p. 84]), would be most welcome. Indeed, though I admire Howes's critical modesty and understatement, I repeatedly found myself, perhaps perversely, wishing for more. Besides a conclusion, my wish list includes some treatment of other, omitted Chaucerian gardens, especially those found in the Shipman's and Squire's *Tales* and the Prologue to *The Legend of Good Women*—or at least a reason for omitting them. Moreover, it sometimes seems an artificial self-limitation to discuss literal gardens but not their figurative reflections—that walking garden the Squire, say, or the flowery opening of *The General Prologue.* For that matter, is it possible to understand gardens fully without understanding the physical and social spaces they distinguish themselves from? (Howes mentions more than once that a medieval garden was often located at some distance from its castle, but it's not clear what this means; more reflection on castles, or the castle-garden dyad, seems called for.) The book's critical apparatus is deliberately focused, or limited, in the same way that the book's argument is. The endnotes are brief and helpful, page numbers and clarifications rather than separate running arguments or surveys of the field; I'm grateful, but at the same time the range of critical reference seems unnecessarily narrow. Secondary work that refers specifically to gardens is amply represented; off the garden path, topics that figure importantly in the argument—such as courtly love, feminist interpretation, Chaucer's use of Italian literature, and the dynamics of lyric and narrative—receive responsible but minimal annotation.

With its argument focused so intently on a set of particular textual gardens, and larger implications left largely implicit, the book must stand or fall on its close reading of particular garden passages. The success of these readings is mixed. Occasionally particular line readings seem tendentious or mistaken. For example, the river in *The Parliament of Fowles* has "floures white, blewe, yelwe, and rede, / And colde welle-stremes, nothyng dede" (lines 186–87). Howes reads this as indicating "the absence of dead fish." But surely *The Riverside Chaucer* is right in seeing "nothyng dede" as an adjectival phrase modifying "welle-stremes"—"not sluggish" (a not unsophisticated litotes). Similarly, I think it's a misreading to say that in *The Book of the Duchess* the knight's first speech to the lady consists of one word, "mercy" (p. 42; see *BD* 1194–220). More typically, my reservations concern matters of emphasis or judgment. At one point Howes sets a descriptive passage from *The Book of the Duchess* against its source in Guillaume de Lorris, and claims that Chaucer's version is more awkward, yet I just didn't see the difference in level of awkwardness. More broadly, I don't think that the narratives in *The Book of the Duchess* and *The Parliament of Fowles* become more coherent when the narrators enter their respective gardens, as Howes states (p. 36 ff.); I would have said the opposite. However, I was surprised how little difference my specific reservations made to my general assent to Howes's conclusions. This, oddly, strikes me as itself a problem. When particular, nuanced readings flow into general conclusions that are hard to quarrel with, the readings, however valuable or debatable in themselves, can end up seeming mere exercises.

The term associated with the generalizing force in Howes's book is "convention," which too often serves as a stopping point for analysis. Convention, despite its frequent appearances, is nearly colorless; though it is said to take different forms (literary, courtly, social), a lack of specific content makes the differences hard to see. There *is* good intertextual interpretation here, notably in the *Troilus* chapter, but the absence of such interpretation is disappointing in other places—notably in the *Canterbury Tales* chapter, where the three gardens appear seriatim, not really engaging with each other or with those of the Squire and Shipman. At the end of the *Troilus* chapter (p. 82) Howes raises the question:

Is there anything, for Chaucer, outside of convention? I think this question poses more of a challenge to her critical project than she acknowledges. If we can't say what forms of discourse fall outside of convention, is "convention" a useful term?

In my polemic against "convention," I fear I have made the book seem more ponderous than it is. The focus is on gardens and the things that happen in them. There is indeed much to value in the specifics here; the comparative horticulture of the *Troilus* chapter, for example, achieves a kind of complexity I have not been able to summarize. And the bigger ideas are well worth thinking through. The image of the dream-narrator entering literary tradition by entering a garden is powerful and memorable. The idea that the gardens of *The Canterbury Tales* represent not merely women or marriage (familiar ideas) but women's roles in particular (p. 84 ff.) makes me somewhat nervous, as "roles" has some of the same bland modern ring as "convention," but the idea is genuinely provocative. It is no slight to say that *Chaucer's Gardens and the Language of Convention* is a provocation, an occasion for meditation, a pleasant spot rather than a map of the world.

THOMAS C. STILLINGER
University of Utah

KARMA LOCHRIE. *Covert Operations: The Medieval Uses of Secrecy.* Middle Ages Series. Philadelphia: University of Pennsylvania Press, 1999. Pp. 304. $45.00.

In Karma Lochrie's deft, judicious, illuminating analysis, the secret is a strange and alluring speech act, and always a covertly dangerous one. Given away as soon as created, it may nevertheless change the relations between people by redistributing the relations of their knowledge and ignorance. When I tell you a secret that you don't know, I become a source of knowledge to you, and you are rendered at least temporarily ignorant. I have something you want and in that lovely moment I am compellingly interesting to you. In the process I create something else—or more usually someone else—as the very object that makes of my knowledge a mastery, revealed only as concealed, casting light only by throwing into darkness. Since it is invariably preferable to bear the secret rather than to be it, secrecy functions to transfer mastery to those who share the secrets of others, in one fell and economical swoop creating the other as the secret and the secret sharers as the manipulators of what there is to be known. Secrets found communities of knowledge and ignorance; their allure lies in their promise of power over one's enemies, over the vagaries of contingency itself, over the bewildering horrors of the sheerly unknowable. In short, secrets allow us the sustaining fantasy that knowing is potent and very often enact alarming scenarios of that potency in their casual re-classifications. As teachers, researchers and fellow gossips we are familiar with these beguiling, sustaining and dangerous pleasures, as makers and breakers of secrets, as traders in the game of knowledge.

But how does secrecy operate in the Middle Ages? The medieval discourse of secrecy, as Karma Lochrie so intelligently and trenchantly analyzes it, is remarkably adaptable. It works to protect the professions, to charge erotically the very transmission of knowledge, to organize the definition of wifely labor (*femme covert*) and so to conceal women's work in the household as not-work, to hide the female sodomite, to create the truth of the Christian subject, to perform, perhaps, a spiritual exercise in which the subject can conceive of him or herself in resistance. Through a wonderfully rich array of discourses (confession, gossip, books of secrets, medieval law and sodomitical discourse) and texts (*Sir Gawain and the Green Knight, The Wife of Bath's Prologue* and *Tale, The Miller's Tale, The House of Fame,* the two sets of texts known as *Secretum secretorum* and *De secretis mulieribus* and Gower's *Confessio Amantis*), Lochrie offers us compelling and thoughtful analyses of the organization of knowledge in medieval culture and some exhilarating new readings of old texts. She organizes each chapter around the analysis of one of these discourses, putting to the test the theorists of the secret—Michel Foucault (on confession), Sissela Bok (on lies and secrets), D. A. Miller and Eve Sedgewick (on the binaries sustained by the practices of secrecy that extend the reach of their domain from the secret itself to the social relations the secret sustains and displaces), and Patricia Meyer Spacks (on gossipy secrets)—and then performs an in-depth reading of an exemplary text.

Foucault has always *required* the Middle Ages—the medieval ship of fools, the torture of Damiens, pre-Tridentine confession—for his brilliant genealogies of modern power. In her first chapter, Lochrie examines the contradictions of Foucault's uses of medieval confession, in which he reduces the subject of confession to sex, equates the flesh with sex, and enacts a nostalgic and unitary picture of the Middle Ages in which sex can be imagined as natural rather than "de-natured." She then examines *Sir Gawain and the Green Knight* as a provocative and deliberate analysis of confessional structure with all its secrecy, moral protocols, and pleasures, reading it as a poem aware of "the trickiness and treachery of confession, both in its narcissistically fashioned truths and in its verbosity" (p. 55). In confession we tell our own secrets; to tell the secrets of others would make us back-biters, informers, spies, judges. In gossip, it is precisely the secret of the other that we tell—were the revelation to be about us it would no longer constitute gossip but confession.

Lochrie's second chapter thus examines the covert links between confession and gossip that both thrive in secret and are similarly irrepressible (p. 57). But gossip is the oral language of the marginalized, its knowledge trivialized as gossip. Untraceable to a single source and incapable of purely individual ascription, it has always been considered at once ethically dodgy and deliciously superficial. Lochrie examines *The House of Fame* as a failed attempt to establish a difference between gossip and poetry, exploring Geffrye's attempt to distance himself from Dido and the "murder by language" she foretells for herself, and the world of masculine gossip in book 3, positing the poem's unsettling conclusion that "oral and written transmission are indistinguishable" (p. 90).

The third chapter explores the interrelationship between secrets and gender ideology by examining the secrets of women as an exchange between men in two pseudo-Aristotelian treatises, and on the binaries that secrets can establish between Greeks and Persians, philosophers and vulgar readers, figurative and literal reading, as well as between men and women. The legal designation of a married woman as *femme covert* designates her work as a secret; indeed her very existence becomes secret, and this is the subject of the fourth chapter. In this chapter's compelling reading of *The Miller's Tale,* Lochrie revisits that tale's play on "*pryvetee,*" seeing the tale finally as a form of literary "*coverture,*" analogous to the rendering secret of women's work in the legal designations. In the last chapter, "Sodomy and Other Female Perversions," Lochrie can turn full circle, but in a different key, to some of her first chapter's Foucauldian preoccupations. Building on the excellent work of Mark Jordan, who has indicated the extent to which the telling category for medieval sexuality is the natural and the unnatural, rather than homosexuality and heterosexuality, Lochrie explores the extent to which some queerers of the Middle Ages have outed a purely imaginary category—the male sodomite rendered kin to the modern homosexual—only to cover over the very existence of female sodomy, and to obscure the functioning of medieval sodomy as a very general category to designate operative categories such as desire, concupiscence, lechery and pleasure. Such medieval categories place what we now think of as heterosexual acts in the same category as homosexual ones and, more to the point, render the designations of homo- and heterosexuality culturally illegible for the Middle Ages, because the proscription of all acts that waste procreative seed as perverse reclassifies most heterosexuals as well as homosexuals as, at least potentially, perverse. Her bold claim is, "Normative heterosexuality did not exist for the Middle Ages," so there is little point in locating it or investigating it (p. 225). Rather, future academic labors would be better spent "tracking . . . the perverse as it slips and shifts from natural to unnatural" (p. 202). She offers her own analysis of Gower's *Confessio Amantis* as being exemplary of such tracking. The categories of natural and unnatural sex, she argues, become hopelessly confused in Genius's dialogue with Amans, as do the inviolability of gender roles (p. 225).

But if the book has a timely, indeed long overdue, analysis of medieval Foucauldianism, making it required reading for those who, like David Halperin, think Foucault is a "fucking saint," it marks its own allegiance to Foucault most indelibly in the way in which two other languages, in which the secret might trace different epistemologies of the closet, become side-lined. Although these are sins of ommission and not commission (and so arguably not even a legitimate focus for the book under review), it is striking, but unsurprising, that a Foucauldian analysis of secrets and power might preclude both theological and psychoanalytic speculations and whatever secrets about the secret their way of seeing the world might bring.

In book 10 of his *Confessions,* Augustine famously exclaims, "O Lord, the depth of man's conscience lie bare before your eyes. Could anything of mine remain hidden from you, even if I refused to confess it?" The awareness of his own utter transparency to God, along with his terrifying opacity to himself ("I have become a problem to myself"), opens up a theology of the secret, for secrets are impossible with God but unavoidable for the cavernous, opaque human unconscious, whose capacities for self-mystification seem both limitless and unavoidable. There are those secrets, then, hidden even to ourselves. They are, or they become after Augustine, part of what it means to be a Christian subject, but also part of what it means to be a subject, a psychoanalytic subject, with a historical unconscious haunted by the phantom secrets passed down from the unconscious of the parents to the unconscious of the children, molded, that is, by the things our ancestors did not know about themselves, by their longings and the claims of those longings on our futures. It is such conceptualizations of the secret that might effect the very way in which historical transmission is conceptualized. Such thoughts are precluded by the parameters of power as they are defined in this work of critical and judicious Foucauldianism. They are in any case stimulated by this captivating, trenchant, brave, indispensably important book.

SARAH BECKWITH
Duke University

DONALD MADDOX and SARA STURM-MADDOX, eds. *Froissart across the Genres.* Gainesville: University of Florida Press, 1999. Pp. 257, 12 b. & w. illustrations.

The essays in this collections were presented at the Amherst Froissart Colloquium held on November 2–5, 1995. The participants of the colloquium were outstanding specialists in Old French literature from the United States, Britain, and France, two historians, and a Middle English specialist.

All the papers of the collection deal with the age of Chaucer, but only one contributor, John M. Flayer, treats specifically "Froissart and Chaucer." He discusses Chaucer's debt to Froissart in *The Book of the Duchess* and analyzes the aspects of the *Paradis d'Amour,* the *Bleu Chevalier,* and the *Voyage en Béarn* in the *Chroniques.* What Flayer stresses is the common tradition of both writers: both were steeped in Ovid. The relationship between Froissart and his contemporaries is discussed by Elspeth Kennedy in "Theory and Practice: The Portrayal of Chivalry in the Prose *Lancelot,* Geoffroy de Charny and Froissart." The links between the prose *Lancelot,* Charny's *Livre de Chevalerie,* and the *Chroniques* are discussed particularly in the light of Orders of Chivalry, those hybrid religious, social, military, and literary creations such as the Order of the Garter, and the short-lived but historically important, French royal *Maison de l'Estoile.*

The *Chroniques* are the subject of four essays. Peter F(roissart) Ainsworth presents in his "Configuring Transience: Patterns of Transmission and Transmissibility in the *Chroniques* (1395–1995)" a rich analysis of the way the chronicler expressed the chief purpose of his endeavor: "the transmission to posterity—through enduring record of the written word—of the deeds and values of the cast he served" (p. 17). Ainsforth is convinced that Froissart worked not only from orally acquired information but also, often, from previously taken notes. He examines one of the means of note taking, wax tablets. Ainsworth's comparison of the chronicler to his admirer, Walter Scott, is illuminating. Charles T. Wood defends Froissart from the (chiefly past) accusations of historical naiveté. In "Froissart, Personal Testimony, and the Peasant Revolt of 1381," he stresses the fact that Froissart relentlessly pursued the sources (both written and oral) and those sources contain the views and attitudes of the class of Froissart's patrons (and informants). Without the *Chroniques,* such views would have been lost to us. In "Froissart's 1389 Travel to Béarn: A Voyage Narration to the Center of the *Chroniques,*" George T. Diller also discusses source gathering. Froissart's travel to Béarn was an occasion to gather the materials for most of his book 3. Diller studies the narration of this travel, he aptly calls "a voyage to its own sources" (p. 31). In "Image and Propaganda: The Illustration of Book I of Froissart's *Chroniques,*" Laurence Harf-Lancner follows the step of Alberto Varvaro in examining the illustrations in the manuscripts of book 1. This rich and detailed study confirms the existence of the two families of manuscripts; Parisian and Flemish. Illustrations—this early indication of reception—show unsurprisingly that the first family tended to be pro-French and the second, pro-English.

Five studies treat Froissart's poetry. William W. Kibler, "*Le joli buisson de Jonece,* Froissart's Midlife Crisis," offers a subtle and penetrating analysis that emphasizes the renovating character of this *dit,* that is to say, a critique of an outmoded model of *courtoisie:* "If [t]he old *courtoisie* was sexually oriented; the new is a sublimated passion for an unattainable lady" (p. 77). Keith Busby studies not *the* but *a* structuring principle of Froissart's esthetics. His "Froissart's Poetic Prison: Enclosure as Image and Structure in the Narrative Poetry" examines most of the narrative *dits* from the point of view of their *locus,* which, while most often *amoenus,* is (almost) always *conclusus.* This is particularly true with regard to

La Prison amoureuse in which enclosure is presented both metaphorically as isolation and historically as the real captivity of Froissart's patron, Wenceslas of Luxembourg. Like Busby, Douglas Kelly also treats several narrative poems. In his masterly "Imitation, Metamorphosis, and Froissart's Use of the Exemplary *Modus tractandi,*" he demonstrates the extraordinary complexity of the allegorical, materials used by Froissart. Whatever their provenance, their principal characteristic is metamorphosis. Rupert T. Pickens concentrates on one *dit.* "History and Narration in Froissart's *Dits:* The Case of the *Bleu chevalier*" a thorough and careful examination of the pseudo-autobiography from the vantage point of heraldry, medieval science, and medicine. For the basic significance of *blue,* it would be helpful to remind ourselves that the original name for the Knights of the Garter—this restored, international Round Table—was "li chevalier dou Bleu Gertier" (*Chroniques,* book 1, ed. Diller [Geneva, 1972], p. 595). Michel Zink returns to the analysis of Froissart's long verse romance. Accepting structural divisions proposed by Peter F. Dembowski's *Jean Froissart and His Meliador: Context, Craft, Sense* (1983) Zink examines in his "*Meliador* and the Inception of a New Poetic Sensibility" Froissart's romance particularly in terms of the long "second prologue," which recounts the history of an ill-conceived love of a typically Froissardian (and uncourtly) character, Camel de Camois. Zink sees manifestations of the new poetic sensibility above all in the "entr'acts" of the *roman,* rather than in its four "acts," its main story.

Philological aspects of *Froissart across the Genres* are sound. Except in Wood's essay, Froissart's works are cited in the original and followed by good translations. Only Flyer uses the Brereton translation, which is inadequate (see, e.g., p. 200). There is one irritating detail due entirely I suspect, to the University Press of Florida. The press editors (as in most of the university presses in this country) decided to accept a uniform rule for the French titles. The French, who indeed have a rule for everything, do not possess uniform rules for the capitalization of the titles. In *Froissart across the Genres,* we encounter systematically such titles as *Le roman de la rose* (p. 95), *L'espinette amoureuse* (p. 167), *L'orloge amoureus* (p. 84) but, surprisingly, *Le joli buisson de Jonece* (p. 163), etc. *Jonece* is a personification-allegory and so is *Buisson, Espinette, Rose, Orloge,* etc., and, as such, should be capitalized despite press editors' passion for order.

Since this collection stresses the multigenre aspect of Froissart, I feel that the virtual absence of discussion of the *Orloge amoureus* is unfortunate. (It is very briefly mentioned on pp. 84–85 by Busby.) This *dit* is most interesting from the genre point of view. Written in a "uncourtly" meter (decasyllables couplets), it is a faithful description of a real clock and as such has earned its permanent place in the histories of clock making as one of the first of such descriptions. But, at the same time, it is a sustained allegory on the working of a lover's heart, that ends with an homage to Albius Tibulus. An essay on the multigeneneric character of the *Orloge* would enhance this outstanding collection studies of Froissart.

For *Froissart across the Genres* is indeed an outstanding collection: sober, free of jargon and of fashionable overstatements. This brief review cannot possibly render justice to these essays.

PETER F. DEMBOWSKI
University of Chicago

VINCENT P. MCCARREN and DOUGLAS MOFFAT, eds. *A Guide to Editing Middle English.* Ann Arbor: University of Michigan Press, 1998. Pp. xii, 338. $47.50.

Different kinds of editing require different kinds of editorial skills. Editing a reader's guide—a volume intended as a text book or manual for graduate students and postdoctoral researchers—is distinct both from editing a medieval text and from editing a collection of theoretical essays intended for advanced scholars in a specific discipline. In many respects *A Guide to Editing Middle English* is a well produced volume. The essays have been meticulously read at the copy and proof stages, and the presentation is impeccable. Furthermore, the editors' and contributors' competence in editing medieval works is unparalleled. However, as the book would seem to prove, experience and expertise in one field do not necessarily translate into another.

This book is primarily intended—as the title indicates—to instruct the uninitiated in the mysteries of editorial practice. At the same time, the editors hope that it will make readers more conscious of the nature of the edited texts from which they work, thus enabling them to make a considered evaluation of their merits, and that it will contribute to larger academic debates. In my view, this book most adequately fulfills the second of these avowed aims:—the reader cannot but come away from *A Guide to Editing* with an awareness of the limitations and pitfalls of various editorial practices. Nor can the attentive reader be unaware of the conflicts and disagreements within Middle English editing, given the range of opinions expressed. However, although it might be argued that lack of consensus in editorial practice is in fact a strength rather than a weakness, this is, as a number of the contributors acknowledge, a moot point. More important, what this book surely fails to do is to encourage any scholar to take up the editorial gauntlet.

One of my principal objections to *A Guide to Editing* is to the tenor of the writing. Hieatt, in her excellent piece on "Editing Middle English Culinary Manuscripts," embraces her successors, asserting that "We badly need some qualified new recruits to carry on a study that is just beginning to pay off" (p. 140). Yet I find it hard to believe that her attitude is shared by some of her fellows. Indeed, even the opening sentence of the editors' preface is off-putting. We are told, "The purpose of this volume is to raise the standard of scholarly editing for Middle English texts" (p. v). The editors may intend to suggest by this that *A Guide to Editing* will rally the troops, drawing forth a new wave of bright young academics willing and able to defend the beleaguered ramparts of learning. But what they succeed in conveying is that they deplore the state of current scholarship. This impression is furthered when they continue, "our perception is that many who have undertaken the editing of Middle English texts in the past have been unable or unwilling to shoulder all of the many burdens that fell to them." McCarren and Moffat conclude their first paragraph thus: "At the very least we hope this volume will provide prospective editors with an indication of the magnitude of they work they would undertake." Hardly a battle cry intended to urge soldiers into the field.

Like most medievalists, I have a certain sympathy with the concerns McCarren and Moffat express in their preface. While increasing numbers of graduate students are now working in our area, relatively few receive extensive instruction in bibliography, manuscript studies, textual criticism, and paleography. Even those who choose to follow the time-worn path of producing an edition as part or all of their doctoral dissertation may not be lucky enough to be supervised by an expert. Rather than restrict knowledge about editing practices to a privileged elite, it would be a service to everyone if the secrets of the trade were made freely available. A book that succeeds in doing so will therefore be extremely welcome. Unfortunately, *A Guide to Editing* might best be characterized as a half-hearted attempt. Quite simply, this book promises far more than it delivers.

Four of the five main sections of the guide include indispensable essays that, taken individually, cannot be faulted, and that fall into convenient subgroups and follow a fairly logical order. In the second section (concerned primarily with "literary" texts), Blake writes on editorial issues and *The Owl and the Nightingale, Piers Plowman,* and *Sir Gawain and the Green Knight;* Cooper on editing Chaucer; and Edwards on problems specific to alliterative verse. In the third section, there are four excellent introductions by Keiser, Mooney, Hieatt, and McCarren to editing scientific, astrological, culinary, and glossographical works. Section 4 incorporates essays by Edwards and Moffat, as well as Lucas, Mills, and Hamel, on such basic but essential topics as working with manuscripts, the treatment of language, using *The Linguistic Atlas of Late Mediaeval English,* source study, annotation, and making a glossary. The novice editor will surely find appendix A ("A Practical Guide to Working with Middle English Manuscripts") a godsend. Similarly, the forward-looking essays in section 5 by Robinson and Baker on computer technology and the production of electronic critical editions will prove essential reading for experienced editor and technopeasant alike.

Unfortunately, some aspects of the book's structure seem inexplicable. What rhyme or reason, for example, can lie behind the decision to place the editors' fine study of authorial and scribal intentions after the chapters by Jacobs and Fellows? What is more, *A Guide to Editing* lacks many of the tools a reader might reasonably expect to find. The three-page preface is an inadequate substitute for a full introduction, which would most usefully have included an overview of the topic, a detailed account of the volume's structure and contents, and clear instructions on how to use the guide. The editors themselves must take final responsibility for many of the problems in the coherence and readability of the volume. There is insufficient dialogue between the various contributors. It would, for example, have been rewarding to have known (rather than simply to have to try to infer) the responses of Robinson or Baker to Cooper's concern that "by making the full range of manuscript readings and misreadings accessible to every Chaucerian critic, [electronic methods of editing] might also allow a process of pick-your-own-text without any of the established editorial controls, such as could invite critical anarchy" (p. 83). The volume is marked by a considerable amount of repetition between essays and insufficient cross-referencing. Frequently, technical terms (such as "copy text" and "variorum edition") or specific well-known editorial "cases-studies" (such as the debate over the relative merits of the "Hengwrt" and "Ellesmere" manuscripts of *The Canterbury Tales*) are introduced or alluded to early on in the book, but are not actually explained until much later. While a few essays append reference and source lists, their inclusion seems to have been at the discretion of the individual author, and their presence is not signaled in the list of contents. More significantly, there is no general bibliography whatsoever, far less a sectioned and annotated guide to further reading. A glossary of technical terms is an equally inexplicable omission, especially given Moffats's own observations about the irritation the reader feels on turning to the back of a work and not finding one (p. 237). This oversight is particularly unforgivable given the risible attempt at an index, which is only two pages long and omits far more key names and editorial terms than it includes.

In summary, one of the volume's main failings is that it is not user-friendly. Another is that the project seems to have been inadequately planned and unevenly executed. No work of editing will ever be unproblematic. As Greetham's postduction explains—in introspective and unnecessary detail—the editors of this volume encountered more problems than most. A well-edited text will explain the practical and theoretical difficulties that have been faced and hopefully overcome in the course of its production. It will be reflective and self-conscious. But at the end of the day, the reader will want to have finished text, not one in which the seams show. *A Guide to Editing Middle English* is, then, something of a patchwork: made of fine fabric but sewn together roughly and frayed around the edges.

DIANE WATT
University of Wales, Aberystwyth

MURRAY MCGILLIVRAY, ed. *Geoffrey Chaucer's* Book of the Duchess: *A Hypertext Edition.* Calgary: University of Calgary Press, 1997. 1 CD-ROM. $25.00

Murray McGillivray's hypertext edition of *The Book of the Duchess* takes on the ambitious task of presenting not only a new critical edition of the poem but also all the textual material McGillivray used in creating his edition, so that readers can evaluate the evidence for themselves and form their own judgments about his editorial decisions. In fact, McGillivray invites users to suggest corrections or improvements to the project, making it (in the long run, one can imagine) rather like *The Book of the Duchess* itself—not a single fixed text but a series of revised versions unfolding over time. It explores the possibilities offered by modern technology to associate electronic texts and images in ways not easily accomplished with their printed counterparts and in the process creates a collection of resources that has something to offer to both undergraduates and advanced scholars.

The CD-ROM brings together a variety of texts and images useful for studying the poem's relations to its sources and its preservation in manuscript and early print versions. It contains a critical edition of *The Book of the Duchess* with textual notes; a reading edition with links to a glossary, explanatory notes, and sound files of the poem recited in Middle English; complete transcriptions of all the witnesses to the text (Bodleian Library manuscripts Tanner 346, Fairfax 16, and Bodley 638, plus William Thynne's 1532 edition); electronic images of every page of the poem in each of the witnesses (full-color photographs of the manuscript pages in small and enlarged versions, scanned images of Thynne); plus several works thought to have influenced Chaucer's composition of *The Book of the Duchess,* each provided in the original Old French or Latin with selected passages translated by McGillivray into modern English. Full texts are provided of Guillaume de Machaut's *Jugement dou roy de Behaingne,* the *Fonteinne amoreuse,* selected Machaut lyrics, and Froissart's *Paradis d'amour.* Excerpts are included of the *Roman de la rose,* Machaut's *Remede de Fortune,* the eleventh book of Ovid's *Metamorphoses,* the *Ovide moralisé,* and Statius's *Thebaid.* McGillivray guides the user through all the CD has to offer in a general introduction and explains the manuscript history of *The Book of the Duchess* in a separate introduction to the poem.

The best way to describe what the CD allows one to do is to give an example. Take the scene where the little dog approaches the dreamer and leads him to the Black Knight. In the reading edition, the browser window is broken into three frames. The poem appears in the left-hand frame, a glossary in the upper-right frame, and the explanatory notes in the lower right. A JavaScript box lets the reader jump directly to line 388, where the scene begins. Otherwise, one can scroll through the poem, which is broken into 200-line chunks. Clicking on the word "founed" in line 389 brings up its glossary definition ("fawned on") in the upper-right-hand frame, while clicking on the asterisk to the left of the line pulls up an explanatory note in the frame below. Within this lengthy note is a hyperlink to a scene in Machaut's *Jugement dou roy de Behaingne* where a small dog acts as the catalyst for a meeting between the narrator and the lady. The Old French text comes up in the frame where the explanatory notes appear. Clicking on the line number of the Old French text in turn brings into that frame the modern English translation of the passage. If the reader wishes to consult a manuscript image or transcription of the passage, there are sigla along the left margin of the poem that act as hyperlinks to any of the manuscript or print witnesses. Clicking on the "F" near the passage brings the transcription of the relevant folio of the Fairfax manuscript into the lower-right frame. From within the transcription one can click on yet another hyperlink that will call up a photograph of the folio. Just to round things off, there are links throughout the poem that play sound files of McGillivray reciting *The Book of the Duchess* (in 10- to 15-line segments) in Middle English.

It's easy to get a bit lost with all the pages trailing off each other, and finding one's way back to wherever one started from can involve a lot of clicking on the browser's "Back" button. The critical edition is more straightforward, with the poem in an upper frame and the textual notes in the frame below. McGillivray's stated goal in creating this edition is to give a rough approximation of the archetype of the four surviving witnesses. To this end he uses Tanner as his base text instead of Fairfax, the usual choice of editors, because it is probably older than Fairfax and less altered by the "improvements" of scribes. A convenient color-coding scheme lets the reader know how well supported a given reading is by the witnesses: black text indicates agreement among all four witnesses, blue text for three, purple text for two, red text for one, and bright red-orange for readings that are based purely on McGillivray's own conjecture. The textual notes detail exactly where all the discrepancies lie.

One feature that really takes advantage of the electronic medium is the ability to open two to six frames simultaneously, each displaying the user's choice of text or images for easy side-by-side comparison. It is possible to view simultaneously, say, a given passage in the reading edition, a related passage in one of the Old French sources, plus the modern

English translation of that source. Or one could choose to view the Tanner and Bodley transcriptions along with images of both manuscripts. (A bit of restraint in the multiplying of frames is called for, though. With six frames open on a seventeen-inch monitor at 800 × 600 resolution, each frame is only 5.75″ × 2″, so viewing its contents involves a good bit of scrolling both horizontally and vertically.) Any file on the CD can also be opened in a window by itself by clicking on its link in the main menu.

Anyone with a working knowledge of how to use a Web browser to surf the Internet has all the computer literacy required; to get started, simply launch the browser and use it to open the files on the CD. Users can search for particular words or phrases by using the "Find" feature of the Web browser. Cutting and pasting blocks of text into a word-processing program is a cinch, and all texts and images can be printed directly from the CD, though the images need to be resized first to fit onto a standard (8.5″ × 11″) sheet of paper. This is easily done by saving the image to the hard drive, editing it in a program like PhotoShop, then sending it to the printer.

A few inconsistencies give the CD the feel of a beta version. (In fact the outdated "readme" file still identifies this as beta version 1.2 with a planned release for midsummer 1997, while the title page says it is release 1.0 from December 1997.) Sources are not always cited for the Old French and Latin texts. The link for 103v in the list of images for the Tanner manuscript points to 103r instead. There are faulty hyperlinks in the English version of the *Ovide moralisé* so that clicking on every tenth line (35, 45, 55, etc.) takes the user to line 4140 in the Old French. The file containing the transcription of Tanner 346 is improperly coded, so that clicking on its sigla in the reading edition points to the beginning or end of the transcription, not to the particular line in question (an error acknowledged by McGillivray on the CD's Web site). The same thing happens with some of the sigla for Thynne's edition. Rather distracting is the tendency for titles to be spelled or capitalized differently in different places. (For example, there's *Jugement du roi de Behaigne* in the main menu but *Le jugement dou Roy de Behaingne* in the Old French transcription; *Fonteine amoreuse* in the main menu but *Fonteinne amoreuse* in the Old French and English texts; *Paradis d'amour* in the main menu but *Paradis d'Amour* in the general introduction). Such errors ought to be corrected in the next version, which hopefully will be available by the time this review gets into print.

The University of Calgary Press hosts a Web site <http://www.ucalgary.ca/ucpress/online/pubs/duchess/> that contains a pared-down version of the CD's contents for evaluation—SGML files for Thynne's edition and the *Fonteinne amoreuse* plus updates that can be downloaded for free. The contents of the CD may be accessed directly from a CD-ROM drive without copying any files onto a local hard drive, but doing so makes using the updates rather problematic. For example, the Calgary Web site has a corrected copy of the Tanner transcription available for downloading, but as the CD itself cannot be modified the only way to replace the bad version is to copy all the files from the CD onto a hard drive, replace the flawed file with the corrected one, then run the program from the hard drive. I tested this method and it works, but be warned that the entire contents of the CD eat up 324 MB of disk space, a considerable amount of storage for someone who may want to use the CD primarily on a home computer. Other than this space consideration, the CD makes very few demands on the computer and can be used on either a Windows 3.1/95/NT PC or a Macintosh with a minimum of 16 megabytes of RAM (to accommodate the sizable enlarged manuscript images) and running either Netscape Navigator 3.0 or higher (including Communicator) or Microsoft Internet Explorer 3.0 or higher.

Planned improvements include a bibliography and further SGML versions of the transcriptions, critical edition, and source texts on the Web site, revised explanatory notes, and hyperlinks between the critical edition and its textual notes. In its present form, the hypertext *Book of the Duchess* is a worthwhile experiment in making widely scattered but related scholarly materials available in one densely interwoven package. It will be interesting to see what innovations find their way into its later incarnations.

Susan Arvay
Rutgers University

David Mills. *Recycling the Cycle: The City of Chester and Its Whitsun Plays.* Toronto: University of Toronto Press, 1998. Pp. xiii, 281. $55.00.

The majority of his scholarly career having been focused on the task of documenting, editing, and analyzing the social and dramatic records of medieval Chester, David Mills brings that career to impressive summation in *Recycling the Cycle: The City of Chester and Its Whitsun Plays.* Although in part a recycling and synthesizing of his many previously published notes and articles, this lucid, trustworthy, and highly readable compendium will be a great service to students of medieval drama and medieval culture for decades to come. A conservative scholar who eschews "speculative" or "theoretical" interpretations of empirical data, Mills's major purpose is not to re-interpret the Chester Plays themselves but rather to position them inside the "local context" of their city. This context includes the city's urban geography, its major religious and secular buildings, its social networks (most notably its guild alliances), its calendar of secular and sacred celebrations, and its influential local historians and political personages—all seen in light of the city's changing economic, political, social, and religious circumstances from the fourteenth until the late seventeenth century. Because only a very few early documents survive, however, *Recycling the Cycle* is mainly an indepth profile of Tudor Chester, the city's many late documents providing sometimes reliable, sometimes antiquarian, and sometimes politically expedient accounts of the city's and the plays's earlier history. Acknowledging that such an ambitious project requires that certain matters be "simplified" and "tailored," Mills succeeds nevertheless in providing a rich sense of the Tudor city and the central importance of such Cestrian documents as the *Life of St. Werburg,* Ranulph Higden's *Polychronicon,* Rogers's Breviary, as well as the plays's pre-Reformation and post-Reformation Banns. Mills is equally informative in his scrupulous accounting for the plays's eight surviving manuscripts, characterizing their scribes, copyists, and owners, and evaluating the cycle's editorial history from the Deimling/Matthews EETS edition (1892/1916) to Mills's and Robert Lumiansky's magesterial EETS edition and commentary (1974/1986).

The scholar whom Mills invokes as his model is none other than E. K. Chambers. Like Chambers, Mills is generously interested in all forms of entertainment, such as popular sports: tennis, fooball, quoits, dice, casting of stones, kailes, and tables (all of which were prohibited to servingmen, laborers, and apprentices); hawking and hare-coursing (carried on in the city's environs); cock-fighting, bear-baiting and bull-baiting (sites of frequent spectator violence); and archery, Cheshire's most prized sport, which was encouraged by city regulators as "an edifying pursuit of the upper classes and the civilized citizen" (p. 73). The popular entertainment most closely linked to the Whitsun Plays was the Midsummer Show. Held on Midsummer Day, the dominant feature of this "pagan festival" (p. 79) was a guild procession which displayed spectacularly constructed figures including a unicorn, dromedary, lynx, camel, ass, dragon, lions, and "sixe hobby horses & sixteenth naked boyes" (p. 88). It is apparent that late in their history certain popular figures from the Whitsun Plays also appeared in the Show, such as devils, shepherds, "Christe in stringes," and "A man in womans apparell with a divuel waytinge on his horse" (from the "Harrowing of Hell"). But in what fashion contemporary citizens "'read' these biblical characters in the context of the Show" (p. 95) and to what extent the Show in turn influenced the perceived valence of the plays is, as Mills allows, quite "difficult to assess."

The only disappointing passage in *Recycling the Cycle* is the author's low-energy interpretation of the Whitsun Plays themselves. In a modest-length chapter which gestures in the direction of the plays's "structure and theme," its "wonders" and "signs," and the city's role as an implicit "actor," Mills adds little to our understanding of the plays as a distinctive form of medieval biblical drama. Mills's strengths, by contrast, reside in his many astute readings of the disparate and often enigmatic surviving records relating to the plays in their final years, some of which have been published (most notably in Lawrence Clopper's 1979 *Chester*) and many of which remain unpublished. Mills's star document is a major new find, a letter-book belonging to the Cestrian Puritan Christopher Goodman containing Goodman's letters to religious and political dignitaries (such as the Archbishop of York) complaining about mayor John Hanky's 1572 decision to mount the Whitsun plays despite strong objections from certain quarters. Mills's unravelling of the production, editing, and re-writing of the Whitsun Plays in the third quarter of the sixteenth century and his interpretation of the plays's revalorized significance in light of ongoing religious and political struggles, both local and national, constitute an extremely insightful account of the mystery play's final days. Mills's manner of interpreting drama, ritual entertainment, and social performance is strikingly distinct from comparable studies such as Sarah Beckwith's articles on the York Cyle, Leah Marcus's analysis of the "politics of mirth," or Jody Enders's explorations of the medieval theater of cruelty. But it is precisely the uncomplicated clarity of Mills's scrupulous form of "empirical" scholarship that makes *Recycling the Cycle* such an admirable critical study in its own right.

PETER W. TRAVIS
Dartmouth College

JAMES J. PAXSON, LAWRENCE M. CLOPPER, and SYLVIA TOMASCH, eds. *The Performance of Middle English Culture: Essays on Chaucer and the Drama in Honor of Martin Stevens.* Cambridge: D. S. Brewer, 1998. Pp. ix, 198. $75.00.

The subject of the eleven essays in this collection in honor of Martin Stevens is, as James Paxson states in the introduction, "the theatrically charged world of late medieval England" (p. 1), a world in which theatricality manifests itself not only in such obvious places as mystery and morality plays, feasts, tournaments, and other public spectacles but also, and more unexpectedly, in poetry, particularly poetry written by Chaucer. Implicitly echoing the handful of studies of Chaucerian theatricality, Paxson argues that *The Canterbury Tales* and *Troilus and Criseyde* "hinge on metaphors and images, explicit and implicit, of stagecraft, public spectacle, and histrionic or dramatic characterization" (p. 1) and are grounded in urban and civic ritual. The aim of the collection is to explore the cultural interdependence of the expressive forms dominant in late medieval England and to examine "the pervasive cultural macrometaphor of performance" (p. 2), which embraced productions as seemingly opposed as Chaucer's writings and the York cycle plays. This is certainly an important goal, one with large consequences for our understanding of late medieval culture and the position of literary and dramatic production within it.

While pursuing this goal, many of the essays unfortunately run afoul of entrenched disciplinary divisions. The result is that instead of consistently bringing the textual into intersection with the performative, the literary into orbit with the dramatic, the essays tend unintentionally to reinforce the separateness of those categories. Thus, more or less on the drama side of the divide, we get a cultural reading of the York cycle plays by Kathleen Ashley; an argument for redrawing the boundaries between "medieval" and "renaissance" drama by Richard Emmerson; an exploration of gender and power in *Wisdom* by Marlene Clark, Sharon Kraus, and Pamela Sheingorn; and a study of civic culture by John Ganim focusing on the descriptions of London by William Fitz Stephen in the twelfth century and John Stow in the sixteenth. On the Chaucer side, we find Richard Daniels's reading of textual pleasure in *The Miller's Tale;* Warren Ginsberg on Petrarch, Chaucer, and the construction of the Clerk's identity; Robert Hanning on the crisis of mediation in Chaucer's *Troilus and Criseyde;* Peter Travis on the mock-exemplum opening of *The Nun's Priest's Tale;* and William McClellan on *The Clerk's Tale* and Maxine Hong Kingston's "No Name Woman."

Although the essays by Ashley and Emmerson respond to the collection's call to examine the theatricality of late medieval English culture by rethinking prevailing interpretive paradigms and pointing to ways in which English drama can be productively read as part of broader cultural processes, the only essays to address explicitly the intersection of literary and theatrical cultures are Alfred David's examination of Noah's wife in *The Miller's Tale* and the cycle plays and Seth Lerer's analysis of Chaucer's deployment of theatricality. It is Lerer's essay that best lives up to the promises made in the collection's introduction and that best shows both how rich a vein the collection has tapped into and how much more work needs to be done to mine it.

Lerer argues that Chaucer's references to theatricality, particularly in the Knight's and the Miller's *Tales,* serve to locate his project among "competing and potentially disruptive forms of dramatic public expression" (p. 60), including royal and provincial drama. Perhaps not unexpectedly, Lerer reads Theseus's tournament as an affirmation of a Ricardian theatricality that was "public and consolidative in polemic, classicizing and dynastic in theme" (p. 62), and, more interestingly, sees *The Miller's Tale* as a provincial parody of civic pageantry and London royal spectacles (p. 69). The silenced guildsmen of *The General Prologue,* Lerer claims, represent what Chaucer would have seen as sponsors of a rival literary form—provincial and communal civic drama—that was "radically other" to court poetry (p. 60), a literary form that might have seemed as distant or different to Chaucer as it does to us today. So while *The Knight's Tale* offers a treatment of familiar theatricality—royal, public, metropolitan—*The Miller's Tale* turns on a theatricality alien to city and court, a theatricality, moreover, that is "violent and decentering" (p. 74). Noting that what distinguishes the forms of drama in Chaucer's day is "their place in the politics of social consolidation or revolt" (p. 76), Lerer concludes that the various forms of theatricality in the late fourteenth century are the backdrops "against which Chaucer stages his own authorial self-construction—one continually striving to adjudicate between the patron and the reader, the historically immanent and the transhistorically literary" (p. 76).

Lerer's essay demonstrates what I, for one, wish had been accomplished throughout the collection. He provides a compelling account of emergent ideologies of authorship and literary production in late medieval England situated against the various forms of theatricality that formed the late medieval cultural dominant, each of which had its own ideological and material aims, which were often in conflict with each other as well as with other modes of cultural production, including poetry. Such an account has important implications for the writing of literary and cultural history as well as for Chaucer studies more particularly. Chaucer undoubtedly was immersed in the theatricality of Ricardian culture and perhaps actively participated in it, as the Smithfield tournament, the *Complaint of Mars* (which may have been written for a court disguising), and the probable oral performance of some of his poetry suggest. Looking more closely at Chaucer's involvement in that culture of performance would tell us more about literary production and consumption in the fourteenth century. Similarly, scholars of medieval drama might well profit from Ashley's charge to take more seriously the textuality of the plays, which has tended to be lost in the best recent criticism with its bent toward social and ideological critique. In the end, then, what the reader is left with is perhaps the sense that there are more books yet to be written, books that would reread Chaucer, medieval drama, and indeed all of Ricardian culture through the lens of theatricality. In gesturing toward those books, this collection has to be rated a success. Its invitation to rethink the expressive cultures of late medieval England is one that I hope will be taken up, and soon.

CLAIRE SPONSLER
University of Iowa

FLORENCE PERCIVAL. *Chaucer's Legendary Good Women.* Cambridge Studies in Medieval Literature 38. Cambridge: Cambridge University Press, 1998. Pp. 338. $69.95.

Scholars often consider Chaucer's *Legend of Good Women* to be a text that marks Chaucer's rejection of the court and its literary productions. However diverse their interpretations of the *Legend* ultimately may be, such critics as Robert Frank, Elaine Hansen, and Lee Patterson all concur that Chaucer registers in the poem his desire for liberation from the aristocratic discourse of *fin amor.* The *Legend* constitutes for these readers a kind of bridge text in Chaucer's literary career, a work that segues from court-identified pieces such as the *Troilus* to the sort of writing exemplified by *The Canterbury Tales.* In *Chaucer's Legendary Good Women,* Florence Percival offers a different take on the *Legend,* which for her does not reject but instead embraces the court and, in particular, its investment in ludic debate over Woman. Taking as her topic Chaucer's self-authorization as a vernacular writer, Percival emphasizes the status of the *Legend* as a palinode that brilliantly participates in a tradition of recreational courtly debate interested not in taking a stand per se on the question of female fidelity, but in playfully exploiting "the competing interests of the disputants" (p. 3).

For Percival, readers for whom Chaucer takes a stand on the topic of female virtue are missing the point. The "surface of the text," admits Percival, "is cheerfully biased" against woman, as the medieval "joke hinted at" in the poem is that while we may dream of good women, "in practice none was likely to be found" (p. 15; p. 7). Yet above all, for Percival, "the fictional debate about women is only an excuse to discuss the poetic craft" and display Chaucer's literary prowess (p. 11). Chaucer's seeming defense of Woman is really a defense of Chaucer, a "declaration of the English poet's own sense of worth and social value" as a court writer (p. 13). Aiming to provide the reader with an understanding of how the *Legend* would have resonated within the courtly milieu for which it was written, Percival offers a wide-ranging account of both the Prologue and the Legends in light of their historical and literary contexts.

The organization of the poem itself roughly dictates the ordering of Percival's book, which begins with two sections on the Prologue and spends the bulk of its second half on six Legends (those of Ariadne,

Medea, Cleopatra, Dido, Lucrece, and Phyllis). The question of Chaucer's authorial self-fashioning dominates Percival's initial discussion of the Prologue. A reading of the daisy motif against the work of Machaut, Froissart, and others suggests Chaucer's self-conscious insertion of his vernacular poetry into the illustrious Marguerite literary tradition; consideration of the Alceste myth in light of its analogues demonstrates the richness and originality of Chaucer's legendary goddess; and, finally, analysis of Alceste's defense of Chaucer demonstrates how the writer uses the goddess to craft himself as at once a learned poet possessed "of social responsibility" and a *grand translateur* (p. 129). A proximate second to the theme of Chaucer as author is that of Chaucer's ironic stance toward female virtue in the Prologue. In chapter 3, for example, Percival points to a "climate of scepticism" in the opening that qualifies the poet's outright praise of the daisy and Alceste (p. 68). What is hinted at, for Percival, in the first twenty-eight lines of the Prologue, becomes manifest later in the "flippant" tone the narrator assumes with regard to the question of believing "more than one can see or prove," namely that "cardinal tenet of courtly orthodoxy, *la louange des dames*" (pp. 68–69). Contra H. C. Goddard's critics, Percival cites evidence from Lydgate and other fifteenth-century poets to demonstrate that "no anachronism need attach to the suggestion that Chaucer is proposing . . . sympathy with the ordinary man whose everyday experience leads him to be sceptical about the faithfulness of women" (p. 73). In a similar vein, chapter 4 situates the ambiguities of Chaucer's Eros against the equally ambiguous literary history of the God of Love; and chapter 5 contends, among other things, that the God of Love's accusation "is in the end a comic speech" in which the antifeminist works cited by the God of Love undermine his role as Woman's defender (p. 112).

Percival distinguishes herself throughout the book by extreme methodological caution. When she takes up the long-standing problem of whether Eros and Alceste may refer to historical personages, for example, Percival carefully avoids drawing clear parallels. Engaging with evidence in the F Prologue that has encouraged critical speculation "that Chaucer was covertly advising Richard II" through Alceste, Percival ultimately concludes by not concluding: ". . . it cannot be assumed in the state of current scholarship that there is a definite reference to Richard in Prologue F of the *Legend of Good Women.* It cannot be assumed either that there is no such allusion" (pp. 92–94). Even when Percival asserts her own opinion—as she does when she argues that "Chaucer briefly speaks . . . in his own voice" when the narrator defends himself in the Prologue—she is compelled to acknowledge the merits of an opposing view; closely on the heels of the above quote she writes, "No doubt, however, we would be on safer ground to see it as yet another stance adopted by the narrator/poet's persona" (p. 133). Percival's unusually cautious approach undoubtedly will please readers weary of tendentiousness in contemporary scholarship; yet that careful methodology just as surely will frustrate readers interested in bold approaches to medieval texts. This is not a book for radical Chaucerians.

When she turns to the Legends themselves, Percival marshals the contradictory critical history of the *Legend* to support her argument that the Chaucer deliberately styled the *Legend* as an ambiguous work that would "promote partisan, gender-biased argument in his original audience" (p. 325). Following the work of Sheila Delaney and others on obscene punning in the *Legend,* Percival points to Chaucer's use of sexual innuendo to burlesque ostensibly pathetic and virtuous heroines such as Ariadne and Cleopatra. For Percival, Chaucer's trivialization of his heroines reflects what is now a commonplace in feminist scholarship: the androcentric linkage of woman and matter in Western thought since Aristotle. Chaucer, that is, trivializes the plights of Dido, Medea, and other abandoned women in the *Legend* by suggesting how these women are betrayed less by men such as Aeneas or Jason than by their "own feminine nature"—a fundamental carnality and sensuality that render them "only too anxious to be seduced" (pp. 252, 249). Chaucer's engagement with what Percival calls "the matter of Woman" informs his representation not only of his heroines in the *Legend* but also of his own authorial identity. Adopting Carolyn Dinshaw's insights on how "Woman's close affinity with things material" resulted in her identification with the very literary "matter" that medieval writers reworked, Percival emphasizes Chaucer's production of himself as a literary analogue to the male seducers he depicts (p. 14). By radically censoring such details as Medea's necromancy and sorcery from her well-known story, Chaucer "like Jason plunders [Medea] of all that is properly her own" and suggests his "power to make of his matter what he willed" (p. 219). Similarly, "by choosing only the best bits," Chaucer "deflowers Phillis's letter" in Ovid's *Heroides* and, like Demophon, "'piked of hire al the good he myghte'" (p. 287).

Even as Woman's identification with matter helps explain Chaucer's rebellion against Eros, it also accounts for those moments when the writer appears to retract sincerely his previous sardonic representations of Woman. Noting how the word *pathos* is "connected with the more material aspects of a person's being," Percival points out how "Woman, in all her materiality and liability to suffering, is thus the natural vehicle of the pathetic" in medieval literature and indeed performs this function throughout the *Legend* (p. 254). Forasmuch as such figures as Ariadne and Dido elicit laughter, then, they also elicit sympathy. Above all, according to Percival, Lucrece demands empathy because she, more than any other heroine, is portrayed as a pathetic figure by Chaucer, in accordance with the tradition of commentary that views Lucretia as a kind of "protomartyr" (p. 264). Yet, for Percival, even Lucrece's status as a good woman par excellence is complicated by "many problematic details, none of them perhaps conclusive in themselves, yet in total quite substantial," that recall Augustine's query whether Lucrece's suicide was motivated by an excessive concern for her honor or by a need to punish herself for enjoying her rape by Tarquin (p. 280).

Percival uses previous critical work on the *Legend* to great advantage in *Chaucer's Legendary Good Women,* finding support in work on the *Legend* by such critics as Delaney, Frank, Kiser, and D. W. Rowe. Some may query the originality of a book so reliant on previous work. Yet it is, paradoxically, the very thoroughness of Percival's engagement with the modern critical reception of Chaucer's text that underlies her most original contention: that only by embracing that critical history in its entirety—contradictions and all—can we begin to understand Chaucer's intentions in writing the *Legend.* According to Percival, the critical tendency "to produce either a seriously pathetic reading or a wholeheartedly humorous or ironic one" results from the "indisputable" fact that "for at least a century, most people have found humour antithetic to pathos" (p. 326). Such was hardly the case in Chaucer's day, when, writes Percival, "the tearshedding, the laughter and shocked debate caused by Chaucer's stories about women all had high entertainment value" (p. 325). While they may appear incompatible to our modern minds, parody and pathos worked together to produce pleasure for the premodern court. Yet while her emphasis upon Chaucer's original recreational and courtly audience leads Percival to accommodate certain contradictions in the critical history of the *Legend,* that same emphasis compels Percival to occlude what she terms a "socio-feminist" analysis (p. 19). As a poem partaking in a "humorous antifeminist/feminist debate" (p. 19), the *Legend,* according to Percival, deals above all "with a literary construct of

Woman, Woman as an ancient topic for discussion, and is not primarily concerned with the problems that real women faced" (p. 328). Does the humorous nature of a written work, however, permit us to sever the textual from the social? As scholarship as early as Henri Bergson's *Le Rire* contends, laughter is a social practice. Moreover, as work on humor and the sex/gender system by Nancy A. Walker, Regina Barreca, Mahadev L. Apte, and others demonstrates, laughter as a social practice in the West traditionally has had unfortunate consequences for actual women. A deeper engagement with the politics of Chaucer's joke at Woman's expense would have enriched Percival's study. But despite this limitation, *Chaucer's Legendary Good Women,* with both its fine synthesis of critical work on the *Legend* and its comprehensive account of the sources and analogues of the poem, is a commendable achievement.

KATHY LAVEZZO
University of Iowa

S. H. RIGBY. *Chaucer in Context: Society, Allegory and Gender.* Manchester Medieval Studies. Manchester: Manchester University Press, 1996. Pp. xii, 205. $59.95 cloth, $24.95 paper.

Much of the study of Chaucer in the last decade has been shaped by a historical criticism heavily influenced by a sense of growing proximity between the disciplinary projects of historians and literary critics. For many in literature this proximity has been enabled by a certain exchange—by the supersession of notions of the distinctiveness of "poetic language" in favor of the "text," an object including both the literary sphere and documentary culture in the same interpretive framework. Similarly, for many historians the positivistic faith in the unique testimonial value of the document has given way to a sense of the importance of structural and narrative models in making proper sense of documentary evidence. The promise of the current rapprochement between literature and history thus lies not in some new negotiation of the relation between these fields, but rather in the fact that we share, perhaps more than ever before, a similar set of analytical objects and interpretive tools.

Stephen Rigby's *Chaucer in Context* is a significant new entry to this interdisciplinary conversation. Rigby's previous work, such as his *En-*

glish Society in the Later Middle Ages: Class, Status and Gender (New York: St. Martin's Press, 1995), has been notably adventurous in its combination of scrupulous historical research and bold structural interpretation. In much of its argument, *Chaucer in Context* shows a similar intellectual flair, not only in its ambition to speak of Chaucer as a historian but also in its careful synthesis of social and intellectual history with a thorough sense of the current stakes in Chaucer studies and in relevant literary theory.

The book is organized into four chapters, with a concluding epilogue. Rigby's method is dialectical, presenting in each chapter two diametrically opposed interpretive stances and then adjudicating between them. First, in "Chaucer: Real-Life Observation versus Literary Convention," he weighs the balance between realism and literary convention in *The Canterbury Tales,* offering the conclusion that "the pilgrims and the characters within their tales are best seen as active reinterpretations of reality in terms of the literary conventions, scientific doctrines and stock social satires of the day" (p. 15). In his second chapter, "Monologic versus Dialogic Chaucer," Rigby turns to Bakhtin's distinction between monologic and dialogic texts, using these categories as a way of separating out what are, for him, the two underlying versions of Chaucer in twentieth-century criticism: on the one hand a monologic, or essentially "conservative," Chaucer; and on the other a "heterodox" Chaucer whose works offer a "challenge to the official world-view of his age" (p. 18). Rigby argues here that the apparent contradiction between dialogic and monologic readings of Chaucer's work is a function of a misperception, that although "Chaucer himself intended his work to buttress the hierarchial, official world-view of his day, such intentions could come into conflict with the dialogic potential inherent in his story-telling contest and with his adoption of a literary form . . . ill equipped to constrain later interpretations" (p. 72). His third chapter, "Allegorical versus Humanist Chaucer," presents the conflict between the inheritors of E. Talbot Donaldson and D. W. Robertson, concluding, somewhat against the grain of current opinion, that a truly historicist reading should be based on a modified patristic criticism. In his most extended chapter, "Misogynist versus Feminist Chaucer," Rigby examines the depiction of women in Chaucer's texts and argues that although "it *is* possible to describe Chaucer as a 'feminist' writer" in contrast with "the stentorian voice of medieval misogyny," this description can be accepted only if one speaks of a feminism "in which women are confined to the role of respected inferior," a feminism "unlikely to appeal to modern feminists" (p. 163). Rigby then ends with a brief methodological conclusion.

This book has many virtues. Rigby makes use of a wide range of references in his account of recent Chaucerian criticism, demonstrating a familiarity not only with recent work on Chaucer but also with relevant theoretical discussions. The book is also written in a clear and energetic style, particularly given the requirements of summary placed upon him by the bounds of his project. And perhaps most impressively, true to his aim "to survey competing approaches to understanding medieval literature in its historical context" and "to put the case for each of them in as persuasive a fashion as possible" (p. ix), Rigby's summaries of previous opinion are remarkably balanced and fair. This book might thus be well recommended to undergraduate readers as a lucid and even-handed introduction to a number of important cruxes in Chaucerian interpretation.

Alongside these virtues, however, there are also perhaps moments at which the zeal to adjudicate between competing interpretations seems to nudge these chapters a bit rapidly toward conclusion and resolution. If there is an overriding polemic to this book, it is less an argument against any particular reading of Chaucer than it is an attempt to prune back the interpretive weeds that have grown up around Chaucer's texts, to assist those readers who find themselves "assailed by a host of mutually exclusive interpretations" (p. 167). Rigby's warrant for this project is his sense that "any intellectual discipline with claims to producing knowledge of the world, and this includes the discipline of literary criticism, is obliged to make such choices between conflicting propositions" (p. 169); his technique is the reduction of interpretation into a series of contradictions to be resolved through the application of historical knowledge. The danger here is that this a priori suspicion of interpretive fecundity leads Rigby, despite his care, into assigning to historical knowledge the disciplinary mission of chastising an errant and overproductive interpretive faculty.

This imperative to resolve contradiction produces two problems. First, although Rigby's preface contains an exemplary discussion of the slipperiness of "context" as a guide to interpretation ["the provision of a context in which to understand any work is itself the result of a process of interpretation" (p. xi)], there are still a number of moments in his arguments at which interpretive quandaries are dissolved by reference to "nonliterary" texts whose meaning is taken to be self-evident, univocal, and, most important, uncomplicatedly expressive of the worldview of an age. For example, we find the thorny question of whether to read Theseus as hero or tyrant put to rest by an assertion that "the dominant view in the Middle Ages" would have had no place for modern suspicions of the will to domination hidden within idealized political terminologies (p. 58). The authorities cited to substantiate this dominant view (Giles of Rome and Philippe de Mézières) are relevant and the connection to Theseus is illuminating, but one might still wonder whether even the joint testimony of these two theorists can convince us that a more cynical reading of Theseus's language could not possibly have been available to Chaucer or his readers. Giles and Philippe may have believed the state to be a perfect community, but is their belief sufficient guarantee for Chaucer's position on the subject?

Similarly, another difficulty in taking contradiction as a problem to be resolved is that such a formulation risks simplifying the ideological history to which Rigby devotes frequent and subtle attention (particularly in his meditations on dialogic and monologic discourse). It is one of the lessons of Marxist cultural criticism that the oppositions bound up with the logical form of the contradiction are often not simply the result of lax thought, but are also the (mediated and distorted) expressions of concrete social form. Rigby's own conclusion, with a paraphrase of Althusser on the imaginary resolution of real problems (p. 171), is only one of many moments suggesting his own commitment to teasing out such contradictions, but his determination to resolve conflicting lines of interpretation also leads him occasionally to dissolve such social contradictions as though they were simply logical error. For example, when Rigby argues that we must understand the Wife of Bath to have been an object of Chaucer's satire because "the Wife's arguments against the clerics' exaltation of virginity are beside the point" and thus meant simply to indicate her error, one is reminded of Rigby's own evocation of Margery Kempe's terror that she would be damned for her sexuality, and one might wonder whether Kempe would not have seen the Wife's concerns as being very much to the point (pp. 143, 131). In other words, a given cultural moment may contain both a Margery Kempe who fears damnation for her sexuality and an ecclesiastical annotator who understands the theological errors in the Wife of Bath's defense of her sexuality. As the careful debates in so much of *Chaucer in Context* can remind us, such conflicting testimony is the very stuff of knowledge, though such contradictions may often require less resolution than further unraveling.

ETHAN KNAPP
The Ohio State University

J. STEPHEN RUSSELL. *Chaucer and the Trivium: The Mindsong of the* Canterbury Tales. Gainesville: University Press of Florida, 1998. Pp. x, 266. $49.95.

The impact of Chaucer's education on his oeuvre is a well-worn topic, so Russell's choice to focus upon the cognitive effects of pedagogy appears sound. In his view Chaucer's training demonstrated the opacity of "natural languages" while allowing that "truth was at least theoretically attainable" in linguistic form. Chapter 1 explores "what Chaucer might have taken from his education," proposing that "medieval education produced people who *thought differently* from the way you and I do," and that these cognitive differences have vast implications for Chaucerians. Russell's argument is restricted to what he terms the "elementary curriculum," a muddled category for historians of medieval schooling within which he includes the grammar school curriculum as well. Much of the chapter focuses on logic, arguing for strict oppositions between the "agent intellect" and the "passive intellect" and stressing the variety of models available to teachers, such as Porphyry's Tree and Aristotle's *Categories.*

Chapter 2 examines *The General Prologue*'s reliance upon medieval habits of categorization, the Knight providing an idealized example of Aristotelian parataxis, the "categorial taxonomy" breaking down in the portrait of the Monk. Chapter 3 argues that Chaucer's Knight narrates his story for the edification of his son, the Squire, employing the "strategies of definition" found in nominalist theories of cognition. Chapter 4 treats legal rhetoric in the story of Constance, suggesting that the tale constitutes "a wide-ranging examination of language and rhetoric delivered in the person of an accomplished practitioner of the forensic arts," while chapter 5 reads *The Clerk's Tale* as a meditation on the "wife-making and freedom-making abilities" of Walter and the creative powers of language. A conclusion extends Russell's approach to the Merchant, the Wife, and Melibee.

Unfortunately Russell's version of "what we know of medieval education" is based on an extremely limited range of sources. While his intended audience is "students of Chaucer and Middle English literature," this does not excuse the numerous omissions and factual errors in the book's treatment of its subject. One problem is Russell's delimited treatment of rhetoric. Two pages of the long background chapter are devoted to this part of the trivium while logic gets thirty-one; rhetoric is stripped down to "verbal arts" and "persuasion," eviscerated of the numerous creative faculties—translation, *actio,* and so on—that scholars such as Rita Copeland, Jody Enders, and Marjorie Curry Woods have restored to it since James Murphy's *Rhetoric in the Middle Ages.* The result is a number of claims about preuniversity education that are simply untrue: for example, "other parts of rhetoric in the modern sense—composition, audience analysis, conventions—were not regular parts of the elementary curriculum at all . . . little extended writing was part of the grammar school program." Aside from its conflation of the "elementary curriculum" and the "grammar school program," this claim contradicts the available scholarship. Nicholas Orme showed long ago that exercises resembling *dictamen* were taught in grammar schools throughout England, while Martin Camargo has revealed that the practice was much more influential at all educational levels than the few sources Russell cites would suggest. Worse yet, earlier in the chapter, Russell quotes verbatim Murphy's observation that some teachers of elementary grammar "appropriated for themselves the right to teach the *ars dictaminis.*" Which of these statements is to be believed by our students: that there was almost no composition in early education, or that grammar masters were themselves often teaching the rhetoric of prose composition? (This general neglect of the *ars dictaminis* perhaps explains Russell's declension confusion: twice he identifies it as the *ars dictamini*). As Jo Ann Hoeppner Moran points out, writing schools were common in London by the late fourteenth century; and Latin education in the late medieval grammar school entailed the teaching of both speech *and* written composition.

Such bibliographical oversights are not simple omissions; they go to substantive matters of scholarly reliability. At times they are quite serious. This reader wonders what Russell's analysis of grammar education would look like had he consulted Tony Hunt's *Teaching and Learning Latin in Thirteenth-Century England* (Cambridge, 1991), a work that appears nowhere in Russell's notes but that undermines his most basic claims about Latin pedagogy, such as the following: "The 'rhetoric' that survives this diaspora"—i.e., once the parts of rhetoric that Russell chooses not to treat have been eliminated—"is limited to a few texts of Cicero, the *Rhetorica ad Herennium,* Horace's *Ars Poetica,* and a few 'modern' poetic texts such as those of John of Garland and Matthew of Vendome. The black hole of the medieval school yields little about how these texts were taught (if at all)." Yet Hunt's work showed very clearly that such texts were in fact taught often and carefully in pedagogical contexts. Some knowledge of Hunt's study would have helped Russell avoid the repeated imposition of simplistic divisions between Latin clarity and vernacular opacity upon the period: "it is relatively difficult to be ambiguous in Latin unless you are actually working at it"; "the transparency of Latin made it an unlikely medium for personal expression." Such all-encompassing pronouncements sweep aside the diversity of the Latin literature of the Middle Ages and its complex role in pedagogical practices.

The supposed "black hole of the medieval school" that Russell bemoans is entirely of his own invention. If it existed in the middle of the twentieth century, it has since been laboriously filled by a generation of scholars whose books and editions are strangely absent from *Chaucer and the Trivium.* Such oversights lead as well to misunderstandings of specific Chaucerian passages: "Education began . . . in the 'song schools' with the alphabet and then Latin recognition and pronunciation through drills in prayers, psalms, and hymns. These texts were sometimes read, but typically they were simply memorized and then either recited or sung by rote, never construed. . . . Only in later years in 'grammar school' would students begin to learn Latin grammar." These assertions support a reading of *The Prioress's Tale* that presents the clergeon's older "felawe" as a student of song who will—according to Russell—be advanced to the study of Latin grammar. The reading is based on scholarship that has since been corrected by historians such as William J. Courtenay and Moran. By Chaucer's time, institutionally separated schools existed for reading and song, and it is wrong to assume that song masters were teaching their students how to read, or that elementary teachers of reading were always instructing their charges in song; many song schools existed without instruction in reading. And some of the song schools that *did* teach reading also taught grammar, despite Russell's claim that Latin was "never construed" by this population.

While such neglect of current scholarship presents grave problems, the interpretations of the individual tales in *Chaucer and the Trivium* should be well received. While the relevance of medieval preuniversity education to the book's discrete readings of Chaucerian texts is not always apparent, Russell's study is sure to provoke further work on the topic.

BRUCE HOLSINGER
University of Colorado, Boulder

NIGEL SAUL. *Richard II.* Yale English Monarchs Series. New Haven and London: Yale University Press, 1997. Pp. xii, 514. $40.00 cloth, $18.00 paper.

That, at the end of the twentieth century, the Yale English Monarchs should have become (or so its dust jacket proclaims) "a classic series, arguably *the* classic series in historical biography"—indeed, that such a series should have been thought of at all—might have surprised an earlier generation of historians. Writing before there was even such a thing as an "*Annales* school," Eileen Power suggested that though "we still praise famous men . . . we praise them with due recognition of the fact that not only great individuals, but people as a whole, unnamed and undistinguished masses of people, now sleeping in unknown graves, have been part of the story"; there is no need, then, to espouse one of the wilder brands of French historiography ("history without people," "immobile history") in order to feel that there is something rather parochial about this whole enterprise. That said, Nigel Saul's biography of *Richard II* fills a distinct gap. With the notable exception of Armitage-Smith, older writers of late medieval political biography (such as Wylie, Vickers, and Schofield) evidently found the fourteenth century less attractive than the fifteenth, and the previous standard life of Richard (Anthony Steel's) is a slight thing by comparison. Steel's was, in fact, a political history in the narrowest sense (as Galbraith noted with approval), and those seeking a more extended view of Richard's reign had either to turn to the last 150 pages of May McKisack's *Fourteenth Century* or to supplement their reading with more specialized studies such as Ruth Bird's or Gervase Mathew's. If I have some reservations about Saul's success, then, they should be read in this context; he has attempted the first comprehensive modern biography of Richard II and his achievement is considerable: the historical scholarship is generally painstaking, the writing on the whole lucid, and the scope, given the limitations imposed by the genre, impressive. It will doubtless serve as the standard account of the reign for many years to come, and readers of this journal, searching out historical background for the literary texts they are working on, will find much of value in it.

My main reservation is with the way Saul handles the central problem his subject presents him with, the enigmatic and protean character of the king himself. *The Westminster Chronicle* (one of the most important sources for the period 1381–94, and one that Saul himself relies upon heavily) offers us, according to its most recent editor, Barbara Harvey, two distinct Richards: the early one, temperamental and vainglorious, and the later one, temperate and conciliatory. Had the chronicler continued on to the end of the reign he might well have had to portray yet a third Richard, the arrogant and vindictive tyrant of the final years, 1397–99. How are we to account for this royal chameleon? We might put it down to the incompetence, ignorance, or bias of the chronicler (or chroniclers), but this is an explanation Harvey herself rejects, attributing the change in the king to the harsh schooling of the Merciless Parliament and its aftermath; he had to learn "the necessity of often dissembling, proceeding adroitly and biding his time." Harvey's Richard, however (in essence, a Richard whom Steel would have recognized), is certainly not Saul's.

When Saul's Richard sheds "the brittle and inflexible behaviour of his adolescent years" and assumes "the character of a mature and reasonable young ruler" (p. 201), he does so in earnest. Here is no calculating temporizer, no "smylere with the knyf under the cloke," but a man responding quite intelligibly to a new set of circumstances: "the sudden changes in Richard's behaviour can be seen as shifts from one psychological environment to another, the periods of stability in between as responses to a basic stability of environment" (p. 202). This smacks strongly of behaviorist psychology; Saul, indeed, describes Richard's behavior as "situation dependent" and finds it subject to a degree of operant conditioning: "to the extent that he was rewarded for his more amenable manner, he was encouraged to reproduce it in a variety of other settings and it became his uniform style" (p. 202). Such a claim is vulnerable to the kind of objection Noam Chomsky (in his famous review of B. F. Skinner's *Verbal Behavior*) raised to all such behaviorist explanations: "the insights that have been achieved in the laboratories of the reinforcement theorist, though quite genuine, can be applied to complex human behavior only in the most gross and superficial way." As objective assessment, Saul's argument is clearly counterintuitive (Richard is at his most stable when he is in the greatest danger and at his most irrational when least threatened), and as subjective analysis, it plainly assumes what it seeks to prove (Why did Richard's behavior change? Because his "psychological environment" altered. How do we know his psychological environment altered? Because his behavior changed). In either case its explanatory force is weak.

Perhaps it is some sense of the limitations of his own analysis that leads Saul later in the book to turn to a quite different psychological paradigm—the neo-Freudianism of Erich Fromm—for a psychic template. Richard's personality, we now learn, was essentially narcissistic: "narcissism describes a condition in which only the person himself—his own body, his own needs and feelings—are experienced as fully real: everybody and everything else lacks reality or interest" (p. 459). The difficulty with this (quite apart from the genuine problems inherent in any attempt to apply the terminology of modern psychoanalysis to psyches long dead) is that it contradicts the earlier account. How can the behaviorist Richard, so responsive to his "psychological environment," be made to square with the neo-Freudian Richard, so out of touch with reality? (Of course, it might be claimed that the psychological environment itself was a mental construct, but in that case it loses all claim to providing an objective standard.) Though Saul follows Galbraith in criticizing Steel for his diagnosis of Richard as a neurotic (pp. 462–63), it is difficult to see how Steel's neurotic Richard differs substantially from Saul's narcissistic one: "a schizoid mind of Richard's type," wrote Steel, "suffers in times of mental stress from feelings that the outer world has less and less reality; it will become a mirror which reflects only what the subject wants to see—in Richard's case the sacred mystery and unfettered nature of royal power." Certainly Saul's Richard is far less indolent and fatalistic than Steel's, but Galbraith, who took Steel to task for failing to account for all the facts, could quite as justly have leveled the same charge against either one of Saul's psychological constructs.

Contemplating his behaviorist Richard, Saul speculates, "had there been no further change in psychological environment [after 1388] it is possible that he would have continued to act in this way [with moderation] and would never have suffered the unhappy fate of deposition. But towards the end of the 1390s it seems that a further change did occur, and as a result there was a second major shift in his behaviour" (pp. 202–3). We must wait 160 pages to learn what this major change was, but when we do it is with a strong sense of anticlimax: "in the early part [of 1397] the political consensus that had prevailed since 1389 began to break down. For the first time in a decade the king was being subjected to outspoken criticism" (p. 368). But what, we might ask, did this outspoken criticism consist of? The answer is Haxey's petition in the January parliament and a putative plot among the older appellants in June. Of the four clauses in Haxey's petition, however, three contain nothing new (and indeed, as Saul knows [p. 369], restate some complaints that had been raised during the unthreatening psychological environment of 1389–96) and the fourth, which objects to an excessive number of bishops and ladies at court, hardly seems so grave a threat to the stability of the realm as to send the king into a panic. The possibility of a new appellant conspiracy proves to be even more of a red herring, for (as Saul again knows [p. 372]) Palmer showed twenty years ago that the only real evidence for such a plot (in the French *Traison et mort*) is a complete fabrication. We are left with the weak claim that "if the reality was that no plot existed in 1397 there was reason to believe that there might be one" (p. 372; cf. p. 391). Such a possibility was not unique to 1397, however (indeed it might have seemed far stronger at the time of the northern rebellions of 1393), and though the three senior appellants had plenty of reason to resent the king in that year, the fact remains that their fortunes were at a low ebb and they had precious little chance of doing much about it. The conventional explanation looks far more plausible: with Warwick sickly, Arundel in financial difficulties, and Gloucester less likely to be protected by John of Gaunt (his brother, incidentally, not his uncle [p. 372]), Richard saw this as an opportune moment to avenge the affronts of the Merciless Parliament.

As regards his narcissistic Richard, Saul's representation of the facts is even more questionable. "Richard may have acted strangely from 1397, but it is doubtful if he was suffering from a split personality. His behaviour did not exhibit any of the usual symptoms of schizophrenia. *At no time is there any indication that he lost self-control*". . . . (pp. 463–64;

my italics). Richard might, I suppose, be conceivably described as imperturbable during the last two years of his reign, but a footnote at this point referring to the apocryphal status of *The Westminster Chronicle*'s story of his throwing his hat and shoes out of the window in a fit of temper (in 1384) shows that Saul means his remark to be applied more generally. But imperturbability is certainly not a characteristic of the Richard of *The Westminster Chronicle,* nor indeed of some of the other accounts. In fact, Saul is here contradicting his previous statement that "in the earlier part of the chronicle [the Monk of Westminster] sees the king as a rather petulant, hot tempered young man, quick to lose self-control: his abuse of Lancaster is recorded, and so too is his threat to draw his sword on the Archbishop of Canterbury" (p. 314). (As a matter of fact, three of Richard's own courtiers were so alarmed by this last display of rage that they jumped off the royal barge.) Weeping in public might be argued to be a socially constructed activity, so perhaps we should not put Richard's several recorded bouts of lachrymosity down to a loss of self-control, but the same can hardly be said of his public displays of anger. According to *The Westminster Chronicle,* when the king flared up at the Earl of Arundel in the Salisbury Parliament (*excanduit rex et totus versus in furorem ac torvo vultu . . . dixit . . .*), all the onlookers were so embarrassed that John of Gaunt had tactfully to break an awkward silence. Saul is completely silent about another occasion on which Arundel provoked the king to fury, indeed to an actual physical assault (at Queen Anne's funeral); this is a particularly significant omission since the incident occurred during the period when Richard was supposedly ruling with reason and moderation. Perhaps Saul feels that the chronicle source here (the *Annales*) is not to be trusted, but there are certainly times when he himself might be faulted for treating his sources uncritically. On the strength of Jean Creton's testimony, for instance, we are told that the captive Richard was handed over to the sons of Gloucester and Arundel for safe keeping at Chester (p. 417); no doubt Creton would have appreciated the grim irony of such a situation, but the fact is that Gloucester's son was almost certainly not present and may well have been dead by this time.

For literary scholars, the most interesting chapter of this biography will be "The King and His Court" (pp. 327–65). Saul may perhaps be right to claim that "it was painting and architecture that attracted [Richard], not letters" (p. 365), but this hardly justifies the allocation of a mere six pages in this lengthy book to the literary and intellectual life of the Ricardian court (pp. 359–65). (Incidentally, painting does no better and neither Herman Scheere nor John Siferwas is even mentioned.) Saul's lack of interest in the subject is reflected in a couple of careless slips (we are told that Thomas Usk was a poet [p. 360] and that *The Tale of Melibee* is a poem [p. 362]), but it has wider consequences. He could not, of course, have known of the new insights into Queen Anne's role at court offered by David Wallace's *Chaucerian Polity* (which appeared in the same year) or Andrew Taylor's article in the 1998 issue of this journal, but nevertheless an awareness of Chaucer's celebrated allusion to "oure firste lettre" at the beginning in *Troilus* or of his proposal to present *The Legend of Good Women* to "the quene . . . at Eltham or at Sheene" at the end of the F Prologue (to say nothing of the character of Alceste in *The Legend*) might have helped Saul to flesh out his rather meager portrait of Richard's consort (pp. 455–56). Similarly, familiarity with Gower's reference to "the newe guise of Beawme" might have made him less skeptical about the influence of Bohemia on Ricardian court culture (pp. 347–49). But such details represent only the tip of an iceberg; I hope it is not unduly partial to suggest that a detailed reading of modern historicist critics such as Patterson, Strohm, and Wallace could have provided Saul with a wealth of material with which to enrich and modulate his biography.

I do not wish to sound monotonously critical of this book, for it contains much to admire. As one might expect of a historian who has worked primarily on the gentry, Saul is particularly good where his story moves out into the shires—on the response of the countryside to the Peasants' Revolt, for example, or on Richard's cultivation of a power base among the gentry after the Merciless Parliament. His discussion of the way Richard manipulated the vocabulary and iconography of kingship to advance his own ends is also excellent and will be of great value to literary scholars working on the Ricardian court. And his ingenious reading of the legal context of the succession question (pp. 396–97) has been amply born out by Michael Bennett's fascinating discovery (published in the *English Historical Review* in 1998) of Edward III's entail on the English crown. Nevertheless, in the final analysis I must confess to a feeling of disappointment. I began by suggesting that straight political biography looks somewhat dated after a century of economic, institutional, legal, social, and cultural history, and I will end with a specific instance. In his last chapter Saul raises an interesting question: "Richard's attempt to establish a new political consensus was thus ultimately unsuccessful. But does it follow from this that the policies he pursued never stood any hope of success?" (p. 439). As he justly points out, many of these same policies were to prove highly effective in the hands of Yorkist and early Tudor monarchs, so where, then, did Richard go wrong? Even when he has made allowance for the rather different political climate of the late fifteenth century, Saul still seems to believe that it was simple political misjudgment (the way his favoring of Cheshiremen created factionalism in the countryside, for example) that cost Richard his crown. He seems oblivious to the larger forces at work against this Renaissance prince *avant la lettre.* Or almost: "in Richard's reign," Saul concedes, "the instruments of autocracy were less highly developed than they were to be later" (p. 441); and again, "the nature of the late fourteenth century polity . . . made it difficult for Richard to achieve the ends that he was seeking" (p. 442). Well, yes; precisely!

RICHARD FIRTH GREEN
University of Western Ontario

PAUL STROHM. *England's Empty Throne: Usurpation and the Language of Legitimation, 1399–1422.* New Haven: Yale University Press, 1998. Pp. xiv, 274. $35.00.

In this elegantly written book, Paul Strohm explores what he calls the "process of symbolization" (p. xi) and the "representational regimes" (p. 154) by which the Lancastrians sought to legitimize their usurpation of the English throne. His procedure is to explore in a series of essays the deep structures of a variety of textual events. The first essay begins with an interesting discussion of the role of prophecy and concludes with an account of the petition to the 1406 Parliament urging that both Lollards and believers in Richard's continued survival be silenced. For Strohm this petition aimed at a far-reaching thought control: the Lancastrians meant to deprive their subjects of the "powers to form mental images of things not experienced, to constitute hypothetical alternatives to the present disposition of things, to engage . . . in moral reflection across time. . . . It harbors a political wish which exceeds any finite objective: the annihilation of the utopian imagination by superimposition of its own sanctioned symbolism on the individual capacity to image alternatives" (pp. 30–31). Consequently, "functioning as a political unconscious, the oppositional imagination produces an unending stream of representations alternative to every established or agreed-upon signification" (p. 31), since the imagination operates "under the permissive domain of the pleasure principle" (p. 31).

As this summary suggests, Strohm's preferred interpretive method is psychoanalytic, and it is deployed throughout the book to a single end. Over and over we are shown how the Lancastrians' effort to impose a single set of beliefs or "desires" upon the nation was thwarted by either history itself or the unruly psyches of their subjects. Chapter 2 argues that the Lollards were not a genuine political threat to the regime but an opportunity for the rulers to adopt a posture of orthodoxy. Yet it also claims (paradoxically) that they posed a symbolic danger: by rejecting the official doctrine on transubstantiation, they broke a crucial link in the "chain of sacramental signification" (p. 61) and allowed entrance to the thought that not even anointment with holy oil could turn a duke into a king. Strohm then describes both the Oldcastle rebellion of 1414 and the Southampton plot of 1415 as stage-managed or "invented" by the Lancastrians, with the "repressed" guilty knowledge—that the earl of March was Richard's legitimate heir—not returning until 1460 with Richard of York's genealogical claim to the throne. Richard II himself, in the next essay, is carefully reinterred by Henry V in an attempt to bury the dead and appropriate his "aura," and once again it is in 1460 that the repressed symbolic "return[s] from the 'real'" (p. 127). Chapter 5 returns to Lollards and the claim by the confessed counterfeiter William Carsewell that he was in league with Oldcastle. This event too is read as a challenge to the "obsessional" Lancastrian belief in the possibilities of transformation, for while real counterfeiters can be apprehended, "imaginary counterfeiters"—and Strohm assures us that such people (whoever they might be) "were everywhere in this society"—used their powers (whatever they were) as "a site in which resistance can be thought about" (p. 151). Henry V's appropriation of the dowry of his stepmother, Joanne of Navarre, through the device of accusing her of sorcery is then subjected to the same scheme, but now we have to wait until, 35 years later, a romanticized biography of Joanne's son, Arthur of Brittany, presents a conventional scene of misrecognition that allows Joanne to be revealed as a "stubborn" resistant "uninstructed in the necessity of forgoing or subordinating her own wishes" (p. 171). The last chapter is on Hoccleve and Lydgate. "Determined in no respect to offend" (p. 179), "unabashedly partisan" (p. 181), and doing what they can "to adjust obstinate circumstances and putative enemies to the requirements" of their Lancastrian masters (p. 191), these poets nonetheless—and against their wills—produced ambivalent texts because of the pressure of what Strohm would call "the 'real,'" i.e., history. In a coda on the "amnesiac text," Strohm concludes with an ingenious reading of an exemplum from Hoccleve's *Regement:* an empty chest that is thought to be full expresses the Lancastrians' obsessive fear of the emptiness of their own dynastic claims.

Summarized in this way, the book can be seen to display the virtues for which Strohm is well known: careful archival research is combined with an overall interpretation that, in its celebration of the resistance to illegitimate power, accords with our contemporary sympathies. But when read in detail, the book is surprisingly disappointing. One familiar annoyance is the fact that citations from theoretical heavyweights are often simply banalities tricked out in pretentious jargon: an egregious example is Lacan's vapid observation that a person condemned to die suffers two deaths, the condemnation and its execution, an idea Strohm likes so much he repeats it three times (pp. 82, 102, 124). But a much more serious problem is the frailty of the evidence upon which the book's large claims rest. How do we know that the Lancastrians "sought to curb imagining—or to substitute for unruly imagining a more officially approved and structured imagination?" (p. 29). Because the petition of 1406 says that the church's endowments are possessed "as it has been best considered and imagined [*avisee ou ymaginee*] by the Laws and Customs of your [the king's] realm" (cited, p. 30). On the slender thread of that one "ymaginee" (which could just as plausibly be translated as "conceived" as "imagined") hangs the whole of Strohm's claim that the Lancastrians sought to impose a Stalinist-like conformity of thought (here Koestler's *Darkness at Noon* is invoked [p. 91]). Another example is the discussion of the Lollards. Although first arguing that the arcane issue of transubstantiation was forced upon them by opponents determined to entrap them, Strohm then reverses his ground by arguing that denying transubstantiation is equivalent to denying the legitimacy of a royal coronation. Does any Lollard actually say such a thing? No, but Roger Dymmock does, in one sentence of his 1395 attack against the Lollards. Is it true that women in the Lancastrian regime were trapped "in their complete subservience to processes of male fantasy?" (p. 161). The career of Joan Beaufort, the duchess of Westmorland, would suggest otherwise: the king's aunt and the second wife of the immensely powerful Ralph Nevill, she persuaded her husband to disinherit his heir in favor of the eldest of *her* sons.[1] Strohm is very hard on the historians of a century ago for accepting the Lancastrian account of the so-called Oldcastle rebellion of 1414, but he ignores more recent work that has already demonstrated the historiographical sleights of hand by which this enigmatic event became part of the legend of Henry V's kingly foresight.[2]

The overall effect of the book is to present the history of Lancastrian England as enacted by puppets subject to impulses that are unrecognized by them but transparent to the sophisticated modern observer. The one place where this presumption cannot function is in the treatment of Hoccleve and Lydgate, who are after all capable of speaking for themselves. The result is the weakest chapter in the book. It is far from accurate to present Hoccleve as an obsequious time server; rather he was, as James Simpson has shown, "Nobody's Man."[3] And in an essay cited by Strohm, I argued that Lydgate had good and entirely conscious reasons for the deep doubts about Henrician ambitions that he expresses in the *Siege of Thebes,* doubts that the poem makes eminently clear.[4] For a reader who can tease meanings out of the most recondite texts, Strohm seriously underreads this familiar poetry.

In the treatment of "the Lancastrians" themselves—by which Strohm seems finally to mean simply the two Henries—the fashionable politics of heroic resistance are most persistently invoked. For Strohm the Lancastrian rule is characterized by "usurpation, tyranny, and terror" (p. 195), and the first two decades of the century are marked by "Henry IV's murderous usurpation, the benefits to orthodoxy in burning English

[1] K. B. McFarlane, *The Nobility of Later Medieval England* (Oxford: Clarendon Press, 1973), p. 67.

[2] Annabel Patterson, *Reading Holinshed's* Chronicles (Chicago: University of Chicago Press, 1994), pp. 130–53; Annabel Patterson, "Sir John Oldcastle and Reformation Historiography," in Donna B. Hamilton and Richard Strier, eds., *Religion, Literature, and Politics in Post-Reformation England, 1540–1688* (Cambridge: Cambridge University Press, 1996), pp. 6–26.

[3] James Simpson, "Nobody's Man: Thomas Hoccleve's *Regement of Princes,*" in Julia Boffey and Pamela King, eds., *London and Europe in the Later Middle Ages* (London: Queen Mary and Westfield College, 1995), pp. 149–80.

[4] "Making Identities in Fifteenth-Century England: Henry V and John Lydgate," in Jeffrey N. Cox and Larry J. Reynolds, eds., *New Historical Literary Study: Essays on Reproducing Texts, Representing History* (Princeton, N.J.: Princeton University Press, 1993), pp. 69–107.

subjects as Lollard heretics, and the path to peace through rapine and seizure in France" (p. 191). This account of the reigns of the Henries is seriously unbalanced. To give just one example, Strohm says that "the normal Lancastrian way of cherishing the Church is to apprehend and burn heretics" (p. 194) but never mentions the Lancastrian religious foundations, Henry IV's pre-1400 crusading or post-1400 acts of contrition and even self-humiliation, or Henry V's famous piety and his plans to reform the monastic houses. Indeed, readers of the recent historiography of the period by McFarlane, Harriss, McNiven, and Allmand, among others, will recognize that Strohm's caricature of these "savage" (p. 68) and "obscene" (p. 213) rulers is possible only by ignoring much of the historical record. The reason must be that Strohm has little sympathy for the often harsh realities of medieval and specifically English kingship. Hence, for instance, he is shocked—shocked!—that Arundel and Henry IV should have colluded in bringing about the exemplary burning of William Sautre in 1401, and equally appalled that Henry V should have had spies who kept him well informed of the rebellion of 1414 so he could manage it to his own advantage. The result is less an analysis of historical texts than a morality play, with the monstrous "Lancastrians" on one side, plotting to control all around them by the most devious of symbolic strategies, and on the other, heroically resistant "texts," which pluckily imagine that perhaps things could be other than they are—perhaps even like 1397–99, when good King Richard ruled?

LEE PATTERSON
Yale University

M. TERESA TAVORMINA and R. F. YEAGER, eds. *The Endless Knot: Essays on Old and Middle English in Honor of Marie Borroff.* Cambridge: D. S. Brewer, 1995. Pp. x, 252. $90.00.

Celebrating the retirement of Marie Borroff—Sterling Professor of English at Yale University—this Festschrift offers sixteen essays penned by distinguished Anglo-Saxonists and medievalists. Especially vital to this collection are key themes (style, poetics) and authors (Langland,

Gower, Chaucer, the *Pearl* poet) appealing to Borroff throughout her scholarly career.

At least five essays call attention to explorations of style, including grammar, language, and prosody. While Eric Stanley's "Paradise Lost of the Old English Dual" focuses on the use of the pronominal construction ("the two of us/you") in Old English prose and verse works, R. F. Yeager's essay ("Ben Jonson's *English Grammar* and John Gower's Reception in the Seventeenth Century"), however, emphasizes the frequent appearance of Gower selections (thirty-two references) in the *English Grammar.* Then revealing how and why Jonson employed Gower, Yeager argues that the medieval poet embodied significant virtues, "ideals Jonson and his circle proposed for themselves" (p. 238). Accordingly, Gower represented for the Renaissance writer authority fused with humaneness, "a man of letters whose classicism and ethical poetic" served as beacons in a benighted world "to light the way for kindred spirits yet to come" (p. 239).

Following these scholarly forays into grammar and its influences, Melissa M. Furrow ("Latin and Affect") elucidates how and why Latin—"the primary language of religious observance . . . , [the tongue] heard from infancy by every Christian" (p. 30)—is used by Gower, Langland, and Chaucer. Such poets, Furrow argues, employed Latin to generate emotional power. Two final explorations of style are found in Stephen A. Barney's "Langland's Prosody: The State of Study" and in Ralph Hanna III's "Defining Middle English Alliterative Poetry." While Barney investigates alliterative meter generally and surveys "recent theories of the alliterative long line and of Langland's prosody" (p. 85), Hanna attempts to decode the ciphers of alliterative verse. Noting the limited critical visions of what truly constitutes alliterative poetry, Hanna contends that scholars must scrutinize extant texts more meticulously and fashion "a more carefully nuanced model of 'alliterativity' than has pertained in the past" (p. 57).

Because of limitations of space, the remainder of this review will be devoted to the artistry of three fourteenth-century Middle English poets—Langland (one essay), Chaucer (selected discussions), and the *Pearl* poet (two analyses). In "Conscience's Dinner," for instance, Traugott Lawler provides "a literal narrative reading . . . of Conscience's dinner in *Piers Plowman* B.13" (p. 87) through characterization and through the properties of the romance mode. Then exploring "the interplay of characters" (p. 88)—Conscience, Patience, Clergy, along with the friar and

Will—Lawler highlights a comic narrative "informed by biblical allusion" (p. 88), thereby shaping "a deepened and charged literal meaning" (p. 88).

Of the seven essays devoted to Chaucer, five are of special interest to this reviewer. J. A. Burrow's "Elvish Chaucer," for example, analyzes the "elvyssh contenaunce" of Chaucer the pilgrim in the Prologue (1. 703) to *Sir Thopas.* Perceiving Chaucer's behavior as placing him in the realm of elves and fairies, Burrow suggests that the pilgrim is "absent" and "reserved," guarding "his authorial privacy and privilege against readerly intrusion" (p. 106). In "Alceste the Washerwoman," however, Anne Higgins explicates *The Legend of Good Women,* a poem infused with the values of "the real world of equivocation, ambivalence, duplicity" (p. 113). Focusing on the character of Alceste, "the God of Love's *quene*" (p. 115), Higgins views this key personage as an amalgam of a classical figure and a fourteenth-century woman—Alice Chester, a laundress in Edward III's household. Similarly, M. Teresa Tavormina (". . . Musical Topicality in the Reeve's and Miller's Tales") offers historical buttressing for the musical leitmotif in Chaucer's *Reeve's Tale.* She hypothesizes that Chaucer coined the names of his Northumbrian clerks "to remind his audience of a noted English composer" (p. 142). Such a musician was "John Aleyn, a clerk of Edward III's royal household chapel from 1361 until his death in 1373" (p. 142).

The remaining two essays on Chaucer explore individual *Canterbury Tales* in terms of other medieval works. Elizabeth Archibald's "Contextualizing Chaucer's Constance," for instance, analyzes *The Man of Law's Tale* in the context of medieval "family romances." Within such literary modes "some or all members of a nuclear family are separated and then reunited after various adventures" (p. 161). Central to *The Man of Law's Tale,* Archibald claims, is subversion of the romance convention of the "happy ending," especially since the narrative calls into question the traditional patriarchal fashioning of family values (p. 162). In Sherry L. Reames's "Artistry, Decorum and Purpose . . . ," the author examines three Middle English renarrations of the St. Cecilia legend—one in the *Northern Homily Cycle,* another in the *South English Legendary,* and a final version in Chaucer's *Second Nun's Tale.* Reames contends that the last half of *The Second Nun's Tale* skewers contemporary authorities whose behavior reflects "the sins of . . . ancient Roman persecutors" (p. 198). Since such rulers—including Parliament members and bishops—held positions of power, Chaucer was circumspect in his account. "Hence the solution of the ancient saint's legend—a genre which provided an ideal screen for potentially dangerous ideas . . . because it was so closely identified with orthodoxy and yet so full of material that did not necessarily uphold the late medieval status quo" (p. 199).

The final essays to be discussed, those dealing with *Pearl,* focus partly on the dreamer. In "Invention, Mnemonics, and Stylistic Ornament in *Psychomachia* and *Pearl,*" for instance, Mary J. Carruthers pinpoints the dreamer's role as "maker of *ornaments* [her emphasis]" (p. 202) and the link "between ornament and invention" and how their tie is fashioned "through the cognitive procedures of mnemonics" (p. 202). Finally, in "The Anatomy of a Mourning: Reflections on the *Pearl* Dreamer," Elizabeth D. Kirk contends that the dreamer's loss does not evaporate but "is subsumed into . . . the realities that surround those who still live in the cycle of nature and of the sacraments" (p. 225). Even though the separation between the dreamer and the maiden remains a central part of *Pearl,* at the end of the poem the dreamer's egotism and stubbornness gradually are "replaced by an image of sacred and secular joined together like the members of a family" (p. 225).

While the Borroff festschrift contains a *Tabula Gratulatoria,* the collection includes no index, comprehensive bibliography, or bibliography of the honoree's published works (except indirectly through the notes penned by the volume's contributors).

ROBERT J. BLANCH
Northeastern University

Books Received

Ashton, Gail. *Chaucer:* The Canterbury Tales. The Analyzing Texts Series. New York: St. Martin's Press, 1998. Pp. viii, 206. $55.00 cloth, $19.95 paper.

Bartlett, Anne Clark, and Thomas Bestul, eds. *Cultures of Piety: Medieval Devotional English Literature in Translation.* Ithaca, N.Y., and London: Cornell University Press, 1999. Pp. 256. $16.95 paper.

Bartlett, Anne Clark, Thomas Bestul, Janet Goebel, and William F. Pollard, eds. *Vox Mystica: Essays on Medieval Mysticism in Honor of Valerie M. Lagorio.* Cambridge: D. S. Brewer, 1995. Pp. xiv, 235. $81.00 cloth.

Bawcutt, Priscilla. *The Poems of William Dunbar.* 2 vols. Association for Scottish Literary Studies, vols. 27 and 28. Glasgow: Association for Scottish Literary Studies, 1998. Pp. x, 277; 621. $107.18 cloth.

Biddick, Kathleen. *The Shock of Medievalism.* Durham, N.C.: Duke University Press, 1998. Pp. x, 315. $49.95 cloth, $17.95 paper.

Biggs, J. H., ed. *The Imitation of Christ.* Early English Text Society, no. 309. (Oxford: Oxford University Press, 1997. Pp. lxxxix, 249. $65.00 cloth.

Boitani, Piero, and Adele Cipolla, eds. *Alessandro Nel Medioevo Occidentale.* Verona: Fondazione Lorenzo Valla, 1997. Pp. xii, 714. $22.23 cloth.

Boitani, Piero, and Anna Torti, eds. *The Body and the Soul in Medieval Literature.* The J. A. W. Bennett Memorial Lectures, 10th ser., Perugia, 1998. Cambridge: D. S. Brewer, 1999. Pp. xi. 211. $75.00 cloth.

Bornstein, George, and Theresa Tinkle, eds. *The Iconic Page in Manuscript, Print and Digital Culture.* Ann Arbor: University of Michigan Press, 1998. Pp. x, 294. $49.50 cloth.

Brewer, Derek. *A New Introduction to Chaucer.* 2d ed. London: Longman, 1998. Pp. xii, 426. $17.99 paper.

Brown, Peter. *Reading Dreams: The Interpretation of Dreams from Chaucer to Shakespeare.* New York: Oxford University Press, 1999. Pp. x, 194. $45.00 cloth.

Burnett, Charles, ed. *Adelard of Bath, Conversations with His Nephew on the Same and the Different, Questions on Natural Science, and On Birds.* Cambridge: Cambridge University Press, 1998. Pp. lii, 287. $80.00 cloth.

Burton, T. L., ed. *Sidrak and Bokkus, vol. 2: Books III–IV, Commentary, Appendices, Glossary, Index.* Early English Text Society, os. 312. Oxford: Oxford University Press, 1999. Pp. 941. $85.00 cloth.

Carruthers, Mary. *The Craft of Thought: Meditation, Rhetoric, and the Making of Images, 400–1200.* Cambridge Studies in Medieval Literature, vol. 34. Cambridge: Cambridge University Press, 1998. Pp. xvii, 399.$59.95 cloth.

Condren, Edward I. *Chaucer and the Energy of Creation: The Design and Organization of the* Canterbury Tales. Gainesville: University Press of Florida, 1999. Pp. 295. $49.95 cloth.

Cowan, Alexander. *Urban Europe 1500–1700.* London: Arnold, 1998. Pp. ix, 229. $75.00 cloth, $19.95 paper.

Cullen, Dolores L. *Chaucer's Host: Up-So-Doun.* Santa Barbara: Fithian Press, 1998. Pp. 208. $14.95 paper.

Dahl, Gunnar. *Trade, Trust and Networks: Commercial Cultures in Late Medieval Italy.* Lund: Nordic Academic Press, 1998. Pp. 355. $60.00 cloth.

Damico, Helen, Donald Fennema, Karmen Lenz, eds. *Medieval Scholarship, Biographical Studies on the Formation of a Discipline, Volume 3: Philosophy and the Arts.* New York and London: Garland Publishing, 2000. Pp. xiv, 339. $90.00 cloth.

Doran, Susan. *England and Europe in the Sixteenth Century.* British History in Perspective Series. New York: St. Martin's Press, 1999. Pp. xvii, 145. $55.00 cloth.

Echard, Siân. *Arthurian Narrative in the Latin Tradition.* New York: Cambridge University Press, 1998. Pp. xi, 256. $69.95 cloth.

Ellis, Steve. *Geoffrey Chaucer.* Writers and Their Work. Plymouth: Northcote House, 1996. Pp. xi, 80. $19.95 paper.

Frantzen, Allen J., and John D. Niles, eds. *Anglo-Saxonism and the Construction of Social Identity.* Gainesville: University Press of Florida, 1997. Pp. 242. $49.95 cloth.

Gillespie, James L., ed. *The Age of Richard II.* New York: St. Martin's Press, 1997. Pp. vii, 256. $55.00 cloth.

Goodman, Jennifer R. *Chivalry and Exploration 1298–1630.* Woodbridge: Boydell Press, 1998. Pp. 234. $63.00 cloth.

Hanawalt, Barbara, and David Wallace, eds. *Medieval Crime and Social Control.* Medieval Cultures, vol. 16. Minneapolis: University of Minnesota Press, 1999. Pp. xvi, 259. $49.95 cloth, $19.95 paper.

Hebron, Malcom. *The Medieval Siege: Theme and Image in Middle English Romance.* New York: Oxford University Press, 1997. Pp. ix, 191. $58.00 cloth.

Hindsley, Leonard P. *The Mystics of Engelthal: Writings from a Medieval Monastery.* New York: St. Martin's Press, 1999. Pp. xxii, 234. $45.00 cloth.

Holloway, Julia Bolton. *Jerusalem: Essays on Pilgrimage and Literature.* AMS Studies in the Middle Ages, no. 24. New York: AMS Press, 1998. Pp. 277. $55.00 cloth.

Jaeger, C. Stephen. *Ennobling Love: In Search of a Lost Sensibility.* Philadelphia: University of Pennsylvania Press, 1999. Pp. xi, 311. $45.00 cloth, $19.95 paper.

Kanno, Masahiko, Hiroshi Yamashita, Masatoshi Kawasaki, Junko Asakawa, and Naoko Shirai. *Medieval Heritage: Essays in Honor of Tadahiro Ikegami.* Tokyo: Yushodo Press Co., 1998. Pp. x, 657.

Kaeuper, Richard W. *Chivalry and Violence in Medieval Europe.* New York: Oxford University Press, 1999. Pp. xi, 338. $45.00 cloth.

Kieckhefer, Richard, ed. *Forbidden Rites: A Necromancer's Manual of the Fifteenth Century.* University Park: Penn State University Press, 1997. Pp. 384. $60.00 cloth, $19.95 paper.

Leech-Wilkinson, Daniel, ed. and R. Barton Palmer, trans. *Guillaume de Machaut: Le Livre dou Voir Dit (The Book of the True Poem).* New York: Garland Publishing, 1998. Pp. 188. $135.00 cloth.

Manlove, Colin. *The Fantasy Literature of England.* Houndmills: MacMillan Press; New York: St. Martin's Press, 1999. Pp. vi, 222. $49.95 cloth.

McCarl, Mary Rhinelander, ed. *The Plowman's Tale: The c. 1532 and 1606 Editions of a Spurious Canterbury Tale.* The Renaissance Imagination Series. New York: Garland Publishing, 1997. Pp. 318. $80.00 cloth.

McEntire, Sandra J., ed. *Julian of Norwich: A Book of Essays.* Garland Medieval Casebooks, vol. 21. New York and London: Garland Publishing, 1998. Pp. xxi, 341. $70.00 cloth.

Minnis, A. J., Charlotte C. Morse, and Thorlac Turville-Petre, eds. *Essays on Ricardian Literature in Honour of J. A. Burrow.* Oxford: Clarendon Press, 1997. Pp. xv, 358. $85.00 cloth.

Montgomery, Thomas. *Medieval Spanish Epic: Mythic Roots and Ritual Language.* University Park: Penn State University Press, 1998. Pp. viii, 176. $42.50 cloth.

Mooney, Catherine M., ed. *Gendered Voices: Medieval Saints and Their Interpreters.* Philadelphia: University of Pennsylvania Press, 1999. Pp. xi, 276. $39.95 cloth, $19.95 paper.

Newman, Barbara, ed. *Voice of the Living Light: Hildegard of Bingen and Her World.* Berkeley: University of California Press, 1998. Pp. ix, 287. $48.00 cloth, $19.95 paper.

Norri, Juhani. *Names of Body Parts in English, 1400–1550.* Humaniora. Saarijarvi: The Finnish Academy of Science and Letters, 1998. Pp. 470.

Osborn, Marijane. *Romancing the Goddess: Three Middle English Romances about Women.* Urbana and Chicago: University of Illinois Press, 1998. Pp. xii, 311. $46.95 cloth, $19.95 paper.

Pahta, Päivi. *Medieval Embryology in the Vernacular: The Case of* De spermate. Mémoires de la Société Néophilologique de Helsinki, vol. 53. Helsinki: Société Néophilologique, 1998. Pp. xi, 328. $45.00 paper.

Palmer, Caroline, comp. *The Arthurian Bibliography, Vol. 3: 1978–1992: Author Listing and Subject Index.* Cambridge: D. S. Brewer, 1998. Pp. xxii, 768. $210.00 cloth.

Palmer, R. Barton, ed. *Chaucer's French Contemporaries: The Poetry/Poetics of Self and Tradition.* New York: AMS Press, 1999. Pp. xxxi, 360. $55.00 cloth.

Percival, Florence. *Chaucer's Legendary Good Women.* Cambridge: Cambridge University Press, 1998. Pp. xii, 338. $69.95 cloth.

Pinti, Daniel J., ed. *Writing after Chaucer: Essential Readings in Chaucer and the Fifteenth Century.* Basic Readings in Chaucer and His Time, vol. 1. New York and London: Garland Publishing, 1998. Pp. vi, 279. $70.00 cloth.

Prendergast, Thomas A., and Barbara Kline, eds. *Rewriting Chaucer: Culture, Authority and the Idea of the Authentic Text, 1400–1602.* Columbus: Ohio State University Press, 1999. Pp. 301. $55.00 cloth, $26.00 paper.

Pryce, Huw, ed. *Literacy in Medieval Celtic Societies.* Cambridge Studies in Medieval Literature, vol. 33. Cambridge: Cambridge University Press, 1998. Pp. xiii, 297. $59.95 cloth.

Richards, Earl Jeffrey. *Christine de Pizan and Medieval French Lyric.* Gainesville: University Press of Florida, 1998. Pp. 224. $55.00 cloth.

Roberts, Anna, ed. *Violence against Women in Medieval Texts.* Gainesville: University Press of Florida, 1998. Pp. 304. $49.95 cloth.

Russell, Stephen J. *Chaucer and the Trivium: The Mindsong of the* Canterbury Tales. Gainesville: University Press of Florida, 1998. Pp. x, 265. $49.95 cloth.

Sautman, Francesca Canade, Diana Conchade, and Giuseppe Carlo di Scipio, eds. *Telling Tales: Medieval Narratives and the Folk Tradition.* New York: St. Martin's Press, 1998. Pp. ix, 320. $49.95 cloth.

Scase, Wendy, Rita Copeland, and David Lawton, eds. *New Medieval Literatures.* New York: Oxford University Press, 1998. Pp. vi, 278. $70.00 cloth.

Shahar, Shulamith. *Growing Old in the Middle Ages: "Winter Clothes Us in Shadow and Pain."* New York: Routledge, 1997. Pp. ix, 243. $75.00 cloth.

Singman, Jeffrey L. *Robin Hood: The Shaping of the Legend.* Westport and London: Greenwood Press, 1998. Pp. 208. $55.00.

Sinnreich-Levi, Deborah M., ed. *Eustache Deschamps French Courtier Poet: His Work and His World.* New York: AMS Press, 1998. Pp. xix, 281. $55.00 cloth.

Smith, E. A. *George IV.* Yale English Monarchs. New Haven and London: Yale University Press, 1999. Pp. xiv, 306. $35.00 cloth.

Somerset, Fiona. *Clerical Discourse and Lay Audience in Late Medieval England.* Cambridge: Cambridge University Press, 1998. Pp. ix, 241. $64.95 cloth.

Stillinger, Thomas C., ed. *Critical Essays on Geoffrey Chaucer.* Critical Essays on British Literature Series. New York: G. K. Hall, 1998. Pp. ix, 272. $49.00 cloth.

Stone, Gregory B. *The Ethics of Nature in the Middle Ages: On Boccaccio's Poetaphysics.* The New Middle Ages Series. New York: St. Martin's Press, 1998. Pp. 250. $45.00 cloth.

Szarmach, Paul E., M. Theresa Tavormina, and Joel T. Rosenthal. *Medieval England: An Encyclopedia.* New York: Garland Publishing, 1998. Pp. 936. $135.00 cloth.

Talbot, C. H., ed. *The Life of Christina of Markyate: A Twelfth Century Recluse.* Toronto: University of Toronto Press, 1998. Pp. ix, 204. $14.95 paper.

Tavormina, M. Teresa, and R. F. Yeager, eds. *The Endless Knot: Essays on Old and Middle English in Honor of Marie Borroff.* Cambridge: D. S. Brewer, 1995. Pp. ix, 252. $90.00 cloth.

Tavormina, M. Theresa. *Kindly Similtude: Marriage and Family in* Piers Plowman. Piers Plowman Studies, vol. 11. Cambridge: D. S. Brewer, 1998. Pp. xix, 262. $81.00 cloth.

Thomas, Alfred. *Anne's Bohemia: Czech Literature and Society, 1310–1420.* Medieval Cultures, vol. 13. Minneapolis: University of Minnesota Press, 1998. Pp. 232. $49.95 cloth, $19.95 paper.

Thomson, John A. F. *The Western Church in the Middle Ages.* New York: Oxford University Press, 1998. Pp. 293. $60.00 cloth, $19.95 paper.

Torti, Anna, ed. *Il Testamento di Cresseida.* Milan: Luni Editrice, 1998. Pp. 97. $7.41 paper.

Usk, Thomas. *The Testament of Love.* Ed. R. Allen Shoaf. TEAMS. Kalamazoo, Mich.: Medieval Institute Publications, 1998. Pp. xiv, 455.

van Houts, Elizabeth. *Memory and Gender in Medieval Europe, 900–1200.* Toronto and Buffalo: University of Toronto Press, 1999. Pp. xii. 196. $50.00 cloth, $19.95 paper.

Wallace, David, ed. *The Cambridge History of Medieval English Literature.* Cambridge: Cambridge University Press, 1999. Pp. xxv, 1043. $100.00 cloth.

Weisl, Angela Jane. *Conquering the Reign of Femeny: Gender and Genre in Chaucer's Romance.* Chaucer Studies, vol. 22. Cambridge: D. S. Brewer, 1995. Pp. 133. $63.00 cloth.

An Annotated Chaucer Bibliography
1998

Compiled and edited by Mark Allen and Bege K. Bowers

Regular contributors:

Bruce W. Hozeski, *Ball State University* (Indiana)
George Nicholas, *Benedictine College* (Kansas)
Martha S. Waller, *Butler University* (Indiana)
Marilyn Sutton, *California State University at Dominguez Hills*
Larry L. Bronson, *Central Michigan University*
Glending Olson, *Cleveland State University* (Ohio)
Jesús Luis Serrano Reyes (*Córdoba*)
Winthrop Wetherbee, *Cornell University* (New York)
Elizabeth Dobbs, *Grinnell College* (Iowa)
Brian A. Shaw, *London, Ontario*
Masatoshi Kawasaki, *Komazawa University* (Tokyo, Japan)
William Schipper, *Memorial University* (Newfoundland, Canada)
Daniel J. Pinti, *New Mexico State University*
Erik Kooper, *Rijksuniversiteit te Utrecht*
Amy Goodwin, *Randolph-Macon College* (Virginia)
Cindy L. Vitto, *Rowan College of New Jersey*
Richard H. Osberg, *Santa Clara University* (California)
Margaret Connolly, *University College, Cork* (Ireland)
Juliette Dor, *Université de Liège* (Belgium)
Mary Flowers Braswell and Elaine Whitaker, *University of Alabama at Birmingham*
Denise Stodola, *University of Missouri–Columbia*
Cynthia Gravlee, *University of Montevallo* (Alabama)
Gregory M. Sadlek, *University of Nebraska at Omaha*
Cynthia Ho, *University of North Carolina, Asheville*
Richard J. Utz, *University of Northern Iowa*
Thomas Hahn, *University of Rochester* (New York)

Norman F. Blake, *University of Sheffield* (England)
Rebecca Beal, *University of Scranton* (Pennsylvania)
Stanley R. Hauer, *University of Southern Mississippi*
Mark Allen, *University of Texas at San Antonio*
Joerg O. Fichte, *Universität Tübingen* (Tübingen, Germany)
Andrew Lynch, *University of Western Australia*
Joyce T. Lionarons, *Ursinus College* (Pennsylvania)
John M. Crafton, *West Georgia College*
Robert Correale, *Wright State University* (Ohio)
Bege K. Bowers, *Youngstown State University* (Ohio)

Ad hoc contributions were made by the following: Paul Alessi (*University of Texas at San Antonio*); Brother Anthony (Sogang University, South Korea); Kathleen A. Bishop (*Brooklyn, N.Y.*); Shannon O. Cotrell (*University of Texas at San Antonio*); Andrew James Johnston (*Freie Universität* [Berlin]); and Juliet Sloger (*University of Rochester*).

The bibliographers acknowledge with gratitude the MLA typesimulation provided by the Center for Bibliographical Services of the Modern Language Association; postage from the University of Texas at San Antonio Division of English, Classics, and Philosophy; and assistance from the library staff, especially Susan McCray, at the University of Texas at San Antonio.

This bibliography continues the bibliographies published since 1975 in previous volumes of *Studies in the Age of Chaucer.* Bibliographic information up to 1975 can be found in Eleanor P. Hammond, *Chaucer: A Bibliographic Manual* (1908; reprint, New York: Peter Smith, 1933); D. D. Griffith, *Bibliography of Chaucer, 1908–53* (Seattle: University of Washington Press, 1955); William R. Crawford, *Bibliography of Chaucer, 1954–63* (Seattle: University of Washington Press, 1967); and Lorrayne Y. Baird, *Bibliography of Chaucer, 1964–73* (Boston: G. K. Hall, 1977). See also Lorrayne Y. Baird-Lange and Hildegard Schnuttgen, *Bibliography of Chaucer, 1974–1985* (Hamden, Conn.: Shoe String Press, 1988).

Additions and corrections to this bibliography should be sent to Mark Allen, Bibliographic Division, New Chaucer Society, Division of English, Classics, Philosophy, and Communication, University of Texas at San Antonio 78249–0643 (fax: 210-458-5366; e-mail: MALLEN@LONESTAR.JPL.UTSA.EDU). An electronic version of this bibliography (1975–97) is available via the New Chaucer Society Web page <http://ncs.rutgers.edu> or via TELNET connection

(UTSAIBM.UTSA.EDU; type "library" at the applications prompt, "cho chau" at the request for a database, and "stop" to exit the database). Authors are urged to send annotations for articles, reviews, and books that have been or might be overlooked.

Classifications

Abbreviations of Chaucer's Works

ABC	*An ABC*
Adam	*Adam Scriveyn*
Anel	*Anelida and Arcite*
Astr	*A Treatise on the Astrolabe*
Bal Compl	*A Balade of Complaint*
BD	*The Book of the Duchess*
Bo	*Boece*
Buk	*The Envoy to Bukton*
CkT, CkP, Rv–CkL	*The Cook's Tale, The Cook's Prologue, Reeve–Cook Link*
ClT, ClP, Cl–MerL	*The Clerk's Tale, The Clerk's Prologue, Clerk–Merchant Link*
Compl d'Am	*Complaynt d'Amours*
CT	*The Canterbury Tales*
CYT, CYP	*The Canon's Yeoman's Tale, The Canon's Yeoman's Prologue*
Equat	*The Equatorie of the Planetis*
For	*Fortune*
Form Age	*The Former Age*
FranT, FranP	*The Franklin's Tale, The Franklin's Prologue*
FrT, FrP, Fr–SumL	*The Friar's Tale, The Friar's Prologue, Friar–Summoner Link*
Gent	*Gentilesse*
GP	*The General Prologue*
HF	*The House of Fame*
KnT, Kn–MilL	*The Knight's Tale, Knight–Miller Link*
Lady	*A Complaint to His Lady*
LGW, LGWP	*The Legend of Good Women, The Legend of Good Women Prologue*
ManT, ManP	*The Manciple's Tale, The Manciple's Prologue*
Mars	*The Complaint of Mars*
Mel, Mel–MkL	*The Tale of Melibee, Melibee–Monk Link*
MercB	*Merciles Beaute*

MerT, MerE–SqH	*The Merchant's Tale, Merchant Endlink–Squire Headlink*
MilT, MilP, Mil–RvL	*The Miller's Tale, The Miller's Prologue, Miller–Reeve Link*
MkT, MkP, Mk–NPL	*The Monk's Tale, The Monk's Prologue, Monk–Nun's Priest Link*
MLT, MLH, MLP, MLE	*The Man of Law's Tale, Man of Law Headlink, The Man of Law's Prologue, Man of Law Endlink*
NPT, NPP, NPE	*The Nun's Priest's Tale, The Nun's Priest's Prologue, Nun's Priest's Endlink*
PardT, PardP	*The Pardoner's Tale, The Pardoner's Prologue*
ParsT, ParsP	*The Parson's Tale, The Parson's Prologue*
PF	*The Parliament of Fowls*
PhyT, Phy–PardL	*The Physician's Tale, Physician–Pardoner Link*
Pity	*The Complaint unto Pity*
Prov	*Proverbs*
PrT, PrP, Pr–ThL	*The Prioress's Tale, The Prioress's Prologue, Prioress–Thopas Link*
Purse	*The Complaint of Chaucer to His Purse*
Ret	*Chaucer's Retraction {Retractation}*
Rom	*The Romaunt of the Rose*
Ros	*To Rosemounde*
RvT, RvP	*The Reeve's Tale, The Reeve's Prologue*
Scog	*The Envoy to Scogan*
ShT, Sh–PrL	*The Shipman's Tale, Shipman–Prioress Link*
SNT, SNP, SN–CYL	*The Second Nun's Tale, The Second Nun's Prologue, Second Nun–Canon's Yeoman Link*
SqT, SqH, Sq–FranL	*The Squire's Tale, Squire Headlink, Squire–Franklin Link*
Sted	*Lak of Stedfastnesse*
SumT, SumP	*The Summoner's Tale, The Summoner's Prologue*
TC	*Troilus and Criseyde*

Th, Th–MelL	*The Tale of Sir Thopas, Sir Thopas–Melibee Link*
Truth	*Truth*
Ven	*The Complaint of Venus*
WBT, WBP, WB–FrL	*The Wife of Bath's Tale, The Wife of Bath's Prologue, Wife of Bath–Friar Link*
Wom Nob	*Womanly Noblesse*
Wom Unc	*Against Women Unconstant*

Periodical Abbreviations

Æstel	*Æstel* (Seattle, Wash.)
Anglia	*Anglia: Zeitschrift für Englische Philologie*
Anglistik	*Anglistik: Mitteilungen des Verbandes deutscher Anglisten*
ANQ	*ANQ: A Quarterly Journal of Short Articles, Notes, and Reviews*
Archiv	*Archiv für das Studium der Neueren Sprachen und Literaturen*
BAM	*Bulletin des Anglicistes Médiévistes*
BWVACET	*Bulletin of the West Virginia Association of College English Teachers*
CarmP	*Carmina Philosophiae: Journal of the International Boethius Society*
Chaucer Yearbook	*Chaucer Yearbook: A Journal of Late Medieval Studies*
ChauR	*Chaucer Review*
CHum	*Computers and the Humanities*
CL	*Comparative Literature* (Eugene, Ore.)
CLAJ	*College Language Association Journal*
CLAQ	*Children's Literature Association Quarterly*
CLS	*Comparative Literature Studies*
Cynge	*Le Cynge: Bulletin of the International Marie de France Society: Abstracts, Notes, and Queries*
DAI	*Dissertation Abstracts International*
Disputatio	*Disputatio: An International Transdisciplinary Journal of the Late Middle Ages*
ÉA	*Études Anglaises: Grand-Bretagne, États-Unis*
EHR	*English Historical Review*
ELH	*ELH*
ELN	*English Language Notes*
EMS	*English Manuscript Studies, 1100–1700*
Envoi	*Envoi: A Review Journal of Medieval Literature*
ES	*English Studies*
ESC	*English Studies in Canada*

Exemplaria	*Exemplaria: A Journal of Theory in Medieval and Renaissance Studies*
Expl	*Explicator*
FCS	*Fifteenth-Century Studies*
Florilegium	*Florilegium: Carleton University Papers on Late Antiquity and the Middle Ages*
FMLS	*Forum for Modern Language Studies*
Genre	*Genre: Forms of Discourse and Culture*
ING	*In Geardagum: Essays on Old and Middle English Language and Literature*
JEAL	*Journal of East Asian Linguistics*
JEGP	*Journal of English and Germanic Philology*
JEngL	*Journal of English Linguistics*
JFR	*Journal of Folklore Research* (Bloomington, Ind.)
JMEMS	*Journal of Medieval and Early Modern Studies*
L&LC	*Literary and Linguistic Computing: Journal of the Association for Literary and Linguistic Computing*
LeedsSE	*Leeds Studies in English*
Library	*The Library: The Transactions of the Bibliographical Society*
MÆ	*Medium Ævum*
Mediaevalia	*Mediaevalia: An Interdisciplinary Journal of Medieval Studies Worldwide*
Mediaevistik	*Mediaevistik: Internationale Zeitschrift für Interdisziplinäire Mittelalterforschung*
MedPers	*Medieval Perspectives*
MES	*Medieval English Studies*
MFN	*Medieval Feminist Newsletter*
MLR	*The Modern Language Review*
MP	*Modern Philology: A Journal Devoted to Research in Medieval and Modern Literature*
N&Q	*Notes and Queries*
Neophil	*Neophilologus* (Dordrecht, Netherlands)
NLH	*New Literary History: A Journal of Theory and Interpretation*
NM	*Neuphilologische Mitteilungen: Bulletin of the Modern Language Society*
NMS	*Nottingham Medieval Studies*
NOWELE	*NOWELE: North-Western European Language Evolution*
OT	*Oral Tradition*
PBA	*Proceedings of the British Academy*

PBSA	*Papers of the Bibliographical Society of America*
PMLA	*Publications of the Modern Language Association of America*
ProverbiumY	*Proverbium: Yearbook of International Proverb Scholarship* (Burlington, Vt.)
R&L	*Religion and Literature* (Notre Dame, Ind.)
Renascence	*Renascence: Essays on Value in Literature*
RenQ	*Renaissance Quarterly*
RES	*Review of English Studies*
RLAn	*RLA: Romance Languages Annual*
RMR	*Rocky Mountain Review of Language and Literature*
SAC	*Studies in the Age of Chaucer*
SAP	*Studia Anglica Posnaniensia: An International Review of English*
SELIM	*SELIM: Journal of the Spanish Society for Medieval English Language and Literature*
SIcon	*Studies in Iconography*
SiM	*Studies in Medievalism*
SMART	*Studies in Medieval and Renaissance Teaching*
SN	*Studia Neophilologica: A Journal of Germanic and Romance Languages and Literatures*
Soundings	*Soundings: An Interdisciplinary Journal*
SP	*Studies in Philology*
Speculum	*Speculum: A Journal of Medieval Studies*
SSEng	*Sydney Studies in English*
Style	*Style* (DeKalb, Ill.)
Text	*Text: Transactions of the Society for Textual Scholarship*
TLS	*Times Literary Supplement* (London, England)
TMR	*The Medieval Review* <http://www.hti.umich.edu/b/bmr/tmr.html>
YES	*Yearbook of English Studies*
YWES	*Year's Work in English Studies*
YLS	*The Yearbook of Langland Studies*

Bibliographical Citations and Annotations

Bibliographies, Reports, and Reference

1. Allen, Mark, and Bege K. Bowers. "An Annotated Chaucer Bibliography, 1996." *SAC* 20 (1998): 355–438. Continuation of *SAC* annual annotated bibliography (since 1975); based on 1996 *MLA Bibliography* listings, contributions from an international bibliographic team, and independent research. A total of 350 items, including reviews.

2. Allen, Valerie, and Margaret Connolly. "Middle English: Chaucer." *YWES* 76 (1995): 159–207. A discursive bibliography of Chaucer studies for 1995, divided into four subcategories: general, *CT, TC,* and other works.

3. ———. "Middle English: Chaucer." *YWES* 77 (1996): 210–49. A discursive bibliography of Chaucer studies for 1996, divided into four subcategories: general, *CT, TC,* and other works.

4. Oizumi, Akio. "A New Rhyme Concordance to Chaucer's Poetical Works." In Jacek Fisiak and Akio Oizumi, eds. *English Historical Linguistics and Philology in Japan* (*SAC* 22 [2000], no. 115), pp. 287–95. Describes the technology and principles of concordancing that underlie *The Rhyme Concordance of the Poetical Works of Geoffrey Chaucer* (SAC 19 [1997], no. 6).

Recordings and Films

5. Gallagher, Joe, dir. *Chaucer Reads Chaucer: The* Miller's Tale. Films for the Humanities, no. 1742. Princeton, N.J.: Films for the Humanities and Sciences, 1993. VHS videocassette; 58 min. Originally produced by Caritas Productions, 1988. *MilT* read in Middle English by Joe Gallagher (with modern subtitles) before an audience in medieval costume. Audience reactions emphasize meaning and humor.

6. Gedalof, Alan, and Michael Moore. The Wife of Bath *by Geoffrey Chaucer.* A Guide to Understanding Literature. Films for the Humanities, no. 6691. Princeton, N.J.: Films for the Humanities and Sciences, 1996. VHS videocassette; 28 min. Originally produced by TVOntario, 1993. Gedalof and Moore discuss the Wife of Bath and *WBPT* in their social and literary contexts, especially as they reflect issues of male-

female relations. Illustrations from historical manuscripts and paintings and from contemporary visual interpretation. Includes selections from *WBPT,* read in Middle English with modern subtitles.

7. Moulton, Carroll, writer; Stephen Mantell, prod. *Geoffrey Chaucer and Middle English Literature.* Princeton, N.J.: Films for the Humanities, 1985; 1988; 1993. Videocassette; 28 min. Introduces the themes and genres of major works of Middle English, with special emphasis on Chaucer and *CT.* Narrated by Protase Woodford.

8. Myerson, Jonathan, exec. dir. *The Canterbury Tales: "Arriving at Canterbury"—Three More Tales.* Cardiff: S4C, with HBO and BBC Wales, 1998. Videocassette; 60 min. Animated adaptation/retelling of *MerT, PardT,* and *FranT,* with interspersed selections from *GP,* each dramatized in a different style of animation. The *Tales* are shortened, reduced to simplified plots. Two versions are included, one in modern English and one in Middle English.

9. ———, exec. dir. *The Canterbury Tales: "Leaving London"—The First Three Tales.* Cardiff: S4C, with HBO and BBC Wales, 1998. Videocassette; 60 min. Animated adaptation/retelling of *NPT, KnT,* and *WBT,* with interspersed selections from *GP,* each dramatized in a different style of animation. The *Tales* are shortened, reduced to simplified plots. Two versions are included, one in modern English and one in Middle English.

10. Richmond, Velma, writer. *Prologue to Chaucer.* Princeton, N.J.: Films for the Humanities, 1988. Videocassette; 29 min. Parallels various features of *CT* with late-medieval English social history.

11. Rush, Pauline. *Geoffrey Chaucer: The* Canterbury Tales. Films for the Humanities, no. 8657. Princeton, N.J.: Films for the Humanities and Sciences, 1998. VHS videocassette; 33 min. Produced by Cromwell Productions. Introduction to the social and cultural milieu of *CT,* with narration by Roy Cane and discussion by Christiana Whitehead and Peter Mack. Includes selected readings in Middle English (by Vanessa Adye) and historical illustrations.

12. Thwaite, Anthony, writer; Richard Mervyn, prod. and dir. *Chaucer, 1340–1400.* [Princeton, N.J.]: Films for the Humanities, [1988]. Videocassette; 28 min. An introduction to Chaucer, with a reading of *GP* in Middle English (with modern subtitles) and a dramatization of *PardT* in the modern translation of Nevill Coghill. Narrators include John Gielgud, Gary Watson, Brian Coburn, Nicholas Gecks, Gerrard McArthur, and Ian Richardson.

13. Venning, Christopher, prod. *The Canterbury Tales.* Penguin Audiobooks, PEN 138. London: Penguin, 1996. 6 audiocassettes; 72 pp. Readings of selections from *CT,* translated by Nevill Coghill, including *GP, KnT, MilPT, RvPT, PrPT, PardPT, WBPT, FrPT, SumPT, MerPT,* and *Ret.* Read by Richard Breers, Alan Cumming, James Grout, Alex Jennings, Geoffrey Matthews, Richard Pasco, Tim Pigott-Smith, Andrew Sachs, Prunella Scales, and Timothy West. Accompanying booklet reprints selections from Brian Stone's *Chaucer* (*SAC* 13 [1991], no. 84).

14. Wakefield, Emma, dir. *Chaucer: The* General Prologue *to the* Canterbury Tales. Films for the Humanities, no. 4081. Princeton, N.J.: Films for the Humanities and Sciences, 1993. VHS videocassette; 20 min. Originally produced by Thames Television, titled *Middle English, Knowledge about Language: Chaucer,* 1991. Combines dramatized readings of sections of *GP* (in Middle English with modern subtitles) with discussion of these selections by schoolchildren of Bannockburn School, London. Then dramatizes *PardT* in modern English, acted by the schoolchildren in an outdoor setting.

Chaucer's Life

15. Hobday, Charles. *A Golden Ring: English Poets in Florence from 1373 to the Present Day.* London: Peter Owen, 1997. 360 pp. Chapter 1 (pp. 15–31) describes Chaucer's 1373 visit to Florence, a great industrial and financial center declining into political factionalism. Italian meters influenced Chaucer's rhyme royal. Boccaccio taught him the potential of romance; Dante provided a model of mixed high and low style.

16. Kelly, Henry Ansgar. "Meanings and Uses of *Raptus* in Chaucer's Time." *SAC* 20 (1998): 101–65. Examines civil and criminal documentary evidence of the meanings of the term "rape," reconsidering their applicability to Cecily Champain's 1380 claim against Chaucer. The "inherent ambiguity" of the term and its "very wide range" of legal and literary uses encourage caution in trying to understand what the term means in Chaucer's life-records and his fiction. The term may have meant sexual violation in Chaucer's case, but there is more evidence that it meant abduction. An appendix includes twelve documents from the Public Record Office.

17. Kennedy, Ruth. "Re-creating Chaucer." In Warwick Gould and

Thomas F. Staley, eds. *Writing the Lives of Writers.* Houndsmill, Basingstoke, and London: Macmillan; New York: St. Martin's Press; in association with the Centre for English Studies, School of Advanced Study, University of London, 1998, pp. 54–67. Like other biographies, those of Chaucer have been constructed in light of the biographers' assumptions and images. Surveys biographies and biographical comments on Chaucer and suggests that modern commentary neglects the transcendent in his works.

18. Quinn, William A. "The Rapes of Chaucer." *Chaucer Yearbook* 5 (1998):1–18. Briefly discusses some of the critical responses to Chaucer's alleged raptus of Cecilia Champaigne and how this incident may have influenced certain works, particularly *TC, PF,* and *HF.* Also suggests that the penitential tone of *Mel, SNT,* and *Astr* possibly "reflects concerns regarding the Cecilia Champaigne episode."

19. Serrano Reyes, Jesús L. "John of Gaunt's Intervention in Spain: Possible Repercussions for Chaucer's Life and Poetry." *SELIM* 6 (1996): 117–45. Surveys scholarship pertaining to Chaucer's 1366 visit to Spain and Gaunt's 1386–87 campaign in Spain, commenting on historical events and Chaucer's involvement with them. Chaucer's diplomatic mission was a success. He reflects his familiarity with political and topographical features of Spain in *HF, Mel,* and *MkT.* Philippa Chaucer may have died in Spain.

See also nos. 52, 102, 167, 193, 246, 262, 287.

Facsimiles, Editions, and Translations

20. Andrew, Malcolm, and A. C. Cawley, eds. *Geoffrey Chaucer: Comic and Bawdy Tales.* London: J. M. Dent, 1997. xxii, 100 pp. Revised edition of Cawley's Everyman text of *GP, MilT, RvT, CkT, ShT,* and *NPT,* with a brief descriptive introduction, glosses, and comments on pronunciation, grammar, and versification.

21. Baker, Peter S. "The Reader, the Editor, and the Electronic Critical Edition." In Vincent P. McCarren and Douglas Moffat, eds. *A Guide to Editing Middle English* (*SAC* 22 [2000], no. 30), pp. 263–83. Suggests that "hypertextuality" is the only major advantage of electronic texts over books and indicates an ideal system for a critical edition in electronic format by examining a "working model" of such editions of *Beo-*

wulf and *Battle of Brunanburh.* Illustrates the differences between electronic and print editions through an example from *TC* (2.85–86).

22. Blake, Norman F. "Editing the *Canterbury Tales:* Preliminary Observations." *Anglia* 116 (1998): 198–214. Referring to *The Wife of Bath's Prologue on CD-ROM* (*SAC* 20 [1998], no. 11), Blake concludes that Hengwrt should be used as the base text for the *Canterbury Tales* Project. He proposes three areas in which Hengwrt might be emended against other witnesses: the addition to Hengwrt of substantial passages found in some other manuscripts; emendation of minor omissions and deletions from Hengwrt; and correction of the spelling of Hengwrt.

23. Cooper, Helen. "Averting Chaucer's Prophecies: Miswriting, Mismetering, and Misunderstanding." In Vincent P. McCarren and Douglas Moffat, eds. *A Guide to Editing Middle English* (*SAC* 22 [2000], no. 30), pp. 79–93. Describes the problems of editing Chaucer's works (especially *CT*), observing that modern editions tend to ignore them. Comments on editing practices from Urry onward, focusing on how treatments of meter, punctuation, and glossing in recent editions tend to simplify the text of Chaucer.

24. Dane, Joseph A. "The Chaucerian Reception of Henry Bradshaw." *Archiv* 235 (1998): 48–64. Suggests that Bradshaw looked at *CT* as an early book in terms of quire structure, which he tried to reconstruct, rather than a topologically real pilgrimage. Outlines the editorial history of *CT,* which after Bradshaw reflected the twentieth-century aesthetics of New Criticism. The recent return to a process of fragmentation is documented by both the *Variorum Chaucer* and the CD-ROM edition.

25. Forni, Kathleen. "The Value of Early Chaucer Editions." *SN* 70 (1998): 173–80. The black-letter editions of Chaucer from 1532 to 1721 are "valuable books with worthless texts." However, their financial value may give some indication of their readers and their readers' socioeconomic status. Argues that their selling price was not so high that it put them out of the reach of a wider readership; these editions were read by more than just the very rich.

26. Goldbeck, Janne. "The Absent Father: Translating Chaucer's *Canterbury Tales.*" *Rendezvous* 32.1 (1997): 87–93. Translations of Chaucer's works, especially *CT,* into modern English reflect individual translators' valuations of Chaucer's poetic virtues, whether "freshness," modernity, humor, irony, or something else. Suggests that when read in translation, Chaucer should be read in multiple versions.

27. Graver, Bruce E., ed. *Translations of Chaucer and Virgil by William Wordsworth.* The Cornell Wordsworth. Ithaca, N.Y., and London: Cornell University Press, 1998. xxviii, 583 pp. Scholarly edition of Wordsworth's modernization of selections from Chaucer (*PrT, ManT* and part of *ManP,* a portion of *TC,* and the apocryphal *Cuckoo and the Nightingale*) and portions of Virgil's *Aeneid* and *Georgics,* including full apparatus and manuscript facsimiles. In his "Introduction" to the Chaucer section (pp. 3–29), Graver surveys modernizations of Chaucer from Dryden to Wordsworth—commenting on Wordsworth's efforts to maintain Chaucerian flavor by archaism—and clarifies the chronology of Wordsworth's translation and its publishing history. Wordsworth's distaste for Dryden's translation resulted from the availability of Tyrwhitt's edition.

28. Kinney, Clare R. "Thomas Speght's Renaissance Chaucer and the *Solaas* of *Sentence* in *Troilus and Criseyde.*" In Theresa M. Krier, ed. *Refiguring Chaucer in the Renaissance* (*SAC* 22 [2000], no. 73), pp. 66–84. Examines the identification of proverbs and sententiae in Speght's 1602 edition of Chaucer's works, focusing on *TC.* The introduction of maniples (pointing hands) enabled Speght to, in effect, preselect nuggets of Chaucerian wisdom for a Renaissance commonplace book, despite the irony of indicating proverbs in a work preoccupied with the instability of human utterance.

29. Kuskin, William. "William Caxton and the English Canon: Print Production and Ideological Transformation in the Late Fifteenth Century." *DAI* 59 (1998): 164A. Explores how Caxton's technical and mechanical modifications of *CT, Bo,* Malory's *Morte Darthur,* and the *Boke of Eneydos* claim authority for these texts and help to shape their audience.

30. McCarren, Vincent P., and Douglas Moffat, eds. *A Guide to Editing Middle English.* Ann Arbor: University of Michigan Press, 1998. x, 338 pp. Nineteen essays by various authors that together seek to "raise the standard of scholarly editing for Middle English texts," describing theories and problems of editing and offering practical recommendations on how to edit. The contributors explore the notion of an authorial text, the functions of parallel-text editions, and perspectives on meter and pedagogy as they relate to editing. They suggest ways to deal with the difficulties of particular kinds of texts: scientific, astrological, culinary, and glossographical. They discuss the tools of editing, including computer technology, and explain what is desirable in a glossary, notes, and a text itself. The collection includes a "Practical Guide" to working

with manuscripts and lists available facsimiles and useful dictionaries. Frequent references to Chaucer's works throughout. For essays that focus in part or wholly on Chaucer's works, see nos. 21, 23, 34, and 40.

31. McGillivray, Murray, ed. *Geoffrey Chaucer's* Book of the Duchess: *A Hypertext Edition.* Alberta: University of Calgary Press, 1997. CD-ROM. An electronic edition of *BD* that includes a reading text (with glossary, notes, and audio recording), a critical edition (with textual notes), facsimiles and transcriptions of the four witnesses to the text of the poem (three manuscripts and Thynne's edition of 1532), and texts and translations of all its major sources (works by Machaut, Froissart, Ovid, and Statius, plus the *Roman de la Rose*—some excerpted). The CD also provides SGML versions of the transcriptions, the critical edition, and the source texts, and it enables simultaneous access to up to six of the texts included. Requires access to the Internet.

32. Mowat, Barbara A. "Constructing the Author." In R. B. Parker and S. P. Zitner, eds. *Elizabethan Theater: Essays in Honor of S. Schoenbaum.* Newark: University of Delaware Press; London: Associated University Presses, 1996, pp. 93–110. Assesses how the sixteenth-century editions of Chaucer by Thynne and Speght helped to create and monumentalize a view of the writer. Renaissance notions of authors, evident in Speght's Chaucer, Holland's Livy, and Harrington's Ariosto, are not the same as those theorized by Foucault and Barthes, but they mark a stage in the development of such a view of authorship.

33. Raffel, Burton. "Gawain, Chaucer and Translatability." *Disputatio* 3 (1998): 1–15. Discusses various levels of difficulty in translating *CT* and *Sir Gawain and the Green Knight* into Modern English.

34. Robinson, Peter M. W. "The Computer and the Making of Editions." In Vincent P. McCarren and Douglas Moffat, eds. *A Guide to Editing Middle English* (*SAC* 22 [2000], no. 30), pp. 249–61. Argues that computer technology is changing "what scholars do as they edit," drawing examples from the activities of the *Canterbury Tales* Project to describe the new questions raised about visual reproduction of manuscripts, representation of transcription, and choices of collation software and delivery systems.

35. Robinson, Peter, and Kevin Taylor. "Publishing an Electronic Textual Edition: The Case of *The Wife of Bath's Prologue on CD-ROM.*" *CHum* 32 (1998): 271–84. Describes the process of bringing to publication *WBP* in CD-ROM format (*SAC* 20 [1998], no. 11), focusing on technical and textual difficulties, provisional solutions, and the success

of the venture. Comments on the future of highly sophisticated electronic editions and suggests that electronic publication of this sort is still in its infancy.

36. Wolf, Helmut, ed. *Sir Francis Kynastons Übersetzung von Chaucers* Troilus and Criseyde*: Interpretation, Edition und Kommentar.* Bibliotheca Humanistica. Frankfurt: Peter Lang, 1997. 493 pp. Edits Kynaston's 1639 Latin translation of Chaucer's *TC.* The introduction surveys research on Kynaston; discusses his life and literary œuvre; describes the printed text of 1635 and the manuscript of 1639; discusses Kynaston's commentary on Chaucer's *TC* (divided into six topics: astronomy/astrology, medicine, nature, technology, human behavior, and *varia*); and analyzes the language, metrics, and concept of translation (pp. 16–121). The edition (pp. 122–334) and commentary (pp. 335–462) follow. Also includes a bibliography and three appendices, which contain Kynaston's dedicatory poems, excerpts from two of his other poems, and various plates.

37. Woodward, Daniel, and Martin Stevens, eds. *Geoffrey Chaucer: The* Canterbury Tales*: The New Ellesmere Chaucer Monochromatic Facsimile (of Huntington Library MS EL 26 C 9).* San Marino, Calif.: Huntington Library; Tokyo: Yushodo, 1997. n.p. A full-size monochromatic facsimile of the Ellesmere manuscript of *CT,* from the same transparencies used to produce the full-color version (*SAC* 19 [1997], no. 30).

See also nos. 40, 79, 85, 202, 223, 293, 305, 333.

Manuscripts and Textual Studies

38. Blake, N. F. "Geoffrey Chaucer and the Manuscripts of *The Canterbury Tales.*" *Journal of the Early Book Society* 1 (1997): 96–122. Describes uncertainties related to the manuscripts of *CT* and surveys critical efforts to resolve them—uncertainties about the state of Chaucer's papers at the time of his death and the circulation of *Tales* before his death, the order and authenticity of the *Tales,* and the dates and chronological sequence of the manuscripts. Argues that Hengwrt and perhaps other manuscripts should be dated before Chaucer's death in 1400, suggesting that the author may have overseen revision of his works.

39. Connolly, Margaret. *John Shirley: Book Production and the Noble Household in Fifteenth-Century England.* Aldershot, Hants; Brookfield, Vt.: Ashgate, 1998. xii, 247 pp.; 17 b&w fig. A biography of John Shir-

ley (d. 1456) that examines available life-records and assesses his scribal output and influence. Shirley was a scribe of several important manuscripts that include works by Chaucer, Lydgate, and Gower; a collector and translator; and a servant of Richard Beauchamp, earl of Warwick. His life offers a window to the relations between literary activity and social-political activity in the first half of the fifteenth century, and his access to many literary exemplars seems to have resulted from affiliation with the Beauchamp family. This study includes codicological analysis of Shirlean manuscripts and assesses his habits as a translator, scribe, and annotator, arguing that his audience was aristocratic. Appendices include a description of Shirley's language and transcription of his verse prefaces.

40. Greetham, David. "'Glosynge Is a Glorious Thyng, Certayn.'" In Vincent P. McCarren and Douglas Moffat, eds. *A Guide to Editing Middle English* (*SAC* 22 [2000], no. 30), pp. 287–302. Comments on theories that underlie the practice of editing Middle English texts, using Chaucer's Summoner as an extended analogue for such a commentary.

41. Harris, Kate. "Unnoticed Extracts from Chaucer and Hoccleve: Huntington MS HM 144, Trinity College, Oxford MS D 29 and *The Canterbury Tales*." *SAC* 20 (1998): 167–99. The compiler-editor-scribe of the prose history in Trinity College, Oxford MS D 29 used *ParsT* and *Mel* as a source in six passages. The same scribe included *Mel* and *MkT* in Huntington MS HM 144. Harris describes the scribal adjustments of Chaucer's texts in these two late-fifteenth-century manuscripts, identifying them as efforts at explanation or clarification. They are based on different copy texts.

42. Horobin, S. C. P. "The 'Hooked G' Scribe and His Work on Three Manuscripts of the *Canterbury Tales*." *NM* 99 (1998): 411–17. The similar scribal features of three manuscripts of *CT* (Devonshire; Trinity College, Cambridge R.3.3; and Bodleian Rawlinson Poetry 223) have sometimes been attributed to a group of scribes and supervisors. This attribution has been used to support the "bookshop theory" (concerning centralized and commercial production of literary manuscripts). The coherent linguistic forms of these three manuscripts (and of associated manuscripts of Gower and Lydgate), however, point to their being the work of a single scribe, likely an émigré to London from Kent.

43. ———. "A New Approach to Chaucer's Spelling." *ES* 79 (1998): 415–24. Chaucer's spelling habits are still uncertain. Reasons for disagreement among scholars lie in approaches to the problem. Anal-

ysis of the spelling *ayein/ayeyn* in Hengwrt and Ellesmere and related manuscripts suggests that studies based on the spelling system of a single text across its entire manuscript tradition will allow for the construction of complete linguistic profiles of single scribes.

44. Machan, Tim William. "The Consolation Tradition and the Text of Chaucer's *Boece*." *PBSA* 91 (1997): 31–50. Examines the textual tradition of *Bo* in light of the twelfth- to fifteenth-century textual tradition of Boethius's *Consolation of Philosophy,* suggesting that the best text of *Bo* is Cambridge University Library ii.iii.21.

45. Olson, Mary Catherine. "Words into Images: Textualizing the Visual and Visualizing the Textual in Medieval Illustrated Manuscripts." *DAI* 58 (1998): 4645A. Seeks to explain how and in what ways illustrations affect reading, discussing the manuscripts of the Harley Psalter, the Old English Illustrated Hexateuch, the Marvels of the East, and the Ellesmere manuscript of *CT.* Ellesmere raises questions about orality and literacy.

46. Partridge, Stephen. "Questions of Evidence: Manuscripts and the Early History of Chaucer's Works." In Daniel Pinti, ed. *Writings after Chaucer: Essential Reading in Chaucer and the Fifteenth Century* (*SAC* 22 [2000], no. 77), pp. 2–26. Focusing on manuscripts of Chaucer's works, Partridge assesses the habits of scribes and book owners in the fifteenth century, showing how variants among texts alter meaning and how fifteenth-century readers, aware of such variants, made "corrections" to the texts for various reasons. However, some of the changes reflect Chaucer's own revisions. Includes a bibliography of further reading.

47. Scott, Kathleen L. *Later Gothic Manuscripts, 1390–1490.* 2 vols. Volume 1: *Texts and Illustrations.* Volume 2: *Catalogue and Indexes.* A Survey of Manuscripts Illuminated in the British Isles, no. 6. London: Harvey Miller, 1996. 1: 296 pp; 17 color plates; 36 b&w figs.; 505 b&w illus. 2: 434 pp. Descriptions of 140 late-medieval manuscripts, selected for their representative value and focusing on their styles and programs of illustration. The introduction (1:23–78) assesses the production, use, texts, style, format, coloration, and iconography of late-medieval British illustration, as well as its relations with Continental traditions. Entries in the catalogue include brief codicological descriptions of individual manuscripts and extensive descriptions of their drawing, illustration, historiation, and other decoration; provenance, bibliography, and exhibition history are also given. Also includes a glossary and several tables and indexes of pictorial cycles, subject matter, and topics. Manuscripts

related to Chaucer include Huntington Library MS EL 26 C 9 (the Ellesmere manuscript); Cambridge, University Library MS Gg 4.27(1); and British Library MS Harley 4866.

48. Solopova, Elizabeth. "Editing All the Manuscripts of All *The Canterbury Tales* into Electronic Form: Is the Effort Worthwhile?" In W. Speed Hill, ed. *New Ways of Looking at Old Texts, II: Papers of the Renaissance English Text Society, 1992–1996.* Medieval & Renaissance Texts & Studies, no. 188. Tempe, Ariz.: Medieval & Renaissance Texts & Studies, with the Renaissance English Text Society, 1998, pp. 121–32. A description of questions raised in the process of producing the first installment of the computer-assisted *Canterbury Tales* Project (*SAC* 20 [1998], no. 11), and a justification of the project. The first installment made possible Solopova's analyses of meter and punctuation in *WBP* and clarified something of Chaucer's process of revision, in particular his excision of the so-called added passages from *WBP.*

49. Spevack, Marvin. "James Orchard Halliwell and Friends: X. Frederick James Furnivall. XI. William Aldis Wright and William George Clark." *Library,* 6th ser., 20 (1998): 126–44. Reviews Furnivall-Halliwell correspondence, which is concerned mainly with the affairs of the New Shakespeare Society, but also includes accounts of Furnivall's work on Chaucer manuscripts.

See also nos. 22, 23, 30, 34, 62, 178, 180, 223, 305, 312, 334, 335.

Sources, Analogues, and Literary Relations

50. Besserman, Lawrence. *Chaucer's Biblical Poetics.* Norman: University of Oklahoma Press, 1998. xiii, 338 pp. Argues that the Bible is a far more pervasive influence on Chaucer than has been previously recognized. Chaucer uses the Bible or the glosses in most of his writings, responding—through quotation, paraphrase, or allusion—to traditional notions of biblical authority and contemporary concerns about this authority. Because Chaucer was torn between the church's traditional stance that the Bible should not be available to the laity and his feeling that the laity should have direct access to the Bible, it was easy for critics of the sixteenth and seventeenth centuries to claim him as their ancestor.

51. Boitani, Piero. "Chaucer e Boccaccio da Certaldo a Canterbury: Un panorama." *Studi sul Boccaccio* 25 (1997): 311–29. Demonstrates the

influence of Dante, Petrarch, and Boccaccio on Chaucer and, in turn, on English literary tradition, employing an extended metaphor that equates Italian tradition with the town of Certaldo and English tradition with Canterbury.

52. Calin, William. "Deschamps's 'Ballade to Chaucer' Again, or, The Dangers of Intertextual Medieval Comparatism." In Deborah M. Sinnreich-Levi, ed. *Eustache Deschamps, French Courtier-Poet: His Work and His World* (*SAC* 22 [2000], no. 151), pp. 73–83. Contrary to earlier critical opinion, the "Ballade to Chaucer" demonstrates very little about Chaucer's renown outside court circles in southern England; it cannot necessarily be read as a sincere expression of Deschamps's opinion of Chaucer the poet.

53. Davenport, W. A. *Chaucer and His English Contemporaries: Prologue and Tale in* The Canterbury Tales. New York: St. Martin's Press, 1998. x, 257 pp. Chaucer was influenced by his English contemporaries, particularly John Gower, William Langland, Thomas Chester, and the *Gawain* poet; yet he chose to seek new literary directions. Chaucer was on a pilgrimage of self-discovery and a quest for literary adventure. Departing from conventional methods of composing prologues and tales, he investigated possibilities for shaping multivalent narratives from traditional genres, while exploring the role of the author in relation to text and audience. The retrospective *Ret,* appended to *CT* at the culmination of his career, may be a rejection of fictions and/or a transition from the earthly to the spiritual journey. Davenport briefly addresses Chaucer's major works but focuses on *CT,* with special attention to *WBT, MLPT,* and *Ret.*

54. Hanna, Ralph, III, and Traugott Lawler, eds., using materials collected by Karl Young and Robert A. Pratt. *Jankyn's Book of Wikked Wyves. Vol. 1: The Primary Texts. Walter Map's "Dissuasio," Theophrastus' "De Nuptiis," Jerome's* Adversus Jovinianum. The Chaucer Library. Athens and London: University of Georgia Press, 1997. xiii, 282 pp. Critical edition of the three Latin antifeminist works that influenced Chaucer most significantly, especially his *WBP, MerT,* and *FranT.* Includes a complete version of Map's "Dissuasio Valerii ad Rufinum" and the portions of Jerome's *Adversus Jovinianum* that Chaucer used, including Theophrastus's "Golden Book of Marriage," here attributed to Jerome. No extant manuscript reflects Chaucer's actual source, but the material edited here is central to the tradition from which he drew. In their introduction, the editors trace the development of this tradition and discuss

the edited texts, medieval commentaries on these texts, and related materials; they discuss Chaucer's relations with this tradition. Collations of variants, textual notes, and explanatory notes accompany the texts. The volume includes a checklist of manuscripts known to contain portions of the edited texts, a subject index, and an index indicating where Chaucer used these texts.

55. Mooney, Linne R., ed. and trans. *The Kalendarium of John Somer.* The Chaucer Library. Athens: University of Georgia Press, 1998. xii, 224 pp. Referred to by Chaucer in *Astr,* Somer's *Kalendarium* may have been a source for a number of the poet's astrological references. This facing-page edition and English translation of the Latin *Kalendarium* includes descriptions of the manuscripts; discussion of Somer's works, biography, and influence; and appendices of Middle English versions of the "Canon" (part of the *Kalendarium*), Somer's star catalog, and descriptions of other scientific works attributed to Somer. Elaborate layout emulates some of the complexities of text and graphics in the original.

56. Sinnreich-Levi, Deborah M. "The Feminist Voice of the Misogynist Poet: Deschamps's Poems in Women's Voices." In Deborah M. Sinnreich-Levi, ed. *Eustache Deschamps, French Courtier-Poet: His Work and His World* (*SAC* 22 [2000], no. 151), pp. 123–30. The misogynist female voices in a number of Deschamps's poems seem to share common sources with *WBPT* and *MerT.*

57. Taylor, Paul Beekman. *Chaucer Translator.* Lanham, Md., New York, and Oxford: University Press of America, 1998. [x], 209 pp. Twelve essays that pertain to Chaucer's "translative" use of source material, exploring less the influence of others on him than the "*affluence* his imagination sets flowing in the process of reshaping material." Recurrent issues include the ways new contexts alter the meanings of utterances and narratives, "translative" relations between the worldly and the spiritual, the hierarchy of language, nominalism and realism, linguistic play, and Chaucer's uses of Scripture, Jean de Meun, Petrarch, Boccaccio, Machaut, Guillaume de Deguileville, and others. Nine of the essays are revisions of previously published discussions. For newly printed essays, see nos. 59, 204, and 268.

58. ———. *Sharing Story: Medieval Norse-English Literary Relationships.* AMS Studies in the Middle Ages, no. 25. New York: AMS Press, 1998. 281 pp. Seventeen essays by Taylor on the conjoining of Christian with native pagan thought in Norse and English medieval literary contexts. Chapter 16, "Norse Story in *The Canterbury Tales*" (pp. 233–44),

discusses two folk-tale versions of Nordic mythological materials that appear in Chaucer. Part 1 of the chapter, "The Pardoner's Old Man and the One-eyed God," demonstrates the Old Man's similarities to the Odin tradition, while part 2, "The Wife of Bath and the Snowshoe Goddess," discusses Alisoun's indebtedness to the motifs of the Icelandic Skadi.

59. ———. "Translating Two Guillaumes." In Paul Beekman Taylor. *Chaucer Translator* (*SAC* 22 [2000], no. 57), pp. 155–69. Compares Antigone's song in *TC* to Machaut's *Paradis; ABC,* to Guillaume de Deguileville's *Le pèlerinage de la vie humaine.* Explores the ironies of Antigone's song, especially those extending from the possibility that the "goodlieste mayde" (2.880) who made the song may be Cassandra. Chaucer's additions to *ABC* appear later in *SNP, PrP,* and elsewhere, exemplifying how translation was for Chaucer a spur to creative imagination.

See also nos. 15, 80, 119, 139, 169, 171, 205, 210, 217, 219, 232, 237, 240, 247, 252, 255, 261, 264, 268, 279, 285, 288, 289, 294, 295, 299, 301–3, 306, 309, 310, 317, 318, 320, 325–27, 330, 332.

Chaucer's Influence and Later Allusion

60. Anderson, Judith H. "Narrative Reflections: Re-envisaging the Poet in *The Canterbury Tales* and *The Faerie Queene.*" In Theresa M. Krier, ed. *Refiguring Chaucer in the Renaissance* (*SAC* 22 [2000], no. 73), pp. 87–105. Chaucer, especially *GP,* inspired Spenser's poetic identity in *The Faerie Queene.* Through allegory, Spenser manifests Chaucer's ironic doubleness, and he decenters his dominant narration through various forms of "impersonation," emulating Chaucer's blurring of "character and characterizer."

61. Berry, Craig A. "'Sundrie Doubts': Vulnerable Understanding and Dubious Origins in Spenser's Continuation of the *Squire's Tale.*" In Theresa M. Krier, ed. *Refiguring Chaucer in the Renaissance* (*SAC* 22 [2000], no. 73), pp. 106–27. Assesses Spenser's appeal to Chaucer and his continuation of *SqT* as an aspect of the Renaissance poet's doubt about his place in English poetry. Chaucer "revels in the multiplication of doubt," but Spenser sought to work out his doubts about his poetry and his career.

62. Bowers, John M. "Controversy and Criticism: Lydgate's *Thebes* and the Prologue to *Beryn.*" *Chaucer Yearbook* 5 (1998): 91–115. Treats

Thebes and the Prologue to *Beryn* (here called *The Canterbury Interlude*) as "efforts to write what Chaucer had left unwritten" and to confront contemporary controversies. Lydgate's work rebukes those who would critique monasticism and diminish the status of Saint Thomas à Becket. The *Beryn* Prologue (and the two-way journey of the Northumberland manuscript in which it appears) asserts orthodox acceptance of pilgrimage in the face of contemporary Lollard challenges.

63. Cooper, Helen. "Jacobean Chaucer: *The Two Noble Kinsmen* and Other Chaucerian Plays." In Theresa M. Krier, ed. *Refiguring Chaucer in the Renaissance* (*SAC* 22 [2000], no. 73), pp. 189–209. Renaissance dramatic adaptations of Chaucer's works often resolve tensions left reverberating in his narratives (e.g., John Fletcher's *Women Pleased* and *WBT;* Fletcher's *Four Plays* and *FranT*). But Fletcher and Shakespeare's *Two Noble Kinsmen* intensifies the conflict between love and friendship seen in *KnT* and replaces its vision of comic order with the insidiousness of mercantilism.

64. Decicco, Mark. "What Vergil Really Wrote: A Study of Gavin Douglas's 'Eneados,' Books I–IV." *DAI* 59 (1999): 2489A. Completed in 1513, Douglas's was the first and only full translation of the *Aeneid* into an English vernacular until Dryden's. The status of Middle English as a literary vehicle had been established by Chaucer. Douglas did the same for Middle Scots to make it a vehicle for great poetry.

65. Delany, Sheila. *Impolitic Bodies: Poetry, Saints, and Society in Fifteenth-Century England. The Work of Osbern Bokenham.* New York and Oxford: Oxford University Press, 1998. xii, 236 pp. Reads Bokenham's *Legends of Holy Women* as a parody of Chaucer's *LGW,* itself a parody of hagiography. By inverting Chaucer's parody, Bokenham critiques Chaucer's emphasis on the classics and reasserts an Augustinian emphasis on Christian aesthetics and ideals. Bokenham structures his work in imitation of *LGW,* but he reflects a more distinct concern with the female body and its parts. Supported by wealthy female patrons of Clare Abbey, Bokenham wages a "modest struggle" against the antifeminism of traditional hagiography. Through its Yorkist partisanship, his work casts light on contemporary concern with dynastic succession, especially as transmitted through females.

66. DeVoto, Marya. "The Hero as Editor: Sidney Lanier's Medievalism and the Science of Manhood." *SiM* 9 (1997): 148–70. Lanier in the early 1880s produced versions of Malory, Froissart, the Percy ballads, and other works aimed at exposing boys to the chivalry and simple piety

of the Middle Ages. The introduction to *The Boy's Froissart* cites Chaucer as a "large and beautiful soul" whose stance and language, exemplified by the envoi to *Sted,* provide a model of literary manhood.

67. Evans, William Dansby. "T. S. Eliot's Harvard College Senior Year: The Medieval Curriculum." *DAI* 59 (1998): 1175A. Examines Eliot's senior-year courses at Harvard for their medieval focus (in art, literature, and philosophy) in the light of primary materials (including Eliot's annotated Chaucer textbook). Compares and contrasts *CT* and *The Waste Land* and analyzes medieval elements in Eliot's œuvre.

68. Fradenburg, Louise O. "The Scottish Chaucer." In Roderick J. Lyall and Felicity Riddy, eds. *Proceedings of the Third International Conference on Scottish Language and Literature (Medieval and Renaissance)* (*SAC* 22 [2000], no. 135), pp. 177–90. Questions the nature and extent of Chaucer's influence on the "Scottish Chaucerians," since most medieval literature is simultaneously derivative and innovative. The *Kingis Quair* of James I (viewed here in the context of the Selden manuscript) is not so much derived from Chaucer as it is a result of a "richly complicated process of historical revisionism."

69. Fyler, John M. "Froissart and Chaucer." In Donald Maddox and Sara Sturm-Maddox, eds. *Froissart across the Genres.* Gainesville: University Press of Florida, 1998, pp. 195–218. Despite Chaucer's early borrowings from Froissart, the two poets diverged as their careers developed. Contrasts the "Voyage en Béarn" section of Froissart's *Chroniques* with *SqT* and *FranT,* arguing that Froissart is "in some respects even more Ovidian than Chaucer."

70. Hieatt, A. Kent. "Room of One's Own for Decisions: Chaucer and *The Faerie Queene.*" In Theresa M. Krier, ed. *Refiguring Chaucer in the Renaissance* (*SAC* 22 [2000], no. 73), pp. 147–64. Books 3–4 of *The Faerie Queene* are a meditation on the nature of sexual passion, deeply influenced by *FranT* (which Spenser paraphrases in part) and its emphasis on companionship as a brake on sexual passion. Spenser develops the meditation in his continuation of *SqT,* incorporating features of *KnT* to acknowledge his son/father relation with Chaucer.

71. Johnston, Andrew James. "Chaucer, Galilei, Brecht: Sprache und Diskurs im Leben des Galilei." In Walter Delabar and Jörg Döring, eds. *Bertolt Brecht (1898–1956).* Berlin: Weidler, 1998, pp. 239–64. Assesses Brecht's portrayal of Galileo Galilei, comparing it with Chaucer's attitudes to scholastic science and scientific language in *SqT* and *Astr,* Lydgate's assessment of Chaucer's scientific writing, Petrarch's view of

scholastic philosophy and science, and Galileo's antischolastic aesthetics. Brecht's portrait is more democratizing than the historical Galileo or his predecessors.

72. Kohl, Stephan. "Henryson's *Testament of Cresseid:* Part of the Chaucerian Tradition?" In Roderick J. Lyall and Felicity Riddy, eds. *Proceedings of the Third International Conference on Scottish Language and Literature (Medieval and Renaissance)* (*SAC* 22 [2000], no. 135), pp. 285–98. Argues that in its depiction of love Henryson's *Cresseid* is more a Renaissance poem than a medieval one. Though its subject matter and verse form follow Chaucer, the poem gives license "to love a human being for his or her own sake—not for God's sake."

73. Krier, Theresa M., ed. *Refiguring Chaucer in the Renaissance.* Gainesville: University Press of Florida, 1998. viii, 240 pp. Ten essays by various authors on the sixteenth- and seventeenth-century reception of Chaucer, as reflected in editing practice, growth of the canon, and poetic imitation and emulation. In "Introduction: Receiving Chaucer in Renaissance England," Krier theorizes the "gratitude" expressed in Renaissance culture for the "generosity" of Chaucer and his works, focusing on Francis Thynne's "Animadversions." For the other nine essays, see nos. 28, 60, 61, 63, 70, 79, 286, 293, and 304.

74. Lee, Sung-Il. "On Robert Henryson's *Testament of Cresseid.*" *MES* 5 (1997): 201–16. Henryson's emulation of Chaucer is evident in his adoption of the stanza form of *TC* for his *Testament,* yet he expresses his "rivalry" with his predecessor by offering a different conclusion.

75. Matthews, David O. "Speaking to Chaucer: The Poet and the Nineteenth-Century Academy." *SiM* 9 (1997): 5–25. Uses the Hoccleve portrait of Chaucer as a focal point for examining the nineteenth-century image of Chaucer. Viewed at first as the one "modern" author of his time, Chaucer becomes, through the work of the Chaucer Society and the edition of Skeat, an illustration of the importance of the study of medieval English, which in turn plays an important role in the development of English studies.

76. Pearsall, Derek. *John Lydgate (1371–1449): A Bio-Bibliography.* English Literary Studies, no. 71. Victoria: University of Victoria, 1997. 95 pp. A documentary biography of Lydgate that prints and places in context his life-records and includes a bibliography of his major works, modern editions, and essential secondary studies. The biography includes recurrent mention of where and how Lydgate's works reflect Chaucer's influence.

77. Pinti, Daniel, ed. *Writings after Chaucer: Essential Reading in Chaucer and the Fifteenth Century.* Basic Readings in Chaucer and His Times, no. 1. New York and London: Garland, 1998. xiv, 279 pp. Reprints eleven essays or book chapters pertaining to Chaucer's reception, with topics such as scribal habits, Chaucer's influence on later poets, Chaucerian apocrypha, and others. For the one essay not previously published, see no. 46.

78. Ward, Antonia. "'My Love for Chaucer': F. J. Furnivall and Homosociality in the Chaucer Society." *SiM* 9 (1997): 44–57. Argues that the impulse behind Furnivall's Chaucer scholarship was homosocial, a desire to become as close to Chaucer as possible and to share his love of the poet with other men as a way of bringing them closer together. This homosocial element has been a recurrent feature of medieval English studies.

79. Watkins, John. "'Wrastling for This World': Wyatt and the Tudor Canonization of Chaucer." In Theresa M. Krier, ed. *Refiguring Chaucer in the Renaissance* (*SAC* 22 [2000], no. 73), pp. 21–39. Examines allusions to Chaucer's poetry in works by Thomas Wyatt. Thynne's edition of Chaucer shows how he was appropriated for the crown's political agenda, while the Devonshire manuscript reflects subversive appropriation. Wyatt capitalized on this fragmentation of Chaucer's "cultural authority" to express his own poetic and political struggles.

See also nos. 41, 108, 144, 243, 282, 286, 300, 304, 333.

Style and Versification

80. Borroff, Marie. "Chaucer's English Rhymes: The *Roman,* the *Romaunt,* and *The Book of the Duchess.*" In Peter S. Baker and Nicholas Howe, eds. *Words and Works: Studies in Medieval English Language and Literature in Honour of Fred C. Robinson* (*SAC* 22 [2000], no. 95), pp. 223–42. Defines kinds of rhyme by their varying degrees of "richness," from "simple rhymes" to "triple rhymes" (in which three successive terminal syllables rhyme). Although Chaucer's rhymes in *Rom* and *BD* are less various and rich than those in the *Roman de la Rose,* his rhyme "systems" achieve formal and thematic richness, particularly the recurrent rhyming of *rowthe* and *trowthe* in *BD.*

81. Chickering, Howell. "Chaucer by Heart." In David Sofield and Herbert F. Tucker, eds. *Under Criticism: Essays for William H. Pritchard.* Athens: Ohio University Press, 1998, pp. 91–108. Considers the peda-

gogical value of memorizing verse and comments on exercises in retention for students of Chaucer's poetry. Includes close reading of several stanzas of *PF.*

Language and Word Studies

82. Besserman, Lawrence. "Chaucer's Multi-Word Verbs: An Historical Introduction and Illustrative Sample." *NOWELE* 34 (1998): 99–153. Historical assessment of Chaucer's multi-word (or phrasal) verbs, assessing the syntax and semantics of such verbs, the drift to postpositioning of the particles in these verbs (e.g., "wente forth" rather than "forth wente"), and the effects of meter on the use of the verbs. Includes as an appendix an exhaustive list of Chaucer's multi-word verbs containing the particles "about," "away," "out," "down," and "up."

83. Calle Martín, Javier. "Stereotyped Comparisons in the Language of Geoffrey Chaucer." *SELIM* 6 (1996): 64–84. Traces the classical and colloquial origins of Chaucer's stereotyped comparisons (e.g., "as stille as any ston," "white as chalk"); describes their syntax; and assesses the functions of grammar, alliteration, and prosody in the development of terms of comparison.

84. Higuchi, Masayuki. "The Roles of the ME Preverbal *y-,* with Special Reference to Chaucer's English." *JEngL* 26 (1998): 199–208. In Chaucer's prose, where usage is unaffected by metrical considerations, the presence or absence of the *y-* prefix in past participles is not random. Chaucer uses *y-* for stylistic variation and to convert nouns to verbs, and it almost always occurs in grammatical environments in which the participle has verbal rather than adjectival force.

85. Jimura, Akiyuki. "Notes on the Word Order in Chaucer's English." *Hiroshima University Studies, Faculty of Letters* 58 (1998): 155–75 (with Japanese abstract). Charts word order in various editions of *CT* and *TC* with reference to the manuscripts on which they are based. Although the evidence in *CT* is obscure, Root's edition of *TC* shows a marked tendency toward modern subject-verb-object syntax.

86. Kanno, Masahiko. *Word and Deed: Studies in Chaucer's Words.* Tokyo: Eihosha, 1998. xi, 275 pp. Collects previously printed essays, all here translated into English. The essays explore various relationships between diction and characterization as the key to Chaucer's literary craft. Concludes that Chaucer composed poetry as if he were building a cathedral.

87. Lay, Ethna Dempsey. "The Romance Vocabulary of Chaucer's

Romances." *DAI* 58 (1998): 4667A. Using the electronic Glossarial Database of Middle English, Lay analyzes Chaucer's habits of combining native English vocabulary with Romance vocabulary in doublets and puns, a reflection of his bilingual imagination. Explores the tradition of such collocations in rhetorical tradition and compares Chaucer's usage with that of analogous English and Continental narratives.

88. Nagucka, Ruta. "Spatial Relations in Chaucer's *Treatise on the Astrolabe.*" In Jacek Fisiak, ed. *Middle English Miscellany: From Vocabulary to Linguistic Variation* (*SAC* 22 [2000], no. 114), pp. 233–44. Assesses the spatial prepositions in *Astr,* arguing that the availability of the instrument to the audience of *Astr* made it possible for Chaucer to use imprecise indicators of space, that the prepositions used are "semantically transparent," and that *Astr* marks a stage in the conceptual separation of "in" and "on."

89. Staczek, John J. "Đin in Late Middle English and Its Contemporary Reflex in Instructional Settings." In Jacek Fisiak, ed. *Middle English Miscellany: From Vocabulary to Linguistic Variation* (*SAC* 22 [2000], no. 114), pp. 245–52. Argues that certain English pronominal forms are "durable over time" when used in instructions. Assesses cookbooks and *Astr* as Middle English samples and compares their usage with that of modern American cookbooks.

90. Tajima, Matsuji. "The Gerund in Chaucer, with Special Reference to Its Verbal Character." In Jacek Fisiak and Akio Oizumi, eds. *English Historical Linguistics and Philology in Japan* (*SAC* 22 [2000], no. 115), pp. 323–39. Like most of his contemporaries, Chaucer used gerunds primarily as nominals. Yet his usage is marked by a penchant for "determiner + gerund + *of*-adjunct" and by an unusual number of gerunds with verbal properties, especially in his prose. A revision of an essay originally published in *Poetica* (Tokyo) 21–22 (1985).

91. Yonekura, Hiroshi. "On the Productivity of the Suffixes *–ness* and *–ity:* The Case of Chaucer." In Jacek Fisiak and Akio Oizumi, eds. *English Historical Linguistics and Philology in Japan* (*SAC* 22 [2000], no. 115), pp. 439–53. Summarizes the distribution of the two suffixes and compares their semantic functions. A revision of an essay originally published in *Studies in Modern English* 19 (1993): 1–25.

See also nos. 43, 103, 114, 115, 130, 170, 204, 227, 232, 268, 324, 329, 331.

Background and General Criticism

92. Akehurst, F. R. P., and Stephanie Cain Van D'Elden, eds. *The Stranger in Medieval Society.* Medieval Cultures, no. 12. Minneapolis and London: University of Minnesota Press, 1997. xii, 149 pp. Nine essays by various authors on representation of and attitudes toward strangers in medieval literature and society. Topics include merchants as strangers, Jews in France, Wolfram von Eschenbach's *Wolfram, Renaut de Montaubon,* the German poet Kelin, and renown as a form of identity in *Sir Gawain and the Green Knight.* For an essay that pertains to Chaucer, see *SAC* 22 [2000], no. 272). See also no. 339.

93. Allman, Wendy West. "Chaucerian 'Rekenynges': Modeling Authority." *DAI* 58 (1998): 2642A. Chaucer's uses of political discourse intersect with his concerns about poetic authority. In *PF,* "commune profyt" represents both an equivocal political ideal and an idealized community of readers. In *KnT,* just as Theseus aestheticizes his reign, the narrator casts his narrative as a foundation myth. *ClT* comments on political tyranny and the tyranny of poetic authority.

94. An, Sonjae (Brother Anthony). *Literature in English Society before 1660. Volume 1: The Middle Ages.* Seoul: Sogang University Press, 1997. 214 pp. A traditional literary history of Britain from the arrival of the Anglo-Saxons until 1500, introducing major writers (including Chaucer) and works, with summaries and brief quotations. Includes a brief outline of French and Italian backgrounds. Designed as an introduction for Korean students. See also no. 340.

95. Baker, Peter S., and Nicholas Howe, eds. *Words and Works: Studies in Medieval English Language and Literature in Honour of Fred C. Robinson.* Toronto, Buffalo, and New York: University of Toronto Press, 1998. xi, 310 pp. Seventeen essays by various authors, focusing primarily on Old English language and literature. For three essays that pertain to Chaucer, see nos. 80, 199, and 269.

96. Beidler, Peter G., ed. *Masculinities in Chaucer: Approaches to Maleness in the* Canterbury Tales *and* Troilus and Criseyde. Chaucer Studies, no. 25. Cambridge; and Rochester, N.Y.: D. S. Brewer, 1998. xii, 252 pp. An introduction by the editor, plus seventeen essays by various authors. The collection includes one essay on the Host, thirteen on *CT,* and three on *TC.* For specific essays, see nos. 166, 194, 198, 206, 216, 225, 241, 247, 250, 254, 262, 266, 267, 273, 308, 311, and 320.

97. Bertolet, Craig E. "Chaucer's Envoys and the Poet Diplomat."

ChauR 33 (1998): 66–89. Chaucer's envoys should be examined not within the context of history but within the context of the art of letter writing, the medieval concept of friendship, and the description of late-medieval diplomacy. Chaucer's is a "public stance," which simultaneously imparts council, not policy, and allows the moral messages of his texts to suggest possible solutions.

98. Biddick, Kathleen. *The Shock of Medievalism.* Durham, N. C., and London: Duke University Press, 1998. x, 315 pp. Explores the "contemporary consequences of the methods used to initiate medieval studies as an academic discipline in the nineteenth century," particularly how the discipline is "still intimately bound" to the "fathers" of medieval studies. Includes discussion of *WBPT* as medieval discourse that resists or disrupts the distinction between commentary and documentary writing theorized by Steven Justice (*SAC* 18 [1996], no. 95).

99. Bisson, Lillian M. *Chaucer and the Late Medieval World.* New York: St. Martin's Press, 1998. x, 294 pp. Reads Chaucer's works for the ways they reflect the "conflicting realities he confronted in his world." An opening section on "The Poet and His World" introduces the "double vision" of the intellectual world Chaucer inherited and describes his balanced "conception of his task as a poet." Subsequent sections introduce social and historical backgrounds to the following topics and then examine how the subtopics are reflected in Chaucer's works: Religion (hierarchy and heresy, quest for perfection, and popular religion), Class and Commerce (chivalry, social unrest, and economy), and Gender and Sexuality (views of women, love, and marriage). Bisson focuses on *CT* and *TC* but mentions all of Chaucer's major works, concluding that *CT* is especially marked by the carnivalesque tensions between high and low, sacred and profane, and serious and comic characteristics of Chaucer's age. See also no. 350.

100. Blum, Martin Albert. "Body Politics: Otherness and Representation of Bodies in Late Medieval Writings." *DAI* 59 (1998): 163A. Examines various ways gender, ethnicity, and disease interact with social class in selected texts. In *MLT,* race is less important than place in salvation history. The tale of Lucrece (*LGW*) seeks to keep women virginal for marital traffic. Erotic fabliaux like *MilT* warn elite young men of transgressive boundaries. Blum also discusses leprosy in Henryson's *Cresseid.*

101. Bradbury, Nancy Mason. *Writing Aloud: Storytelling in Late Medieval England.* Urbana and Chicago: University of Illinois Press, 1998.

x, 247 pp. Explores how Middle English metrical romances reflect "proximity to orally transmitted legends." Treats the *Tale of Gamelyn* and related outlaw ballads as "fragmentary remains of a predominantly oral tradition," *Havelock the Dane* as an early experiment in literary retelling of oral material, *The Seege of Troye* as a failed effort to assimilate oral story to literary form, and *King Alisaunder* as a successful application of oral-based method to literary material. Chapter 5 ("Chaucerian Minstrelsy: *Troilus and Criseyde*," pp. 175–201) assesses ways *TC* was "profoundly influenced by English minstrel-style romance," considering relations between oral story and "old books" as a significant theme of the work. Also assesses how *Th* reflects Chaucer's and his audience's knowledge of the conventions of metrical romance.

102. Brewer, Derek. *A New Introduction to Chaucer.* 2d ed. London and New York: Longman, 1998. xiv, 426 pp. A "radical revision" (xi) of Brewer's 1984 *Introduction to Chaucer* (*SAC* 8 [1986], no. 55a); like its predecessor, a general introduction intended for specialists and first-time readers of Chaucer alike. Carried over from the first edition, the biographical and social history is retained largely intact. The expanded discussions of Chaucer's works are marked by Brewer's interests in social anthropology and his belief in what is "common to human nature." Brewer views Chaucer as a great artist and a sensitive and humane person. See also no. 353.

103. Burnley, David. *Courtliness and Literature in Medieval England.* London and New York: Longman, 1998. xiv, 241 pp. Historical survey of the language and actions of courtly behavior as evident in Anglo-Norman and Middle English writings, with some corroboration from Latin. Traces the emergence of aristocratic courtliness in the eleventh century through to its appropriation by the merchant class in the fourteenth and fifteenth centuries, examining intersections between courtliness and ideals of personal beauty, notions of nobility, individualism, courtly love, and religion. Focuses on concepts such as pity, graciousness, largesse, honesty, measure, reverence, service, and (by contrast) villainy. Contains frequent references to Chaucer's works, including *Rom, BD,* and several lyrics, as well as *TC* and *CT.* Also treats several French and English romances, courtesy books, hunting manuals, and didactic works, including the Auchinleck manuscript and works by Chrétien de Troyes, Marie de France, John Gower, and others. See also no. 354.

104. Carruthers, Leo, ed. *Rêves et prophéties au Moyen Âge.* AMAES, no. 22. Paris: Publications de l'Association de Médiévistes Anglicistes

de l'Enseignement Supérieur, 1998. 150 pp. Eight essays by various authors examining medieval dreams and prophecies in literature and society. For three essays that pertain to Chaucer, see nos. 275, 288, and 297.

105. ———, ed. *La ronde des saisons : Les saisons dans la littérature et la société anglaises au Moyen Âge.* Cultures et civilisations médiévales, no. 16. Paris: Presses Universitaires de Paris–Sorbonne, 1998. 120 pp. Ten essays by various authors exploring the four seasons in medieval English literature and society. Includes an essay by Sandra Gorgiewski about David Fincher's movie *Seven* in relation to *ParsT* and Dante. For an essay that pertains directly to Chaucer, see no. 110.

106. Cowgill, Jane. "Chaucer's Missing Children." *EMS* 12 (1995): 39–53. As in late-medieval lyrics and drama, the suffering of mothers and children in Chaucer's works is presented as analogous to the suffering of Mary and Jesus. Surveys the presence and absence of references to children in Chaucer's works.

107. Crépin, André. *Chaucer et les cultures d'expression française: Catalogue de l'exposition en Sorbonne, juillet 1998.* AMAES, Hors Série, no. 4. Paris: Publications de l'Association des Médiévistes Anglicistes de l'Enseignement Supérieur, 1998. 72 pp. Catalogue of the exhibition at the Eleventh International Congress of the New Chaucer Society, held at the Sorbonne. Lists books and objects that illustrate the "boundless influence of French-speaking cultures on Chaucer" and the "scholarly contribution in French to Chaucerian studies." Facing-page English and French.

108. ———, and Hélène Taurinya Dauby. *Histoire de la littérature anglaise du Moyen Âge.* Fac. Littérature. Paris: Nathan, 1993. 254 pp. An introduction to literature written in England from Gildas's Latin chronicle to Sir Thomas Malory, including, among others, separate chapters on Chaucer (pp. 148–61) and Chaucer's influence and apocrypha (pp. 187–201). The chapter on Chaucer emphasizes his relations with Continental literature and his modernity.

109. Damico, Helen, ed. *Medieval Scholarship: Biographical Studies on the Formation of a Discipline. Volume 2: Literature and Philology.* Garland Reference Library of the Humanities, no. 2071. New York and London: Garland, 1998. xxx, 465 pp. Thirty-two essays by various authors, sketching the biographies and intellectual achievements of scholars who have helped shape medieval studies. Of greatest interest to Chaucerians are the essays on Frederick J. Furnivall (by Derek Pearsall), Walter William Skeat (Charlotte Brewer), George Lyman Kittredge (John C.

McGalliard), and John Matthews Manly and Edith Rickert (Elizabeth Scala).

110. Dauby, Hélène. "Les saisons et les mets à la fin du Moyen Âge en Angleterre et en France." In Leo Carruthers, ed. *La ronde des saisons: Les saisons dans la littérature et la société anglaises au Moyen Âge* (*SAC* 22 [2000], no. 105), pp. 101–10. Examines the diet of the poor widows in *CT* and the extravagant menus of the Franklin, the numerous recipes in *Le ménagier de Paris,* and *The Boke of Nurture* by John Russell. Describes various ways of preparing dishes, preserving food, and producing food and drink, emphasizing the importance of season, weather, geography, religion, and tricks to bypass inconveniences.

111. Dougill, John. *Oxford in English Literature: The Making, and Undoing, of "The English Athens"*. Ann Arbor: University of Michigan Press, 1998. xii, 363 pp. Surveys depictions of and reactions to Oxford in English literature, from legends of St. Frideswide to modern fiction and screenplays. Treats *MilT* (pp. 19–26) as "the first Oxford novel"; its wealth of details and Chaucer's sympathetic representation of Oxford clerks reflect the poet's familiarity with the medieval town and university.

112. Ellis, Steve. "Popular Chaucer and the Academy." *SiM* 9 (1997): 26–43. Shows that the steady growth in understanding of the historical context of Chaucer's poetry has coexisted with a tendency, on the part of scholars as well as popularizers, to view Chaucer as the jovial poet of "merrie England."

113. Federico, Sylvia. "Old 'Stories' and New Trojans: The Gendered Construction of English Historical Identity." *DAI* 58 (1998): 3125A. Examines fictional representations of Troy as England's mythic ancestor in *TC, HF,* Gower's *Vox Clamantis, Sir Gawain and the Green Knight,* and other works. Since Troy was thought to have led to later empires only through its fall, the city is an ambivalent ideal, providing authors with a fantasy space, which they interpreted and adapted to their goals.

114. Fisiak, Jacek, ed. *Middle English Miscellany: From Vocabulary to Linguistic Variation.* Poznan: Motivex, 1996. [iv], 283 pp. Fifteen essays by various authors from the 1994 conference on Middle English held in Rydzyna, Poland. Individual essays consider lexicographical topics such as Middle English sexual vocabulary, plant names, and words associated with fate; morphological studies of weak verbs, plural markers, locatives, and the relations between derivational and inflectional endings;

and comparative studies of Anglo-French/Middle English relations and Middle English reflexes in modern English. For two essays that pertain to Chaucer, see nos. 88 and 89.

115. ———, and Akio Oizumi, eds. *English Historical Linguistics and Philology in Japan.* Trends in Linguistics, Studies and Monographs, no. 109. Berlin and New York: Mouton de Gruyter, 1998. x, 464 pp. Twenty-five essays by various authors and a select, annotated bibliography of Japanese studies of English historical linguistics from 1950 to 1995. For four essays on Chaucer not previously annotated in *SAC,* see nos. 4, 90, 91, and 316.

116. Fradenburg, Louise O. "Analytical Survey 2: We Are Not Alone: Psychoanalytic Medievalism." *New Medieval Literatures* 2 (1998): 249–76. Questions the claim that psychoanalytical medievalism is insufficiently historical. Surveys a selection of articles that may consciously or unconsciously use psychoanalytical principles, including articles that address *TC* and portions of *CT.*

117. Frantzen, Allen J. *Before the Closet: Same-Sex Love from* Beowulf *to* Angels in America. Chicago and London: University of Chicago Press, 1998. x, 369 pp. Examines same-sex love in English literature and culture between 600 and 1200, with commentary on later tradition. Contains recurrent references to Chaucer's works, including *GP, RvT, ParsT,* and, especially, *MLT.* Although Chaucer "made nothing of" the love between Custance and Hermengyld, "it *is* same-sex love."

118. Giancarlo, Matthew Christopher. "'Al Nys but Conseil': The Medieval Idea of Counsel and the Poetry of Geoffrey Chaucer." *DAI* 58 (1998): 4264A. Describes classical, biblical, and patristic notions of "counsel" as background to Chaucer's "transcendentalizing notion of counsel." Considers counsel in *BD, PF, Mel, TC, KnT, NPT, WBPT, MerT, ManT,* and *ParsT,* arguing that Chaucer aligns human counsel with *consilium Dei* and that he indicates human inability to achieve this ideal.

119. Grinnell, Natalie. "Reflecting Pools: The Thematic Construction of Gender in Medieval Romance." *DAI* 58 (1998): 2644A. Analyzes the motif of the reflecting pool in works by Chrétien de Troyes, Guillaume de Lorris, Jean de Meun, Chaucer, and John Gower. These works indicate that gender stereotypes become more rigid through time and that representations of feminine power faded in Western tradition.

120. Harwood, Britton J. "The Political Use of Chaucer in Twentieth-Century America." In Richard Utz and Tom Shippey, eds.

Medievalism in the Modern World: Essays in Honour of Leslie J. Workman. Turnhout, Belgium: Brepols, 1998, pp. 379–92. Recent works of Chaucer scholarship depict a bourgeois Chaucer articulating contemporary American ideology; thus, they work to reproduce that ideology.

121. Henderson, Arnold Clayton. "Moralized Beasts: The Development of Medieval Fable and Bestiary, Particularly from the Twelfth through the Fifteenth Centuries in England and France." *DAI* 59 (1999): 2489A. Fables present a worldlier view than do Christian bestiaries, and neither genre presented a worldview full enough for Chaucer or other writers. Fable became more Christian, developing witty moralization, sharply drawn personae, and more vivid style (shown in a wide variety of English and French writers).

122. Hoenen, Maarten J. F. M., and Lodi Nauta, eds. *Boethius in the Middle Ages: Latin and Vernacular Traditions of the* Consolatio Philosophiae. Studien und Texte zur Geistesgeschichte des Mittelalters. Leiden, New York, and Köln: Brill, 1997. viii, 376 pp; 3 b&w plates. Twelve essays by various authors on the reception of Boethius's *Consolatione Philosophiae*—its medieval glosses, commentaries, and translations. Four essays pertain to the Middle Dutch tradition. Passim references to Chaucer's *Bo;* see no. 282.

123. Holloway, Julia Bolton. *Jerusalem: Essays on Pilgrimage and Literature.* New York: AMS Press, 1998. [iv], 277 pp.; 11 b&w illus. Ten essays and a personal testimony by the author on the interrelated topics of pilgrimage and exile in works from Homer and Plato to James Joyce. Focuses on the Middle Ages, with essays on female saints and mystics, *Song of Roland,* Dante, Langland, and Chaucer. Includes two essays on Chaucer: a revision of a previously published essay (*SAC* 12 [1990], no. 125) and a newly printed one. See no. 180.

124. Johnson, Ian. "Language and Literary Expression." In Chris Given-Wilson, ed. *An Illustrated History of Late Medieval England.* Manchester and New York: Manchester University Press, 1996, pp. 127–51. A survey of genres and topics in Middle English literature, including Chaucer's "diversity of literary forms and [the] strategies he took to negotiate literary authority." See also no. 373.

125. Kamyabee, Mohammad Hadi. "'And out of Fables Gret Wysdom Men May Take': Middle English Animal Fables as Vehicles of Moral Instruction." *DAI* 59 (1998): 2036A. Discusses how the narrative strategies and implied audiences of animal fables produce the didactic impact of the tales, assessing *The Owl and the Nightingale* and fables by

Chaucer (*NPT* and *ManT*), Gower, Langland, Lydgate, and Henryson. Also explores the history of the genre.

126. Kerby-Fulton, Kathryn, and Steven Justice. "Langlandian Reading Circles and the Civil Service in London and Dublin, 1380–1427." *New Medieval Literatures* 1 (1997): 59–83. Argues that William Langland's readership may have been more like Chaucer's (and John Gower's) than has been assumed in the past, presenting evidence that readers of these authors included scribes and bureaucratic clerks such as Thomas Usk, Thomas Hoccleve, James le Palmer, John But, James Yonge, and others. These clerks make up the coteries of the poets.

127. Kim, Myoung-ok. "The Medieval Concepts of the Poet, Narrator, and Reader Related to the Poet, Narrator, and Reader Found in Chaucer's Poetry." *MES* 5 (1997): 107–44 (in Korean). Examining passages from *BD, TC,* and *CT,* Kim contrasts Chaucer's uses of multiple narrative voices with the ways other medieval writers write themselves and their readers into their texts.

128. Kline, Daniel T. "'Narwe in Cage': Teaching Medieval Women in the First Half of the British Literature Survey." *MFN* 25 (1998): 25–31. Recommends incorporating *MilT* and *WBPT* into a sophomore-level survey of early British literature. Along with works by Margery Kempe and Julian of Norwich, these *Tales* can help make writings about and by medieval women "an essential part of what we teach."

129. Lee, Brian S. "Seen and Sometimes Heard: Piteous and Pert Children in Medieval English Literature." *CLAQ* 23 (1998): 40–48. Examines the diverse portrayals of children in medieval literature, commenting on how Chaucer questions the innocence of the "clergeoun" in *PrT* and how in *LGW* and *MkT* his pathos is more restrained than in his sources.

130. Lehr, John. "Hoccleve and the National Language." *MES* 5 (1997): 243–82. Compares the multilingual conditions of late-medieval England with modern conditions in Korea, Kenya, and Quebec. Then argues that Hoccleve's poetic career resulted from Lancastrian encouragement of a national English language imitating Chaucer's model.

131. Liang, Sun-Chieh. "Chaucer, Joyce, Lacan, and Their 'We-Men.'" *DAI* 58 (1998): 2669A. Both Chaucer and Joyce are incapable of depicting women because the language they use is solipsistically male and logocentric. Liang uses the theories of Jacques Lacan and Jacques Derrida to explore the intrinsic ambiguity of logocentrism, the inter-

penetrability it prompts, and analogies between such interpenetrability and incest.

132. Lindahl, Carl. "Chaucer." In John Miles Foley, ed. *Teaching Oral Traditions.* New York: Modern Language Association, 1998, pp. 359–64. Despite his bookishness, Chaucer is an oral poet, trained in medieval rhetorical tradition, which is rooted in oratory, and successful in his efforts to render oral narratives in literature. Includes several suggestions for teaching Chaucer as an oral poet.

133. Lindley, Arthur. *Hyperion and the Hobbyhorse: Studies in Carnivalesque Subversion.* Newark: University of Delaware Press; London: Associated University Presses, 1996. 197 pp. Assesses how select literary works "encode subversive possibilities within orthodox gestures." An opening essay explores the possibilities of the carnivalesque within an Augustinian framework, and subsequent essays examine such possibilities in *WBT* (revised reprint of *SAC* 16 [1994], no. 193); *Sir Gawain and the Green Knight;* Marlowe's works, especially *Tamburlaine* and *Dr. Faustus;* Elizabethan tragedy, especially *Hamlet* and *The Revenger's Tragedy;* and *Antony and Cleopatra.*

134. ———. "Inducing the Hole: Paratactic Structure and the Unwritten *Canterbury Tales.*" In Robert J. C. Young, Ban Kah Choon, and Robbie B. H. Goh, eds. *The Silent Word: Textual Meaning and the Unwritten.* Singapore: University of Singapore and Word Scientific, 1998, pp. 103–18. Argues that gaps and "narratorial subversions" make Chaucer's works (and much of medieval aesthetic theory) "postmodern," comparing them with the definition of postmodernism by Ihab Hassan. Unreliable signs and indeterminate language compel Chaucer's audience to produce meaning. Lindley discusses the Pardoner's sexuality, the sketch of the Prioress, *WBP,* and *Ret.*

135. Lyall, Roderick J., and Felicity Riddy, eds. *Proceedings of the Third International Conference on Scottish Language and Literature (Medieval and Renaissance). University of Stirling 2–7 July 1981.* Stirling/Glasgow: Department of Scottish Literature, University of Glasgow, 1981. 456 pp. Twenty-eight essays by various authors on Scottish language and literature of the Middle Ages and Renaissance. For two essays that pertain to Chaucer, see nos. 68 and 72.

136. Matsuda, Takami. *Death and Purgatory in Middle English Didactic Poetry.* Woodbridge, Suffolk; and Rochester, N.Y.: D. S. Brewer, 1997. x, 278 pp. Traces the development of the doctrine of purgatory

in medieval art and literature, focusing on Middle English homiletic and didactic writings on death and the necessity of intercession for souls in purgatory. Such works encourage pragmatic, prudential preparation before death to alleviate postmortem suffering. Occasional references to Chaucer's works, particularly *PardPT.* See also no. 391.

137. McGerr, Rosemarie P. *Chaucer's Open Books: Resistance to Closure in Medieval Discourse.* Gainesville: University Press of Florida, 1998. x, 210 pp. Argues that all of Chaucer's major works "play with medieval concepts of closure" and that the inconclusiveness of these works self-consciously indicates that readers generate their own meanings. Through play with (non)closure and (in)conclusiveness, Chaucer explores the goals of fiction and enables us to understand our limitations. Open literary forms, closure, and conclusiveness were topics of concern for medieval theorists as well as for more modern ones.

138. Mehl, Dieter. "A Canon of Middle English Literature? Of Some Problems of Writing a Survey of the Age of Chaucer." In Bernardo Santano Moreno, Adrian R. Birtwhistle, and Luis Gustavo Girón Echevarría, eds. *Papers from the VIIth International Conference of the Spanish Society for Medieval English Language and Literature* (*SAC* 19 [1997], no. 120), pp. 187–205. Comments on changes in the "canon" of fourteenth-and fifteenth-century English literature, including the rise in importance of *LGW.*

139. Miller, Miriam Youngerman, and Jane Chance, eds. *Approaches to Teaching* Sir Gawain and the Green Knight. Approaches to Teaching Masterpieces of World Literature. New York: Modern Language Association of America, 1986. xii, 256 pp. Twenty-four brief essays on pedagogical approaches to teaching *Sir Gawain and the Green Knight,* arranged by class level and course design. Includes a section of "Materials" for teaching the poem, i.e., critical, textual, and audiovisual aids. Recurrent references to Chaucer help indicate approaches to teaching his works and clarify relations between the two poets.

140. Na, Yong-Jun. "Nature and Vision in the Poems of Chaucer, Langland, and Spenser." *DAI* 58 (1998): 3146A. Examines personifications of Nature in representative works to argue that allegory is a powerful tool of visionary literature.

141. Paxson, James J., and Cynthia A. Gravlee, eds. *Desiring Discourse: The Literature of Love, Ovid through Chaucer.* Selinsgrove, Penn.: Susquehanna University Press; London: Associated University Presses, 1998. 239 pp. An anthology of essays by various authors on aspects of

medieval love literature. The introduction, by Paxson, discusses literary depictions of love in light of postmodern theories of the "psychological, phenomenological, and gendered bases" of desire. The twelve essays address aspects of love and desire in works such as *Roman d'Eneas, Pamphilus,* commentaries on Ovid, troubadour lyrics, and the *Lais* of Marie de France. For four essays that pertain to Chaucer, see nos. 197, 244, 324, and 325.

142. ———, Lawrence M. Clopper, and Sylvia Tomasch, eds. *The Performance of Middle English Culture: Essays on Chaucer and the Drama in Honor of Martin Stevens.* Cambridge: D. S. Brewer, 1998. ix, 198 pp. Eleven essays by various authors on medieval theatricality as a cultural process, including discussion of dramatic images and ludic energy in Chaucer and the social and ideological "performativities" of the mystery and morality plays. For the six essays that pertain to Chaucer, see nos. 182, 200, 231, 235, 274, and 315.

143. Pearsall, Derek. "The Future of Chaucer Studies." *Poetica* (Tokyo) 50 (1998): 17–29. Describes three recent schools of Chaucer criticism: "identity formation," New Historicism, and (three phases of) feminism. Opines that reading Chaucer, and English literary study generally, will be replaced by media studies in the near future, even though literature has the "secret weapon" of pleasure to forestall this process.

144. ———. "Language and Literature." In Nigel Saul, ed. *The Oxford Illustrated History of Medieval England.* Oxford: Oxford University Press, 1997, pp. 245–76. Surveys English language and literature from the Anglo-Saxon invasions to Thomas Malory, briefly discussing Chaucer as a court poet and as the one who brought "England fully into the stream of contemporary French and Italian poetry," making English "part of the whole medieval Latin and vernacular tradition."

145. Plumer, Danielle Cunniff. "Langland, Kempe, and Chaucer, and the 'Makynges' of Authority." *DAI* 59 (1999): 2490A. Fourteenth-century English dialogue between Wycliffite heresy and religious orthodoxy brought a redefinition of authorship and authority. Langland and Chaucer developed their own "authorial identities, or bibliographic egos," and sometimes altered their works to avoid being claimed by heretical groups. Kempe, writing later, absents herself as author. All represent their works as divinely inspired.

146. Reed, Teresa P. "Reading Contingencies: Marian Figuration in Middle English Literature." *DAI* 57 (1997): 3930A. Representations of Mary in medieval literature are paradoxical, often underscored by her

opposition to Eve. *MLT* and the hagiography *Seinte Marherete* seek to present a unified view of Mary but ultimately fail; *WBPT* and *Pearl* are more sensitive to the implications of the paradox.

147. Roberts, Anna. *Violence against Women in Medieval Texts.* Gainesville: University Press of Florida, 1998. viii, 254 pp. Ten essays by various authors, including discussions of Ælfric's female saints, *Emaré,* English translations of Christine de Pizan, and other topics. Includes a slightly revised reprint of Carolyn Dinshaw's "Rivalry, Rape, and Manhood: Gower and Chaucer" (*SAC* 15 [1993], no. 36), and one other essay on Chaucer; see no. 186.

148. Robertson, Kellie Paige. "'Sethe That Babyl Was Ybuld': Translation and Dissent in Later Medieval England." *DAI* 58 (1998): 4645A. Explores conflicts between theories and practice of translation from Geoffrey of Monmouth to Thomas Hoccleve, focusing on how Lollard debates about translation provoked orthodox claims that the vernacular was "pestilential." Assesses in this context Chaucer's claim to be translating from Latin in *TC* and his revisions to *LGW.*

149. Root, Jerry. *"Space to Speke": The Confessional Subject in Medieval Literature.* American University Studies, ser. 2, Romance Languages and Literatures, no. 225. New York: Peter Lang, 1997. [viii], 271 pp. Examines how the confessional mandate of the Fourth Lateran Council provoked the rise of vernacular penitential manuals, and their impact on literary characters from Chaucer, Machaut, and the *Libro de buen amor.* Revision of the author's 1991 dissertation (*SAC* 15 [1993], no. 128). Chapter 4, "Chaucer and the 'Space to Speke' the Private," is a revision of *SAC* 18 (1996), no. 189.

150. Sholty, Janet Poindexter. "Into the Woods: Wilderness Imagery as Representation of Spiritual and Emotional Transition in Medieval Literature." *DAI* 58 (1998): 2645A. Neoplatonism is the root of medieval depictions of wilderness as a metaphoric landscape of psychological transition and spiritual conversion. Examines select medieval works, including Dante's *Divine Comedy, Beowulf, Pearl, Sir Gawain and the Green Knight, BD, PF,* and *TC,* comparing them with depictions in the visual arts.

151. Sinnreich-Levi, Deborah M., ed. *Eustache Deschamps, French Courtier-Poet: His Work and His World.* New York: AMS Press, 1998. xix, 281 pp. Thirteen essays reexamining Deschamps's work and life. While critics in the first half of the century saw Deschamps as a possible source for Chaucer and as an admirer of Chaucer's work, these essays investigate

a wider context for his work, including Christine de Pizan and *Roman de la Rose.* For essays pertaining to Chaucer, see nos. 52 and 56.

152. Snodgrass, Mary Ellen. *Encyclopedia of Fable.* ABC-CLIO Literary Companion. Santa Barbara, Calif.: ABC-CLIO, 1998. xvi, 451 pp.; 47 b&w figs. An alphabetical dictionary of the "world fable," i.e., the beast fable and related narratives in various international traditions, both as stand-alone narratives and as exempla in larger works. Includes entries on national and ethnic traditions, authors, subgenres, and motifs; also includes a timeline, lists of authors and sources, a bibliography, and an index. The entry on Chaucer (pp. 70–78) provides biographical information and comments on *NPT* and *ManT.* Also includes a separate entry on Chauntecleer (pp. 78–81).

153. Spearman, Robert Alan. "Towards a Rhetoric of Youth: Readings in Augustine and Selected Medieval Narratives." *DAI* 58 (1998): 4672A. Constructs an Augustinian "rhetoric of youth" to assess the depictions of infancy, childhood, and youth in Boethius's *De consolatione philosophiae,* Innocent III's *De miseria condicionis humane,* and the *Roman de la rose.* Then considers how Chaucer resists this tradition in *BD, PF, HF,* and *TC.*

154. Stillinger, Thomas C., ed. *Critical Essays on Geoffrey Chaucer.* Critical Essays on British Literature. New York: G. K. Hall; London: Prentice Hall International, 1987. x, 272 pp. Eleven essays by various authors. In his introduction, Stillinger characterizes Chaucer studies up to the 1980s as a great debate between New Criticism and exegetical criticism; he says that he selected the essays in the volume for the ways they go beyond the debate. Nine of the essays were published previously, five as chapters in books. For the two essays that are newly published here, see nos. 192 and 330.

155. Strohm, Paul. *England's Empty Throne: Usurpation and the Language of Legitimation, 1399–1422.* New Haven and London: Yale University Press, 1998. xiv, 274 pp. Combines New Historicism and cultural psychoanalysis to explore how the Lancastrian dynasty and its supporters responded to and helped to construct a response to Henry Lancaster's usurpation of Richard II's throne. Interrogates the indeterminacies of literary and historical texts to formulate a "series of perspectives on the relations between textuality and political process," examining how such perspectives contributed to "Lancastrian self-legitimation" (xiii). Lancastrian dynastic texts are particularly "amnesiac," since their aim was often to repress information, but such amnesia is endemic in all texts.

Recurrent references to various chronicles, prophecies, Lollard texts, and works by Hoccleve and Lygate; occasional references to Chaucer.

156. Szarmach, Paul E., M. Teresa Tavormina, and Joel T. Rosenthal, eds. *Medieval England: An Encyclopedia.* Garland Encyclopedias of the Middle Ages, no. 3. Garland Reference Library of the Humanities, no. 907. New York and London: Garland, 1998. lxix, 882 pp.; 156 b&w figs. An alphabetical encyclopedia from "Abbo of Fleury" to "York Virgin and Child." Written by members of a team of contributors, the entries provide fundamental, descriptive information and bibliographies for further reading. The volume is cross-referenced and indexed and includes maps, genealogies, and several glossaries of specialized terminology. The entry on Chaucer (pp. 172–75) is by Helen Cooper; on Chaucerian apocrypha (pp. 175–76), by Kathleen M. Hewett-Smith.

157. Thomas, Susanne Sara. "*Lex Scripta et Lex Non Scripta:* Tensions Between Law and Language in Late Fourteenth-Century England and Its Literature." *DAI* 58 (1998): 2645A. Examines how Chaucer and the *Gawain* poet explore the legal power of written and spoken words. *Sir Gawain and the Green Knight* challenges the potency of oral oaths, *WBT* parodies courtroom rhetoric, the *GP* sketch of the Sergeant of Law exposes legal subversion of land law, *PardPT* abuse and fetishize texts, and *CYPT* depicts the fearful prospect that texts are empty and language inauthentic.

158. Truscott, Yvonne J. "Chaucer's Children and the Medieval Idea of Childhood." *CLAQ* 23 (1998): 29–34. Refutes claims that children were ignored during the Middle Ages. Chaucer wrote *Astr* to his son. In *Th,* he adopts a "childish identity," complemented by the pedagogy of *Mel.* The narrators of *HF, PF,* and *BD* are childlike.

159. Utz, Richard. "'Cleansing' the Discipline: Ernst Robert Curtius and his Medievalist Turn." In Richard Utz and Tom Shippey, eds. *Medievalism in the Modern World: Essays in Honour of Leslie J. Workman.* Turnhout, Belgium: Brepols, 1998, pp. 359–78. Curtius sought to "cleanse" the study of medieval texts from emerging aesthetic and sociological readings by demonstrating the superiority of philological scholarship in his extensive review of Hans H. Glunz's study, *Die Literarästhetik des Europäischen Mittelalters: Wolfram—Rosenroman—Chaucer—Dante* (1937).

160. ———. "Literary Nominalism in Chaucer's Late-Medieval England: Toward a Preliminary Paradigm." *European Legacy* 2.2 (1997): 206–11. Argues that recent attention to the late-medieval shift from

realism to nominalism is attributable to a parallel shift in modern critical assumptions. Inspired by postmodern views of the world as "recalcitrant to universals, contingent, and supportive of . . . free will," critics have studied late-medieval nominalism as a source of linguistic and philosophical attitudes in the works of Chaucer and his contemporaries and as a bridge between medieval and modern views.

161. Waters, Claire McMartin. "Doctrine Embodied: Gender, Performance, and Authority in Late-Medieval Preaching." *DAI* 59 (1999): 4423A. Focuses on the association of preaching and the preacher's body in medieval tradition, exploring the association through traditional identification of women and the body. Women preachers of hagiographic tradition and various exemplary women (including Constance of *MLT,* Griselda of *ClT,* and Philosophy of *Bo*) reflect the struggles of women to educate or preach. Elsewhere in *CT,* Chaucer's own body is a secular version of the struggle.

162. Wilsbacher, Gregory James. "Art and Obligation: Reading, Ethics, and Middle English Poetry." *DAI* 59 (1999): 3448A. Examines ethical questions raised by medieval literature for modern readers in the light of modern philosophical studies (Jean-François Lyotard, Emmanuel Levinas, Jean-Luc Nancy), as shown in *LGW* (literature and history), *Piers Plowman* (fourteenth-century poverty and critics), and *PrT* (anti-Semitism and critics). Modern readers may experience a sense of obligation not easily dealt with.

163. Winstead, Karen A. *Virgin Martyrs: Legends of Sainthood in Late Medieval England.* Ithaca, N.Y., and London: Cornell University Press, 1997. xiv, 201 pp. Divides Middle English saints' lives about virgin martyrs (ca. 1200–1450) into three subgroups and examines how each reflects the cultural conditions of its reception. Addressed to monastic audiences, the earliest are dominated by didacticism and devotional concerns; the Katherine group is a primary example. The second group focuses on the disruptive power of the martyrs, reflecting the social concerns of Chaucer, William Paris, Margery Kempe, and others. The third group returned to the earlier monastic style, satisfying bourgeois conservatism and the desire for a politically safe religion found in Osbern Bokenham, John Lydgate, and versions of the life of Queen Katherine of Alexandria. Assesses how *SNT,* like the fabliau dynamics of *WBP,* relies upon invective to challenge authority.

164. Yeager, R. F., ed. *Re-Visioning Gower.* Asheville, N.C.: Pegasus Press, 1998. xii; 303 pp.; 15 b&w figs. Fifteen essays by various authors,

each essay originally presented at the annual meeting of the John Gower Society between 1992 and 1997. Revised for publication, the essays explore issues of Gower's poetics and methods, his political concerns, and the texts and manuscripts of his works. Recurrent references to Chaucer, with one essay that contrasts the two poets. See no. 210.

165. Zieman, Katherine Grace. "Reading and Singing: Liturgy, Literacy, and Literature in Late Medieval England." *DAI* 59 (1998): 818A. Late-medieval liturgical activities—especially benefactions and the education that lay behind them—resulted from a variety of conditions and motives and produced a volatile environment that influenced the rise of vernacular literacy. Langland's *Piers Plowman,* Gower's *Vox Clamantis,* and *HF* and *MilT* reflect this volatility in various ways, with Chaucer claiming authority for the vernacular.

See also no. 53.

The Canterbury Tales—General

166. Allen, Mark. "Mirth and Bourgeois Masculinity in Chaucer's Host." In Peter G. Beidler, ed. *Masculinities in Chaucer: Approaches to Maleness in the* Canterbury Tales *and* Troilus and Criseyde (*SAC* 22 [2000], no. 96), pp. 9–21. In the transformation from Deduit in the *Roman de la Rose* to the Host of *CT,* and in the actions of the Host during the pilgrimage, we can see intersections of gender and class as Chaucer constructs the Host's distinctively "bourgeois masculinity."

167. Ashton, Gail. *Chaucer:* The Canterbury Tales. Analysing Texts. New York: St. Martin's Press, 1998. viii, 206 pp. An introduction to *CT,* designed to enable students to approach the poem on their own. Includes sections on style and narrative technique; voice, narration, and form; and themes, tensions, and ambiguities—each with explanatory discussion, summary of Chaucer's techniques, and suggestions for further reading. Also includes sections on Chaucer's life, the context of his work, and analytic discussions of brief excerpts from several critical studies of Chaucer's works.

168. Biebel, Elizabeth M. "Pilgrims to Table: Food Consumption in Chaucer's *Canterbury Tales.*" In Martha Carlin and Joel T. Rosenthal, eds. *Food and Eating in Medieval Europe.* London and Rio Grande, Ohio: Hambledon Press, 1998, pp. 15–26. Surveys references to food in *CT,* arguing that they capitalize on traditional associations of the "feminized

Christ" and butchered animals. In general terms, references to food recall the spiritual associations of pilgrimage and indicate character: individuals who eat vegetables are depicted as more upstanding than meat eaters.

169. Bishop, Kathleen A. "Classical and Medieval Influences on Chaucer's Fabliau Comedy." *DAI* 58 (1998): 4643A. Explores how classical comedy (especially Plautus and Ovid) and medieval elegiac comedies influenced Chaucer's fabliaux and the fabliau elements of *ManT, WBP, TC,* and the Prologue to the apocryphal *Tale of Beryn.*

170. Boehme, Timothy Howard. "'Speketh So Pleyn': Elements of the Realist/Nominalist Debate in Selected 'Canterbury Tales.'" *DAI* 60 (1999): 121A. Analysis of *WBPT, FrT, SumT, ClT, FranT,* and *Ret* indicates that Chaucer was "a realist with regard to religion and a nominalist with regard to language and epistemological issues."

171. Brosamer, Matthew James. "Medieval Gluttony and Drunkenness: Consuming Sin in Chaucer and Langland." *DAI* 58 (1998): 4643A. Assesses gluttony in *CT* and *Piers Plowman,* arguing that each presents consumption as both an occasion of the sin and part of its symbolic apparatus. In these works and in scriptural and patristic traditions, gluttony signifies human potential for all sins.

172. Carruthers, Leo. "*Know Thyself:* Criticism, Reform and the Audience of *Jacob's Well.*" In Jacqueline Hamesse et al., eds. *Medieval Sermons and Society: Cloister, City, University: Proceedings of International Symposia at Kalamazoo and New York.* Textes et études du Moyen Âge, no. 9. Louvain-la-Neuve: Fédération Internationale des Instituts d'Études Médiévales, 1998, pp. 219–40. Shows how the Middle English sermon series *Jacob's Well* reflects many aspects of contemporary society. Carruthers likens its audience to that of *CT.*

173. Cote, Mary Kathleen Hendrickson. "Feminine Dialectic and the Problem of Salvation in Chaucer's 'Canterbury Tales.'" *DAI* 58 (1998): 2665A. *WBT, PrT,* and *SNT* all confront the masculine authority of books, the nature of love and marriage, and the nature of feminine authority—issues of female identity and agency. They assert a feminine response to masculine discourse in *CT,* culminating in the balance between *SNT* and *ParsT.*

174. Cullen, Dolores L. *Chaucer's Host: Up-So-Doun.* Santa Barbara, Calif.: Fithian Press, 1998. 207 pp. Allegorical reading of the *CT* Host as an image of Christ, a figure of the Eucharist associated with joy, heroism, and omnipotence. The Host is a guide of others and the only pil-

grim not in need of penance. His name, his language, and his leadership reveal his identity with Christ. His wife, Goodelief, is a figure of the recalcitrant Church. Argues that Chaucer and his audience were accustomed to seeking "hidden meaning" and derives the fourteenth-century notion of Christ from various sources, including Corpus Christi plays, the liturgies of Corpus Christi and Lent, *Cursor mundi,* and others.

175. DeVries, David. "Chaucer and the Idols of the Market." *ChauR* 33 (1998): 391–99. Despite David Wallace's assertion that London is "absent" in Chaucer, and D. W. Robertson's contention that medieval Londoners were content within "an hierarchical classless society," *CT* depicts London as an "underworld" where unscrupulous characters tell unreliable tales. Chaucer's London is, in fact, a mercantile place that "mirrors in a perverse image the order of the ideal."

176. Doltas, Dilek. "The Discussion of Love and Marriage in 'The Canterbury Tales.'" *Hacettepe Bulletin of Social Sciences and Humanities* 3 (1971): 157–75. While depicting love and marriage in the Marriage Group, Chaucer presents the "delights of both the flesh and the soul." The group opens with *Mel; WBPT, ClT,* and *MerT* offer extreme but lively views. *FranT* presents an ideal secular solution, while *ParsT* presents a religious ideal.

177. Ellis, Steve, ed. *Chaucer: The* Canterbury Tales. Longman Critical Reader. London and New York: Longman, 1998. xiv, 241 pp. An anthology of twelve previously published essays and excerpts from longer works that apply modern critical theory to *CT.* Ellis's introduction assesses the contributions of the essays to a postmodern understanding of *CT.* Includes essays by H. Marshall Leicester Jr. (on *GP*), Mark A. Sherman (*KnT*), Peggy Knapp (*MilT*), Carolyn Dinshaw (*MLT*), Arthur Lindley (*WBPT*), Elaine Tuttle Hansen (*ClT*), Carolyn P. Collette (*MerT*), John Stephens and Marcella Ryan (*WBT* and *FranT*), Lee Patterson (*PardT*), Elizabeth Robertson (*PrT*), Britton J. Harwood (*NPT*), and Paul Strohm (styles of *CT*).

178. Forni, Kathleen. "'Queynte' Arguments: The Ellesmere Order May Be the Most 'Satisfactory' but Is It Chaucer's?" *Chaucer Yearbook* 5 (1998): 79–90. Claiming "there is no clear textual evidence for the assertion that [the Ellesmere order] reflects Chaucer's intention," Forni questions the authority of the Ellesmere order and examines how that order was canonized as Chaucerian. She contends that it is impossible to determine the order in which Chaucer intended the fragments to be read.

179. Haas, Kurtis Boyd. "Rhetoric, Romance and the Structure of

Authority in the 'Canterbury Tales.'" *DAI* 59 (1999): 2970A. Unlike other authors of chivalric romance of his time, Chaucer manipulates medieval theories of rhetoric to reveal how the relations of authority and discourse define both the pilgrim narrators and the characters in their tales. Treats *WBPT, KnT, SqT, FranT,* and *Th.*

180. Holloway, Julia Bolton. "Perverse Pilgrims: Chaucer's Wife and Pardoner." In Julia Bolton Holloway. *Jerusalem: Essays on Pilgrimage and Literature* (*SAC* 22 [2000], no. 123), pp. 173–94. Assesses the Wife of Bath (in contrast to the Clerk) and the Pardoner (in contrast to the Parson) as "Chaucer's Diptych of Eve and Adam," commenting on their depictions in the Ellesmere manuscript and reading them as inversions of the ideals of pilgrimage. Focuses on the Wife's association with Bath and her contrast with the Samaritan woman; considers the Pardoner's distortions of "the Emmaus tale" and his affiliations with the figure of Renart.

181. Kensak, Michael Alan. "Dante, Alain de Lille, and the Ending of the 'Canterbury Tales.'" *DAI* 59 (1998): 817A. Entry into heaven and the approach to God properly conclude a pilgrimage, as represented by Dante and Alain de Lille. In *ManPT,* Chaucer inverts the topos to show logic and language vitiated (not transcended) as the Cook becomes literally drunk (not spiritually inebriated), and "the Host rededicates the pilgrimage to Bacchus."

182. Lerer, Seth. "The Chaucerian Critique of Medieval Theatricality." In James J. Paxson, Lawrence M. Clopper, and Sylvia Tomasch, eds. *The Performance of Middle English Culture: Essays on Chaucer and the Drama in Honor of Martin Stevens* (*SAC* 22 [2000], no. 142), pp. 59–76. In the beginning of *CT,* Chaucer's references and allusions to late-fourteenth-century theater indicate the potentially disruptive nature of dramatic public expression. *CT* defines the cycle plays as radically other—provincial, civic, and communally produced.

183. Pappano, Margaret Ann. "The Priest's Body: Literature and Popular Piety in Late Medieval England." *DAI* 59 (1999): 2490A. Explores the sociocultural influence of sacerdotal celibacy on literature. Capable of performing the Mass, the "special body" of the priest became a literary icon, aligned with the Latin language in opposition to Lollardy. Lay writing emerged against clerical restraint, as seen in the concept of the "priest's body" in *CT,* the play *Mankind,* and works of Margery Kempe and Margery Baxter.

184. Russell, J. Stephen. *Chaucer and the Trivium: The Mindsong of the* Canterbury Tales. Gainesville: University Press of Florida, 1998. x, 265

pp. Argues that medieval language theory and the arts of grammar, logic, and rhetoric inform *CT.* They provided Chaucer with his fundamental awareness of the slipperiness of language—its inability to represent truth and reality and its ability to distort as well as convince. Also, as the source of Chaucer's understanding of human cognition, the *trivium* gave Chaucer the "mechanism for consciously evoking an image of the human individual" (203). Summarizes medieval education and its "implications" and discusses *GP, KnT, MLT,* and *ClT* as works in which the influence of the *trivium* on Chaucer's imagination and techniques is particularly clear. Includes brief discussion of *WBP, MerT, FranT,* and *Mel.*

185. Silar, Theodore Irvin. "Feudal Land Law Terminology in Selected Works of Geoffrey Chaucer." *DAI* 58 (1998): 4283A. Legal terminology pertaining to land law is dense in Fragments 1 and 2 of *CT* and in *TC.* Chaucer used the terms in informed ways and expected his audience to be familiar with their implications.

186. Weisl, Angela Jane. "'Quiting Eve': Violence Against Women in the *Canterbury Tales.*" In Anna Roberts, ed. *Violence against Women in Medieval Texts* (*SAC* 22 [2000], no. 147), pp. 115–36. Though Chaucer grants women agency in *CT,* they act against a background of violence that is often ignored or mitigated. The fabliaux, the romances, and the religious narratives all present violence against women as a normal part of society. *WBT* comes closest to challenging such violence, and *ClT* is the most antipathetic to women.

187. Wodzak, Victoria Lee. "Reading Dinosaur Bones: Marking the Transition from Orality to Literacy in *The Canterbury Tales, Moll Flanders, Clarissa,* and *Tristram Shandy.*" *DAI* 59 (1998): 500A. Assesses the status of *CT* and three eighteenth-century novels as "transitional texts" between orality and literacy, examining such features as voicing, framing devices, and insecurity about the social and moral roles of the texts.

188. Yager, Susan. "Boethius, Philosophy and Chaucer's 'Marriage Group.'" *CarmP* 4 (1995): 77–88. With the exception of Dorigen, the women in the Marriage Group (*WBPT, ClT, MerT, FranT*) are similar to Boethius's character Philosophy: they assume authoritative roles, echo some of her sentiments, and sometimes recall her voice. Dorigen's behavior is more similar to that of the character Boethius in the *Consolation of Philosophy.*

See also nos. 7, 10, 11, 13, 20, 22–24, 26, 29, 33, 34, 37, 38, 42, 45, 53, 67, 99, 103, 110, 127, 137, 161, 200, 207, 336.

CT—The General Prologue

189. Gastle, Brian W. "Chaucer's 'Shaply' Guildsmen and Mercantile Pretensions." *NM* 99 (1998): 211–16. The portrait of the five guildsmen in *CT* is a critique of "petty bourgeois pretensions to political power." Though each was "shaply for to been an alderman," the guildsmen were not members of the professions from which aldermen were elected. Their dress, like their wives' aspirations for social climbing, makes them subjects for derision.

190. Hardwick, Paul. "Chaucer: The Poet as Ploughman." *ChauR* 33 (1998): 146–56. If the Parson represents the church, the Ploughman represents lay piety in brotherhood with the church. This is how Chaucer perceives the poet's role: as a "'trewe swynkere,' working 'for Cristes sake, for every povre wight' in accordance with the exemplary model provided by the Church."

See also nos. 8, 9, 12, 14, 60, 117, 157, 166, 184.

CT—The Knight and His Tale

191. Brewer, Derek. "Chaucer's *Knight's Tale* and the Problem of Cultural Translatability." In George Hughes, ed. *Corresponding Powers: Studies in Honour of Professor Hisaaki Yamanouchi.* Woodbridge, Suffolk; and Rochester, N.Y.: D. S. Brewer, 1997, pp. 103–12. Reads *KnT* as an expression of Chaucer's own outlooks, i.e., his sympathetic views of chivalry and ritual.

192. Fowler, Elizabeth. "The Afterlife of the Civil Dead: Conquest in the *Knight's Tale.*" In Thomas C. Stillinger, ed. *Critical Essays on Geoffrey Chaucer* (*SAC* 22 [2000], no. 154), pp. 59–81. In *KnT,* Chaucer questions force as a basis for government. Conquest "dissolves voluntary social bonds" and fails to produce the consent necessary to a good society. An agent of force, Theseus uses rhetoric to control others, and his final speech is "loose reasoning." Arcite's body is a locus in which the deleterious effects of conquest are evident.

193. Hallissy, Margaret. "Writing a Building: Chaucer's Knowledge of the Construction Industry and the Language of the *Knight's Tale.*" *ChauR* 33 (1998): 239–59. A close reading of passages in *KnT* reveals Chaucer's close familiarity with the medieval construction industry. Although Chaucer supervised building rather than creating buildings, as a poet, he is supreme master over his own creative process.

194. Ingham, Patricia Clare. "Homosociality and Creative Masculinity in the *Knight's Tale.*" In Peter G. Beidler, ed. *Masculinities in Chaucer: Approaches to Maleness in the* Canterbury Tales *and* Troilus and Criseyde (*SAC* 22 [2000], no. 96), pp. 23–35. Examines masculine suffering and Theseus's stoic masculinity, particularly how it demands the suffering of the ruler's soldiers and the sorrowing of women. Concludes that the *Tale* depicts Theseus's creative power as specifically masculine.

195. O'Brien, Timothy D. "Fire and Blood: 'Queynte' Imaginings in Diana's Temple." *ChauR* 33 (1998): 157–67. In *KnT,* Chaucer's use of the word "queynte," the dying and quickening fires in the temple, and the spurting and spewing of the flames to "suggest parturition, life's uncertainty and tenuousness and even menstruation." Emelye's tears at the sight of the fires may indicate her "elemental fear of entry" into a world in which these aspects are a part.

196. Park, Youngwon. "Providence and the Planetary Gods in the *Knight's Tale.*" *MES* 6 (1998): 163–95. *KnT* reveals a providential pattern that is both Boethian and Pauline—"all things work together for the good." The gods of the *Tale* are pagan, but the outcome of the story shows Christian Providence.

197. Stein, Robert M. "The Conquest of Femenye: Desire, Power, and Narrative in Chaucer's *Knight's Tale.*" In James J. Paxson and Cynthia A. Gravlee, eds. *Desiring Discourse: The Literature of Love, Ovid Through Chaucer* (*SAC* 22 [2000], no. 141), pp. 188–205. As the Miller refuses to allow easy closure to *KnT,* so the *Tale*'s opening is rooted in the uneasy conquest of Femenye. Throughout the *Tale,* patterns that suggest resolution fail to reach their hoped-for conclusion, indicating the ongoing nature of desire and conflict.

See also nos. 9, 63, 70, 93, 118, 179, 184, 185, 199, 204, 267.

CT—The Miller and His Tale

198. Blum, Martin. "Negotiating Masculinities: Erotic Triangles in the *Miller's Tale.*" In Peter G. Beidler, ed. *Masculinities in Chaucer: Approaches to Maleness in the* Canterbury Tales *and* Troilus and Criseyde (*SAC* 22 [2000], no. 96), pp. 37–52. John, Nicholas, and Absolon are, each in his own way, feminized in *MilT,* while Alison is masculinized and thereby escapes punishment.

199. Boyd, David Lorenzo. "Seeking 'Goddes Pryvete': Sodomy, Quitting, and Desire in *The Miller's Tale.*" In Peter S. Baker and Nicholas Howe, eds. *Words and Works: Studies in Medieval English Language and Literature in Honour of Fred C. Robinson* (*SAC* 22 [2000], no. 95), pp. 243–60. In medieval tradition, sodomy was associated with misinterpretation. When seen in this light, Absolon's sodomizing of Nicholas in *MilT* both reinforces traditional heteronormativity and decries the system upon which it is based. The Miller's reference to "Goddes pryvete" (*MilP* 1.3164) is part of his rebellion against the Knight and the order he embodies.

200. Daniels, Richard. "Textual Pleasure in the *Miller's Tale.*" In James J. Paxson, Lawrence M. Clopper, and Sylvia Tomasch, eds. *The Performance of Middle English Culture: Essays on Chaucer and the Drama in Honor of Martin Stevens* (*SAC* 22 [2000], no. 142), pp. 111–23. In *MilT,* Chaucer transformed a bawdy joke into pleasing narrative art, producing in the sexual scenes moments when a reader might feel *jouissance.* Includes some notes toward a materialist reading of the *Tale* as a representation of the poetic and narrative structures that make up *CT* as a whole.

201. Dove, Debra Magai. "Violence at the Borders in Early English Literature." *DAI* 59 (1998): 1175A. Violence, induced by the impermissible crossing of borders, involves clashing social codes and evokes varying attitudes: *Beowulf* authorizes it; *Juliana* opposes it; *Sir Gawain and the Green Knight* and *MilT* develop its ambiguities. *Sir Gawain* poses a "reading lesson," while *MilT* shows emotion in conflict with reason to challenge the audience's view of morality.

202. Mack, Peter, and Chris Walton, eds. *Geoffrey Chaucer: The Miller's Tale.* Oxford Student Editions. Oxford: Oxford University Press, 1995. viii, 167 pp. Textbook edition of the Miller's sketch from *GP, MilPT,* and *RvP,* including glosses and discursive notes, and a discussion of "approaches" to the works—sources and analogues, character analysis, assessment of theme and topic, and analysis of poetic technique. Includes basic contextual materials (6 b&w illus., summaries of two analogous tales, etc.) and suggestions for classroom activities and discussion.

203. Novelli, Cornelius. "Sin, Sight, and Sanctity in the *Miller's Tale:* Why Chaucer's Blacksmith Works at Night." *ChauR* 33 (1998): 168–75. The blacksmith is an ambiguous figure. Medieval blacksmiths often worked at night because the temperature was cooler, but ordi-

nances forbade them to do so. Furthermore, although the medieval blacksmith was a symbol of the devil, he was also a symbol of the preacher and of St. Gervasius, who restored sight to the blind. In *MilT,* a burlesque preacher has left a burlesque penitent, Absolon, spiritually blind.

204. Taylor, Paul Beekman. "Translating Spiritual to Corporeal in the Dusk of the *Miller's Tale.*" In Paul Beekman Taylor. *Chaucer Translator* (*SAC* 22 [2000], no. 57), pp. 39–50. Reads *MilT* as a dim, worldly "eschatological drama" in which providential order is turned to disorder and "spiritual grace to secular disgrace." Analyzes various words and details ("ba," "stone," the ring, etc.), the concern with Noah's Flood, and the activities in the darkness, arguing that *MilT* "translates" the Knight's high ideals to a "comedy of errors" and reduces spiritual secrets to mundane deception.

See also nos. 5, 100, 111, 128, 165, 185, 197.

CT—The Reeve and His Tale

205. Finlayson, John. "Of Leeks and Old Men: Chaucer and Boccaccio." *SN* 70 (1998): 35–39. *RvP* is a psychological study of the bitterness and frustrations of old age, as well as a quiting of the Miller. Chaucer borrowed the leek–old age simile from Boccaccio's *Decameron* and adapted it to his own purpose. The simile is not proverbial.

206. Pigg, Daniel F. "Performing the Perverse: The Abuse of Masculine Power in the *Reeve's Tale.*" In Peter G. Beidler, ed. *Masculinities in Chaucer: Approaches to Maleness in the* Canterbury Tales *and* Troilus and Criseyde (*SAC* 22 [2000], no. 96), pp. 53–61. Connects the violence implicit in the performance of the *Tale* with physical violence and argues that *RvT* portrays the perversion of masculine power.

See also nos. 117, 185.

CT—The Cook and His Tale

207. Kang, Ji-Soo. "The (In)completeness of the *Cook's Tale.*" *MES* 5 (1997): 145–70. Explores medieval theories of narrative closure in Matthew of Vendome, Geoffrey of Vinsauf, Brunetto Latini, and John of Garland to argue that if "inconclusiveness" is a thematic goal, the end

of a work is the "natural place to accent it." As an ending to the degenerative movement of Fragment 1, *CkT* is an appropriate conclusion to several thematic patterns: characterization of females, male competition, geography, social strata, and the theme of love and courtesy.

CT—The Man of Law and His Tale

208. Barefield, Laura D. "Reproducing the Past: Gender and History in Later Middle English Romance and Popular Chronicle." *DAI* 59 (1999): 2489A. At the crux of chronicle and romance, Geoffrey of Monmouth's *Historia* provides much of the basis for later literature. The work emphasizes women not only as child bearers but also as speakers who could uphold or deny legitimacy. Barefield discusses Nicholas Trevet, Mary of Woodstock, *MLT,* the prose *Brut,* and *Sir Gawain and the Green Knight.*

209. Breeze, Andrew. "The Celtic Gospels in Chaucer's *Man of Law's Tale.*" *ChauR* 33 (1998): 335–38. The "Britoun book, written with Evaungiles," on which Constance's false accuser swears before being struck dead, is likely to have been a Latin gospel book illuminated in Celtic. Such a book (like the Gospel of Gildas) was said to have the power to shorten the life of anyone convicted of perjury.

210. Bullón-Fernández, María. "Engendering Authority: Father and Daughter, State and Church in Gower's 'Tale of Constance' and Chaucer's 'Man of Law's Tale.'" In R. F. Yeager, ed. *Re-Visioning Gower* (*SAC* 22 [2000], no. 164), pp. 129–46. In Gower's version of the Constance story, incest is a metaphor for the relationship between the Church and the crown, a means to critique the two. In contrast, *MLT* "tries to avoid suggesting any tension between lay and clerical power."

211. Goldstein, R. James. "'To Scotlond-ward His Foomen for to Seke': Chaucer, the Scots, and the *Man of Law's Tale.*" *ChauR* 33 (1998): 31–42. Because Chaucer's work is almost free of references to things Scottish, his mention of Scottish footmen in *MLT* stands out as a pointed reference to contemporary relations between the English and the Scots and posits Henry IV as "another Alla" who would put the Scots in their "proper place."

212. Landman, James. "Proving Constant: Torture and *The Man of Law's Tale.*" *SAC* 20 (1998): 1–39. In *MLT,* the torment of Constance is explicitly linked with the judicial torture of Alla's messenger. A notion of a "single, certain truth" underlies the concern with torture in the

Tale, also reflected in the attitude toward fiction expressed in *MLP* and threatened by the inscrutability of women in *MLT.* Landman surveys medieval English legal attitudes toward torture and argues that the Man of Law is a "particularly appropriate narrator" who subscribes to a "logic of torture." *MLT* reflects this logic more clearly than *SNT* or *ClT.*

213. Nolan, Maura Bridget. "Past Imagined, Future Retold: English Poetry, 1350–1450." *DAI* 60 (1999): 123A. The poetry of the age demonstrates the construction and manipulation of history, while popular culture reflects the changing relations of ruler and laws. Thus "Wynnere and Wasture" treats the 1352 Statute of Treasons. Chaucer's *MLT,* a poetic revision of history, showed his successors (especially Lydgate) the means of assimilating ever-changing political situations.

214. Reed, Teresa P. "Shadows of the Law: Chaucer's *Man of Law's Tal*e, Exemplarity and Narrativity." *Mediaevalia* 21 (1997): 231–48. Parallels between Mary and Constance exist not only in details but also in narrative strategy, since both women are subject to the complexities and contradictions of the exemplary mode. In addition, Constance is presented through metaphors of death, revealing the limits of law and the Man of Law's narrative capacity.

See also nos. 53, 100, 117, 146, 157, 161, 184, 185.

CT—The Wife of Bath and Her Tale

215. Biebel, Elizabeth M. "The Lion, the Lady, and the Curtain: Alisoun's Transformation under Feminist Criticism." *DAI* 59 (1998): 1564A. Feminist criticism has changed perceptions of the Wife of Bath. Feminist critics perceive her not as a superficial and "garish caricature" of womanhood but as a serious person attempting to establish her identity, rejecting antifeminist tradition, interpreting masculine monopoly of the written word, and then providing a message on queenship. Explores pedagogical uses of *WBPT.*

216. ———. "A Wife, a Batterer, a Rapist: Representations of 'Masculinity' in the *Wife of Bath's Prologue* and *Tale.*" In Peter G. Beidler, ed. *Masculinities in Chaucer: Approaches to Maleness in the* Canterbury Tales *and* Troilus and Criseyde (*SAC* 22 [2000], no. 96), pp. 63–75. *WBT* reveals the Wife's idealized vision of society. The *Tale* answers her society's gender inequities, which victimize both men and women, by de-

picting a world wherein ultimately women and men are recognized as individuals.

217. Bowers, Robert. "The Frame Is the Thing: Gower and Chaucer and Narrative Entente." *InG* 19 (1998): 31–39. Awareness of narratological levels helps us understand differences in intent in Gower and Chaucer. Comparison of Gower's "Tale of Florent" and Chaucer's *WBT* illustrates these differences. Overall, Gower has a purpose and achieves closure; Chaucer conceals his purpose and evades closure. With *Ret,* Chaucer "is just beginning what Gower has ended" (38).

218. Choi, Yejung. "Sermon and Wycliffite Thought in the Wife of Bath." *MES* 5 (1997): 171–200 (in Korean). Links between *WBP* and Wycliffite thought indicate that Chaucer was sympathetic to the movement.

219. Heffley, Sylvia Patricia. "Lovers and Their Critics: The Medieval Marriage and Sexuality Debates." *DAI* 59 (1999): 3446A. Although Christian marriage was well defined by theologians in the twelfth through the thirteenth centuries, the proper role of sexuality remained debatable, as shown in the west portal of Senlis Cathedral, in Jean de Meun's introduction of the subject into vernacular literature in *Roman de la Rose,* and in Chaucer's varying treatment in *WBP* and *WBT.*

220. Rivera, Alison Bucket. "Motherhood in the *Wife of Bath.*" *SELIM* 6 (1996): 103–16. Considers medieval family structures, attitudes toward sexuality, and marital practices to argue that the Wife of Bath "almost definitely had no children." Unlike Margery of Kempe, she may have been sterile.

221. Salla, Sandra M. "Disappearing Fairies in the *Wife of Bath's Tale.*" *Mediaevalia* 21 (1997): 281–93. In *WBT,* the first mention of fairies—the Wife's lament for their disappearance—is linked to and introduces the other fairy scenes. The knight's experience demonstrates that even in her first mention of fairies the Wife associates them with happiness, sexual satisfaction, and education—notions supported by numerous medieval ballads and romances.

222. Seaman, Myra. "Speech In/Action: Gender and Discourse in Medieval English Romance." *DAI* 59 (1998): 1156A. Medieval romance generally assumes that action is inherently a masculine activity and speech feminine, with both supporting patriarchy. Various English romances examine these assumptions (sometimes ambiguously). *WBT* employs them to subvert not only the clichés of romance and chivalry but also the values of patriarchy itself.

223. Tinkle, Theresa. "The Wife of Bath's Textual/Sexual Lives." In George Bornstein and Theresa Tinkle, eds. *The Iconic Page in Manuscript, Print, and Digital Culture.* Ann Arbor: University of Michigan Press, 1998, pp. 55–88. Despite Chaucer's efforts to create a stable "poetic self-fashioning," *WBPT* takes different forms in its different redactions in the Hengwrt and Ellesmere manuscripts and in Thynne's 1532 edition. The textual variants of the manuscripts, especially the so-called added passages of *WBP,* and the glosses to the manuscripts reflect how open the text was. Thynne's version of the Wife "manifests the hegemonics" of his literary tradition.

See also nos. 6, 9, 35, 48, 53, 54, 56, 58, 63, 98, 118, 128, 133, 134, 146, 149, 157, 163, 169, 173, 176, 179, 180, 184, 186, 188.

CT—The Friar and His Tale

224. Godfrey, Mary P. "Only Words: Cursing and the Authority of Language in Chaucer's *Friar's Tale.*" *Exemplaria* 10 (1998): 307–28. Psychoanalytic argument that the old woman's curses are pivotal to the workings of hostility, manipulation, and eroticism in *FrT.* The summoner, the devil, and the woman reenact a patriarchal version of the Oedipal scenario, disrupted by the woman's appropriation of masculine discourse in her own defense.

225. Jost, Jean E. "Ambiguous Brotherhood in the *Friar's Tale* and *Summoner's Tale.*" In Peter G. Beidler, ed. *Masculinities in Chaucer: Approaches to Maleness in the* Canterbury Tales *and* Troilus and Criseyde (*SAC* 22 [2000], no. 96), pp. 77–90. Analyzes the fraternal and potentially sexual attraction between the Friar and the Summoner by focusing on Chaucer's conception of brotherhood and the male relationships in *FrPT* and *SumPT.*

226. Kline, Daniel T. "'Myne by Right': Oath Making and Intent in *The Friar's Tale.*" *PQ* 77 (1998): 271–93. Assesses the scenes of swearing and oath making in *FrT,* arguing that the *Tale* is not only a theological exemplum but also a reflection of "cultural anxiety concerning the nature of changing social and economic relations as mediated by new forms of legal alliance that were superseding traditional feudal relationships." The summoner fails to recognize that legal, contractual relations do not banish the hierarchy of theology.

CT—The Summoner and His Tale

227. Lim, Hye-Soon. "'Glosyng' in 'The Summoner's Tale.'" *MES* 6 (1998): 199–223 (in Korean, with English abstract). Deriving from the Greek word for "tongue" and from Scandinavian "superficial luster," "glosing" is the central notion of *SumT.* Chaucer uses it to disclose fraternal hypocrisy and distortion of Scripture.

228. Olson, Glending. "On the Significance of Saint Simon in the *Summoner's Tale.*" *ChauR* 33 (1998): 60–65. The reference to "Symoun" alludes not to Simon Magus (as previously suggested) but to Simon the Apostle, whose connections with sin and confession advance some of the larger themes of *SumT.*

See also nos. 40, 225.

CT—The Clerk and His Tale

229. Aers, David. "Faith, Ethics, and Community: Reflections on Reading Late Medieval English Writing." *JMEMS* 28 (1998): 341–69. Argues that Griselda of *ClT* is not a type of Christ, because not all depictions of human suffering imitate Christ's passion. Texts by authors from Aquinas to Wycliffe, Arundel, and William Thorpe indicate that passive suffering is one of many competing models of faith, suggesting that Chaucer's religious tales may not affirm unquestioning faith and obedience.

230. Ashton, Gail. "Patient Mimesis: Griselda and the *Clerk's Tale.*" *ChauR* 33 (1998): 232–38. Griselda's response to Walter at crucial points in the narrative—when he has "killed" her children and when he has banished her from the palace so he can take another "wife"—underscores his appalling behavior and demonstrates the ways outward patience is "confoundingly deceptive."

231. Ginsberg, Warren. "Petrarch, Chaucer and the Making of the Clerk." In James J. Paxson, Lawrence M. Clopper, and Sylvia Tomasch, eds. *The Performance of Middle English Culture: Essays on Chaucer and the Drama in Honor of Martin Stevens* (*SAC* 22 [2000], no. 142), pp. 125–41. Assesses how the Host's address to the Clerk reflects effort to shape the identity of the Clerk as a tale teller, so that even before the Clerk speaks, literary, philosophical, and spiritual discourses compete to define his subjectivity.

232. Godorecci, Barbara J. "Re-Writing Griselda: Trials of the Grey Battle Maiden." *RLAn* 8 (1996): 192–96. Assesses the modifications of Boccaccio's tale of Griselda (*Decameron* 10.10) in the translations of Petrarch and Chaucer, focusing on the uses and nuances of the verb "provare" (to prove) and its associations with "probus" (good). In *ClT,* Chaucer's uses of "assaye," "tempte," and "preve" subtly reorient the meaning of the narrative.

233. Harding, Wendy. "Griselda's 'Olde Coote' and Textual Variance." *Chaucer Yearbook* 5 (1998): 187–92. Examines *ClT* 911–17 and concludes that, because of textual ambiguities, it is difficult to know whether Griselda has physically changed upon returning to her former home or, as Harding seems to believe, her "olde coote" is no longer fit to be worn.

234. ———. "Griselda's 'Translation' in the *Clerk's Tale.*" In Roger Ellis, René Tixier, and Bernd Weitemeier, eds. *The Medieval Translator/ Traduire au Moyen Âge,* vol. 6. [Turnhout, Belgium]: Brepols, 1998, pp. 194–210. Assesses Chaucer's transformation of *ClT* in his process of translating his sources, focusing on the imagery of clothing. Through his alterations of the clothing motif, Chaucer disclaims the traditional notion that translation is merely superficial change and makes the story his own.

235. McClellan, William. "A Postmodern Performance: Counter-Reading Chaucer's *Clerk's Tale* and Maxine Hong Kingston's 'No Name Woman.'" In James J. Paxson, Lawrence M. Clopper, and Sylvia Tomasch, eds. *The Performance of Middle English Culture: Essays on Chaucer and the Drama in Honor of Martin Stevens* (*SAC* 22 [2000], no. 142), pp. 183–96. Both *ClT* and Kingston's "No Name Woman" reveal how patriarchal culture operates to disguise male complicity in women's repression, and both connect issues of knowledge and power with the construction of subjectivity, showing how these are intimately tied up with the construction of sexual difference. The Clerk takes issue with Petrarch's religious moral that erases gender, and argues that clerks—the class that controls knowledge—choose not to tell of women's suffering and forbearance. Kingston tells the story despite familial collusion in her father's desire to erase her aunt's existence.

236. McKinley, Kathryn L. "The *Clerk's Tale:* Hagiography and the Problematics of Lay Sanctity." *ChauR* 33 (1998): 90–111. The concept of piety was complex and problematic during the Middle Ages, and Chaucer's refusal to align himself with one side or the other in *ClT* is

distressing. Griselda is neither a paradigm for lay sanctity nor an ironic or satiric character.

237. Newman, Florence. "The Man with Two Wives: Female Rivalry and Social Power in a Medieval Motif." *Cygne* 2 (1996): 19–22. An abstract of a paper that considers *ClT* and Petrarch's version of the Griselda tale in comparison with *Laxdaela Saga* and Marie de France's *Le Fresne.* In all, the central female figure "possesses a greater value than may at first appear."

238. Newton, Allyson. "The Occlusion of Maternity in Chaucer's *Clerk's Tale.*" In John Carmi Parsons and Bonnie Wheeler, eds. *Medieval Mothering.* New York and London: Garland, 1996, pp. 63–77. Classical and medieval theories of sexual reproduction privilege the male role as active and occlude the female as passive. This occlusion is paralleled by the plot and language of *ClT,* in which mothering is subordinated to paternalistic concerns with lineage.

239. Paris, Bernard J. "'The Clerk's Tale.'" Chapter 5 in *Imagined Human Beings: A Psychological Approach to Character and Conflict in Literature.* New York and London: New York University Press, 1997, pp. 82–92. Psychoanalyzes Walter of *ClT* as one who tests Griselda's submissiveness to assure his own freedom and to vindicate his choice of her as a wife. Griselda seeks personal glory in her subservience. They are "two sick people in a pathological relationship, and Chaucer seems aware of this."

See also nos. 93, 161, 176, 184, 186, 188, 212.

CT—The Merchant and His Tale

240. Baker, Joan, and Susan Signe Morrison. "The Luxury of Gender: *Piers Plowman* and *The Merchant's Tale.*" *YLS* 12 (1998): 31–63. *MerT* is a direct response to passus 9 of the B version of *Piers Plowman,* presenting an "unkyndely similitude" of marriage in contrast to the ideal expressed in Langland's poem.

241. Everest, Carol A. "Sight and Sexual Performance in the *Merchant's Tale.*" In Peter G. Beidler, ed. *Masculinities in Chaucer: Approaches to Maleness in the* Canterbury Tales *and* Troilus and Criseyde (*SAC* 22 [2000], no. 96), pp. 91–103. From the perspective of medieval psychology, January's pretensions to youth and sexual vigor are ridiculous and

potentially fatal, since his sexual overactivity diminishes vital spirits and, among other effects, causes blindness and eventually death.

242. Lucas, Angela M. "The Mirror in the Marketplace: Januarie through the Looking Glass." *ChauR* 33 (1998): 123–45. January's comparison of looking for a bride to reflections in a mirror evokes associations of limited and distorted vision, of two-dimensional representations, and of reversals of left and right. This image of "imperfect vision" is reflected in January's own blindness and in his misperception of May in *MerT.*

See also nos. 8, 54, 56, 118, 176, 184, 188.

CT—The Squire and His Tale

243. Stubblefield, Jay. "A Note on Spenser's *Faerie Queene IV* and Chaucer's *Squire's Tale.*" *ELN* 36.1 (1998): 9–10. Suggests that Spenser was influenced by the structure of *SqT* as well as by its subject matter.

See also nos. 61, 69–71, 179.

CT—The Franklin and His Tale

244. Gravlee, Cynthia A. "Presence, Absence, and Difference: Reception and Deception in *The Franklin's Tale.*" In James J. Paxson and Cynthia A. Gravlee, eds. *Desiring Discourse: The Literature of Love, Ovid through Chaucer* (*SAC* 22 [2000], no. 141), pp. 177–87. Argues that the "horizon of expectations" (a concept derived from Hans Jauss) of *FranT* is never fulfilled by the narrative. Although the Franklin strives to meet social and generic expectations, he leaves his *Tale* open-ended—Chaucer's means of encouraging his readers to seek beyond the limited assumptions of his narrator.

245. Lipton, Emma. "'Affections of the Mind': The Politics of Marriage in Late Medieval English Literature." *DAI* 60 (1999): 123A. Influenced by literature, the meaning of marriage changed radically in late-medieval England. Replacing the celebration of celibacy as reflecting union with Christ, earthly marriage validated itself in bourgeois ideology, as shown by *FranT,* Gower, the "Mary Plays from the N-Town Cycle," and Margery Kempe.

246. Purdon, Liam O., and Julian N. Wasserman. "The Franklin,

Food, and the Freemen of York." *ChauR* 33 (1998): 112–15. Chaucer's somewhat unusual association of his Franklin with food may reflect the frequent migration of the Exchequer from Westminster to York and the prioritizing of the York food trade as a result. The Franklin may have been a York franklin who profited from the frequent moves.

247. Rossi-Reder, Andrea. "Male Movement and Female Fixity in the *Franklin's Tale* and *Il Filocolo.*" In Peter G. Beidler, ed. *Masculinities in Chaucer: Approaches to Maleness in the* Canterbury Tales *and* Troilus and Criseyde (*SAC* 22 [2000], no. 96), pp. 105–16. Like Boccaccio in *Il Filocolo,* Chaucer in *FranT* contrasts men and women by emphasizing men's mobility and women's fixity. Men are depicted as publicly and physically active, while women are privately and intellectually active.

248. Wright, Michael J. "Isolation and Individuality in the *Franklin's Tale.*" *SN* 70 (1998): 181–86. *FranT* is set in a pre-Christian age, but Dorigen prays to God and thus achieves the status of a good pagan. She is portrayed as an individual rather than a socially rule-bound wife. Chaucer celebrates individuality through her, but he also recognizes the social and personal cost resulting from that individuality.

See also nos. 8, 54, 63, 69, 70, 110, 176, 179, 184, 188.

CT—The Physician and His Tale

249. Kline, Daniel Thomas. "'My Sacrifice with Thy Blood': Violence, Discourse, and Subjectivity in the Representation of Children in Middle English Literature." *DAI* 58 (1998): 3125A. Works such as *Pearl, PhyT, PrT,* and Lydgate's *Siege of Thebes* present children as transgressive social agents whom society represses through ill treatment to stabilize traditional hierarchies.

See also no. 250.

CT—The Pardoner and His Tale

250. Burger, Glenn. "Doing What Comes Naturally: The *Physician's Tale* and the Pardoner." In Peter G. Beidler, ed. *Masculinities in Chaucer: Approaches to Maleness in the* Canterbury Tales *and* Troilus and Criseyde (*SAC* 22 [2000], no. 96), pp. 117–30. The actions of the Host and the Pardoner in Fragment 6 connect *PhyT* and *PardT* and their re-

spective tellers, bringing "the male body into view to an extent not seen elsewhere" in *CT.* The fragment's representation of gendered bodies sheds "the harshest possible light [on] the oppressive force of the essentialized gender system lying behind medieval politics."

251. Little, Katherine Clover. "Reading for Christ: Interpretation and Instruction in Late Medieval England." *DAI* 59 (1999): 5136A. Examines Wycliffite sermons and the opposing views of William Thorpe and Nicholas Love to compare Lollard and orthodox views of narrative and of the individual. Chaucer's awareness of the conflict, his refusal to take sides, and the futility of claiming absolute truth are revealed in *PardPT.*

252. Pedrosa, José. "Existe el Hipercuento?: Chaucer, una leyenda andaluza y la historia de el tesoro fatal (AT 763)." *Revista de Poética Medieval* 2 (1998): 195–223. Explores analogues to *PardT,* including sixteenth- and seventeenth-century Spanish versions. Focuses on a modern Andalusian legend from Priego de Córdoba.

253. Saito, Isamu. "The Old Man in *The Pardoner's Tale.*" *English Studies in Doshisha University* 67 (1996): 1–25. Compares the old man and the three rioters in *PardT,* reading the old man as an Everyman figure with the problem of old age as he searches for permission from God to be penitent.

See also nos. 8, 12, 14, 58, 134, 136, 157, 180.

CT—The Shipman and His Tale

254. Beidler, Peter G. "Contrasting Masculinities in the *Shipman's Tale:* Monk, Merchant, and Wife." In Peter G. Beidler, ed. *Masculinities in Chaucer: Approaches to Maleness in the* Canterbury Tales *and* Troilus and Criseyde (*SAC* 22 [2000], no. 96), pp. 131–42. Compares *ShT* with *Decameron* 8.1 to assess the negative and positive characteristics of masculinity portrayed in the monk and merchant of the *Tale.* The wife is given traits identified with men in the Middle Ages, perhaps because of the *Tale*'s original assignment to the Wife of Bath.

CT—The Prioress and Her Tale

255. Caspi, Mishael M., with Debra Snyder. "The Respected Oral Tradition Which Promoted the Calumny of the Jews." In Mishael M.

Caspi, ed. *Oral Tradition and Hispanic Literature: Essays in Honor of Samuel G. Armistead.* New York and London: Garland, 1995, pp. 81–109. Because of oral anti-Jewish tales of blood libel, *PrT,* in attitude and some details, was for Chaucer's audience a familiar account. *PrT* and the ballad "The Jew's Daughter" (first recorded in the eighteenth century) indicate how literary and oral accounts interacted to produce medieval anti-Semitism.

256. Hanawalt, Barbara A. "Narratives of a Nurturing Culture: Parents and Neighbors in Medieval England." *EMS* 12 (1995): 1–21. Examines various fourteenth- and fifteenth-century historical and literary texts to demonstrate that law and tradition encouraged parental and communal responsibility for the proper raising of children. Mentions *PrT* and the hagiography of Hugh of Lincoln.

257. Johnson, Willis Harrison. "Between Christians and Jews: The Formation of Anti-Jewish Stereotypes in Medieval England." *DAI* 59 (1998): 917A. Anatomizes the development of anti-Jewish sentiments in medieval England, arguing that the prejudices of Chaucer and his late-medieval contemporaries, which returned to traditional, exegetical stereotypes, were less malicious than those of the thirteenth century.

258. Kaplan, Philip Benjamin. "We All Expect a Gentle Answer: 'The Merchant of Venice,' Antisemitism, and the Critics." *DAI* 59 (1999): 3465A. Defines anti-Semitic art as any work that employs pejorative stereotypes about Jews without repudiating them. Focuses on Shakespeare's *Merchant of Venice* but also considers *PrT* and Marlowe's *The Jew of Malta.*

259. Maleski, Mary A. "The Culpability of Chaucer's Prioress." *Chaucer Yearbook* 5 (1998): 41–60. Debates whether Chaucer's Prioress is childlike or simply childish, and questions why she is on a pilgrimage. Also discusses the extent of Chaucer's understanding of medieval religious women.

260. Russell, J. Stephen. "Song and the Ineffable in the *Prioress's Tale.*" *ChauR* 33 (1998): 176–89. By electing not to include the exact text of *O Alma Redemptoris Mater* (of which there were several versions) in *PrT,* Chaucer forces the audience to think through issues of verbal prayer vs. prayers of the heart that express the intent behind the spoken words.

261. Tejera Llano, Dionisia. "The Matter of Israel: The Use of Little Children in the Miracles of the Holy Virgin during the Middle Ages." *SELIM* 5 (1996): 7–17. Compares *PrT* with Gonzalo de Berceo's

thirteenth-century "Judiezno" (Little Jewish Child) from his *Los Milagros de Nuestra Señora.* Featuring a Jewish child who has a vision of Mary, Berceo's tale reflects a more tolerant attitude toward Jews than does Chaucer's. The attitude in Berceo's tale is consistent with Spanish social history.

See also nos. 27, 59, 129, 134, 162, 173, 249.

CT—The Tale of Sir Thopas

262. Cohen, Jeffrey Jerome. "Diminishing Masculinity in Chaucer's *Tale of Sir Thopas.*" In Peter G. Beidler, ed. *Masculinities in Chaucer: Approaches to Maleness in the* Canterbury Tales *and* Troilus and Criseyde (*SAC* 22 [2000], no. 96), pp. 143–55. One of the dominant themes of Fragment 7 of *CT* is the "gendering of male bodies." The theme plays out through the shrinking masculinity of Thopas and the absence of menacing sexuality in his encounter with Olifaunt. It parallels the diminution of masculine threat in Chaucer's fictional accounts of rape and in the accusation of rape against Chaucer himself.

263. Wright, Glenn. "Modern Inconveniences: Rethinking the Parody in 'The Tale of Sir Thopas.'" *Genre* 30 (1997): 167–94. Examines biographical, textual, and comparative approaches to *Th* to show how dependent they are on modern notions of author and text. Argues that medieval textuality and authorship pose methodological problems for understanding *Th* as parody, a genre that postdates the poem.

See also nos. 101, 158.

CT—The Tale of Melibee

264. Hartman, Roland. "Boethian Parallels in the *Tale of Melibee.*" *ES* 79 (1998): 166–70. Suggests a clear parallel between Boethius and Melibee: both have suffered an injustice, which is seen as a symptom of an illness that has to be cured and that has moved them away from God to where Fortune rules. They are thus subjected to punishment and correction from God.

265. Moore, Stephen Gerard. "A Shifting Paradigm: The Act of Reading Actors in Medieval Allegorical Narrative." *DAI* 59 (1998): 2014A. Readers of medieval allegory look for meaning but find themselves obliged by many factors to revise their interpretations. Even the literal sense proves highly complex, seeming to shift as it develops, so that readers must reconsider. Moore analyzes *Mel,* various works by Henryson, and *Piers Plowman* (B text, passus 18) from this perspective.

266. Rubey, Daniel. "The Five Wounds of Melibee's Daughter: Transforming Masculinities." In Peter G. Beidler, ed. *Masculinities in Chaucer: Approaches to Maleness in the* Canterbury Tales *and* Troilus and Criseyde (*SAC* 22 [2000], no. 96), pp. 157–71. Places *Mel* in the context of Richard II and his detractors in the 1380s and 1390s and examines the competing kinds of masculinity in the *Tale* as argued by Prudence and allegorized in the character of Sophie.

See also nos. 18, 19, 41, 118, 158, 176, 184, 262.

CT—The Monk and His Tale

267. Sharp, Michael D. "Reading Chaucer's 'Manly Man': The Trouble with Masculinity in the *Monk's Prologue* and *Tale*." In Peter G. Beidler, ed. *Masculinities in Chaucer: Approaches to Maleness in the* Canterbury Tales *and* Troilus and Criseyde (*SAC* 22 [2000], no. 96), pp. 173–85. *MkT* critiques secular masculinity, represented by the Host and the Knight; their comments about the *Tale* disclose more about themselves than about the *Tale* or its teller. Against these two figures, the "Monk remains a figure of resistance."

268. Taylor, Paul Beekman. "Redressing Nero's Array." In Paul Beekman Taylor. *Chaucer Translator* (*SAC* 22 [2000], no. 57), pp. 105–18. Assesses Chaucer's alterations of his sources (Jean de Meun and Boethius) in the Nero account of *MkT.* Through selection and emphasis, especially emphasis on clothing, Chaucer "forges a link between the emperor's name and his deeds," associating Nero with knitting (Latin *nere*) and cutting (French *nairon*). In Chaucer, Nero's name is his fortune.

269. Wenzel, Siegfried. "Why the Monk?" In Peter S. Baker and Nicholas Howe, eds. *Words and Works: Studies in Medieval English Language and Literature in Honour of Fred C. Robinson* (*SAC* 22 [2000], no. 95), pp. 261–69. Surveys attempts to explain how *MkT* is appropriate to the Monk as teller, and cites examples from monastic preaching of

associations of "the monastic profession and an interest in historical examples of misfortune."

See also nos. 19, 41, 129.

CT—The Nun's Priest and His Tale

270. Finlayson, John. "The 'Povre Widwe' in the *Nun's Priest's Tale* and Boccaccio's *Decameron.*" *NM* 99 (1998): 269–73. The vivid details of *Decameron* 7.3 (the story of Friar Rinaldo)—the corrupt clergy, their obesity and sweating faces, their rich foods and wine, together with the simplicity of the widow's life—suggest that Boccaccio's work may have inspired *NPT* as a pointed satire of the clergy's failure (especially the Monk's) to meet the needs of lay people.

271. Mooney, Linne R. "'A Woman's Reply to Her Lover' and Four Other New Courtly Love Lyrics in Cambridge, Trinity College MS R.3.19." *MÆ* 67 (1998): 235–56. Prints the lyric "My lefe ys faren in a lond," referred to by Chaucer in *NPT* 7.2879.

272. Pearsall, Derek. "Strangers in Late-Fourteenth-Century London." In F. R. P. Akehurst and Stephanie Cain Van D'Elden, eds. *The Stranger in Medieval Society* (*SAC* 22 [2000], no. 92), pp. 46–62. Explores the nuances of "strange" and "stranger" in Middle English, arguing that noncitizens, immigrants from the provinces, and merchants were considered strangers in London. Comments on the 1381 massacre of Flemings and Chaucer's allusion to it (*NPT* 7.3394–97).

273. Thomas, Paul R. "'Have Ye No Mannes Herte?': Chauntecleer as Cock-Man in the *Nun's Priest's Tale.*" In Peter G. Beidler, ed. *Masculinities in Chaucer: Approaches to Maleness in the* Canterbury Tales *and* Troilus and Criseyde (*SAC* 22 [2000], no. 96), pp. 187–202. Differences between *NPT* and *Roman de Renart* indicate how Chaucer's *Tale* depicts a mock-heroic masculinity through its scenes with the cock and the hen and the cock and the fox, as well as in the chase scene.

274. Travis, Peter W. "Reading Chaucer *Ab Ovo:* Mock-*Exemplum* in the *Nun's Priest's Tale.*" In James J. Paxson, Lawrence M. Clopper, and Sylvia Tomasch, eds. *The Performance of Middle English Culture: Essays on Chaucer and the Drama in Honor of Martin Stevens* (*SAC* 22 [2000], no. 142), pp. 161–81. In the opening of *NPT,* Chaucer investigates the exemplary form, both honoring the aesthetic persuasion of Geoffrey of Vinsauf and of Horace and—through parody—undercutting prescrip-

tive notions that narrative must have a predominant sense and readers' expectations that it will.

275. Zeitoun, Franck. "Le rêve prophétique dans le *Conte du Prêtre de Nonnains.*" In Leo Carruthers, ed. *Rêves et prophéties au Moyen Âge* (*SAC* 22 [2000], no. 104), pp. 99–112. The dissonant echoes within and between Chauntecleer's dream narrative and the subsequent *disputatio* prevent any clear idea of the veracity of the dream's apparently prophetic nature. In the confrontation between the cock and the fox, the dogmatism of the characters makes mutual understanding impossible. *NPT* throws light on Chaucer's humanistic viewpoint, revealed here as a belief in human free will.

See also nos. 9, 110, 118, 121, 125, 152, 290.

CT—The Second Nun and Her Tale

276. Arthur, Karen. "Equivocal Subjectivity in Chaucer's *Second Nun's Prologue* and *Tale.*" *ChauR* 32 (1998): 217–31. Chaucer's choice of this version of the saint's life allows him to portray the interests of a female teller and to fuse masculine and feminine ideals. We hear Cecilia's strident voice and experience her powers of articulation. Further, the hair shirt under the golden robe suggests that she conforms overtly while continuing her self-assertion.

277. Børch, Marianne. "Chaucer's 'Second Nun's Tale': Record of a Dying World." *Chaucer Yearbook* 5 (1998): 19–40. Views *SNT* as a "generic experiment" built "upon an epistemological premise whose axiomatic status was crumbling." Discusses analogical, hermeneutical, and hagiographic elements of the *Tale* as well.

See also nos. 18, 59, 163, 173, 212.

CT—The Canon's Yeoman and His Tale

278. Abraham, Lyndy. *A Dictionary of Alchemical Imagery.* Cambridge: Cambridge University Press, 1998. xii, 249 pp.; 50 b&w figs. Alphabetical arrangement of alchemical terms and images from "ablution" to "zephyr." The entries define the terms and illustrate the images, citing works in which they appear, including *CYPT.*

279. Landman, James H. "The Laws of Community, Margery

Kempe, and the 'Canon's Yeoman's Tale.'" *JMEMS* 28 (1998): 389–425. Both *CYPT* and *The Book of Margery Kempe* raise questions about community and selfhood. In each, an individual criticizes his or her community to the members of a different, markedly less local community. The two texts suggest the precariousness of individual and community self-definitions, and their tensions complicate the distinction between "medieval" and "modern," suggesting the possibility of a distinctly "late medieval" selfhood.

See also no. 157.

CT—The Manciple and His Tale

See nos. 27, 118, 125, 152, 169, 181.

CT—The Parson and His Tale

See nos. 41, 105, 117, 118, 176, 190, 336.

CT—Chaucer's Retraction

See nos. 53, 134, 217.

A Treatise on the Astrolabe

280. Eisner, Sigmund. "Chaucer as a Teacher." *CLAQ* 23 (1998): 35–39. Suggests that Chaucer "creates a persona from his son (Lewis Chaucer) to be the initial audience" of *Astr* and argues that Chaucer's prose style is pedagogic, written to be easily understood by children.

281. Laird, Edgar. "Astrolabes and the Construction of Time in the Late Middle Ages." *Disputatio* 2 (1997): 51–69. Considers *Astr* and three other treatises on the astrolabe, exploring what they reflect about medieval notions of time. The treatises describe practical uses of the astrolabe, and they also describe operations that had ethical and moral implications. However, they do not speculate about the nature of cosmic time, as do theoretical treatises. Laird claims that "lyte Lowis" was not Chaucer's only intended audience.

See also nos. 18, 55, 71, 88, 89, 158.

Boece

282. Johnson, Ian. "Placing Walton's Boethius." In Maarten J. F. M. Hoenen and Lodi Nauta, eds. *Boethius in the Middle Ages: Latin and Vernacular Traditions of the* Consolatio Philosophiae (*SAC* 22 [2000], no. 122), pp. 217–42. Helps clarify the place and meaning of John Walton's translation of Boethius's *Consolatione Philosophiae* (1410) by contrasting it with Chaucer's *Bo.*

See also nos. 44, 122, 161, 188, 264.

The Book of the Duchess

283. Bolens, Guillemette, and Paul Beekman Taylor. "The Game of Chess in Chaucer's *Book of the Duchess.*" *ChauR* 33 (1998): 325–34. At the beginning of *BD,* the Black Knight has an inaccurate conception of how chess is played. The misconception must be corrected by the narrator as the poem progresses and before the castle bell strikes midday and the game, the hunt, and the poem all end.

284. Jember, Gregory K. "Two Notes on Chaucer and Cultural Tradition." *InG* 19 (1998): 1–17. In *BD* and *HF,* Chaucer uses the "symplegades" or "clashing rocks" motif, which is related to the "Cliff of Death" theme in Germanic literature, as identified by Donald K. Fry. However, in Chaucer's texts, the motif reflects the "polarity between knowledge and ignorance" (17) rather than movement between life and death. Chaucer's concern with boundaries places him in a "liminal tradition" (1).

285. Palmer, R. Barton. "Rereading Guillaume de Machaut's Vision of Love: Chaucer's *Book of the Duchess* as *Bricolage.*" In David Galef, ed. *Second Thoughts: A Focus on Rereading.* Detroit: Wayne State University Press, 1998, pp. 169–95. Argues that in reading *BD* medieval audiences would also have reread Machaut's *Fonteinne Amoureuse* and recalled other works by Chaucer's predecessor. Chaucer's derivative version of the account of Seys and Alcyone "thematizes the story as a rereading," and, drawn from sections in Machaut spoken by women, the Black Knight's complaints feminize him, a radical "translation."

286. Steinberg, Glenn. "Idolatrous Idylls: Protestant Iconoclasm, Spenser's *Daphnäida,* and Chaucer's *Book of the Duchess.*" In Theresa M. Krier, ed. *Refiguring Chaucer in the Renaissance* (*SAC* 22 [2000], no. 73),

pp. 128–42. Reads Spenser's *Daphnäida* as a "refiguration and response" to *BD,* modified by Spenser's Protestant outlook. Compares and contrasts the two poems, considering tone, idiom, and faith in the ability of art to console.

287. Thundy, Zacharias P. "The Dreame of Chaucer: Boethian Consolation or Political Celebration?" *CarmP* 4 (1995): 91–109. Suggests that as an example of several kinds of prophetic dream described by Macrobius, as an expression of wish fulfillment, and on the authority of Thynne, *BD* should be called "The Dream of Chaucer." Argues that the poem was probably recited for the last time in celebration of the ascendancy of Henry IV and that it existed in several versions, the last version dated 1399. Cites to support the date the reference to Gaunt as "seynt John" and an identification of the king of the chess game as Henry.

288. Yvernault-Gamaury, Martine. "Le rêve révélateur dans *Le livre de la Duchesse* de Chaucer: Étude des mécanismes de la révélation." In Leo Carruthers, ed. *Rêves et prophéties au Moyen Âge* (*SAC* 22 [2000], no. 104), pp. 69–98. Focuses on the function of reality and fiction in Chaucer's *BD* as influenced by Ovid, Boccaccio's *Amorosa visione,* Guillaume de Machaut's *Dit de la Fonteinne Amoureuse,* and *Jugement du roy de Behaigne.* Topics include the relations among sight, vision, and illusion; the nature of oral exchanges (narrative, dialogue, confession, revelation); and how staging represents the vision and its images. The Black Knight's experience gradually awakens his poetic potential and a more perceptive vision of the truth of human living.

See also nos. 31, 80, 103, 118, 127, 137, 150, 152, 158.

The House of Fame

289. Boitani, Piero. "Un'Idea Inglese della Manica nel Medioevo." *Rivista di Letterature Moderne e Comparate* 51 (1998): 251–69. Uses the "chunnel" as a metaphor of the literary and cultural interconnections between England and the European continent, assessing classical and medieval influences on *HF:* Virgil, Ovid, and Claudian, along with medieval writers of Italy, France, and Spain.

290. Brewer, Melody Light. "Chaucer's *House of Fame* as a Menippean Satire on the Philosophical/Theological Ideas of the Fourteenth Century." *DAI* 59 (1999): 4136A. The clash of realist Thomistic Christianity (Dante) and nominalism (Ockham) provides the basis of Chau-

cer's exuberant satire on philosophy, linguistics, classical tradition, the state of the church, and other late-fourteenth-century issues. *HF* contrasts with treatment of the same matter in *TC* (serious) and *NPT* (comic).

291. Choi, Yejung. "An Apology of Poetry: Chaucer's Poetics in *The House of Fame.*" *MES* 6 (1998):131–61 (in Korean, with English abstract). In *HF,* Chaucer defends poetry, indicating that despite its fictional nature and relativity, poetry is as valid as theology or philosophy.

292. Klitgård, Ebbe. "Chaucer's Narrative Voice in the *House of Fame.*" *ChauR* 33 (1998): 260–66. Chaucer writes in a "highly literate cultural code of poetry," which reveals the evolving persona of the poet. It is possible that he read *HF* aloud in installments and that the original ending—reflecting, no doubt, some crisis at court—was subsequently lost.

293. Martin, Carol A. N. "Authority and the Defense of Fiction: Renaissance Poetics and Chaucer's *House of Fame.*" In Theresa M. Krier, ed. *Refiguring Chaucer in the Renaissance* (*SAC* 22 [2000], no. 73), pp. 40–65. Assesses the presentation of *HF* in Speght's edition as an example of "Renaissance uneasiness" with the poem. Explains this uneasiness by contrasting *HF* with Sidney's *Apologie for Poetrie* (and Boccaccio's *Genealogie deorum gentilium libri*), arguing that Chaucer's rhetoric-based and "paradox-oriented" poetics differ from Sidney's more confident and philosophical theory of poetry.

294. McTurk, Rory. "Chaucer and Giraldus Cambrensis." *LeedsSE* 29 (1998): 173–83. Several studies have suggested Chaucer's indebtedness to works by Giraldus Cambrensis. Comparison of passages from the *Topographia Hibernie* and *HF* support the claim that Chaucer used this particular Latin source.

295. Meecham-Jones, Simon. "'Betwixen Hevene and Erthe and See': Seeing Words in Chaucer's *House of Fame.*" In Neil Thomas and Françoise Le Saux, eds. *Unity and Difference in European Cultures.* Durham Modern Language Series. Durham, N.C.: University of Durham, 1998, pp. 155–71. *HF* is a response to the "creative anxiety inherent in seeking to continue a literary inheritance believed to have already reached its highest peaks of achievement." In his presentation of a desert landscape, Chaucer partially resists Continental models and indicates that English is outside the "impermeable" system of European language and culture.

See also nos. 18, 19, 113, 137, 153, 158, 165, 284.

The Legend of Good Women

296. Aloni, Gila. "Brèches et murs élevés dans *La légende de Thisbé.*" *BAM* 53 (1998): 33–34. Explores the metaphoric and symbolic value of walls and gaps in the Thisbe account in *LGW.*

297. ———. "Le rêve de femmes vertueuses de Chaucer." In Leo Carruthers, ed. *Rêves et prophéties au Moyen Âge* (SAC 22 [2000], no. 104), pp. 53–68. Examines the allegorical purpose of *LGWP,* assessing the dream structure and the importance of the dreamer's awakening at the end of the G version. The poet grants the notion of authority its due place and appears to submit to it, while at the same time seeking a way to override it, symbolically at least. Chaucer thus creates a new kind of space—at once dreamlike and realistic.

298. Crane, Susan. "Maytime in Late Medieval Courts." *New Medieval Literatures* 2 (1998): 159–79. Suggests that "maying" shapes participants' sexuality, thereby furthering the "ritual's enactment of social status." Uses *LGW* as an example of the mirroring of human qualities in the natural world.

299. Kim, Chong-Ai. "Gower's Good Women: *Confessio Amantis.*" *MES* 5 (1997): 59–82 (in Korean). Compares the treatment of women in *Confessio Amantis* and *LGW.* In each case, the frame of the poem and the male-authored perspective disallow true praise of women.

300. Mahoney, Dhira B. "Middle English Rendering of Christine de Pizan." In Douglas Kelly, ed. *The Medieval "Opus": Imitation, Rewriting, and Transmission in the French Tradition.* Amsterdam and Atlanta: Rodopi, 1996, pp. 405–27. Discusses medieval English translations of Christine's works, focusing on Hoccleve's translation of *L'Epistre au Dieu d'Amours.* Also considers the influence of *LGW* on Hoccleve's translation.

301. Percival, Florence. *Chaucer's Legendary Good Women.* Cambridge: Cambridge University Press, 1998. xii, 338 pp. Chaucer's *LGW* testifies to the disparate views of women prevalent in the Middle Ages. A complex medieval notion of Woman informs the structure of the poem: in the *Prologue,* Chaucer praises conventional ideas of female virtue, while in the legends he shows a humorous skepticism, apparently influenced by contemporary antifeminist traditions. The debate Chaucer promotes could be relied on to entertain many medieval readers, while at the same time demonstrating how the vernacular translator-poet could handle language wittily and play with authoritative texts. A close

reading of the poem in light of literary, historical, political, and social texts.

302. Simpson, James. "Ethics and Interpretation: Reading Wills in Chaucer's *Legend of Good Women*." *SAC* 20 (1998): 73–100. Reads *LGW* as a work about "voluntarist" hermeneutics, reflected in Cupid's "cupidinous," tyrannical understanding of *TC* and in the narrator's telling of the legends as a "testamentary document of a dying author." Modeled on Ovid's *Heroides*, *LGW* represents the suppression of authorship by interpretive aggressiveness, suggesting a need for readers to be aware of the validity of an author's intent as well as their own.

See also nos. 65, 100, 129, 137, 138, 148, 162.

The Parliament of Fowls

303. Cooney, Helen. "The *Parlement of Foules:* A Theodicy of Love." *ChauR* 33 (1998): 339–76. *PF* offers an example of Chaucer's intertextuality. The two "olde bokys" mentioned—Macrobius's commentary on *Somnium Scipionis* and Alain de Lille's *De planctu naturae*—inform the themes of suffering in love and the limitations of natural law in the poem.

304. Krier, Theresa M. "The Aim Was Song: From Narrative to Lyric in *The Parlement of Foules* and *Love's Labours Lost*." In Theresa M. Krier, ed. *Refiguring Chaucer in the Renaissance* (*SAC* 22 [2000], no. 73), pp. 165–88. *PF* and *Love's Labours Lost* develop similar relations between lyrics and poetic or dramatic narratives. Shakespeare emulated Chaucer's movement from narrative to song—a psychoanalytic release from courtly or social constraint into "cosmic, creative eros."

305. Mukai, Tsuyoshi. "Richard Pynson's 1526 Edition of *The Parliament of Fowls*." *Poetica* (Tokyo) 49 (1998): 49–62. Pynson's (1526?) edition of *PF* was the first printed version of the poem to establish the text from multiple sources. The copy text seems to have been of the δ subgroup of group B manuscripts, closest to Bodleian Library MS Bodley 638, and perhaps corrected against a manuscript that underlies the later (1530) edition supervised by Robert Copland for Wynken de Worde.

306. Smarr, Janet. "The *Parlement of Foules* and *Inferno* 5." *ChauR* 33 (1998): 113–22. Like *Inferno* 5, *PF* contains references to Earthly Paradise and Hell, the dream, and the fate of those who attend to private

lusts. Dante compares the plight of souls to that of several kinds of birds, including three of the four bird categories in *PF.* The descriptions of the lovers painted on the wall in the Venus temple contain six additional names derived from *Inferno* 5, and like Dante's narrator, Chaucer's "I" is only an observer.

See also nos. 18, 81, 93, 118, 137, 150, 153, 158.

Troilus and Criseyde

307. Andretta, Helen Ruth. *Chaucer's* Troilus and Criseyde: *A Poet's Response to Ockhamism.* New York: Peter Lang, 1998. viii, 240 pp. *TC* is a poetic response to several aspects of Ockhamism, the philosophy of William of Ockham. He claimed that all truths are probable; that man's [sic] reasoned truth can be in conflict with revealed truth; that man is vulnerable to the whims of his Creator in his quest for salvation; that man can merit salvation without God's grace; that God foresees the actions of men and predestines or reprobates them according to this knowledge; and that universals, including love, goodness, justice, and mercy, are only concepts in the mind, not realities.

308. Brewer, Derek. "Troilus's 'Gentil' Manhood." In Peter G. Beidler, ed. *Masculinities in Chaucer: Approaches to Maleness in the* Canterbury Tales *and* Troilus and Criseyde (*SAC* 22 [2000], no. 96), pp. 237–52. According to Chaucer's conception of "manhood," as distinct from the somewhat anachronistic term "masculinity," Troilus is to be seen as "manly" and virtuous in his behavior, as well as worthy of the reader's sympathy. He is an "idealized and idealistic" example of a young man in the kind of society in which he lives.

309. Brody, Saul N. "Making a Play for Criseyde: The Staging of Pandarus's House in Chaucer's *Troilus and Criseyde.*" *Speculum* 73 (1998): 115–40. Assesses Pandarus's house and its literary functions in light of architectural details of fourteenth-century houses such as the *privy, stewe,* and *trappe* and in relation to conventions of medieval dramatic staging. Pandarus, leading Troilus through the trap, may be reminiscent of stage devils emerging from hell. Pandarus acts as director and author of the scene, while Criseyde serves as the audience.

310. Cigman, Gloria. "The Seasons in Late Medieval Literature: Mutability and Metaphors of Good and Evil." *ÉA* 51 (1998): 131–42.

Depictions of the seasons in late-medieval literature are loci for considerations of good and evil, mutability and human responsibility. The conventional representations of the seasons are reversed in *Sir Gawain and the Green Knight,* the Townley Nativity play, Chaucer's *TC,* and Henryson's *Testament of Cresseid:* spring brings sorrow, and winter brings hope.

311. Dietrich, Stephanie. "'Slyding' Masculinity in the Four Portraits of Troilus." In Peter G. Beidler, ed. *Masculinities in Chaucer: Approaches to Maleness in the* Canterbury Tales *and* Troilus and Criseyde (*SAC* 22 [2000], no. 96), pp. 205–20. The characterization of the male hero in the four portraits of Troilus exhibits "gender slippage" through "linguistic slippage." The second and third portraits show Chaucer subverting gender assumptions, while the other two are more "essentialized" depictions of masculinity.

312. DiMarco, Vincent. "'Renewing' *Troilus,* 1.890–96: *Si Erravit Scriptor, Debes Corrigere, Lector.*" *Chaucer Yearbook* 5 (1998): 61–78. Attempts to "rehabilitate the status and reputation of lines 1.890–96," which some authorities have viewed as an insertion that breaks the continuity of Pandarus's encomiums for Criseyde. Starting from the supposition that these lines were composed by the poet on a separate slip of paper or written somewhere in the margin, DiMarco suggests that Chaucer intended the lines to follow, rather than precede, *TC* 1.897–903.

313. Dobbs, Elizabeth A. "Seeing through Windows in Chaucer's *Troilus.*" *ChauR* 33 (1998): 400–22. *TC* contains a series of images of windows both open and closed, which are added to (or changed from) Chaucer's sources and which provide a commentary on the relationships between the lovers. Views out of windows are limited views, or "fictions," representing and summarizing one meaning of the poem.

314. Gasse, Rosanne. "Deiphebus, Hector, and Troilus in Chaucer's *Troilus and Criseyde.*" *ChauR* 33 (1998): 422–39. In *TC,* Deiphebus serves as an important foil to Troilus. He exposes Troilus not only as weak and inadequate but also as human, something Hector is not.

315. Hanning, Robert W. "The Crisis of Mediation in Chaucer's *Troilus and Criseyde.*" In James J. Paxson, Lawrence M. Clopper, and Sylvia Tomasch, eds. *The Performance of Middle English Culture: Essays on Chaucer and the Drama in Honor of Martin Stevens* (*SAC* 22 [2000], no. 142), pp. 143–59. In *TC,* the narrator and Pandarus are mediators—purveyors of desired commodities (women or love stories) to a desig-

nated recipient (Troilus; the audience assembled for the occasion). Hanning examines the "crisis of mediation" of late-medieval translators in relation to the poem's problematic presentation of desire.

316. Jimura, Akiyuki. "An Approach to the Language of Criseyde in Chaucer's *Troilus and Criseyde.*" In Jacek Fisiak and Akio Oizumi, eds. *English Historical Linguistics and Philology in Japan* (*SAC* 22 [2000], no. 115), pp. 91–110. A revised, abridged version of three previous essays: see *SAC* 17 (1995), no. 257 (parts 1 and 2), and *SAC* 19 (1997), no. 306 (part 3).

317. Kawasaki, Masatoshi. "Chaucer's Mutability Topos: The *Troilus* and Boethius." *JBAL* 33 (1998): 1–11 (in Japanese). Assesses the importance of Troilus's apotheosis, emphasizing Chaucer's debt to Boethius and considering the poet's uses of juxtaposition and his fusion of classical and medieval ideas.

318. Kaylor, Noel Harold, Jr. "The Influence of Boethius and Dante upon Chaucer's *Troilus and Criseyde.*" *MES* 5 (1997): 83–105. The influence of Boethius and Dante "gives shape and universal meaning" to *TC.* The operation of Fortune and her wheel, the four "Classical cardinal emotions," Dante's three spiritual realms, and the code of knighthood are evident in the deep structure of the narrative.

319. Keller, Kimberly Anne. "Recognition and Regression in Chaucerian Love Poetry." *DAI* 60 (1999): 122A. A psychoanalytic, Lacanian study of the lover's complaint reveals the fragmented lover as seeking at once wholeness through recognition of his "trouthe" by the lady and union with her. Treats lovers' fantasies and failures in *TC,* Lydgate, Hoccleve, and Chaucerian apocrypha.

320. McInerney, Maud Burnett. "'Is This a Mannes Herte?': Unmanning Troilus through Ovidian Allusion." In Peter G. Beidler, ed. *Masculinities in Chaucer: Approaches to Maleness in the* Canterbury Tales *and* Troilus and Criseyde (*SAC* 22 [2000], no. 96), pp. 221–35. Chaucer plays with Ovid's *Metamorphoses* in his characterization of Troilus in book 3, examining the nature of masculinity by depicting Troilus as a "man trapped between two literary modes of loving."

321. Moore, Marilyn L. Reppa. "Assumptions of Gender: Rhetoric, Devotion, and Character in Chaucer's *Troilus and Criseyde.*" *DAI* 58 (1998): 2644A. Rejects psychological characterizations of Troilus and Criseyde, arguing that they are better seen in light of rhetorical and devotional traditions. Associates Troilus with the ethos of petition and devotion and Criseyde with the pathos.

322. Moore, Marilyn Reppa. "Who's Solipsistic Now? The Character of Chaucer's Troilus." *ChauR* 33 (1998): 43–59. Troilus's character should be viewed not in the light of medieval romance but within the context of medieval "devotion," such as that advocated in Saint Anselm's *Proslogion.* It is more important to realize that Troilus learned to love with constancy than to know that his love affair ended badly.

323. Papka, Claudia Rattazzi. "Transgression, the End of Troilus, and the Ending of Chaucer's *Troilus and Criseyde.*" *ChauR* 33 (1998): 267–81. Chaucer refuses to allow closure in *TC,* either for Troilus or for the poem itself. For Chaucer, transgression is inevitable, closure is impossible, and the poet seems to "celebrate" this fact.

324. Paxson, James J. "The Semiotics of Character, Trope, and Troilus: The Figural Construction of the Self and the Discourse of Desire in Chaucer's *Troilus and Criseyde.*" In James J. Paxson and Cynthia A. Gravlee, eds. *Desiring Discourse: The Literature of Love, Ovid through Chaucer* (*SAC* 22 [2000], no. 141), pp. 206–26. Reads *TC* as "an autocritique of the sophisticated rhetorical devices used by medieval poets to create the literature of desire." Examines several instances of apostrophe, pragmapoeia, ethopoeia, and sermocinatio in the poem, exploring relations between human language and noise or emotive utterance and arguing that Chaucer uses devices often associated with allegory.

325. Reale, Nancy M. "Reading the Language of Love: Boccaccio's *Filostrato* as Intermediary between the *Commedia* and Chaucer's *Troilus and Criseyde.*" In James J. Paxson and Cynthia A. Gravlee, eds. *Desiring Discourse: The Literature of Love, Ovid through Chaucer* (*SAC* 22 [2000], no. 141), pp. 165–76. In *TC,* Chaucer poses a tension between "Boccaccio's interest in the persuasive powers of linguistic skills to create private realities" and Dante's depiction of poetry as a means to transcendent enlightenment. This tension makes *TC* a poem "that appears to speak against itself."

326. Rigg, A. G. "Calchas, Renegade and Traitor: Dares and Joseph of Exeter." *N&Q* 243 (1998): 176–78. Outlines the history of the defection of Calchas from Troy to the Greeks as found in Latin narratives that predate *TC.*

327. Sanok, Catherine. "Criseyde, Cassandre, and the *Thebaid:* Women and the Theban Subtext of Chaucer's *Troilus and Criseyde.*" *SAC* 20 (1998): 41–71. Explores the allusions to Statius's *Thebaid* in *TC* and identifies several structural similarities between the poems. Criseyde's reading of the epic and Cassandre's summary of it depict female con-

sciousness of history and awareness of the significance of martial violence. In some ways like both Amphiaraus and Hypsipyle of the *Thebaid,* and linked genealogically with "*both* sides of the Theban war," Criseyde reflects the poignancy of historical contingency.

328. Sanyal, Jharna. "The Reader as Author: Influence of Anxiety?" *Indian Journal of American Studies* 23.1 (1993): 65–74. Discusses *TC,* Henryson's *Testament of Cresseid,* Shakespeare's *Troilus and Cressida,* and Dryden's *Troilus and Cressida, or Truth Found Too Late,* arguing that each treatment of Criseyde reflects how its author responds to literary tradition. In these "Criseyde-texts," she is the primary object of interpretation, the "axis round which the life-world of the texts revolve."

329. Silar, Theodore I. "An Analysis of the Legal Sense of the Word *Fin* (*Finalis Concordia*) in *Piers Plowman, Sir Gawain and the Green Knight,* Chaucer's Works and Especially the Ending of *Troilus and Criseyde.*" *ChauR* 33 (1998): 284–309. The repetition of "fin" (the settlement of a fictitious suit) at the ending of *TC* has many legal overtones. It evokes "landholding," "harmonization of contrary positions," and "legal fiction," as in a legal suit for which there is, as in *TC,* a "preordination," a "foreknowledge of the outcome."

330. Wetherbee, Winthrop. "Dante and the Poetics of *Troilus and Criseyde.*" In Thomas C. Stillinger, ed. *Critical Essays on Geoffrey Chaucer* (*SAC* 22 [2000], no. 154), pp. 243–66. An analysis of the end of *TC* that reads Troilus's ascent (itself inherently meaningless) as a stage in the progress of the narrator's recognition of the relations between Christian poetry and classical tradition. Dante mediates Chaucer's engagement with the classics; in particular, the transformation of Chaucer's narrator at the end of *TC* parallels Dante's transformation of Statius from pagan to Christian poet. Wetherbee provides close reading of parts of the end of *TC.*

331. Wilson, E. "The Sense of 'Directe' in Chaucer's *Troilus* V.1856: A Correction." *N&Q* 243 (1998): 24–27. The word *directe* has been taken to mean "to dedicate," and critics have assumed that the poem was dedicated to Gower. But "ye loveres," Gower and Strode, are sent the poem for correction, especially in morals and philosophy. The word *directe* means "to direct, address," a sense Chaucer would have come across in his bureaucratic affairs.

332. Yoshiko, Kobayashi. "Chivalry, Power, and Justice in Three Medieval Romances." *DAI* 58 (1998): 3144A. Argues that Benoît de Sainte-Maure's *Roman de Troie* is a critique of chivalry; Chaucer in *TC*

and Gower in *Confessio Amantis* adapted the subversive message of their predecessor to comment negatively on the Hundred Years' War and its consequences.

See also nos. 18, 21, 27, 28, 36, 59, 72, 74, 99, 101, 103, 113, 118, 127, 137, 148, 150, 153, 169, 185, 290, 302.

Lyrics and Short Poems

See no. 103.

An ABC

See no. 59.

The Complaint of Chaucer to His Purse

333. Prendergast, Thomas A. "Politics, Prodigality, and the Reception of Chaucer's 'Purse.'" In William F. Gentrup, ed. *Reinventing the Middle Ages and the Renaissance: Constructions of the Medieval and Early Modern Periods.* Arizona Studies in the Middle Ages and the Renaissance, no. 1. [Turnhout, Belgium]: Brepols, 1998, pp. 63–76. Surveys "legends" about Chaucer's prodigality, from Thomas Usk's *Testament of Love* to early editions of *Purse* and modern critical reception of the poem. Editions of the poem and critical responses to it seek to defend Chaucer "from charges of political opportunism," casting him variously as a prodigal, a "'pure' unsullied poet," and a "self-serving though loyal subject."

Chaucerian Apocrypha

334. Boffey, Julia, and A. S. G. Edwards. "'Chaucer's Chronicle,' John Shirley, and the Canon of Chaucer's Shorter Poems." *SAC* 20 (1998): 201–18. Assesses John Shirley's role in construction of the canon of Chaucer's shorter poems, using as test cases three poems attributed to Chaucer by Shirley but not by modern tradition: "The Chronicle [of Nine Women] Made by Chaucer" (Bodleian Library MS Ashmole 59) and "The Balade of a Reeve" and "The Plowman's Song" (British Library MS Additional 16165). Modern editors reject the three, seemingly because of muddled details or obscenity. However, Shirley's attributions

and the relations of the poems to *LGW* and *CT* should encourage editors to recognize that the evidence for attributing most of the shorter poems is indeterminate. Includes an edition of each of the three poems.

335. Costomiris, Robert. "Bodleian MS Tanner 346 and William Thynne's Edition of Clanvowe's 'Cuckoo and the Nightingale.'" *The Library,* 6th ser., 20 (1998): 99–117. Uses correspondences between the Tanner text of Clanvowe's poem and that printed in Thynne's 1532 edition of Chaucer to argue that Thynne's dependence on this manuscript was greater than scholars have avowed.

336. Taylor, Andrew. "The Curious Eye and the Alternative Endings of *The Canterbury Tales.*" In Paul Budra and Betty A. Schellenberg, eds. *Part Two: Reflections on the Sequel.* Toronto, Buffalo, and London: University of Toronto Press, 1998, pp. 34–52. Reads the *Tale of Beryn* and Lydgate's *Seige of Thebes* as acts of resistance to Chaucer's dissolution of his fiction in the meditation that is *ParsT.* These continuations of *CT* seek to keep alive the drama of *CT* through visualization, a form of *curiositas* that shares features with the visualization necessary for successful meditation.

See also nos. 27, 62, 108, 156, 169, 319.

The Romaunt of the Rose

337. Spreuwenberg-Stewart, Allison Dean. "The Representation of Clothing in Renaissance Poetry: The Material of Desire." *DAI* 58 (1998): 3542A. Considers issues of gender, identity, and sexuality in depictions of clothing in poetry by Chaucer (*Rom*), Marlowe, Donne, Samuel Butler, and Milton. Through dress, *Rom* depicts the richness of desire and the roles of art and culture in both seduction and natural beauty.

See also nos. 80, 103.

Book Reviews

338. Aers, David, and Lynn Staley. *The Powers of the Holy: Religion, Politics, and Gender in Late Medieval English Culture* (*SAC* 21 [1999], no. 244). Rev. T. L. Burton, *ES* 78 (1998): 565–66; Jo Ann McNamara,

TMR, Mar. 8, 1998; H. L. Spencer, *RES,* n. s., 49 (1998): 349–51; Nicholas Watson, *SAC* 20 (1998): 219–22.

339. Akehurst, F. R. P., and Stephanie Cain Van D'Elden, eds. *The Stranger in Medieval Society* (*SAC* 22 [2000], no. 92). Rev. Cynthia Ho, *TMR,* 2 Nov., 1998.

340. An, Sonjae (Brother Anthony). *Literature in English Society Before 1660. Volume 1: The Middle Ages* (*SAC* 22 [2000], no. 94). Rev. Yoon Minwoo, *MES* 5 (1997): 301–7 (in Korean).

341. Arn, Mary-Jo, ed. *"Fortunes stabilnes": Charles of Orléans's English Book of Love* (*SAC* 19 [1997], no. 76). Rev. Helen Phillips, *Journal of the Early English Book Society* 1 (1997): 158–61.

342. ———, ed. *Medieval Food and Drink* (*SAC* 19 [1997], no. 77). Rev. Evelyn Mullally, *Journal of the Early English Book Society* 1 (1997): 154.

343. Ashby, Cristina, Geoff Couldrey, Susan Dickson, et al., developers. *Chaucer: Life and Times CD-ROM* (*SAC* 19 [1997], no. 3). Rev. Michael Delahoyde, *RMR* 52.2 (1998): 75–77.

344. Astell, Ann W. *Chaucer and the Universe of Learning* (*SAC* 20 [1998], no. 112). Rev. Paul Beekman Taylor, *SAC* 20 (1998): 226–29.

345. ———. *Job, Boethius, and Epic Truth* (*SAC* 18 [1996], no. 72). Rev. Daniel J. Pinti, *TMR,* May 16, 1995.

346. Baswell, Christopher. *Virgil in Medieval England: Figuring the* Aeneid *from the Twelfth Century to Chaucer* (*SAC* 19 [1997], no. 292). Rev. Ralph Hexter, *TMR,* Mar. 3, 1996; Richard Thomas, *TMR,* Mar. 2, 1996; Barbara Nolan, *MP* 96 (1998): 65–69.

347. Beer, Jeanette, ed. *Translation Theory and Practice in the Middle Ages* (*SAC* 21 [1999], no. 83). Rev. Joan Tasker Grimbert, *TMR,* Feb. 6, 1998.

348. Beidler, Peter G., ed. *Geoffrey Chaucer:* The Wife of Bath (*SAC* 20 [1998], no. 165). Rev. Michael Calabrese, *TMR,* Aug. 1, 1996.

349. Benson, Larry D. *Contradictions: From Beowulf to Chaucer.* Andersson, Theodore M., and Stephen A. Barney, eds. (*SAC* 19 [1997], no. 78). Rev. Ebbe Klitgård, *ES* 78 (1998): 90–91.

350. Bisson, Lillian M. *Chaucer and the Late Medieval World* (*SAC* 22 [2000], no. 99). Rev. Steven Rigby, *TMR,* Oct. 8, 1998.

351. Blamires, Alcuin. *The Case for Women in Medieval Culture* (*SAC* 21 [1999], no. 85). Rev. Leo Carruthers, *ÉA* 51.1 (1998): 85; Gloria Cigman, *RES,* n. s., 49 (1998): 348–49.

352. ———, ed., with Karen Pratt and C. W. Marx. *Woman De-*

famed and Woman Defended: An Anthology of Medieval Texts (*SAC* 16 [1994], no. 68). Rev. Lesley Smith, *TMR,* May 9, 1995.

353. Brewer, Derek. *A New Introduction to Chaucer,* 2d ed. (*SAC* 22 [2000], no. 102). Rev. Hélène Dauby, *BAM* 54 (1998): 70–72.

354. Burnley, David. *Courtliness and Literature in Medieval England* (*SAC* 22 [2000], no. 103). Rev. Claes Schaar, *ES* 78 (1998): 472–73.

355. Burrow, J. A., and Thorlac Turville-Petre. *A Book of Middle English,* 2d ed. (*SAC* 20 [1998], no. 68). Rev. Neil Cartlidge, *NM* 99 (1998): 230–32.

356. Calabrese, Michael A. *Chaucer's Ovidian Arts of Love* (*SAC* 18 [1996], no. 34). Rev. Teresa Kennedy, *TMR,* Feb. 12, 1997.

357. Calin, William. *The French Tradition and the Literature of Medieval England* (*SAC* 18 [1996], no. 35). Rev. Ardis Butterfield, *MÆ* 67 (1998): 144–45; Judith Weiss, *YES* 28 (1998): 299–300.

358. Cohen, Jeffrey Jerome, and Bonnie Wheeler, eds. *Becoming Male in the Middle Ages* (*SAC* 21 [1999], no. 92). Rev. Laurie Finke, *TMR,* Feb. 11, 1998.

359. Coleman, Joyce. *Public Reading and the Reading Public in Late Medieval England and France* (*SAC* 20 [1998], no. 72). Rev. J. P. Conlan, *Journal of the Early Book Society* 1 (1997): 150–51; Joel T. Rosenthal, *TMR,* July 3, 1997; Kristen Mossler Figg, *JEGP* 97 (1998): 236–39; Richard Firth Green, *SAC* 20 (1998): 237–40.

360. Cooper, Helen. *The Canterbury Tales,* 2d ed. (Oxford Guides to Chaucer) (*SAC* 20 [1998], no. 113). Rev. Richard Newhauser, *JEGP* 97 (1998): 418–20.

361. Cox, Catherine S. *Gender and Language in Chaucer* (*SAC* 21 [1999], no. 97). Rev. D. Burnley *N&Q* 243 (1998): 488–89; James M. Dean, *MFN* 26 (1998): 33–35; Robert S. Sturges, *TMR,* July 10, 1998.

362. Craun, Edwin D. *Lies, Slander, and Obscenity in Medieval English Literature: Pastoral Rhetoric and the Deviant Speaker* (*SAC* 21 [1999], no. 98). Rev. Siegfried Wenzel, N&Q 243 (1998):106–7.

363. Dean, James M. *The World Grown Old in Later Medieval Literature* (*SAC* 21 [1999], no. 100). Rev. André Crépin, *ÉA* 51 (1998): 338–39; Míceál Vaughn, *YLS* 12 (1998): 189–94; Lawrence Warner, *TMR,* Jan. 9, 1998.

364. Delany, Sheila. *The Naked Text: Chaucer's* Legend of Good Women (*SAC* 18 [1996], no. 265). Rev. Nicola F. McDonald, *TMR,* Sept. 2, 1995; Kathryn L. Lynch, *Chaucer Yearbook* 4 (1997): 98–102;

Juliette Dor, *Archiv* 235 (1998): 415–17; R. W. Frank, *Speculum* 73 (1998): 502–4; Peter Travis, *MFN* 26 (1998): 49–52.

365. DeLooze, Laurence. *Pseudo-Autobiography in the Fourteenth Century: Juan Ruiz, Guillaume de Machaut, Jean Froissart, and Geoffrey Chaucer* (*SAC* 21 [1999], no. 260). Rev. J. A. Burrow, *N&Q* 243 (1998): 487–88; George D. Greenia, *TMR,* June 11, 1998; Hans R. Runte, *FR* 72 (1999): 748–49.

366. Dillon, Janette. *Geoffrey Chaucer* (*SAC* 17 [1995], no. 84). Rev. L. Anne Clark Doherty, *Chaucer Yearbook* 4 (1997): 108–10.

367. Evans, Ruth, and Lesley Johnson, eds. *Feminist Readings in Middle English Literature: The Wife of Bath and All Her Sect* (*SAC* 18 [1996], no. 86). Rev. Anne Clark Bartlett, *TMR,* Oct. 2, 1995; Jennifer Summit, *MFN* 25 (1998): 63–66.

368. Farrell, Thomas J., ed. *Bakhtin and Medieval Voices* (*SAC* 19 [1997], no. 94). Rev. James J. Paxson, *SAC* 20 (1998): 249–56.

369. Ferster, Judith. *Fictions of Advice: The Literature and Politics of Counsel in Late Medieval England* (*SAC* 20 [1998], no. 77). Rev. Lorraine Attreed, *TMR,* Dec. 1, 1996; Derek Pearsall, *SAC* 20 (1998): 256–59.

370. Fisher, John H. *The Importance of Chaucer* (*SAC* 16 [1994], no. 35). Rev. Paul R. Thomas, *Chaucer Yearbook* 4 (1997): 111–15; Mary Blockley, *MP* 96.2 (1998): 217–21.

371. Fradenburg, Louise Olga. *City, Marriage, Tournament: Arts of Rule in Late Medieval Scotland* (*SAC* 15 [1993], no. 272). Rev. Richard J. Moll, *Chaucer Yearbook* 4 (1997): 116–19.

372. Gellrich, Jesse M. *Discourse and Dominion in the Fourteenth Century: Oral Contexts of Writing in Philosophy, Politics, and Poetry* (*SAC* 19 [1997], no. 168). Rev. Robert Sturges, *TMR,* Nov. 1, 1997; Steven Justice, *RenQ* 51 (1998): 246–47.

373. Given-Wilson, Chris, ed. *An Illustrated History of Late Medieval England* (*SAC* 22 [2000], no. 124). Rev. Bradford Eden, *TMR,* July 6, 1998.

374. Grudin, Michaela Paasche. *Chaucer and the Politics of Discourse* (*SAC* 20 [1998], no. 84). Rev. E. D. Craun, *MÆ* 67 (1998): 137–38; Roberta Davidson, *TMR,* June 8, 1998; Mary F. Godfrey, *SAC* 20 (1998): 262–65.

375. Hanna, Ralph, III. *Pursuing History: Middle English Manuscripts and Their Texts* (*SAC* 20 [1998], no. 22). Rev. Charlotte Brewer, *YLS* 12 (1998): 204–6; David Greetham, *SAC* 20 (1998): 269–77.

376. Havely, Nicholas R., ed. *Chaucer:* The House of Fame (*SAC* 19 [1997], no. 22). Rev. J. M. Fyler, *Speculum* 73 (1998): 488–89.

377. Honegger, Thomas. *From Phoenix to Chauntecleer: Medieval English Animal Poetry* (*SAC* 21 [1999], no. 109). Rev. Ebbe Klitgård, *ES* 78 (1998): 91–92; Helen Phillips, *NMS* 42 (1998): 153–54.

378. Howes, Laura L. *Chaucer's Gardens and the Language of Convention* (*SAC* 21 [1999], no. 112). Rev. Jeffrey Cain, *RMR* 52.2 (1998): 84–86; Carol A. N. Martin, *TMR,* Aug. 6, 1998.

379. Jager, Eric. *The Tempter's Voice: Language and the Fall in Medieval Literature* (*SAC* 18 [1996], no. 208). Rev. Richard K. Emmerson, *TMR,* June 7, 1994; Eugene Vance, *TMR,* Oct. 8, 1994.

380. Justice, Steven. *Writing and Rebellion: England in 1381* (*SAC* 18 [1996], no. 95). Rev. James B. Given, *TMR* 12 May 1995; Stephen Stallcup, *TMR,* Sept. 3, 1995.

381. Kanno, Masahiko. *Studies in Chaucer's Words: A Contextual and Semantic Approach* (*SAC* 20 [1998], no. 56). Rev. Ebbe Klitgård, *ES* 78 (1998): 92–93.

382. Kelly, Henry Ansgar. *Chaucerian Tragedy* (*SAC* 21 [1999], no. 297). Rev. Noel Harold Kaylor, Jr., *SAC* 20 (1998): 281–83; Edward Wilson, *RES,* n.s., 49 (1998): 499–500.

383. ———. *Ideas and Forms of Tragedy from Aristotle to the Middle Ages* (*SAC* 18 [1996], no. 98). Rev. Eugene Vance, *TMR,* Dec. 3, 1993.

384. Kimmelman, Burt. *The Poetics of Authorship in the Later Middle Ages: The Emergence of the Modern Literary Persona* (*SAC* 20 [1998], no. 91). Rev. Anne Berthelot, *TMR,* Mar. 12, 1997; Amy W. Goodwin, *SAC* 20 (1998): 283–88.

385. Klassen, Norman. *Chaucer on Love, Knowledge and Sight* (*SAC* 19 [1997], no. 103). Rev. C. David Benson, *RES,* n. s., 49 (1998): 347–48; Peter Brown, *YES* 28 (1998): 297−98.

386. Kruger, Steven F. *Dreaming in the Middle Ages* (*SAC* 16 [1994], no. 101). Rev. Laurel Amtower, *Chaucer Yearbook* 4 (1997): 162–65.

387. Laskaya, Anne. *Chaucer's Approach to Gender in the* Canterbury Tales (*SAC* 19 [1997], no. 149). Rev. Janette Dillon, *MLR* 92.4 (1997): 941–42; Laura L. Howes, *SAC* 20 (1998): 288–90.

388. Lerer, Seth. *Chaucer and His Readers: Imagining the Author in Late-Medieval England* (*SAC* 17 [1995], no. 50). Rev. William A. Quinn, *Chaucer Yearbook* 4 (1997): 177–80; Tim William Machan, *JEGP* 97 (1998): 418–20.

389. ———. *Reading from the Margins: Textual Studies, Chaucer, and*

Medieval Literature (*SAC* 20 [1998], no. 97). Rev. Nicola F. McDonald, *TMR*, Jan. 5, 1996; Nicholas H. Clulee, *RenQ* 51 (1998): 1025–26; Stephen Partridge, *SAC* 20 (1998): 291–96.

390. Linden, Stanton J. *Darke Hierogliphicks: Alchemy in English Literature from Chaucer to the Restoration* (*SAC* 21 [1999], no. 256). Rev. Lyndy Abraham, *JEGP* 97 (1998): 114–16; Elizabeth Holtze, *RMR* 52.1 (1998): 79–80.

391. Matsuda, Takami. *Death and Purgatory in Middle English Didactic Poetry* (*SAC* 22 [2000], no. 136). Rev. *Eigo Seinen* 144.2 (1998): 110–11; Siegfried Wenzel, *N&Q* 243 (1998): 487–88.

392. McCarl, Mary Rhinelander, ed. *The Plowman's Tale: The c. 1532 and 1606 Editions of a Spurious Canterbury Tale* (*SAC* 21 [1999], no. 309). Rev. B. Boyd, *Speculum* 73 (1998): 1156–57.

393. Meale, Carol M., ed. *Women and Literature in Britain, 1150–1500* (*SAC* 17 [1995], no. 105). Rev. Laura L. Howes, *TMR*, Jan. 4, 1996.

394. Minnis, A. J., with V. J. Scattergood and J. J. Smith. *The Shorter Poems* (Oxford Guides to Chaucer) (*SAC* 19 [1997], no. 112). Rev. Winthrop Wetherbee, *TMR*, May 6, 1997; Julia Boffey, *JEGP* 97 (1998): 112–14; Helen Phillips, *MÆ* 67 (1998): 330–32.

395. Morse, Ruth. *The Medieval Medea* (*SAC* 20 [1998], no. 257). Rev. N. McDonald, *N&Q* 243 (1998): 107–8; R. F. Yeager, *SAC* 20 (1998): 300–302.

396. Newhauser, Richard G., and John A. Alford, eds. *Literature and Religion in the Later Middle Ages: Philological Studies in Honor of Siegfried Wenzel* (*SAC* 19 [1997], no. 114). Rev. James H. Morey, *TMR*, Dec. 8, 1996.

397. Pask, Kevin. *The Emergence of the English Author: Scripting the Life of the Poet in Early Modern England* (*SAC* 20 [1998], no. 4). Rev. Stephen Partridge, *Envoi* 7.1 (1998): 64–71.

398. Quinn, William A. *Chaucer's "Rehersynges": The Performability of* The Legend of Good Women (*SAC* 18 [1996], no. 267). Rev. Alan T. Gaylord, *Chaucer Yearbook* 4 (1997): 192–99; Alexandra H. Olsen, *RMR* 52.2 (1998): 83–84.

399. Rex, Richard. *"The Sins of Madame Eglentyne" and Other Essays on Chaucer* (*SAC* 19 [1997], no. 118). Rev. Catherine Batt, *YES* 28 (1998): 296.

400. Rigby, S. H. *Chaucer in Context: Society, Allegory, and Gender* (*SAC* 20 [1998], no. 124). Rev. Howard Kaminsky, *TMR*, Aug. 8,

1998; Nicola F. McDonald, *RES,* n.s., 49 (1998): 496–97; Helen Phillips, *NMS* 42 (1998): 153–54.

401. Robinson, Peter, ed., with contributions from N. F. Blake, Daniel W. Mosser, Stephen Partridge, and Elizabeth Solopova. *The Wife of Bath's Prologue on CD-ROM* (*SAC* 20 [1998], no. 11). Rev. Mark Allen, *SAC* 20 (1998): 318–23.

402. Rudd, Niall. *The Classical Tradition in Operation: Chaucer/Virgil, Shakespeare/Plautus, Pope/Horace, Tennyson/Lucretius, Pound/Propertius* (*SAC* 18 [1996], no. 37). Rev. Ralph Pite, *JEGP* 97 (1998): 578–80.

403. Saunders, Corrine J. *The Forest of Medieval Romance: Arvernus, Broceliande, Arden* (*SAC* 17 [1995], no. 114). Rev. Ruthmarie H. Mitsch, *TMR,* Jan. 2, 1995.

404. Seymour, M. C. *A Catalogue of Chaucer Manuscripts: Volume 1, Works Before the* Canterbury Tales (*SAC* 19 [1997], no. 7). Rev. H. Phillips, *MÆ* 67 (1998): 330–32; Walter Scheps, *ANQ* 11.1 (1998): 34–37.

405. ———. *A Catalogue of Chaucer Manuscripts: Volume II,* The Canterbury Tales (*SAC* 19 [1997], no. 7). Rev. N. F. Blake, *The Library,* 6th ser., 20 (1998): 372–73; A. S. G. Edwards, *MÆ* 67 (1998): 332–33.

406. Sigal, Gail. *Erotic Dawn-Songs of the Middle Ages: Voicing the Lyric Lady* (*SAC* 21 [1999], no. 145). Rev. Keith Busby, *SAC* 20 (1998): 331–33; Laura Kendrick, *MP* 96.2 (1998): 221–26.

407. Singman, Jeffrey L., and Will McLean. *Daily Life in Chaucer's England* (*SAC* 19 [1997], no. 124). Rev. Philip Niles, *Speculum* 73 (1998): 260–61.

408. Stillinger, Thomas C. *The Song of Troilus: Lyric Authority in the Medieval Book* (*SAC* 16 [1994], no. 314). Rev. Karla Taylor, *JEGP* 97 (1998): 110–12.

409. Taylor, Paul Beekman. *Chaucer's Chain of Love* (*SAC* 21 [1999], no.177). Rev. Richard J. Utz, *SAC* 20 (1998): 334–36.

410. Thompson, N. S. *Chaucer, Boccaccio, and the Debate of Love: A Comparative Study of* The Decameron *and* The Canterbury Tales (*SAC* 20 [1998], no. 128). Rev. George D. Economou, *SAC* 20 (1998): 336–39; Nick Havely, *MLR* 93.4 (1998): 1082–99; Janet Smarr, *JEGP* 97 (1998): 241–43.

411. Tinkle, Theresa. *Medieval Venuses and Cupids: Sexuality, Hermeneutics, and English Poetry* (*SAC* 20 [1998], no. 111). Rev. Andrew Galloway, *JEGP* 97 (1998): 239–41; Laura Kendrick, *MP* 96.2 (1998): 221–26; Judy Kronenfeld, *RenQ* 52 (1998): 690–91; Helen Phillips, *SAC* 20 (1998): 340–43.

412. Wallace, David. *Chaucerian Polity: Absolutist Lineages and Associational Forms in England and Italy* (*SAC* 21 [1999], no. 155). Rev. Louise M. Bishop, *TMR,* May 2, 1998; Peter Brown, *RES,* n.s., 49 (1998): 497–99.

413. Whitaker, Muriel, ed. *Sovereign Lady: Essays on Women in Middle English Literature* (*SAC* 19 [1997], no. 133). Rev. Elizabeth Walsh, *TMR,* Dec. 11, 1996.

414. Windeatt, Barry. *Troilus and Criseyde* (Oxford Guides to Chaucer) (*SAC* 16 [1994], no. 320). Rev. Thomas C. Stillinger, *Chaucer Yearbook* 4 (1997): 203–8.

Author Index—Bibliography

INDEX